D0103180

The Catholic
Theological Union
LIBRARY
Chicago, Ill.

DISCOVERIES IN THE JUDAEAN DESERT · XXIII

QUMRAN CAVE 11

II

DISCOVERIES IN THE JUDAEAN DESERT

EMANUEL TOV, EDITOR-IN-CHIEF

DISCOVERIES IN THE JUDAEAN DESERT · XXIII

QUMRAN CAVE 11

II

11Q2–18, 11Q20–31

BY

FLORENTINO GARCÍA MARTÍNEZ
EIBERT J. C. TIGCHELAAR
AND
ADAM S. VAN DER WOUDE

INCORPORATING EARLIER EDITIONS BY

J. P. M. VAN DER PLOEG, O.P.

WITH A CONTRIBUTION BY

EDWARD HERBERT

CLARENDON PRESS · OXFORD

1998

Oxford University Press, Great Clarendon Street, Oxford OX2 6DP
Oxford New York
Athens Auckland Bangkok Bogota Bombay
Buenos Aires Calcutta Cape Town Dar es Salaam
Delhi Florence Hong Kong Istanbul Karachi
Kuala Lumpur Madras Madrid Melbourne
Mexico City Nairobi Paris Singapore
Taipei Tokyo Toronto Warsaw
and associated companies in
Berlin Ibadan

Oxford is a trade mark of Oxford University Press

Published in the United States
by Oxford University Press Inc., New York

British Library Cataloguing in Publication Data
Data available

Library of Congress Cataloging in Publication Data
Data available

ISBN 0 19 826959 5

1 3 5 7 9 10 8 6 4 2

Printed in Great Britain
on acid-free paper by
St. Edmundsbury Press, Bury St Edmunds

DEDICATED TO

THE ASHTON FAMILY FOUNDATION

IN APPRECIATION

OF ITS CONTINUED SUPPORT

OF QUMRAN SCHOLARSHIP

CONTENTS

TABLE OF PLATES

FOREWORD

THE present volume, *DJD* XXIII, is the second containing texts found in cave 11. This volume completes the publication of all the manuscripts found in that cave, with the exception of two large texts published elsewhere: Y. Yadin, *The Temple Scroll*, vols. 1–3 (Jerusalem 1983); D. N. Freedman and K. A. Mathews, *The Paleo-Hebrew Leviticus Scroll (11QpaleoLev)* (Winona Lake, IN, 1985). Most of the texts presented in this volume were published preliminarily, but over the course of the years the understanding of some manuscripts has changed significantly. The names of some texts have been changed; likewise, the numbering and arrangement of the fragments has also been altered. All these revisions are duly recorded in the appropriate places in the volume.

This volume presents the joint labour of three authors from Groningen, Prof. A. S. van der Woude, the founder and ex-director of the Qumran-Instituut at the University of Groningen, Prof. F. García Martínez, the present director of the Instituut, and Dr. E. J. C. Tigchelaar. It is an agreeable duty to thank these three authors for their work, and it was a pleasure working with them. The present volume is the lengthiest published thus far in the *DJD* series, and its scope certainly reflects the enormous amount of work invested in it over the course of many years.

The volume was read carefully by M. Morgenstern and S. Chavel of the Hebrew University, both of whom improved the manuscript in many details.

The bulk of the volume was typeset in Groningen by Dr. Eibert J. C. Tigchelaar, who skillfully translated into English many texts that had been previously published in French and German, and prepared the corresponding *DJD* versions. The complete volume was copy-edited in Jerusalem by Janice Karnis and Valerie Carr Zakovitch. Further typing and proof-reading were carried out by Eva Ben-David and Sarah Presant-Collins. The camera-ready copy was produced by Janice Karnis. The production was coordinated by Claire Pfann who, together with Valerie Carr Zakovitch, also finalized the preparation of the plates.

As in the past, we are grateful to the various members of the staff at Oxford University Press for their professional production of the complete volume, including the high-quality plates.

The in-context concordances were prepared by Stephen and Claire Pfann of the Center for the Study of Early Christianity, Jerusalem. The correcting and formatting of the concordances for this volume was supported by the Foundation for Ancient Research and Mormon Studies in Provo, Utah.

As always, we are indebted to the Israel Antiquities Authority for its constant encouragement and for the network of support services it supplies, including public relations, access to archival materials, production of photographic plates, and the on-going task of preservation of the scrolls. In particular we wish to thank the Director, General (ret.) Amir Drori, Ayala Sussmann, Director of Publications, Tsila Sagiv, photographer, and Lena Libman, conservator. By the same token, we owe a debt of gratitude to the Advisory Committee of the Israel Antiquities Authority for its active involvement in the reorganization of the Dead Sea Scrolls Publication Project over the past six years, which has contributed to the present accelerated rate of progress in the publication of the *DJD* volumes.

The Qumran Project of the Oxford Centre for Hebrew and Jewish Studies is to be thanked for its support for the typesetting of this volume and for the work of the international Dead Sea Scrolls Publication Project as a whole.

Jerusalem
September 1997

EMANUEL TOV
EDITOR-IN-CHIEF

PREFACE

THIS volume contains all the manuscripts acquired from the Bedouin in 1961 and 1962 by the Palestine Archaeological Museum (PAM) with funds provided by the Koninklijke Nederlandse Akademie van Wetenschappen (KNAW) and the Nederlandse Organisatie voor Zuiver-Wetenschappelijk Onderzoek (ZWO). The majority of these manuscripts were apparently found by the Bedouin in January 1956, in what was later known as cave 11, together with the scrolls acquired by the PAM on 19 May 1956 (**11Q1**, **11Q5**, and some other unidentified fragments); only a small number of them were found *in situ* by the archaeological expedition conducted by R. de Vaux in February 1956 (see *RB* 63 [1956] 574).

A letter from R. de Vaux, President of the Board of Trustees of the PAM, to J. P. M. van der Ploeg, written on 7 June 1959, in which he set out in detail 'les conditions les plus favorables que j'ai pu obtenir du gouvernement [jourdanien]', which was found attached to a memorandum to the KNAW written by Profs. Th. C. Vriezen and W. C. van Unnik on 10 July 1959, is the earliest indication in the KNAW archives of the involvement of the Dutch Academy in the negotiations which would finally lead to the acquisition from the Bedouin of the materials found in cave 11. These conditions, repeated in the two 'agreements' signed by both parties, concern the property rights to the documents ('the manuscripts will stay in Jordan as the property of the Jordanian Government'), the exclusive rights of study ('the Academy is granted the exclusive right to study the manuscripts and to prepare their publication'), the method of publication of the manuscripts ('Publication of the texts . . . may, if the Academy wishes so, be included in the series Discoveries in the Judaean Desert . . . Such publication does not preclude other publications by the Academy'), and the manner in which the manuscripts should by exhibited ('The manuscripts, although the property of the Jordanian Government, will be registered, kept and exhibited at the Museum with the legend 'Donation of the Royal Netherlands Academy of Sciences and Letters').

The two separate agreements by the representatives of the PAM and the KNAW describe in detail the manuscripts in question and, in both, the origin of the manuscripts is specified as 'found at Qumran, Cave 11'. The first, signed 23 December 1961, concerns exclusively the 'Aramaic Targum of Job'. The second, signed 12 December 1962, pertains to all the remaining materials; some of these are specified in detail in the agreement ('Unopened scroll and fragments containing Aramaic text about the New Jerusalem'; 'Unopened scroll and fragments containing a text provisionally denoted "ʿOlat ha-Shabbat"'), while others are vaguely designated as 'Numerous fragments containing biblical texts in square Hebrew and non-biblical texts', or 'small scrolls and fragments also found in Cave 11'.

The KNAW, using the prerogatives granted in the agreements, entrusted the study and publication of the manuscripts to Profs. J. P. M. van der Ploeg and A. S. van der Woude. With the assistance of B. Jongeling, they jointly produced the *editio princeps* of **11Q10** (11QtgJob), the first manuscript secured by the KNAW, and separately they published several preliminary editions of many of the manuscripts acquired on the basis of the second agreement (sections of 11Q**2**, 11Q**6**, 11Q**7**, 11Q**11**, and 11Q**20** were published by van der Ploeg; 11Q**12**, 11Q**13**, 11Q**14**, and 11Q**17** were published by van der Woude). In 1985, van der Ploeg and van der Woude entrusted the undersigned with the publication of the remainder of the texts (mainly 11Q**18** and 11Q**20**). In 1987, J. Strugnell, then editor-in-chief of the *DJD* series, charged me with the task of preparing the manuscript of the whole 'Dutch share of Cave 11' for publication in the series, on the basis of the previous publications.

In the present publication, the undersigned, A. S. van der Woude, and E. J. C. Tigchelaar share equal responsibility. A. S. van der Woude was actively involved in the revision of the texts published by him and commented on several drafts of the manuscript of the volume. In 1995–96, E. J. C. Tigchelaar was actively involved in the editing of the earlier publications. This work included the translation into English of the publications in French and German, as well as the standardization and updating with more recent studies. Dr. Tigchelaar was instrumental in discovering new joins between fragments, making new identifications, proposing new readings, and evaluating others with critical acumen; therefore, it is only fair that he be given full recognition as a co-author of the volume. J. P. M. van der Ploeg was instrumental in involving the KNAW in the acquisition of the manuscripts; he produced many fundamental contributions to the understanding of the scrolls, and was very active in stimulating research of the Dead Sea Scrolls in the Netherlands. At the same time, Prof. van der Ploeg notified us that he no longer wished to be involved in the publication of the manuscripts. We acknowledge our great debt to his preliminary editions, and while sadly missing his expertise, have respected his wish; therefore we take full responsibility for the publication of the manuscripts originally edited by him.

It is a pleasant duty to thank the many individuals and institutions, both in the Netherlands and elsewhere, who have assisted in and contributed to the completion of this volume. First and foremost, we thank the Koninklijke Nederlandse Akademie van Wetenschappen, which not only took the necessary steps to secure the acquisition of the manuscripts but has also been unfailing in its support of the research necessary for the publication of this volume. Equally unfailing has been the support of the Theological Faculty of the Rijksuniversiteit Groningen, the academic home of the three co-authors, within which its Qumran-Instituut has established ideal conditions for research.

The Dead Sea Scrolls Foundation and its executive director Dr. Weston W. Fields, have been most helpful, providing funding not only for the work of Dr. E. J. C. Tigchelaar, but also for the necessary computer facilities, new photographic reproductions, and supplementary funds for working at the Rockefeller Museum, etc. Without this active help, the preparatory work would have taken a great deal longer.

It is also a pleasure to thank the 'Direccíon General de Investigación y Desarrollo' of the Spanish Ministry of Education and Science, which funded my stay for a sabbatical semester in 1997 at the Universidad Complutense of Madrid, allowing me to complete the manuscript and to prepare the plates for this volume.

Among the colleagues who have worked with these texts following their preliminary publication and who have freely contributed their time and expertise, I should like to single out É. Puech; his publications of 11Q**11** and 11Q**13** have fundamentally contributed to our understanding of these texts and have been used often, more than footnotes can acknowledge; his willingness to share his insights has been unfailing since our first joint publication of part of the last column of 11Q**10** in 1978; his expertise in palaeography and his critical acumen have been a source of continual help. The readiness of Lena Libman and her team of conservators at the Rockefeller Museum to comply with all our requests is also gratefully acknowledged.

Finally, it is a most agreeable duty to acknowledge the patient guidance and constant encouragement of Prof. Emanuel Tov, the editor-in-chief of the *Discoveries in the Judaean Desert* series. His personal involvement in all phases of the production of the manuscript secured uninterrupted progress and encouraged us to lay aside other obligations in order to complete this work. He and his staff, especially Janice Karnis, Valerie Carr Zakovitch, and Claire Pfann, who coordinated the work, deserve the gratitude of the public as well as that of ourselves. The critical remarks by Simcha Chavel and Matthew Morgenstern have helped us to sharpen our formulations. The care invested by Valerie Carr Zakovitch, Janice Karnis, Sarah Presant-Collins, and Eva Ben-David in the preparation of the camera-ready copy has improved the final result and earned our gratitude.

Although cave 11 was discovered in 1956 and the manuscripts here published were acquired only in 1961 and 1962, it seems fitting that this 'Dutch volume', completed during the fiftieth anniversary year of the discovery of the manuscripts of cave 1, is presented to the public as a token of the continuous involvement of the Netherlands in research on the scrolls.

Madrid FLORENTINO GARCÍA MARTÍNEZ
July 1997

2. 11QLeviticus^b

(PLATE I)

Previous discussion: J. P. M. van der Ploeg, 'Lév. IX 23–X 2 dans un texte de Qumran', *Bibel und Qumran. Beiträge zur Erforschung der Beziehungen zwischen Bibel- und Qumranwissenschaft. Hans Bardtke zum 22.9.1966*, ed. S. Wagner (Berlin: Evangelische Haupt-Bibelgesellschaft, 1968) 153–5 + plate; ibid, 'Les manuscrits de la Grotte XI de Qumrân', *RevQ* 12/45 (1985) 9–10; F. García Martínez, 'Texts from Cave 11', *The Dead Sea Scrolls: Forty Years of Research,* eds. D. Dimant, E. Rappaport (STDJ 10; Leiden: E. J. Brill, 1992) 20.

Physical Description

THE skin, somewhat thicker than average, is dull brown in colour. Only frgs. 2 and 6 are well preserved and legible with the naked eye. The other fragments have darkened to a deep grey, with only a few characters or traces remaining visible on the original fragments. The back of frg. 7a (Mus. Inv. 1016) is a light greyish-brown colour.

Horizontal and vertical ruling is apparent on most fragments. The tetragrammaton is written in palaeo-Hebrew characters.

Frg. 1 preserves an intercolumnar margin; frg. 5 preserves a right margin. A bottom margin of up to 1.7 cm is preserved on frgs. 5 + 6.

The average number of letter-spaces per reconstructed line is *c*.40 (slightly fewer in frg. 3, slightly more in frg. 7). The approximate width of the columns is calculated at 9–10 cm.

The only indication for the height of the columns is given by frg. 1. If the reading of the sparse letters is correct, there are 17–20 lines missing between frg. 1 i 2 and frg. 1 ii 2 (the calculation is based upon 𐤉𐤄𐤅𐤄 written *plene*, assuming an average line length of 40 letter-spaces and a *vacat* or blank line before Lev 8:1; frg. 1 ii 2 may correspond to any of the three examples of וישם in Lev 8:8-9). Since the distance between the horizontal lines is *c*.0.9 cm, the height of the inscribed section of the column would have measured 15–18 cm.

Contents

TABLE 1: *Contents of 11Q2 Lev^b*

Frg.	Lev.	Frg.	Lev.
1 i	7:34-35	4	14:16-17
1 ii	8:8 or 9	5 + 6	15:18-19
2	9:23–10:2	7	25:31-33
3	13:58-59	8, 9	not identified

Palaeography

The hand is a fine example of the late Herodian fomal bookhand (*c*.50 CE), written elegantly with a pen which allowed both thick and very thin strokes.

Orthography and Morphology

The preserved parts of the manuscript are written *plene* in all cases where possible. Of interest is the spelling of פושתים] in frg. 3 4 (Lev 13:59), with *waw* instead of the /*i*/ of the Tiberian tradition. The only preserved example of כי is spelled כיא (frgs. 5 + 6 2). The manuscript does not use the lengthened forms of the 3rd masc. pl. suffixes.

Textual Character

The fragments of **11Q2** exhibit a textual character somewhere between 𝔐 and 𝔊. The unique readings are grammatically awkward. **11Q2** agrees with 𝔊 against 𝔐 in the following cases:

9:23 (2 1) כו[ל 𝔊] > 𝔐𝔪

10:1 (2 4) שׁ[ני 𝔊] > 𝔐𝔪𝔊[A]

10:1 (2 7) 𐤉𐤄𐤅[𐤄 𝔊] > 𝔐𝔪.

11Q2 corresponds to 𝔐 against the majority of 𝔊 manuscripts in the following cases:

10:1 (2 5) בה[ן 𝔐𝔪𝔊[A] ἐπ' αὐτά] 𝔊 ἐπ' αὐτό

25:31 (7 1) לו[11Q1 𝔐𝔪] αὐταί 𝔊[F*Madefi-z]𝔖; > 𝔊

25:33 (7 3) ממכר 11Q1 𝔐𝔪𝔊[GMabceklmorsu-xzb2]] ἡ διάπρασις αὐτῶν 𝔊; > 𝔙

The following cases contain readings unique to **11Q2**:

9:24 (2 3) החלב השלמ[ים] החלבים 𝔐𝔪𝔊

25:33 (7 3) ביתו עׄ[יר] בית ועיר 11Q1 𝔐𝔪𝔖; οἰκιῶν πόλεως (= בתי עיר ?) 𝔊

Cf. also the loss of the article in frg. 3:

13:59 (3 4) צמר] הצמר 𝔐𝔪

13:59 (3 4) פושתים]] הפשתים 𝔐𝔪

13:59 (3 5) עור 𝔐] העור 𝔪

Mus. Inv. 566, 567, 577, 615, 1016, 1032
PAM 42.175, 42.176, 42.177*, 42.178, 42.180, 43.794*, 43.978*, 44.007*, 44.011*, 44.114*
IAA 525009, 525011, 525015, 563769

Frg. 1 i Lev 7:34-35

1 [ ]בׄני
2 [ישראל 35זואת משחת אהרון ומשחת בניו מ]אשי

Mus. Inv. 577
PAM 42.178, 43.978*

NOTES ON READINGS

Col. i could also be reconstructed according to Lev 6:11 or 10:14-15; however, no plausible texts can be found in these cases which fit column ii (a correspondence with 10:20 וישמע would give a rather short column).

L. 1 (7:34/10:14)]בׄני. The dark dot at the edge, if ink, may be a remnant of a *bet*. A faint stroke to the right of the base of the *nun* also shows that the preceding letter has faded away.

Frg. 1 ii Lev 8:8 or 9

2 ויש]ם

NOTES ON READINGS

The left-hand part of the fragment, with *yod* and *šin*, is only visible in the oldest photograph, PAM 42.178, having broken off subsequently. It is not likely that the word should be reconstructed ויש]חט as in Lev 8:15, since that would make the column very long.

L. 1 (10:20) ויש]ם. The last letter is a *šin*, or, less likely, an *ʿayin*.

Frg. 2 Lev 9:23–10:2

1 [ ]את כו[ל]הׄעׄם[וירא כבוד 𐤉𐤄𐤅𐤄]
2 [אל כול העם 24ותצ]א אש מלפנׄי 𐤉𐤄𐤅𐤄[ותאכל על]
3 [המזבח את העו]לה ואת החלב השלמ[ים וירא כול]
4 [העם וירנו ויפולו]על פניהם 10:1ויקחו שׄ[ני בני אהרון]
5 [נדב ואביהוא א]יש מחתתו ויתנו בה[ן אש וישימו]

6]עליה קטורת ו[יק֯ר֯יבו לפני 𐤉𐤄𐤅[𐤄 אש זרה אשר[

7]לוא צוה 𐤉𐤄𐤅[𐤄 אותם[2]ותצא[אש מלפני 𐤉𐤄𐤅𐤄[

8]ותאוכל אותם וימותו [ל]פני 𐤉𐤄𐤅𐤄

Mus. Inv. 566
PAM 42.180, 43.978, 44.011*

NOTES ON READINGS

Frg. 2 has several tears, folds, and holes. It has now become flattened. Small pieces from the bottom were lost after PAM 42.180 was taken. Frg. 8, a small fragment with]על[, was superimposed upon the left edge of line 3. It is unclear whether it should be joined to frg. 1 (a join at the right side of line 3 is unlikely), or whether it belongs to another layer of the scroll.

L. 1 (9:23)]את. Parts of all three strokes of *ʾalep* are visible.

L. 1 (9:23) כו[ל]ה֯עם[. Van der Ploeg read כו[ל ה]עד[ה, but that reading is very difficult. Firstly, the traces which are interpreted as *ʿayin* are unlike any other *ʿayin* in the preserved fragments. Secondly, one must assume a large space between כו[ל and ה]עד[ה, but two traces compatible with *he* (a dot, and a stroke which is only visible in PAM 42.180) above the *yod* of מלפני in line 2 contradict this assumption. The traces read as *ʿayin* and the leg of *dalet* appear on a small fragment, but it is impossible to ascertain from the photographs whether the fragment had become completely detached or was still attached at its bottom left-hand part. It seems advisable to rotate the fragment *c.*20 degrees clockwise and read a final *mem* preceded by *nun*, *ṣade*, or *taw*. Yet in that case, the position of the fragment in this line is problematic.

L. 2 (9:24) מלפ֯ני. A minute dot from the curve in the middle of the downstroke of *nun* is visible. The base of *nun* should be visible on the fold which covers the lower part of *yod*.

L. 3 (9:24) העו[לה. Parts of the upper arm of a *lamed* and of the crossbar and left leg of *he* are visible in the dark part of the fragment. Frg. 8 (with]ע֯ל[) might be joined here, but the defective spelling העלה is not likely.

L. 3 (9:24) השלמ[ים. The last two letters were obscured in the older photographs by the small fragment with]על[.

L. 4 (10:1) ש֯[ני. The trace near the ceiling line indicates *šin* or *ʿayin*. PAM 44.011 seems to show another trace near the baseline, but the older photographs show that this is merely a shadow.

L. 8 (10:2) וימותו]ל[פני. A piece of skin at the bottom right of the fragment is visible in PAM 42.180, but has disappeared in the later photographs. Some of the dark strokes in the photographs may perhaps be the tops of letters of וימותו. PAM 42.180 still shows the horizontal stroke and part of the hook of the *lamed*; the later photographs preserve only the upper arm.

COMMENTS

L. 2 (9:24) 𐤉𐤄𐤅𐤄[. Other biblical texts with the tetragrammaton written in the palaeo-Hebrew script are 2Q**3** (Exod[b]), 4Q**26b** (Lev[g]), 4Q**57** (Isa[c]), and 11Q**5** (Ps[a]).

L. 3 (9:24) החלב השלמ[ים. The variant has no other textual support and is grammatically unusual, as the clause seems to be in a construct state with a determined *nomen regens*. The addition of השלמ[ים apparently means to explicate that the 'fat' does not belong to the burnt-offering, but to the peace-offerings mentioned in verse 22. For חלבי השלמים, cf. Lev 6:5; 2 Chr 7:7; 29:35.

VARIANTS

9:23 (1) כו[ל 𝔊] > 𝔐𝔰
9:24 (3) החלב השלמ[ים] החלבים 𝔐𝔰𝔊
10:1 (4) ש֯[ני 𝔊] > 𝔐𝔰$𝔊^{A}$
10:1 (5) בה[ן 𝔐𝔰$𝔊^{A}$ ἐπ' αὐτά] 𝔊 ἐπ' αὐτό
10:1 (6) ו]י֯קר֯י֯ב֯ו $𝔰^{mlt}$] ויקרבו 𝔐𝔰
10:1 (7) [paleo-Hebrew] 𝔊] > 𝔐𝔰
10:1 (8) [אותם]] אתם 𝔐𝔰

Frg. 3 Lev 13:58-59

1]◦ ◦[
2 [הע]רב או כו֯[ל כלי העור אשר]
3 [תכבס וסר מהם]ה֯נגע ו֯כבס שנית[וטהר 59זואת]
4 [תורת נגע צרעת ב]גד צמר או פושתי֯ם[או שתי]
5 [או ערב או כול כ]ל֯י עור לטהרתו או [לטמאו]
6 [ ] *vacat* [ ]

Mus. Inv. 615
PAM 42.175, 44.007*

NOTES ON READINGS

L. 1]◦ ◦[. The traces of ink are too minute for identification.

L. 3 (13:58)]ה֯נגע[. On the edge, the bottom half of a downstroke (the left leg of a *he*) is visible.

L. 4 (13:59) פושתי֯ם[. The *waw* might also be *yod*, but the typical characteristics of *yod* are not present.

L. 5 (13:59) כ]ל֯י. The trace on the edge of the fragment may belong to a *lamed*. The other dark trace along the diagonal edge of the fragment, partially below the head of the *yod*, is not ink.

L. 5 (13:59) [לטמאו]. The *lamed* is attested indirectly by the blank space at the bottom of the line.

L. 6] *vacat* [. The horizontal dry line shows that the bottom of the fragment is a blank line, and not the bottom margin.

COMMENTS

Ll. 3–5 (13:59) זואת תורת נגע צרעת ב]גד צמר או פושתי֯ם[או שתי או ערב או כול כ]ל֯י עור לטהרתו או [לטמאו]. 11QLev[b] differs from both 𝔐 and 𝔰 in the use of the article. 𝔰 reads הצרעת and העור, where 𝔐 has צרעת and 𝔐 and 11QLev[b] have עור. Yet, both 𝔐 and 𝔰 have the article with צמר and פשתים, where it is absent in 11QLev[b]. 𝔐 seems to take an intermediate position between 𝔰 and 11QLev[b]. In the reconstruction, the article is also omitted before שתי and ערב (where 𝔐 and 𝔰 read השתי and הערב).

L. 4 (13:59)]פושתי֯ם֯. The reading]פישתים֯ is not only palaeographically more difficult, but also orthographically: the *yod* does not represent a short *i*.

L. 5 (13:59) לטהרתו. The action noun is used more often in Leviticus (cf. 13:7, 35; 14:23, 32; 15:13). The word is probably not the *qotlāh* type of infinitive which should have been spelled *plene* לטוהרתו.

L. 6] *vacat* [. The *vacat* corresponds to the *petuḥa* in 𝔐.

VARIANTS

13:58 (2) כו֯]ל] 𝔐𝔖 כל
13:59 (4) צמר] 𝔐𝔖 הצמר
13:59 (4)]פושתי֯ם֯] 𝔐𝔖 הפשתים
13:59 (5) 𝔐 עור] 𝔖 העור
13:59 (5) לטהרתו] 𝔐 לטהרו

Frg. 4 Lev 14:16-17

1]בא[צ֯בעו ש[בע פעמים לפני יהוה [17]ומיתר השמן אשר[
2]על כ[פ֯ו

Mus. Inv. 1032
PAM 42.177*
IAA 563769

NOTES ON READINGS

The letters of the first line may correspond to either Lev 14:16 or 16:19, but a reconstruction based on Lev 16:19-20 (line 2]מכ[פ֯ר) would give a line rather longer than average.

L. 2 כ]פ֯ו. The bottom part of the fragment has broken off, and nothing remains of the trace. The trace, as it appears in the photograph, is peculiar. It looks like the top half of a slanting oval form. *Ṭet* or *pe* is possible, but the few examples of these letters in 11QLev[b] are written with a more angular head.

VARIANTS

14:16 (1)]בא[צבעו 𝔐𝔊] > 𝔖; +]הימני[ת 11Q1 paleoLev[a]

Frg. 5 + 6 Lev 15:18-19

1]איש אתה שכבת זר[ע ו֯]רחצו במים וטמאו עד הערב[
2 [19]ואשה כי֯א֯[תהיה [זבה דם[

bottom margin

Mus. Inv. 567, 577
PAM 42.176, 43.978*, 44.114*
IAA 525015

NOTES ON READINGS

Frg. 5 + 6 is composed of two fragments, both preserving the bottom margin.

L. 1 (15:18) זר[ע. Or זר[עו֯. PAM 44.114 suggests a downstroke slightly fainter than the traces of *ʿayin*, but the new IAA photograph of the fragment, which has lost a tiny piece at the top, does not confirm the *waw*.

VARIANTS

15:19 (2) כיא֯]] כי 𝔐𝔪

Frg. 7 Lev 25:31-33

[ת]ה֯[יה]לו ובׄי֯ו֯[בל יצא 32 וערי הלויים בתים]
[ערי אחוזת]ם֯ גאולת עולם ת[היה ללויים 33 ואשר יגאל]
[מן הלויים וי]צא ממכר ביתו ע֯[יר אחוזתו ביובל כיא]
[בתי ערי ה]ל֯[ויים

Mus. Inv. 567
PAM 43.794*, 44.114*
IAA 525015

NOTES ON READINGS

Frg. 7 is composed of two fragments which can be joined. Frg. 7b has since broken into several pieces. The horizontal placement of the fragment within the column is tentative.

L. 1 (25:31) ת]ה֯[יה. The tip of a leg probably belongs to *he*, but *taw* or *yod* cannot be ruled out.

L. 1 (25:31) ובׄי֯ו֯[בל. The remains of a *yod* or *waw* should also be visible on the fragment, but the microfiche is not clear enough to read with certainty.

COMMENTS

L. 3 (25:33) ביתו ע֯[יר. The variant may have arisen from the uncertainty as to whether the *waw* belonged to בית or עיר.

VARIANTS

25:31 (1) לו[11Q1 𝔐𝔪] αὐταί 𝔊$^{\text{F*Madefi-z}}$𝔖; > 𝔊
25:31 (1) ובׄי֯ו֯[בל 𝔐𝔪𝔊 (וביבל)] ביובל 11Q1 𝔊^{dfiprt}𝔗
25:32 (2) גאולת] גאלת 11Q1 𝔐𝔪

25:33 (3) ממכר 11Q1 𝔐⅏$𝔊^{GMabceklmorsu\text{-}xzb_2}$] ἡ διάπρασις αὐτῶν 𝔊; > 𝔙

25:33 (3) ביתו עׄ]יר] בית ועיר 11Q1 𝔐⅏S; οἰκιῶν πόλεως (= בתי עיר ?) 𝔊

Unidentified Fragments

Frg. 8

]על[1

Mus. Inv. 566
PAM 42.180, 43.978, 44.011*

NOTES ON READINGS

The fragment was superimposed on frg. 2.

Frg. 9 i

]◦ׄכׄ◦ס 1

]◦ׄי 2

]לׄ 3

Mus. Inv. 567
PAM 44.114*
IAA 525009, 525011, 525014

NOTES ON READINGS

The colour of the fragment and its thickness indicate that it originates from **11Q2**, and certainly not from **11Q20**. The distance between the lines is also consistent with **11Q2**, but the few certain letters do not allow for a positive identification.

L. 1]◦ׄכׄ◦ס. The first trace could be one of many letters. The space between the *kap* and the *samek* also allows for two narrow-to-medium letters. A possible reading might be כׄבׄס◦ׄ, since the *bet* in 11Q2 is rather wide.

L. 2]◦ׄי. The photograph does not clearly show the letter before the *yod* (or *waw*) and the traces have broken away from the fragment, which is illegible to the naked eye.

Comments

A possible placement for the right column of the fragment might be Lev 6:20-22, reading]יׄכבׄס (cf. 𝔊, or else תׄכבׄס with 𝔐),]בׄו and כו]ל, which would result in lines of similar length to those of the identified fragments.

Frg. 9 ii

וׄמ°[1

°[2

Mus. Inv. 567
PAM 44.114*
IAA 525009, 525011, 525014

Notes on Readings

L. 1 וׄמ°[. It is not at all certain that the first trace, looking most like a *waw*, is ink at all. The last letter might be a *bet*, but it is not sure which traces are ink.

L. 2 °[. A trace beneath the *mem* of line 1 resembles the head of *reš*.

3. 11QDeuteronomy

(PLATE II)

Previous discussion: J. P. M. van der Ploeg, 'Les manuscrits de la Grotte XI de Qumrân', *RevQ* 12/45 (1985) 10; F. García Martínez, 'Texts from Cave 11', *The Dead Sea Scrolls: Forty Years of Research*, eds. D. Dimant, E. Rappaport (STDJ 10; Leiden: E. J. Brill, 1992) 20–21.

Physical Description

THE only well-preserved fragment, frg. 1, is a light brown colour. Frgs. 2 and 3 are darker and not legible to the naked eye. The letters עבר of בעבר on frg. 1 are covered with white spots, possibly salt crystals (cf. 11Q**10** for discussion of similar white powderings on the ink).

Horizontal and vertical dry lines are clearly visible. The distance between the horizontal lines is 0.8 cm. The reconstructed lines of frgs. 1 and 2 indicate a column width of *c.*13 cm.

The manuscript is written in the late Herodian formal bookhand (*c.*50 CE). The thickness of the strokes hardly varies.

The spelling עישו in frg. 2 2 suggests that the manuscript had a *plene* writing. Apart from this orthographic variant, the manuscript agrees with 𝔐; since the versions do not have variants in the preserved parts, however, nothing can be said regarding the textual character.

Mus. Inv. 576, 1016
PAM 42.176, 43.794*, 44.003*

Frg. 1 Deut 1:4-5

1 [סיחון מלך האמורי אשר יושב בחשבו]ן֯ ו֯את עוג
2 [מלך הבשן אשר יושב בעשתרות ב]אדרעי 5 בעבר
3 [הירדן בארץ מואב הואיל מושה ב]אר את התו֯ר[ה]

Mus. Inv. 576
PAM 42.176, 44.003*

NOTES ON READINGS

The first line of the fragment is the eighth one of the column, if the column started with Deut 1:1.

L. 3 (1:5) ב]אר. Only the bottom part of the left leg of *ʾalep* remains.

L. 3 (1:5) התו֯ר֯[ה]. The head of what must be *waw* is clear. The very thin traces on the bottom edge are possibly remains of *reš*.

Frg. 2 Deut 2:28-30

1 [[ו֯שת֯[יתי]

2 [רק אעברה ברגלי [29]כאשר עשו לי [ב֯ני עישו

3 [היושבים בשעיר והמואבים היו[שבים

4 [בער עד אשר אעבור את הירד[ן אל הארץ֯

5 [אשר יהוה אלוהינו נותן לנו [30]ולוא אב[ה סיח֯[ון]

Mus. Inv. 1016
PAM 43.794

NOTES ON READINGS

The rather large space after היו[שבים in line 3 may indicate that the fragment belonged to the left-hand side of the column. Line 3 is rather short in transcription, but may have fit in the original. There is some overlap with 4QDeut[d] I.

VARIANTS

2:29 (2) עישו] עשו 𝔐

Frg. 3 i

2]ת̇

2a]°

3]א֯ב

4]°

Mus. Inv. 1016
PAM 43.794

NOTES ON READINGS

The fragment is very darkened and the reading is based upon the photograph. The shape of the fragment is identical (except for the right edge) to frg. 2, including corresponding tears or cracks, which indicates that the two fragments stem from corresponding positions in the scroll, most probably from subsequent revolutions. The darker colour of frg. 3 might indicate that it covered frg. 2.

L. 2a ○[. The head of a letter, e.g. of *bet* or *reš* written intralinearly or supralinearly.

L. 3 אׄב[. The diagonal trace before the *bet* must belong to *ʾalep* or *gimel*. Note, however, that the left leg of the *gimel* in frg. 1 1 is written less diagonally than the trace here.

COMMENTS

The location of the preserved traces is problematic. The traces of line 3 can only correspond to מו[אב in Deut 2:8, 9, or 17, or to אר[גב or האר[גב in Deut 3:4, 13, or 14. Since *gimel* is more difficult than *ʾalep*, and ארגב would probably have been written *plene*, the most likely reading is מו[אׄב. This would locate the trace in e.g. Deut 2:8, מאיל[תׄ /]ומעציון גבר ונפן ונעבור דרך מדב[ר מו[אׄב. However, it is difficult to locate the traces of the second column of this fragment in the text following this, or one of the other occurrences of מואב in 𝔐.

Frg. 3 ii

]○[ ] 1

]○○ 2

]○ד○ 3

] 4

]○ 5

Mus. Inv. 1016
PAM 43.794

NOTES ON READINGS

The only legible letter is the perfectly clear *dalet*. It is not of the same height as the corresponding letters of the right column, but for a similar height difference in biblical texts cf. 1QIsa[a] XIII and XIV. Some other traces of ink are visible along the left and bottom edge, but in view of the position of the *dalet* it may be assumed that most of the ink has faded away.

L. 1]○[ ]. Only a trace at the edge remains, the bottom tip of a slanting downstroke (*ʾalep* is very difficult). Unless the right margin were ragged, this is not the first letter of the line.

L. 2]○○. Or]○[ ], or]○. It is difficult to determine which traces are ink.

L. 3]°ד°. The dark diagonal stroke before *dalet* may be ink, e.g. a remnant of the tick of *yod*. The trace after *dalet* need not be ink.

L. 4]. Or *vac*]*at*.

COMMENTS

The search for a *dalet* as the first or second letter of a word in a plausible position between frg. 3 i and frg. 2 only results in יד (Deut 2:15) or עד (Deut 2:22 and 23). Neither of these identifications is entirely convincing.

4. 11QEzekiel

(PLATES II, LIV)

Previous discussion: W. H. Brownlee, 'The Scroll of Ezekiel from the Eleventh Qumran Cave', *RevQ* 4 (1963) 11–28; H. J. Plenderleith, *Examination and Dissection of a Rigid Dead Sea Scroll*, unpublished report to the Palestine Archaeology Museum (Jerusalem, 1962).

11QEZEKIEL, when discovered, represented approximately 35 percent of a scroll which had survived as a dense, unopenable mass. P. Skehan salvaged frgs. 2 and 6 from the surface of the scroll, and in 1960 identified it as a scroll of Ezekiel. The scroll was purchased by the Claremont Graduate School for William Brownlee to study. It proved, however, to be unopenable due to its poor state of preservation. Consequently, H. J. Plenderleith, the director of the Rome Center for Conservation of Antiquities, a branch of UNESCO, was invited to Jerusalem to advise concerning the opening of the document. Plenderleith's (unpublished) report giving his assessment of the scroll and an account of his actions in seeking to reclaim fragments from it was submitted in March 1962. This date finds confirmation both in Plenderleith's report and Brownlee's preliminary publication, but is surprisingly at variance with the photographer's logbook, which dates photographs taken before and after Plenderleith's dissection to March 1961 (see E. Tov and S. J. Pfann, *Companion Volume to the Dead Sea Scrolls Microfiche Edition*, 2nd ed. [Leiden: E. J. Brill, 1995] 162).

Physical Description

The scroll is a heavy solid lump; it is like charcoal in both colour and texture, and is very brittle. At one time, the skin must have been sufficiently soft for the cylindrical shape of the scroll to have collapsed, resulting in the scroll's current, somewhat flattened, shape. Plenderleith noted that, since then, the scroll has become 'solidified into a pitch-like lump which breaks with a jet-black lustrous or resinous fracture' (*Examination*, 1). This black material appears to be the product of gelatinization and later congealation. The inner layer of the scroll physically resembles the black material at the end, a fact that Plenderleith ascribed to 'the prolonged action of water running through the scroll, as if through a tube, and doubtless coupled with bacterial action and followed later by a long period of desiccation' (*Examination*, 1). This would also account both for the interior of the scroll being filled with fine sand, and for the presence of sand grains embedded in the inner layers of the scroll. The skin of the few salvaged fragments is very thin, being *c.*0.18 mm (of the six measured fragments, four measured 0.18 mm, and the others 0.36 mm and 0.38 mm, the latter two presumably representing two thicknesses of leather). Many such layers can be seen in the wad represented by frg. 10. These fragments were of dark brown appearance with the ink being hard to detect without the aid of infra-red photography. Plenderleith suggested that the scroll was probably made of parchment rather than raw or tanned skin.

Since the 1960s, the processes of disintegration and gelatinization have progressed somewhat, with gelatinization now being apparent around the cut as well as at the original edges of the scroll. The recovered fragments, being very fragile, have also deteriorated substantially, so that they have been largely reduced to a sort of gelatinous dust. Consequently, the photographs taken in the early 1960s have had to be used in this volume. The scroll is now in such condition that it is impossible to unroll without causing more damage. It is to be hoped that technological advances (e.g. enabling the writing on the underside of one or more layers to be read without unrolling the scroll) may, at some future date, allow the remaining scroll to yield up its secrets.

Recovery of Readable Texts

Neither alcohol, ethyl ether, nor paraffin affected the scroll. Water caused gelatinization, and acetone tended to dissolve some brown matter without softening the skin. This left excision as the primary means of recovering fragments. Frg. 7 was removed using a scalpel, and was identified by Brownlee as containing text from Ezek 7:9ff. Three fragments were rendered temporarily legible by being bleached by a drop of ether containing hydrogen peroxide vapor, but within less than twenty minutes the material had turned to a sticky gelatin. The original state was seemingly recoverable by drying through the evaporation of a drop of alcohol containing ether. According to Brownlee (p. 13), the first (unphotographed) fragment (frg. 5) 'read clearly' תאכלנ ב (Ezek 4:10). The second fragment (frg. 8) was less distinct, but seemed to him to contain the words נתתה and תאכלנו (Ezek 4:9) on consecutive lines, although he then noted that 'the vestige of this fragment which appears in an infra-red photograph seems rather to support NTT . . . LHM, so that the identity of this fragment remains in doubt' (p. 13, n. 4). The third fragment (which may be frg. 4 or one of the miscellaneous fragments), according to Brownlee, contained the letters אש preceded by a space, although he noted that the space had crumbled from the beginning of the fragment before being photographed.

Frg. 3 was obtained by applying a piece of the thinnest white silk to the scroll surface with polyvinyl acetate emulsion adhesive while the adhesive was tacky. After fifteen minutes, when quite dry, the silk was carefully removed with many fractured and discontinuous fragments of scroll attached.

Next, Plenderleith sought to expose the inside surface, on which he hoped to find writing. He made three cuts using 'the finest rotary steel saw of the thinness of tissue as used in dental surgery' (p. 3). Two parallel cuts were made along the edges of the flattened cylinder in a longitudinal direction, as though to cut the scroll into two half cylinders. These appear to have been deep enough to cut through the layers of scroll, but not the sand inside. One transverse cut was also made, although the precise nature of this cut is not certain. From the photographs (the actual fragments have disintegrated to such a degree that the photographs now provide the clearest evidence), it seems probable that this third cut was made after the longitudinal cuts and parallel to the angle of the base of the scroll, thereby severing a relatively thin disk from the base. This seems to be confirmed by Plenderleith's comment that 'the saws met with an insuperable resistance on reaching black material. The fragments had to be separated at the resin boundary', which more easily relates to the top of the scroll. This reconstruction of Plenderleith's actions, however, results in three fragments, whereas only two have been photographed, and ignores Brownlee's comment that the transverse cut was made 'below the gelatinized knob at the top of the scroll' (p. 13). As a result of the dissections, some thin fragments flaked off, and the inside of the scroll was cleansed of sand. Neither these fragments, however, nor the scroll interior revealed any traces of writing when submitted to infra-red photography.

Contents

The identified fragments are as follows:

TABLE 1: *Contents of 11QEzek*

Frg.	Ezekiel	Reconstructed Column
1	1:8-10	I
2	4:3-5	III
3a	4:6	III
4–5	4:9-10	III
3b, 6	5:11-17	IV
7	7:9-12	V

Reconstruction Method

All measures of the amount of space occupied by a section of text have been made using 'reconstructed lengths' rather than the more traditional letter-counts, in order to take account of the varying sizes of the different letters of the Hebrew alphabet. For this purpose, the average width of each letter of the Hebrew alphabet was calculated on the basis of measurements of the actual widths of letters in the extant scroll fragments. For those few letters of which no extant example has survived, the average width was estimated as being 80 percent of the average for that letter in 1QM, a scroll with similar general letter shapes but written 25 percent larger than those for 11QEzek. The reconstructed length of a section of text is then calculated as the sum of the average widths of the letters which make up the text, and corresponds to the amount of space that the text could be expected to occupy if the scribe were writing each letter in an average fashion. For further details of the average letter widths for 1QM and the method for calculating average letter widths and reconstructed widths, see E. D. Herbert, *A New Method for Reconstructing Biblical Scrolls, and its Application to the Reconstruction of 4QSam[a]* (Ph.D. diss., Cambridge University, 1995) 6–29, 58–66 (forthcoming, E. J. Brill, Leiden). The resulting average letter widths in millimetres for 11QEzek (items in parentheses indicate that the average letter width was estimated using 1QM data) are: א 2; ב 1.7; ג 1.5; (ד 1.8); ה 2.2; ו 1.1; (ז 0.8); ח 2.1; ט 2.5; י 1.2; כ 1.4; ך 1.8; ל 1.6; מ 1.7; ם 2.1; נ 1.3; (ן 1); ס 2.3; ע 2.2; פ 1.5; (ף 2); (צ 2.2); (ץ 2.1); (ק 2.8); ר 1.6; ש 2.7; ת 2; space 0.8.

Use of reconstructed widths provides a more accurate measure of the line length than is possible with letter-counts. It can also help occasionally to identify likely margin positions where these are not extant, since the amount of text between the right margin and a vertical line drawn through an extant fragment should be similar for each line of the fragment. Such data, together with general considerations concerning the approximate position of each of the extant parts of cols. I, III, IV and V (see COLUMNS AND MEASUREMENTS, below), enabled the approximate margin positions of most of the identified fragments to be estimated.

Calculations of reconstructed line lengths (measured between the corresponding extant points on two consecutive lines, reconstructing the non-extant parts of the line on the basis of 𝔐) are shown in TABLE 2.

TABLE 2: *Line Lengths Reconstructed on the Basis of 𝔐*

Col.	Frg.	Line	Reconstructed Line Lengths (mm)	Notes
I	1	1–2	103.2	
		2–3	103.7	
III	2	1–2	73.8	*setuma* in 𝔐
		2–3	112.7	
	4–5	1–2	108.4	
IV	3b, 6	1–2	102.8	
		2–3	105.6	
		3–4	110.9	
		4–5	84.5	suggests deviation from 𝔐
		5–6	108	
		6–7	104.8	
		7–8	108.4	
V	7	1–2	102.4	
		2–3	104.7	
		3–4	101.7	

Apart from frg. 2 1–2, which probably includes a paragraph division (*setuma* in 𝔐), and frgs. 3b, 6 4–5, the consistency of reconstructed line lengths is striking, not only within columns but between columns as well. This indicates that, for each reconstructed *lacuna*, excepting frgs. 3b, 6 4–5, it is possible that 11QEzek followed the text of 𝔐. It is, of course, equally true that alternative reconstructions which do not involve significant changes to the overall amount of reconstructed text are possible. Consequently, where 𝔊 deviates from 𝔐 in a way that involves a minimal change in the amount of Hebrew text indicated, no judgement can be made as to which of these 11QEzek is more likely to have reflected. On the other hand, where 𝔊 suggests a Hebrew text which is substantially longer or shorter than that of 𝔐, a judgement will be made as to whether the overall line length is compatible with the plus or minus of 𝔊. In general terms, a deviation from the average line length of a column by more than 12 percent is considered as too great to be accounted for by a left margin not being justified together with variations in the size of the scribe's writing. For a more sophisticated method for determining the degree of variation in line length which should be allowed for before a reconstruction should be viewed as implausible, see Herbert, *New Method*, 58–66.

Columns and Measurements

Frg. 3 consists of a number of small fragments from more than one layer of the scroll which stuck to Plenderleith's piece of silk (see RECOVERY OF READABLE TEXTS). The presence of material from Ezek 4:6 and 5:15-16 in frg. 3 confirms that the fragments include material from corresponding points in different (almost certainly consecutive) columns. For the purpose of determining correspondence, the count of BHS-lines is the number of lines that would have been required if no stichometric arrangement had been used. There are 43.5 BHS-lines between the extant material of 4:6 and 5:16. Since the 4:6 material is one scroll-line lower than that of 5:16 (one scroll-line is approximately 1.5 BHS-lines), 45 BHS-lines between corresponding points of the two columns is suggested. Brownlee noted that all of the readable scroll fragments were obtained from the same side of the scroll, and it is quite likely that the main fragments have come from broadly corresponding points on successive revolutions. This corresponds with what is actually found, since the last extant material of Ezek 7:9-12 (frg. 7) is 39 BHS-lines after the extant material of 5:16, and the first extant material of 1:8-10 (frg. 1) is 91.5 BHS-lines before that of 4:3-5. As such, it is almost certain that the extant parts of chaps. 4, 5, and 7 are from consecutive columns and that the fragments preserving parts of chapter 1 come from two columns before those from chapter 4. The above data also suggests an average column-length of *c*.44 BHS-lines per column, based upon the average of the four columns between chapters 1 and 7. This is similar to the 45 BHS-lines which were estimated to be between corresponding points in consecutive columns from frg. 3. The extant fragment from chapter 1 suggests that the extant fragments are from the upper half of the scroll. This receives support from the fact that it is the upper half of the scroll which has survived. The data also suggests that the scroll, assuming that it contained the full text of Ezekiel, would have occupied approximately 44 columns. Examination of the scroll and of some of the large lumps that have been separated from it (presumably by Plenderleith) suggests that many of the columns (possibly all, since frg. 1 appears to preserve part of col. I) have been preserved. In light of this, Brownlee's reference to a mere seven visible layers (p. 12) is enigmatic.

The average lengths calculated for lines within each of the columns are between 102 mm and 111 mm (103.5 mm, 110.6 mm, 106.8 mm, and 102.9 mm, for cols. I, III, IV, and V, respectively; see RECONSTRUCTION METHOD), suggesting that each column, including its left margin gap, occupies approximately 120 mm. Since the circumference of the scroll is *c*.165 mm, each column, at least in the outer part of the scroll, occupies approximately three-quarters of a turn of the scroll. Reconstructing the scroll on this basis, it is only possible for the extant materials from cols. I, III, IV, and V to be directly above each other in the scroll if the material from col. III is from the right-hand third of the column, that from col. IV from the middle third of its column, and that from cols. I and V from the left-hand third of their columns. While such calculations are inevitably only approximate, especially since the extant fragments are not necessarily directly above each other, it is nonetheless a reasonable representation, yielding an arrangement of the fragments within their columns which is consistent with the available data. For each of the main fragments, a vertical line was drawn through the fragment, and an attempt was made to find possible positions of the fragment relative to the right margin for which the reconstructed widths of the right-hand section (i.e. the material between the right margin and the vertical line) were as similar as possible for the various lines of the fragment. For col. III, it has been noted that the extant fragments should be in the right-hand third (i.e. *c*.40 mm) of their respective columns. Within this range, the greatest consistency of reconstructed widths of the right-hand section is *c*.35 mm for frg. 2 (col. III). Moreover, such a position places the beginning of a new paragraph after a paragraph division at the start of line 2, adding to the likelihood that the suggested fragment location relative to the margin is correct. This positioning of frg. 2 would suggest a location for the main fragment of col. IV (frg. 6) at approximately 75 mm from the right margin, yielding a reasonable degree of consistency of reconstructed widths for the right-hand section (indeed, there is only one other margin position which would yield any comparable measure of consistency—approximately 26 mm to the right of that which is being suggested as most likely). The placement of frgs. 1 and 7 near the left margin of cols. I and V respectively places frgs. 1, 2, 6, and 7 (the main extant fragments in each column) roughly one above the other. The general consistency with the evidence that is obtained on the basis of the above makes it probable that the suggested fragment locations relative to the margins of the respective columns are correct. Nevertheless, although these fragment positions are likely, they are not certain. Interestingly, if frg. 1 were identified as 10:11-12 rather than 1:8-10 (see NOTES ON READINGS *ad loc.*) the margin position estimates for cols. III, IV and V would remain unchanged, and frg. 1 would be *c*.35 mm from the right margin of col. VII. The fragments have been placed in the suggested positions in the following reconstructions; however, due to the uncertainty, the positions have not been used as data towards decisions concerning the text to be reconstructed.

Given the estimate of 120 mm for the approximate column-width including inter-column gap, and assuming that the scroll contained the full text of 𝔐 Ezekiel, the length of the scroll can be estimated at 5–5.5 metres. Based upon an average line width of 105.9 mm (excluding lines 1–2 of frg. 2, and lines 4–5 of combined frgs. 3b and 6) and an average width of characters of 1.53 mm, a column in 11QEzek probably contained approximately thirty-one to thirty-two lines (cf. 1QIsa[a] with 28–32 lines in a column). The average line height (i.e. the gap between the tops of consecutive lines) is

5.3 mm. Assuming a top margin of 2 cm and a bottom margin of 3 cm (as in 1QIsa[a]), one may estimate a scroll height of *c*.21.5 cm. Since the extant scroll was only *c*.8 cm high, *pace* Plenderleith (p. 1) and Brownlee (p. 11) who measured it as 7.5 cm, one may estimate that, in 1962, perhaps 35 percent of the scroll had survived, while subsequent disintegration has reduced it even further. The above estimate of the length of the scroll is compatible with the 7.5 mm width between the outer and inner extant revolutions. This supports the generally Masoretic character of 11QEzek, although the imprecision of the calculations necessitates caution. On the basis of this evidence alone, it is not possible to rule out completely the possibility that 11QEzek might have contained a truncated text such as that reflected in 𝔊.

Palaeography and Date

The script in 11QEzek is mid-Herodian or possibly late early-Herodian. A date of *c*.10 BCE–30 CE is suggested on the basis of the typological sequences established by F. M. Cross, 'The Development of the Jewish Scripts', *The Bible and the Ancient Near East: Essays in Honor of William Foxwell Albright*, ed. G. Ernest Wright (Garden City, NY: Doubleday, 1961) 33–202. A Herodian dating is indicated by the baseline of *bet* being written with a separate pen stroke, by the broad head of final *kap*, and by the relatively wide shoulder of some (but not all) of the *lameds*. A mid-Herodian date rather than an early Herodian date is suggested by the basic *keraiai* at the top of the right arm of some (but not all) of the *ʾaleps*, and especially by medial *mem* with its left diagonal stroke written first as the beginning of a continuous motion which also draws the right downstroke and the baseline; the inconsistent occurrence of the late forms of *ʾalep* and *lamed* noted above makes a late Herodian date unlikely. The right arm of *šin* curves, with a thickened end which does not closely approach the central arm, suggesting that the date range be expanded to include the possibility of late early-Herodian as well as the more likely mid-Herodian dating; thus *c*.10 BCE–30 CE is probable. Brownlee's dating of the scroll (pp. 19–28) to *c*.55–25 BCE is too early.

Orthography, Paragraph Division, and Scribal Character

11QEzek preserves the following orthographic variations from 𝔐:

TABLE 3: *Orthography*

Frg.	Line	Ezekiel	11QEzek	𝔐
3b	5	5:15	והית	והיתה
3b	7	5:16	אׄתׄם	אותם

In both orthographic variations of 11QEzek from 𝔐, the scroll attests defective spellings, although in the first case it is unclear whether the scroll's reading is a defective spelling of the 2nd masc. sing. form found in 𝔊𝔗𝔖𝔙, or of the 3rd fem. sing. reading found in 𝔐 (see VARIANTS below).

Only in frg. 1 1–2 is there any evidence of a paragraph division in the extant parts of 11QEzek. This corresponds to a *setuma* in 𝔐, which is the only paragraph division in 𝔐 for a passage that is extant in 11QEzek.

No scribal errors or corrections are apparent in the recovered text.

Textual Character

Brownlee noted a number of instances where 11QEzek followed the text of 𝔐, especially where 𝔊 substantially deviated from 𝔐 (e.g. in the order of verses in Ezekiel 7). He also noted three occasions where, in his opinion, 11QEzek probably broadly followed 𝔊 against 𝔐. It has been noted above, however, that 11QEzek did not follow 𝔊 in two cases (the omission of the copula of ובתכחות in Ezek 5:15, and the putative omission of two words in Ezek 5:13), and the third case (והית in Ezek 5:15) remains unclear. This does not mean that 11QEzek always followed the text of 𝔐, as the absence of the copula in Ezek 5:15 and the evident lack of sufficient text from 𝔐 to fill the available space in frg. 6 3–4 demonstrate. There appears, however, to be no evidence for the agreement of 11QEzek with 𝔊 against 𝔐, since, *pace* Brownlee (p. 15), the absence of the copula in Ezek 15:5 is best viewed as unrelated to its absence from 𝔊. In light of the above, 11QEzek should be viewed as broadly Masoretic in that it does not show evidence of agreement with 𝔊, but not in the sense that it is incapable of deviating from 𝔐.

Mus. Inv. 1010, 1013, 1013A
PAM 43.731, 43.732*, 43.742, 43.743, 43.744*, 43.745*, 43.745A*, 43.750B

Frg. 1 Ezek 1:8-10

1] א]רׄבעתׄ[
2 9]]סׄבו בלכׄ[תם
3 10] לארב[עתׄ]ם

NOTES ON READINGS

Frg. 1 should be placed at or near the left margin. This has not been adequately represented above, since the actual column is significantly wider than the printed page allows. Technically, frg. 1 could be identified as Ezek 10:11-12, which would then yield viable reconstructed line widths of 103.2 mm and 103.7 mm for lines 1–2 and 2–3 respectively. Moreover, it would be in the upper part of col. VII in a position fully consistent with the positions of the other fragments of col. V). It is, however, improbable that this fragment would have been salvaged from two layers *beneath* the extant remains of col. V (which were obtained by the elaborate mechanism described in RECOVERY OF READABLE TEXTS, without Plenderleith indicating how he had obtained the fragment). If, however, frg. 1 is indeed from col. I, then it may have been separated from the scroll without difficulty, thus explaining Plenderleith's silence on the matter.

L. 3 (10:12)]עׄתׄ[. Brownlee blacked out the remnant of line 3, 'because this fragment is wrongly placed in the photograph' (p. 16, n. 8). The clear compatibility of line 3 on the plate with לארבעתם in the middle of 1:10, and the resulting reconstructed length for lines 2–3 (103.7 mm) being so close to that for lines 1–2 (103.2 mm) make the positioning look probable. Since it would appear that Brownlee did not place it there, the most natural explanation for its placement in that position is that it is (or at least was) actually connected to the rest of frg. 1, although certainty on this point is not possible.

Frg. 2 Ezek 4:3-5

1]]וׄצרת עליהׄ[

2]4 השמ]אׄלי ושׂמ[ת

3] 5 נת]תי לךׄ[

NOTES ON READINGS

Frg. 2 consists of two separate fragments, which meet in line 2. The positioning of the fragment relative to the right margin, as shown here, is probable, since it yields the greatest measure of consistency of reconstructed lengths for the right-hand section that is obtainable whilst keeping the fragment in or near the right-hand 40 mm of the column, as suggested above (see COLUMNS AND MEASUREMENTS). This positioning is more likely, since it results in a new paragraph (v 4) beginning at the start of a new line (line 2).

POSSIBLE RECONSTRUCTION

4:4 (2b) הימים 𝔐𝔊^{pc}ℭ𝔖𝔙] των ημερων πεντηκοντα και εκατον 𝔊 (= חמשים ומאה יום*?).

If 𝔊's plus were present in 11QEzek, the reconstructed length of lines 2–3 would increase by 14.4 mm to 127.1 mm—too long compared with the column average of 110.6 mm to be plausible.

Frg. 3a Ezek 4:6

] ל]שנה נׄתׄתיו לךׄ[

NOTES ON READINGS

This is the lower line of the main body of frg. 3, which, together with material from Ezek 5:15-16, adhered to Plenderleith's piece of silk. The fragment has been placed approximately 40 mm closer to the right margin than the extant material in frg. 3b (whose position relative to the right margin can be estimated), since frgs. 3a and 3b lie one revolution apart, with a revolution being *c.*160 mm—approximately equivalent to a column plus 40 mm.

Frgs. 4–5 Ezek 4:9-10

] לל]חם[

] [10]ומאכל]ךׄ אש]ר [תאכלנו ב[משקול

NOTES ON READINGS

Frg. 5 (תאכלנו ב) has been recorded solely on the basis of Brownlee's account of it (p. 13), since the fragment was not photographed and has since disintegrated. Since Brownlee did not indicate where letters were unclear, it is possible that some uncertainty of readings existed. It is also unclear whether Brownlee's description (p. 13) of a fragment that contained the letters אש preceded by a space relates to frg. 4.

POSSIBLE RECONSTRUCTION

4:9 (1b) שלש מאות ותשעים 𝔐𝔊^{pc}𝔗𝔖𝔙] ενενηκοντα και εκατον 𝔊 (= מאה ותשעים*).

If the latter reading were present in 11QEzek, the reconstructed length of lines 1–2 would be reduced by 8.7 mm to 99.7 mm. Whilst this would be significantly lower than the 110.6 mm average line length for col. III, it is not low enough for the possibility to be discounted.

Frgs. 3b and 6 Ezek 5:11-17

] ו]גם אני אׄ[גרע

] [12] יכ]לוׄ בתׄוׄכך וה[שלשית

3] אחר]יהם [13]וכלה אפי[

4] חמ]תי בם [14]ואתנך[

5] עוב]ר [15]והית חרפה וג]דופה]מוסר ומ]שמה

6] באף ובח]מה בתכחות חמה אני יהוה ד]ברתי

7 [16]] ל]משחית א]שר א]של]ח]אתם לשחת]כם

8] וש]לחתי על]יכם[17]

Notes on Readings

In the above reconstruction, frgs. 3b and 6 are placed approximately 5 mm (3 characters) closer to the right margin than they are believed to have been. The suggested positioning results in a high degree of consistency of reconstructed line lengths, and yields reasonably consistent reconstructed widths for the right-hand section for frg. 2, when it is placed within its column, *c*.40 mm to the right of where frg. 6 is positioned within its column.

L. 2 (5:12) בתוכך. *Waw* is clearly present, *pace* Brownlee (pp. 14–15).

L. 5 (5:15) מוסר ומ]שמה. Breaks in the skin and the shifting of parts of the letters makes a reading difficult. While the remnants fit the suggested reading, the reconstruction remains uncertain. Nevertheless, Brownlee's identification of these remains as גדופ of וגדופ]ה (p. 14) is implausible, both because it is incompatible with the extant remains in frg. 3b and because it overlooks the significant *lacuna* between the extant start of וגדופה in frg. 6 and the remains here.

L. 6 (5:15) אני. The *yod* of אני has split lengthways along the stroke, so that its left part together with the very bottom of *nun* and the left leg of *ʾalep* have moved significantly leftwards.

L. 7 (5:16)]אתם. The top of the *taw* of אתם, together with *ʾalep*, have shifted upwards and to the right of the rest of the word.

Variants

5:15 (5) והית **]** והיתה 𝔐; והיית* 𝔊ℭ𝔖𝔙

11QEzek could preserve either a defective spelling (only one *yod*) of 𝔊ℭ𝔖𝔙's 2nd masc. sing. form, as Brownlee (p. 15) suggests, or a defective orthographic variation of 𝔐's 3rd fem. sing. reading.

5:15 (5) מוסר ומ]שמה 𝔐𝔊^{mlt}α′σ′θ′ℭ𝔖𝔙 **]** > 𝔊

Even if one disputes this reading, 11QEzek could not have lacked these two words with 𝔊, since that would reduce the length of lines 5–6 by 18.1 mm to 89.9 mm, producing a line too short compared with the average line length for col. IV of 106.8 mm.

5:15 (6) באף ובח]מה 𝔐𝔊^{pl}σ′ℭ𝔖𝔙 **]** > 𝔊

5:15 (6) בתכחות 𝔊^{pc} **]** ובתכחות 𝔐𝔊^{pl}ℭ𝔖𝔙.

Although it too lacks the *waw*, 𝔊 also lacks the two preceding words (באף ובחמה) to which the *waw* of ובתכחות was linked, so that it cannot be said to reflect the reading of either 11QEzek or 𝔐, *pace* Brownlee (p. 15), who views the absence of the copula in these witnesses as reflecting 11QEzek's reading.

5:16 (7–8) אׄ[שר א]שׄל[ח]אׄתם לשחׄתׄ[כם ורעב אסף עליכם 𝔐𝔊^{pl}θ′ℭ𝔖𝔙] >𝔊

Reconstructed Variants

5:12 (2a) וברעב 𝔐ℭ𝔖𝔙] και το τεταρτον σου εν λιμω (וארבעתיך ברעב*)𝔊.

If 11QEzek reflected 𝔊's reading but otherwise followed 𝔐, the length of lines 1–2 would increase by 13.3 mm to 116.1 mm—sufficiently high compared with the average line length of 106.8 mm for col. IV to make it unlikely, but insufficient to allow 𝔊's use of four 'quarters' in v 12 instead of 𝔐ℭ𝔖𝔙's three 'thirds' to be discounted on the basis of space considerations.

5:13 (3–4) והנחותי חמתי בם והנחמתי 𝔐α′σ′θ′ℭ𝔖𝔙] και η οργη μου επ αυτους και παρακλη-θησομαι (וחמתי בם והנחמתי*) 𝔊^{pl}; και η οργη μου επ αυτους (וחמתי בם*) 𝔊

If 11QEzek followed 𝔐 except for missing either והנחותי or והנחמתי (with 𝔊), the reconstructed length of lines 3–4 would be reduced by 10.7 mm and 12.4 mm respectively, to line lengths of 100.2 mm and 98.5 mm, respectively, or 87.8 mm if both words were absent, compared with an average line length of 106.8 mm for col. IV. The absence of one of these words is therefore possible, although reconstruction on the basis of 𝔐 yields a length that is closer to the column average. The possibility that both are lacking can be discounted with confidence. Brownlee (p. 15) sees the absence of one or both of these words as required since he calculates space using letter-counts rather than reconstructed widths. A case such as this, where the line has a particularly high proportion of narrow letters, demonstrates the benefit of using reconstructed letter widths when assessing the amount of space available for reconstruction.

5:14 (4–5) ולחרפה בגוים אשר 𝔐𝔊^{pc}σ′ℭ𝔖𝔙] και τας θυγατερας σου (ובנותיך*) 𝔊; + κυκλω σου και τας θυγατερας σου (+ סביבותיך ובנותיך*) 𝔊^{pl}θ′

While it is certain that 11QEzek contained a longer text than is found in either 𝔐 or 𝔊, since these result in line lengths for lines 4–5 of only 84.5 mm and 69.1 mm, respectively, it is quite likely that 11QEzek reflected the reading of 𝔊^{pl}θ′ or something similar, since, assuming that 11QEzek followed 𝔐 elsewhere in the line, this would result in a reconstructed length of 109.3 mm, which is close to the column average of 106.8 mm.

5:16 (7a) הרעים 𝔐𝔊^{mlt}θ′(ℭ)𝔖𝔙] >𝔊

1QEzek reflected the minus of 𝔊, but reflected 𝔐 elsewhere in the line, the reconstructed width would be reduced by 10.1 mm to 93.7 mm. The resulting line would be too short compared with the 106.8 mm average line length for col. IV to be plausible.

Frg. 7 Ezek 7:9-12

1] 9 ת]ח֯ו֯ס ע֯י[ני

2] [יהוה מכ֯ה֯] 10

3] 11]למטה רשע לא מ[הם

4] 12 י]שמ[ח

Notes on Readings

Frg. 7 should be placed at or near the left margin, i.e. approximately 40 mm to the left of the positioning of frg. 6. This has not been adequately represented above, since the actual column is significantly wider than the printed page allows.

Reconstructed Variants

7:9-10 (2–3) $\mathfrak{G}$ placed vv 3-5 of $\mathfrak{MCSV}$ between vv 9 and 10. 11QEzek follows $\mathfrak{MCSV}$, for the space is not available to fit three extra verses between the extant parts of lines 2 and 3.

7:11 (3–4) . . . לא מ[הם $\mathfrak{M}\mathfrak{G}^{pl}\mathfrak{SV}$] $\mathfrak{G}$ reflects only two of the four negative phrases of $\mathfrak{M}$. It is unlikely that 11QEzek lacked any of the four negative phrases of $\mathfrak{M}$, and almost certain that it did not lack two, since, even when reconstructed with all four, the reconstructed length is slightly below the column average.

Unidentified Fragments

Frg. 3, which comprises a range of tiny fragments which adhered to Plenderleith's piece of silk, includes materials from cols. III and IV (frgs. 3a and 3b above), together with a plethora of mostly tiny unidentified fragments. Brownlee (p. 17), however, identified פניך אל ב, by asserting that three fragments on the right side of frg. 3 which have been twisted in a variety of directions (אל which has been twisted clockwise by 90 degrees, a possible final *kap* which has been twisted by 180 degrees, and פנ֯י֯) were originally contiguous. These readings are plausible (אל is certain), and Brownlee's juxtaposition is possible, although his assumption that the word after אל begins with a *bet* appears not to be based on ink from the same layer of the scroll. On the basis of the reading (including the *bet*), he identifies these fragments as being from Ezek 13:17. This is improbable, since it would place these fragments in col. X or XI, though no other fragments that adhere to the silk were outside of cols. III and IV. Indeed, the extant אל that is on a stratum that appears lighter in colour is at least one layer *behind* the extant material from 5:15-16, as Brownlee observes (p. 17), but this requires that אל be closer to the outside of the scroll rather than, as Brownlee assumes, nearer the inside. If Brownlee's juxtaposition of the three little fragments is correct, as it may well be, this might suggest their identification as being from Ezek 4:3. Although there appears to be a space after אל, which would be problematical for this identification, the general disfigurement and fragmentation of both skin and ink apparent in frg. 3 makes the existence of this space uncertain. Nevertheless, the uncertainty concerning the identification of Ezek 4:3 is sufficient for it not to be included as a positive identification.

The moderately large fragment on the lower left side of frg. 3 is the result of overlapping letters presumably from different layers of the scroll coupled with displacements and disfigurements. Although much ink has survived, the overlaps and disfigurements make it hard to read any character combinations except what appear to be two *lameds* (לל) adjacent to each other in the middle of the fragment.

Frg. 8

1]]נ̊תת[ה

2]]הם ל[

NOTES ON READINGS

Frg. 8 is actually comprised of two smaller fragments, with most of *lamed* and the left tip of final *mem* having become separated from the main fragment. Using a drop of ether containing hydrogen peroxide vapour, Brownlee (p. 13) noted that 'it seemed to have upon it a small vertical section out of two lines containing the words NTTH . . . T'KLNW from 4,9', but then notes (p. 13, n. 4) that 'the vestige of this fragment which appears in an infra-red photograph seems rather to support NTT . . . LHM, so that the identity of this fragment remains in doubt'. Despite Brownlee's comments, the infra-red photograph makes the bottom line clear as reading]הם ל[, raising significant difficulties with his identification of the fragment as being from Ezek 4:9.

Frg. 9

1]]ג̊[

5. 11QPsalms^{a}, Fragments E, F

(PLATES IV–V)

Previous discussion: Y. Yadin, 'Another Fragment (E) of the Psalms Scroll from Qumran Cave 11 (11QPs^{a})', *Textus* 5 (1966) 1–10, Plates I–V; J. A. Sanders, *The Dead Sea Psalms Scroll* (Ithaca, New York: Cornell University Press, 1967) 155–65.

SUBSEQUENT to the publication of 11QPs^{a} in *DJD* IV, two further fragments have become known. Frg. E was published preliminarily by Y. Yadin, 'Another Fragment', while the tiny frg. F is published here for the first time.[1]

Physical Description

The fragments are, like the scroll, tanned animal skin, brown in hue, considerably darker than the infra-red photographs would indicate. Frg. E is just less than 1 mm thick, and at its widest points measures 13.5 long and 36.5 cm wide.

The line spacing of frg. E corresponds to that of the main body of the scroll and varies from 0.85 cm to 1 cm; the column margins between the ruled vertical lines are 2.1 cm.

Frg. E contains the remains of three columns; those on the right (col. i) and the left (col. iii) are defective at their right and left sides respectively, while in the centre column (col. ii) both margins have been preserved. All three columns lack the bottom parts and considerable portions of their top parts which were eaten away.

Contents

Frg. E i preserves remains of: Ps 118:24-29 and 104:1-6; frg. E ii: Ps 104:22-35 and 147:1-2; frg. E iii: Ps 147:18-20 and 105:1*, 1–11. Frg. F perhaps contains Ps 147:3.

Palaeography

A detailed description of the palaeography of 11QPs^{a} has been given by Sanders in *DJD* IV, 6–9. The hand of frgs. E and F is identical to the hand of the main body of the scroll. It may be noted that this hand differs from those of the other 11Q manuscripts, and that the identification of frg. F was based first of all on the characteristics of the script.

Orthography

For the orthography of 11QPs^{a}, cf. Sanders's discussion in *DJD* IV, 9–13. In frg. E *plene* writing with *waw* is consistent, whereas the use of *yod* is consistent with the

[1] The re-edition of frg. E is based upon Yadin's publication, but revisions have been made where necessary.

orthography of 𝔐 (except for דויד and ירושלים). The 2nd masc. sing. perfect affix, and pronominal suffix are written with final *he*. Final *he* also occurs in col. ii 5 (Ps 104:25) שמה against 𝔐 שם (cf. COMMENTS), but not with the 3rd masc. pl. suffix. Remarkable is the inconsistent use of *nun paragogicum* in col. ii 6–9 (Ps 104:26-30): יהלכון, ישברו, וילקטון, ישבעו, ויגועו, ישובו, ויבראון, where 𝔐 has the *nun* in all these cases. In view of the consistency of the *plene* orthography with *waw*, and the long forms of the 2nd masc. sing., this orthography has also been used in the reconstruction of the text.

Frg. E and 11QPs[a]

11QPs[a], as published by Sanders, consists of four fragments and the main body of the scroll. As stated by Sanders, and clearly indicated by his facsimiles, 'the four fragments . . . probably derive from the sheet or sheets immediately preceding the extant sections of the scroll' (*DJD* IV, 3). Yadin demonstrated that since frg. E terminates with Ps 105:11, and Sanders's col. I begins with Ps 105:24, frg. E should be placed immediately before col. I. Psalm 119, which is copied in the scroll in the alphabetic acrostic arrangement of eight verse-lines to the letter with a blank line-space between the groups, makes it clear that each column of the scroll had twenty-five lines. This number of lines fits frg. E exactly, since the bottom of frg. E iii can be reconstructed as eight lines containing Ps 105:12-24.

Frg. E also sheds some more light on the beginning of the scroll. The appearance of Psalm 104 in frg. E i 6–ii 14 indicates that frg. C II 12 preserves the beginning of Psalm 103, and not of Psalm 104. Likewise, the appearance of Psalm 105 in frg. E iii, shows that Sanders's suggestion (*DJD* IV, 21) that 'Ps. 105 could have followed directly' after Psalm 109 on frg. D should be dismissed.

With regard to the reconstruction of the beginning of the scroll, the following facts can be established. The reconstruction of the lines of frgs. A, B, C II shows that Psalm 101 started at the beginning of the column. This may indicate that Psalm 101 was the first Psalm of the scroll, but cf. col. III which starts with Psalm 121, albeit preceded by a *vacat*. The Masoretic text of Psalms 103 and 109:1-21 fits between the bottom of frg. C II and frg. D if one reconstructs between those fragments an extra column with a slightly larger width than frg. D. It is therefore possible that the first four columns of the scroll contained Psalms 101-103, and 109.

The position of frg. D in relation to frg. E is less certain. The Masoretic text of Ps 118:1-24 is too long to fit exactly between frg. D and frg. E i: line 25 of the column beginning with frg. D line 1 would have ended with Ps 118:20 or 21. Though it is possible that the text of 11QPs[a] was shorter than the Masoretic text, the possibility that one or more columns between frgs. D and E have been lost should be considered too.

The loss of one or more columns between frgs. D and E cannot be excluded, as is shown by the loss of a complete column between frg. C II and frg. D. In this edition we will not discuss the possible contents of such missing columns, but point out some material aspects of the fragments in relation to the scroll and the possible implications.

It is clear that the shape of frg. E is not consistent with the pattern of damage visible in the four separate leaves recovered from the main body of the scroll (cols. I–VI): 'decomposition along one side of the rolled scroll had destroyed the three or so layers of skin which had originally been continuous' (*DJD* IV, 3). Frg. E, on the other hand, preserves two full revolutions of the scroll without this decomposition which affected the scroll, implying that frg. E had become detached from the scroll before this particular damage occurred. Sanders's description of the disintegration of the fine threads connecting the sheets offers a plausible explanation for this detachment: frg. E (as well as the more exterior fragments) may have loosened from the scroll if frg. E and 11QPs[a] I belonged to two different sheets which were separated by the disintegration of the connecting thread. The assumption that 11QPs[a] I was the first column of a sheet is corroborated by the pattern of the ruling lines of cols. I-VII. The sheet consisting of cols. I–VII is longer than any of the following sheets (seven columns, *c.*98 cm), but not much more than the sheet consisting of cols. XIV–XIX (six columns, 87 cm). Hence, frg. E preserves the last three columns of a sheet.

Much more problematic is frg. D. One should note that the assumption that the line ending with ש]מכה כי טוב is the first line of the column is uncertain. Above this line there are traces which may indicate two more lines. In that case the text of Psalms 103 and 109 may still fit in a missing column of the same width as frg. C II. It is, however, clear that the reconstruction of the lines of frg. D results in a column width of 11–11.5 cm, whereas cols. A+B+C I, C II, and E i–iii all measured *c.*13 cm. Comparison with the other sheets shows that, except for the last sheet, narrower columns occur at the end of the sheet (frg. E iii measures *c.*12.5 cm, as opposed to *c.*13.5 cm in frg. E i–ii; col. VII is less wide than col. VI; cols. XII and XIII are more than 2 cm narrower than the preceding columns; cols. XVIII and XIX measure 1 cm less than cols. XIV–XVII; col. XXIV also is 1 cm less wide than cols. XX–XXIII). Hence, one may assume that frg. D belongs to the final or penultimate column of a sheet. Since all sheets consist of at least five columns (the last sheet has four columns and a large handling page), one is inclined to assume at least two lost columns between frg. D and frg. E.

The transliteration is based upon the combined evidence of the infra-red photographs taken before (SHR 6213, 6214, 6216, 6222) and after (SHR 6221) the cleaning of the fragment, since both sets of photographs reveal traces which are less visible, or not at all visible in the other. The non-infra-red photograph, sent to Yadin before he aquired the fragment, shows in addition at the bottom left (frg. E iii 15–16), a piece which does not appear on the infra-red photographs (cf. Yadin, Plate I).

Mus. Inv. 614B, 976
PAM 44.008*
SHR 6213, 6214, 6216*, 6221, 6222

Frg. E i Ps 118:25-29; Ps 104:1-6

top margin ?

]ונשמחה בו 118:25אנא 𐤉𐤄𐤅𐤄 [הושיעה נא אנא 𐤉𐤄𐤅𐤄

]הצליחה נ[א֯ 26ברו֯ך֯[ה]בא֯ בׄשם 𐤉𐤄𐤅𐤄 ברכנוכם {בׄשׄםׄ}

]מבית [𐤉֯𐤄𐤅𐤄 27אל 𐤉𐤄𐤅𐤄 ויאר לנו אסורי֯ חג בעבותים

]עד קר[נות המזבח 28אלי אתה ואודכה אלוהי ארוממכה

5 [29הודו]ל֯𐤉𐤄𐤅𐤄 כי טוב כי לעולם חסדו *vacat*

6 [*vacat*] *vacat* לדויד 104:1ברכי נפשי

7 [את 𐤉𐤄𐤅𐤄 𐤉𐤄]𐤅𐤄 אלוהינו גדלתה מואדה ה֯ו֯ד

8 [והדר לבשתה 2עוטה א]ור כשלמה נוטה שמים כיריע֯ה֯

9 [3המקרה במים עליותיו ה]שם עבים רכובו המהלך על

10 [כנפי רוח 4עושה מלאכיו ר]ו֯ח֯[ות מ]ש֯ר֯ת֯יו אש לוהטת

11 [5יסד ארץ על מכוניה בל תמוט עולם ו]ע֯ד֯ 6ת֯הום

Mus. Inv. 976
SHR 6213, 6216*, 6221, 6222

NOTES ON READINGS

Yadin argued that line 1 is the first line of the column, as attested to by the lack of any signs of a possible previous line at the top. However, there may be some traces at the very top, even if it is not sure whether these are ink. On the other hand, the available space between frg. E and Sanders's col. I is consistent with the placement of the fragment at the top of the column.

L. 1 אנא 𐤉𐤄𐤅𐤄. In the infra-red photograph of the fragment taken before the cleaning, some of the letters (א 𐤉𐤄) are partially covered by a small piece of skin which, erroneously, had not been removed when the photograph was taken. These letters on this piece of skin, stuck upside down on the fragment, can be read]◦ ת֯מ֯י֯ד֯[, and if this small fragment stems from one of the columns of frg. E, it should be placed in frg. E iii 11.

L. 2 (118:25-26) נ]א֯ ברו֯ך֯[ה]בא֯. Yadin's transliteration (נא] ברו[ך הבא) disregards minute remains of letters.

L. 2 (118:26) {ב֯ש֯ם֯}. The word was cancelled by dots above the letters. Later the letters themselves were erased. Cf. frg. E iii 13.

L. 3 (118:27) אסורי. The broader head of the last letter suggests *yod* rather than *waw*, but the distinction is not always consistent.

L. 7 (104:1) ה֯ו֯ד. Yadin claimed that careful examination shows the reading to be definite, but the first letter especially is difficult in the photographs.

L. 10 (104:4) מלאכיו ר]ו֯ח֯[ות. Certainly not מל[א]כיו רוחות (Yadin).

COMMENTS

L. 2 (118:26) {ב֯ש֯ם֯}. By mistake the scribe wrote בשם after ברכנוכם and then erased it. In any case the position of 𝔐𐤉𐤄𐤅𐤄 (line 3) at the end of the verse demands מבית to precede it.

L. 3 (118:27) אסורי חג. If we read אסורו חג (cf. דרושו for 𝔐 דרשו in Ps 105:4), the reading conforms with 𝔐 and the versions, and the difficulties emanating from this *hapax legomenon* remain (cf. the commentaries, particularly ICC). However, on palaeographical grounds, a strong, although admittedly not decisive case can be made for reading אסורי. This reading implies that the object of the verse is the festal animals, and the עבותים are actual ropes as in Judg 16:11 ואסרוני בעבתים; *ib.*, 15:13 ויאסרהו בשנים עבתים; Ezra 3:25 נתנו עליך עבתים ואסרוך בהם.

L. 5 (118:29) [הודו]. The reconstruction according to 𝔐 is slightly too short for the available space.

L. 11 (104:5) Even though the gap is very long, and the letters and spaces might be expanded, the text of 𝔐 seems two to three letters too short. Possible variant readings are יוסד, הארץ, or לעולם.

Variants

118:27 (3) אסורי] אסרו 𝔐
104:1 (6) לדויד 𝔊] > 𝔐
104:1 (7) אלוהינו] אלהי 𝔐𝔊
104:4 (10) לוהטת] להט 𝔐; πῦρ φλέγον 𝔊

Frg. E ii Ps 104:21-35; Ps 147:1-2

1 [חיתו יער [104:21]הכפירים ש]אֿגֿ[ים לטרף ולבקש מאל אוכלם [22]תזרח]
2 השמש ויאספון ואֿל מעונותיהם [ירבצון [23]יצא אדם]
3 לפועלו ולעבודתו עד ערב [24]מה רבו מעשֿ[י]כֿ[ה 𐤉𐤄𐤅𐤄]
4 כולם בחוכ^מה עשיתה מלאה הארץ קנינכה [25]הים גֿ[דול]
5 ורחב ידים שמה רמש הרבה ואין למספר חיות קטֿנֿ[ות]
6 עם גדולות [26]שם אוניות יהלכון לויתן זה יצרתה לשחק
7 בו [27]כולם אליכה ישברו לתת להם אוכלם בעתו [28]תתן להם
8 וילקטון תפתח ידכה ישבעו טוב [29]תוסף רוחכה ויגועו
9 ואל עפרם ישובו [30]תשלח רוחכה ויבראון ותחדש פני
10 אדמה [31]ויהי כבוד 𐤉𐤄𐤅𐤄 לעולם ישמח 𐤉𐤄𐤅𐤄 במעשיו
11 [[32]המ]בֿיט אל הארץ ותרעד יגע בהרים ויעשֿו [33]אשירה
12 [ל𐤉𐤄]𐤅ֿ𐤄 בחיי אזמרה *vac* לאלוהי בעודי [34]יערב עליו שיחי
13 [אנוכי אשמח ב]𐤉ֿ𐤄𐤅𐤄 [35]כאשר יתמו חוטאים מארץ
14 [ורשעים עוד אינם *vac?* ב]רֿכֿי נפשֿי אתֿ 𐤉𐤄𐤅𐤄 הללויה
15 [[147:1]הללויה *vacat* [*vacat*
16 [כי טוב זמרה אלוהינו כי נעים נאוה ת]הלה [2]בונה ירושלים

Mus. Inv. 976
SHR 6213, 6214, 6216*, 6221, 6222

Notes on Readings

There is a slight possibility that frg. F should be placed at the end of line 17 (cf. discussion below).

L. 1 (104:21) ש]אֿגֿ[ים. Yadin identified with certainty a trace of *šin* in the infra-red photograph taken before cleaning (in the photograph taken since the cleaning, the protrusion has broken off), but the identification of the first angular trace with the *šin* of ולבקש disregards the following traces and implies a *vacat* at the end of the line. However, comparison with 𝔐 suggests the traces should correspond to שאגים. The three vertical strokes may be the two legs of *ʾalep* and the right leg of *gimel*, whereas the dot at the very right part of the protrusion may be the bottom left tip of *šin*. If this identification is correct, the line would have continued into the margin.

L. 4 (104:24) בחוכ֯ה. The *mem* was added by the scribe above the *he*.

L. 11 (104:32) ויעשׁ֯ו. The *nun* was added by the scribe above the *waw*.

L. 12 (104:33) לאלוהי *vac.* The word is written after a short blank space due to a flaw in the skin.

COMMENTS

L. 5 (104:25) שמה. The spelling of שם in 11QPs^a is not consistent. It appears as שם, as in 𝔐, in line 6 (104:26), col. VI 8 (132:17), col. XX 1 (139:10), and 17 (137:1), but as שמה in col. III 9 (122:4) and col. XXIII 10 (133:3). 𝔐 שמה (122:5) is broken in col. III 10: ש֯[.

L. 13 (104:35) מארץ. Note that in the two cases where 11QPs^a overlaps with 𝔐, the preposition מן is joined to the next word with assimilation of the *nun*, and that מן as a separate word is not attested at all in 11QPs^a. Cf. col. II 1 משמים against 𝔐 מן השמים.

L. 15 (147:1) הללויה]. The entire missing text of the beginning of Psalm 147 does not fit in the gap of line 16. Therefore one must assume either a shorter variant reading, an omission, or that הללויה was written on a separate line, as in 𝔐. This last possibility is the most elegant, but note that such a procedure is not attested in the remainder of 11QPs^a.

VARIANTS

Ps 104:22 (2) ויאספון 𝔊] יאספון 𝔐
Ps 104:22 (2) מעונותיהם Cf. Jer 21:13; Job 37:8] מעונתם 𝔐.
Ps 104:23 (3) עד] עדי 𝔐
Ps 104:25 (4) הים] זה הים 𝔐𝔊
Ps 104:25 (5) שמה] שם 𝔐
Ps 104:25 (5) הרבה] > 𝔐𝔊
Ps 104:25 (5) למספר] מספר 𝔐
Ps 104:27 (7) להם] > 𝔐𝔊
Ps 104:28 (8) וילקטון] ילקטון 𝔐𝔊
Ps 104:29 (8) >] תסתיר פניך יבהלון 𝔐𝔊
Ps 104:29 (8) רוחכה] רוחם 𝔐 𝔊
Ps 104:29 (8) ויגועו 𝔊] יגועון 𝔐
Ps 104:30 (9) ויבראון 𝔊] יבראון 𝔐
Ps 104:31 (10) ויהי] יהי 𝔐𝔊
Ps 104:32 (11) אל הארץ] לארץ 𝔐
Ps 104:35 (13) כאשר] > 𝔐
Ps 104:35 (13) חוטאים] חַטָּאִים 𝔐
Ps 104:35 (13) מארץ] מן הארץ 𝔐

Frg. E iii Ps 147:18-20; Ps 105:1*, 1–11

[18]ישלח דבר֯ו֯] וימסם ישב רוחו יזלו מים [19]מגיד דברו ליעקוב[
חוקיו ומשפטיו ל֯]ישראל [20]לוא עשה כן לכול גוי[
משפטים בל הודיע֯ם] הללויה *vacat* [

[105:1*]הודו ל𐤉𐤄𐤅𐤄 כי טוב כי] לעולם חסדו [1]הודו ל𐤉𐤄𐤅𐤄 קראו]
בשמו הודיעו בעמים עלי]לותיו [2]שירו לו זמרו לו שיחו]
בכול נפלאותיו [3]התהללו בשם ק]ודשו ישמח לב מבקש]
רצונו [4]דרושו 𐤉𐤄𐤅𐤄 ועוזו בקשו] פניו]תמיד [5]ז]כורו]
נפלאותיו אשר עשה מופתיו ומשפט]י פיו [6]זרע אברהם]
{עֹבֹוֹדֹ} עבדיו בני יעקוב בחירו [7]כי הוא 𐤉]𐤄𐤅𐤄 ובארץ]
משפטיו [8]זכר לעולם בריתו דבר צוה לאלף] דור [9]אשר כרת]
עם אברהם שבועתו לישחק [10]ויעמידה לי]עקוב לחוק]
לישראל ברית עולם [11]לאמור לכם אתן את א]רץ כנען]
]חב]ל[נחלתכם [12]בהיותם מתי מספר כמעט וגרים בה]

Mus. Inv. 976
SHR 6213, 6214, 6216*, 6221

NOTES ON READINGS

The four missing lines at the top of the column contained Ps 147:14-17 as well as a part of v 13. A careful calculation of the space of the lost bottom of the column (lines 18–25) proves that it contained vv 13-23 of the Psalm, thus preceding col. I of Sanders' text.

L. 11 (105:4-5)]תמיד ז]כורו]. A tentative placement of the small fragment which was stuck on frg. E i 1.

L. 13 (105:6) {עֹבֹוֹדֹ}. The scribe cancelled the letters by *puncta extraordinaria*. Later they were erased, perhaps by the scribe himself.

L. 13 (105:7) 𐤉]𐤄𐤅𐤄. The stroke at the edge of the fragment is probably the right tip of the palaeo-Hebrew *yod*. Note that the right oblique of the *yod* is often written very close to the preceding word. Cf. e.g. frg. E ii 10 (twice).

L. 15 (105:10) לי]עקוב. Cf. Yadin, Plate I.

L. 16 (105:11) את א]רץ. Cf. Yadin, Plate I.

L. 17 (105:11)]חב]ל[נחלתכם. Only the top of the *lamed* remains. One would also expect to see the top of the *lamed* of נחלתכם, but there is no clear trace which can be identified as such.

L. 17 (105:12) בהיותם. There may be a remnant of the head of *bet* in SHR 6216.

COMMENTS

L. 8 (105:1*) הודו ל𐤉𐤄𐤅𐤄 כי טוב כי] לעולם חסדו. Cf. Ps 106:1; 118:1, 29; 136:1; 11QPs[a] XVI 1, 5–6. Apparently this is the beginning of the Psalm.

L. 13 (105:7) כי הוא 𐤉]𐤄𐤅𐤄 ובארץ]. The gap at the end of the lines is far too short for a reconstruction according to 𝔐, כי הוא 𐤉]𐤄𐤅𐤄 אלוהינו בכול הארץ], which would require 2.5 cm more space than any of the other lines. כי הוא 𐤉]𐤄𐤅𐤄 ובארץ] results in a normal line length.

VARIANTS

Ps 147:20 (7) משפטים] ומשפטים 𝔐; ומשפטיו 𝔊

Ps 147:20 (7) הודיעם 𝔊 ℭ 𝔖] ידעום 𝔐

Ps 105:1* (8) הודו ל𐤉𐤄𐤅𐤄 כי טוב כי] לעולם חסדו] > 𝔐; הללויה 𝔊

Ps 105:3 (10–11) רצונו [ישמח לב מבקש 𝔊 1 Chr 16:10 ζητοῦσα τὴν εὐδοκίαν αὐτοῦ] ישמח לב מבקשי יהוה 𝔐𝔊.

Ps 105:6 (13) עבדיו 𝔊] עבדו 𝔐

Ps 105:6 (13) בחירו 𝔐^{2} MSS] בחיריו 𝔐𝔊

Ps 105:7 (13) כי] > 𝔐𝔊

Ps 105:9 (15) עם] את 𝔐

Ps 105:9 (15) שבועתו] ושבועתו 𝔐𝔊

Ps 105:11 (16) לכם] לך 𝔐𝔊

Frg. F Ps 147:3 (?)

1]עצבוני֯[

Mus. Inv. 614B
PAM 44.008

Notes on Readings

L. 1]עצבוני֯[. The vertical part of the right arm of *ʿayin* has been lost. The vertical stroke of the last preserved letter has no distinct tip, thereby making the reading *yod* uncertain. The very light spot on the upper edge of the fragment, to the right of *ʿayin*, appears at exactly the place where one would expect the bottommost trace of a preceding *lamed*, in which case one might transcribe]ל֯עצבוני֯[.

Comments

The preserved word has no exact correspondence with 𝔐, but, in view of the many additions and variants in 11QPs[a], this need not be surprising. A possible, but difficult, location for the fragment is in Ps 147:3 (𝔐 לעצבותם), in which case it might be placed at the end of line 17 of frg. E ii, even though the join is not precise. If this is correct, the word may be reconstructed ל]עצבוני֯[הם, with the plural of עצבון instead of עצבת. In order to fit the words of 𝔐 into frg. E ii 17, the letters must have been written compactly, as in line 9 of the same column, and ל]עצבוני֯[הם would have continued into the margin.

6. 11QPsalms[b]

(PLATE III)

Previous discussion: J. P. M. van der Ploeg, 'Fragments d'un manuscrit de Psaumes de Qumran (11QPs[b])', *RB* 74 (1967) 408–12, pl XVIII; J. P. M. van der Ploeg, 'Fragments de Psaumes de Qumrân', *Intertestamental Essays in Honour of Józef Tadeusz Milik*, ed. Zdzisław J. Kapera (Qumranica Mogilanensia 6; Kraków: Enigma Press, 1992) 233–7; F. García Martínez and E. J. C. Tigchelaar, 'Psalms Manuscripts from Qumran Cave 11: A Preliminary Edition', *RevQ* 17 (1996) 74–81, pls 8–9.

Physical Description

THE skin, of a slightly less than average thickness, has a tan to reddish-brown colour. Frg. 1 is slightly lighter in colour than the other fragments, and frg. 7 is somewhat darker. The skin of frg. 1 is thicker than that of the others, resembling that of 11Q7. The grain is less smooth than that of 11Q7. In some places, the surface has rubbed off. Only in frgs. 3–5 are the lines visible, though faint.

The physical characteristics are less compelling than the palaeographical evidence in identifying the manuscript to which the first fragment belonged.

Measurements and Columns

The seven largest fragments of 11QPs[b] come from six or, less probably, seven columns. Two reconstructed lines are missing between frgs. 4 and 5, preserving part of the *Plea for Deliverance*. It is therefore possible, though not likely, that these fragments come from two different columns.

Calculation of the average number of letter-spaces per line cannot be precise, since the extant material is scanty. Additionally, some reconstructions are uncertain (especially in frg. 4), and *vacat*s and irregular left margins must be taken into account. The reconstruction of the extant lines of frgs. 1 and 2 suggests an average of 46 letter-spaces per line. The tentative reconstruction of frgs. 4 and 5 points to a similar average line length, but considerably shorter and longer lines make the reconstruction and calculation questionable. The two fully reconstructed lines of frg. 6, without *vacat*s. suggest a slightly longer length of *c.*50 letter-spaces per line. Reconstruction shows that the inscribed width of these columns measured 10–11 cm.

The distance between horizontal ceiling lines (not visible in the photographs) is *c.*0.8 cm, except for frg. 5, where it is 0.7 cm.

Reconstruction of the columns of the manuscript is not easy in view of the small number of fragments, the absence of unambiguous points of material correspondence, and the varying line lengths. Note though, that it is plausible that frg. 6 should be placed to the right of frg. 7 (although there is no neat join), in which case one should be able to calculate the height of the column.

Two margins have been preserved: the left margin of frg. 6 and the right margin of frg. 7.

Palaeography

The hand is early Herodian, showing mainly formal, but also semi-formal features. The letters are not uniform, and the few *keraiai* are rudimentary. Some letters have forms which correspond more closely to the developed Herodian hand, suggesting a hand of the beginning of the first century CE. The transitional character of the hand (early to developed) is also shown from the differing width of certain letters, e.g. *dalet* and *taw*, ranging from narrow to wide.

A comparison of the hands of 11QPs^{b} (11Q**6**) and 11QPs^{c} (11Q**7**) clearly shows that frg. 1 (Ps 77:18–78:1) has the same hand as the other fragments of 11QPs^{b} and differs considerably from 11QPs^{c}. The *ductus* is less regular and slightly thinner than in 11QPs^{c}, which shows a more uniform and 'square' character, with letters of the same size. The most conspicuous difference is the form in which the *lamed* has been drawn. In 11QPs^{c} the *lamed* is almost always written with two strokes, the hook protruding to the left and crossing the descending stroke. In 11QPs^{b}, the *lamed* seems to have been written in one stroke. Four of the six *lamed*s of frg. 1 are certainly written in one stroke; the others are most probably written in the same way. Another clear difference is the medial *mem*. In 11QPs^{b}, the left oblique ends at half the height of a letter, whereas in 11QPs^{c} the oblique is much more diagonal, stretching down to the baseline. The *ʾalep* seems to be written in one movement in 11QPs^{b}, with the axis joining the left leg near to the top, whereas in 11QPs^{c} the axis is joined to the left leg halfway to the top.

Textual Character

The extant fragments indicate that 11QPs^{b} and 11QPs^{a} (11Q**5**) represent two copies of the same composition.[1] 11QPs^{b} 3 agrees with 11QPs^{a} XVI 1–2 in the order of the verses of Ps 118:1, 15-16; 11QPs^{b} 4 preserves part of the 'Plea of Deliverance' also found in 11QPs^{a} XIX; 11QPs^{b} 6 preserves two words of the 'Apostrophe to Zion', cf. 11QPs^{a} XXII 4–5; 11QPs^{b} 7 (Psalms 133, 141, and 144) displays the same sequence and readings as in 11QPs^{a} XXIII.

The differences between the two copies of this Qumran Psalter are minimal. In cases where both manuscripts preserve the 3rd masc. pl. pronominal suffix, 11QPs^{b} uses the form הם-, as opposed to המה- in 11QPs^{a}. The divine name is written in the square script in 11QPs^{b}, but in palaeo-Hebrew characters in 11QPs^{a}.

[1] References to 11QPs^{a} are to J. A. Sanders, *The Psalms Scroll of Qumrân Cave 11 (11QPs^{a})* (DJD IV; Oxford: Clarendon, 1965).

TABLE 1: *Correspondence between 11QPs[b] and 11QPs[a]*

11QPs[b] (frg.)	11QPs[a] (col.)	Contents
1		Ps 77:18–78:1
2	XIII 15–17	Ps 119:163-165
3	XVI 1-2	Ps 118:1, 15-16
4–5	XVIII–XIX 15	Plea for Deliverance
6	XXII 4–5	Apostrophe to Zion
7	XXIII 6–13	Ps 141:10; 133; 144:1-2

TABLE 2: *Differences between 11QPs[b] and 11QPs[a]*

11QPs[b] (frg., line)		11QPs[a] (col., line)	
4–5 4	יודכה	XIX 2	יודה
4–5 5	להם	XIX 3	להמה
4–5 8	מהם	XIX 6	מהמה
7 4	שיורד	XXIII 9	שירד

Mus. Inv. 576, 606, 613, 614, 621B, 1032
PAM 42.176, 42.177, 43.980*, 44.003*, 44.005*, 44.006*, 44.117*
IAA 563769

Frg. 1   Ps 77:18–78:1

top margin

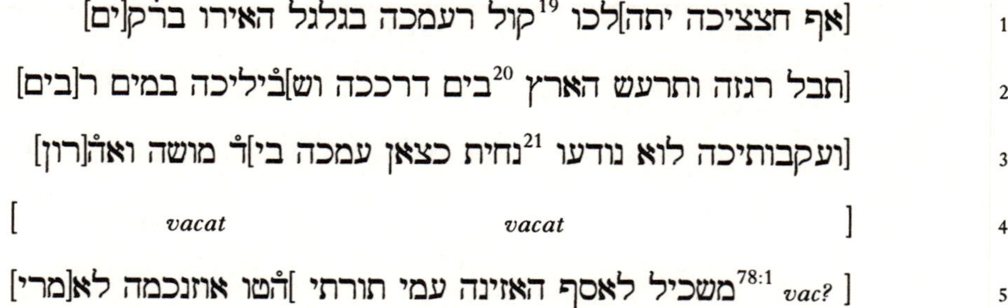

1 [אף חציציכה יתה]לכו 19קול רעמכה בגלגל האירו בר̊ק[ים]

2 [תבל רגזה ותרעש הארץ 20בים דרככה וש]ב̊יליכה במים ר[בים]

3 [ועקבותיכה לוא נודעו 21נחית כצאן עמכה בי]ד̊ מושה ואה̊[רון]

4 [*vacat* *vacat*]

5 [*vac?* 78:1משכיל לאסף האזינה עמי תורתי]ה̊טו אוזנכמה לא[מרי]

Mus. Inv. 606
PAM 42.177, 43.980*

NOTES ON READINGS

L. 5 (78:1) אוזנכמה. The reading is certain in spite of the partial abrasion of the lower part of the *nun;* the second letter is *waw*; there is no *yod* between *nun* and *kap*.

COMMENTS

Van der Ploeg included this fragment with 11QPs^{c} on the basis of a superficial similarity between it and 11QPs^{c} 8. However, the scribal hand of frg. 1 bears a marked affinity with that of 11QPs^{b} and is dissimilar to that of 11QPs^{c} (cf. PALAEOGRAPHY of 11QPs^{b} and 11QPs^{c}). In addition, the line length of frg. 1 matches that of 11QPs^{b}, and not that of 11QPs^{c}.

This conclusion is not without importance for the discussion of the character of 11QPs^{a} and 11QPs^{b} as liturgical compositions or as Psalms scrolls, because it shows that these scrolls do not necessarily limit themselves to the last part of the Psalter.

L. 1 (77:19) בר̊ק[ים]. Alternatively, reconstruct בר̊ק[יכה] (cf. VARIANTS), for which cf. Ps 97:4 האירו ברקיו תבל. The left part of lines 1–2 has broken off from the original.

L. 5 *vac?*. The *vacat* is suggested by the *vacat* at the beginning of Psalm 144 (cf. frg. 7).

L. 5 (78:1)]ה̊טו. A scrap of skin superimposed on the bottom edge of the fragment obscures the leg of the *waw*.

VARIANTS

77:19 (1) רעמכה] רעמך 𝔐

77:19 (1) בר̊ק[ים] 𝔐] αἱ ἀστραπαί σου 𝔊𝔖𝔙

77:20 (2) וש]ב̊יליכה] ושביליך 𝔐; αἱ τρίβοι σου 𝔊

77:21 (3) מושה] משה 𝔐

78:1 (5) אוזנכמה] אזנכם 𝔐; pl. 𝔖

Frg. 2 Ps 119:163-165

Parallel: 11QPs[a] XII 15–16 (underline)

[[163]שקר שנאתי וא]תעבה *vac* [ותורתכה אהבתי]

[[164]שבע ביום אה]ללכה *vac* על[משפטי צדקכה]

[[165]שלום רב לאוהבי] תור[תכ]ה̊[

Mus. Inv. 614
PAM 42.176, 44.006*

NOTES ON READINGS

L. 3 (119:165) תור[תכ]ה̊[. The ink at the bottom of the fragment appears where the scribe should have written the crossbar of the *he*.

COMMENTS

This small fragment, not published by van der Ploeg, but written by the same hand as 11QPs[b], is placed here on the basis of the parallel with 11QPs[a], where Psalm 119 precedes Ps 118:1, 15-16. One may assume that the text was written as in 11QPs[a], each verse beginning on a new line. The *vacat*s visible in lines 1 and 2 separate the two hemistichs. For other Psalms scrolls written in a stichometric format, cf. 1QPs[a]; 5QPs; 4QPs[b]; 4QPs[d]; 4QPs[l]; 8QPs; MasPs[a]; for Psalms scrolls written with each verse beginning a new line cf. 4QPs[g]; 4QPs[h].[2]

L. 2 (119:164) על[משפטי צדקכה]. Cf. 𝔐 על משפטי צדקך, but the few traces of 11QPs[a] XIII 16, transcribed by Sanders as ל[ ] שׄפׄטׄיׄ[, may suggest another reading. The first hemistich, שבע ביום אה]ללכה, is too short for the lacuna at the beginning of 11QPs[a] XIII 16, if the preserved *lamed* belongs to על. The lacuna between ל[and שׄפׄטׄיׄ[is too large for the reconstruction ע]ל[מ]שׄפׄטׄיׄ; the traces read as שׄפׄטׄיׄ[are close to the end of the line, and there is only room for צדקכה in the left margin.

VARIANTS

119:164 (2) אה]ללכה] הללתיך 𝔐𝔊

[2] Cf. P. W. Flint, *The Psalters at Qumran and the Book of Psalms* (Ph.D. diss., Notre Dame, 1993) 39–49. For a longer list and analysis, cf. E. Tov, 'Special Layout of Poetical Units in the Texts from the Judean Desert', *Give Ears to My Words, Psalms and Other Poetry in and around the Hebrew Bible*, ed. J. Dijk (Amsterdam, 1996) 115–28.

Frg. 3 Ps 118:1, 15-16

Parallel: 11QPs^a XVI 1–3 (underline)

[1הודו ליהוה כי טוב כי לעול]ם̊ חסדו 15ק̇[ול רנה וישועה]
[באהלי צדיקים ימין יהוה ע]שׂה חיל 16ימ̇[ין יהוה רוממה]

Mus. Inv. 613
PAM 42.176, 44.005*

NOTES ON READINGS

L. 1 לעול]ם̊. The final *mem* is written in the dark area of the fragment and only the left downstroke is distinct.

L. 2 ע]שׂה. Faint traces of the upper oblique show that the first visible letter is *śin*.

COMMENTS

In 11QPs^a XVI, Ps 118:1, 15, 16, 8, 9, and 29 (as well as an unknown stich) are placed between Psalms 136 and 145. 11QPs^a E (see 11Q**5** above), which preserves Ps 118:25-29, shows that the verses in 11QPs^a XVI do not represent the whole of Psalm 118 in the Psalter, but are an additional anthology (a 'catena').

Frgs. 4–5 'Plea for Deliverance'

Parallel: 11QPs^a XIX 1–16 (underline)

[ ]∘∘[
[ ]ודל אנוכי כי [
[1כי] לוא רמה תודה לכ̊[ה]
[ולוא תספר חסדכה תולעת 2ח]י̊ חי יודכה לכה יודו[לכה]
[כול מוטטי רגל בהודיעכה] 3חסדכה להם וצדקתכ[ה]
[תשכילם כי בידכה נפש כול 4ח]י נשמת כול בשר אתה [נתתה עשה]
[עמנו יהוה 5כטובכה כרוב רחמ]יכה וכרוב צדקותיכ[ה שמע]
[6יהוה בקול אוהבי שמו ולוא ע]ז̊ב חסדו מהם 7בר[וך יהוה]
[עושה צדקות מעטר חסידיו]8חסד ורחמים שאג[ה]
[נפשי להלל את שמכה להודות]ברנה 9חסדיכה לה[גיד]

]אמונתכה לתהלתכה אין חקר למות [10]הייתי בחטאי ועוונותי[11

]לשאול מכרוני ותצילני [11]יהוה כרוב רחמיכה וכרוב צדקותיכה[12

]גם אני את [12]שמכה אהבתי ובצלכה]חׄסיתי בזוכׄ[רי עוזכה יתקף[13

][13]לבי ועל חסדיכה אני נסמכת]י סלחה יהוה לחׄ[טאתי [14]וטהרני[14

]מעווני רוח אמונה ודעת ח]וׄנׄני אל אתקלה [15]בע[ויה אל[15

]תשלט בי שטן ורוח טמאה]מׄכׄאׄ[וב ויצר [16]רע אל ירשו[16

Mus. Inv. 576
PAM 42.177, 44.003*

NOTES ON READINGS

Frgs. 4a (lines 1–9) and 4b (lines 9–10) are shown separately in PAM 42.177, but are joined in PAM 44.003. A gap of probably two, but possibly three, lines separates frg. 5 (lines 13–16) from frg. 4b. From line 3 on, the preserved text overlaps with 11QPs^{a} XIX (line numbers of col. XIX entered in the text). The lines have been reconstructed on the basis of that text, though in one or two lines, the text of 11QPs^{a} XIX may have been longer than in 11QPs^{b}. The positioning of the fragments within the column is tentative, but the reconstruction of the lines suggests the fragments belonged to the left part of the column.

L. 1]∘∘[. The upper part of the fragment has broken off and no traces are left on the original.

L. 4 יׄ[ח. The reading is based upon 11QPs^{a}, but the traces on the edge, because of the darkening of edge not visible on the original, are not typical of *yod*.

L. 9 ורׄחמים. Most of *waw* has disappeared, only two dots remaining.

L. 16]מׄכׄאׄ[וב. All that remains are the upper parts of three letters. The reading is more likely than other possibilities suggested by 11QPs^{a} XIX.

TRANSLATION

1.] [
2. [ ] and weak am I, for [
3. [for] a maggot cannot give yo[u] thanks
4. [and a worm cannot tell of your kindness. The liv]ing, the living can praise you, even can praise [you]
5. [all those who stumble. By revealing] your kindness to them, and through yo[ur] righteousness
6. [you enlighten them. For in your hand is the soul of every liv]ing being, you [have given] to all flesh its breath. [Deal]
7. [with us, YHWH, according to your goodness, according to the abundance of] your [compassion] and according to the abundance of your righteous deeds.
8. [YHWH has heard the voice of those who love his name, and he has not de]nied them his kindness. Bles[sed be YHWH,]
9. [who performs righteous deeds, who crowns his devout with] kindness and compassion.
10. [My soul cried out to praise your name, to give thanks] with shouts for your kind deeds, to pro[claim]

11. [your faithfulness, to the praise of you there is no end. Because of my sins I was near to death, and my iniquities]
12. [have sold me to Sheol, but you, YHWH, saved me, according to the abundance of your compassion, and according to the abundance of your righteous deeds.]
13. [I, too, have loved your name, and in your shelter] I have found refuge. When [I] reca[ll your power]
14. [my heart is strengthened, and I rely upon your kind deeds.] Forgive [my] si[n,] YHWH, [and cleanse me]
15. [from my iniquity. Be]stow on me [a spirit of faith and knowledge.] Let me not stumble in trans[gression. Let not]
16. [Satan rule over me, nor an evil spirit; let neither] pai[n nor an evil inclination take possession]

COMMENTS

Apart from the beginning, the so-called 'Plea for Deliverance' is preserved in 11QPs[a] XIX 1–18. The text of frgs. 4–5, beginning with line 3, corresponds closely to 11QPs[a] XIX. The words of line 2 should have belonged to the last line of 11QPs[a] XVIII. Since 11QPs[b] is fragmentarily preserved, in contrast to 11QPs[a] XIX, comments will be restricted to differences between the two texts.

L. 2]ודל אנוכי. Reconstruct אביון or עני before]ודל. Cf. Ps 70:6; 86:1; 109:22.

L. 4 יודכה לכה. Most probably an error (originated by the recollection of Isa 38:19, as van der Ploeg notes) for יודה לכה in 11QPs[a] XIX 2.

Ll. 6–7 [נתתה עשה] / [עמנו יהוה כטובכה כרוב רחמ]יכה. The text of 11QPs[a] XIX 4–5 is too long for the gap of one line here. One must surmise that the scribe omitted a word (e.g. כטובכה).

Ll. 11–13 A reconstruction of the lines between the two fragments on the basis of 11QPs[a] XIX is somewhat problematic. In the reconstruction offered above, lines 12–13 are slightly longer than average, but a reconstruction with lines of average length would bring the second fragment closer to the right margin of the column, which is even more problematic.

L. 15 אתקלה. *Nipʿal* of תקל, with the meaning 'to stumble'. Cf. Sir 15:12.

Frg. 6 'Apostrophe to Zion'

Parallel: 11QPs[a] XXII 4–5 (underline)

1] [4]המ[תאוים

2 [ליום ישעך וישישו ברוב כבודך [5]זיז כבודך י[ׄ]נקו

Mus. Inv. 621B
PAM 42.176, 44.117*

NOTES ON READINGS

The fragment, not published by van der Ploeg, may preserve the bottom margin, but it is also possible that line 3 was shorter than line 2. The verse numbers were given by Sanders in 11QPs[a] XXII.

L. 1 המ]תאוים. A trace of the crossbar shows the first letter cannot be *nun*. The dot to the right may be the bottom tip of the right leg of *taw*.

L. 2 י֯[ינקו. Part of the base of *nun* has disappeared. A faint stroke on the edge may be the remnant of the second *yod*.

TRANSLATION

1. [[4]Those who y]earn
2. [for the day of your salvation, may they rejoice in the greatness of your glory. [5]Your full breast they may] suckle

COMMENTS

Cf. the discussion by Sanders, *Psalms Scroll*, 85–9.

Frg. 7a–e Ps 141:10; 133; 144:1-2

Parallel: 11QPs^a XXIII 6–13 (underline)

[רשעים יחד אנוכי עד]אעבור [*vacat*] 1

[*vac* 133:1 שיר המעל]ות לדויד הנה מה֯ ט֯[וב ומה נעים שבת אחים] 2

[גם יחד 2 כשמן] הטוב על הרואש[יורד על הזקן זקן אהרון] 3

שיורד על פי מדיו 3 כטל חרמון שיור[ד על הר ציון כי שמה צוה] 4

י[ה]וה את הברכה[עד עו]ל֯ם֯ שלום על֯[ישראל *vacat*] 5

vac[*at*] [144:1 ברוך יהוה צו]ר֯י המלמ[ד ידי לקרב ואצבעותי] 6

למלחמה [2 חסדי ומצודתי משג]ב֯י ומפל[ט לי מגני ובו חסיתי הרודד] 7

עמ֯[ים 3 תחתי אלוהים מה אדם ותדעהו בן אנוש ותחושבהו] 8

◦[9

Mus. Inv. 576, 621B
PAM 42.176, 42.177, 44.003*, 44.117*

NOTES ON READINGS

Frgs. 7b, 7c, and 7d were already joined by van der Ploeg. Frg. 7a preserves the right margin of lines 4–5. Frg. 7e no longer shows the remains of lines 8 and 9. Both the wording and the order of the text correspond to 11QPs^a XXIII.

L. 4 (133:2) מדיו. Traces of *dalet* are preserved on frgs. 7b and 7c.

L. 5 (133:3) י[ה]וה. A tiny dot after *yod*, may, if ink, represent the upper right part of the first *he*.

L. 5 (133:3) הברכה]. The crossbar of the final *he* is preserved at the very bottom of the upper frg. 7c.

L. 6 *vac[at]*. Cf. the large blank space at the bottom of frg. 7b.

COMMENTS

The preserved text of this column differs only in minor aspects from 11QPs[a]. Because of the similarity, the reconstruction follows the text and orthography of 11QPs[a], rather than that of 𝔐.

L. 5 (133:3) הברכה] עד עו[לם. The size of the lacuna indicates the same text as 11QPs[a] XXIII 10–11. There is no room for 𝔐 חיים.

L. 5 (133:3) שלום על] ישראל. Cf. Ps 125:5; 128:6.

L. 6 (144:1) The blank space at the bottom of frg. 7b shows that 11QPs[b], like 11QPs[a] XXIII 12, cannot have had the heading לדויד. Note that 11QPs[a] XXIII 12 has no indentation in this line at the beginning of the new Psalm.

VARIANTS

133:2 (2) לדויד 11QPs[a] XXIII 7] לדוד 𝔐
133:2 (3) הרואש] 11QPs[a] XXIII 8] הראש 𝔐
133:2 (4) שיורד] שירד 𝔐 11QPs[a] XXIII 9
133:2 (4) מדיו 11QPs[a] XXIII 9] מדותיו 𝔐; sg. 𝔊𝔖𝔙
133:3 (4) שיור[ד 11QPs[a] XXIII 10] שירד 𝔐
133:3 (5) עד עו[לם שלום על] ישראל] 11QPs[a] XXIII 10–11] חיים עד העולם 𝔐
144:1 (6) > 11QPs[a] XXIII 12] לדוד 𝔐; + πρὸς τὸν Γολιαδ 𝔊𝔙

Frg. 8 Ps 109:3-4 or 11QPs[a] XVIII 14 (?)

1 [ה֯◦]
2 [ם תח֯ת֯]

Inv. No. 1032
IAA 563769

NOTES ON READINGS

L. 1 [ה֯◦]. There may be a space before *he/ḥet*. It is not certain that the faint trace after *he/ḥet* is ink, but if so, it might be the bottom part of *lamed*, or, with more difficulty, part of the right arm of *ṣade*.

L. 2 תח֯ת֯]. The downstroke of the last letter could also belong to *mem* or several other letters.

COMMENTS

The sequence of letters in line 2 corresponds to Ps 109:3-4 חנ[ם תח֯ת֯] and to 11QPs[a] XVIII 14 טובי[ם תחמ֯]ל. In both cases, it is difficult to identify the traces of line 1.

Frg. 9

] וׄ°[1

Mus. Inv. 1032
IAA 563769

NOTES ON READINGS

Identification of the fragment is based on the form of the head of *waw*.

L. 1] וׄ°[. The first trace may belong to *ḥet* or, with more difficulty, to *qop*.

7. 11QPsalms^{c}

(PLATE VI)

Previous discussion: J. P. M. van der Ploeg, 'Fragments d'un Psautier de Qumrân', *Symbolae Biblicae et Mesopotamicae Francisco Mario Theodore de Liagre Böhl Dedicatae*, eds. M. A. Beek *et alii* (Studia Francisci Scholten Memoriae Dicata IV; Leiden: E. J. Brill, 1973) 308–9; J. P. M. van der Ploeg, 'Fragments de Psaumes de Qumrân', *Intertestamental Essays in Honour of Józef Tadeusz Milik*, ed. Zdzisław J. Kapera (Qumranica Mogilanensia 6; Kraków: Enigma Press, 1992) 233–7; F. García Martínez and E. J. C. Tigchelaar, 'Psalms Manuscripts from Qumran Cave 11: A Preliminary Edition', *RevQ* 17 (1996) 82–92, pls 10–11.

Physical Description

THE skin has a deep tan to brown colour with some reddish spots, turning to deep brown on the deteriorated edges. At some places, the top layer has peeled off, revealing a light brown colour. The grain is smooth and the surface is well prepared. There is occasional shrinkage of the skin. Horizontal and vertical ruling is clearly visible. The letters often cross over the horizontal ruling.

Three margins are preserved, albeit incompletely: frg. 4 preserves a left margin (0.7 cm); frg. 8 preserves a right margin (1 cm); frg. 11 preserves a right margin (1.1 cm).

Measurements

The height of the inscribed part of the columns measures about 28 cm (reconstructed for 36 lines on the basis of frg. 8, with a height of 13.5 cm and containing 18 lines).

In frg. 8, the width of the column (without margin) measures 13 cm, 12.2 cm of which is extant and the remaining 0.8 cm reconstructed.

TABLE 1: *Average Number of Letter-Spaces per Line*

Frgs.	Letter-Spaces
1–2	63
3	62
4–7	59
8	53
10	52
11	56
Average	58

Calculation of the numbers of lines per column is based upon the material points of correspondence between frgs. 1–2, frg. 3, frgs. 4–7, and frg. 8. Reconstruction of the column on the basis of 𝔐 requires 36 lines from frg. 3 1 to frg. 5 1 (the first line of the right fragment) and another 36 lines from frg. 5 1 to frg. 8 1. A column length of 36 lines is consistent with the placement of frg. 10. It starts *c.*50 lines after frg. 8 1, and its material point of correspondence is with the lower right part of frg. 8.

A length of 36 lines per column, however, does not seem to agree with the beginning of the scroll. A reconstruction according to 𝔐 would place frg. 3 1 at approximately the sixty-fifth line, that is, near the bottom of the second column of the scroll. This is quite unlikely in view of the correspondence of its shape with that of frgs. 5 and 8. Rather, one would expect it to be placed near the top of the third column of the scroll. This is possible, if the width of the second column was considerably smaller than that of the first and third column, or if the first column had ten lines more than 𝔐. Perhaps the scroll did not begin directly with Ps 1:1, but had an introduction of some kind.

A reconstruction of the scroll based upon a line length of 36 lines per column implies that one column is missing between frgs. 1–2 and frg. 3, and another between frgs. 10 and 11. The distance between the fragments shows that they belong to the outer section of the scroll. Because of the uncertainty regarding the place of frg. 9, a full reconstruction of columns is avoided, and most references are to fragments.

TABLE 2: *Tentative Reconstruction of the Beginning of the Scroll*

Frgs.	Cols.	Psalm(s)
1–2	I	2:1-8
	one column missing	
3	II	9:3-7
4–7	III	12:5–14:6
8	IV	17:9–18:12
10	V	19:4-8
	one column missing	
11	VI	25:2-7

Contents

TABLE 3: *Contents of 11QPs^c^*

Frgs.	Psalm(s)
1–2	2:1-8
3	9:3-7
4–7	12:5–14:6
8	17:9–18:12
9	18:15-17?
10	19:4-8
11	25:2-7

Palaeography and Dating

The hand of the manuscript is Herodian and displays features of the types classified by Cross as early Herodian round semi-formal hand and developed Herodian formal script. The manuscript can therefore be dated to the first half of the 1st century CE. The letters are more square and of a more uniform size than those of 11QPs[b].

Several letters have characteristic forms, making it easy to identify the fragments of this manuscript. The oblique of the *ʾalep* is joined halfway up the left leg. *He* is almost square, with a slightly slanting right leg, and a very thick head. *Lamed* is written in two strokes, the horizontal stroke of the hook almost always extending beyond the descending line of the upper arm. The left oblique of medial *mem* stretches towards the baseline, and the base stroke of *mem* sometimes is written beneath the baseline. The same goes for the base stroke of medial *ṣade*, which is mostly written well beyond the baseline. Very typical is the writing of final *mem*: the two vertical strokes and the bottom stroke seem to have been written in one movement, like a triangle with a rounded top; a large, thickening separate stroke at the left is joined to the top of this 'triangle', suggesting the horizontal head stroke.

Orthography and Morphology

Plene spellings are consistently used, together with ה- for the 2nd masc. sing. pronominal suffix and the 2nd masc. sing. affix of the perfect.

2:4 (1–2 3) אדוני] אדני 𝔐[L]
2:6 (1–2 4) קודשי֯] קדשי 𝔐
9:3 (3 1) ב֯כ֯ה֯] בך 𝔐

9:4 (3 2) עשי]תה] 𝔐 עשית
9:5 (3 2) ושבתה] 𝔐 ישבת
12:6 (4–7 2) יואמר] 𝔐 יאמר
12:7 (4–7 3) טה]ורות] 𝔐 טהרות
12:7 (4–7 4) מזוקׄ]ק] 𝔐 מזקק
13:5 (4–7 8) יואמר] 𝔐 יאמר
13:5 (4–7 8) אויב[י]] 𝔐 איבי
13:6 (4–7 9) בי]שׁ[ועת]כה] 𝔐 בישועתך
14:5 (4–7 14) שׁׄמׄהׄ] 𝔐 שם
17:12 (8 3) יושב] 𝔐 ישב
17:13 (8 4) פ]לט] 𝔐 פלטה
17:13 (8 4) ח]רבכה] 𝔐 חרבך
17:14 (8 4) ממותׄ]ים]מׄיׄד[כה]] 𝔐 ממתים ידך
17:14 (8 5) וצפׄ]ונכ[ה] 𝔐^{k} וצפינך (𝔐^{q} וצפונך)
18:1 (8 9) כול] 𝔐 כל
18:1 (8 9) אויביו] 𝔐 איביו
18:2 (8 9) ו]יׄ[ו]אמר] 𝔐 ויאמר
18:4 (8 11) אקראה] 𝔐 אקרא 2 Sam 22:4 𝔐
18:4 (8 11) ומאויבי 2 Sam 22:4 𝔐 (ומאיבי)] 𝔐 ומן איבי
18:7 (8 13) אלוהי] 𝔐 אלהי
19:7 (10 3) מ]קׄצי] 𝔐𝔊 מקצה (orthographic or textual variant)
25:5 (11 3) באמתכה] 𝔐 באמתך
25:6 (11 4) רחמיכה] 𝔐 רחמיך 5/6Ḥev1b

Textual Character

In general, the text of the extant fragments corresponds to 𝔐, but, in view of the limited size of the preserved text, the number of variants is rather large. Most of the variants are unique, not being attested in the versions; thus frg. 3 2 (Ps 9:5) שפטתה; frgs. 4–7 3 (Ps 12:6) אל צדי]קׄיׄם]; 4 (Ps 12:7) עיל[ ]; frg. 8 1 (Ps 17:9) דרשׁׄ]וני; frg. 9 2 (Ps 18:16) ישל]ח. Such variants might suggest a separate textual tradition, or a liberal interpretative treatment of the text. The variant גרשוני in frg. 8 2 (Ps 17:11), which corresponds to 𝔊, shows that not all the variants can be regarded as idiosyncracies of the manuscript.

2:6 (1–2 4) קודשׁׄי] 𝔐𝔖 קדשי; τὸ ἅγιον αὐτοῦ 𝔊𝔙
9:5 (3 2) שפטתה] 𝔐𝔊𝔖𝔙 שפט
9:7 (3 3) 𝔐𝔊𝔙 האויׄבׄ] 𝔖 ܒܥܠܕܒܒܐ
12:6 (4–7 3) אל צדי]קׄיׄם]] > 𝔐𝔊𝔖𝔙
12:7 (4–7 4) עיל לארץ[ ] 𝔐 בעליל לארץ 5/6Ḥev1b; δοκίμιον τῇ γῇ 𝔊𝔖𝔙; χωροῦν τῇ γῇ α′; *separatum a terra* Hier
17:9 (8 1) דרשׁׄ]וני] 𝔐𝔊 שדוני
17:11 (8 2) 𝔊 גרשוני (ἐκβαλλοντές με)] 𝔐σ′ אשרינו (μακαρίζοντές με) 𝔖 (ܛܘܒܢܝ = אשרוני)

17:14 (8 4) ממוׄת[ים]מׄיׄד[כה]] ממתים ידך 𝔐α′ (ἀπὸ τεθνηκότων); ἀπὸ ἐχθρῶν τῆς χειρός σου 𝔊𝔙
18:8 (8 15) לו 𝔐] αὐτοῖς 𝔊𝔖𝔙
18:11 (8 17) רוח 𝔐] הרוח ℭ
18:12 (8 18) ח]שכות] חשכת 𝔐; חשרת 𝔐^{ms} 2 Sam 22:12 𝔐
18:16? (9 2) ישׄל]ח] > 𝔐 (transposition of stichs?)
19:8 (10 4) תור]וׄת (?)] תורת 𝔐𝔊
25:5 (11 3) למׄ]דני] ולמדני 𝔐𝔊

Mus. Inv. 606, 614, 621B, 1027
PAM 42.176, 42.177, 43.980*, 44.006*, 44.117*
IAA 522908*

Frgs. 1–2 Ps 2:1-8

1 [1למה רגשו גוים ולאומים יהגו רי]קׄ 2יתׄ[יצבו מלכי ארץ ורוזנים נוסדו יחד]
2 [על יהוה ועל משיחו]3ננתק[ה את]מׄוסדרות[ימו ונשליכה ממנו עבותימו 4יושב]
3 [בשמים ישחק]אדוני ילעׄגׄ למׄו 5אׄז[י]דׄבר אלׄ[ימו באפו ובחרונו יבהלמו 6ואני]
4 [נסכתי מלכי על צ]יׄון הר קודשׄי 7אספׄרׄה אׄ[ל חוק יהוה אמר אלי בני אתה]
5 [אני היום ילדתיכה 8שא]לׄ[מ]מׄ[ני ו]אׄתׄ[נה

Mus. Inv. 606
PAM 42.176, 43.980*

NOTES ON READINGS

The column is composed of two fragments which almost join; no more than 1 or 2 mm are missing in line 3 between the two fragments. The reconstruction of the lines is based upon the assumption that the psalm began at the right margin.

L. 1 (2:1) רי]קׄ. The vertical stroke on the edge is consistent with the tail of *qop*.

L. 2 (2:3)]מׄוסדרות[ימו. Van der Ploeg suggested]אׄנׄו סדרות[ימו as an alternative reading, but there is no space between *waw* and *samek*, the stroke before *waw* is too diagonal to be the base of *nun*, and a spot of the lower stroke of *mem* is still visible.

L. 2 (2:3)]ננתק[ה. The *qop* is preserved in PAM 42.176, though lost in PAM 43.980.

L. 3 (2:4-5) ילעׄגׄ למׄו אׄז[י]דׄבר. The surface of the skin has peeled off in various spots, and few letters have survived completely.

L. 5 (2:8) שא]לׄ[מ]מׄ[ני ו]אׄתׄ[נה. The bottom edge of the fragments preserves the upper parts of some letters.

COMMENTS

L. 2 (2:3)]מֹוסדרות[ימו. The word מוסדרה is unknown. One must assume either a strange error (a kind of dittography), or a form derived from סדר in the sense of 'battle array', as does van der Ploeg.

VARIANTS

2:3 (2)]מֹוסדרות[ימו] מוסרותימו 𝔐

2:4 (3) אדוני] אדני 𝔐^{L}; יהוה ℭ$^{mlt\ mss}$; > 𝔐^{A} (erasure)

2:6 (4) קודשׁי] קדשי 𝔐𝔖; τὸ ἅγιον αὐτοῦ 𝔊𝔙

Frg. 3 Ps 9:3-7

1 [3אשמחה ואעל]צֹהֹ בֹכֹהֹ אזמֹ[רה שמכה]עֹ[לי]וֹן 4בשוב אויב[י אחור יכשלו ויאבדו]

2 [מפניכה 5כי עשי]תה משפטי ודיני ושֹבתה לכסא שפטתה צֹ[דק 6גערתה גוים אבדתה]

3 [רשע שמם מחיתה]לעולם ועד 7האויבֹ תֹמֹ[ו חרבות]לנֹ[צח וערים נתשתה אבד]

4 [זכרם המה 8ויהוה לעו]לֹ[ם ישב

Mus. Inv. 606
PAM 42.176, 43.980*

NOTES ON READINGS

The placement of the fragment within the column is tentative. In this reconstruction, the missing first part of the psalm fits in the line preceding line 1.

L. 1 (9:3) ואעל]צֹהֹ בֹכֹהֹ אזמֹ[רה. Only the tips of the legs or the base strokes of most letters are preserved. These remnants of letters are entirely consistent with the reading of 𝔐.

L. 1 (9:3)]עֹ[לי]וֹן. A faint stroke on the top edge of the fragment is consistent with the base of ʿayin. Two dots may be remnants of the *waw*.

L. 2 (9:5) ושבתה. The first letter is almost certainly *waw*, not *yod* (which in this hand usually has a larger tip).

L. 2 (9:5) צֹ[דק. The two preserved strokes are compatible with the downstroke and the right arm of *ṣade*, but there is no trace of its base.

L. 3 (9:7) תֹמֹ[ו חרבות]לנֹ[צח. All along the bottom edge of the fragment are faint strokes representing the upper tips of letters. One might transcribe תֹמֹוֹ חֹרֹבֹ[ו]תֹ לנֹ[צח, or possibly תֹמֹוֹ חֹ[ו]רֹבֹ[ו]תֹ לנֹ[צח.

L. 4 (9:8) לעו]לֹ[ם. More likely than]לֹ[עולם, since there is no trace of a second *lamed*.

VARIANTS

9:3 (1) בֹכֹהֹ] בך 𝔐

9:5 (2) עשי]תה] עשית 𝔐

9:5 (2) ושבתה] ישבת 𝔐

9:5 (2) שפטתה] שפט 𝔐𝔊𝔖𝔙

9:7 (3) האויבֹ 𝔐𝔊𝔙] ܒܥܠܕܒܒܐ 𝔖

Frgs. 4–7 Ps 12:5–14:6

1 [כול שפתי חלקות לשון מדברת גדולות 5אשר אמרו ללשו]ננו נגביר שפתינו

2 [אתנו מי אדון לנו 6משוד עניים מאנקת אביונים עתה אקו]ם֯ יואמר יהוה

3 [אל צדי]ק֯י֯ם אש֯[ת בישע יפיח לו 7אמרות יהוה אמרות טה]ורות כסף צרוף

4 [ ]עיל לארץ מזוק֯[ק שבעתים 8אתה יהוה תשמרמה תצרנ]ו מן הדור זה֯

5 [לעו]ל֯[ם 9סבי]ב֯ ר֯ש[עים יתהלכון כרום זולות לבני אדם] *vacat*

6 [13:1למנצח מזמור לדויד 2עד אנה יהוה תשכחני נצח עד אנ]ה ת֯ס֯תיר֯[את פניכה]

7 [ממני 3עד אנה אשית עצות בנפשי יגון בלבבי יומם עד] אנה ירום [אויבי]

8 [עלי 4הביטה ענני יהוה אלוהי האירה עיני פן אישן המות 5פן] יואמר אויב[י]

9 [יכלתיו צרי יגילו כי אמוט 6ואני בחסדכה בטחתי יגל לבי בי]ש[ועת]כה

10 [אשירה ליהוה כי גמל עלי *va* [*cat*

11 [14:1למנצח לדויד אמר נבל בלבו אין אלוהים השחיתו ה]תעיב֯[ו]עולה֯[אין]

12 [עושה טוב 2יהוה משמים השקיף על בני אדם לראות ה]יש מ֯[ש]כ֯י֯ל[דורש]

13 [את אלוהים 3הכול סר יחדו נאלחו אין עושה טוב אין גם]אחד [4הלוא]

14 [ידעו כול פועלי און אוכלי עמי אכלו לחם יהוה לוא]קר֯[או] 5ש֯מ֯ה֯

15 [פחדו פחד כי אלוהים בדור צדיק 6עצת עני תבישו כי] י֯הו֯ה֯ מח֯[סהו]

Mus. Inv. 606, 614
PAM 42.176, 43.980*, 44.006*

NOTES ON READINGS

The column is composed of four fragments. Frgs. 4 + 5 correspond to Ps 12:5–13:6, frg. 5 at the right side of the column (lines 3–5), frg. 4 at the left, preserving part of the left margin, with the vertical ruling visible on lines 1–3.

Frg. 4 with Ps 12:5–13:6 should be joined to frgs. 6 + 7 which preserve Ps 13:6–14:3, the join running horizontally through the head of the *he* of בי]ש[ועת]כה.

L. 3 (12:6) צדי]ק֯י֯ם. Before the final *mem*, there are the bottom parts of two downstrokes. The first clearly descends beneath the baseline.

L. 3 (12:6) אש֯[ת. After the *šin*, the bottom part of a downstroke is visible.

L. 6 (13:2) אנ]ה. Perhaps the utmost tip of the *nun* is present on the edge.

L. 6 (13:2) פניכה]. This could also be positioned at the beginning of the next line.

L. 8 (13:5) יואמר. The distinction between *waw* and *yod* in this hand rules out ויאמר.

L. 9 (13:6) בי֯ש֯[ועת]כה. Frg. 4 preserves the *šin* and the top part of the head of *he*. Frg. 6 has כה.

L. 11 (14:1)]עולה֯[. After *lamed*, a downstroke with a head or the beginning of a crossbar is visible. Other letters than *he* are also possible.

L. 12 (14:2) ה֯]יש. Two faint spots may be traces of the *he*.

L. 15 (14:6) י֯הו֯ה. PAM 43.980 shows a dark stroke on the baseline, but this stroke should not be interpreted as part of a letter.

COMMENTS

L. 3 (12:6) [אל צדי]ק֯י֯ם. The reconstruction is uncertain, since this is a variant not attested by other versions.

L. 4 (12:7) [ ]עיל. 𝔐 בעליל is usually explained as the preposition *bet* with the *hapax* עליל, 'furnace'. The versions either did not understand the word or read a different text. It is not clear how one might reconstruct the broken word.

L. 4 (12:8) זהׄ. Here, as in Ps 17:9, our manuscript has זה instead of the uncommon זו of 𝔐.

L. 11 (14:1) ה]תעיב֯[ו]עולה֯[. Cf. Ps 53:2 והתעיבו עול.

VARIANTS

12:6 (2) יואמר] יאמר 𝔐

12:6 (3) [אל צדי]ק֯י֯ם] > 𝔐𝔊𝔖𝔙

12:7 (3) טה]ורות] טהרות 𝔐

12:7 (4) [ ]עיל לארץ] בעליל לארץ 𝔐 5/6Ḥev1b; δοκίμιον τῇ γῇ 𝔊𝔖𝔙; χωροῦν τῇ γῇ α′; *separatum a terra* Hier

12:7 (4) מזו֯]ק] מזקק 𝔐

12:8 (4) זהׄ] זו 𝔐

13:5 (8) יואמר] יאמר 𝔐

13:5 (8) אויב]י[ ] איבי 𝔐

13:6 (9) בי֯ש֯[ועת]כה] בישועתך 𝔐

14:1 (11)]עולה֯[𝔗^mss עילא = עול cf. Ps 53:2] עלילה 𝔐

14:5 (14) שׁ֯מ֯ה] שם 𝔐

Frg. 8 Ps 17:9–18:12

[9]מפני רשעים זה דר֯ש֯[וני אויבי בנפש יקיפו עלי [10]חלבמו סגרו פימו] 1

דברו בגאות [11]גרשוני עתה סבב֯[וני עיניהם ישיתו לנטות בארץ] 2

[[12]דמינו כאריה יכ]סוף לטרוף וככפיר יושב ב[מסתרים [13]קומה יהוה] 3

[קדם פניו הכריעהו פ]לט נפשי מר[שע ח]רבכה [14]ממו֯ת֯[ים]מ֯י֯ד֯[כה] 4

[יהוה ממתים מחלד ח]לקם בחייה֯[ם] וצפ֯[ונכ]ה ת֯מלא בטנם י֯[שבעו] 5

[בנים והניחו יתרם לעוללי]הם [15]אני ב֯צדק֯ אח֯[זה]פ֯ניכה אשב֯ע֯ה בהקי֯[ץ] 6

7 [תמונתכה vac[at

8 [18:1 למנצח לעבד יהוה לדוי]ד אשׁ̇ר דבר ליהו̇ה[את]ד̊ברי השירה̇[הזואת]

9 [ביום הציל יהוה אותו מכ]ף כול אויביו ומיד שאו[ל 2 ו]י̊[ו]אמר רחמ̊[תיכה]

10 [יהוה חזקי 3 יהוה סלע]י̊ ומצ[ו]ד̇תי ומפלטי אלי צורי אחס[ה]

11 [בו מגני וקרן ישעי משגבי]4 מ̊ח̊[ו]לל אקראה יהוה ומאויבי או̊[שע]

12 [5 אפפוני חבלי מות ונחלי בליעל יב]עתוני 6 חבלי שאול סבבוני

13 [קדמוני מוקשי מות 7 בצר לי אק]ר̊א יהוה ואל אלוהי אשו[ע ישמע]

14 [מהיכלו קולי ושועתי לפניו תבוא בא]זניו 8 ותגעש ותרעש[הארץ]

15 [ומוסדות השמים ירגזו ויתגעשו] כי חרה לו 9 על[ה] עשן[באפו ואש]

16 [מפיו תואכל גחלים בערו ממנו 10 וי]ט̊ שמים וירד וער̇[פל תחת]

17 [רגליו 11 וירכב על כרוב ויעוף וידא]ע̊ל כנפי רוח *va]cat* [

18 [12 ישת חושך סתרו סביבותיו סוכתו ח]שכות מים [

Mus. Inv. 606
PAM 42.176, 43.980*

NOTES ON READINGS

Parts of the surface of the skin have worn off in lines 3–10. Some letters have completely disappeared; of others only minute traces remain. The first letters of lines 3–6 are not legible on the original.

L. 1 (17:9) דר̊ש̊[וני. The second letter is *dalet* or *reš*. The third letter can be *ṭet*, *ʿayin*, or *šin*.

L. 2 (17:11) סבב̊[וני. Minute traces of the downstroke and base of the second *bet* seem to be present on the edge.

L. 4 (17:13) פ[לט. The reading is certain; פ[ל]ט[ה, of the edition of van der Ploeg, is excluded by the almost completely preserved *ṭet* on the edge.

L. 4 (17:14) ממו̇ת̊[ים. The downstroke in ligature with the second *mem* must belong to *waw* or *yod*, since the vicinity of the next trace excludes other letters. The next two traces seem to be the tip of the right leg and the short base stroke of *taw*.

L. 4 (17:14)]מ̊י̊ד̇[כה]. The traces can be interpreted as the left diagonal of *mem* attached to the downstroke of *yod*. The position of the small dot at the right is consistent with the left tip of the base of *mem*. The traces of a leg are compatible with *dalet*.

L. 5 (17:14) בחיי̇ה̇[ם]. The head of the second *yod* is somewhat irregular (the upper right part seems to be lost); the final *mem* has completely disappeared.

L. 6 (17:15) אשב̊ע̊ה. A tip of *ʿayin* may be attached to the right leg of *he*. Otherwise, read אשב̊[ע]ה.

L. 9 (18:1) מכ]ף. The trace on the right edge appears where one expects the *mem*, but it is not really compatible with *mem*.

L. 9 (18:2) ו]י̊[ו]אמר. Rather than]ו̇[י]אמר.

L. 9 (18:2) רחמ֯[תיכה]. Like all the letters on the dark part of the left edge, the width of the *reš* is compressed. The tick on the left side of the head shows the reading is certain. The vertical trace on the edge after *ḥet* can belong to many letters.

L. 11 (18:4)]מ֯ח֯[ו]לל. This is one of the few cases where the original fragments have better traces than PAM 43.980. A trace before *mem* may be *waw*.

COMMENTS

L. 1 (17:9) זה. For זה where 𝔐 has זו, cf. also Ps 12:8.

L. 1 (17:9) דר֯ש֯[וני. Probably a case of a replacement of a rare poetic word (שדוני 𝔐) by a more common one, as suggested by van der Ploeg.

L. 2 (17:11) גרשוני. Again (cf. line 1), 11Q7 seems to preserve a common word against a rare, poetic one in 𝔐 (אשרני); 𝔊, which often uses ἐκβάλλειν to render גרש, sides with 11Q7.

L. 3 (17:13) קומה יהוה]. Reconstruct, perhaps, קום יהוה] (cf. next note).

L. 4 (17:13) [קדם פניו הכריעהו פ]לט. A reconstruction following 𝔐 is a trifle too long. We suggest קדם instead of 𝔐 קדמה, since 11Q7 reads פ]לט where 𝔐 has פלטה.

L. 4 (17:14) ממו֯ת֯[ים]מ֯י֯ד֯[כה]. Proposed as a conjecture by BHS.

L. 5 (17:14) ממתים מחלד. Thus 𝔐, but other reconstructions are possible.

Ll. 9–10 (18:2-3) רחמ֯[תיכה] / [יהוה חזקי יהוה סלע]י֯. The text of 𝔐 is somewhat short for the beginning of line 10, but רחמ֯[תי] / [אותכה יהוה חזקי יהוה סלע]י֯ would be too long.

L. 11 (18:3) [בו מגני וקרן ישעי משגבי. The text of 𝔐 may be somewhat too short.

Ll. 14–15 (18:8) ותרעש[הארץ] / [ומוסדות השמים ירגזו ויתגעשו] כי חרה לו. Cf. 2 Sam 22:8. 𝔐 reads ומוסדי הרים, but that phrase is definitely too short for the lacuna.

VARIANTS

17:9 (1) זה] זו 𝔐
17:9 (1) דר֯ש֯[וני] שדוני 𝔐𝔊
17:11 (2) גרשוני 𝔊 (ἐκβαλλοντές με)] אשרינו 𝔐σ′(μακαρίζοντές με) 𝔖 (ܛܘܒܢܝ = אשרוני)
17:12 (3) יושב] ישב 𝔐
17:13 (4) פ]לט] פלטה 𝔐
17:13 (4) ח]רבכה] חרבך 𝔐
17:14 (4) ממו֯ת֯[ים]מ֯י֯ד֯[כה]] ממתים ידך 𝔐α′ (ἀπὸ τεθνηκότων); ἀπὸ ἐχθρῶν τῆς χειρός σου 𝔊𝔙
17:14 (5) בחייה֯[ם] 𝔊𝔙] בחיים 𝔐𝔖
17:14 (5) וצפ֯[ונכ]ה] וצפינך 𝔐^{k} (וצפונך 𝔐^{q})
18:1 (9) כול] כל 𝔐
18:1 (9) אויביו] איביו 𝔐
18:2 (9) ו]י֯[ו]אמר] ויאמר 𝔐
18:2 (9) רחמ֯[תיכה]] ארחמך 𝔐
18:4 (11) אקראה] אקרא 𝔐 2 Sam 22:4 𝔐
18:4 (11) ומאויבי 2 Sam 22:4 𝔐 (ומאיבי)] ומן איבי 𝔐
18:7 (13) אלוהי] אלהי 𝔐
18:8 (15) לו 𝔐] αὐτοῖς 𝔊𝔖𝔙
18:11 (17) רוח 𝔐] הרוח ℭ
18:12 (18) ח]שכות] חשכת 𝔐; חשרת 𝔐^{ms} 2 Sam 22:12 𝔐

Frg. 9 Ps 18:15-17?

16 ובר]ק֯י֯[ם 1

17 מוסד]י֯ תבל ישל[ח 2

]ממ֯רום ויק֯ח֯[ני 3

Mus. Inv. 614
PAM 42.176, 44.006*

NOTES ON READINGS

L. 1 (18:15) ובר]ק֯י֯[ם. The tentative reading is based upon the different lengths of the downstrokes.

L. 2 (18:16) מוסד]י֯. Only the bottom tip of the last letter remains. The trace seems to be vertical, which rules out מוסד]ו֯ת֯.

L. 3 (18:17) ויק֯ח֯[ני. Only the heads of the third and fourth letters are visible. The traces are compatible with *qop* and *ḥet*, but other readings are possible as well.

COMMENTS

The words תבל and ממ֯רום indicate that the fragment is related to Ps 18:15-17, even though the sequence תבל ישל[does not correspond to 𝔐. The nature of the variant reading is unclear. Possible are a rephrasing of 𝔐 v 16aγ-b, or perhaps a change in the order of the stichs, although neither rephrasings nor changes in the order of stichs are attested in the fragments where identifications are certain. The hand of the fragment (see especially *lamed*) corresponds to that of 11QPs^c.

VARIANTS

18:16 (2) מוסד]י֯] מוסדות 𝔐

18:16? (2) ישל[ח] > 𝔐 (transposition of stichs?)

Frg. 10 Ps 19:4-8

]דעת [4]אין אומר ואין דברים בלי [נ֯]שמע קולמה [5]בכול הארץ יצא[1

]קום ובקצי תבל מליהמה לשמש [שם או֯ה֯]ל בהמה [6]והוא כחתן יוצא[2

]מחופתו ישיש כגבור לרוץ אורח [7]מ]ק֯צי ה[שמים מוצאו ותקופתו[3

]על קצותמה ואין ונסתר מחמתו [8]תור]ת֯ יה[וה 4

Mus. Inv. 621B
PAM 44.117

Notes on Readings

The reconstruction of the scroll indicates that frg. 10 belongs to the left part of the column.

L. 2 (19:5)]שׂם. The slant of the downstroke and faint traces of what seems to be the upper oblique suggest *šin*.

L. 2 (19:5) אוה֯[ל. The *waw* (or *yod*) is rather certain. אח֯[and את֯[are far more difficult, whereas אה֯[is excluded. The tip on the left edge may belong to *he* or to another letter with a downstroke.

L. 3 (19:7) מ[ק֯צי. The traces of *qop* are blurred.

L. 3 (19:7) ה[שמים. The trace after *he* in the photograph is not ink.

L. 4 (19:8) תור[ו֯ת. *Waw* is written almost diagonally, but other readings are unlikely.

L. 4 (19:8) יה[וה. The trace after *he* in the photograph is not ink.

Comments

L. 3 (19:7) מ[ק֯צי. Cf. the quotation of Deut 13:8 in 11Q**20** (Temple[b]) XVI 4, where 𝔐 מקצה is written מקצי. The form מקצי may be singular (orthographic variant of מקצה) or plural.

L. 4 (19:8) תור[ו֯ת יה[וה. A change to the plural is possible. Cf. 4Q**89** (Psalms[g]; Ps 119:44) תורתיך for 𝔐 תורתך.[1] Another possibility would be עד[ו֯ת יה[וה, assuming a change of the order of the stichs of 𝔐.

Variants

19:7 (3) מ[ק֯צי] מקצה 𝔐𝔊

19:8 (4) תור[ו֯ת (?)] תורת 𝔐𝔊

Frg. 11 Ps 25:2-7

1 אל אבושה֯[אל יעלצו אויבי לי [3]גם כול קויכה לוא יבושו יבושו]

2 הבוגדים ר֯[יקם [4]דרכיכה יהוה הודיעני אורחותיכה למדני [5]הדריכני]

3 באמתכה למ֯[דני כי אתה אלוהי ישעי אותכה קויתי כול היום [6]זכור]

4 רחמיכה [י]ה֯[וה וחסדיכה כי מעולם המה [7]חטאות נעורי ופשעי]

5 [אל]ת֯ז֯כ֯[ור

Mus. Inv. 1027
PAM 42.177
IAA 522908*

Notes on Readings

PAM 42.177 shows the left side of frg. 11 covered by sand; the fragment was cleaned in 1996 and rephotographed (IAA 522908), but the traces on the left, illegible on the original, are still very faint.

[1] P. W. Skehan, 'Qumran and Old Testament Criticism', *Qumrân, Sa piété, sa théologie et son milieu*, ed. M. Delcor (BETL XLVI; Paris-Gembloux: Duculot; Leuven: University Press, 1978) 179.

L. 1 (25:2) אבושה̊[. After *šin*, only a downstroke is visible; the rest is covered by a fold in the skin.

L. 4 (25:6) [י]ה̊[וה. IAA 522908 shows no trace of the *yod*, but there is just enough space for it, and the letter may have faded away.

Variants

25:5 (3) באמתכה] באמתך 𝔐

25:5 (3) למ̊[דני] ולמדני 𝔐𝔊

25:6 (4) רחמיכה] רחמיך 𝔐 5/6Ḥev1b

8. 11QPsalms^{d}

(PLATES VII–VIII)

Previous discussion: J. P. M. van der Ploeg, 'Fragments de Psaumes de Qumrân', ***Intertestamental Essays in Honour of Józef Tadeusz Milik***, ed. Zdzisław J. Kapera (Qumranica Mogilanensia 6; Kraków: The Enigma Press, 1992) 233–7; F. García Martínez and E. J. C. Tigchelaar, 'Psalms Manuscripts from Qumran Cave 11: A Preliminary Edition', *RevQ* 17 (1996) 92–101 and pls 12–13; S. Talmon, 'קטעי כתבים עבריים בלתי מזוהים מעזבונו של יגאל ידין', ***Tarbiz*** 66 (1996–97) 113–16.

Physical Description

THE skin is of a creamy yellow colour, with frequent dark stains. Dry lines, both horizontal and vertical, are clearly visible and sometimes have a slightly reddish colour. In many lines, the letters are written slightly beneath the dry lines. The distance between horizontal lines varies between 0.7–0.75 cm. Frg. 15 is glossy and dark brown in colour, rather than creamy yellow. However, the hand and the ruling are consistent with 11Q**8**, and the different colour need not indicate a separate manuscript. Five margins have been preserved, albeit incompletely: right margins on frg. 4 (0.6 cm) and frg. 14 (1.2 cm); a left margin on frg. 8 (0.3 cm); top margins on frg. 7 (1.7 cm) and frg. 8 (1.8 cm).

Reconstruction of the columns is uncertain due to the fragmentary state of 11QPs^{d}. The most important indication is the material correspondence between the shapes of frgs. 7 and 8, which suggests that they stem from successive revolutions, and that the column beginning with frg. 7 had 32–34 lines if the text agreed with 𝔐. Frgs. 13 and 14 probably correspond materially, as well, but the average line-length cannot be based upon the reconstruction of the lines of these fragments. It is, however, plausible that one column was missing between the columns preserved by those fragments. Frgs. 10 and 11 may belong to the same column or to two successive columns.

In addition to the preserved fragments of the scroll, cave 11 has yielded an indirect witness to the manuscript. PAM 44.012 contains a picture of a clay object on which an inscription has been preserved in reverse. According to the catalogues, this object has not been kept with the other written materials of cave 11, and it is possibly stored in a different section of the Rockefeller Museum, or elsewhere. Since the object itself has not been located, and no other description of it has been given elsewhere, for example, in the excavation report, the description must be based solely upon the photograph.

The object, with a maximal height and width of *c.*2.3 cm, is possibly composed of some type of clay, and consists of two pieces. Two lines of writing are preserved on the object. A crack is apparent just above line 2 of the reverse inscription, running through the top of *mem* and *waw*. The surface has eroded at the edges.

The object should probably be compared to 7Q**19**, which consists of three clay blocks preserving a Greek inscription in reverse. Baillet (*DJD* III, pp. 45 and 145 attributes the reverse writing to prolonged contact between the clay and papyrus fragments, resulting in a transference of the inscription from the papyrus to the clay, along with an impression of the horizontal fibres of the papyrus.

The identification of the text with Ps 6:2-4, and the correspondence with the hand of 11Q8, indicate that the object has been in contact with part of **11Q8** Psalms[d]. The main difference between the impression and the **11Q8** fragments is the slightly wider space between the lines on the impression (0.9 cm).

Contents

TABLE 1: *Contents of 11QPs[d]*

Frg.	Psalm(s)
1	6:2-4
2	9:3-6
3	18:26-29
4	18:39-42
5	36:13 – 37:4 (5?)
6	39:13 – 40:2
7	43:1-3
8	45:6-8
9	59:5-8
10	68:1-5
11	68:14-18
12	78:5-12
13	81:4-9
14	86:11-14
15	115:16 – 116:1
16	78:36-37 (?)
17	60:9 (?)

Palaeography

The hand is of a developed to late formal Herodian, indicating a date from the middle of the 1st century CE. The hand is clearly distinct from 11QPs[b] and 11QPs[c], both of which preserve a less developed, formal Herodian script.

Orthography

The use of the vowel letter *waw* is irregular. Frg. 12 corresponds exactly with 𝔐, with four defective and one *plene* spelling. Frg. 9 has two defective spellings, one of those ירצון (as in 𝔐^{A}) where 𝔐^{L} spells ירוצון *plene*. Similarly, frg. 5 has two defective spellings, including יבלון against 𝔐 יבולון. Frg. 10 2 כהנדף need not be a defective spelling. Frgs. 1, 4, 8, 11, 13, 14, and 15 display the usual *plene* writing, once, in frg. 8, supralinearly: מישׁ֯ר. The *plene* writing of /ī/ with *yod* against the defective spelling in 𝔐 occurs in frg. 5 לדויד. The expanded orthography כה- for the 2nd masc. sing. suffix appears twice, in frgs. 13 and 14.

6:3 (1 1) 𝔐 חנני] חונ̇[ני
6:4 (1 2) 𝔐 מאד]]מואדה[
18:39 (4 1) 𝔐 יפלו] יׄפׄו[לו
37:1 (5 2) 𝔐 לדוד] לדויד
37:2 (5 4) 𝔐 יבולון] יבלון
45:7 (8 2) 𝔐 מישר] מישׁ֯ר
59:5 (9 2) 𝔐^{L} ירוצון] 𝔐^{A} ירׄצון
68:16 (11 2) 𝔐 אלהים] אלוהים
68:16 (11 3) 𝔐 גבננים] ג]בנונים
81:5 (13 2) 𝔐 יעקב]]יעקובׄ[
81:8 (13 5) 𝔐 ואחלצך] וא]חׄלצכה
86:11 (14 1) 𝔐 באמתך] באמתכׄ]ה
86:12 (14 2) 𝔐 אלהי] אלוהי
86:14 (14 4) 𝔐 אלהים] אׄל[ו]הים[
115:17 (15 2) 𝔐 ולא]]ולוא[

Textual Character

Apart from spelling differences, the text of the fragments disagrees with 𝔐 in four cases. Twice, in frg. 13, it concerns a difference between singular and plural forms. Twice the manuscript seems to have had an addition, but, in both cases, the variant letters do not permit an evaluation of the nature of this addition. In frgs. 5, 13, and 14, a reconstruction according to 𝔐 results in lines of considerably different lengths. This may indicate a divergent text (cf. the proposed reconstruction of frg. 14 2–3), but frg. 12, with its ragged left margin, shows that this need not be the case.

45:6-7 (8 1) 𝔐𝔊ℭ𝔖𝔙 <] אלף
68:16 (11 2) 𝔐 הר בשן] ז[
81:6 (13 3) 𝔐𝔊ℭ𝔖𝔙 שפת] שפות
81:7 (13 4) 𝔐𝔊ℭ𝔖𝔙 כפיו] כפו
86:13 (14 3) 𝔐 חסדך גדול עלי] (?) גדול ע]לי חסדכה

Mus. Inv. 569, 580, 581A, 619, 621, 621B, 1025, 1032
PAM 42.175, 42.176, 42.177, 43.976, 43.980, 44.004, 44.005, 44.006, 44.007, 44.008, 44.012, 44.115, 44.117
IAA 563757, 563765, 563769
WSR 629 = JWS 98 (Frg. 3)

Frg. 1 Ps 6:2-4

[ואל בהמתכה]תׄיסרני [3]חונ֯[ני כי אמלל אני רפאני יהיה כי נבהלו]
[עצמי [4]ונפשי נבהלה]מואדה֯[

PAM 44.012

COMMENTS

L. 1 (6:3) חונ֯[ני. A *plene* spelling with *waw* representing *qameṣ ḥaṭuf*. Cf. the same spelling throughout 11QPs[a].

VARIANTS

6:3 (1) חונ֯[ני] 𝔐 חנני
6:4 (2)]מואדה֯[ ] 𝔐 מאד

Frg. 2 Ps 9:3-6

עליו֯ן֯[[4]בשוב אויבי אחור יכשלו ויאבדו מפניכה [5]כי עשית]
משפטי֯[ודיני ישבת לכסא שופט צדק [6]גערת גוים]
א[ב]ד֯תׄ[

Mus. Inv. 1025
IAA 563765

NOTES ON READINGS

The fragment was cleaned and first photographed in 1997.

L. 1 (6:3) עליו֯ן֯[. Faint discolourations may be indicative of *waw* and *nun*. Otherwise read עלי[ון.

Frg. 3 Ps 18:26-29

top margin

תתחסד גבר תמי]ם תתמם [27]עם נבר תתברר[

ועם עקש תתפתל [28]כי[אתה עם עני תושיע ועינים[

רמות תשפיל [29]כי אתׄ]ה האיר נרי יהוה אלהי יגיה[

]ח[שׄ]כי

WSR 629 (JWS 98)

This fragment, found in Y. Yadin's legacy, was published preliminarily by S. Talmon in *Tarbiẓ* 66 (1996–97) 113–16 without any specific identification.

Frg. 4 Ps 18:39-42

יׄפׄוׄ]לו תחת רגלי [40]ותאזרני חיל למלחמה תכריע קמי[

תחׄ]תי [41]ואויבי נתתה לי עורף ומשנאי אצמיתם [42]ישועו ואין[

מוׄ]שיע על יהוה ולוא ענם

Mus. Inv. 619
PAM 42.175, 44.004*

NOTES ON READINGS

The hand, size of the letters, interlinear distance, and colour all suggest that the fragment is part of 11QPs^{d}. The fragment corresponds to Psalm 18, but in view of the scarcity of the remains, the identification cannot be considered certain.

L. 1 (18:39) יׄפׄוׄ]לו. The first downstroke may belong to *waw*, *yod*, or perhaps *dalet* or *reš*. It cannot be the right leg of *taw*, as the following base stroke is too long. The base of the second letter and the leg of the third letter have been preserved.

L. 2 (18:40) תחׄ]תי. The right part of the second letter is consistent with *dalet*, *he*, and *ḥet*. If the faint stroke at the edge of the fragment is ink, it should be the left leg of *he* or *ḥet*.

L. 3 (18:42) מוׄ]שיע. The short length of the leg of the second letter suggests *yod*, but *waw* cannot be excluded. Other letters, like *reš*, are far more difficult.

VARIANTS

18:39 (1) יׄפׄוׄ]לו] יפלו 𝔐

18:42 (3) מוׄ]שיע 𝔐] ὁ σῴζων 𝔊

Frg. 5 Ps 36:13–37:4 (5?)

1 קו]ם *va]cat*

2 *va[cat* [1]לדויד א]ל תתחר במרעים

3 א]ל תקנׄא בעש]י עולה [2]כי כחציר מהרה ימלו וכירק

4 ד]שׄא יבלון [3]בט]ח ביהוה ועשה טוב שכן ארץ

5 ורע]הׄ אׄמׄונה [4]והׄ]תענג על יהוה ויתן לכה

6]לׄ[

Mus. Inv. 621B
PAM 42.175, 44.117*

Notes on Readings

The lines cannot be reconstructed on the basis of 𝔐. The fragment is placed at the beginning of the line, and the words of 𝔐 are written to the left.

L. 5 (37:3) אׄמׄונה. The *nun* is clear in PAM 42.175.

Comments

L. 2 (37:1) לדויד *va[cat*. The Psalm begins after a *vacat* at the beginning of the line, whereas in frg. 6 the new psalm seems to start at the right margin.

L. 2 (37:1) The text of 𝔐 seems rather short for this line.

L. 6 (37:4/5)]לׄ[. The *lamed* must have belonged to v 4, לבכה, or v 5, גול, or perhaps to v 5, על, depending on the length of the line.

Variants

37:1 (2) לדויד] לדוד 𝔐𝔊𝔗; ψαλμὸς τῷ Δαυιδ 𝔊^{2046} $^{L'}$𝔙^{VDΩs}; εἰς τὸ τέλος ψαλμὸς τῷ Δαυιδ 𝔊^{A} La^{G}

37:2 (4) יבלון] יבולון 𝔐; ταχὺ ἀποπεσοῦνται 𝔊𝔙 (ἀποπεσοῦνται is probably a translation of יבולון, not of יפולון; cf. also 𝔊 Isa 40:7); ταχὺ ἀποξηρανθήσονται 𝔊^{2046} (*ex* 37:2a)

37:3 (5) אׄמׄונה 𝔐] ἐπὶ τῷ πλούτῳ αὐτῆς 𝔊; ἐν τῷ πλούτῳ αὐτῆς 𝔊^{2046}𝔙 (*in divitiis eius*)

Frg. 6 Ps 39:13–40:2

1 [האזי]נׄהׄ] אל דמעתי אל תחרש כי גר אנוכי עמכה]

2 תׄושב] ככול אבותי [14]השע ממני ואבליגה בטרם אלך]

3 ואינׄ]י *vacat* [

4 [40:1]למנצ]ח [

5 [ ]◦[

Mus. Inv. 569
PAM 44.006*, 44.115

Notes on Readings

The margin has not been preserved; nevertheless, the fragment may preserve the first words of the lines. The fragment could not be located on Mus. Inv. 569.

L. 5]◦[ ]. The small trace on the bottom tip of the fragment can belong to almost any letter.

Comments

L. 2 (39:13) תֿושב[. There seems to be no space for an additional *waw* between the assumed right margin and *taw*.

L. 5]◦[ ]. If the text corresponded to 𝔐, one may reconstruct [ו]שׁ֯[שמע.

Variants

39:13 (2) תֿושב[𝔐ℭ] ותושב 𝔊𝔖

Frg. 7 Ps 43:1-3

top margin

1 [מרמה וע]ולה תפלטני [2]כי[אתה אלוהי מעוזי למה זנחתני למה]

2 [קודר א]תהלך בל[חץ אויב [3]שלח אורכה ואמתכה המה ינחוני]

3 [יביאוני א]ל[הר

Mus. Inv. 569
PAM 42.176, 43.980, 44.115*

Notes on Readings

The placement of the fragment within the column is uncertain and can only be calculated on the basis of a reconstruction of the scroll.

L. 1 (43:1) וע]ולה. The traces of *he* are faint but visible.

L. 2 (43:2) א]תהלך. The fragment may have preserved part of the left leg of *ʾalep*.

Variants

43:1 (1) [מרמה וע]ולה 𝔐] ἀδίκου καὶ δολίου (transposition) 𝔊𝔖𝔙

Frg. 8 Ps 45:6-8

top margin

בלב אוי]ב̊י המלך אלף]

[7]כסאכה אלהים עולם ועד ש]ב̊ט מיש̇ר]

]שבט מלכותכה [8]אהבת צדק ותשנא רשע על כן משחכה א]ל[הים

Mus. Inv. 621B
PAM 44.117

NOTES ON READINGS

The reading המלך in line 1 followed by שבט מיש̇ר in line 2, as well as the physical similarity to the fragment preserving Ps 43:1-3, indicates that the fragment corresponds to Ps 45:6-8. The black traces on the upper right part of the fragment, visible in the photograph, are probably tears.

L. 1 (45:6) אוי]ב̊י. The head of *yod* is visible. The two dots to the right of *yod* may be the left tips of the head and base of *bet*.

L. 1 (45:6) המלך אלף. The space between the words is larger than usual.

L. 1 אלף. There is a small space between the *lamed* and the final *pe*, and one may also transcribe אל ף.

COMMENTS

L. 1 אלף. The meaning of the word ('thousand'? or אל followed by final *pe*?) is not clear. It may be the first word of a new clause. None of the versions confirms an addition, but cf. Theodoretus's commentary: μεθυπερβατα εστι τα ρηματα . . . τα βελη σου γαρ ηκονημενα, δυνατε, εν καρδια των εχθρων του βασιλεως, τουτων δε τρωθεντων λαοι υποκατω σου πεσουνται.

L. 3 א]ל[הים. The *lamed* might also belong to the following אלהיכה.

VARIANTS

45:6-7 (1) אלף] > 𝔐𝔊ℭ𝔖𝔙

45:7 (2) מיש̇ר] מישר 𝔐

Frg. 9 Ps 59:5-8

]◦ [ ]

י̊רצון וי]כוננו עורה לקראתי וראה [6]ואתה יהוה אלהים צבאות[

אלהי ישר]אל הקיצה לפקד כל הגוים אל תחן כל בגדי[

4 אוןֿ סלה֯[[7]ישובו לערב יהמו ככלב ויסובבו עיר [8]הנה יביעון]

5 ב֯פיהם [

Mus. Inv. 569
PAM 42.176, 43.980, 44.115*

NOTES ON READINGS

A tiny fragment seems to be attached to the left side of line 3, but the traces of two letters (the second probably *waw* or *yod*) shows it does not belong there. The dry line of the right margin is not visible, but probably coincided with the right edge of the fragment.

L. 1]◦ [. Dots of ink on what should be the baseline can be seen, preceded by a space without dots.

L. 2 (59:5) י֯רצון. The dot representing the *yod* is visible in PAM 44.115.

COMMENTS

L. 1]◦ [. One may perhaps read א֯ר֯]בו [הנה], but then the line is some seven letter-spaces longer than the others.

L. 2 (59:5) י֯רצון. The defective spelling does not imply that the copyist interpreted the word as a form of רצה (van der Ploeg); cf. 𝔐^{A} and the *plene* and defective spelling in Joel 2:4, 7, and 9.

VARIANTS

59:5 (2) י֯רצון 𝔐^{A}**]** ירוצון 𝔐^{L}𝔊 (ἔδραμον); 𝔙 *cucurri* (interpreting ἔδραμον as a 1st sing.); + ܪܗܛܬ 𝔖

59:6 (4) סלה֯[𝔐𝔊𝔙^{CQ} **]** > 𝔙$^{W\phi G^{*}G^{*}VD\Omega}$

Frg. 10 Ps 68:1-5

1 [[1]למנצח לדוד מזמו]ר שי֯[ר [2]יקום אלהים יפוצו אויביו]

2 [וינוסו משנאיו מפניו][3]כ֯הנדף [עשן תנדף כהמס דונג מפני]

3 [אש יאבדו רשעים]מפני [אלהים [4]וצדיקים ישמחו יעלצו]

4 [לפני אלהים וישישו] בשמח֯ה֯[[5]שירו לאלהים זמרו שמו סלו]

5 [לרכב בערבות ביה ש]מו ועל[זו לפניו

Mus. Inv. 569
PAM 42.176, 44.005, 44.006, 44.115*

NOTES ON READINGS

The oldest photograph, PAM 42.176, shows the two fragments still partially attached. Placement of the fragment within the column is tentative.

Frg. 11 Ps 68:14-18

[בירקר]ק֯[חרוץ 15בפרש שדי מלכים בה תשלג בצלמון] 1

[16הר] אלוהים ז[ה הר בשן הר גבננים הר בשן 17למה תרצדון] 2

[הרים ג]בנונים ה[הר חמד אלהים לשבתו אף יהוה ישכן] 3

[לנצ]ח 18רכב אל֯[והים 4

Mus. Inv. 569
PAM 42.177, 44.007, 44.008, 44.115*

NOTES ON READINGS

Two fragments, which were still attached to one another in PAM 42.177, comprise frg. 11. Eight to nine lines are missing between frg. 10 (Ps 68:1-5) and this fragment. The placement of the fragment at the right side of the column is uncertain.

L. 1 (68:14) [בירקר]ק֯[. PAM 42.177 shows a dot to the left of the top of the upper arm of the *lamed* of אלוהים (line 2), perhaps being the tip of the tail of a letter; cf. the *qop* of נושקי and the *lamed* of אלהים in frg. 12 5–6 (Ps 78:9-10). The reconstruction of the lines suggests it is one of the two *qop*s of בירקרק.

L. 2 (68:16) ז[. The remains are clearly *zayin* and not the right part of *he*.

L. 3 (68:17) ג]בנונים. The head of *bet* is visible in PAM 44.115, and the base is visible in PAM 42.177 and 44.008.

COMMENTS

L. 2 (68:16) ז[. It is unclear what the text could have read. The reading ז[ה הר בשן הר גבננים הר בשן למה תרצדון would just fit in the line, but the use of זה instead of הוא as a copula is not very usual. Alternatively, the text may have deviated from 𝔐, e.g. הר אלוהים ז[ה שכן בו הר גבננים הר בשן למה תרצדון (cf. Ps 74:2). The only other word beginning with *zayin* which might fit in the context is the old poetic זו which, in 11Q7 8 1, has been replaced precisely by זה.

VARIANTS

68:16 (2) אלוהים] אלהים 𝔐
68:16 (2) ז[ה] > 𝔐
68:16 (3) ג]בנונים] גבננים 𝔐

Frg. 12 Ps 78:5-12

לבני]ה֯ם [6למען ידעו]] 1

[דור אחרון בנים יולדו יקמו וי]ספרו לבנ֯[יהם 7וישימו] 2

3 [באלהים כסלם ולא ישכחו מ]עׄללי אל ומ֯[צותיו ינצרו]
4 [8ולא יהיו כאבותם דור סורר ו]מרה דור לא הכין
5 [לבו ולא נאמנה את אל רוחו 9בני]א֯פרים נושקי
6 [רומי קשת הפכו ביום קרב 10לא]שמרו ברית אלהים ובתור[תו]
7 [מאנו ללכת 11וישכחו עלילותיו] ונפלאותיו אשר
8 [הראם 12נגד אבותם עשה פלא באר]ץ מׄצׄרׄים ש[דה

Mus. Inv. 569, 621B
PAM 42.176, 44.004*, 44.005*, 44.006, 44.008, 44.115*, 44.117*

NOTES ON READINGS

Frg. 12 is composed of seven fragments, three of which (frgs. c, d, e) are joined in PAM 44.115. On Mus. Inv. 569, frg. b (PAM 44.004) has been joined to these three fragments. Three other fragments have been joined to the top, left, and bottom left of the four already joined fragments. Frg. f (PAM 44.117) shows that the left margin was very ragged. The dry line is not visible on that fragment, so one cannot know whether ובתור[תו] was written in the intercolumnar margin.

L. 3 (78:7) מ]עׄללי. Parts of the base of the *ʿayin* are preserved on two fragments.

L. 8 (78:12) מׄצׄרׄים. In view of the perfect join the reading is certain, although none of the letters is preserved completely.

VARIANTS

78:6 (2) ויׄ[ספרו 𝔐𝔊[S,2054] La[G]𝔖𝔗] + αὐτὰ 𝔊
78:9 (5) נושקי 𝔐] נוקשי 𝔐[mss]
78:12 (8) ש[דה 𝔐] ἐν πεδίῳ 𝔊𝔖𝔗

Frg. 13 Ps 81:4-9

1 [בכסה ל]יום [חגנו 5כי חוק לישראל הוא משפט]
2 [לאלוהי]יעקוב֯[6עדות ביהוסף שמו בצאתו על]
3 [ארץ מצרי]ם שפות ל֯[וא ידעתי אשמע 7הסירותי]
4 [מסבל ש]כמו כפו מ֯[דוד תעברנה 8בצרה]
5 [קראת וא]ח֯לצכה א[ענכה בסתר רעם אבחנכה על]
6 [מי מריבה]ס֯לה֯ 9שׄ[מע

Mus. Inv. 569
PAM 44.005, 44.115*

NOTES ON READINGS

The placement of the fragment within the column is tentative.

L. 4 (81:7) מ֯[דוד. The tiny trace at the edge is compatible with the bottom right stroke of *mem*. The reading *bet* is excluded.

VARIANTS

81:5 (2)]יעקוב֯[ ] יעקב 𝔐
81:6 (3) שפות] שפת 𝔐𝔊ℭ𝔖𝔙
81:7 (4) כפו] כפיו 𝔐𝔊ℭ𝔖𝔙
81:7 (4) מ֯[דוד 𝔐] ἐν τῷ κοφίνῳ 𝔊𝔙 = בדוד
81:8 (5) וא]ח֯לצכה] ואחלצך 𝔐

Frg. 14 Ps 86:11-14

באמתכ֯[ה יחד לבבי ליראה שמכה 12אודכה אדני] 1
אלוהי ב[כול לבבי ואכבדה שמכה לעולם 13כי] 2
גדול ע[לי חסדכה והצלת נפשי משאול תחתיה] 3
14א֯ל[ו]הים] 4

Mus. Inv. 621B
PAM 42.177, 44.117*

NOTES ON READINGS

Frg. 14 was originally ascribed to 11Q**9** (Psalms[e]), but the hand is the same as that of 11Q**8** (Psalms[d]). Most important, this fragment has a pattern of damage in its lower and left part similar to that of frg. 13, suggesting that they come from superimposed layers.

L. 4 (86:14) א֯ל[ו]הים]. The space between *lamed* and *he* is the same as in line 2 אלוהי.

COMMENTS

Ll. 2–3 (86:13) כי] / גדול ע[לי חסדכה. The reconstruction of the lines suggests that חסדכה was placed after גדול ע[לי, and not before it, as in 𝔐; cf. Ps 108:5 כי גדול מעל שמים חסדך.

VARIANTS

86:11 (1) באמתכ֯[ה] באמתך 𝔐
86:12 (2) אלוהי] אלהי 𝔐

86:13 (3) חסדך גדול עלי](?) גדול ע[לי חסדכה 𝔐
86:14 (4) אלהים] אׄל[ו]הים[𝔐

Frg. 15 Ps 115:16–116:1

[עושה שמים וארץ 16השמים שמים]ליהוׄ[ה והארץ נתן] 1
[לבני אדם 17לוא המתים יהללו יה]ולוא[כול יורדי] 2
[דומה 18ואנחנו נברך יה מעתה וע]ד ע[ולם הללו יה] 3
[*vacat*]*vac*[*vacat*] 4
[116:1אהבתי כי ישמע יהוה את קולי תחנ]וׄני [2כי חטה] 5
[ ]◦ ◦[ ] 6

Mus. Inv. 581A
IAA 563757

NOTES ON READINGS

The fragment, which was flattened and first photographed in 1997, is a glossy dark brown, different from the other 11QPs[d] fragments, but both ruling and hand conform to 11Q**8**. The identification is based on the assumption that the *vacat* in line 4 indicates the beginning of a new psalm in line 5.

L. 1 (115:16)]ליהוׄ[ה. After *he*, the fragment is very dark, but strong light shone from behind the photograph reveals traces of *waw*.

L. 6]◦ ◦[. Both traces are on the edges of the fragment. The second trace has the slant of *waw*, but it is difficult to read the first trace as *taw*, ruling out the reading מו[תׄ וׄ]מצרי.

VARIANTS

115:17 (2) ולא 𝔐]]ולוא[

Unidentified Fragments

Frg. 16 Ps 78:36-37 (?)

יכזבׄ]ו לו ולבם לא נכון עמו 1
] [ל] 2

Mus. Inv. 580
PAM 43.976

NOTES ON READINGS

Frg. 16 has previously been viewed as part of 11Q**20** (Temple[b]; Yadin, García Martinez, Wacholder), but the colour of the skin, the reading and the intralinear space suggest it belongs to another manuscript. The hand is compatible with 11QPs[d], and it might correspond with Ps 78:36. However, the *lamed* in line 2 does not fit in the reconstruction of the line according to 𝔐. An identification with the apocryphal psalm preserved in 4Q**88** (Psalms[f]) IX may also be possible, in which case one must assume that the *lamed* corresponds to that in 4QPs[f] IX 15.

L. 1 יכזב֯]. The first letter is almost certainly *yod*, which excludes the reading וכזב֯]ח (Ps 83:12).

L. 2 [ ]ל]. There is space before *lamed* for *waw* or *yod*.

COMMENTS

L. 2 [ ]ל]. It is not clear to which word of 𝔐 the letters correspond. [ו]ל[בם would imply a large *vacat* in line 1, but [ו]ל[וא, corresponding to ולא of v 37, would also give a somewhat shorter line 1 than elsewhere in the manuscript.

Frg. 17 Ps 60:9 (?)

1 [ד֯ ול֯י֯]

Mus. Inv. 1032
IAA 563769

NOTES ON READINGS

The hand and the clearly visible ruling strongly suggest 11Q**8**.

L. 1 [ד֯ ול֯י֯]. The first letter may also be *reš* or final *kap*. The shortness of the stroke of the last letter suggests *yod*. After *yod* no traces are visible, but this might be due to the ink having faded.

COMMENTS

The preserved traces fit in Ps 19:3 אמ]ר֯ ול֯י֯[לה and Ps 60:9 לי גלע[ד֯ ול֯י֯]מנשה. The blank area of skin following *yod* may indicate the latter.

9. 11QPsalms[e]?

(PLATE VIII)

11QPsalms[e]? is a small fragment comprising remnants of Psalm 50:3-7. The two fragments formerly named 11QPsalms[e] are now identified as 11QPsalms[d] (frgs. 8, 14).

The fragment, 2.9 cm in height and 2.3 cm in width, is, like most fragments belonging to Mus. Inv. 1016, illegible to the naked eye. Its colour, like that of the other fragments on this museum plate (belonging to such different manuscripts as 11Q**2**, 11Q**3**, and 11Q**20**), is dark brown, with a greyish hue. The upper part of the fragment appears to be uninscribed, although this could be accidental (see the very faint traces of lines 1 and 3).

The small size of the script, with letters no higher than 2 mm, the narrowly spaced lines (0.5 and 0.6 mm), as well as the apparently uninscribed upper section, might suggest that the fragment preserves an intercolumnar addition to one of the already identified Psalms scrolls. The hand displays some similarities to that of 11QPsalms[c], especially with regard to the slant of the letters, but the forms of the few distinct letters in this fragment do not exactly correspond to those of 11QPsalms[c]. Moreover, if the identification of the traces of lines 1 and 3 is correct, the lines would have measured *c.*10.5 cm. There are examples of multiple intralinear lines spilling over into the intracolumnar margin (cf. e.g. 4QJer[a] III), but since the fragment differs both physically and palaeographically from the other Psalms scrolls, it is more likely that 11Q**9** is the only preserved fragment of a fifth Psalms scroll from cave 11.

Mus. Inv. 1016
PAM 43.794*

Ps 50:3-7

1]לפניו תא[כׄל וסביביו נשערה מאד 4יקרא אל השמים מעל ואל הארץ לדין עמו 5אספו לי[
2]חסידי כר[תׄ]י [בׄ]ר[יתי עלי זבׄ]ח 6ויגידו שמים צדקו כי אלהים שפט הוא סלה 7שמעה עמי[
3]ואדברה י[שׂראׄלׄ] ואעידה
4 [◦]

NOTES ON READINGS

L. 1 (50:3) תא[כׄל. The only clear traces on the line suggest *kap* or *bet*, but it cannot be ascertained if these traces are indeed ink.

L. 2 (50:5) כר]תׄי [בׄ[ר]יתי. A dark trace, if indeed ink, is compatible with the head of *bet*. The last letter of בׄ[ר]יתי may be either *waw* or *yod*. Very faint traces, if from ink, may be remnants of *yod* and *reš*.

L. 3 (50:7) י[שׂרׄאׄל]. The traces on this line are fainter than those at the end of line 2, and may be interpreted differently. The upper arm of *lamed* slants slightly to the right, and the dark trace to the left, which resembles the upper arm of *lamed*, may be a supralinear *waw* of ואעידה, if actually ink.

L. 3 (50:7) ואעידה. There are no certain traces of this word, although it would fit on the fragment. The dark stroke after י[שׂרׄאׄל] might be a supralinear *waw*, and a horizontal stroke further to the left could agree with the head of *dalet*.

L. 4]◦[. Several traces at the lower edge of the fragment are possibly ink, but any identification is impossible.

10. 11QtargumJob

(PLATES IX–XXI)

Preliminary editions: J. P. M. van der Ploeg, O. P., A. S. van der Woude (avec la collaboration de B. Jongeling), *Le Targum de Job de la Grotte XI de Qumrân* (Leiden: E. J. Brill, 1971) = *ed. princ.*; M. Sokoloff, *The Targum to Job from Qumran Cave XI* (Ramat-Gan: Bar-Ilan University, 1974); B. Jongeling, C. J. Labuschagne, A. S. van der Woude, *Aramaic Texts from Qumran with Translations and Annotations* (SSS New Series 4; Leiden: E. J. Brill, 1976) 1–73 = *ed. ATQ*; É. Puech, F. García Martínez, 'Remarques sur la colonne XXXVIII de 11 Q tg Job', *RevQ* 9/35 (1978) 401–7; K. Beyer, *Die aramäischen Texte vom Toten Meer* (Göttingen: Vandenhoeck & Ruprecht, 1984) 280–98; B. Zuckerman, S. A. Reed, 'A Fragment of an Unstudied Column of 11QtgJob: A Preliminary Report', *The Comprehensive Aramaic Lexicon Newsletter* 10 (1993) 1–7; K. Beyer, *Die aramäischen Texte vom Toten Meer: Ergänzungsband* (Göttingen: Vandenhoeck & Ruprecht, 1994) 133.

Textual discussions (selection): S. A. Kaufman, 'The Job Targum from Qumran', *JAOS* 93 (1973) 317–27; F. García Martínez, 'Nuevas lecturas de 11QtgJob', *Sefarad* 36 (1976) 241–9.

Bibliography: W. E. Aufrecht, 'A Bibliography of the Job Targumim', *Newsletter for Targumic and Cognate Studies*, Supplement 3 (1987).

Physical Description

THE remnants of the scroll consist of the so-called small scroll, twenty-eight large fragments belonging to subsequent revolutions of the original scroll, and a large number of additional fragments, twenty-two of which were numbered in the *editio princeps*. In addition to the fragments printed in the *editio princeps*, and the fragment published by Zuckerman and Reed (frg. 6a), this edition comprises some fragments of Mus. Inv. 567 (PAM 44.114) and all fragments of Mus. Inv. 625 (PAM 44.116), most of which have broken into many small pieces. Only one of those fragments has been identified (cf. col. XVII). This edition maintains the system of numbering introduced in the *editio princeps*. The numbers of the reconstructed columns I–XXXVIII are those given in the *editio princeps*. Four columns located between the columns presented in the *editio princeps* are referred to in this edition as cols. IA, IIIA, VIIA and VIIB. The large fragments stemming from subsequent revolutions are numbered 1 to 27, whereas the fragment published by Zuckerman and Reed, preserving the revolution between frgs. 6 and 7, is numbered frg. 6a. The *editio princeps* assigned the sigla A1–A5 to the small fragments that were presented to the editors as separate fragments, and B–R to the fragments that became detached from the small scroll while it was being unrolled. This edition adds the sigla A6–A19 for the fragments of Mus. Inv. 567 and 625, and S–W for other fragments which became detached from the small scroll but were not numbered in the *editio princeps*. Frgs. B–W can no longer be located in the museum

The skin of the scroll is 0.3–0.4 cm thick, smooth and very well prepared, with the writing on the hair side. The colour of the skin ranges from tan to dark brown; in most of the fragments and the small scroll, the edge, to a depth of 0.2 to 0.5 cm, has darkened to the point of being almost black, and there are no longer any visible letters. Examination of the small scroll and fragments in December 1995 revealed that parts of the corroded areas have broken away, and that, in some cases, the oxidation of the skin has progressed further; a number of traces on the edges discernible in the photographs are no longer visible on the fragments and scroll in the Rockefeller Museum.

Several sheets display different characteristics. The skin of sheet 4 (cols. VIII–X; frgs. 7 ii–9) is of a lighter colour, has a smoother surface, and does not show the border deterioration of the preceding and following sheets. The colour of the skin of sheet 5 (cols. XI–XIV; frgs. 10–12) is darker, the grain is coarser, and the deterioration of the edges appears again, as in the first fragments. Sheets 6 and 7 have the same colour, texture, and preparation. The skin of sheet 8 (cols. XX–XXII; frgs. 17 ii–19) is a lighter hue of the same basic brown, and is smoother and shinier. The skin of sheets 12 and 13 is smoother and of a finer grain; the colour is a little lighter. The thickness of each separate sheet has not been measured. The fragments on Mus. Inv. 567 and 625 have darkened to a large extent, but some fragments on Mus. Inv. 625 have turned ash grey instead of black.

The leather has been carefully ruled, both vertically and horizontally. In the first nine preserved sheets (cols. I–XXV; frgs. 1–23), the ruling has left deep indentations in the skin. As a result, these rulings are clearly visible and are of a darker colour. In the following sheets, however, the horizontal ruling especially is faint and often invisible. Sometimes only a shiny reflection is visible; the clearest vertical rulings on those sheets are on frg. 26, but even there the rulings are different from those found in the first sheets.

Stitching between sheets has been preserved on several fragments and in the small scroll. On frg. 17 more than 5 cm of the thread that attached the sheet has been preserved. A few millimetres of leather have been folded on each side prior to the stitching (best visible on frg. 7). The stitching has been made on the fold, so that no holes are visible on the surface of the scroll as attested by frg. 17. Frg. 15 allows for a measurement of the distance between the holes: 0.6 cm. As the fragments are now glued to rice paper, it is not possible to measure the distance between the holes in the other cases, nor is it possible to ascertain the dimensions of the fold.

The ink is deep black and the contours of the letters are sharp and well defined. On some fragments, in some words more than others, a white powdery substance is visible in the ink, but is not seen on the skin itself. According to L. Libman (oral communication) this substance could be salt crystals contained in the water used for the preparation of the ink.

Margins Preserved

Col.	Right	Left	Top	Col.	Right	Left	Top
I				XIX	•	•	•
II	•		•	XX	•		•
III			•	XXI	•		•
IV	•		•	XXII			•
V			•	XXIII	•	•	•
VI		•	•	XXIV	•	•	•
VII	•		•	XXV	•		•
VIIA			•	XXVI	•	•	•
VIIB		•	•	XXVII	•	•	•
VIII	•		•	XXVIII	•	•	•
IX			•	XXIX	•	•	•
X		•		XXX	•	•	•
XI		•	•	XXXI	•	•	
XII	•	•	•	XXXII	•	•	
XIII	•		•	XXXIII	•	•	
XIV			•	XXXIV	•	•	
XV			•	XXXV	•	•	
XVI		•	•	XXXVI	•	•	
XVII		•	•	XXXVII	•	•	
XVIII	•	•	•	XXXVIII	•	•	

Measurements

Height of the Inscribed Sections of the Sheets (excluding Margins)

Sheet 2 — *c*.10.5 cm (reconstructed for 18 lines on the basis of an average distance between the horizontal lines of 0.6 cm; 17 x 0.6 + 0.3)

Sheet 6 — *c*.10.8 cm (reconstructed for 15 lines on the basis of an average distance between the horizontal lines of 0.75 cm; 14 x 0.75 + 0.3)

Sheet 7 — *c*.10.8 cm (reconstructed for 16 lines on the basis of an average distance between the horizontal lines of 0.7 cm; 15 x 0.7 + 0.3)

Average Number of Letters per Line

Col. XVI	30	Col. XXXII	38
Col. XXVI	38	Col. XXXIII	39
Col. XXVII	42	Col. XXXIV	37
Col. XXVIII	38	Col. XXXV	34
Col. XXIX	40	Col. XXXVI	36
Col. XXX	41	Col. XXXVII	33
Col. XXXI	40	Col. XXXVIII	37

Margins between Columns

VI–VII	1.2 cm
XI–XII	1.5 cm
XII–XIII	1.4 cm
XVIII–XIX	1.9 cm
XXIII–XXIV	1.5 cm (note the extra vertical ruling in the intercolumnar space at 1 cm from the left ruling of col. XXIII)
XXIV–XXV	1.5 cm
XXVI–XXVII	1.5 cm
XXVII–XXVIII	1.5 cm
XXIX–XXX	1.7 cm
XXX–XXXI	1.4 cm
XXXII–XXXIII	1.4 cm
XXXIII–XXXIV	1.3 cm
XXXIV–XXXV	1.5 cm
XXXVI–XXXVII	1.5 cm
XXXVII–XXXVIII	1.8 cm
XXXVIII–blank handle page	1.8 cm

Right Margins (from Stitching to Ruling)

Col. VIII	1 cm
Col. XVIII	1.3 cm
Col. XX	0.7 cm
Col. XXXII	1 cm
Col. XXXVI	0.7 cm

Left Margins (from Ruling to Stitching)

Col. VIIB	1 cm
Col. XVII	0.9 cm
Col. XIX	1–1.2 cm
Col. XXXI	1 cm
Col. XXXV	0.7 cm

Top Margins

Col. XX	1.3 cm (complete)
Col. XXI	1.3 cm (complete)

Preserved Stitchings between Sheets

Sheet 3–4	Cols. VIIB–VIII
Sheet 6–7	Cols. XVII–XVIII
Sheet 7–8	Cols. XIX–XX
Sheet 11–12	Cols. XXXI–XXXII
Sheet 12–13	Cols. XXXV–XXXVI

Width of Sheets and Columns

Sheet	Total Width (cm)	Col.	Width without Margins (cm)
1			
		I	*c.*7.5 ? (2.5)
		[IA]	*c.*7.5 ? (0)
2	*c.*42.5 (10.8)	II	*c.*9 (3.1)
		III	*c.*9 (3.7)
		[IIIA]	*c.*9 (0)
		IV	*c.*9 (3.6)
.3	*c.*45–45.5 (15)	V	*c.*8–8.5 (4.3)
		VI	*c.*7.5 (1.9)
		VII	*c.*7.5 (2)
		VIIA	*c.*7.5 (4.8)
		VIIB	*c.*7.5 (0.1)

Sheet	Total Width (cm)	Col.	Width without Margins (cm)
4	*c*.31.0 (12.8)	VIII	*c*.8.5 (2.4)
		IX	*c*.8.5 (4.4)
		X	*c*.8.5 (4.4)
5	*c*.42.5–43.0 (17.1)	XI	*c*.9 ? (3.2)
		XII	*c*.8.7 (1.6)
		XIII	*c*.9.1 (3.8)
		XIV	*c*.8–8.5 (5.6)
6	*c*.28.0 (13.2)	XV	*c*.8.3 (5.2)
		XVI	*c*.7.3 (4.4)
		XVII	*c*.7.3 (1.7)
7	*c*.21.5 (10.7)	XVIII	*c*.8.7 (3.2)
		XIX	*c*.8.7 (3.2)
8	*c*.29.5 (13.6)	XX	*c*.7.7 (2.5)
		XXI	*c*.8.5 (4.8)
		XXII	*c*.8.5 (5.1)
9	*c*.36.5 (22.1)	XXIII	*c*.10.3 (5.7)
		XXIV	*c*.10.5 (6.5)
		XXV	*c*.10.5 (5.9)
10	*c*.34.5 (27.3)	XXVI	*c*.10 (7.7)
		XXVII	*c*.10 (8)
		XXVIII	*c*.9.5 (7.9)
11	*c*.32.6 (32.4)	XXIX	9.2
		XXX	9.3
		XXXI	9
12	39.3	XXXII	8.3
		XXXIII	8.5
		XXXIV	8.1
		XXXV	8.2
13	37.7	XXXVI	7.9
		XXXVII	7.7
		XXXVIII	7.3
		blank handle page	9.5

Figures preceded by *c*. are calculated or estimated. Other figures (whether or not in parenthesis) are extant.

Distance between Horizontal Lines (in cm)

Sheet	Oscillating between	Average
2	0.5–0.7	0.60
3	0.6–0.8	0.70
4	0.4–0.7	0.65
5	0.5–0.7	0.60
6	0.6–0.8	0.75
7	0.6–0.8	0.70
8	0.5–0.7	0.60
9	0.5–0.8	0.65
10	0.5–0.7	0.60
11	0.5–0.7	0.60
12	0.5–0.7	0.60
13	0.5–0.7	0.60

Revolutions

The width of a revolution rapidly increases in col. XXXVIII from 3.5 to 3.9, and to 4.3 cm. This indicates that the first revolution of the scroll (not visible in the photograph in the *editio princeps*) was *c.*3 cm; therefore, the empty diameter in the scroll was less than 1 cm. In the ten revolutions from the left, stitched part of col. XXXV to the right margin of col. XXIX, the revolution increases from 5.8 cm to 8 cm (including one stitching). This shows that the very beginning of the scroll was somewhat less tightly wrapped, and that the average increase per revolution is about 0.2 cm, with stitchings (as, here, the skin is folded) giving an extra increase. The 28 fragments covering cols. I–XXVIII represent 28 consecutive revolutions in which nine stitchings should be placed (including that between cols. XXVIII and XXIX). Hence, the width of the revolution between frgs. 1 and 2 measured at least 15.2 cm (revolution of col. XXIX + 27 revolutions with an average increase of *c.*0.2 cm + 9 stitchings of a minimum of 0.2 cm).

Columns

Comparison with 𝔐 suggests that the numbers of lines per column varied between 15 and 18. For example, 9 missing lines may be reconstructed in addition to the 9 preserved lines in col. IV where the average distance between the horizontal lines is 0.6 cm. This would correspond to a total of 16 lines in those sheets where the average line distance is 0.7 cm. Thus, the inscribed height of the scroll may be calculated to be *c.*10.5 cm (the figures given in the *editio princeps*, p. 2, i.e. 16–17 lines and an inscribed height of *c.*9.5 cm, are slightly too low). The top margin measured 1.3 cm. The size of the bottom margin is unknown. Assuming the bottom margin was at least the same size as the top margin, the total height of the scroll would have been *c.*14 cm.

Col. VII begins with Job 22:16, which according to the Masoretic annotation is the middle of the book (in verses, not in words). From here to the end, the scroll has 34 columns with a reconstructed width of *c*.350 cm. Hence, the complete scroll would have contained about 68 columns and have measured *c*.700 cm without the blank handle sheets.

The distinctive pattern of decay of the scroll, the presence of many margins and several stitches on the loose fragments, differences in the skin texture and rulings, all make it easy to reconstruct the scroll, although calculations tend to be less exact towards the beginning of the scroll. These calculations show that one column has been lost between cols. I and II, and another between III and IV. The pattern of decay indicates that these columns were not preserved, and that there is no hope for a reappearance as in the case of frg. 6a. The same goes for col. VIIB of which only 0.1 cm of the left side has survived.

Only one uncertainty remains regarding the sheets to which the columns belong. The lost column IA may have been situated on sheet 1 or sheet 2, but since none of the other sheets is longer than *c*.45 cm, we assume that sheet 2 began with col. II.

At least in one case the reconstruction of the scroll is of help to the reconstruction of columns. The reconstruction in the *editio princeps* (p. 38) of col. XIV is certainly incorrect, and a reconstruction giving longer lines is to be favoured.

Contents

TABLE 1: *Contents of 11QtgJob*

Col.	*Job*	Col.	*Job*	Col.	*Job*
I	17:14–18:4	XI	27:11-20	XXV	34:24-34
[IA]	[18:15 (?)–19:10]	XII	28:4-13	XXVI	35:6-15
II	19:11-19	XIII	28:20-28	XXVII	36:7-16
III	19:29–20:6	XIV	29:7-16	XXVIII	36:23-33
[IIIA]	[20:15 (?)–21:2]	XV	29:24–30:4	XXIX	37:10-19
IV	21:2-10	XVI	30:13-20	XXX	38:3-13
V	21:20-27	XVII	30:25–31:1	XXXI	38:23-34
VI	22:3-9	XVIII	31:8-16	XXXII	39:1-11
VII	22:16-22	XIX	31:26-32	XXXIII	39:20-29
VIIA	23:1-8	XX	31:40–32:3	XXXIV	40:5-14 (15?)
[VIIB]	[23:15(?)–24:11]	XXI	32:10-17	XXXV	40:23-31
VIII	24:12-17	XXII	33:6-16	XXXVI	41:7-17
IX	24:24–26:2	XXIII	33:24-32	XXXVII	41:25–42:2; 40:5; 42:4-6
X	26:10–27:4	XXIV	34:6-17	XXXVIII	42:9-12

Palaeography

The hand is of a developed to late formal Herodian type, indicating a date from the middle of the 1st century CE. In a few cases, the writing is very neat and the letters almost calligraphic (cf. especially col. XV: noteworthy is the *keraia* of the *ṣade* in col. XV 6, an embellishment not present in the rest of the manuscript), but, in general, the writing is rather inconsistent. The width and height of letters varies considerably, and one finds *qop*s with very short downstrokes, or *lamed*s with short upper arms. The *ʾalep* and *šin* are usually written elegantly, with clear *keraiai* and an alternation of thin and thick strokes, but other letters such as *ʿayin* or medial *pe* lack such finesse, and the impression is gained that the nib of the pen was too wide in relation to the size of the letters. The scribe did not always keep to the horizontal ruling lines, and some words are written too high or too low. The spacing between letters and words is sometimes irregular; the space between two letters within a word may be larger than a word-dividing space. Generally *waw* and *yod* are distinct (except in ligatures), but because of the general irregularity of the size of letters, it is not always clear whether a small *waw* or a large *yod* should be read. The base of *bet* does not always extend clearly to the right of the downstroke, and sometimes *bet* and *kap* are indistinguishable. Likewise, some forms of *ḥet* can be mistaken for *he*.

Orthography

The vowel letters ʾalep and he

ʾAlep is used as an internal vowel letter for [*ā*] in באשושה (col. XX 2), and for [*ē*] in גאפה (col. XXXV 2).

At the end of words, *ʾalep* and *he* are used as vowel letters for final [*ā*] or [*ē*]. There is no clear-cut distinction between these letters, although some grammatical categories and words are predominantly written with an *ʾalep*, and others with a *he*. Thus, the final [*ā*] of the determined state is mostly written with *ʾalep*, whereas *he* represents the final [*ā*] of the feminine ending. Likewise, in the majority of cases the final vowels of III-*yod* verbs are represented by *ʾalep*; the *he* is used only in a few imperfect forms. Other grammatical categories with these final vowels occur less often in the preserved text, and a predominance of *ʾalep* or *he* may be incidental. This may be the case with regard to the 1st pl. pronominal suffixes and verbal endings, where the preserved text more often employs *ʾalep*. Some words are attested in only one spelling, e.g. מא (but למה), הא, נא, and the 1st sing. independent pronoun אנה, but the numeral חדה and the adverb כחדה are written with *he* or *ʾalep*.

The determined state of the noun is represented by *he* instead of *ʾalep* in ארע[ה̊ (col. III 6); לנורה̊] (col. VIII 3); מ]מ[ונ]ה and קש̇טה (col. XI 8); באשושה (col. XX 2); דתאה (col. XXXI 5); פראה (col. XXXII 4); קרבה (col. XXXIII 6); דינה (col. XXXIV 4); באישתה (col. XXXVIII 6). The exceptions דתאה and פראה suggest that the sequence אא- was avoided. An *ʾalep* instead of *he* expresses the feminine ending in למלא̊] (col. I 5); מלא (col. X 5); קריא (col. XIV 1; XXXII 6); חטא (col. XX 1); כימא (col. XXXI 8); חכא (col. XXXV 4). The few III-*yod* forms written with *he* are ו[א]חוה (col. XXI 9); ותשוה (col. XXX 7); תמנ]ה̊ (col. XXXII 1); יתלה (col. XXXIII 4); יחדה (col. XXXIII 7); תכסה (col. XXXIV 9). The infinitives of the derived conjugations are written with either *ʾalep* or *he*. The attested forms are: מללא (col. XIV 3); הוכחה (col. VIIA 5); באסיא̇] (col. XXIII 4); לחבל{ה̊}א (col. XXIV 5); להלבש{ו}א (col. XXIX 7); להנחתה (col. XXXI 3); להסבעה (col. XXXI 4); ולהנפקה (col. XXXI 5); בהתחננה (col. XXXV 6). All the examples of 1st pl. pronominal suffixes and verbal endings are דמינא] (col. I 6); לנא (cols. VII 3; XXVI 5); באדנינא and שמענא (col. XIII 3); חיבנא (col. XXI 5); עבדנה and לנצבתנא (col. XXVI 5); פרשנא (col. XXVI 6); חכמנה (col. XXVI 7). Demonstrative pronouns: ד]נ̊א (col. XVIII 3); דא (cols. XXIII 9; XXIX 5). Adverbs: כחדה (cols. V 6; XXX 5); כחדא (col. XXX 5); צדא (col. XXIV 6); תמה (col. XXVI 7); תנא (col. XXX 8); היכא (col. XXXI 2). Numerals: בחדא (col. XXII 8); לחדה (col. XXXVI 2); חדה (cols. XXXVII 5; XXXVIII 7); תלתה (col. XXIII 8). Other forms: לא (*passim*); מא (ten times); כמא (col. XXI 6); למה (cols. XI 2; XXI 4); הא (cols. XXIII 7; XXVIII 3; XXXIV 5).

The vowel letters waw and yod

The *waw* and *yod* are commonly used to indicate original long vowels or contracted diphthongs, though occasionally words are written defectively. *Waw* is sometimes used in final closed syllables to indicate an original short vowel; *yod* is used only with the pronominal suffix הין. A few times these vowel letters represent original short vowels in non-final unstressed syllables.

A large number of the supralinear additions involve *waw* and *yod*. This may indicate that the scribe had a tendency to write defectively. Cf. the following cases: קש'טה (col. XI 8); ש'זבת (col. XIV 6); לה'ן (cols. XIV 7; XXVII 3); ית'בון (col. XXVII 4); י]ש'ח (col. XXVIII 10); עליה'ן (col. XXIX 6); אח'דון (col. XXX 4); י]ר'ח'הין (col. XXXII 1).

Defective writings of original long vowels and contracted diphthongs are ימהון (col. XXVII 5); ואשתד̇ר̇ (col. XXXI 1; but אשתדור in XXXIII 6); ירטון (col. XXXVI 5); and possibly עקה (col. XXIX 9). Examples of the *plene* writing of a short vowel in ultimate position are ינ]ע̇ו̇ל (col. VIIA 7; י]נעול in col. XXXVI 2), ויפרוס (col. XXXIII 7), ותשוב (col. XXXI 2) and the 3rd fem. pl. pronominal suffix הין. *Plene* writing of short vowels in other positions occurs in איתחד (col. XI 10); עולים (col. XXIII 3); חותלוהי (col. XXX 7); אוריך (col. XXXII 9).

Orthographic ʾalep

The word הוא in col. XV 7 is the 3rd masc. pl. perfect *Peʿal* of הוא. The spelling indicates [ō]. In other texts, the word is spelled הוו or הווא. The other examples of וא- indicate [ū]. Cf. מלוא (col. VIIA 3, 7) and תבוא (col. XXXII 3). The spelling יא- occurs in שויא (cols. XXIX 6; XXXI 2).

The spelling of original /ś/

In a few cases only the scribe employs ש to represent etymological /ś/: ישבעון (col. XI 5); י]ש'ח (col. XXVIII 10); שם (col. XXX 3); בשרה (col. XXXVI 8). In more than twenty cases the scribe writes ס; so for all forms derived from סגא, הסתכל and פרס, but also סימו (col. IV 4) and להסבעה (col. XXXI 4).

Hapʿel and Hitpeʿel/Hitpaʿal forms

The general tendency is for *he* to be written at the beginning of the word (perfect, imperative, infinitive) and dropped in the imperfect. Note, however, the following forms: איתחד (col. XI 10); אסת̇ח̇רת (col. XIII 2); אתכפפת (col. XVI 3); יאקפוני (col. XVI 6); אחתוני (col. XVI 9); אתקצרת (col. XVIII 5); יהכן (col. XXVIII 5). The only (probable) participle is ממתין (col. XXVII 8). יה[ימנון (col. XV 1) may indicate that הימן was regarded as a quadriliteral verb.

Elision of ʾalep in I-ʾalep verbs

Elision of the *ʾalep* occurs in the imperfect of אתא (cols. II 2; XVI 1, 2) and in היבא (col. XXXII 8). The *ʾalep* is retained in all forms of אמר (including the noun מאמר) and in יאחדון (col. XVI 8); יאכ̊[ל (col. XVIII 1); יאבדון (col. XXVII 7).

The *ʾalep* is assimilated to *taw* in איתחד (col. XI 10) but not in תתאשד (col. XVI 5).

Assimilation of nun and dissimilation by means of nun

In more than half of the cases, I-*nun* verbal forms show assimilation, but the many exceptions show this was not a rule. In one case, the *nun* has been added supralinearly, י̇ׄנׄחתו̇ן̇ (col. XXVIII 5). The preposition מן is usually written separately, but again there are some exceptions. Several nouns also contain assimilation of *nun*. In this text the *nun* is retained (or secondarily dissimilated) in the dual אנפין, but assimilated in the sing. אף.

Dissimilation of a geminated consonant occurs in all imperfect forms of ידע and in the nouns מנדע (except in col. XXIX 8) and אנתה. Dissimilation of the imperfect forms of עלל is indicated in cols. VI 3 and XXXVI 2.

Assimilation of taw

Regressive assimilation of *taw* occurs in הטמרו (col. XIV 4). Progressive assimilation may explain the erasure in הׄתׄע̇ט{ו̊}ת̇ו̇ן̇] (col. V 8).

Mus. Inv. 567, 581, 621, 623–638
PAM 42.176, 43.796–799, 43.800–824*, 44.114*, 44.116*
SHR 6215*
IAA 525015

Col. I (Frgs. 1a, 1b) Job 17:14–18:4

[top margin]

1] תו]לׄעׄה 15ומא אפו אׄ[

2] 16[הׄעמי לשאול תׄ[נחתון]

3]או כחדה על עפר נ]שׄכׄב *va]cat*

4 *vacat*] 18:1ענ]א בלדד שוחאׄ]ה

5] 2עד אמת]ׄ תשוׄא סוף למלאׄ[

6] 3 לב]עירא דמינא[

7 4] [העל דבׄ]רתך

8] [מן את]רה 5

Mus. Inv. 635
PAM 42.176, 43.797, 43.824*

NOTES ON READINGS

Col. I is presented in two small fragments: 1a (lines 1–5) and 1b (lines 5–8). Though the fragments themselves have deteriorated, the join is still apparent in the oldest photographs, PAM 42.176 + 43.797, where the *taw* of frg. 1b 1 supplies the first letter of the first word on frg. 1a 5. The black colour at the bottom edge of frg. 1b probably has been caused by oxidation of the skin. PAM 43.797 shows that parts of frg. 1a have become detached, but no certain traces can be discerned on the lost parts. The comparison with frgs. 2 and 3 shows that line 1 is the first line of the column. The fragments are likely to have belonged to the left side of the column, if the lost col. IA had an average width.

L. 1 (17:14) תו]לׄעׄה. PAM 43.824 preserves only one distorted letter before *he*. It may be a *taw* (*ed. princ.*, p. 12, תולע]תה); however, the thin trace which looks like the left leg of *taw* may not, in fact, be ink, and the curve of the right leg can only be explained by a distortion of the skin. An *ʿayin* (or *mem*) is no more difficult. This letter is almost completely hidden in the fold in PAM 43.797, but to the right are traces of what probably is a *lamed*.

L. 2 (17:16) תׄ[נחתון]. The *taw* is virtually certain in PAM 43.797.

L. 3 (17:16) נ]שׄכׄב. Only the bottom parts of the two first letters have been preserved. The second is probably *kap*. The traces of the first letter are consistent with *šin*.

L. 4 (18:1) ענ]א. Traces of the *nun* may be visible in PAM 43.797.

L. 4 (18:1) שוחאׄ]ה. A tiny spot at the edge of frg. 1a touches the *ḥet*. If this spot is ink, it could be the right tip of the *keraia* of the right arm of *ʾalep*.

L. 5 (18:2) למלאׄ[. The trace at the end of the line may be the *keraia* of *ʾalep*.

L. 7 (18:4) דבׄ]רתך. After *dalet* there is a trace of the upper right part of a letter, consistent with *bet*.

L. 8 (18:4) מן את]רה. The two words are written without a space between them.

TRANSLATION

1. [wo]rm. [15]And what then [
2. [ ] [16]Will you [descend] with me to Sheol? [
3. [or shall we] lie down [together in the dust?] *vac[at*
4. [*vacat* [18:1]Then] Bildad [the] Shuhite [answer]ed [
5. [[2]Whe]n will you stop speaking? [
6. [[3]] do we resemble [ca]ttle? [
7. [[4]] is it for [your] sa[ke
8. [ ] from [its] pla[ce.

COMMENTS

L. 1 (17:14) תו]לׄעׄה. Cf. 𝔐 לרמה. לׄ[ר]מׄה is also possible (cf. 𝔖 ܠܪܡܬܐ; *Tg. Isa* 14:11; *Tg. Neof.* Exod 16:24).

Ll. 1–2 (17:15-16) הׄעמי[ ] / אׄ]. Reconstruct e.g. הׄעמי[וסברתי מן יחזנה] / [אׄ]סבר] (*ed. ATQ*, 12).

L. 2 (17:16) [תׄ]נחתון]. Or fem. [תׄ]נחתן]. Cf. 𝔐 תרדנה; 𝔖 ܢܚܬܘܢ; 𝔊 καταβήσονται.

L. 3 (17:16) או כחדה על עפר נ]שׄכׄב]. Cf. 𝔐 אם יחד על עפר נָחַת. For או, see COMMENTS on col. XXXII 8 (39:9). Read נֵחֻת instead of 𝔐 נָחַת; cf. 𝔊 καταβησόμεθα. After נ]שׄכׄב, the line is blank, since Job has concluded his answer.

L. 4 (18:1) ענ]א. Not וענ]א. Cf. col. VIIA 1 (23:1); IX 3 (25:1); XXXVII 3 (42:1).

L. 4 (18:1) שוחאׄ]ה. Cf. 𝔐 השחי; 𝔊 ὁ Σαυχίτης; 𝔖 ܫܘܚܝܐ; ℭ דמן שוח. The readings שוח]י or שוחׄי] are rather unlikely. On the form שוחאה, cf. G. Dalman, *Grammatik des Jüdisch-Palästinischen Aramäisch nach den Idiomen des palästinischen Talmud des Onkelostargum und Prophetentargum und der Jerusalemischen Targume*, 2d ed. (Leipzig: J. C. Hinrichs, 1905) 177; H. Bauer and P. Leander, *Grammatik des Biblisch-Aramäischen* (Halle: Max Niemeyer, 1927) § 13 h–k.

L. 5 (18:2) עד אמת]ׄי. Cf. 𝔐 עד אנה. We may perhaps reconstruct the gap between lines 4 and 5 as: שוחאׄ]ה] / [ואמר לאיוב עד אמת]ׄי. For the addition of לאיוב, cf. col. III 3 (20:1).

L. 5 (18:2) תשואׄ. Cf. 𝔐 תשימון. The sing. is found also in 𝔊 παύσῃ.

L. 6 (18:3) לב]עירא דמינא]. Cf. 𝔐 נחשבנו כבהמה, and בעׄ]ירי in col. XXVI 6 (35:11) as the rendering of 𝔐 בהמות. The preposition *lamed* is employed with the verb דמא.

L. 7 (18:4) העל דבׄ]רתך [. Cf. 𝔐 הלמענך, 'is it for your sake'. For the reconstruction, cf. col. XXXIV 4 (40:8).

VARIANTS

17:16 (2) הׄעמי[𝔊 ἢ μετ' ἐμοῦ] בדי 𝔐

[Col. IA Job 18:15(?)–19:10]

Col. II (Frg. 2) Job 19:11-19

top margin

[[11]ותקׄ]ף עלי רגזה וח]שבני [12]כחדה] 1

[י]תׄון חתפוהי וכבשו] 13-14? 2

3 הׄרחקו וידעי ב◦[15

4 ביתי אמתי לנכר[י

5 [16]לעבדי קרית ולא עׄ[נא

6 [17]רוח המכת לאנתתי[18

7 רשיעין יסגפׄ[ונני 19

8 כל אנש די[

Mus. Inv. 627
PAM 43.797, 43.823*

NOTES ON READINGS

The column is preserved on frg. 2. The top of the fragment is visible in PAM 43.797. It seems that the top left part has crumbled and broken off. No traces of the vertical right ruling are visible, but the preserved text belongs to the right edge of the column. This is clear not only from the beginnings of lines 4–8, and the reconstruction of lines 1–3, but also from the calculation of the position of the fragments within the scroll.

L. 2 (19:12) [י]תֿון. It is possible to see the bottom part of the left leg and the angular base of *taw*. The middle of the following *waw* is damaged, but the small vertical stroke beneath the broken part shows it is not *yod*; hence the reading [א]תֿין is not possible. There is not enough space for [יא]תֿון.

L. 3 (19:13-14) ב◦[. Only part of the vertical stroke has been preserved from the letter following *bet*. No horizontal strokes can be detected, even when the fragment is examined under a microscope.

L. 4 (19:15) ביתי. The first *yod* is somewhat longer than usual and touches the base of the preceding *bet*. An abrasion on the skin, evidenced by a change in the colour of the leather, explains the loss of the left part of the head of the *yod*.

L. 7 (19:18) יסגפׄ[ונני. The remnants of the last letter suggest *pe*. The possibility of *ʾalep* must be ruled out.

TRANSLATION

1. [[11]And] his anger [fla]red up against me, and He c[ounted me [12]Together]
2. His raiders [co]me and tread [[13–14?]
3. have moved away, and those who know me [[15]
4. my house. My maidservant as a strang[er
5. [16]I summon my slave, but he does not an[swer
6. [17]I lowered (my) spirit before my wife [[18]
7. the wicked affl[ict me [19]
8. all the people who [

COMMENTS

L. 1 (19:11) [ותק]ף. Cf. 𝔐 ויחר. ℭ also reads ותקף.

L. 1 (19:11) [וח]שבני. Cf. 𝔐 ויחשבני; ℭ וחשבנני.

L. 2 (19:12) חתפוהי. This is a pronominal suffix added to the pl. participle of חתף (usually written חטף, but חתף in 𝔐 Job 9:12 and ℭ Job 9:12; cf. also Prov 23:28; Sir 32:21; 50:4).

L. 2 (19:12) וכבשו[. Cf. 𝔐 ויסלו. ℭ and *Tg. Isa* 40:3 also use כבש to render סלל. The third hemistich of Job 19:12 seems to be missing.

L. 3 (19:13) ב°[. Perhaps a rendering of 𝔐 אך־זרו (reconstruct ברׄ[חו?). However, 𝔐 19:14 has completely disappeared in the missing part of the manuscript. It is possible that the scribe's eye skipped from וידעי (v 13) to מידעי (v 14).

L. 4 (19:15) אמתי. This is singular (unless the *he* of the normal pl. has been dropped), whereas 𝔐 reads the plural: ואמהתי; 𝔊 θεράπαιναι (without καί); 𝔖 ܐܡܗ̈ܬܝ.

L. 4 (19:15) לנכר[י. The indeterminate form (cf. 𝔐 לזר) is more likely than לנכר[יא (𝔖 ܐܝܟ ܢܘܟܪܝܐ).

L. 6 (19:17) המכת. Probably the 1st sing. *Hapʿel* of מכך.

L. 7 (19:18) יסגפׄ[ונני. Cf. 𝔐 מאסו; סגף, 'to afflict', also occurs in ℭ 30:11.

VARIANTS

19:13 (3) הׄרחקו 𝔊 ἀπέστησαν 𝔖 ܐܪܚܩܘ] הרחיק 𝔐

Col. III (Frg. 3) Job 19:29–20:6

top margin

1] בׄאיש[*v]acat*
2] *va[cat* *va]cat*
3 20:1 [ענא צפר נעמתיא ואמר לאיו]ב 2 לכן לבבי י[
4] 3 ק]לׄלתי אשמע ורו[ח]
5] 4 יד]עת מן עלמא מן דׄ[י]
6] ארע]הׄ 5 ארו מבע רשיעׄ[ין]
7] לעבע תעדא [6 הן]
8 [תסוק לשמיא גאותה ואנ]פה לענניא]

Mus. Inv. 627
PAM 43.823

NOTES ON READINGS

The reconstruction of the scroll indicates that frg. 3, the only preserved fragment of col. III, is close to the left margin of the column, the broken words at the end of lines 3–6 being the last words of the lines. The reconstructions of lines 2 and 6 demand a column width of 9 cm, or slightly more. After line 1 there is a blank line which separates Job's speech from Zophar's answer.

L. 1 (19:29) בׄאיש[. Before *ʾalep* there is a trace which may be the upper left part of *bet*. There is also a dark spot where one expects the left end of its base, but this spot need not be ink.

L. 4 (20:3) ק]ל̊לתי. The leather is very dark. Therefore, it is hard to recognize traces of the first *lamed* in the photographs. However, the small tip protruding from the dark area might be the bottom left tip of the hook of *lamed*. Nothing of the first *lamed* can now be seen on the fragment, not even under a microscope.

L. 5 (20:4) ד̊[י]. The downstroke of *dalet* is rather short, but this is often the case with *dalet* and *reš* in these columns.

L. 6 (20:4) ארע]ה̊. The trace at the right edge of the fragment as seen in PAM 43.823, if it is ink, could be the left tip of the head of *he*, sloping down somewhat more than is usual. No traces remain on the fragment itself.

L. 8 (20:6) אנ]פה. The letter preceding *he* is *pe*. Both its head and the left end of the base are recognizable.

TRANSLATION

1. [ ] evil *vaca*[*t*
2. [*vac*]*at* *vac*[*at*
3. [[20:1]Zophar the Naamathite answered and said to Jo]b: [2]Indeed, my heart [
4. [[3]] my [dis]grace I hear and the spir[it]
5. [[4]] you [kn]ow from of old, sin[ce]
6. [ ] the [earth,] [5]that the rejoicing of the wick[ed]
7. [ ] passes away quickly. [[6]Though]
8. [his pride rises up to heaven, and] his [fa]ce the clouds [

COMMENTS

L. 1 (19:29)]ב̊איש. באיש has no equivalent in 𝔐. Perhaps it is in apposition to 𝔐 דין.

L. 3 (20:1) [ענא צפר נעמתיא ואמר לאיו]ב. This reconstruction (which adds לאיו]ב to 𝔐) fits in the maximum width of the column. The alternative reconstruction, [ענא צפר נעמתיא והתי]ב, is rather short, even for the minimum width of the column.

L. 3 (20:2) י̊[. Probably the first letter of a verbal form. The reconstruction י̊[תיבנני] (cf. 𝔐 ישיבוני) is too long.

L. 4 (20:3) ק]ל̊לתי. Cf. 𝔐 כלמתי, both words meaning 'disgrace, shame'.

L. 6 (20:5) ארו. Several times, ארו corresponds to 𝔐 כי, which functions as a subordinating conjunctive, e.g. cols. XXVII 3 (36:9) and XXVIII 1 (36:24). In those cases, ארו seems merely to convey the meaning 'that', as די in col. XXXVII 3 (42:1).

L. 6 (20:5) מבע. Cf. 𝔐 רננת. It is an infinitive of the verbal root בוע, 'to shout, rejoice'. ℭ reads בועת.

L. 7 (20:5)]לעבע. This word, 'at once', 'in a hurry', is also attested in 1QapGen ar XX 9 (לעובע). Cf. the different spelling (לעבק) in the Aramaic papyri from Elephantine (AP 26 and 42), and עבק in *Aḥiqar* 103. The clause לעבע תעדא is a free rendering of 𝔐 עדי־רגע.

Ll. 7–8 (20:6) [הן] / [תסוק לשמיא גאותה ואנ]פה. The length of the reconstruction corresponds with that of line 3.

L. 8 (20:6) אנ]פה. The reconstruction אנ]פה is grammatically awkward (one expects אנפוהי).

[Col. IIIA Job 20:15(?)–21:2]

Col. IV (Frg. 4) Job 21:2-10

top margin

1 [ ]א לי להות◦[3

2 מׄנדעי תמיקׄ[ון 4

3 ארו אפו לא ת[קצר רוחי 5

4 סימו ידיכון על [פם 6

5 ותמהא אחד לי 7 הׄ[יך

6 והסגיו נכסין 8 זרעׄ[הון

7 לעיניהון 9 בתיהון[

8 אלהא עליהוׄ[ן 10

9 הריתהון פׄל[טת

Mus. Inv. 628
PAM 43.797, 43.822*

NOTES ON READINGS

Frg. 4 contains the beginnings of nine lines of col. IV. The vertical right ruling is visible in lines 7–8.

L. 1 (21:2) א[ ]. The distance to the right margin of the column allows for one or two letters preceding *ʾalep*.

L. 1 (21:2) להות◦[. After the *taw*, there are traces of one or two unidentifiable letters.

L. 2 (21:3) מׄנדעי. In the photographs, the horizontal black line in the carbonized area looks like the base of *mem*. It is no longer visible in the fragment; even part of the *nun* has disintegrated.

L. 2 (21:3) תמיקׄ[ון. After *qop* there are some dark stains, which may or may not be *waw* and final *nun*. No marks remain on the fragment itself.

L. 4 (21:5) על [. The small stroke protruding from the carbonized area after על does not seem to be part of a letter. The fragment now shows no traces.

L. 8 (21:9) אלהא. Inexplicably, the first *ʾalep* is 3 mm out of alignment with the right margin of the column.

L. 9 (21:10) פׄל[טת. At the left end of the line, the upper arm of *lamed* is easily discernible. The traces of the preceding letter show the top of a slightly slanting downstroke and a curved, though not completely angular, head. *Pe* is probable; *kap* possible, but less likely.

TRANSLATION

1. [ ] for me [3
2. my knowledge you may mock [4
3: Behold, [my spirit] is not [impatient. 5
4. Put your hands over [(your) mouth(s). 6

5. and astonishment takes hold of me. [7]H[ow
6. and accumulate possessions? [[8]Their] progeny [
7. before their eyes. [9]Their houses [
8. God upon the[m. [10]
9. Their pregnant (cow) calv[es

COMMENTS

L. 1 (21:2)]◦א[לי להות]. Unless the targumist combined the two hemistichs of 21:2 in one clause, this line corresponds to the second hemistich of 𝔐 ותהי זאת תנחומתיכם. 𝔊 renders ἵνα μὴ ᾖ μοι παρ' ὑμῶν αὕτη ἡ παράκλησις. A possible reconstruction is therefore: ל[מ]א לי, but one might also consider ו[ד]א, corresponding to 𝔐 זאת. The reading and meaning of]◦להות is disputed. Jongeling and Kaufman propose a noun derived from the verbs להא (להות) or לאא (להות[א]), 'to be tired, annoyed'. However, the traces immediately after להות do not resemble ʾalep. Beyer suggests]להיתיה̊, but then a confusion between *waw* and *yod* must be assumed.

L. 2 (21:3) תמיק[ון. Cf. 𝔐 תלעיג. The plural is rather likely: cf. 𝔊 καταγελάσετέ μου; 𝔖 ܬܒܙܚܘܢ; and the plural סימו in line 4.

L. 3 (21:4) ארו אפו. Cf. 𝔐 ואם מדוע. Apparently the question of 𝔐 has been turned into a statement.

L. 3 (21:4) ת[קצר רוחי. Cf. 𝔐 תקצר רוחי. Or reconstruct ת[תעיק רוחי (cf. 𝔗 𝔖 ܬܬܥܩܐ).

L. 5 (21:7) ה̊[יך. Cf. 𝔐 מדוע. In col. VII 6 (22:20), היך, 'how', corresponds to 𝔐 אם.

L. 9 (21:10) הריתהו[ן. The fem. participle of הרא with the 3rd masc. pl. suffix: 'their pregnant (cow)'. Perhaps both the translator and 𝔊 (αὐτῶν ἐν γαστρὶ ἔχουσα) interpreted 𝔐 פרתו, 'his cow', as a fem. participle of פרה, 'to be fruitful' (Jongeling). However, הרית might also be a noun meaning 'pregnancy', and hence 'fetus'.

Col. V (Frg. 5) Job 21:20-27

top margin

[20] ע]י̊נ̊והי במפלתה ומח̊[מת מרא ישתא]
[21]ארו מא]צ̇בו לאלהא בביתה ו̇[
] מני]ן ירחוהי גזירין [22]הלא̇[לדהא
[מנדע ו]ה̇וא רמיא מדין [24]אבר̊[והי
]]ן גרמוהי [25]דן ימות בנפ̇[ש
] ל]א̇ אכל [26]כחדה על [
] ע]ליהון [27]ארו ידעת̇[
]]◦ ה̇י̇ע̇ט{ו̊}ת̇ו̇ן[

Mus. Inv. 628
PAM 43.822

Notes on Readings

Frg. 5 should be positioned in the middle of the column, probably somewhat closer to the right margin than to the left.

L. 1 (21:20) ומח̊]מת. The letters are distorted. The last letter consists of a vertical stroke, and traces of a head. In any case, it is not final *nun*.

L. 2 (21:21) ו̊]. At the end of the line, a thin vertical stroke can be seen in the PAM photograph. Since it breaks through the bottom line, *waw* is most likely. The mark is no longer preserved on the fragment itself.

L. 3 (21:21) מני[ן. A small dot before the final *nun*, if ink, might be the extreme left tip of the base of medial *nun*. A *yod* may fit between these two letters. Only the head of the final *nun* is partially visible on the edge of the fragment.

L. 4 (21:24) אבר̊]והי. The partially preserved last letter could be *reš* or *taw*, or, less probably, *dalet*, *he*, or *ḥet*.

L. 5 (21:24)]ן. The vertical stroke on the right edge of the line is not the left leg of *ḥet*, but final *nun*.

L. 7 (21:27) ידעת̊]. A small black spot at the left edge of the line is the remainder of *taw*.

L. 8 (21:27)]י̊. The trace at the beginning of the line could be the upper part of *yod*. However, the absence of any trace of the upper arm of *lamed* rules out the reconstruction על]י̊.

L. 8 (21:27) ה̇ע̇ט{ו}ת̊ו̊ן̊]. A thin letter (e.g. *waw*, *yod*, or *nun*) left of *ṭet* has been erased. The last three letters are badly damaged. Nothing can be seen now on the fragment.

Translation

1. [[20]] his own [ey]es his downfall, and [let him drink] of [the] w[rath of the Lord.]
2. [[21]For what] concern has God in his house and [
3. [the numbe]r of his months is cut down? [22]Is for G[od
4. [knowledge,] He who judges the exalted ones? [24][His] member[s
5. [ ] his bones. [25]That one dies with a sou[l
6. [ ] he has [no]t tasted. [26]Together in [
7. [ ] them. [27]Behold, I know [
8. [ ] you have plotted [against] me. [

Comments

L. 1 (21:20) ע]י̊נ̊והי]. The reconstruction [יחזון ע]י̊נ̊והי is somewhat short, but may be correct.

L. 1 (21:20) במפלתה. מפלתה, 'his fall' (cf. σ′ πτῶσιν) is the interpretation or translation of the *hapax legomenon* כידו (perhaps the translator and σ′ read פידו or אידו).

L. 1 (21:20) ומח̊]מת מרא ישתא]. Or ומר̊]גז. We reconstruct מרא as rendering of 𝔐 שדי because אלהא might make the line too long.

L. 2 (21:21)]צבו לאלהא. This is the targumist's interpretation of 𝔐 חפצו.

L. 2 (21:21) ו̊]. This introduces an expansion on 𝔐.

L. 3 (21:21) מני[ן. 𝔐 מספר. This reconstruction is based upon ℭ מניין and 𝔖 ܡܢܝܢܐ.

Ll. 4–5 (21:24) There is not enough space for a translation of the four hemistichs of 21:23-24. Most likely, verse 23 has been omitted.

L. 4 (21:24) אבר̊]והי. Cf. 𝔐 עטיניו. This *hapax legomenon* has been interpreted differently. 𝔊 translates with 'intestines', whereas in Mishnaic Hebrew it means '(dripping) olives'. Both אבר and עטינים can be designations of the male genitals (cf. R. Gordis, *The Book of Job. Commentary, New Translation, and Special Studies* [Moreshet Series 2; New York: The Jewish Theological Seminary of America, 1978] on עטינים, p. 232). If the translator meant to use a euphemism, he also may have used the sing. אברה.

L. 5 (21:24)]ן גרמוהי[ ]. The translation is not a literal rendering of 𝔐 ומח עצמותיו ישקה. The verb is either missing, or transferred. Note that the word before גרמוהי is not מח, 'marrow', but ends with final *nun*.

L. 8 (21:27) הׄתׄעׄט{ו}תון. The erasure may be explained as a correction of a spelling in which *taw*, of the suffix -תון, had been assimilated to the final *ṭet* of the root. The reading of the corrected word raises some problems. The text reads הׄתׄעׄט{ו}תון[, but some interpreters prefer the reading הׄתׄיעט{ו}תון[. It is argued that lack of space caused the scribe to write *yod* after *ʿayin*. This argument is very unlikely: the scribe could have written *yod* above *ʿayin*, next to *taw*, instead of between *ʿayin* and *ṭet*. The verb corresponds to 𝔐 תחמסו. This is perhaps the only occurrence in 𝔐 of II חמס, 'to consider, devise', in which case התעיטתון should be considered as a parallel form of התיעטתון, both verbs meaning 'to consider', 'to take counsel', hence 'to plot'. Otherwise, התעיטתון might mean 'to be angry' (cf. ܐܬܚܡܬ), a rather liberal translation of חמס, 'to be violent'.

Col. VI (Frg. 6 i) Job 22:3-9

top margin

1] [3] לא]להא
2] אׄרחך[
3] [4] יׄ]נׄעל עמך
4] [5] ל]א איתי
5] [6] א]חיך מגן
6] [7] צהא לא[
7] ל]חׄם [8] ואמרת
8] א]נׄפוהי
9] [9]]◦נׄה

Mus. Inv. 636
PAM 43.821

NOTES ON READINGS

Frg. 6 i preserves the remains of col. VI.

L. 3 (22:4) יׄ]נׄעל. The letter in front of *lamed* is clearly *ʿayin*. The black dot to the bottom right of *ʿayin* could be the left end of the base of *nun*. It is, however, no longer visible on the fragment.

L. 8 (22:8) א]נׄפוהי. The peculiar trace of the first letter in the photograph (the stroke first drops down from the ceiling line, then curves slightly down to the left, and breaks through the bottom line) is not the left leg of an *ʾalep*, but a scrap of the skin. On the fragment, only the top of a letter, compatible with *nun*, is visible.

L. 9 (22:9) ◦נֹה[. The reading רי[קֹנה, though it corresponds nicely to 𝔐 ריקם, is impossible. The remainder of the first letter of the line is a downstroke beginning from the ceiling line. There is absolutely no trace of the head of *qop*. The letter is most likely *waw*, *yod*, or (the left leg of) *taw*.

TRANSLATION

1. [[3] to G]od
2. [ ] your way.
3. [[4] he/it] enters with you
4. [[5]] there is [n]o
5. [[6]] your [br]others without reason
6. [[7]] the thirsty shall not
7. [br]ead. [8]And you said:
8. [ ] his [f]ace
9. [[9]]

COMMENTS

L. 1 (22:3) לא[להא. Cf. 𝔐 לשדי. In col. XXIV 7 (34:12) the translator employs מרא to render שַׁדַּי.

L. 3 (22:4) י[נֹעל. If the black dot to the bottom right of the *ʿayin* is a trace of *nun*, then י[נֹעל, an example of dissimilation, should be reconstructed. Otherwise reconstruct י[על.

L. 6 (22:7) צ̇הא[. 'Thirsty', instead of 𝔐 עָיֵף, 'exhausted'. Cf. 𝔊 διψῶντας.

L. 7 (22:8) ואמרת. An interpretative addition missing in 𝔐. Job 22:8 is formulated in the 3rd person and interrupts Eliphaz's direct address to Job. The statements of this verse should be read as Job's philosophy of life according to Eliphaz.

L. 9 (22:9) ◦נֹה[. A possible reconstruction is וימ[ינֹה, as a rendering of 𝔐 וזרעות. ℭ and 𝔖 employ a sing. form.

VARIANTS

22:3 (2) 𝔐 דרכיך] 𝔊* אֹ[רחך

Col. VII (Frg. 6 ii) Job 22:16-22

top margin

1 [16]די מיתו בֹ[לא … [17]
2 אמרין ל[אלהא
3 לנא אלה[א [18]
4 ועטת רש[יעין … [19]
5 ויחאכון ו̇[
6 [20]היך לא [
7 [21]הסתכל[
8 [22]קבל[
9 ◦[

Mus. Inv. 636
PAM 43.797, 43.821*

NOTES ON READINGS

Frg. 6 ii preserves the remains of col. VII.

L. 1 (22:16) בْ]לא. There are some traces of a letter in the carbonized area at the end of the line. Visible are a vertical downstroke slanting slightly to the right, and a long base slanting downwards to the left. The letter must be *bet* or *mem*.

L. 4 (22:18) רש]עין. The *šin* is clearly visible in PAM 43.797.

TRANSLATION

1. [16]Who died while [not [17]
2. said to [God:
3. God for us [[18]
4. the counsel of the wick[ed [19]
5. and they laugh, and [
6. [20]How ( ) not [
7. [21]Consider [
8. [22]Receive [
9. [

COMMENTS

L. 1 (22:16) די מיתו בْ]לא. Cf. 𝔐 אשר קמטו ולא עת, 'who were cut off before their time'. Reconstruct e.g. with 𝔗 בْ]לא עדנהון.

L. 3 (22:17) אלה]א. Here again, as in col. VI 1 (22:3), אלהא renders 𝔐 שדי.

L. 5 (22:19) ויחאכון. *Pe*ʿ*al* of the verb חאך, 'to laugh'.

L. 7 (22:21) הסתכל]. 𝔐 reads הסכן, probably meaning 'to become familiar'. The translator uses the verb הסתכל to render several Hebrew verbs: בין col. VIIA 6 (23:5); התבונן cols. X 6 (26:14) and XXIX 5 (37:14); השכיל col. XXV 3 (34:27).

VARIANTS

22:17 (3) לנא 𝔊S] למו 𝔐𝔗

Col. VIIA (Frg. 6a) Job 23:1-8

top margin

] *va[cat* [1]ענא איוב ואמْ[ר]

[[2]אף יומא דן] מן טלל שעותי די

] תנ]חתי [3]מלוא אנדע ואשכْ[חנה]

[ואתא עד]אתר מדרה [4]אמלל קדמ[והי]

] ופמ]י אמלא הוכחה [5]ואנדע

[ ]ואסתכל מא יאמר לׄיׄ 6
[6]ינ]עׄוׄל עמי מלוא עדׄ[7
[ ]7 ארו קשט ודת[8
[ ]∘ 8 הן לקדׄ]ם 9
[ ]לׄ[10

SHR 6215

Notes on Readings

Frg. 6a, previously published by B. Zuckerman, is now situated in the Rockefeller Museum but has not yet been assigned an inventory number. It is curved and cannot be measured at this time. The texture and colour of the skin, though lighter than that of the previous fragments, leave no doubt that it comes from the same sheet as col. VII. The back was found to be smooth and well prepared. The abrasions on the fragment are caused by the stitchings of frg. 7.

L. 3 (23:3) ואשכׄ]חנה[. The last letter on the line is only partially preserved and can be read as *kap*, *nun*, or *mem*.

L. 5 (23:4) ופמ]יׄ. Only the head of the first letter in the line can be seen. It could be read as *waw* or *yod*.

L. 6 (23:5)]ואסתכׄל. The top of the head of the first letter is visible. *Kap* is partially obscured in a surface abrasion.

L. 6 (23:5) לׄיׄ. The trace after *lamed* suggests *waw* or *yod*.

L. 7 (23:6) ינ]עׄוׄל. The traces at the beginning of the line can be read as *taw*, *nun*, or *ʿayin*. The next letter can be *waw* or *yod*. The last letter of the line is heavily abraded, but *dalet* is likely.

L. 8 (23:7) קׄשט. The head of *qop* is lost because of the skin abrasion.

L. 9 (23:7)]∘. In the preliminary report, the editors noted that a trace of the first letter in the line could be seen. On the basis of the context, they reconstructed דינ]יׄ, although, as they admit, *yod* is rather unlikely. With the naked eye nothing can be seen on the edge, because the fragment has not yet been flattened. No microscope examination has been possible.

L. 9 (23:8) לקדׄ]ם. Only the right part of the head of a letter can be seen. The trace is consistent with *dalet*.

Translation

1. [*vac*]*at* 23:1 Job answered and sai[d:]
2. [2 Today] because of my complaint which
3. [ ] my [groa]ning. 3 If only I would know to fi[nd him,]
4. [that I could come to] the place of his dwelling. 4 Before [him] I would speak
5. [and] my [mouth] I would fill (with) reproof, 5 and I would know
6. [ ] and I would understand what He would say to me.
7. [6 will he] proceed against me. If only [
8. [ ] 7 For truth and judgement [
9. [ ] 8 If forwa[rd
10. [ ] [

COMMENTS

L. 1 (23:1) *va* [*cat*]. The dialogue introductory formula is indented, as in col. IX 3 (25:1).

L. 2 (23:2) מן טלל. ‘Because of’. Cf. בטלל in the Egyptian Aramaic papyri and in 1QapGen ar, as well as מטול and מיטול in Jewish and Christian Palestinian Aramaic. It does not correspond to any phrase in 𝔐.

L. 2 (23:2) שעותי. Cf. 𝔐 שחי. 𝔖 ܫܘܥܝܬܝ.

L. 3 (23:2) תנ]חתי]. 𝔐 reads אנחתי; 𝔗 תונחתי; 𝔖 ܬܢܚܬܝ. Though the noun אנחתא is attested in Aramaic, it is far less common than תנחתא (written in several ways). The space at the beginning of the line is too small for a literal rendering of 𝔐.

L. 3 (23:3) מלוא. Cf. 𝔐 מי יתן. מלוא is related to the emphatic particle -ל, לו, or לוא. Cf. also Hermopolis 1 7 (מלא). In a Christian Palestinian Aramaic biblical MS of Exod 16:3, לוא is utilized to render מי יתן.

L. 3 (23:3) אנדע ואשכ̇[חנה]. Cf. 𝔐 ידעתי ואמצאהו. 𝔗 has the same translation as this text.

L. 4 (23:3) ואתא עד] אתר מדרה]. אתר מדרה renders 𝔐 תכונתו. Cf. 𝔗 מדור בית מוקדשיה. Note that 𝔗 MS ד reads אתר instead of מדור.

L. 4 (23:4) אמלל קדמ[והי]. Cf. 𝔐 אערכה לפניו.

L. 5 (23:4) ופמ̇[י]. The reconstruction [דין ופמ]י is approximately two letters too short. Another word may be reconstructed (but דין is the usual rendering of משפט), or a short word added, e.g. [דין ואף פמ]י.

L. 5 (23:4) הוכחה. A *Hapʿel* infinitive. Cf. 𝔐 תוכחות.

Ll. 5–6 (23:5) [ ] / ואנדע. Cf. 𝔐 אדעה מלים יענני. The translation should be אנדע מליא יתיבנני, but this hardly fits: ואנדע is written close to the left margin. It possibly is the last word and one may at best add a short word like מא to line 5. Reconstruct e.g. [יתיבנני] / [מא] ואנדע rather than [מא יתיבנני] / ואנדע.

L. 6 (23:5) לי̇. This is probably the last word, though a short word could have followed.

L. 7 (23:6) ינ[עׄוׄל]. Cf. 𝔐 יריב. The word may be reconstructed י[עׄוׄל and analysed as a *Paʿel* of עול, ‘to pervert, do wrong’ (in which case it would be a Hebraism), or as י[עׄיל, an *Apʿel* form with the same meaning as in Syriac. Yet, it is preferable to reconstruct the imperfect of עלל, ‘to enter’, with the forensic meaning: ‘to enter a lawsuit’, ‘to proceed against’. In col. VI 3 (22:4), עלל is used to render 𝔐 בוא in the expression בוא במשפט. 𝔊 reads ἐπελευσέται (ἐπέρχομαι meaning ‘to proceed against’). One can reconstruct e.g. [הבחיל ינ]עׄוׄל.

L. 7 (23:6) מלוא. Cf. 𝔐 לא אך, though the translator probably rephrases the hemistich.

L. 7 (23:6) עדׄ[. Does it belong to the construction with מלוא, or is it a preposition used with the missing verb? All the versions have a noun absent in 𝔐: 𝔊 ἐν ἀπειλῇ; 𝔖 ܕܚܠܬܐ; 𝔗 תגרא. Perhaps 𝔊 read the text as follows: לא אך הוא זעם בי שם.

L. 8 (23:7)]ארו קשט ודת[. Cf. VARIANTS. 𝔗 has two main variants: תמן תריצתא ותקין and תמן תריצא יתקון. In this context, as a rendering of נוכח, דת should probably not be interpreted as ‘law’, but as ‘judgement’.

L. 9 (23:8) לקדׄ[ם. Cf. 𝔐 קדם. Reconstruct either לקדׄ[ים ‘to the East’ (cf. 𝔗 למדינחא), or לקדׄ[ם ‘forward’ (cf. 𝔊 and 𝔖).

VARIANTS

23:7 (8)]ארו קשט ודת[𝔊 (ἀλήθεια γὰρ καὶ ἔλεγχος)] 𝔐 שם ישר נוכח

[Col. VIIB (Frg. 7 i)]

Mus. Inv. 636
PAM 43.821

NOTES ON READINGS

Frg. 7 i, now separated from frg. 7 ii, preserves the left margin of col. VIIB which began around Job 23:15. The skin has the same colour as that of frg. 6. Ten holes for the stitching are still visible, at a distance of *c*.0.6 cm. The last three preserve part of the thread, also visible in the back of the next column. Parts of the ruling of the left margin can still be seen between lines 5 and 6. At the end of lines 2 and 6 there are traces of what might be ink. The position of the trace at the end of line 2, between the ceiling lines, is rather odd. The gap between frgs. 6a and 7 i can be calculated to be at least 9.2 cm. The lost column measured *c*.7.5 cm.

Col. VIII (Frg. 7 ii) Job 24:12-17

top margin

1 12מן קריהון]
2 תקבל אלהא] 13
3 קדמוהי לנורה]
4 בשבילוהי 14ל]
5 ומסכן ובלי[ליא 15
6 קבל למא[מר
7 ויחטא 16ח[תר
8 בבאיש[תהון
9 17להון]

Mus. Inv. 636
PAM 43.821

NOTES ON READINGS

Frg. 7 ii, now separated from frg. 7 i, contains the beginnings of the first nine lines of col. VIII. A distance of approximately 28.5 cm is measured from the right ruling of col. VIII to the left ruling of col. X (frg. 9). Assuming that the two intervening margins have an average width of 1.5 cm, this would result in a width per column of 8.5 cm. This assumption implies that the reconstruction במרו]מה] in col. IX 5 is the first word of the line.

L. 1 (24:12)] קריהון. Only the top of *waw* has been preserved. Both the top and the lower part of the leg of final *nun* are visible near the hole.

L. 3 (24:13) לנורה֯]. The trace at the left edge of the line cannot belong to *ʾalep*. The vertical stroke should be interpreted as the right leg of *he*.

L. 7 (24:15-16) ויחט֯א ח֯]תר. The supralinear *ʾalep* is placed exactly above the space between ויחט and ח֯].

L. 8 בבאיש֯]תהון. The junction of downstroke and base shows the first letter is *bet*, not *kap*.

TRANSLATION

1. [12]From their cities [
2. it complains: God [[13]
3. before Him to the fire. [
4. in his/its paths. [14]At [
5. and the needy; and at nig[ht [15]
6. darkness, say[ing:
7. and he sins. [16]He br[eaks in
8. in [their] evil [
9. [17]To them[

COMMENTS

L. 1 (24:12) מן קריהו֯ן. 𝔐 מעיר has no suffix.

L. 2 (24:12) תקבל. Cf. 𝔐 תשוע. Cf. the similar use of קבל in the Aramaic fragments of *1 Enoch* and the *Book of Giants*.

L. 2 (24:12) אלהא]. The omission of the copula before אלהא shows that the translator understood the third hemistich to be the contents of the complaint.

L. 3 (24:13) לנורה֯]. The translator interpreted 𝔐 אוֹר, 'light', as אוּר, 'fire'. The text differs from 𝔐, which reads המה היו במרדי אור.

L. 6 (24:15) קבל. Cf. 𝔐 נשף, 'early morning'.

L. 7 (24:15-16) ויחט֯א ח֯]תר. The proposal to read ויחט֯א ח֯]שכא, 'and in the dark he breaks in' (cf. 𝔐 24:16), should be dismissed. There is no evidence that חטט means 'break through'; the Qumran Hebrew case of a prosthetic *ʾalep* in אבית is not an example of a prepositional *ʾalep*. The suggestion that ויחט֯א is an addition to the end of 24:15 is more plausible.

L. 8 בבאיש֯]תהון. The word on this line is not found in 𝔐.

Col. IX (Frg. 8) Job 24:24–26:2

top margin

1] התכ]פפו כיבלא יתקפצון א֯[ו

2 [25] מ]ן אפו יתיבנני פתגם ויש֯[וא

3] *vac*[*at* [25:1]ענא בלד֯]ד שוחאה ואמר]

4 [2]ארו ש]לטן ורבו עם אלהא ע[בד שלם]

5 [במרו]מה [3]האיתי רחצן להש[

6]] או על מן לא תקו֯ם [[4]

[ ]אׄלהא ומא יצדקׄ[5

[ ]זׄכי וכוכביא לאׄ[6

[רמתא וב]רׄ אנש תולעׄ[תא *vacat*]

[26:1ענא איוב ואמ]רׄ 2העדׄ[רת

Mus. Inv. 633
PAM 43.820

NOTES ON READINGS

Frg. 8 contains part of the first ten lines of col. IX. The calculation of the width of the columns of this sheet suggests that the column measured 8.5 cm, and that the reconstruction [במרו]מה (line 5) was the first word of the line.

L. 1 (24:24) כיבלא. *Bet* and *lamed* are damaged, but the fragment indicates that the reading is certain.

L. 2 (24:25) וישׁׄ[וא. After *yod*, there is a small trace which, if ink, rules out any letter with a (right) vertical stroke. The position of the trace is compatible with *šin*.

L. 5 (25:3) להשׁ[. The *šin* is damaged, but virtually certain. Nothing can now be seen on the fragment.

L. 6 (25:3) או על. Note the lack of space between או and על. This is not the only case in which there is hardly any space between או and the following word. Apparently, the scribe optionally treated או as -ו.

L. 7 (25:4) יצדקׄ[. Only the right tip of the head of *qop* can be seen.

L. 9 (25:6) וב]רׄ אנש. Note the lack of space between *reš* and אנש. This suggests that בראנש was perhaps written as a single word.

L. 10 (26:1) ואמ]רׄ. A faint horizontal trace at the bottom edge of the fragment may be the remains of the head of *reš*.

L. 10 (26:2) העדׄ[רת. The top halves of *he* and *ʿayin* rule out any other identification. In view of the context, the last letter (the vertical stroke and part of the head remaining) must be *dalet*.

TRANSLATION

1. [ ]they are [b]ent [down], they shrivel like the cynodon, o[r
2. [25 wh]o then will give me an answer, and ma[ke
3. [*vac*]*at* 25:1Bild[ad the Shuhite] answered [and said:]
4. [2Behold, do]minion and greatness are with God. He ma[kes peace]
5. [in] his [high p]lace. 3Is there security for[
6. [ ] or upon whom does not rise [4
7. [ ] God, and how can one be just [5
8. [ ] pure, and the stars are not [6
9. [a maggot, and a so]n of man, a wor[m. *vacat*]
10. [26:1Job answered and sai]d: 2Did [you] he[lp

COMMENTS

L. 1 (24:24) התכ]פ̇פו]. Cf. 𝔐 והמכו. The verb התכפף also occurs in col. XVI 3 (30:15) where it translates 𝔐 הפך. If the calculation of the width of the column and the reconstruction of the beginnings of lines 4–5 and 9–10 are correct, one can only add a two-letter word before התכ]פ̇פו ([והתכ]פ̇פו is too short). One may reconstruct [או התכ]פ̇פו, but this is not very elegant since the next hemistich also begins with אׄ[ו.

Other possible reconstructions are [ואף התכ]פפו or [ואף יתכ]פפו. The reconstruction [ואף התכ]פפו may be slightly too long. For ואף as rendering of 𝔐 ו-, cf. cols. XX 8 (32:3) and XXVII 2 (36:8).

L. 1 (24:24) כיבלא. The plant יבלא is identified by Löw, *Aramäische Pflanzennamen*, (Leipzig: Engelmann, 1881; Hildesheim: Georg Olms, 1973) 183 §141, and *Die Flora der Juden* I (Wien and Leipzig, 1928; Hildesheim: Georg Olms, 1967) 697–9, as *cynodon dactylum*. The corresponding word in 𝔐 is ככל. Gordis argues that here, as in 2 Sam 17:3, כל is 'grass'. 𝔊 reads ὥσπερ μολόχη (μολόχη is μαλάχη, *malva silvestris*, mallow).

L. 1 (24:24) א֯ו[. Cf. 𝔐 ו; 𝔊 ἤ. Cf. also line 6 (25:3) where או corresponds to 𝔐 ו.

L. 2 (24:25)] מ]ן אפו. Cf. 𝔐 ואם לא אפו מי. The lacuna at the beginning does not allow for a literal translation of 𝔐: [והן לא מ]ן אפו is too long, and [לא מ]ן אפו / [והן] too short. One may reconstruct e.g. [וארו מ]ן אפו, a liberal rendering of 𝔐.

L. 4 (25:2) עם אלהא. 𝔐 עמו and the versions do not add אלהא.

L. 5 (25:2) במרו]מה]. Cf. 𝔐 במרומיו. Since the MS prefers to employ *ʾalep* as the indicator of the determined state, *he* is likely to express the pronominal suffix. Cf., however, 𝔊 ἐν ὑψίστῳ.

Ll. 5–6 (25:3) The space needed for the translation of Job 25:3 is approximately one and a half times as much as that used for vv 2, 4, 5, and 6. The translator elaborated on 𝔐, or rendered a longer Hebrew text.

L. 5 (25:3) האיתי רחצן להש[. The translation differs from 𝔐 היש מספר לגדודיו, 'Is there any number to His armies?'. 𝔊 reads μὴ γάρ τις ὑπολάβοι ὅτι ἔστιν παρέλκυσις πειραταῖς, 'for who would assume that there might be a delay for brigands?' In *ed. princ.* (p. 29) it is suggested that ὑπολάβοι and רחצן, 'hope', are comparable, and that the idea of παρέλκυσις might be expressed in the verbal form following רחצן. Hence להש[היה (*Hapʿel* infinitive of שהא), 'to delay', in *ed. princ.* However, רחצן usually means 'security', 'safety', or 'confidence', not 'hope'.

L. 6 (25:3) או על מן לא תקום̇]. 𝔐 ועל, 'and upon', has been changed to או על, 'or upon' (the two words are written together). תקום̇ corresponds to 𝔐 יקום. The fem. form תקום̇ suggests that the translator did not read 𝔐 אורהו, 'his light' (Aramaic נהורה, masc.), but either interpreted 𝔐 as 'his fire' (נור can be masc. as well as fem.), or read a variant similar to 𝔊 ἔνεδρα παρ' αὐτοῦ, 'his ambush' (Heb. אורבו).

Ll. 6–7 (25:4) תקום̇ [ ] / / [א̇להא. Reconstruct e.g. תקום̇ [נורה ומה יזכא] / [אנש ב]א̇להא.

L. 8 (25:5) זכי[. זכי is an adjective, since the masc. sing. participle of III–*yod* verbs is elsewhere spelled with *ʾalep*. On זכי as an interpretation of 𝔐 יאהיל, cf. 𝔖 ܢܕܟܐ. Reconstruct e.g. [ארו לא]זכי.

L. 10 (26:2) העד̇רת. The verb with interrogative *he* corresponds to 𝔐 מה עזרת. The introductory formula is not indented here, as in line 3.

Col. X (Frg. 9) Job 26:10–27:4

[top margin]

1 [ ] על̊[סי]פי חסוך̇

2 [ ]11 י]ז̊יע ויתמהון מן

3 [ ]12]ימא ובמנדעה קטל

4 [ ]13 הד]נח חללת ידה תנין ערק̇

5 [14 שבילו]הי מא עטר מלא נש̇[מע]

6 [ ]יסתכל *vacat*

7] vac[at

8 [27:1]]ואמר ^{2}חי אלהא[

9]]לנפשי ^{3}הן לכמ[א

10] ב]אפי ^{4}הן ימל[לן

Mus. Inv. 633
PAM 43.820

NOTES ON READINGS

Though no top margin is visible, the first line of frg. 9 must have been the first of the column. The left margin ruling is clearly visible at lines 2 and 3. The width of the column must have been *c*.8.5 cm.

L. 1 (26:10)]על֯[[. Several scholars read]עו֯ or ע]ד. Although this interpretation corresponds nicely to 𝔐, it does not conform to the preserved traces. After the *ʿayin* there is a small trace that resembles the remains of *lamed* (compare על of col. IX 6, where the *lamed* also starts below the ceiling line), or even a *šin*. The photograph shows more traces to the right of the *ʿayin*, which, if they are ink, are not consistent with any letter. These traces are not visible on the fragment.

L. 1 (26:10) ס]י[פי. Before *pe*, a very minute trace can be detected in the photograph, which might be the remnant of a letter, but on the fragment nothing can be seen.

L. 1 (26:10) חסוך֯. The second letter cannot be *šin*. The head of *samek* stretches from the right downstroke almost up to the left upstroke before it extends beyond the edge of the fragment. This head cannot be mistaken for an extremely long *keraia* of *šin*. Moreover, the alleged trace of the upper oblique of *šin* is absent.

L. 5 (26:14) שבילו]הי. The first letter must be interpreted as *he*, not *ḥet*. The protruding left part of the *he* joins the *yod*.

L. 8 (27:1) אלהא]. The dot above the *lamed* is visible in the photograph, though not on the fragment.

L. 9 (27:2)]לנפשי הן. The *yod* is not a supralinear addition. The scribe disregarded the ceiling line and, after *nun*, each letter was a little more raised. After *yod*, he noticed his mistake and dropped down, back to the ceiling line.

L. 10 (27:3) ב]א֯פי. The edge of the left leg is the only remnant of *ʾalep*.

L. 10 (27:4) ימל֯[לן. The only remainder of *yod* is a speck of ink.

TRANSLATION

1. [ ] at the [en]ds of the limit
2. [^{11} He] causes to tremble, and they are stunned at
3. [^{12}] the sea, and by his knowledge He killed
4. [^{13} He caused to sh]ine. His hand pierced the fleeing serpent.
5. [^{14} of] his [ways]. What small thing do we he[ar!]
6. [ ] understands? *vacat*
7. [*va*]*cat*
8. [$^{27:1}$] and said: ^{2}As God lives [
9. [ ] my soul, ^{3}Verily, as long [as
10. [in] my nose, ^{4}if [t]he[y] spea[k

COMMENTS

L. 1 (26:10) על̇]סי[פי חסוך̇ [. 𝔐 reads עד תכלית אור עם חשך. ℭ renders תכלית by סוף. The unknown word חסוך̇ (but cf. Syriac) should be derived from the verb חסך, 'to withhold'. Here we may have a case of a double translation: the translator interpreted 𝔐 תכלית as a derivation of both כלה and כלא.

L. 2 (26:11) י[ז̊יע. A *Hapʿel* form. The subject in 𝔐 ('the pillars of heaven') has become the object of God's actions. Cf. line 4.

L. 4 (26:13) הד[נח. A *Hapʿel* form. As in line 2, the translator changes the subject of the verb. According to modern commentators, 𝔐 שפרה is not a noun, but should be vocalized as a *Piʿel* (the subject is רוחו; *bet* should be deleted as a dittography). Gordis (p. 280–1) refers to the Akkadian root *šuparruru*, 'spread out (a canopy)'. The 𝔐 stich should therefore be translated 'his breath spread out the heavens'. It is not clear which text the translator read. In any case, he interpreted שפרה in the sense of 'fairness' or 'to make fair'.

L. 4 (26:13) תנין ערק̇. Cf. the similar understanding of 𝔐 ברח in 1QIs[a] 27:1: נחש בורח.

L. 5 (26:14) שבילו[הי. Cf. 𝔐 דרכו, 𝔐[q] דרכיו. Since the pl. of ארח is ארחן, construct state ארחת, and with a suffix ארחתה (cf. Dan 4:34), one may reconstruct שבילו[הי.

L. 5 (26:14) עטר. Cf. 𝔐 שמץ, which is interpreted either as a 'whisper' or as a 'fraction', a 'small thing'. Since the verb עטר means 'to smoke', the substantive עטר must denote 'smoke, haze'. Both 𝔐, 'a whisper of a word', and here, 'a haze of a word', would be expressions meaning 'a faint echo'. Sokoloff (p. 118), however, connects עטר with the Targumic Aramaic verb עטר (*Peʿal*), 'to be gone, cease entirely'. The expression מא עטר מלא would mean: 'what small thing'.

Col. XI (Frg. 10 i) Job 27:11-20

top margin

1] [11] בי]ד̇ אלהא ועבד

2] [12] כ]לכון חזיתון למה

3] [13]]אנש רשיעין

4] מן]ק̇דמוהי ינסון [14]הן

5] חר]ב יפצון ולא ישבעון

6] [15]]ן̊ וארמלתה לא

7] [16]]ז̇ו̇זיא כטינא יסגא

8] [17] מ]מ[ונ]ה קש̇ט̇ה יפלג

9 [18]]]°°ן כקטותא

10] [19] ש]כב ולא איתח̣ד

11] [20]]כ̇מ̇י̇ן באי̇ש̇[

Mus. Inv. 637
PAM 43.819

NOTES ON READINGS

Frg. 10 i has preserved the left part of the first lines of col. XI. This column, the first one of a new sheet, measured approximately 9 cm. The fragment has three holes which correspond exactly to the holes of smaller dimension which appear in frg. 11.

L. 3 (27:13) אנש[. The *nun* clearly breaks through the ceiling line. The surface of the skin is abraded at this point and it is difficult to see whether there has been a correction.

L. 6 (27:15) ן̊[. The photograph (but not the fragment) shows the remains of a vertical stroke at the right edge of the fragment. This stroke is written very close to the next word, but note that the scribe uses very small spaces in this column.

L. 8 (27:17) מ[מו]נ[ה. The first visible letter is clearly *mem*, then, in the hole of 0.4 cm, there is space for two more letters between *mem* and *he*.

TRANSLATION

1. [[11] by the ha]nd of God, and the work of
2. [[12] a]ll of you have seen (it). Why
3. [[13]] the wicked,
4. [ ] will carry away [from] before Him: [14]If
5. [swo]rd, they will open (their mouths), and not be satisfied
6. [[15]] and his widows will not
7. [[16]] money like clay amasses
8. [[17]] the [mo]ne[y] the innocent will divide.
9. [[18]] like a hut
10. [[9] go]es to bed and it is not taken away
11. [[20]] evil like water[

COMMENTS

L. 1 (27:11) ועבד. The substantive, 'work', corresponding to 𝔐 אשר עם.

L. 3 (27:13) אנש רשיעין[. Since אנש is a collective noun, it may take *ad sensum* a pl. adjective or verb.

L. 4 (27:13) ינסון. Cf. 𝔐 יקחו. The verbal root is נשי. Other Aramaic texts from Qumran employ the verb נסב instead.

L. 5 (27:14) יפצון. 𝔐 reads וצאצאיו, 'and his offspring', but the translator has changed the sentence. The expression פצה פה, 'to open one's mouth (to eat, or to speak)', is common in Hebrew, but quite unusual in Aramaic. The dictionaries list only ℭ 35:16. Here פם is missing (an ellipse?), but the meaning 'to open (one's mouth)' is the only one which makes sense.

L. 6 (27:15) ן̊[. The word probably corresponds to 𝔐 יקברו. Reconstruct e.g. יתקברו[ן̊.

L. 7 (27:16) זוזיא. Cf. 𝔐 כסף. Although זוז may designate various coins, the context suggests the simple translation 'money'.

L. 7 (27:16) יסגא. A *Hapʿel* form.

L. 8 (27:17) מ[מו]נ[ה. Or מ[מנ]ה. Sokoloff suggests ו]מ[צו]ה], 'and charity' (the expression פלג מצוה, *Paʿel*, 'to distribute charity', is common in Galilean Aramaic).

L. 9 (27:18) ן°°[. כגו[נ̊]י̊ן (cf. 𝔖 ܐܝܟ ܓܢܘܢܐ) corresponding to 𝔐 כעש (*ed. princ.*, p. 33) may perhaps be reconstructed.

L. 9 (27:18) כקטותא. Cf. 𝔐 כסכה. The word קטותא elsewhere means 'branch, switch'. One may tentatively argue that it can also mean a 'hut (built from branches)', but it is more likely that קטותא (<*קטונתא) is a variant of קיטון, 'chamber, small room', derived from Greek κοιτών.

L. 10 (27:19) ש]כב. Since the following perfect איתחד corresponds to a 𝔐 imperfect, one may assume that a perfect ש]כב (𝔐 ישכב) should be reconstructed.

L. 10 (27:19) איתחד. The form is probably a perfect *Itpaʿal* or *Itpeʿel* of אחד. The assimilation of *ʾalep* is possible (cf. e.g. אתחד[ו], Cowley 34, line 4), but the *plene* spelling of the -את prefix as אית is unusual for this period (another example is Mur **18** 2). The *Itpaʿal* corresponds to 𝔐 יאסף (*Nipʿal*), and not to the more likely reading יסיף, which is also suggested by 𝔊 προσθήσει.

L. 11 (27:20) באיש̇]. Cf. 𝔐 בלהות, 'terrors'. Hence a pl. form באיש̇]תא can be expected. However, the verb in 𝔐 is sing., and therefore the translator could have employed a sing. form.

Col. XII (Frgs. 10 ii, 11 i) Job 28:4-13

top margin

1 רגל̇] 5 [
2 וחליף̊] 6את]ר̇י
3 ספירא̊] 7 [
4 לא י̊] 8לא הד]רʾה
5 תני̇] 9 יד]ה̇
6 עק̇]ר 10 טי]פ̊ין
7 בז]ע 11 כ]לא
8 ו̇] 12? ◦[
9] 13 אנ]ש

Mus. Inv. 637
PAM 43.819

NOTES ON READINGS

Frgs. 10 ii and 11 i are the vestigial remains of col. XII. The identification of the text is made possible by ספירא̊] in line 3.

L. 1 (28:4) רגל̇]. Part of the hook of *lamed* can be seen.

L. 1 (28:5) [. The small black mark visible on the right edge of frg. 11 in PAM 43.819 is in fact a crack in the skin, parallel to the hole behind the margin.

L. 2 (28:5) וחליף̊]. The *yod*, which is partially written above the ceiling line, has been inserted apparently as a correction, but just within the ruling. A small black mark at the edge of the fragment, below the bottom line, might be a remnant of the tail of final *pe*. The trace cannot be seen on the fragment.

L. 3 (28:6) ספירא̊]. The trace after ספיר could be the remains of the *keraia* of the right arm of *ʾalep*, but it is not completely clear how to interpret the space between *reš* and *ʾalep*. Thus, read ספירא̊] or, with more difficulty, ספיר א̊]בניה.

L. 3 (28:7) [. The fragment shows no trace here.

L. 4 (28:8) הד]רכה. The supralinear *kap* seems to have been written by another hand, but the skin is abraded and perforated, perhaps necessitating the writing of the *kap* above the ruling line.

L. 5 (28:9) יד]ה֯. The left end of a crossbar or head at the end of the line could belong to *dalet*, *reš*, or *he*.

L. 6 (28:9) עק֯]ר. The letters are no longer visible on the fragment.

L. 6 (28:10) טי]פ֯ין. The left end of the base of a letter is clearly recognizable before *yod*.

L. 7 (28:10) בז]ע. The upper part of *zayin* is visible in PAM 43.819. The letters are no longer visible on the fragment.

L. 8 (28:11) ו֯]. Visible in PAM 43.819, but no longer on the fragment, is the lower part of a tapering vertical stroke.

Translation

1. foot [5]
2. And are chan[ged 6Plac]es of
3. sapphire [7]
4. do not [8No] serpent [has set f]oot
5. on it [9] his [hand]
6. he upro[ots 10 chan]nels
7. he he[ws out, 11 he restr]ains
8. and [12?]
9. [13 ma]n

Comments

L. 2 (28:5) וחליף֯]. A *Peʿil* form of חלף, 'to change', as a translation of 𝔐 נהפך. Cf. *Tg. Isa* 1:7, which renders 𝔐 מהפכת by אתחלפת.

L. 2 (28:6) את]ר֯י. It is likely that the word ending with רי corresponds to 𝔐 מקום, thus e.g. מש]ר֯י, 'resting-place', or את]ר֯י (pl.), 'places'.

L. 4 (28:7) לא]י֯. לא is likely to correspond to the negative particle in the first hemistich of 𝔐 Job 28:7. The trace at the left edge of frg. 10 ii might be *yod*, suggesting a reconstruction of י֯]נדע (imperfect) or י֯]דע (perfect) or the like.

L. 4 (28:8) הד]רכה. Cf. 𝔐 הדריכהו. The translator turned the phrase into the singular.

L. 5 (28:8) תנין]. Cf. 𝔐 בני שחץ, literally 'sons of pride', and generally rendered 'proud (or: wild) beasts'.

L. 6 (28:9) עק֯]ר. Cf. 𝔐 הפך משרש.

Ll. 6–7 (28:10) טי]פ֯ין בז]ע. Cf. 𝔐 יארים בקע. ℭ reads נהרין בזע, and 𝔖 ܦܠܓ ܢܗܪ̈ܘܬܐ, but the base of the letter before *yod* rules out נהר]ין. טיף is a common word for 'channel' in the targums.

L. 7 (28:11) כ]לא. Cf. 𝔐 חבש.

L. 9 (28:13) אנ]ש. Cf. 𝔐 אנוש. The *šin* at the end of the line occurs where one expects a translation of the first hemistich of 𝔐 Job 28:13.

Col. XIII (Frg. 11 ii) Job 28:20-28

top margin

אתר ערימותא [21]אׄ[רו 1

צפרי שמיא אסתׄ[תרת [22] 2

באדנינא שמענא שׄ[מעה [23] 3

בה ארו הוא יצ[[24] 4

לקצוי ארעא י◦[5

[25]במעבדה לרוחא[6

במכילה [26]במעבד[ה למטרא דת וארח לעננין] 7

קלילין [27]באדיׄןׄ[8

[28]ואמר לבני[אנשא 9

ומסטיאׄ[10

Mus. Inv. 637
PAM 43.819

NOTES ON READINGS

The beginnings of the first ten lines of col. XIII have been preserved on frg. 11 ii.

L. 1 (28:21) אׄ[רו. The remains suggest *ʾalep*, rather than *waw*.

L. 2 (28:21) אסתׄ[תרת. *Taw* is barely readable.

L. 3 (28:22) שׄ[מעה. In view of 𝔐, the small trace at the end of the line is likely to be *šin*.

L. 4 (28:23) יצ[. *Ṣade* is absolutely certain (almost identical to the *ṣade* in the next line). The strange stroke which touches the left arm of the *ṣade*, as seen in PAM 43.819, is in reality a crack in the edge of the skin.

L. 5 (28:24) י◦[. The letter at the end of the line is *pe*, *ṭet*, or *mem*.

L. 10 (28:28) ומסטיאׄ[. The vertical stroke of *yod* nearly joins the *ṭet*. The small space between the letters can be seen in clear prints of the PAM photograph. Of *ʾalep*, only the *keraia* can be seen.

TRANSLATION

1. the place of wisdom? [21]F[or
2. the birds of the heaven [she] is con[cealed. [22]
3. With our ears we have heard a ru[mour of it. [23]
4. in (?) her. For He [[24]
5. to the ends of the earth he [
6. [25]When He made for the wind [
7. by its measure. [26]When He made [a law for the rain, and a way for the]
8. light [clouds.] [27]Then [

9. [28]And said to the sons of [men
10. And the turning [

Comments

L. 1 (28:21) א̊]רו. As in line 4 (28:23), ארו renders explicative *waw*.

L. 2 (28:21) צפרי שמיא. This is the rendering of 𝔐 עוף השמים, even though the exact equivalent, עוף שמיא is good Aramaic (cf. e.g. Dan 2:38). Sokoloff suggests that the translator sometimes tries to avoid exact equivalents, e.g. rendering Hebrew רב by Aramaic שגיא, and vice versa.

L. 3 (28:22) ש̊]מעה. This is the noun שמע with the 3rd fem. sing. pronominal suffix; cf. 𝔐 שמעה.

L. 4 (28:23) בה. There is nothing in the first hemistich of Job 28:23 which corresponds to בה. One can surmise that the translator changed 'her way' (𝔐 דרכה) to 'her'. In that case, the first hemistich may be reconstructed ארו אסתכל אלהא] / בה, 'God understands her'. The translator uses אסתכל to render הבין in col. VIIA 6 (23:5). The object of אסתכל is expressed by means of the preposition *bet*. ארו is added because the reconstruction of line 3, ש̊]מעה אסתכל אלהא], is too short.

L. 4 (28:23) יצ]. Many readings and reconstructions have been proposed: יצ̇ר̊ ('he has created'), יצ]ף ('he cares [for]'), יצ]פא ('he spies').

L. 5 (28:24) לקצוי ארעא. Cf. 𝔐 לקצות הארץ. The expression קצוי ארץ occurs in Ps 48:11, 65:6, and Isa 26:15, but קצוי (pl. construct form of *קצה) is not attested in Aramaic.

L. 5 (28:24) י◦]. The broken word at the end of the line corresponds to 𝔐 יביט, but no convincing reconstruction can be put forward.

Ll. 7–8 (28:26) במעבד]ה למטרא דת וארח לעננין] / קלילין. The second hemistich of 𝔐 Job 28:26 (ודרך לחזיז קלות) recurs in 38:25. The latter occurrence is translated in col. XXXI 3 as וארח לעננין קלילין. Apparently the translator interpreted 𝔐 קלות as a fem. pl. of the adjective קל. For דת as a rendering of 𝔐 חק, cf. col. XXX 8 (38:10).

L. 9 (28:28) לבני] אנשא. Cf. 𝔐 לאדם. In col. XXVIII 2 (36:25), בני אנשא corresponds to 𝔐 אנוש.

L. 10 (28:28) ומסטי̇א]. The form can be analysed as the emphatic state of the infinitive *Peʿal*. S also has an infinitive (ܘܠܡܣܛܐ).

Col. XIV (Frg. 12) Job 29:7-16

top margin

1 [ב]צ̇פרין בתרעי קריא בשוק[א

2 [[8]ו]ח̇זוני עלומין טשו וגברין ח◦[

3 [[9]ו]רבר⌜ב⌝ין חשו מללא וכף ישו[ן

4 [10]ק̇ל סגנין הטמרו לחנך דב̇[ק [11]

5 [ת]שמע אדן שבחתני ועין ח̇[זת

6 [[12]א]רו אנה ש̓זבת לענא מן ◦[

7 [ד]י̇ לא עדר להו̇ן [13]ברכת א̇[בד

8 [בפ]ם ארמלה הוית לצלו̊[[14]

9 [לבש]תני וככתון לבשת [15

10 [ו]ר֯גלין לחגיר [16

11 [ל]א֯ י֯ד֯ע֯[ת

Mus. Inv. 632
PAM 43.818

Notes on Readings

Frg. 12 preserves the remains of col. XIV. Most probably the right margin of the column should be located *c*.3 mm to the right of the right edge of the fragment. This supposition is based upon the fact that, in lines 1–3 and 5–6 (or 1–7), one letter should be added to the right. The width of the column must have been somewhat smaller than usual, since a comparison with 𝔐 shows that only one or two words are missing in each line. Its width measured *c*.8–8.5 cm (the exact position of the left ruling is unknown). The two insertions (lines 3 and 7) were made by the same hand.

L. 2 (29:8) ח°[. The first letter is definitely *ḥet* (not *he*). The remains of the next letter belong to *dalet*, *he*, *reš*, or *taw*.

L. 4 (29:10) ק֯ל. Only a small part of *qop* remains.

L. 8 (29:13) [בפ]ם. Not [בפ]ו֯ם. No *waw* is visible in the photographs. This is also the spelling used in 1QapGen ar XX 8.

L. 8 (29:13) לצלו֯[. Only the faintest trace of a letter, no longer visible on the fragment, is distinguishable at the left edge.

L. 10 (29:15) לחגיר [. לחגיר[א is not possible, as traces of the *ʾalep* would have been visible.

L. 11 (29:16) ל]א֯. Only the tip of the diagonal of *ʾalep* remains.

Translation

1. [in] the mornings to the city gates, in [the] square [
2. [[8]And] (when) youths saw me, they hid, and men [
3. [[9]And] great men refrained from speaking and placed (their) hand [
4. [10]Leaders concealed (their) voice, to (their) palate stu[ck
5. [[11](When) an ear [h]eard (me), it praised me, and (when) an eye s[aw
6. [[12]F]or I saved the poor man from [
7. [wh]o had no helper. [13]The blessing of the d[ying
8. [In the mou]th of a widow I was a prayer.[[14]
9. [cloth]ed me, and as with a tunic I clothed myself [[15]
10. [and] feet to the lame. [[16]
11. [I] did [no]t know [

Comments

L. 1 (29:7) בשוק[א. Cf. 𝔐 ברחוב (S ܒܦܠܛܝܐ). Hebrew רחוב can be translated by Aramaic רחוב, פתאה, or שוק (cf. e.g. *Tg. Prov* 1:20; 7:12; 22:13; 26:13).

L. 2 (29:8) [ו]ח֯זוני. Cf. 𝔐 ראוני. *Ed. ATQ* (p. 30) suggests [י]חזוני and refers to line 5. Both lines would employ the syntactical construction of an imperfect in the protasis and a perfect in the apodosis. However, this syntactical construction is known only from the Sefire texts.

L. 2 (29:8) עלומין. The manuscript clearly shows עלומין. Nevertheless, some scholars prefer to read the regular עלימין. The word may be irregular, but it is not unique (cf. *Tg. Isa* 54:6 עלומין).

L. 2 (29:8) טשו. Cf. 𝔐 ונחבאו. 𝔖 uses the same root: ܘܐܬܛܫܝܘ.

L. 2 (29:8) וגברין ח◦[. Cf. 𝔐 וישישים קמו עמדו. For 𝔐 ישישים, 'the aged', cf. also Job 12:12; 15:10; 32:6. The broken word cannot be reconstructed to correspond literally to 𝔐 קמו. One might therefore assume that it is an attribute of the preceding גברין. The reconstruction חכ̊[מין (García Martínez, 'Nuevas Lecturas', 243), which is based upon Job 12:12, is doubtful since the last letter is unlikely to be *kap*. More likely is חר̊[שו, 'and they were silent'. 'Silence' is the issue in vv 8-9 (cf. Gordis's interpretation of קמו עמדו: the aged 'stood up in silence').

L. 3 (29:9) [ו]רבר(ב)ין. Cf. 𝔐 שרים, 'chiefs, lords'. Biblical Aramaic uses two different pl. forms of רב: רברבין is the normal pl. of the adjective; the pl. noun רברבנין refers to 'chiefs'.

L. 3 (29:9) חשו מללא. Normally the verb חשא, 'to be silent', is used without an object. It is therefore doubtful whether one should regard מללא as a nominal form. It may also be regarded as an infinitive (*Paʿel*), but then the preposition מן would be expected. Cf. e.g. the similar Hebrew construction in 1 Kgs 22:3 and Sir 41:21. This interpretation entails the supposition of haplography: <מל>מללא.

L. 4 (29:10) קׄל סגנין הטמרו. Probably: 'leaders concealed (their) voice'. הטמרו is a *Hapʿel* form. The absence of a pronominal suffix is not problematic (cf. כף in line 3 and חנך in the next hemistich). Yet, the interpretation 'the voice of leaders was concealed' (cf. the same construction in 𝔐) should not be ruled out. A similar genitive construction, with the genitive in the absolute state, and the whole construction nevertheless determined, occurs in line 1 (בתרעי קריא). In that case הטמרו is a *Hitpeʿel* form.

L. 5 (29:11) [ת]שמע אדן. This reconstruction corresponds to 𝔐 כי אזן שמעה, but the use of the perfect שבחתני after the imperfect [ת]שמע is strange (but cf. COMMENTS on line 2 [ו]חזוני). Yet, the reconstruction [למ]שמע אדן, as in col. XXXVII 7 (42:5), conflicts with the assumption that only one letter fits between the right margin of the column and the right edge of the fragment.

L. 6 (29:12) שׄזבת. The *plene* spelling is in accordance with Biblical Aramaic. Apparently the translator interpreted 𝔐 משוע, 'crying out', as the preposition מן annexed to the noun שוע (cf. Job 34:19). Cf. 𝔊 ἐκ χειρὸς δυνάστου and 𝔖 ܡܢ ܥܘܠܨܢܐ.

L. 7 (29:12) עדר. A participle 'a helper' (cf. 𝔐) or a noun meaning 'help, assistance'. Such sentences do not necessarily employ the particle of existence איתי. איתי is used in cols. XXXI 5 (38:28) and XXXIV 5 (40:9), but not in cols. XXII 3 (33:9) or XXXI 4 (38:26).

L. 9 (29:14) [לבש]תני וככתון לבשת]. It is difficult to reconstruct this line according to 𝔐. [לבש]תני suggests that the translator switched the two verbs of 𝔐, but the space left at the end of line 8 suggests two words, not merely the word 'righteousness'. The structure of the verse is not clear to modern commentators (two hemistichs of three words or three tristichs of two words?).

VARIANTS

29:7 (1) [ב]צׄפרין בתרעי] שער 𝔐 ὄρθριος 𝔊 (שחר). Apparently there was a double reading in the transmitted Hebrew text (שער and שחר), both preserved in 11QtgJob. On such double translations, cf. S. Talmon, 'Double Readings in the Masoretic Text', *Textus* 1 (1960) 144–84.

29:13 (8) [בפ]ם ארמלה הוית לצלו̊ן̊[𝔊 (στόμα δὲ χήρας με εὐλόγησεν)] ולב אלמנה ארנן 𝔐

Col. XV (Frg. 13) Job 29:24–30:4

top margin

1 [ ]24אׄחאך להון ולא יה[ימנון
2 [ ]ון 25בחרת ארחי והוית ר̊[אש
3 [ ]בראש חילה וכגבר די א[בלין ינחם]
4 [30:1וכען ח]אכו עלי זערין מני ביומין[
5 [אבה]ת̊הון מלמהוא עם כלבי ע[ני 2
6 [ידיהון]ל̊א הוא לי צבין ובאכפיׄ[הון
7 [3 כ]פ̊ן רעין הוא ירק ד̊[חשת
8 [ ]בׄאישה 4די אכל[ו
9 [ועיקרי רתמ]ין לחמהוׄ[ן

Mus. Inv. 632
PAM 43.818

Notes on Readings

The remains of nine lines of col. XV can be seen on frg. 13. The scribe has executed his task meticulously; the hand is very neat and the letters are almost calligraphic. It is plausible that the column measured *c*.8.3–8.5 cm, of which *c*.1.4 cm were to the right of the fragment (cf. also the notes on readings on the next column).

L. 2 (29:25) ר̊[אש. A leg and part of a shoulder, no longer visible on the fragment, are visible at the edge of the line.

L. 6 (30:2)]ל̊א. A tiny dot on the edge of the fragment may be part of the arm of *lamed*.

L. 7 (30:3) כ]פ̊ן. Visible is a trace of the left part of the head of *pe*.

Translation

1. [ ]24I smiled on them, and [t]he[y] did not be[lieve it;
2. [ ] 25I chose my path, and I was a c[hief;
3. [ ] at the head of his army, and like a man who [comforts] s[ad ones.]
4. [30:1But now] they [l]augh at me, (men) younger than I in days. [
5. their [father]s from being with the dogs of [my] fl[ock. 2
6. [of their hands] I did not like, and under [their] pressure [
7. [3 a fam]ine they were grazing the verdure of the s[teppe
8. [ ] bad. 4Who ate [
9. [and the root of broom]s was thei[r] bread. [

Comments

L. 1 (29:24) יה]ימנון. Cf. 𝔐 יאמינו and ℭ יהימנון.

L. 2 (29:24) ון[. The letters are undoubtedly the ending of a verb which corresponds to 𝔐 יפילון.

L. 2 (29:25) ארחי. Note the 1st sing. suffix, as opposed to 𝔐 דרכם.

L. 3 (29:25) בראש חילה[. Cf. 𝔐 בגדוד.

L. 5 (30:1) מלמהוא. The infinitive of הוא preceded by the prepositions מן and -ל. The same construction occurs in col. XX 3 (32:1).

L. 6 (30:2) לא הוא לי צבין[. Cf. 𝔐 למה לי, 'what (*scil.* good, or: gain) to me'. The rhetorical question is turned into a negative statement. הוא is likely to be a verbal form.

L. 6 (30:2) ובאכפי]הון. אכף, 'load, weight', 'burden'. The translator interpreted 𝔐 עלימו, 'upon them', as 'their yoke'. This misinterpretation probably forced the translator to alter the rest of the hemistich, too.

L. 7 (30:3) כ]פן רעין הוא ירק ד]חשת. The text deviates somewhat from 𝔐 ובכפן גלמוד הערקים ציה. The first word of the line כ]פן corresponds to 𝔐 בכפן, and the reconstruction of the last word, ד]חשת (cf. col. XXXII 5), to 𝔐 ציה. The word רעין might be interpreted as a noun 'desire': '(their) desire was the vegetation of the desert' (*ed. princ.*, p. 41), but the interpretation of רעין as a pl. participle conforms more to 𝔐. הוא, then, is the 3rd masc. pl. perfect of הוא, which in other Qumran Aramaic texts is written הוו or הווא.

L. 8 (30:3) באישה[. Cf. 𝔐 משאה. In col. XVI 3 (30:14), באישה corresponds to 𝔐 שאה.

L. 8 (30:4) די אכלו]. Cf. 𝔐 הקטפים.

L. 9 (30:4) ועיקרי רתמ]ין לחמהו]ן[. 𝔐 ושרש רתמים לחמם. ℭ also uses רתמין.

Col. XVI (Frg. 14) Job 30:13-20

top margin

] [13]לס]תרי יתון ופצא לא

]איתי להון [14]וכע]ן בתקף שחני יתון

]תחות]באישה אתכפפת [15]התכפפת

]עלי ונדת כ]רוח טבתי ו⌈ר⌉בתי וכענן

]עבר מני פורק]ני [16]וכען עלי תתאשד

]נפשי יאחדונני י]ומי תשב⌈א⌉ יאקפוני

] [17]בלילא] גרמי יקדון ועדק[י]

]לא ישכבון [18]בסגיא]חיל יאחדון לבו[שי]

]כפם כתוני יסנ]פונני [19]אחתוני [לטינא]

] [20] ע]ליך ◦]

Mus. Inv. 631
PAM 43.817

Notes on Readings

The ends of the first lines of col. XVI have been preserved on frg. 14. The handwriting is not as neat as that of the previous column, although it is the same hand. The abrasion on the fragment has been caused by the stitching of frg. 15. The original reconstructions in the *editio princeps*, which were based on lines 2 and 3, would imply a column of hardly more than 6 cm. This is unlikely, because there would remain a gap of 5 cm to the left edge of frg. 13. What is more, the other lines demand a longer reconstruction. There is no material evidence for the position of frg. 13 in col. XV, and the presence of stitching between frgs. 12 and 13 makes calculations more difficult. Yet, the combination of possible reconstructions in cols. XIV–XVI and the assumption that the width of the columns of one sheet did not vary considerably lead to the probability that col. XVI measured *c*.7.3 cm, and that the margin between cols. XVI and XVII was *c*.1.8 cm.

L. 1 (30:13) לס]תׄרי. The horizontal stroke at the bottom before *reš* is most likely a trace of *nun*, *ṣade*, or *taw*, but the possibility that another letter should be read cannot be ruled out completely. No traces remain on the fragment; even the *reš* has disappeared.

L. 3 (30:14)]בׄאישה. The left tip of the base of *bet* has been preserved.

L. 4 (30:15) כ]רׄוח. The left tip of the head of *reš* is visible.

L. 5 (30:15) פורק]ני. The first letter is a *nun*. The trace in PAM 43.817 oriented towards the right is a crack in the skin.

L. 6 (30:16) חשב˺א. The downstroke of the supralinear *reš* joins the tick of the head of *bet*.

L. 9 (30:18) יסנ]פׄונני. At the beginning of the line, at half the normal height of a letter, there is an ink trace that could be the tip of the left part of the head of *pe* (or the left arm of *mem*).

L. 9 (30:19) [לטינא]. PAM 43.817 shows a trace at the end of the line consistent with the hook of *lamed*, in which case one might reconstruct לׄ[טינא]. On the fragment, however, the surface is peeled at this point, explaining the apparent trace in the photograph.

Translation

1. [ ][13]They come [for] my [ru]ination, and [there is] no deliverer
2. [for them. [14]And no]w, forcefully my boils emerge,
3. [under an] evil [ ]I am bent down. [15]I am bent down,
4. [and fled as] the wind are my goodness and my dignity, and as a cloud
5. my [deliveran]ce [has passed from me.] [16]And now is poured out from me
6. [my soul, da]ys of suffering [take hold of me] (and) surround me.
7. [[17]At night] my bones burn (within me), and [my] veins
8. [know no rest. [18]With great] strength they seize [my] gar[ment,]
9. [as by the collar of my tunic] they will [gir]d me. [19]They caused me to descend [in the mire]
10. [[20] t]o you [

Comments

L. 1 (30:13) לס]תׄרי. The reconstruction לס]תׄרי, 'to my ruin', is based upon להותי 𝔐, 'to my downfall'. A noun ܡܣܬܪܐ from the Aramaic root סתר, 'to overthrow', is known in Syriac, but other reconstructions, e.g. לת]בׄרי (cf. *Tg. Ezek* 7:26) are possible as well.

L. 1 (30:13) יתון. The use of יתון suggests that the translator interpreted יעילו 𝔐 as יעלו.

L. 1 (30:13) ופצא. Like עזר 𝔐, פצא should be read as a participle.

L. 2 (30:13) [איתי להון וכע]ן. The logical reconstruction of the beginning of the line would be [איתי להו]ן or [הוא להו]ן. This, however, would leave more than one centimetre of manuscript unaccounted for. Grelot's reconstruction [איתי לי מנהו]ן changes the thrust of 𝔐. The introduction of an extra particle in the tentative reconstruction איתי להון וכע]ן[is plausible in view of the translator's misunderstanding of the first hemistich of v 14.

L. 2 (30:14) בחקף שחני יתון. Cf. 𝔐 כפרץ רחב יאתיו, 'they come as through a wide breach'. פרץ is also translated by חקף in ℭ 16:14 and *Tg. Onq.* Gen 38:29. The noun שחן (cf. Hebrew שחין in Job 2:7), 'boil, inflamed spot', also occurs in 4Q**242** (PrNab) lines 2 and 6. It is difficult, though, to understand the relation between 𝔐 and this translation. The clause can be interpreted in several ways. It can be translated: 'Lorsque mon ulcère (?) est terrible, ils viennent' (*ed. princ.*, p. 43), but it is also possible to regard שחני (pl.) as the subject of יתון, and בחקף as an adverbial expression meaning 'strongly' (cf. *Tg. Onq.* Exod 14:25; Gen 49:9): 'Strongly (i.e. with force) my boils emerge'.

L. 3 (30:14)]בֿאישה אתכפפת. Cf. 𝔐 שאה התגלגלו. Reasons of space demand an additional word in front of]בֿאישה. באישה, both here and in col. XV 8 (30:3), where it corresponds to 𝔐 משאה, may be an adjective, in which case one should reconstruct a noun in both verses. Since 𝔊 reads a 1st sing. passive form (πέφυρμαι), one can interpret אתכפפת as a 1st sing. form (and not 3rd fem. sing.).

L. 3 (30:15) התכפפת. Cf. 𝔐 ההפך.

L. 4 (30:15) טבתי ו֯ר֯ב֯תי. Cf. 𝔐 נדבתי. The versions have rendered נדבתי in several ways (𝔊 μου ἡ ἐλπὶς; 𝔖 ܪܒܘܬܝ). 𝔖 corresponds to the reading of some 𝔐 manuscripts נתיבתי (probably influenced by Job 30:13 נתסו נתיבתי). רבותי seems to be the correct translation of this much disputed word, but the additional טבתי is puzzling. It is interesting to note that Beer already suggested reading טובתי in 𝔐 in the critical apparatus of BHK. This is possibly a case of double translation.

L. 5 (30:15) עבר מני פורק]ני[. Cf. 𝔐 עברה ישעתי. The usual Aramaic equivalent of ישועה is פורקן. Cf. also ℭ פורקני and 𝔖 ܦܘܪܩܢܝ. מני is an addition to 𝔐, added in the reconstruction to fill the gap.

L. 5 (30:16) תתאשד. This word, as well as 𝔐 תשתפך, must have some metaphorical meaning. The meaning 'to be confounded', or 'to be angry', may be intended in Padua Pap. I *recto* 7 (לא תתאשד).

L. 6 (30:16) נפשי יאחדונני י]ומי חשב֯א[. The reconstruction corresponds literally to 𝔐 נפשי יאחזוני ימי עני. In view of both 𝔐 and the following imperfect יאקפוני, one should reconstruct the imperfect יאחדונני.

L. 6 (30:16) חשב֯א. This is likely a noun derived from the verb חשב, 'to suffer', which occurs in an ossuary inscription (J. Naveh, *IEJ* 20 [1970] 33–7). This meaning corresponds to 𝔐 עני.

L. 6 (30:16) יאקפוני. An *Apʿel* of נקף, 'to surround'. Both the *plene* spelling and the ending -וני (instead of -ונני) are exceptional (cf. also the COMMENTS on חזו המ֯ו֯ן in col. XXVIII 2). The word, possibly with a subject at the beginning of the next line, may be a secondary translation of יאחזוני. Cf. 𝔖 ܢܫܘܓܢܢܝ.

L. 7 (30:17) יקדון. 𝔐 reads נקר (*Piʿel* of נקר, 'to bore, to pick'). The difference seems to stem from a confusion between *dalet* and *reš* in the Hebrew text. Cf. also 𝔊 συγκέκαυται (Swete B συγκέχυται).

L. 7 (30:17) ועדק]י[. Cf. 𝔐 וערקי, 'my sinews'. Either ועדק]י[is a scribal error for וערק]י[, or it is a noun meaning 'tendons' derived from עדק, 'to be fastened, to stick to'. Cf. Syriac ܥܕܩܬܐ, 'curl, lock of hair'.

L. 9 (30:18) כפם כתוני יסנ]פ֯ונני[. יסנ]פ֯ונני (cf. ܣܢܦ *Paʿel*) or יאק]פ֯ונני (as in line 6) are tentative reconstructions of the verbal form corresponding to 𝔐 יאזרני.

L. 9 (30:19) אחתוני. This *Apʿel* of נחת may be a somewhat free translation of 𝔐 הרני, 'he threw me'. Like ℭ and 𝔖, the translator retained the pl. of the preceding verse. Yet, there is a possibility that the translator read הרדני, a conjecture for the reading in 𝔐 already proposed by Beer (BHK).

L. 9 (30:19)]לטינא[. Cf. 𝔐 לחמר. טינא is used in ℭ and 𝔖.

L. 10 (30:20) ע]ל֯יך. Cf. 𝔐 אליך. Insufficient space in the first part of the line does not allow for a literal rendering of 𝔐.

VARIANTS

30:17 (7) יקדון 𝔊 συγκέκαυται (Swete B συγκέχυται) (יקד)] נקר 𝔐

30:18 (8) יאחדון 𝔊 ἐπελάβετο (יתפש)] יתחפש 𝔐

Col. XVII (Frg. 15 i, A6) Job 30:25(?)–31:1

top margin

1 [ ]אׄתה
2 [ ]בׄדי
3 [ ]א אתקף ◦[[27]מעיני רת]חׄו ולא
4 [דמו קד]מׄוניׄ יומי עמׄ[לא [28]קדרת ו]הׄלכת
5 [מן שמשא]קׄמׄתׄ[ו]אׄזעקת
6 [[29] לבנ]תׄ יענה
7 [[30]]וׄ מן
8 [[31] אבוב]יׄ
9 [[31:1]]לׄא

Mus. Inv. 567, 631
PAM 43.817*, 44.114*

NOTES ON READINGS

The complete words in frg. 15 i 3–7 correspond to 𝔐, but the identification of the broken words in lines 1–2 is problematic. The column seems to have measured no more than 7.5 cm, and possibly some millimetres less. The stitching holes are at 0.7 cm; ten are preserved, some with the thread in them. The placement of the small fragment A6 (lines 3–5), presently broken into many pieces, between frgs. 14 and 15 is tentative and does not conform with the pattern of damage witnessed in the other fragments. The only available photograph of frg. A6 was taken in a smaller scale.

L. 3 (30:26?)]א. A small faint trace, *c.*0.2 cm above the *keraia* of the *ʾalep*, is compatible with the tick of the upper arm of *lamed*. The broken and darkened state of the fragment makes it impossible to check whether this trace is ink.

L. 3 (30:27) רת]חׄו. The trace at the right edge is part of the left leg or arm of a letter. The correspondence with 𝔐 suggests a *ḥet*.

L. 5 (30:28) ו]אׄזעקת. A trace of ink, still visible on the fragment, appears before *zayin*, and may be the remains of the bottom part of the left leg of *ʾalep*.

L. 6 (30:29) לבנ]תׄ. In view of 𝔐, the traces, no longer visible on the fragment, can possibly be identified as *taw*.

TRANSLATION

1. [ ]
2. [ ]
3. [ ] is strong [[27]My intestines boi]l and do not
4. [rest;] days of afflic[tion come] to meet me. [28][In darkness] I go about

5. [without sun;] I rise up [and] I shout for help.
6. [29 to the ost]riches.
7. [30] from
8. [31] my [flute]
9. [31:1] not

COMMENTS

L. 1 (30:25-26) א̇תה[. The letters cannot be identified unless one hypothesizes that the translator considerably expanded v 26. In that case, the reconstruction י]א̇תה may correspond to the first ויבא of v 26.

L. 3 (30:26) אתקף. The form can be analysed in different ways, as a 3rd masc. sing. perfect *Apʿel* or *Itpeʿel*, or as a 1st com. sing. imperfect of any stem of תקף. 11QtgJob shows a preference for perfect *Hapʿel*/*Hitpeʿel* forms, above *Apʿel*/*Itpeʿel* forms. Targumic תקף usually renders 𝔐 חזק or אמץ. However, אתקף may be part of a circumlocution of Job 30:26 𝔐 ויבא אפל.

L. 4 (30:27) קד]מ̇וני̇ יומי עמ̇[לא. Corresponding to 𝔐 קדמוני ימי עני. Or reconstruct ע̇[לבנא instead of עמ̇[לא.

L. 5 (30:28) ו]א̇זעקת]ק̇מ̇ת̇[. Cf. 𝔐 קמתי בקהל אשוע. Note the *Apʿel* form.

L. 6 (30:29) לבנ]ת̇ יענה. Cf. 𝔐 לבנות יענה.

L. 7 (30:30) ו̇[. The *waw* probably indicates a pl. form of a verb corresponding to 𝔐 חרה. Whereas 𝔐 has a sing. subject עצמי, 𝔊 and 𝔖 have the pl. forms τὰ ὀστᾶ and ܓܪ̈ܡܝ.

L. 8 (30:31) אבוב]י̇. Cf. 𝔐 עגבי. אבוב is the usual translation of עגב in the targums.

Col. XVIII (Frgs. 15 ii, 16 i) Job 31:8-16

top margin

1 יאכ̇[ל 9 פ]ת̇י̇א

2 לבי בא[נתא צ]ד̇ת

3 10 תטחן ל[11 ד]נ̇א רגז

4 והוא חטא̇[12 הי]א̇ עד

5 אבדון ת[אכל]13 הן אתקצרת

6 בדין עב̇[די]14 מ̇א אעבד

7 כדי יק[ום אלהא] 15 ארו

8 עבד̇[ני ח]ד̇ 16 הן

9 אמ̇[נע]ס̇יפת

Mus. Inv. 624, 631
PAM 43.816*, 43.817*

NOTES ON READINGS

The beginnings and ends of col. XVIII 1–9 have been preserved on frgs. 15 ii and 16 i. The ruling of the left margin has been drawn at an angle. The column width varies from *c.*8.6 cm at line 1 to *c.*9 cm at line 9.

L. 1 (31:8) יאכ֯[ל. Part of the bottom stroke of *kap* (no longer on the fragment) has been preserved in PAM 43.817.

L. 1 (31:9) פ]ת֯י֯א. The traces before *ʾalep* (an extended bottom stroke and a trace above its left side) are consistent with *taw* and *yod*.

L. 2 (31:9) צ]ד֯ת. The preserved trace of the letter before *taw* looks like the left end of the head of *reš* or *dalet*. It is definitely not the remains of a *yod*.

L. 3 (31:11) ד]נ֯א. The remainder of a bottom stroke (no longer visible on the fragment) before the *ʾalep* indicates a *nun*, *ṣade*, or *taw*. The discolouration at the edge is caused by peeling of the skin; it should not be interpreted as a *waw*.

L. 4 (31:11) חטא֯[. In PAM 43.817, the *ṭet* seems to have been raised half a letter and written across the ceiling line. This may be the result of a contraction of the skin. The fragment with this letter has become separated from the main fragment and has turned completely black. After *ṭet*, PAM 43.817 shows a minute trace which might be the right part of the *keraia* of an *ʾalep*.

L. 6 (31:14)]מ֯א. 𝔐 suggests this reading, but the trace of the first letter at the edge of the fragment is not entirely consistent with *mem*. The trace is too close to the *ʾalep*, and a remnant of the left arm would be expected to be seen.

L. 8 (31:15) עבד֯[ני. All that remains of *dalet* is the slanting, tapered bottom of the vertical stroke.

L. 8 (31:15) ח]ד֯. The preserved left part of a horizontal stroke may be the left part of the head of a somewhat irregularly written *dalet*. On the fragment the small head seems quite normal.

L. 9 (31:16) אמ֯[נע. All that remains of *mem* is a small dot at the edge of the fragment, but its presence is assured in the fragment.

TRANSLATION

1. Will ea[t][9] has been [en]ticed
2. my heart by a wom[an,] I [have lur]ked.
3. [10]May she grind for [[11] Th]is is (a cause for) anger
4. and it is a sin [[12] i]t is (that) up to
5. Abaddon [consume]s.[ ][13]If I had been impatient
6. with regard to the claim of [my] ser[vant,][14]What shall I do
7. when [God] ari[ses.][15]For
8. He who made [me o]ne. [16]If
9. I re[fused] I ruined.

COMMENTS

L. 1 (31:8) The space between יאכ֯[ל and the end of the line is too large for a literal translation of 𝔐. The translator may have read a different Hebrew text. 𝔊 deviates from 𝔐, and 𝔖 has a totally different reading.

L. 1 (31:9) פ]ת֯י֯א. The last word of the line should correspond to 𝔐 נפתה. The reconstruction פ]ת֯י֯א, a *Peʿil* of פתא, 'to be accessible to influences', 'to open, influence, persuade, entice', shows the same orthographic *ʾalep* as שויא in col. XXIX 6.

L. 2 (31:9) צ]ד֯ת. It is likely that the word at the end of this line corresponds to 𝔐 ארבתי. The usual rendering of ארב is כמן, but *Tg. Prov* 23:28 uses צוד. *Ed. princ.*, p. 46, suggested the reconstruction אטמ]ר֯ת.

L. 3 (31:10) There is not enough room in this line to translate all of v 10. The translator probably understood the sexual connotations and regarded the second hemistich (but apparently not the first) to be offensive and therefore did not translate it.

L. 3 (31:11) ד]נ̊א רגז. The reconstructions הו]א רגז or ה]ו̊א רגז are unlikely (cf. NOTES ON READINGS), in spite of the following והוא חטא̊[. רגז, 'anger', is not a literal translation of 𝔐 זמה, 'infamy, licentiousness'. We should probably understand רגז as 'something which arouses anger'.

L. 4 (31:12) הי]א̇. Cf. 𝔐 היא, which refers to אש. The fem. form ת]אכל shows that the translator also used a fem. noun. Cf. ℭ ארום אשא היא.

L. 5 (31:12) אבדון. Spelled as in 𝔐, instead of the usual spelling of Qumran Aramaic: אבדן.

L. 7 (31:15) ארו. Cf. 𝔐 הלא. The rhetorical sentence is changed into an affirmative one.

L. 8 (31:15) עבד̊]ני. Cf. 𝔐 עשני. ℭ renders (var דעבדני) הלא בכריסא עבדני, and 𝔖 ܘܗܐ ܒܟܪܣܐ ܕܒܪܢ.

L. 9 (31:16) ס̇יפת[. Read ס̇יפת[(*Paʿel*) or ה]ס̇יפת (*Hapʿel*). Cf. 𝔐 אכלה. The semantic ranges of both verbs coincide to a large extent.

Col. XIX (Frgs. 16 ii, 17 i) Job 31:26-32

top margin

1	דנח ולס[הרא	27	ל]ב̊י̊
2	ונשקת ידי לפ̊[מי 28		כד]ב̇ת
3	לאלהא מעל̈[א 29		ה]ללת
4	על באישתה̇[		]◦א
5	לוטי וישמע[		]ברגזי
6	ואחדת א[	30	למחט]א
7	חכי למש̇[אל	31	א]נש
8	ביתי מ[ן		32
9	לא י̊[בית		

Mus. Inv. 624
PAM 43.816

NOTES ON READINGS

The first words of col. XIX 1–9 and the last letters of lines 1–7 have been preserved on frgs. 16 ii and 17 i. The width of the left margin until the sharp edge of the stitching is 1.2 cm in line 1 and 1 cm in line 6, due to the crumbling of the skin. The width of the column was *c*.8.8–9 cm (depending on the thickness of the stitching of frg. 17). Between vv 29 and 30 there are some hemistichs not included in 𝔐.

L. 1 (31:26) ולס]הרא. One would expect to see part of the legs of *he*. The right leg is not visible, but a vertical stroke more to the left could be interpreted as the bottom part of the left leg of *he*. In that case, one should transcribe ולסה̊]רא. Nothing can be seen now on the fragment.

L. 1 (31:27) ל]ב̊י̊. The remnants of the letters are consistent with the reading suggested by 𝔐. All that remains of *yod* is the uppermost left part of the tick.

L. 2 (31:27) ל̊פ̊]מי. To the left of the hook of *lamed* one can see a dark trace on the edge of the fragment, on the spot where one would expect the bottom part of the downstroke of *pe*.

L. 4 א◦[. The horizontal stroke before *ʾalep* looks like the head of *dalet* or *reš* which has dropped down from the ceiling line. Nothing can be seen now on the fragment.

L. 9 (31:32) לא י̊]בית. There is unmistakably a letter at the left edge of frg. 16 ii, probably *yod*.

Translation

1. it shone, and at the mo[on 27] my [he]art
2. and my hand kissed [my] m[outh. 28] I would have [li]ed
3. to God on hi[gh. 29] did I [ex]ult
4. because of his misfortune? [ ]
5. my curse, and he heard [ ]in my anger
6. and I took [30 to si]n
7. my palate, by seek[ing 31 m]en
8. of my household: Wh[o 32
9. did not have to [sleep

Comments

L. 1 (31:26) ולס]הרא. The *lamed* indicates that ס]הרא (cf. 𝔐 ירח) is the direct object of the verb in the preceding hemistich (cf. 𝔐 אראה).

L. 2 (31:28) כד]בת. This is *Paʿel*. 𝔐 כחשתי. 𝔗 (כדביבית with many variant spellings) and 𝔖 (ܟܕܒܬ) also use כדב.

L. 3 (31:29) ה]ללת. The reconstruction of this word is disputable, because of the uncertain meaning of the corresponding 𝔐 והתעררתי and the reading of 𝔊 καὶ εἶπεν (α′ εἶπον) ἡ καρδία μου Εὖγε. However, the completely different reading of 𝔊 probably derives from Ps 35:25. Cf. H. Heater, *Septuagint Translation*, 96.[1] Since the following על באישתה̊] corresponds to 𝔐, but not to 𝔊, one should reject the reconstruction מ]ללת. 𝔐 והתעררתי may mean 'I was stirred up, I was excited', but BHS also suggests the readings והתעדדתי and והתרעעתי, both meaning 'I exulted'. The verb הלל, which occurs in 1QapGen ar XXI 2 and in Syriac, might convey this meaning. Cf. also 𝔗 ויבבית ושבחית, 'I exulted and rejoiced' (with several variant readings), and 𝔖 ܪܘܙܬ.

L. 4 (31:29) על באישתה̊]. Cf. 𝔐 כי מצאו רע.

Ll. 4–6 The text has an addition of three or four hemistichs which are neither in 𝔐 nor in any of the ancient versions. It is not possible to reconstruct, or even to grasp the overall meaning of the addition.

L. 6 (31:29) ואחדת. The lack of context prevents us from determining the mode and person of this verbal form.

Ll. 6–7 (31:30) לחט]א / חכי למש]אל. Cf. 𝔐 לחטא חכי לשאל. We cannot be certain whether one should reconstruct a *Peʿal* or a *Paʿel* infinitive of חטא.

Ll. 7–8 (31:31) א]נש / ביתי. Cf. 𝔐 מתי אהלי. The expression is used a number of times in 1QapGen ar.

L. 8 (31:31) מ]ן. The meaning of 𝔐 מי יתן is disputed. Here, as in 𝔊, 𝔖, and 𝔗, we encounter a literal translation.

---

[1] H. Heater, *A Septuagint Translation Technique in the Book of Job* (CBQMS 11; Washington, DC: The Catholic Biblical Association of America, 1982).

VARIANTS

31:29 (3) 𝔐 והתעררתי] (והתרעעתי) 𝔖ℭ ה]ללת

Col. XX (Frg. 17 ii) Job 31:4–32:3

top margin

1 [40]תחות חטא]

2 באשושה ספ̇[ו 32:1

3 אלין מלהתב̇[ה פתגם

4 הוא איוב זכ̇[י

5 *vac*]*at*

6 [2]אדין רגז] אליהוא בר ברכאל בוזאה מן[

7 זרע רומא̊]ה

8 [3]ואף ע̇[ל

9 מלי̊[ן

Mus. Inv. 624
PAM 43.816

NOTES ON READINGS

Frg. 17 ii contains the beginnings of the first nine lines of col. XX. No stitching holes are visible on the front; on the back nine holes can be counted, with the thread still intact and hanging. This fragment has preserved the complete top margin of the scroll. The top margin is 1.3 cm. The distance from the right margin of col. XX to that of col. XXI is 8.5–8.7 cm. It is possible that the margins, too, were narrower than usual. Hence, we may assume that the column measured *c*.7.5 cm. This fits with the reconstruction of line 6.

L. 3 (32:1) מלהתב̇[ה. Only the downstroke and the right end of the head of *bet* are visible.

L. 4 (32:1) זכ̇[י. The thin, slightly slanting vertical stroke of ink (no longer visible on the fragment) is consistent with *kap*.

L. 7 (32:2) רומא̊]ה. The small trace of ink after *mem* can be interpreted as the remainder of the *keraia* of the right arm of *ʾalep*.

TRANSLATION

1. [40]Instead of wheat [

2. rue. Ended [32:1

3. these from answering [a word
4. Job was right[eous
5. *va[cat*
6. [2]Then [Elihu] became angry, [the son of Barachel the Buzite from]
7. the family of Ruma. [
8. [3]And also ag[ainst
9. word[s.

Comments

L. 2 (31:40) באשושה. Cf. 𝔐 באשה. Löw (*Aramäische Pflanzennamen*, 370–72 § 371; *Die Flora der Juden* III, 507–10) identifies this plant with *Peganum Harmala L.*

L. 3 (32:1) מלהתב̇]ה. Cf. 𝔐 מענות. The missing part of the line is too large for a literal translation of 𝔐 את איוב כי. Since the translator employs both התיב פתגם and התיב with the meaning 'to answer', one may assume that פתגם was used here.

L. 4 (32:1) הוא. Here הוא is not the pronoun used as a copula, but the verbal form. Cf. 𝔊 ἦν γὰρ Ἰὼβ δίκαιος ἐναντίον αὐτῶν. Unfortunately, the word corresponding to 𝔐 בעיניו (𝔖 ܒܥܝܢ̈ܘܗܝ) is missing.

L. 5 A completely blank line separates the conclusion of the preceding discourses from the beginning of the Elihu speeches.

L. 6 (32:2) אדין. The use of אדין (cf. 𝔐 ו) emphasizes the beginning of a new episode.

L. 6 (32:2)]רגז. A verbal form rendering 𝔐 חרה אף. In col. II 1 (19:11) and ℭ, the rendering קצף רגז is used.

Ll. 6–7 (32:2) זרע /]מן. Cf. 𝔐 ממשפחת.

L. 7 (32:2) רומא̊]ה. Cf. 𝔐 רָם. The same name, רם, occurs in 𝔐 Ruth 4:19 and 1 Chr 2:9, 10, 25, 27. 𝔊 and 𝔖 transcribe the name in various ways, but never with an *o* or *u* in the first syllable. In Job 32:2, 𝔊[A] reads Ῥάμα, and 𝔊[C] Ἀραμ. In Ruth 4:19, 𝔊 renders Ἀρραν. In 𝔖, there are several other transcriptions of the same name. This indicates a tendency to replace the unknown 'Rām' with a better known name. It is possible that רומא̊]ה betrays a similar attempt. Perhaps the translator connected 𝔐 רם to the village רומה mentioned in 2 Kgs 23:36. Josephus mentions the same village (Ροῦμα; *J.W.* 3.233), the present-day Khirbet er-Rumeh. ℭ interprets Ram as Abraham.

L. 8 (32:3) ואף ע̇]ל. The words correspond to the conjunction and preposition of 𝔐 ובשלשת.

L. 9 (32:3) מלי̊]ן. Probably a free rendering of 𝔐 מענה.

Col. XXI (Frg. 18) Job 32:10-17

top margin

מלי אף אנה [11]ארו סברת̇[

תסיפון עד תחקרון סוף̇[12

וארו לא איתי מנכון לא̇]יוב

למלוהי [13]די למה תאמרו̊ן[

להן אלהא חיבנא ולא א̊]נש 14

מלין וכמא לא יתיבנה̇[15

7 והחשיו ונטרת מנהון]○ [16]

8 [ו]קׄמו ולא ימללון עודׄ] [17]

9 [וא]חוה מלי אף א]נה

Mus. Inv. 634
PAM 43.815

NOTES ON READINGS

Frg. 18 contains the right part of lines 1–9 of col. XXI. It, too, preserves the upper edge of the scroll. The top margin measures 1.3 cm. The space between the right rulings of cols. XXI and XXII is almost 10 cm. The column probably measured *c.*8.5 cm. The fragment thus preserves more than half the width of the column.

L. 3 (32:12) לאׄ]יוב. At the end of the line, the *keraia* of the right arm of *ʾalep* is visible. In spite of the crack in the edge, traces of ink are clear on the fragment.

L. 4 (32:13) תאמרוןׄ]. The top of final *nun* is visible.

L. 5 (32:13) אׄ]נש. Some minute marks of ink have been preserved on the left edge on both sides of a crack, but not enough to determine whether they stem from the round head of *gimel* (גׄ]בר) or from the *keraia* of *ʾalep*. There is no trace of a right leg of a *gimel*, although the skin has been preserved.

L. 7 (32:15)]○. The dark spot at the extreme edge of the line is ink, but it could belong to any letter.

L. 8 (32:16) [ו]קׄמו. The stroke at the beginning of the line can be the left end of the head of *qop* or *dalet* (or almost anything else).

L. 8 (32:16) עודׄ]. The black spot at the left edge of the fragment is certainly ink and could be the uppermost right end of the head of *dalet*.

L. 9 (32:17) א]נה. A small piece adhering to the surface has been removed from the fragment, and the *keraia* of the *ʾalep* is now clearly visible.

TRANSLATION

1. I too, my words [ ] [11]Behold, I hoped [
2. you had finished, till you had searched out the end of[[12]
3. but behold, J[ob] has nobody among you [
4. to his words. [13] Perhaps you say: [‘
5. but it is God whom we blamed, and not a m[an.’ [14]
6. words, and he does not answer him at all [[15]
7. And they were silent and I withheld from them [[16]
8. And they arose and do not speak any more[[17]
9. [And I] too will display my words [

COMMENTS

L. 1 (32:10) מלי. Here, as well as in line 9 (Job 32:10b and 17b are identical), מלי corresponds to 𝔐 דעי.

L. 1 (32:11) סברת]. סבר has many meanings, but the fact that it corresponds to 𝔐 הוחלתי suggests that the meaning ‘to hope’ was intended.

L. 2 (32:11) תסיפון עד תחקרון סוףׄ]. Neither תסיפון nor סוףׄ is found in 𝔐. It is possible that the introduction of the words expressing ‘finish’ and ‘end’ was prompted by 𝔐 עד before תבונתיכם. The versions display various readings, but S (ܘܨܬܬ ܥܕܡܐ ܕܫܠܡܬܘܢ, 'I listened till you finished') seems to corroborate תסיפון.

L. 3 (32:12) וארו לא איתי מנכון לא]יוב. The translator slightly changed the word order of 𝔐 והנה אין לאיוב . . . מכם. The missing part of the line supposedly contained the verb 'to answer' (cf. 𝔐 עונה), but one can only guess whether it also translated 𝔐 מוכיח.

L. 4 (32:13) די למה. Cf. 𝔐 פן. The two words are written separately as in Ezra 7:23, whereas 1QapGen ar XXII 22 writes דלמא.

L. 5 (32:13) חיבנא. 𝔐 reads ידפנו, 'let (El) drive him', but it is argued that נדף is used in an abstract sense: 'to rebut, rebuke'. The word in 𝔐 is disputed; two 𝔐 MSS read יהדפנו and ירדפנו, whereas modern scholars propose the conjecture ילפנו, '(El) teaches us'. חיבנא may be regarded as the translator's interpretation of a difficult word, but it is also possible that the translator read or interpreted גדפנו, 'we reviled (El)'. חיבנא, 'we blamed (El)', would be a rather accurate rendering of גדפנו.

L. 5 (32:13) א]נש. Cf. 𝔐 איש. In col. XXXVIII 7–8 (42:11), גבר renders איש, and elsewhere the translator uses אנש for 𝔐 אדם and אנוש.

L. 6 (32:14) מלין וכמא לא יתיבנה]. מלין corresponds to the last word of the first hemistich of Job 32:14: ולא ערך אלי מלין, 'and he did not direct words against me' (Elihu seems to be the speaker and Job the subject of ערך, but scholars also venture other possiblities). However, in the translation of the next hemistich, the 3rd masc. sing. יתיבנה renders the 1st sing. 𝔐 אשיבנו. It is therefore probable that the missing translation of the first hemistich also deviated from 𝔐.

L. 7 (32:15) והחשיו ונטרת מנהון. The preserved words are not a literal rendering of 𝔐, which makes it difficult to ascertain to which part of 𝔐 they correspond. The three words may correspond to 𝔐 לא ענו עוד העתיקו מהם, in which case one should interpret נטרת as a defectively written *Peʿil* form, and reconstruct a fem. sing. subject 'speech' after מנהון. This would give a fairly accurate translation of 𝔐 העתיקו מהם מלים. Yet, in all but one case (1QapGen ar XX 14 דברת), *Peʿil* forms are written *plene* in Qumran Aramaic; moreover, the translator normally uses מלין to render מלים. We prefer, instead, to regard נטרת as the 1st sing. *Peʿal*: the translator changed the person, and thus the meaning, of the second hemistich of Job 32:15: 'they were silent, and I withheld from them [e.g. an answer]'. That is more likely than the assumption that נטרת is a free rendering of והוחלתי of v 16.

L. 8 (32:16) ו]קמו. A literal translation of 𝔐 עמדו. 𝔗 reads שתקון קמו (var שתקין and ישתקון), 'they stood up in silence'. שתקון seems to be no more than a targumic addition, brought about by the mention of dumbness in the previous verse. It shows, however, that the alternative reading דמו, 'they were silent', is not impossible.

Col. XXII (Frg. 19) Job 33:6-16

top margin

1 [אנה] 7הן חרגתי לא תסר]דנך לא]
2 [יי]קר 8הך אמרת באדני וק[ל
3 [9זכ]י אנה ולא חטא לי ונקא]
4 10הן עולין השכח אחד לי ה]יך
5 [11י]שוא בסדא רגלי וסכר כ[ל
6 12bארו רב אלהא מן אנשא] 13

7 רׄבברן תמלל ארו בכל פ[תגמוהי
8 [[14]א]רו בחדא ימלל אלה[א
9 [[15]ב]חׄלמין בחדידי לילׄי[א
10 [במנ]מה על משכבה[[16]
11]רׄהׄ[ ]

Mus. Inv. 634
PAM 43.815

NOTES ON READINGS

The remains of col. XXII are found on frg. 19. But for 2 mm, the right edge of the fragment coincides with the right margin of the column (only part of a single letter is missing in lines 6 and 7). In view of the stitching between cols. XXII and XXIII, it is unlikely that the column measured more than 8.5 cm.

L. 1 (33:6) [אנה]. In the discoloured area at the right of the fragment there may be some vertical traces which belong to *he*, but nothing is visible on the fragment.

L. 1 (33:7) חסרׄ[דנך. The dot of ink at the end on the line is likely to be the bottom part of the downstroke of *reš*.

L. 4 (33:10) הׄ[יך. The left edge of the fragment shows the remains of a vertical downstroke and very faint traces of a horizontal stroke. The traces are consistent with *he*.

L. 7 (33:13) בכל. In PAM 43.815, the apparent interlinear insertion after בכל is only a dark spot; no ink is visible on the fragment.

L. 9 (33:15) בחדידי. Although it does not have the rounded head of the left stroke, the second letter is clearly *ḥet*, not *he*.

L. 9 (33:15) לילׄי[א. Nothing can be determined with certainty about the last visible traces, but we are inclined to read *yod* (not *ʾalep*). The only spot of ink which is clear on the fragment has the sharp hook of *yod*. The other traces in PAM 43.815 are shadows from the lower layer of the skin, not ink.

L. 11 (33:16?)]רׄהׄ[. The very bottom of the fragment shows the heads of two letters from line 11.

TRANSLATION

1. [I (too).] [7]Surely, the dread of me will not te[rrify you will not]
2. [be he]avy. [8]Surely, you spoke in my ears and the so[und
3. [[9]'Pu]re am I, and I have no sin; and innocent [
4. [10]If He had found iniquities, he would have considered me a[s
5. [[11]He] puts my feet in the stocks, and blocked up a[ll
6. [12b]Because God is greater than man. [[13]
7. do you speak proud words? For of all [his] a[cts
8. [[14]F]or God speaks once [
9. [[15]In] dreams, during the night [
10. [In] his [sl]eep on his bed. [[16]
11. [ ] [

COMMENTS

L. 1 (33:7) חרגתי. חרגה also renders 𝔐 אימה in *Tg. Onq.* Deut 32:25.

L. 1 (33:7) תסר̊]דנך. Cf. 𝔐 תבעתך. On the basis of ܙܘܥ (*Paʿel*), 'terrify' (not yet attested in Aramaic), *ed. princ.* (p. 54) reconstructs תסר̊]דנך. תסג]פנך (Beyer) is a less likely rendering of 𝔐 תבעתך.

L. 2 (33:7) [יי]ק̇ר. 𝔐 יכבד; ℭ ייקר; 𝔖 ܢܐܩܪ.

L. 2 (33:8) הך. This seems to be the Aramaic equivalent of 𝔐 אך.

L. 3 (33:9) ונקא̊[. Corresponds to 𝔐 חף, 'pure' (*hapax legomenon*). The word נקי is common in Biblical Hebrew, where it means 'innocent'. In the Aramaic dialects its usual meaning is 'clean'.

L. 4 (33:10) ה̇ן. Here, as in 𝔐, הן can be interpreted both as a conditional conjunctive ('if'), or as a demonstrative adverb ('behold').

L. 4 (33:10) עולין. עולין renders 𝔐 תנואות, which is attested only here and in Num 14:34. The precise meaning of *תנואה is unknown. 𝔖 ܥܠܠܬܐ is a translation of תואנות, 'opportunities' (cf. Judg 14:4).

L. 4 (33:10) אחד לי ה̊]יך. Since we do not know what followed, we cannot be sure whether אחד לי is to be taken literally, 'he seized me' (cf. col. IV 5; 21:6), or as an expression conveying the same thought as 𝔐 -יחשבני ל, 'he considered me as'. For this meaning of אחד, cf. the Syriac use of ܐܚܕ in Mark 11:32 (a translation of εἶχον).

L. 5 (33:11) [י]שׂוא. The imperfect (cf. 𝔐 ישם) is somewhat peculiar amid the surrounding perfect forms.

L. 5 (33:11) וסכר. סכר, 'he blocks', is not a literal translation of 𝔐 ישמר, 'he watches', but it continues the line of thought of the previous hemistich.

L. 6 (33:12) The first hemistich of 𝔐 33:12 is missing. Was it missing in the translator's *Vorlage*, or did the translator object to the condemnation of Job? Is it a case of homoioteleuton by a copyist (presuming the translator used ארו for 𝔐 הן in verse 33:12a)?

L. 7 (33:13) ר̇בברן. A scribal error for רברבן. The expression מלל רברבן, 'speak proud words', also occurs in Dan 7:8, 20. Cf. also *As. Mos.* 7:9 *os eorum loquetur ingentia*, and the substantive רברבנותא, 'boast, pride'. Apparently, the translator interpreted 𝔐 ריבות, 'you argued', as a form of the verb רבב, 'to be big'. The verb ריב occurs often in Job, but these instances have not been preserved in the Aramaic text.

L. 9 (33:15) בחדידי לילי̊]א. 𝔐 reads חזיון לילה ($𝔐^{ms}$ בחזיון 𝔖 ܒܚܙܘܐ). The clause is not clear, and one may consider the following explanations: 'in sharp experiences of the nights' (from חדד, 'to be sharp'), 'during the night' (בחדיד is a composite preposition; *חדד, 'to delimit'), בחדי די, 'in the bosom of (the night)', and the emendation בחזו די ליליא, 'in a night vision'. In view of 𝔊 ἐν μελέτῃ νυκτερινῇ (בהגיון לילה?), one may suspect that both translations read a corrupted Hebrew text.

L. 10 (33:15) במנ]מה[. ℭ translates 𝔐 בתנומות with בניומתא. The suffix of משכבה (𝔐 משכב) suggests that the *he* of במנ]מה[is a pronominal suffix too. מנם is either a *maqṭal* noun, or a *Peʿal* infinitive.

L. 11 (33:16)]ר̊ה̊[. Assuming that the translator literally followed 𝔐, the remaining letters belong to a word corresponding to 𝔐 ובמסרם. The remains might therefore be reconstructed as something like ובמוס]ר̊ה̊[ון; cf. col. XXVII 4 (36:10). This reconstruction, however, allows for no more than two or three letters at the beginning of the line.

Col. XXIII (Frgs. 20, 21 i, A4) Job 33:24-32

top margin

1 [24]ויאמר פצהי מן חב]לא]ת̇

2 אשה ישנקנה ויתמלין [גרמוהי מוח [25]]מן

3 עולים ותב ליומי עלימ]ותה [26] ו]ישמענה

4 ויחזא אנפוהי באסיא̇] [[27]וכעבד

5 כפוהי י̇שלם לה ויאמ[ר]ולא

6 כארחי הש̇תלמת [28]פר̇[ק]ה̇

7 בנהור תחזא [29]הא כ̇[ל ג]בר

8 זמן תרין תלתה [30]לא̊[תבה בנהו]ר̊

9 חיי̇ן [31]הצת דא [אמ]לל

10 [[32]הן א]י̊ת̊י̊ מ[לין]

Mus. Inv. 629, 635
PAM 43.814*, 43.824*

NOTES ON READINGS

Col. XXIII is preserved on three fragments. Frg. 20 contains the right half of the lines, and the right margin between lines 2–7. The preserved margin measures 0.8 cm. Frg. 21 i shows the endings of the line, and the intercolumnar margin; this margin has a total width of 1.5 cm, but it has been ruled twice: the first time at only 1 cm from the left margin. Frg. A4 fits at the beginning of lines 8–9. From the right to the left ruling the lines measured 10–10.3 cm. The surface of frg. 20 has peeled away in the middle, slightly affecting lines 5–7; the fragment also preserves four holes, which, inexplicably, have no correspondence in frgs. 19 and 21.

L. 4 (33:26) באסיא̇]. The fragment clearly shows that the extension of the leg of *yod* is not ink, but a discolouration of the skin, which continues to the top of the *mem* in the next line. The clearly visible diagonal trace of ink to the left of the *yod* is part of the *keraia* of *ʾalep*. It definitely is not consistent with *waw*.

L. 5 (33:27) י̇שלם. Part of the *yod* (a spot of ink between the hole and the peeled area of the skin) has been preserved on the fragment on the edge of the hole.

L. 6 (33:27) הש̇תלמת. Apart from the top of the left arm, *šin* is not visible due to an abrasion.

L. 7 (33:29) כ̇[ל. After הא, PAM 43.814 shows only a dark spot at the edge of the fragment, just beneath the ceiling line, but the fragment clearly shows the downstroke, both the ink and the white salt crystals.

L. 8 (33:30) לא̊[תבה. A diagonal trace of ink, part of the *keraia* of *ʾalep* or *ṣade*, has been preserved after *lamed*.

L. 8 (33:30) בנהו]ר̊. The left end of the head of a letter without a left leg (*reš* or *dalet*) has been preserved.

L. 9 (33:30) חיי̇ן. The first two letters can be seen on frg. A4. A minute speck on the edge of frg. 20 is a remnant of the second *yod*.

L. 10 (33:32) [הן א]י̊ת̊י̊ מ[לין. The first traces are consistent with *yod* and *taw*. It is a matter of dispute whether the minuscule black specks after the remains of the possible *taw* are evidence of a second *yod*. One may also transcribe [הן א]י̊ת̊[י] מ[לין.

TRANSLATION

1. [24]And he will say: 'Save him from ha[rm] of
2. fire strangles him. And [his bones] will be filled [with marrow. [25]] than

3. that of a youth, and he will return to the days of [his] you[th. [26] and] He hears him.
4. And he will see his face while he heals,[ ] [27]and according to the work of
5. his hands He will recompense him. And he will sa[y: '] yet not
6. according to my way was I recompensed'. [28]He has deli[vered] his [ ]
7. will see the light. [29]Behold a[ll m]an,
8. once, twice, three times. [30]To br[ing back in the ligh]t
9. of life. [31]Pay attention to this [I will sp]eak
10. [[32]If the]re are w[ords,]

COMMENTS

L. 1 (33:24) פצהי. A *Peʿal* imperative with suffix, it interprets 𝔐 פדעהו (*hapax legomenon*) as פדהו, 'deliver him'.

L. 1 (33:24) חב]לא. In the targums, חבל often corresponds to 𝔐 שחת (the translator omitted 𝔐 מרדת). Cf. 𝔖 ܕܠܐ ܢܚܘܬ ܠܚܒܠܐ.

Ll. 1–2 ת̇[/ אשה ישנקנה ויתמלין [גרמוהי מוח. The text probably has two hemistichs which are missing in 𝔐. One cannot reconstruct them merely on the basis of the three preserved words at the beginning of line 2, but the additions of 𝔊 are of some help. Instead of 𝔐 מצאתי כפר, 𝔊 reads ἀνανεώσει δὲ αὐτοῦ τὸ σῶμα ὥσπερ ἀλοιφὴν ἐπὶ τοίχου, τὰ δὲ ὀστᾶ αὐτοῦ ἐμπλήσει μυελοῦ, 'he will renew his body as plaster on a wall, and he will fill his bones with marrow'. Apparently ὥσπερ ἀλοιφὴν is a misinterpretation of 𝔐 כפר. The general intent of 𝔊 is clear: to reverse the image of v 21. The second part of the addition in 11QtgJob may have corresponded to the second part of the addition of 𝔊, e.g. ויתמלין [גרמוהי מוח.

Ll. 2–3 (33:25) מן[/ עולים ותב ליומי עלימ[ותה. These words correspond literally to 𝔐.

L. 3 (33:26) ו]ישמענה. A rendering of the more specific 𝔐 וירצהו. 𝔖 has both words: ܘܢܬܪܥܐ ܠܗ ܘܢܨܛܒܐ ܒܗ.

L. 4 (33:26) באסיא̇]. An infinitive *Paʿel* of אסא, whereas 𝔐 reads בתרועה. Apparently the translator read or misread בתרופה, a reading not attested in the versions.

Ll. 4–5 (33:26-27) וכעבד / כפוהי ישלם לה. One may consider the clause a free rendering of 𝔐 וישב לאנוש צדקתו, and surmise that the lost text in line 4 contained a translation of the first words of v 27 ישר על אנשים. Another solution is to regard the clause as an addition, after which the first part of v 27 was omitted. Finally, the clause may also be a free rendering of the first part of v 27 if the translator understood ישר as a noun parallel to צדקתו. Note that both this rendering and the occurrence of ארח in line 6 are reminiscent of Job 34:11.

Ll. 5–6 (33:27) ולא[/ כארחי השתלמת. A free rendering of 𝔐 ולא שוה לי.

L. 6 (33:28) פר̇]ק. The translator uses פרק to render 𝔐 פדה, whereas he employed פצא in line 1 (33:24). ℭ and 𝔖 use the verb פרק in both verses.

L. 6 (33:28) ה̇[. The *he* at the end of the line is probably the 3rd masc. sing. pronominal suffix (cf. 𝔐^q וחיתו).

L. 8 (33:29) זמן תרין תלתה. Cf. 𝔐 פעמים שלוש. Since the normal expression for 'twice or three times' would be תרין זימנין ותלתה or תרי תלתה זימנין, the expression here is probably elliptical: '(one) time, two (times), three (times)'.

L. 8 (33:30) לא̊]תבה בנהו[ר̊. The reconstructions correspond to 𝔐 להשיב and באור. There is not enough room for a literal translation of 𝔐 between the two reconstructed words, but the text may have rendered 𝔐 נפשו by a pronominal suffix. In view of the correspondence between 𝔐 החיים and חיין in the next line, the reconstruction נהו[ר̊ is probable.

L. 9 (33:31) הצת דא]. Cf. 𝔐 הקשב. The demonstrative pronoun is an addition. In col. XXIX 5, the same expression renders 𝔐 האזינה זאת.

Col. XXIV (Frgs. 21 ii, 22 i) Job 34:6-17

top margin

1	מן חטא [7]מן]	]א חטיא [8]ומתחבר
2	לעבדי שקראׄ]	רש]ע [9]ארו אמר לא
3	ישנא גבר מיׄ]	ב]תׄר אלהא *vacat*
4	*vacat* [10]כען אנשׁׄ]	]חׄס לאלהא מן שקר
5	ומן לחבל{הׄ}א מׄ]רא [11]	]אנש ישלם לה
6	{ }]	][12]הכען צדא אלהא
7	ישקר ומראׄ]	][13]הׄוׄא ארעא עבד
8	וקשט תבׄ]ל [14]	נשמ]תה עלוהי יכלא
9	[15]וימות]	] ישכבון
10	[16]]	מ]לׄיׄ [17]הׄבׄשקׄרׄ]

Mus. Inv. 621, 629
PAM 43.813*, 43.814*

Notes on Readings

Col. XXIV is preserved on frgs. 21 ii and 22 i. The left part of frg. 22 was folded in PAM 43.813. When unfolded, it revealed the complete intercolumnar margin. The space between the right and left ruling measures 10.5–10.8 cm. This calculation agrees with tentative reconstructions (based on 𝔐 and 𝔗) of lines 1–2 and 4.

L. 1 (34:7) מן]. In the dark area on the left edge of frg. 22 ii, there are some barely recognizable traces which belong to final *nun*. In PAM 43.814 the letter is slightly distorted, probably due to the crumbling of the edge of the fragment. This section is now carbonized, and nothing is visible any longer.

L. 1 (34:7)]א. The two remaining traces can be interpreted only as the bottom parts of the diagonal and left arm of *ʾalep*.

L. 2 (34:8) שקראׄ]. After *reš*, one can see the tip of the *keraia* of *ʾalep*.

L. 3 (34:9) מיׄ]. All that is left of the last letter is a vertical stroke which does not extend completely to the bottom. This suggests *yod*, but the the size of some letters in the column varies considerably, and it is quite possible that the downstroke belongs to e.g. a small *reš* or *taw*.

L. 5 (34:10) לחבל{הׄ}א. The erasure after the second *lamed* suggests that the scribe first wrote a different letter: a small remaining stroke may be the tip of the left leg of *he*.

L. 6 { }. The surface of the skin seems to have been scraped off, as in the case of corrections. No traces of ink can be seen on the fragment, even though only 0.2 cm is scraped in some spots and many of the letters are 0.3 cm in height.

L. 7 (34:13)]הׄוׄא. A minute trace remains of the head of *he*.

L. 10 (34:16-17) מ]לׄיׄ הׄבׄשקׄרׄ]. Apart from *lamed*, *šin*, and the probable *qop*, only the heads of letters have been preserved.

TRANSLATION

1. without sin. [7]Who [ ] sins, [8]and keeps company
2. with wrongdoers [ev]il? [9]For he says: 'No
3. man changes [af]ter God. *vacat*
4. *vacat* [10]Now, men [ ] Far be it from God (to do) wrong,
5. and from [the] L[ord to do harm. [11]] a man, He will recompense him
6. { } [ ][12]Now then, will God really
7. do wrong, and the Lord [ ] [13]It is He who made the earth,
8. and established the wor[ld. [14]] withhold his [brea]th to Himself,
9. [15]then [ ] would die [ ] would lie down
10. [[16]] my [wo]rds. [17]Is it in wrong[

COMMENTS

L. 1 (34:6) מן חטא. Cf. the end of 𝔐 34:6 בלי פשע. For מן as a rendering of בלי cf. COMMENTS on col. XXVII 7 (36:12).

L. 1 (34:7) א[. Reconstruct שת]א (participle) or ישת]א; cf. 𝔐 ישתה.

L. 1 (34:7) חטיא. Whereas in Job 34:6 the translator employs חטא to render 𝔐 פשע, he now uses חטיא to translate 𝔐 לעג, 'blasphemy'.

L. 1 (34:8) ומתחבר. Cf. 𝔐 וארח לחברה.

L. 2 (34:8) לעבדי שקרא̊]. Cf. 𝔐 פעלי און. In ℭ and *Tg. Psalms*, עבדי שקר is the common translation of 𝔐 פעלי און. In line 4 the translator uses שקר to translate רשע. Apparently the semantic range of שקר has expanded, becoming a more general word for 'evil, sin'. A comparable general usage of the word is also found in 𝔐 2 Sam 18:13 and Hos 7:1 (with עשה and פעל). The emphatic state שקרא̊] is somewhat unusual, especially in view of the undetermined רש]ע further on. עבדי שקרא is also found in *Tg. Ps* 53:5.

Ll. 2–3 (34:9) לא / ישנא. Instead of 𝔐 לא יסכן, 'he does not profit'. The diverging interpretations of the ancient versions and ℭ, here and in the other occurrences of the word in Job, suggest that the meaning of סכן was not completely understood. On the other hand, the translator might have thought the expression to be too disrespectful.

L. 3 (34:9) מ̊]. The space between מ̊] and ב]תר אלהא is too large for a verbal translation of 𝔐. It is difficult to propose a reconstruction of מ̊], מר̊], or מת̊], which would correspond to 𝔐 ברצתו. Perhaps the interpretation of סכן as שנא entailed the addition of an extra word.

L. 3 (34:9) ב]תר. The preposition ב]תר may indicate that the translator interpreted ברצתו as an infinitive of רוץ (cf. also ℭ במרהטיה).

L. 4 (34:10) The small *vacat* (9 mm) marks the change of address.

L. 4 (34:10) ח̊ס[. As in the targums, חס corresponds to 𝔐 חללה.

L. 4 (34:10) שקר. שקר renders 𝔐 רשע, whereas ℭ employs שקר to render 𝔐 עול.

L. 5 (34:10) מ̊]רא. 𝔐 שדי.

L. 6 (34:12) הכען צדא[. Cf. Dan 3:14 הצדא. The phrase corresponds to 𝔐 אף אמנם, but the negative statement of 𝔐 has been changed into a rhetorical question.

L. 7 (34:13) הו̊א̊ ארעא עבד[. The reading הו̊א̊ is confirmed by 𝔊. Cf. VARIANTS. ℭ combines both variants: מן פקיד עלוהי למעבד ארעא.

L. 8 (34:14) יכלא. Instead of 𝔐 יאסף.

L. 9 (34:15) ישכבון. Like ℭ, this text reads 'to lie down' (שכב) in the dust, whereas 𝔐 has 'to return' (שוב) to dust.

L. 10 (34:17) ה̊ב̇שק̊ר̊]. This is no corresponding expression in 𝔐.

VARIANTS

34:13 (7) הו̊א̊ ארעא עבד[𝔊 ὅς ἐποίησεν τὴν γῆν] 𝔐 מי פקד עליו ארצה

Col. XXV (Frgs. 22 ii, 23) Job 34:24-34

top margin

1] [24] ר]ב֯רבין די לא סוף ויקים א[חרנין]
2]° [25a] יחכ]ם עבדהון [26aβ] וירמא המון באת֯[ר]
3] [27] אר]חה ובכל שבילוהי לא הסתכ֯[לו]
4 [28] ל]היתיה עלוהי קבילת]מ֯סכנין וקבילת ענין ישמע
5] [29] ויסת]ר֯ אנפוהי מן יתיבנה על ע֯ם
6] [30]]ך֯ אנש רשיעיא התקלו
7] [31]]תו לה איחל [32] בלחודוהי֯
8]]לא אוסף [33] ארו מ°]
9] תב]חר ולא אנה [
10] [34] מ]ל֯ין וג֯ב֯]ר

Mus. Inv. 621
PAM 43.813

NOTES ON READINGS

The remains of col. XXV are found on frgs. 22 ii and 23. The fold on the left side of frg. 22 has now been unfolded, revealing parts of letters in lines 2 and 4 and the right margin, with ruling lines visible on lines 1–5. The calculated distance between the ruling of the right margin of frg. 24 and that of the left margin of frg. 22 is approximately 15.3 cm. Since few columns are larger than 10.5 cm, we must assume a larger than average margin due to the stitching between frgs. 23 and 24. It is rather likely that frg. 23 contains the left side of the column, its right margin being quite close to the left edge of frg. 22. The position of the left ruling is unknown, but the lines must have measured *c.*10–10.5 cm.

L. 2 (34:24?)]°. The unfolded part of frg. 22 shows part of a downstroke, curving to the left. It could represent a *nun*, *mem*, *bet*, or *kap*.

L. 3 (34:27) הסתכ֯[לו]. Only the downstroke and traces of the angular shoulder of *kap* remain.

L. 4 (34:28) ל]היתיה. Remains of the *lamed* are clearly visible on the unfolded part of frg. 22. The reconstruction is offered in order to indicate the calculated distance to the right margin.

L. 5 (34:29) ויסת]ר֯. There is a horizontal trace (certainly ink) just below the ceiling line. The lack of any trace of a downstroke suggests it is the left end of the head of *dalet*, final *kap*, or *reš*.

L. 6 (34:30) ךׄ[. Two traces are visible in PAM 43.813. The first trace at the edge of the fragment, which appears to be part of the upper arm of a *lamed*, is only a crack in the skin. The second, horizontal trace is ink, and cannot belong to any letter but *dalet*, final *kap*, or *reš*.

L. 7 (34:31) תו[. The inclination to the left, both at the top and at the bottom, shows that the downstroke belongs to a *taw*. The downstroke of the next letter is far too long to be *yod*.

L. 7 (34:32) בלחודוהׄיׄ. The trace, read as a vestige of *yod*, might only be a discolouration.

L. 8 (34:33) מ°]. The downstroke after *mem* can belong to many letters. There is a supralinear mark to the left of the downstroke; it cannot be part of *lamed*.

L. 10 (34:34) מ]ליׄן וגׄבׄ[ר. Only the upper parts of the letters of two words are visible. The second word seems to begin with *waw* and *gimel*. In view of 𝔐, one expects וגבר, but the traces after *gimel* do not match the head of a normal *bet*.

TRANSLATION

1. [[24]] the mighty without limitation, and He establishes o[thers]
2. [[25a]He kno]ws their work, [26aβ]and He throws them in the pla[ce of]
3. [[27]] His [wa]y, and [they] did not he[ed] any of His paths,
4. [28]to [bring before Him the complaint of] the poor, that He may hear the complaint of the indigent.
5. [[29] And when He hi]de[s] his face, who can answer Him about a nation
6. [[30]] the wicked. They tripped
7. [[31]] for Him I wait, [32]at Him only
8. [ ] I will do no more. [33]Behold, [
9. [you must deci]de, not I. [
10. [[34] wo]rds, and a ma[n

COMMENTS

L. 1 (34:24) ר]בׄרבין]. In the missing right part one should reconstruct an Aramaic equivalent of 𝔐 ירע, 'He breaks, shatters'. The text of ℭ shows many variants, most of which show a double interpretation of ירע, namely as a form of רוע (Hebrew רוץ), 'to run' (ℭ reads ירהיט and ירהטון), as well as of רעע, 'to beat' (ℭ יבתר). S (ܘܐܒܐܫ) interprets the form as a *Hipʿil* of רעע, 'to harm'.

L. 1 (34:24) לא סוף. Cf. 𝔐 לא חקר, 'innumerable', hence 'unlimited'. For this Hebrew expression, cf. e.g. 1QH[a] XI 20 (III 20) במישור לאין חקר. S renders ܕܠܐ ܡܢܝܢ. The deviating text of 𝔊 is based upon Job 9:10 (cf. Heater, *Septuagint Translation*, 114).

L. 2 (34:24-25) יחכ]ם]. The beginning of the line should correspond to 𝔐 תחתם לכן יכיר. In col. XXXIV 8 (40:12), תחו]תׄיהון renders 𝔐 תחתם. However, a reconstruction like [תחותיהון להן יחכ]ם is two to three letters too short to fill up the calculated lacuna. The reconstruction [מן בתרהון להן יחכ]ם (cf. ℭ) would fit better. The reconstruction יחכ]ם is an appropriate rendering of 𝔐 יכיר.

L. 2 (34:26) וירמא המון. Cf. 𝔐 ספקם, 'he strikes them'; the beginning of 𝔐 v 26, תחת רשעים, is missing in the translation.

L. 3 (34:27) אר]חׄה. This reconstruction presupposes either a free translation of 𝔐 מאחריו, possibly evoked by דרכיו in the next hemistich, or a reading (or misreading) of 𝔐 מארחיו. 𝔊 employs νόμος θεοῦ and δικαίωμα in the two hemistichs. Cf. Job 24:4, 11, and 13, where 𝔊 preserves glosses on דרך, adding some form of δίκαιος in each.

L. 4 (34:28) ל]היתיה עלוהי קבילת [. Cf. ℭ לאיתאה עלוהי קבילתא. The reconstruction is added to indicate the width of the gap.

L. 4 (34:28) מׄסכנין[. The translator uses two plurals (מסכנין and ענין) whereas the first noun in 𝔐 is sing.: דל. The word מסכן also renders 𝔐 אביון (col. VIII 5; 24:14) and עני (col. XXVII 2; 36:8).

L. 5 (34:29) יתיבנה. Cf. 𝔐 ישורנו. Did the translator read ישיבנו?

L. 5 (34:29) על. Instead of 𝔐 ועל. This suggests that the translator took the third hemistich to be the object of יתיבנה.

L. 6 (34:30) ךְ[. In view of 𝔐 ממלך, this word is probably a form of מלך, but any reconstruction remains uncertain. S reads ܘܠܐ ܐܡܠܟ. Hence, one of the possible reconstructions is ולא אמל]ךְ.

L. 6 (34:30) אנש רשיעיא. Cf. 𝔐 אדם חנף. The Aramaic is either a genitive construction ('a man of the wicked ones'), or אנש functions as a collective plural.

L. 6 (34:30) התקלו. Cf. 𝔐 ממקשי. תקל is used to render 𝔐 יקש in *Tg. Onq.* Deut 12:30 and *Tg. Ps* 9:17. The form can be read either as a *Hitpeʿel* or *Hapʿel.* The latter possibility corresponds better to 𝔐.

L. 7 (34:31) תו[. The word cannot be reconstructed on the basis of 𝔐.

L. 7 (34:31) לה איחל. Instead of 𝔐 לא אחבל, 'I will not do wrong'. The difference between לה and 𝔐 לא might stem from a reading in which לא was spelled לוא, and interpreted as לו. The lack of context makes it difficult to understand איחל. The Hebrew verb יחל means 'to wait (for)', but Syriac ܐܘܚܠ (*Apʿel* of ܘܚܠ) 'to despair'.

L. 7 (34:32) בלחודוהי. Cf. 𝔐 בלעדי. The lack of context prevents us from determining whether the translator regarded this word as part of the previous clause or as the beginning of a new one.

L. 8 (34:33) ארו מ◦[. Cf. 𝔐 המעמך (interrogative *he*). This may be one of the cases in which the translator changes a rhetorical question into some kind of statement.

L. 10 (34:34) מ]ליֿן וגֿבֿ[ר. Assuming that the preserved letters correspond to 𝔐 יאמרו לי וגבר, one may reconstruct the first word מ]ליֿן or ימל]לון.

VARIANTS

34:25 (2) > 𝔊] 𝔐 והפך לילה וידכאו

34:26 (2) >] 𝔐 תחת רשעים

Col. XXVI (Frgs. 24, 25 i) Job 35:6-15

top margin

1 [ב]ךְ ובסגיא עויתך מא תֿ[עבד לך 7הן זכי]תֿ מא

2 תתן לה או מא מידך יקבל[8לגבר כות]ך חטיך

3 ולבר אנש צדקתך 9מן סגיא [עשוקיא יז]עקון יצוחון

4 מן קדם סגיאין 10ולא אמר[ין אן הוא]אלהא

5 די עבדנה ודי חלק לנא לֿ[ ]◦ לנצבתנא

6 בליליא 11די פרשנא מן בעֿ[ירי ארעא ומן] צפריא

7 חכמנה 12תמה יזעקון ולאֿ[יענא מן קדם ג]אות

8 [ב]אישין 13ארו שוא יש[מע אלהא ומרא ה]בֿלא

9 [לא] יצתנה 14הן תאמר[

10 [ ]◦ לה 15אֿ[רו

Mus. Inv. 626
PAM 43.812

NOTES ON READINGS

Col. XXVI is preserved on frgs. 24 and 25 i. The assumption that the gap in line 2 contained the words [לגבר כות]ך (cf. 𝔐 לאיש כמוך) matches with the calculation that the gap in line 3 measured *c.*2.3 cm. The faint vertical ruling which marks the left margin of the column runs next to the final *kap* of line 2 and the *taw* of line 7.

L. 1 (35:6) [ב]ך̇. The bottom part of what must be the tail of final *kap* is visible. In itself the letter could also have been *waw* (cf. the very long *waw* in line 7 [ג]אות), but the space between it and the next word strongly indicates final *kap*. The dark spot to the right, at the edge of the fragment, is not ink.

L. 2 (35:7) או מא. There is hardly any space between the words. Cf. NOTES ON READINGS to col. IX 6.

L. 2 (35:8) כות]ך. Not only part of the head, but also the tip of the tail of final *kap* are visible in PAM 43.812 (but no longer on the fragment).

L. 5 (35:10) ◦[. *Ed. princ.* p. 62:]ר̊. The clearly visible traces (*v*-shaped) are difficult to identify. A *reš* is less difficult as no *reš* in the MS has such an angular head.]הׄיׄ (Beyer) is also unlikely: the head of the *yod* would be too round. A *taw* or *qop* is more probable.

L. 7 (35:12) ולא̊[. The speck of ink after *lamed* might be part of *ʾalep*.

L. 8 (35:13) ה]בׄלא. The first letter after the lacuna is almost certainly *bet*, though the possibility of *kap* cannot be ruled out completely.

L. 10 (35:14) ◦[. The rather thick trace might belong to final *nun*. The trace does not go straight down, but tends to slant somewhat downwards to the right, making e.g. *ʿayin* a possibility.

TRANSLATION

1. [by] yourself, and when your iniquities are manifold, what [can] you [do for yourself? [7]If] you [are righteous,] what
2. will you give Him, or what does He receive from your hand? [8]Your sin [affects a man like] yourself
3. and your righteousness a son of man. [9]Because of the great number [of oppressions] t[he]y [c]ry out, they shout for help
4. because of the many. [10]But [they] do not say: [‘Where is] God
5. who made us, and who allotted to us [ ] for our plantation
6. in the night, [11]who distinguished us from the be[asts of the earth, and more than] the birds
7. made us wise?’ [12]There they will cry out, but [He will] not [answer, because of the p]ride of
8. [e]vil men. [13]Behold, [God] he[ars] vanity, [and to ab]surdity [the Lord]
9. pays [no] attention. [14]If you say [
10. [ ] for Him. [15]Be[hold

COMMENTS

L. 1 (35:6) [ב]ך̇ corresponds to 𝔐 בו. The translator has changed the meaning of the hemistich. Now the pronominal suffix refers to Job, not to God. 𝔊 has no equivalent of either בו or לו of the next hemistich. 𝔖 and ℭ agree with 𝔐.

L. 1 (35:6) ובסגיא עויתך. Cf. *Aḥiqar* 106 בשגיא בנן.

L. 1 (35:6) [לך]. The equivalent of 𝔐 לו belongs to the lost part. It could have been either לך (parallel to בך), or לה (as in the next line). In view of the irregular hand of this column, one cannot decide on the basis of the computed measurement of the lines.

L. 2 (35:8) כות]ך. 𝔐 כמוך. Cf. col. XXXIV 5 (40:9) where כותה renders 𝔐 כמהו.

L. 3 (35:9) עשוקיא]. A word corresponding to 𝔐 עשוקים should be reconstructed in the lacuna between the two fragments. ℭ reads טלומין; 𝔖 ܕܛܠܘܡܐ. *Tg. Onqelos* always renders 𝔐 עשק by עשק, whereas *Tg. Psalms*, ℭ, and *Tg. Pseudo-Jonathan* favour טלם. עשק, which is also used in Sefire III 20, in Official Aramaic, and in Qumran Aramaic (4Q**488**), seems to be the older word. Note that the word can be read עשוקים, 'oppressions', or עשוקים, 'oppressors'. The parallelism with סגיאין in the next line would suggest that the translator read the latter.

L. 3 (35:9) יז]עקון. Here, as well as in line 7 (35:12), the translator uses the same word as 𝔐. In col. XXV 4 (34:28), קבילה corresponds to צעקה.

L. 3 (35:9) יצוחון. Cf. 𝔐 ישועו. In col. VIII 2 (24:12), the translator used the verb קבל to render שוע.

L. 4 (35:9) מן קדם. A rather free rendering of 𝔐 מזרוע.

L. 4 (35:9) סגיאין. The translator interpreted 𝔐 רבים as 'numerous' (𝔊 πολλῶν; 𝔖 ܣܓܝܐ̈ܐ), and not as 'mighty' (𝔗 דורבניא, 'haughty leaders'; cf. 𝔗 34:20).

L. 4 (35:10) אמר]ין. In spite of 𝔐, the context (עבדנה and לנה) requires a plural. Cf. 𝔖 ܐܡܪܘܢ. A participle is more fitting than a perfect form.

L. 4 (35:10) אן הוא]. In the gap between the fragments one must reconstruct an equivalent of 𝔐 איה. Since col. XXX 2 (38:4) uses אן for 𝔐 איפה, and because of the relative pronoun די in line 5, one may reconstruct אן הוא.

L. 5 (35:10) חלק. Cf. 𝔐 נתן.

L. 5 (35:10) לנא ל̇[ ]°לנצבתנא. The text adds לנא, 'to us', and probably three more words, whereas 𝔐 reads only זמרות. Apart from the first and last letters, the first two words are missing in the gap, whereas the last word, לנצבתנא, seems to be an explanatory addition. An extra problem is that the trace before לנצבתנא is irregular. Most reconstructions are based upon the supposition that it is *reš*. 𝔐 זמרות is a problematic word, however, which the translator may have interpreted in various ways. Both the versions and modern commentators suggest many possibilities. First, זמרות are 'songs (of praise)'. Thus, e.g. 𝔗 האן אלהא דעבד יתי דמסדרין אנגלי מרומא קדמוהי תושבחתא בליליא, 'Where is God, my Maker, before whom the angels on high arrange songs in the night'. Similarly, Gordon explains the זמרות to be the songs sung by heavenly beings. Following this interpretation of זמרות, one might reconstruct ל̇]שן מזמ[ר̇. The reading of 𝔊 ὁ κατατάσσων φυλακὰς might stem from a confusion of זמר and שמר, but it is also possible that the translation was influenced by 𝔊 Job 7:12. From Ugaritic, however, we know that there is a root זמר, 'to guard', hence 'to be strong' (cf. KBL *sub* III *זמר). Some scholars suggest that לנצבתנא expresses this meaning (cf. נצבתא in Dan 2:41). The reconstruction ל̇]שן מזמ[ר̇ לנצבתנא, then, would render זמרות according to its two-fold connotation. Note, however, that this reconstruction would not fill the gap, leaving room for an additional three letters.

L. 7 (35:12) תמה. This is the older form; other Qumran Aramaic texts employ תמן.

L. 8 (35:13) שוא ישמ]ע. The negative particle לא of 𝔐 is missing, either because the translator or scribe forgot it, or because the translator objected to the idea that there are things which God does not hear. שוא is probably a Hebraism.

L. 8 (35:13) ה]ב̇לא. The word is not in 𝔐.

L. 9 (35:13) [לא] יצתנה. Cf. 𝔐 לא ישורנה. The change of meaning may be due to the translator's wish to mitigate the statement, but one should also note the translator's varying renderings of שור. He does not understand 𝔐 ישר in Job 33:27 (col. XXIII 4–5), and renders יתיבנה in col. XXV 5 (34:29). However, col. XXVIII 2 (36:24) may indicate that he did know the meaning of the word.

L. 10 (35:14) לה. Cf. 𝔐 לו of the end of Job 34:14. This identification concords with the approximate length of the translation of verses of 𝔐. In that case, the following word may be א]רו, corresponding to 𝔐 וכען.

VARIANTS

35:11 (6) פרשנא 𝔊 (διορίζων = מפלנו)] מלפנו 𝔐𝔖 (ܡܠܦ ܠܢ = מלפני)

Col. XXVII (Frgs. 25 ii, 26 i) Job 36:7-16

top margin

למלכין יתבי ע֯[ל כרסיהון וכל ר]ח֯י֯מ֯והי לרחצן ירמון 1

8ואף עם אסירין ב֯[זיקין א]חידין בחבלי מסכניא 2

9ויחוא להׄ[ן עבדיהו]ן ועית]הון ארו התרוממו 10ויגלא 3

אדניהון למוסר וא[מר להון]הן יתׄבון מן באישתהון 4

11הן ישמעון ויעבד֯[ון ישלמון]בטב ימהון ושניהון 5

ביקר ועדנין [12והן לא ישמ]ע֯ון בחרבא יפלון 6

ויאבדון מן מ֯[נדעא 13 ל]בבהון לרגז 7

עליהון 14?ו֯°[מ]דינתהון בממתין 8

15ויפרק מ֯[סכנא] די אדניהון 9

16]]ל֯א֯[[10

Mus. Inv. 626, 630
PAM 43.811*, 43.812*

NOTES ON READINGS

Col. XXVII is preserved on frgs. 25 ii and 26 i. The gap between the two fragments (line 3) measures *c*.2 cm. In frg. 25, the horizontal ruling is not visible.

L. 1 (36:7) למלכין יתבי. At first sight, the two instances of *yod* in יתבי are awkwardly written: the head of the second *yod* seems to start beneath the (not visible) ceiling line, and the downstrokes of both *yod*s stretch down to the bottom line. However, no guide line is visible on the fragment, and the writing appears to slant downwards. This is constant, except for the final *nun* which, as usual, reaches above the ceiling line. This is clearer on the fragment than in the photographs; the distance from the head of the first *lamed* to the top of the *waw* (line 2) is 0.65 cm; the distance from the top of the *yod* of למלכין to the top of the final *mem* (line 2) is 0.6 cm, and the distance from the top of the *taw* to the top of the *samek* (line 2) is 0.55 cm.

L. 1 (36:7) ע֯[ל. PAM 43.812 shows the bottom part of a downstroke (not visible on the fragment any longer), curving into a long base stroke. It could be part of *kap*, but the length of the base should rather be taken as an indication of *ʿayin*.

L. 1 (36:7) ר]ח֯י֯מ֯והי. To the right of *mem* are two unconnected dots at the bottom line, probably the remainder of two downstrokes or legs. The distance between these two dots is too small to allow even for a narrow *ḥet*. It is more likely that the first dot is the tip of the left leg of *ḥet*, and the second dot the tip of the downstroke of *yod*.

L. 2 (36:8) ב֯[זיקין. At the edge of the fragment there are two thin strokes: a downstroke slanting to the right and a horizontal stroke slanting down to the left. The traces really conform more to, e.g. *mem* or *pe*, but *bet*, which seems the most logical choice in view of the context, cannot be totally excluded.

L. 4 (36:10) וא[מר. The photograph is unclear, but the fragment clearly shows the *keraia* of *ʾalep*.

L. 5 (36:11) ויעבדֿ]ון. Two minute traces are left of *dalet*, and can be seen in PAM 43.812; they are no longer visible on the fragment.

L. 6 (36:12) ישמ]עֿון. The trace before *waw* is compatible with the top of the left arm of *ʿayin*.

L. 7 (36:12) מֿ]נדעא. The traces of the first letter consist of the upper part of the downstroke and the remains of a separate diagonal stroke close to the head of the downstroke. This almost certainly indicates *mem*. The distance between the diagonal breaking and the right downstroke is rather small, as, e.g. in *mem* of למוסר in line 4.

L. 7 (36:13) ל]בבהון. One would expect to see part of the arm of *lamed*, but nothing is visible except a tiny speck. Note, however, that the part of the fragment where the trace should be visible is damaged.

L. 8 (36:13 or 14)]°וֿ. The traces either belong to *waw* followed by *yod* or another letter, or to *reš*. It cannot be, e.g. *mem*, because of the long straight downstroke, or any other letter of which the head and downstroke are made with two separate strokes.

L. 9 (36:15) מֿ]סכנא. The traces of the first letter are consistent with *mem*, but also with many other letters.

L. 9 (36:15) די [. The *yod* looks more like a *waw*, but the lack of any trace before *dalet* (only a *nun* written at some distance before *dalet* would leave no trace) suggests the two letters are not the end of a broken word, but are a separate word.

L. 9 (36:15) אדניהון. A small spot of ink is visible above the *ʾalep*.

L. 10 (36:16)]. At the beginning of the line, PAM 43.812 shows three traces of tops of letters which are consistent with ואֿ]ף. However, the fragment shows only small cracks in the skin, and it is possible that these caused the appearance of traces in the photograph.

Translation

1. kings sitting o[n their thrones, and all] his [fr]iends will be exalted in safety.
2. [8]And even with those bound in [chains, hel]d in the cords of the poor.
3. [9]And He shows them the[ir] works [and] their [iniquities] because they exalted themselves. [10]And He will open
4. their ears for instruction, and s[ay to them:] 'If they turn from their evil deeds,
5. [11]If they listen and do[, they shall complete] their days in goodness, and their years
6. in honour and pleasures. [[12]And if] they [do not list]en, they shall fall by the sword
7. and perish without kn[owledge'. [13]]their [h]eart for anger
8. upon them, [14?]and [ ]their [vil]lage by killers.
9. [15]And He delivers [the] p[oor] of their ears.
10. [[16]] not[ ]

Comments

L. 1 (36:7) למלכין יתבי עֿ]ל כרסיהון. The syntactical construction of ואת מלכים לכסא וישיבם 𝔐 is somewhat confusing. 𝔊 renders literally καὶ μετὰ βασιλέων εἰς θρόνον καὶ καθιεῖ αὐτούς, but 𝔖 (ܘܡܘܬܒ ܡ̈ܠܟܐ ܥܠ ܟܘܪܣܝܐ) and 𝔗 (ועם מלכיא תקניא למתב על כורסי מלכותא, 'he will make them sit upon the throne of his kingdom with established kings') connect the verbal form ישיבם with the preceding clause. It is not clear how this text understood 𝔐. The *lamed* before מלכין suggests that the translator interpreted את 𝔐 as the *nota accusativi*, and that we should therefore reconstruct a preceding verb. It is possible that this was a verb corresponding to ישיבם, but יתבי suggests that the translator dealt with the Hebrew clause in a still different way.

L. 1 (36:7) וכל ר]חֿמֿוהי. Whether this reconstruction is correct or not, the word is missing from 𝔐 and the versions. וכל is added in the reconstruction in order to fill the gap.

L. 1 (36:7) לרחצן. A deviation from 𝔐, which reads לנצח, 'for ever'. There is no need to assume that the translator mixed up the expressions לנצח and לבטח, 'in safety'.

L. 2 (36:8) ואף עם אסירין בֿ]זיקין א]חֿידין. The translation differs from 𝔐 in some minor points. ואם 𝔐 is rendered by ואף עם. A participle א]חֿידין is used instead of the imperfect ילכדון of 𝔐. The reconstruction

בֿ]זיקין is based on the fact that a form of שושלא or שלשלתא (cf. 𝕮 בשושלוון and 𝔖 ܒܫ̈ܫܠܬܐ) would be too long for the lacuna.

L. 2 (36:8) בחבלי מסכניא. Like 𝔖 (ܒܚܒܠܐ ܕܡܣܟܢܘܬܐ), the translator understood 𝔐 עני as 'poor' instead of as 'misery, affliction'.

L. 3 (36:9) עבדיהוֿ]ן. Plural (like 𝔊, 𝔖, and 𝕮), instead of the sing. of 𝔐 פעלם. Note, though, that פֹּעַל, except in the construction רב פעלים, is grammatically singular. Cf. English 'behaviour' or 'conduct'.

L. 3 (36:9) ועוית]הֿון. In the lacuna, a word corresponding to 𝔐 ופשעיהם must be reconstructed. 𝔖 reads ܘܣ̈ܟܠܘܬܗܘܢ; 𝕮 ומרדיהון. In cols. XXII 3 (33:9) and XXIV 1 (34:6), חטא renders פשע; in col. XXVI 1 (35:6), the translator uses עויה.

L. 3 (36:9) התרוממו. Instead of, e.g. התגברו (cf. 𝔐, 𝔖, and 𝕮). The choice of this word was probably influenced by the use of the same verb two lines above.

Ll. 3–4 (36:10) ויגלא / אדניהון למוסר וא]מר להון]הן יתֿ'בון מן באישתהון. An almost literal translation of 𝔐. A slight change is the translation of 𝔐 כי by הן. מוסר is probably a Hebrew loan-word.

L. 5 (36:11) ויעבדֿ]ון. Contrary to 𝔐 יעבדו, Aramaic יעבדון does not have the meaning 'to serve'. 𝕮 therefore renders ויפלחון; 𝔖 agrees with this text: ܢܥܒܕܘܢ.

L. 5 (36:11) ישלמון]. Cf. 𝔐 יכלו. One may reconstruct according to 𝕮 ישלמון (𝔖 ܢܫܬܡܥܘܢ).

L. 5 (36:11) ימהון. A scribal error for יומיהון. The two supralinear *waws* in the previous lines might indicate a scribal tendency to write defectively.

L. 6 (36:11) ביקר ועדנין. 𝔐 בנעימים has been rendered with two words.

L. 6 (36:12) בחרבא. Cf. 𝔐 בשלח. Note the different translations in the versions: 𝔙 *per gladium*; 𝔖 ܒܩܪܒܐ; 𝕮 has two variants, בזיני קרב בסרהוביא ל"א בשלהא. The variations indicate that either the exact meaning of שלח, 'javelin', was unknown, or that the translators did not care for a literal translation.

L. 7 (36:12) מן מֿ]נדעא. Cf. 𝔐 כבלי דעת. 𝔐 בלי דעת is also found in Job 35:16, 38:2 and 42:3. 𝕮 translates thrice מדלית מנדעא and, in 42:3: ולא מנדעא. A rendering of 𝔐 בלי פשע is found twice in the preserved text: ולא חטא in col. XXII 3 (33:9), and מן חטא in col. XXIV 1 (34:6). In both cases, 𝕮 employs מדלית. This shows that in this text מן can have the meaning of 𝔐 בלי.

L. 7 (36:13) ל]בבהון לרגז. ל]בבהון corresponds to 𝔐 לב, and רגז is a rendering of 𝔐 אף, but both the addition of the suffix and the continuation of the phrase show that the translator changed the wording of 𝔐.

L. 8 (36:13-14) עליהון ו°[מ]דינתהון. The lacuna is too short for a rendering of both v 13b and 14a. The word after עליהון cannot be ול]א. Therefore it is more likely that ו°[corresponds to the beginning of v 14.

L. 8 (36:14) מ]דינתהון בממתין. A rendering of 𝔐 וחיתם בקדשים. The translator interpreted Hebrew חיה as 'the place where one lives' (cf. Ps 68:11; *Tg. Onq.* Num 32:41 as a rendering of כפרא). The vocalization of 𝔐 בקְּדֵשִׁים refers to 'male prostitutes', and both 𝕮 (היך מרי זנו, 'like lords of prostitution') and 𝔙 (*inter afeminatos*) agree with this interpretation. 𝔊 ὑπὸ ἀγγέλων, however, seems to be a rendering of בקדשים. The translation ממתין is certainly derived from 𝔐 Job 33:22 וחיתו לממתים, where ממתים, 'killers', are often interpreted as 'angels of death'. In view of Job 33:22 (where some MSS of 𝕮 read ממיתיא instead of קטוליא), one should interpret ממתין as an *Ap'el* participle.

L. 10 (36:16)]לאֿ[. The word may correspond to the same word in 𝔐, in which case the translation is somewhat longer than the wording of 𝔐.

Col. XXVIII (Frgs. 26 ii, 27) Job 36:23-33

top margin

עֿבֿ]דת עולה [24]ד]כֿרֿ אֿרו רברבין עבדוהי די 1

חזו המֿ]ון [25]ו]כל אנשא עלוהי חזין ובני אנשא 2

מרחיק̇[עלוה]י̇ יבקון [26]הא אלהא רב הוא ויומוהי
סגיא[לא נג]דע ומנין שנוהי די לא סוף [27]ארו
ענני̊[מין ימנא] וזיקי מטר יהכן [28]ועננוהי י̇חתו̇ן
ט̇[יפי מין על]ע̇ם סגיא [29]הן *vacat* מן פר̇ס̇
ע[נניא די אתרגו]ש̊תה מן טלל [30]ופרס נה̇[ורה]
[כ]סי [31]ארו {◦}בהון ידין ע̇[ממין]
[ ][32]על מאמרה מ[
[ ][33]י]ש̇ח על[והי

Mus. Inv. 623, 630
PAM 43.810*, 43.811*

NOTES ON READINGS

Frg. 26 ii and 27 contain the remains of the col. XXVIII. A faint vertical ruling is visible in frg. 27 2–4. At this point the revolution of the scroll measured *c*.8.4–8.7 cm. The distance between the fragments (in line 3) is therefore 1.3–1.6 cm. The reconstruction of lines 1–7 corresponds to a gap of 1.6 cm in line 3.

L. 1 (36:23) ע̇ב̇[דת. The oblique trace at the beginning of the line (frg. 26 ii) belongs almost certainly to *ʿayin*. The dot to the left of this letter can belong either to *bet* or *waw* (or most other letters).

L. 1 (36:24) ד]כ̇ר̇. The two traces at the beginning of frg. 27, a horizontal bar at the baseline and a downstroke extending to the left end of the horizontal bar, are consistent with the reconstruction based on 𝔐.

L. 1 (36:24) ד̇י̇. Compare the traces with those of די in line 4; in both cases the downstrokes are 0.3 cm apart. The head of the *dalet* would have joined the downstroke of *yod*, of which the lowest part can be seen. It is highly unlikely that another word, e.g. אנש, should be reconstructed at the end of the line. There is no trace at all of a letter. The darkened section, visible in PAM 43.810, has deteriorated; not even the *yod* is visible any longer.

L. 2 (36:24) חזו המ̇[ון. The reading is difficult. The traces actually suggest the reading חזוה ◦[. A larger than usual space follows *he*. At the very edge of the fragment we can see a dot on the baseline. This dot can be the bottom tip of a vertical stroke. Palaeographically, the reading חזוה[ון or חזוה̇[ן is unlikely: normally *waw* is written immediately after *he*.

L. 2 (36:25) ו]כ̇ל. The left end of the base of *kap* extends, as usual, beneath the hook of *lamed*.

L. 3 (36:25) עלוה]י̇. The trace, a short vertical stroke, slants down to the right with a thickened head, most closely resembles a *yod*. The stroke slants slightly more than usual (cf. similar examples on frg. 2, e.g. אמתי in col. II 4). *He* is virtually impossible: the stroke slants too much, the left leg of *he* does not have a thickened head, and there is no trace of a crossbar.

L. 5 (36:27) ענני̊[. A trace of *yod* can be seen on the edge of the fragment.

L. 6 (36:29) פר̇ס̇. The last letter can be only *samek* or *qop*.

L. 7 (36:29) אתרגו]ש̊תה. The trace at the right edge of frg. 27 could be the tip of any broad downstroke or horizontal bar.

L. 7 (36:30) ופרס. The apparently irregular shape of *waw* is caused by a dark spot on the leather.

L. 8 (36:31) {◦}בהון. A letter before בהון has been erased so thoroughly that only faint traces of a right downstroke are to be seen.

L. 8 (36:31) ידין עֿ[ממין]. The second *yod* starts rather below the ceiling line. As a result, its downstroke extends to the baseline. Because of its size it should not be interpreted as *waw*. The trace at the end of the line is consistent with *ʿayin*.

L. 10 (36:33) י]שׁ[ח עלֿ[והי. Only the top halves of the letters have been preserved, but there can be no doubt about their interpretation. The supralinear *yod* is written straight above the right leg of *ḥet*. From the fragment, the bottom part has broken off, so only the supralinear *yod* remains.

TRANSLATION

1. ['You] have don[e wrong'. [24]Re]member that his works are great which
2. they see. [[25]And]every man looks to Him, and the sons of man
3. from afar watch out [for Hi]m. [26]Behold, God is great, and his days are
4. a multitude [we do not kn]ow, and the number of his years is endless. [27]Behold,
5. [He counts] the clouds [of water] and He forms the blasts of rain. [28]And his clouds send down
6. dr[ops of water upon] a numerous people. [29]If *vacat* who spreads out
7. [the] cl[ouds] of his [thund]er from (his) pavilion? [30]and spreads out [his] lig[ht]
8. [co]vers [31]For by them He judges na[tions]
9. [ ][32]At his command [
10. [[33]]speaks about [Him

COMMENTS

L. 1 (36:23) עֿבֿ[דת עולה. Cf. 𝔐 פעלת עולה; 𝔗 עדבתא עילתא; S ܕܥܒܕܬ ܥܘܠܐ. Since the dot to the left of the *ʿayin* can belong to *bet*, there is no need to reverse the order of the words.

L. 1 (36:24) רברבין. Cf. 𝔐 תשגיא, which the translator apparently understood as 'are big'. Cf. 𝔊 μεγάλα ἐστίν; S ܕܡܣܓܐܝܢ ܐܢܘܢ.

L. 1 (36:24) דׄיׄ. The reconstruction די [אנש] would give a more agreeable sentence but is rather unlikely. There is no trace of *ʾalep*, and [אנש] would have been written in the margin.

L. 2 (36:24) חזו המֿ[ון. חזו, *si vera lectio*, renders 𝔐 שררו, but the translator did not interpret it as a *Polel* of שור, 'to sing'. He either derived the word from the verb שור, 'to see', or (in view of the fact that he elsewhere renders this verb שור in different ways) he just gave a translation which seemed to fit the context. It is not certain how to reconstruct this word and the following gap. The alternative reconstruction חזו[הו]ן shows two irregularities. First, there is only one example in the Aramaic of this period of a 3rd pl. suffix added to a verb. This example, however, appears in col. XXIX 3 (יפקדנון). Second, according to the grammatical rules as we know them, the proper form should be חזונון. But again, there is an exception in this text: col. XVI 6 (יאקפוני). The combination of two such irregularities in a reconstructed form may seem too much. This reconstruction, חזו המֿ[ון, has the problem that the words are written together, but that is no exception in the manuscript.

L. 3 (36:25) מרחיקֿ [עלוה]י יבקון. The translator has altered the syntax of 𝔐. Since the word in the lacuna almost certainly ends with *yod*, one may reconstruct עלוה]י, analogous to עלוהי in the previous line.

Ll. 3–4 (36:26) ויומוהי / סגיא[. This is an expansion of 𝔐. Note that רב in the preceding clause אלהא רב הוא is the translation of 𝔐 שגיא. It seems that this Hebrew word, as well as the mention of years in the next hemistich, triggered the expansion. The word סגיא might be a substantive (יומוהי סגיא[, 'his days are a multitude') or an adjective (יומוהי סגיא[יא, 'his days are numerous'). The choice depends largely on the reconstruction of the following lacuna.

L. 4 (36:26)] לא נ[נ]דע. Or perhaps] ולא נ[דע; cf. 𝔐 ולא נדע.

L. 4 (36:26) די לא סוף. Once again the translation of 𝔐 לא חקר. Cf. col. XXV 1 (34:24).

L. 5 (36:27) ענ[נ]ֿ מין. Instead of 𝔐 נטפי מים, 'drops of water'.

L. 5 (36:27) ימנא]. One may tentatively reconstruct ימנא (or ימנה) with 𝔊 and S, against 𝔐 יגרע, 'he draws up'. Note, however, the different constructions of the versions: S ܐܠ ܢܛܦܐ ܕܡܛܪܐ ܥܢܢܐ ܘܡܢܝܢ

ܢܛ̈ܦܝ ܕܡܛܪܐ ܒܠܚܘܕܘܗܝ, ‘When He counts the pillars of heaven, and He alone forms the drops of rain’; 𝔊 ἀριθμηταὶ δὲ αὐτῷ σταγόνες ὑετοῦ; ℭ ארום ימנע טופי מיא.

L. 5 (36:27) וזיקי[. The translator seems to have read וזקי instead of 𝔐 יזקו. The word זיקא can have many meanings, including ‘blast’, ‘wind’, ‘storm’.

L. 5 (36:27) יהכן. Instead of 𝔐 לאדו, the translator added יהכן. This form could be a 3rd fem. pl. imperfect of הוך, ‘to go’, but the masc. זיקא rules out this possibility. Instead, the form should be interpreted as a *Hapʿel* of כון (not attested in Aramaic, but cf. Syriac ܐܟܢ, ‘to form, create’). This word corresponds quite closely to 𝔖 ܢܨܘܪ.

L. 5 (36:28) ועננוהי ינחתון. The translator added a suffix to ‘clouds’: ‘His (i.e. God’s) clouds’. ינחתון renders 𝔐 יזלו (cf. 𝔖 ܘܡܫܠܝܢ). As for the dissimilation of the *nun*, cf. col. XXXI 3 להנחתה. In col. XVI 9 (אחתוני), the scribe did not write the *nun*. Apparently the *nun* was not pronounced in the scribe’s dialect.

L. 6 (36:28) ט]יפי מין על [עם. The broken *ṭet* at the beginning of the line suggests that 𝔐 נטפי מים (36:27), not translated in the previous lines, has found its way to this hemistich. Possibly, these words have been employed as a free translation of 𝔐 ירעפו. There is just enough space in the lacuna for the reconstruction ט]יפי מיא על [עם. It appears that both the translator and 𝔖 have dealt freely with 𝔐 36:27-28, using most of its expressions, but not exactly in the same constructions.

L. 6 (36:29) הן *vacat*. The *vacat* appears where one expects a rendering of 𝔐 יבין.

L. 6 (36:29) מן פרס. Cf. 𝔐 מפרשי. The Aramaic wording does not necessarily imply that the translator understood מפרשי as a combination of the interrogative pronoun and a verbal form. It seems more likely that the *mem* of מפרשי was understood, first, as the preposition מן, and later as מן, ‘who’. Unfortunately, the text does not show whether the line read פרס[י] or פרס.

L. 7 (36:29) ע]נניא די אתרגו[שתה מן טלל. The first word of the line is likely to be a form of ענן, corresponding to 𝔐 עב. The context suggests a pl. form. The lacuna and the following תה מן טלל, then, should correspond to 𝔐 תשאות סכתו. טלל might be a rendering of סכה, which would allow one to fit into the lacuna a word corresponding to תשאות. Van der Woude (*ed. princ.*, p. 67) suggested אתרגו[שתה, this word being the translation of תשאות in *Tg. Isa* 22:2 and ℭ 39:7. The meaning of the reconstructed clause might be: ‘who spreads out the clouds of his noise (i.e. his thunderclouds) from (his? their?) hut’. Of course, in view of both the broken state of the line and the uncertainty about how the translator could have understood the difficult Hebrew expression, other reconstructions or interpretations are possible. Thus, e.g. van der Ploeg (*ed. princ.*, p. 67) suggests the reconstruction: קט]ותה (cf. col. XI 9 where the same word corresponds to 𝔐 סכה in Job 27:18). This reconstruction requires an additional preceding word of three or four letters corresponding to תשאות. מן טלל, in that case, could be an explanatory addition. But it is also possible that the translator interpreted 𝔐 סכתו as a verb with pronominal suffix, and that מן טלל should be understood as ‘who has covered’ or ‘who covers’, either as the beginning of the next clause, or perhaps as the end of the preceding clause with the object being the word ending in תה-. Thus we might also translate: ‘who spreads out his thunderclouds? who covers and spreads out his light?’.

L. 9 (36:32)]על מאמרה. Probably a rendering of 𝔐 על כפים. The translator may have wished to avoid the anthropomorphism of 𝔐. The word מאמר still has its historical spelling, whereas other Qumran Aramaic texts have ממר.

L. 10 (36:33) יש]ח על[והי. Cf. 𝔐 יגיד עליו.

VARIANTS

36:27 (5) 𝔐 יגרע] 𝔊𝔖 ימנא]

Col. XXIX (Small scroll, col. i; Frgs. A2, B, C, S) Job 37:10-19

top margin

על אנפי מין 11אף בהון ימרק ע֯נ֯[ין] וינפק מן
ענן נורה 12והוא אמר ישמעון לה ואזלין לעבדיהון
על כל די ברא יפקדנון על אנפי תבל 13הן למכתש
הן לארעא הן לכפן וחסרנה והן פתגם ח֯ו֯ב להוא
עליה 14הצת דא איוב וקום הסתכל בגבורת אלהא
[15הת]נדע מא שויא אלהא עליה֯ן ו֯[הו]פ֯ע֯ נ֯הור עננה
[16aהתנ]ד֯ע להלבש{ו}א עננה גבורה [17aב]דיל די לבושך
[ ]16bא֯רו הוא ידע מדע֯[א 18העמה ת]נפח ערפ֯לא
[תקיף כמח]ז֯יה עקה 19ינדע֯[ ]ל֯[ ]

Mus. Inv. 635, 638
PAM 43.800, 43.824

NOTES ON READINGS

This is the first column on a small scroll of ten columns from the end of the manuscript. Although no visible traces of stitching have been preserved on the edge of the scroll, col. XXIX most probably belongs to a new sheet. The small fragments reproduced on the top and bottom of PAM 43.800 can no longer be located.

Frg. B fits in line 1, frg. C in lines 5–9, frg. A2 in lines 6–7, and frg. S in line 7. The spacing between the words is very irregular. In several cases, as, e.g. in על אנפי (line 1), the words seem to be written without any space at all. The scribe did not separate words which formed one inseparable expression. Cf., on the other hand, the spacing in line 7 להלבש{ו}א עננה, where there is more space between *šin* and *ʾalep* than between *ʾalep* and *ʿayin*, or על כל at the beginning of line 3, where the distance between *ʿayin* and *lamed* is greater than that between *lamed* and *kap*.

L. 1 (37:11) וינפק [. The first four letters and a tiny piece of *qop* are found on frg. B. The same fragment also shows the top of the upper arm of *lamed* of לעבדיהון from line 2. The left part of the broken *qop* of וינפק appears on the scroll. The edge of the fragment has now deteriorated, and nothing of the *qop* remains.

L. 4 (37:13) פתגם ח֯ו֯ב. At the top right of frg. C the bottom part of final *mem* can be seen; at the top left the bottom right part of *bet*. In between one can see the bottom tips of two vertical strokes. These traces exclude the reading פתגם ט֯ב, since one cannot see any remains of the base of *ṭet*. The reading ר֯י֯ב is also impossible, because the traces are far too close to each other. It is more likely that the first vertical stroke is the left leg of *ḥet*, and the second the remnant of *waw*.

L. 5 (37:14) בגבורת אלהא. The letters גבורת and some traces of the first *ʾalep* of אלהא are found on frg. C.

L. 6 (37:15) עליה͘ן. The trace to the left of the supralinear *waw* is the tip of the head of final *nun* (breaking through the ceiling line). The tail of the final *nun* is visible on frg. A2.

L. 6 (37:15) ו̇[הו]פ̇ע̇. The bottom part of the first *waw* appears on frg. A2. The traces at the beginning of frg. C do not unambiguously confirm *pe* and *ʿayin*.

L. 7 (37:16) להלבש{ו}א. The scribe first wrote *waw*, scraped the skin, and then wrote *ʾalep*, which accounts for its irregular shape.

L. 7 (37:16)] גבורה. A large part of *bet* has been preserved on frg. S. The three last letters are preserved on frg. A2.

L. 9 (37:18) כמח[ז̇]יה. The *zayin* is barely legible (only a small spot of ink is visible on the fragment), but seems likely in view of 𝔐.

Translation

1. on the surface of the water. [11]He also brightens the cloud[s] with them, and He sends forth from
2. a cloud His fire. [12]And He says: 'Let them listen to him'. And they go to (do) their works.
3. He puts them in charge over everything which He created upon the face of the earth, [13]whether for a plague,
4. or for the land, whether for famine and its want, or when there is a case of law-breaking
5. on it. [14]Listen to this, Job, and stand up, consider the mighty works of God.
6. [[15]Do you] know what God has placed upon them, and [(how) He makes] the light of His cloud [sh]ine?
7. [[16a]Do you kn]ow how to clothe His cloud with might? [[17a] Be]cause your dress
8. [ ][16b]Behold, it is He who has knowled[ge. [18]Can you, with Him], inflate the fog
9. [strong like] a pressed [mirr]or? [19]He knows [ ] [

Comments

L. 1 (37:10) על אנפי מין. These words must correspond in some way to the end of 𝔐 ורחב מים במוצק, 'and the width of the sea is frozen'. None of the versions corresponds to the wording of the translation. The first words of 𝔐, מנשמת אל (ℭ מן מימר אלהא), may have called Gen 1:2 to mind: 'the spirit (or wind) of God hovered on the surface of the water'; cf. also Gen 7:18.

L. 1 (37:11) אף בהון. 𝔐 reads אף ברי, which the translator apparently read or interpreted as אף בם. The ancient versions have interpreted the difficult word ברי in various ways: 𝔊 ἐκλεκτόν; 𝔖 ܓܒܝܐ; ℭ בברירותא. On the different modern interpretations of ברי, cf. HAL *sub* רי.

L. 1 (37:11) ימרק. 𝔐 יטריח, 'to load', is a *hapax legomenon*, which 𝔊 (καταπλάσσει) and 𝔖 (ܡܛܥܢ) did not understand. ℭ simply renders מטרח. This text reads ימרק, which suggests that the translator read a form of טהר. מרק ('to polish', 'to cleanse', 'to brighten') does not evoke a very fitting image, but the notion of the brightness of the clouds may be connected to the going forth of fire from the clouds mentioned in the next clause.

Ll. 1–2 (37:11) וינפק מן / ענן נורה. וינפק renders 𝔐 יפיץ, 'he scatters', whereas נורה translates 𝔐 אורו (on the rendering of 𝔐 אור, cf. col. VIII 3). The meaning of 𝔐 is not exactly clear: should one understand 'he scatters the clouds of light' or 'he scatters his lightning from the clouds'? The latter apparently was the understanding of the translator.

L. 2 (37:12) והוא אמר ישמעון לה. The text deviates from the difficult text of 𝔐 (והוא מסבות) on several points. 𝔊 and 𝔖 tried to translate 𝔐 as well as possible, whereas ℭ (which has two variant readings of the verse) has several explanatory additions. והוא, which in 𝔐 must refer to either the clouds (collective sing.) or the light, refers to God in 11QtgJob. The form ישמעון is evidence of the gradual loss of the use of the jussive form (in Official Aramaic, one would expect ישמעו). The expression שמע ל means 'listen to, obey', in contrast to שמע, 'to hear'.

L. 2 (37:12) ואזלין לעבדיהון. The translator gives a free rendering of 𝔐 מתהפך בתחבולתו לפעלם, which expresses the idea that the clouds move under his guidance.

L. 3 (37:12) ברא. One may hypothesize that the translator rendered two variant readings of 𝔐: יצור and יצום.

L. 3 (37:12) יפקדנון. This is an exceptional form because a 3rd pl. pronominal suffix is affixed to a verbal form. More usual would be יפקד המון. Cf. also COMMENTS on col. XXVIII 2.

L. 3 (37:12) על אנפי תבל. The translator omitted 𝔐 ארצה.

L. 3 (37:13) הן למכתש. Cf. 𝔐 אם לשבט. מכתש can be the noun 'plague' or the infinitive *Peʿal*.

L. 4 (37:13) הן לארעא. This renders the awkward 𝔐 אם לארצו, which most scholars regard as corrupt. The Aramaic reading should be regarded as an almost literal translation of 𝔐. Cf. also 𝔊 ἐὰν εἰς τὴν γὴν αὐτοῦ and 𝔖 ܘܐܢ ܠܐܪܥܗ. There is no need to assume that a scribe changed לארעה to לארעא. The alternatives are less likely. It has been suggested that לארעא is an infinitive *Apʿel* of רעע, 'to shatter, break'. The translator would have tried to make sense of 𝔐 לארצו, understanding it as a (causative) form of רצץ. Yet this would be the only preserved infinitive *Apʿel* in the text (other infinitives being *Hapʿel* forms). In addition, the *Apʿel* of רעע is quite rare, in contrast to the *Peʿal* and *Paʿel*. Likewise, it is unlikely that ארעא is here a noun meaning 'accident' (in the plural 'evils, diseases'), derived from the verb ארע (originally ערע as in *Tg. Onqelos*). The problem is that one must assume that the writer of 11QtgJob changed ערע to ארע. The two latter interpretations do give a more coherent text: 'either to smite or to shatter', or 'either for a plague or for a disease', and it is not unthinkable that an Aramaic reader would indeed read the text in this way. However, the translator picked the word which was the logical translation of 𝔐 instead of any other word expressing 'to shatter' or 'evil'. That is, even if he was aware of other possible interpretations, he chose the word which was the translation of 𝔐.

L. 4 (37:13) לכפן וחסרנה. Apparently the translator read לחסר instead of 𝔐 לחסד.

L. 4 (37:13) פתגם חֹוב. The words have no correspondent in 𝔐 or the versions; cf. for this expression *Tg. Onq.* Exod 22:8 פתגם דחוב (𝔐 דבר פשע).

Ll. 4–5 (37:13) להוא / עליה. The Aramaic is probably a free rendering of 𝔐 ימצאהו; it should most likely be taken as an attribute to all of the preceding verse, and not only to פתגם חֹוב. The suffix of עליה refers to תבל in line 3.

L. 5 (37:14) הצת דא איוב וקום הסתכל בגבורת אלהא. The line gives an almost literal translation of 𝔐, differing slightly in the position of the conjunction (וקום הסתכל compared with 𝔐 עמד והתבונן). 𝔊 στῆθι νουθετοῦ has no conjunction at all, whereas 𝔖 ܘܫܠܝ ܘܐܬܒܝܢ has two conjunctions but a different rendering of עמד.

L. 5 (37:14) בגבורת. 𝔐 (נפלאות), 𝔖, and ℭ read a pl.; 𝔊 a sing. δύναμιν. It is unlikely that 11QtgJob reflects a variant in the Hebrew text: נפלאות is commonly plural.

L. 6 (37:15) מא שויא. Cf. 𝔐 בשום; 𝔊 ὅτι . . . ἔθετο; 𝔖 ܕܣܡ ܘܡܦܩ; ℭ כדי ישוי. שויא is a perfect of the *Paʿel*.

L. 6 (37:15) נהור. Note that here the translator correctly renders 𝔐 אור with נהור.

Ll. 7–8 (37:16-17) [התנ]דע להלבש{ו}א עננה גבורה [ב]דיל די לבושך / [ ] ארו הוא ידע מדע[א]. The text deviates from 𝔐. The translator renders v 16, but omits the last two words, which are dealt with after the translation of the first hemistich of v 17.

L. 7 (37:16) להלבש{ו}א. The rendering of 𝔐 על מפלשי. The *hapax legomenon* מִפלש, perhaps meaning 'floating', has not been understood by any of the versions. 𝔊 διάκρισιν and ℭ על מבשקרני ל"א קטרא ('concerning the true nature [of the fogs]') derive the word from פלשׁ. 𝔖 reads ܡܦܩܬܐ (var. ܡܦܩܢܐ), 'end', 'going out', probably referring to the gates of heaven.

L. 7 (37:17) לבושך. Sing. instead of 𝔐 בגדיך.

L. 8 (37:17) [ ]. The reconstruction [חמים] (cf. 𝔐 חמים; 𝔖 ܫܚܝܢ; ℭ שחנין) fits, but because of the deviations from 𝔐 any reconstruction is uncertain.

L. 8 (37:16) ארו הוא ידע מדע[א]. This seems to be a rendering of the last two words of v 16: תמים דעים. 𝔊 (ἐξαίσια δὲ πτώματα πονηρῶν, 'and extraordinary falls of the wicked') reads רעים for דעים. The wording of 𝔊 might also have been influenced by 18:12. 𝔖 regards the words as a qualification of מפלאות; ℭ דשלים מנדעיא takes them to be an epithet of God. The second hemistich of Job 37:17 is missing.

L. 8 (37:18) העמה ת[נפח. In the lacuna there is room for one word. One may reconstruct התנדע למ[נפח (*ed. princ.*, p. 69), but העמה corresponds more to 𝔐 עמו. The verbal form ending in]נפח renders 𝔐 תרקיע. Both 𝔖 and ℭ use the same verbal root as 𝔐.

L. 9 (37:18) תקיף כמח]זיה עקה]. The missing first word of the line most likely corresponded to 𝔐 חזקים (S ܬܩܝܦܐ; 𝔗 תקיפין). The broken second word should have rendered 𝔐 כראי, 'like a mirror'. One can not know for sure whether the translator understood this meaning (𝔊 and S did not), but if he did one may reconstruct כמח]זיה or כח]זיה (cf. ܡܚܙܝܬܐ). If the reconstruction תקיף is right, one should reconstruct כמח]זיה. In that case the word עקה, corresponding to 𝔐 מוצק, is a fem. participle of עוק, 'to press' (עיקה written defectively). The translator interpreted מוצק as a form of צוק (in Aramaic עוק). However, one cannot rule out the possibility that the translator understood the hemistich rather differently, and rendered מוצק by the noun עקה, both words meaning 'distress, trouble'.

L. 9 (37:19) ינדע̇]. Imperfect instead of the imperative הודיענו of 𝔐. 𝔊, S, and 𝔗 also have the imperative, but 𝔊 and S read a 1st sing. suffix.

Col. XXX (Small scroll, col. ii; Frgs. D1, D2) Job 38:3-13

top margin

1 3אסר נא כ̇ג̇בר חלצ̇[י]ך̇ [ואש]אלנ̇ך והתיבני { } פתגם

2 4אן הוית במעבדי ארעא החויני הן ידעת חכמה

3 5מן שם משחתה הן תנדע מן נגד עליה חוטא 6או

4 על מא אשיה אח̇דון או מן הקים אבן חזיתה 7במזהר

5 כחדא כוכבי צפר ויזעק[ו]ן̇ כחדה כל מלאכי אלהא

6 8התסוג בדשין ימא ב[הנ]גחותה מן רחם תהומא

7 למפק 9בשוית ענני̇ן [לבו]שה וע̇רפלין חותלוהי 10ותשוה

8 לה תחומין ודת̇[ל]ימא נגר]י̇ן ו̇[תר]ע̇י̇ן 11ואמרת עד תנא

9 ולא תוסף̇[ג]ללי[ך] 12הביומיך מנית

10] 13]כנפ̇[י]ארע̇[א]

Mus. Inv. 638
PAM 43.801

NOTES ON READINGS

Two small fragments, D1 and D2, can be joined at the bottom left of the scroll (line 10).

L. 1 (38:3) חל̇צ̇[י]ך̇]. *Ed. princ.*, 70: חל[ציך, but the traces after *lamed* are consistent with the left end of the base of *ṣade* and, further on, with the bottom part of the tail of final *kap*.

L. 1 (38:3) פתגם { }. After והתיבני a word of at least three letters has been erased. פתגם follows, written (apart from the *pe*) in the margin. The scraping has peeled the surface of the skin so that no traces of the first word have remained.

L. 4 (38:6) אח֯דון. The letter after *dalet* is clearly *waw*. On the whole, the scribe carefully distinguishes between *yod* and *waw*. The occasional confusions mainly arise when the script is smaller than average (e.g. in col. XXVII 1), or when *waw* or *yod* follows a letter with an extended base, especially, but not exclusively, at the end of words.

L. 7 (38:9) ענני֯ן. The first *nun* is torn into two parts.

L. 8 (38:10)]ודתׄ. The last readable letter is almost certainly *taw*. The form of the bottom of the downstroke excludes the possibility of a base stroke.

L. 8 (38:10) נגר]י֯ן ו֯[תר]ע֯י֯ן. Some letters are preserved in the middle of the lacuna. The final *nun* is certain; the small trace to its right may be interpreted as the tick of *yod*. The downstroke to the left is probably *waw*, since no traces of a crossbar or head are visible. The remnants of letters before ואמרת are very hard to read. The reconstruction is based on the fact that the first letter resembles *ʿayin*.

L. 9 (38:11) ג]לליׄ[ך]. The *yod* is visible in the photographs.

L. 10 (38:13)]כנפׄ[י]אׄרע֯[א]. Frg. D1 shows the left part of the base of *kap*, a *nun*, and part of *pe*. The rest of *pe* appears on the edge of the scroll. The left half of *ʾalep* and almost the complete *reš* are found on frg. D2. The edge of the scroll shows the very top of the diagonal of *ʾalep*. The dark spot at the left bottom edge of the scroll might be the tip of the right arm of *ʿayin*. It certainly is not the left edge of the head of *reš*.

TRANSLATION

1. ³Gird, then, your loin[s] like a man, [and I will a]sk you, and you will answer me { } a word.
2. ⁴Where were you when I made the earth? Tell me if you know wisdom!
3. ⁵Who laid down its measures, do you know? Who stretched the cord over it? ⁶Or
4. on what are its foundations held? Or who erected its boundary stone, ⁷when
5. the morning stars shone together, and all of God's angels shouted together?
6. ⁸Did you hold back the sea with doors, when it [b]roke forth from the womb of the deep
7. to go out, ⁹when the clouds were being made its [dre]ss, and the fog its swaddling clothes? ¹⁰And did you place
8. its bounds and a law [to the sea, bar]s and [doo]rs? ¹¹And did you say: 'Thus far
9. and no further; [your w]aves'? ¹²Have you, in your days, commanded
10. [¹³ the] edge[s of the] earth.

COMMENTS

L. 1 (38:3) אסר נא כ֗בר חלצׄ[י]ך֯[ואש]אלנׄך והתיבני { } פתגם. Apart from the conjunctive *waw* in 𝔐 ואשאלך, the verse is identical to Job 40:7. The translation of that verse in col. XXXIV 2–3 corresponds to this line.

L. 2 (38:4) אן הוית במעבדי ארעא החויני הן ידעת חכמה. The translation has some minor deviations from 𝔐. במעבדי renders the more specific reading of 𝔐 ביסדי. Like 𝔊 and 𝔖, the translator adds the pronominal object ('to me') which is missing in 𝔐 הגד. The translator uses חכמה, and not בינה, to render 𝔐 בינה.

L. 3 (38:5) שם. Elsewhere in the preserved parts of the targum, the translator renders 𝔐 שים with the *Paʿel* of שוא. Here he uses the less common שים.

L. 3 (38:5) מן נ֯גד. Cf. 𝔐 או מי נטה. 𝔐 או has been transposed from v 5a to the beginning of v 6.

L. 4 (38:6) אח֯דון. A perfect *Peʿil* form, which renders 𝔐 הטבעו. The ון- ending of the 3rd masc. pl. perfect forms is irregular in this period, but cf. ובעון in 1QapGen ar XIX 15.

L. 4 (38:6) אבן חזיתה. Cf. 𝔐 אבן פנתה, 'cornerstone'. In Hebrew, חזית has the meaning 'cutting; rough, unfinished side', which, according to Jastrow (444a), might have the extended meaning of 'border-mark' in *B. Bat.* 1.2. But does the fact that חזית functions as a border-mark in that text also imply it is one of the meanings of the word?

L. 4 (38:7) במזהר. במזהר, 'when shone', corresponds to 𝔐 ברן, 'when cried'. This change, as well as the change from 𝔐 בני אלהים to מלאכי אלהא in line 5, and possibly the addition of תהומא in line 6, all seem to serve the purpose of removing the mythological expressions from the text. The same tendency is apparent in 𝔊 (ὅτε ἐγενήθησαν), S (ܒܪܐ), and 𝔗.

L. 5 (38:7) כחדה . . . כחדא. The translator uses this word in both hemistichs, whereas 𝔐 reads יחד only in the first hemistich. 𝔊 does not translate יחד.

L. 5 (38:7) מלאכי אלהא. Apparently the translator did not want to render 𝔐 בני אלהים literally. Cf. 𝔊 ἄγγελοί μου; S ܒܢ̈ܝ ܡܠܐܟ̈ܐ; 𝔗 כיתי מלאכיא.

Ll. 6–8 (38:8-11) התסוג . . . ותשוה . . . ואמרת. The translator has turned the verbal forms of 𝔐 (ויסך . . . ואשבר . . . ואמר) into rhetorical questions, like those of vv 4-5 and 12ff.

L. 6 (38:8) ב[הנ]גחותה. The broken word in the middle of the line corresponds to 𝔐 בגיחו. The gap in the word requires two letters, which rules out the natural reconstruction ב[ה]גחותה (S ܘܐܟܢܫ, whereas 𝔗 has a *Peʿal* form במגחיה). One must assume that we are dealing either with the *Hapʿel* of נגח, a secondary root formation with the same meaning as גיח, or with ב[הת]גחותה, a *Hitpaʿal* of גיח. The fact that many *Apʿel* forms of גיח can also be interpreted as *Apʿel* forms of נגח leads us to favour the first assumption.

L. 6 (38:8) מן רחם תהומא. Cf. 𝔐 מרחם. Perhaps the addition was made to remove the mythological element, but cf. the same expression in Sir 51:5 מרחם [תה]ום; 𝔊 ἐκ βάθους κοιλίας ᾄδου. 𝔗 uses the same two words: מן תהומא ממין רחמא.

L. 7 (38:9) בשוית. Cf. 𝔐 בשומי. The form שוית is the construct state of שויא (infinitive *Paʿel*).

L. 7 (38:9) עננין . . . וערפלין. Pl. forms are used instead of the sing. forms in 𝔐. For a similar change from sing. to pl., cf. col. XXIX 1 (37:11).

L. 7 (38:10) ותשוה. One would expect the word to correspond to 𝔐 ואשבר, a form which many scholars regard as suspect. Cf. 𝔊 ἐθέμην; S ܘܣܡܬ; 𝔗 ופסקית. However, normally שוא renders 𝔐 שים; one may hypothesize that ותשוה renders 𝔐 ואשים.

L. 8 (38:10) תחומין ודת[. This could be a double interpretation of 𝔐 חקי. In any case, it is unlikely that the word beginning with וד is a verbal form: one would expect a 2nd masc. sing. imperfect corresponding to the 1st sing. in 𝔐.

L. 8 (38:10)]. לימא נגר]ין ו[תר]עין. נגר]ין ו[תר]עין corresponds to 𝔐 בריח ודלתים. Cf. 𝔗 נגרין ודשין and, in reverse order, S ܬܪ̈ܥܐ ܘܡܘܟܠܐ. One would, in fact, expect דשין to render 𝔐 דלתים as in line 6 (38:8), but this reconstruction is not consistent with the preserved traces. A word like לימא must be added to fill the rest of the lacuna.

L. 8 (38:11) ואמרת. Cf. 𝔐 ואמר. Since the translator changes the 1st sing. verbal forms of 𝔐 to 2nd masc. sing. ones, we should interpret ואמרת also as a 2nd masc. sing. perfect.

L. 8 (38:11) עד תנא. 𝔐 עד פה תבוא.

L. 9 (38:12) מנית. A *Paʿel* form, it corresponds to 𝔐 צוית.

L. 10 (38:13)]כנפ[י ארע[א]. One may reconstruct למאחד ב]כנפ[י ארע[א]. 𝔐 has לאחז בכנפות הארץ; cf. 𝔗 (alternative targum) למיחד בגדפי ארעא; S ܠܡܐܚܕ ܒܟܢ̈ܦܝܗ ܕܐܪܥܐ.

Col. XXXI (Small scroll, col. iii; Frgs. E, T, U) Job 38:23-34

1 23ד]י מנעת ל]ע̇ד̇ן ע̇[ק]ת̇[א ליום קרב ואשתדר [24?

2 היכא יפק *vac* ותשוב קדמוהי על ארעא 25מן שויא

3 למטרא זמן וארח לענגין קלילין 26להנחתה על ארע

4 מדבר די לא אנש בה 27להסבעה שיתא ושביקה

5 ולהנפקה צמחי דתאה 28האיתי למטרא אב או מן

6 ילד̇ [ע]נני טלא 29 ומן בטן מן נפק גלידא ושיקו[ע שמיא]

7 מ̊[ן ילד]ה̇ 30 כא[בן] מ̇ין התקרמו מנה ואנפי ∘∘ל̊[

8 [31]ע̊∘[ ]כימא או סיג נפילא ת[פתח]

9 [32]∘∘∘א על בניה תיאש 33 ∘[

10 [ ]אר̊עא̊ 34

11 [ ]∘∘∘[

Mus. Inv. 638
PAM 43.802

Notes on Readings

Five stitching holes can be seen at the end of the column; the string is still attached in the upper and lower parts. The stitching has left clear vertical marks at the beginning of the column, damaging several letters, at 8 cm distance to the right of the stitching. Some letters of lines 5–8 are preserved on frg. E, which, placed in the right part of the column, also help us in restoring the lacuna in line 7. All the available photographs reproduce the backside of frg. E. We have not been able to locate the fragment itself, nor have we succeeded in finding the photograph from which frg. E has been reproduced on p. 131 of the *editio princeps*. Its reproduction on plate XXVII is taken from the *editio princeps*. Frg. T (without number in the *editio princeps*) fits at the end of lines 8–9. Frg. U can be joined to the bottom (lines 10–11).

L. 1 (38:23) ד̊[י מנעת ל]ע̊ד̊ן ע̊[קת]א̊. The reading and reconstruction are based upon the sparse remains of letters and on 𝔐. All that remains of the first letter are a downstroke. The tiny speck of ink to the left could be the bottom part of *yod* of ד̊[י. In the photograph black traces seem to appear some six spaces from the beginning of the line along the edges of the scroll; however, these are not ink but a crack in the skin. After ע̊ד̊ן the inclining base typical of *ʿayin* can be seen. After the gap, the edge shows the left arm and part of the diagonal of *ʾalep*.

L. 1 (38:23) ואשתד̇ר̇]. Not ואשתד̇[ו̇]ר. The letter after *dalet* clearly has a long head; moreover, there is no trace of a vertical stroke near this letter.

L. 1 (38:24)]. Above the *mem* of מן in line 2 there is a crack in the skin; it is not ink, as it may appear in the photograph.

L. 2 (38:24) *vac*. This is a real *vacat*; there are no signs of an erasure.

L. 3 (38:26) להנחתה. The head of *taw* is missing.

L. 5 (38:27) ולהנפקה. The final *he* is preserved on frg. E.

L. 6 (38:28) [ע]נני טלא. Frg. E shows]נני ט[.

L. 6 (38:29) ושיקו[ע. Since the bottom half of *waw* is missing, one might also read *yod*.

L. 7 (38:29) מ̊[ן ילד]ה̇. The trace at the beginning of the fragment is consistent with *mem*. The upper left half of *he* is found on frg. E.

L. 7 (38:30) כא[בן]. The first two letters are preserved on frg. E.

L. 7 (38:30) ואנפי. Note the remarkable ligature of *waw* and *ʾalep*.

L. 7 (38:30) ∘∘ל̊[. The traces are problematic. The last letter on the line is either *lamed* or supralinear *waw*. The surface of the skin has peeled off, leaving only some parts of the upper layer of the skin with ink. In the *ed. princ.* (p. 72) the remains were reconstructed מ̊ב̊ל̊[א; while the first letter could be *mem*, there is no room for *bet* between the *mem* and *lamed*. Later some scholars read תה֯ו֯]מא, but this gives us a *taw* with one and a half times its normal width.

L. 8 (38:31)]○ע֯[. The upper parts of two (or three?) letters have been preserved on frg. E. The first might be *ʿayin*; the other traces cannot be identified with any probability.

L. 8 (38:31) נפילא ת]פתח[. The left arm of *ʾalep* and *taw* belong to frg. T.

L. 9 (38:32) א○○○[. In front of *ʾalep* there are remnants of four downstrokes. The first one, on the edge of the fragment, could be *waw*, *zayin*, or the left downstroke of, e.g. *he*, *ḥet*, or *šin*. The second downstroke is almost certainly *waw* or *zayin*, though *yod* cannot be ruled out. The third downstroke slants slightly to the left. Only the head of the last downstroke remains. The proximity of the last two downstrokes suggests that the last one is *yod*, but the two downstrokes might perhaps also be the arms of *ṣade* (if written in the manner of frg. 11). The traces are no longer visible on the scroll. Only the left part of *ʾalep* remains.

L. 9 (38:33)]○. Frg. T shows the remains of a downstroke.

L. 10 (38:33)]ארעא֯[. In the *ed. princ.* (p. 72) the reading is: ע֯נ֯נ֯]ין[. To the right of *ʿayin* there is a trace of the head of a letter. The first trace after *ʿayin* looks more like the *keraia* of *ʾalep* than the top of *nun*. In front of these traces frg. U fits with a clear *ʾalep*, and minute traces which are consistent with *reš*. The join must be based on the photographs since this fragment can no longer be located, and only the head of *ʿayin* remains on the scroll.

L. 11]○○○[. The remnants of letters are on frg. U.

Translation

1. [23]Wh[ich I have reserved for] the time of dis[tress,] for the day of war and battle? [[24?]
2. how does it go out? *vac* And do you blow in front of Him over the earth? [25]Who set
3. a time for the rain, and a way for the light clouds, [26]to bring (them) down on the land
4. of wilderness, where there are no people, [27]that they would satiate thorns and thickets
5. and cause shoots of plants to sprout? [28]Does the rain have a father, or who
6. gave birth to the [cl]ouds of dew? [29]And from whose womb did the ice come forth, and the cove[ring of the heavens]
7. w[ho gave birth to] it? [30]Like a st[one,] water is covered by it, and the surface of [
8. [[31]] [ ] the Pleiades, or can you [open] the fence of Orion?
9. [[32]] can you give up the [ ] with its sons? [33][
10. [ ] the earth. [[34]
11. [ ] [

Comments

L. 1 (38:23) ד֯]י מנעת. Cf. 𝔐 אשר חשכתי. 𝔗 renders here חשכתי by גנזית (var גנזית), but, in the other cases where 𝔐 has חשך, 𝔗 employs the verb מנע.

L. 1 (38:23) ע֯]קת[א֯. Cf. 𝔐 צר and 𝔗 עקתא.

L. 1 (38:23)] ואשתד֯ר֯. This renders 𝔐 מלחמה, as in col. XXXIII 6 (39:25) אשתדור.

L. 1 (38:24)]. At the end of the line there is room for one more word, possibly the subject of יפק in line 2. This might be a word corresponding to 𝔐 אור, but the context suggests a different word. A reconstruction like רוחא is, however, entirely hypothetical.

L. 2 (38:24) היכא יפק *vac*. The incomplete text at the end of line 1 and the *vacat* here make an understanding of the text difficult. 𝔐 reads אי זה הדרך יחלק אור, but most modern commentators do not see the sense of אור; 𝔊 has πάχνη, 'hoar-frost, rime'. Did the translator or scribe leave a space because he was not sure of the text? היכא renders 𝔐 אי זה הדרך. It can be interpreted as 'where', but this is an Eastern Aramaic form. It seems more likely that היכא is an orthographic variant of היך or היכה, 'how'. יפק is a free interpretation of 𝔐 יחלק. It is not clear whether the form is a *Peʿal* or *Apʿel*.

L. 2 (38:24) ותשוב קדמוהי. ותשוב is a free translation of 𝔐 יפץ. קדמוהי can be interpreted as 'in front of him', or as 'his east winds'. 𝔐 קדים would suggest the latter interpretation, but there are several objections: נשב *Pe*ʿ*al* is intransitive, whereas the *Hap*ʿ*el* is used in the transitive sense; the normal writing is קדום; and the change of 𝔐 'the east wind' to a pl. form with the pronominal suffix is rather strange. It seems more likely that the translator misinterpreted 𝔐.

L. 2 (38:25) שויא. For the form שויא, cf. col. XXIX 6 (37:15). The translator either did not understand the image or wording of 𝔐 'who cleft a channel for the floods', or he objected to the image.

L. 3 (38:25) לעננין קלילין. On קלילין as a rendering of 𝔐 קלות, cf. col. XIII 8 (28:26). The translator took 𝔐 חזיז to be 'cloud'. For this tradition, cf. HAL 290, and the Syriac translation of Sir 32:26, where כעת חזיזים is rendered ܐܝܟ ܥܢܢܐ ܕܡܛܪܐ.

Ll. 3–4 (38:26) להנחתה על ארע / מדבר די לא אנש בה. Cf. 𝔐 להמטיר על ארץ לא איש מדבר לא אדם בו. The translator telescoped the two hemistichs of 𝔐 by combining the two expressions לא איש and לא אדם בו into one phrase לא אנש בה, and the two separate words ארץ and מדבר into one construction ארע מדבר.

L. 4 (38:27) להסבעה. This is a phonetic spelling of להשבעה. In col. XI 5 (27:14), ישבעון is written with its original *śin*.

L. 4 (38:27) שיתא ושביקה. Cf. 𝔐 שאה ומשאה, 'the desolate wasteland' (literally: 'devastation and desolation'). 𝔊 renders ἄβατον καὶ ἀοίκητον; 𝔖 ܟܠ ܒܝܪܐ (Brockelmann, LS ܒܝܪܐ *herba inutilis, virgulta, vepres*; but he also refers to Arabic *wa*ʿ*r regio aspera*); ℭ רונשא ואתרגושתא, 'the noisy and wild'. שית is attested in Aramaic in Sefire 2 A 5; it probably is related to Hebrew שית (cf. HAL for a discussion of the meaning). שביקה may perhaps also refer to some kind of vegetation in the desert. שבקא (Syriac ܫܒܘܩܐ) refers to the branches of the vine, whereas Jastrow mentions שביק, 'abandoned; spontaneous growth'. Sokoloff's suggestions that שיתא derives from an original *שהיתא, 'desert', and that שביקה is used elliptically for ארע שביקה, 'abandoned land', are interesting, but lack corroboration.

L. 6 (38:28) [ע]ני. This renders the *hapax legomenon* 𝔐 אגלי; cf. 𝔊 βώλους; 𝔖 ܢܛܦܬܐ; ℭ רסיסי.

L. 6 (38:29) גלידא. This is the Aramaic rendering of 𝔐 קרח, as in *Tg. Onq.* Gen 31:40 and *Tg. Ezek* 1:22.

L. 6 (38:29) ושיקו[ע שמיא]. Both the reconstruction and the translation, 'covering of the heavens', are uncertain. The word beginning with ושיקו[corresponds to 𝔐 וכפר. However, there is no fitting word meaning 'hoar-frost'. One must therefore assume that the translator either translated a different word or that he interpreted כפר e.g. as a 'covering': שיקו[ע]. שיקוע derives from the stem שקע, which means, among other things, 'to cover'. However, the use of שיקוע ('sinking, covering up, depression') in the sense of 'covering' is not attested, and the types of 'covering' of כפר and שקע differ. This reconstruction demands the addition of שמיא which would have been partly written in the margin. Another possibility is that the word is a form of שיקיא, 'irrigation', pl. 'canals, pools'. Beyer reconstructs ושיקי[ה, and takes the reconstructed suffix to refer to the ice. A more logical reconstruction would be ושיקי[שמיא], 'and the pools of the heavens', referring to the heavenly waters. However, this reconstruction fails to explain the relation to 𝔐 כפר.

L. 7 (38:30) התקרמו מנה. This is a rendering of the image, not of the wording of 𝔐 יתחבאו. ℭ, which has many variant readings, uses the verbs קרש ('to congeal') and טמר ('to hide'); cf. 𝔖 ܐܝܟ ܟܐ̈ܦܐ ܡܬܩܡܛܝܢ ܡ̈ܝܐ 'like stones the water hardens'. The verb קרם ('to overlay, form a skin') is also used in the sense of 'forming a layer of ice upon the water' in Sir 43:20 על כל מעמד מים יקרים.

L. 8 (38:31)]◦עׄ[. If the translator gave a literal rendering of 𝔐, then the traces on frg. E should belong to a word corresponding to 𝔐 מעדנות (𝔊 δεσμόν; 𝔖 ܟܐ̈ܦ; ℭ שירי).

L. 8 (38:31) סיג נפילא. Cf. 𝔐 משכות כסיל. ℭ also uses נפילא (or נפלא) to render כסיל, both here and in Job 9:9. 𝔖 reads in both verses ܓܢܒܪܐ, ('the strong one, hero, giant'; in 9:9 the order of ܟܝܡܐ and ܓܢܒܪܐ is reversed), a similar name for Orion.

L. 8 (38:31) ת[פתח]. Cf. 𝔐 תפתח, but another verbal form, e.g. ת[שרא] (cf. ℭ תשרי), is equally possible.

L. 9 (38:32)]◦◦◦א על בניה תיאש. A rendering of 𝔐 ועיש על בניה תנחם, 'and can you guide the Great Bear with its sons?'. Cf. ℭ וזגתא על אפרחהא ועיש על בנהא תדברנון, 'and can you guide the hen clucking over her chickens and the Great Bear with its sons?'; 𝔖 employs the name ܥܝܘܬܐ, but renders the rest of the hemistich differently. אתא, and perhaps יותא, may refer to the constellation עיש, but neither of these names is consistent with the traces at the beginning of the line. The same goes for the reading יׄוׄאׄ, which may perhaps be the Evening Star.

L. 9 (38:31) תיאש. The verb יאש ('desist from, despair of') always refers to a state of mind and is not a fitting rendering of 𝔐 תנחם. It is rather difficult to determine the meaning of תיאש in this context, and one wonders how the translator interpreted תנחם. S ܐܢܬ ܦܣܩܬ regarded it as a form of נוח.

L. 10 (38:33)]אׄרׄעׄא[. This reading, corresponding to 𝔐 בארץ, fits better here than]עׄנׄנׄין[, corresponding to עב from v 34.

Col. XXXII (Small scroll, col. iv; Frg. F) Job 39:1-11

1 יעלי כפאׄ וחׄב[ל]י֯[ ]◦[ ][2]תמנ]הׄ [י]רׄח֯היׄן

2 שלמין ותנדע עדן מולדהין [3]ילדן בניהן ויפלטן

3 וחבליהן תושר [4]יקשן בניהן ויפק{}ן נפקו ולא תבוא

4 עליהן [5]מן שלח פראה ברחרין וחנקי ערדא מן

5 שרא [6]די שוית דחשת ביתה ומדרה בא֯ע מליחה

6 [7]וחאך על מהמא תקף קרׄיׄאׄ ונגשת שליט לא

7 ישמע [8]ויבחר לה טורין לרׄעׄ[יה ו]בתר כל ירוק

8 ירדף [9]היבא ראמׄ[א ל]מפלחך אׄ[ו]היבית על

9 אוריך [10]התקטרׄ[ראמא ב]צׄוריה וילגׄ[ן] בׄבקעה

10 בׄתׄרׄיך ות◦[ ][11]ה]תׄתרחץ ב[ה ארו] סׄגיא

Mus. Inv. 638
PAM 43.803

NOTES ON READINGS

Frg. F fits in the lacuna of lines 7–10.

L. 1 (39:1)]י֯[ל]וחׄב. The top parts of the letters are broken off. The bottom part of *yod* is clearly visible. It is doubtful whether the faint trace between *bet* and *yod* is the lowest part of the hook of *lamed*.

L. 1 (39:2) תמנ]הׄ [י]רׄח֯היׄן. Only the lower part of the final *nun* can still be seen on the fragment. The *yod* of the suffix can also be read as *waw*. Above the left leg of *ḥet* the lower part of a downstroke is visible. It makes sense to regard this as part of a supralinear *yod*. Before *ḥet* there is a horizontal bar approximately at the midpoint of the height of *ḥet*. The trace above *yod* of ילדן in line 2 suggests that the line gradually dropped, but that ח֯הין was written at the original height of the line. The traces before *reš* therefore can be the lower parts of the legs of *he*.

L. 2 (39:2) מולדהין. The *yod* of the suffix is just as long as *waw*. In שלמין, *yod* is long, too, but all other *yod*s in the column are clearly distinct from *waw*.

L. 3 (39:4) ויפק{}ן. Between *qop* and final *nun* a letter has been erased. The space between the two letters suggests *waw*.

L. 6 (39:7) וחאך. The first letter is clearly *waw*, not *yod*.

L. 6 (39:7) קרׄיׄאׄ. Only the tops of the last letters remain. The trace shows that the last letter is *ʾalep*, not *he*.

L. 7 (39:8) טוריׄן. According to the *ed. princ.* (p. 75), the vestige of final *nun* might also indicate *ʾalep* (טוריׄא). This trace appears slightly higher than the heads of the other letters, which is often the case with final *nun*, not with the right arm of *ʾalep*. The edge of the scroll has now broken off and the skin is no longer extant.

L. 7 (39:8) לרׄעׄ]יה. Cf. the top of frg. F. The second letter is not *mem*. Its identification is not easy because of the stains on the fragment. There is a dark smudge where one would expect the base stroke of a letter. The decisive arguments against *mem* and in favour of *reš* are the angle of the shoulder and the straight line of the head. The tip of the right arm of *ʿayin* is visible. Note that there is just enough space for לרׄעׄ]יה. לרׄעׄ]י would fit better, whereas there is not enough space for the reconstructions למׄלׄ]עס or למׄשׁ]רי.

L. 8 (39:9) ראמׄ]א. If the rest of the reconstruction of the line is correct, ראמׄ]א should be reconstructed and not ראםׄ. The latter reading would give an extraordinarily large space, and the traces fit better with a medial *mem*.

L. 8 (39:9) אׄו] היבית. The lower right part of the diagonal stroke of *ʾalep* can be seen on frg. F. The spot appearing just before *he* of]היבית in PAM 43.803 is a crack in the skin, visible on the fragment.

L. 9 (39:10) ב]צׄוריה. The first, broken letter on frg. F is unlikely to be *taw*. The inclination of the downstroke suggests *ṣade*. The reading ב]נׄיריה is not impossible, though, as *yod* sometimes is connected to the base strokes of *nun* and *taw*.

L. 9 (39:10) וילגׄ[ן]. The downstroke of the letter following *lamed* (and clearly separated from it, therefore excluding the reading ויס]דד) slants to the right, thus suggesting *gimel*, and not e.g. *he*.

L. 10 (39:10) בׄתׄריך. Only some minute specks of the tops of the first two letters are visible on the bottom edge of the column. Even so, the first speck shows the reconstruction אׄחׄריך to be impossible.

L. 10 (39:10) ותׄ◦[. The first letter could also be *yod*. The remains of the third letter consist of a horizontal stroke on the ceiling line, inclining slightly to the left.

L. 10 (39:11) ה]תׄתרחץ. Cf. frg. F. Some parts of the letters are extremely faint in the photograph. The two clear downstrokes at the beginning of the fragment are the legs of the second *taw*. To the right of the first downstroke we can just see the upper left end of a letter, presumably *taw*. Frg. G (cf. UNIDENTIFIED FRAGMENTS) may perhaps be placed to the right of frg. F, in which case one should read]יׄנך תׄתרחץ.

TRANSLATION

1. the mountain goats, and [the birth]-pan[g]s [[2]Do you coun]t their [m]onths
2. in full, and do you know the time they give birth? [3]They give birth to their children and cast them out,
3. and can you send away their progeny? [4]They rear their children and send them out; when they have gone out, they will not return
4. to them. [5]Who has set the wild ass free, and the bonds of the onager, who
5. untied them, [6]whose home I made in the desert, and whose dwelling place in salt land?
6. [7]And he laughs at the tumult of the strong city, and the driving of the ruler he does not
7. hear. [8]And he chooses for himself mountains as [his] past[ure, and] after anything green
8. he hunts. [9]Does [the] wild ox want [to] serve you, o[r] will he spend the night in
9. your stable? [10]Can you tie [the wild ox with] his rope, and will he til[l] in the valley
10. behind you, and [[11]Can] you trust in [him because] is great

COMMENTS

L. 1 (39:2) תמנ]הׄ. The reconstruction corresponds to 𝔐 תספר; cf. 𝔗 תמני.

L. 1 (39:2) [י]רׄחׄהין. Note the suffix here and in 𝔊 αὐτῶν μῆνας, whereas there is none in 𝔐, 𝔖, or 𝔗. This may perhaps be a textual variant, but it is more likely that this translator and 𝔊 added the suffix.

Ll. 1–2 (39:2) מולדהי̇ן . . . [י]רח̇הי̇ן. Logically, the suffixes of [י]רח̇הי̇ן and מולדהי̇ן refer to female animals. Grammatically, we should therefore not read the suffix הון-. These are, however, the only two instances in the preserved text where the fem. pl. ending is written *plene*. In the next verse the usual defective spelling is employed. Perhaps the suffixes refer to the חבלי, understood in the sense of the product of the birth-pangs, i.e. their progeny, as in line 3.

L. 2 (39:3) ילדן בניהן. A plain rendering of 𝔐 תכרענה ילדיהן.

L. 2 (39:3) ויפלטן. *Paʿel* or *Peʿal*, rendering 𝔐 תפלחנה; cf. col. IV 9 (21:10).

L. 3 (39:3) וחבליהן. This word, as well as 𝔐 חבליהם and 𝔊 ὠδῖνας, can refer either to birth-pangs, or to its product.

L. 3 (39:3) תושר. Cf. 𝔐 תשלחנה. For the 2nd masc. sing. form, cf. 𝔊 ὠδῖνας αὐτῶν ἐξαποστελεῖς. The *Apʿel* of ישר occurs in Egyptian Aramaic papyri with the meaning 'to send'.

L. 3 (39:4) יקשן בניהן ויפק{}]. The two verbs are fem., and therefore *Apʿel* forms, with בניהן as object, whereas 𝔐 בניהם is the subject of יחלמו and ירבו. יפק{}] corresponds to 𝔐 ירבו בבר. Note, however, that one 𝔐 manuscript has ילכו instead of ירבו.

L. 3 (39:4) תבוא. The *ʾalep* is orthographic and indicates *-ū*.

L. 4 (39:5) ברחרין. 𝔐 חפשי; cf. 𝔗 בר חורי; 𝔖 ܒܢܝ ܚܐܪ̈ܐ.

L. 5 (39:6) דחשת. Cf. 𝔐 ערבה. This is the first occurrence of the Persian loanword דחשת in Aramaic. On this word, cf. the discussions of Greenfield and Shaked, and of Rundgren.[2]

L. 5 (39:6) בא̇ר̇ע מליחה. Cf. 𝔐 מלחה; 𝔗 ארע צדיא, 'the desolate land'; 𝔖 ܒܐܬܪܐ ܡܠܝܚܐ. מליחה is a passive participle, not a substantive.

L. 6 (39:7) מהמא תקף ק̇ר̇י̇א̇. 𝔐 reads המון קריה. המון can mean 'tumult' (𝔗 רגוש) or 'crowd, multitude' (𝔊 πολυοχλία; 𝔖 ܣܘܓܐܐ). Several interpretations of תקף are possible. It may be another word for 'noise', but, if so, why did the translator add it? Or did the translator try to convey the second meaning of המון by means of תקף, 'strength'? On the other hand, תקף can be a 'stronghold', thus תקף קריא meaning 'a strong city'.

L. 6 (39:7) ונגשת שליט. Cf. 𝔐 תשאות נוגש. The root נגש is probably not Aramaic (the dictionaries refer to wrong readings). The word נגשת is therefore probably an *ad hoc* borrowing from 𝔐. In 𝔐, the participle נגש usually refers to taskmasters, rulers, or oppressors (cf. e.g. Job 3:18 לא שמעו קול נגש). The use of the word שליט (cf. 𝔖 ܫ̈ܠܝܛܐ) suggests that the translator interpreted נגש as a ruler, not a driver. 𝔊 translates φορολόγος, 'tax-gatherer', both in 3:18 and 39:7.

L. 7 (39:8) ויבחר. Cf. 𝔐 יתור. Like 𝔗 יאליל and 𝔊 κατασκέψεται, the translator interpreted יתור as the *Qal* of תור, 'to explore'. 𝔖 ܒܣܘܓܐܐ apparently derived the form from יתר (cf. Aramaic יתיר).

L. 7 (39:8) לר̇ע̇]יה. Cf. 𝔐 מרעהו. The reconstruction לר̇ע̇]י is also possible.

L. 8 (39:9) היבא ראמ̇]א ל[מפלחך א̇]ו. The construction of 𝔐, *he* interrogative followed by אם, is rendered here by *he* interrogative followed by או; cf. also cols. XXXIV 3–4 (40:8-9) and XXXV 5–6 (40:27). In the next line, however, the translator employs *waw* instead of או.

L. 9 (39:10) ראמא ב[צוריה. The lacuna is not big enough for a rendering of 𝔐 רים בתלם. In view of the difficult construction of 𝔐 and the need to supply an object, one should reconstruct ראמא.

L. 9 (39:10) ב[צוריה. Cf. 𝔐 עבתו. The ending יה- is an unusual spelling of either the determined masc. pl. noun (elsewhere in the text יא-) or the 3rd masc. sing. pronominal suffix attached to a sing. noun (elsewhere ה-). The suffix 𝔐 עבתו indicates the latter.

L. 9 (39:10) וילגנ[ן]. This is the only sensible reconstruction which corresponds to 𝔐 ישדד, even though the verb לגן is not attested in other texts. *Tg. Isa* 28:25 employs לוגנין to render 𝔐 שׂורה, but the meaning of שׂורה, and therefore of לוגן, is disputed. Whatever its meaning in 𝔐, the translator probably interpreted שורה as 'row, line'. The tilling and planting terminology in Isa 28:24-25, and especially the use of שדד in v 24, strongly suggest that לגן means 'harrowing' or a similar tilling activity.

---

[2] J. C. Greenfield and S. Shaked, 'Three Iranian Words in the Targum of Job from Qumran', *ZDMG* 122 (1972) 38–9; F. Rundgren, 'Aramaica II', *Or.Suex.* 22 (1973) 72–3.

L. 10 (39:10) בׄתׄרׄיך. The reading is based upon 𝔐 אחריך. Note, however, that 𝔊 and 𝔖 have no word corresponding to אחריך.

L. 10]ותׄ֯. The broken word is probably the beginning of a verbal form. The space between this word and the beginning of 39:11 on frg. F indicates one or two missing words: The text had a clause missing from 𝔐 and the versions.

L. 10 (39:11) ה]תׄתרחץ. 𝔐 התבטח; cf. 𝔗 איפשר דתתרחץ.

Col. XXXIII (Small scroll, col. v; Frgs. I, K, L1) Job 39:20-29

[ ] [20]התזיענה בתׄקׄף֯[
בס{֯}רוהי אימה ודחלה [21]וחפר בבקע וירוט ויחדא
ובחיל ינפק לאנפי חרב [22]יחאך על דחלא ולא
יזוע ולא יתוב מן אנפי חרב [23]עלוהי יתלה שלט
שנן ונזך וחרף סיף [25]ולקל קרנא יאמר האח ומן
רחיק יריח קרבה ולנקשת זין וזעקת אשתדור
יחדה { } [26]המן חכמתך יסתער נצא ויפרוס
כנפוהׄי לרוחין [27]או על מאמרך יתגבׄהׄ נׄשׄרא
ועזׄאׄ יׄרׄיׄם קנׄ[ה [28]ב]כׄפא ישכון ויקנׄ[ ]֯ ֯[
] [29]מׄןׄ תׄ[מה י]חׄצׄאׄ מׄאׄכׄל[א

Mus. Inv. 638
PAM 43.803*, 43.804*

NOTES ON READINGS

The lacuna in lines 7–8 can be reconstructed by means of frg. I. Frg. L of the *editio princeps* consists of two partially superimposed fragments. The largest, frg. L1, fits at the end of lines 7–9. Frg. K, with only one trace, fits between frg. L1 and the next column.

L. 1 (39:20) בתׄקׄף֯[. Only the tails of *qop* and final *pe* are visible.

L. 2 (39:20) בס{֯}רוהי. It is clear from the original MS that a letter has been intentionally abraded, and traces of one or two downstrokes are still visible. The abraded space between בס and רוהי is larger than any other space between words in the column, but is exactly the size of *ḥet*. Did the MS originally read בסחרוהי, the *ḥet* being abraded for some unknown reason, or did it originally contain some other letter which was abraded in order to be corrected to *ḥet*?

L. 5 (39:24) שנן ונזך. This is probably a scribal error, to be corrected to ושנן נזך.

L. 7 (39:25-26) { }. Frg. I can no longer be located, but the upper edge of the scroll here, as well as the right edge, shows that the surface of the skin has been scraped and is abraded as in other corrections (from the scroll it seems that the blank abraded space is exactly the same as in col. XXX 1 before פתגם).

L. 7 (39:26) נצא. The dots above and below *nun* are not ink.

L. 7 (39:26) ויפרוס. The bottom left part of *samek* is preserved on frg. L1.

L. 8 (39:26) כנפוה̇י̇ לרוחין. The *yod* of כנפוה̇י̇, and the entire word לרוחין, are preserved on frg. I.

L. 8 (39:27) יתגב̇ה̇ נ̇ש̇רא. Only the uppermost tops of *he* and *nun* are visible. The small scroll preserves the tops of *šin*; frg. L1 preserves the left arm. The base stroke attached to the *reš*, thus suggesting *bet*, is a trace of ink from the writing on the upper fragment. The left leg of *ʾalep* appears on frg. K.

L. 9 (39:27) י̇ר̇י̇ם. Only faint traces of the first three letters can be discerned (frg. I).

L. 10 (39:29)]מ̇ן̇ ת̇]מה י]ח̇צ̇א מ̇אכל[א. Traces of the first three letters can be seen on frg. I. The remains of the first two are very vague. Only the last letter, *taw* or *he*, is fairly clear. The word read as י]ח̇צ̇א̇ is very damaged, but the combination of the traces rules out most reconstructions such as]ח̇פ̇ר̇.

TRANSLATION

1. [ ] [20]Can you make him leap with strength [
2. When he { } there is fright and fear. [21]And he paws in the valley, and gallops and rejoices,
3. and with force he goes out to the sword. [22]He laughs at fear, and neither
4. does he tremble nor turn away from the sword. [23]On him are hanging quiver,
5. sharp-edged lance, and whetted sword. [25]At the sound of the horn he says 'Aha', and from
6. afar he smells the battle, and at the clash of weapons and the battle-cry
7. he rejoices. { } [26]Is it by your wisdom that the falcon soars and spreads
8. his wings to the winds? [27]Or is it at your command that the eagle mounts,
9. and the black eagle builds [its] nest up high? [[28]On] the cliff it dwells and nests [ ] [
10. [ ][29]From the[re it] picks out [the] food [

COMMENTS

L. 1 (39:20) התזיענה. A literal translation of 𝔐 התרעישנו (cf. 𝔖 ܡܙܝܥ ܐܢܬ ܠܗ).

L. 1 (39:20) בתקף̇[. Probably an explanatory addition. At the end of the line one should reconstruct a rendering of 𝔐 כארבה; cf. 𝔗 היך גובאי; 𝔖 ܐܝܟ ܩܡܨܐ. The rendering of 𝔊, περιέθεκας δὲ αὐτῷ πανοπλίαν, shows that the translator did not understand the simile. The hemistich in 𝔊 is based upon v 19.

L. 2 (39:20) בס{ם}רוהי. Cf. 𝔐 הוד נחרו, literally 'the splendour of his snort'. One is tempted to surmise that בסחרוהי was either the original word, or, more likely, the intended word. The hitherto unattested verb סחר must be a cognate of the Arabic verb *šaḫara*, 'to snore; to snort; to neigh, whinny'. 𝔊 and 𝔖 did not understand נחרו.

L. 2 (39:20) אימה ודחלה. Cf. 𝔐 אימה. This is hardly a case of multiple translation, but rather of reinforcement.

L. 2 (39:21) וירוט. An addition to 𝔐.

L. 3 (39:21) ובחיל. Like 𝔊, the translator regards 𝔐 בכח as part of the second hemistich.

Ll. 3–4 (39:22) יחאך על דחלה ולא / יזוע. The stems דחל and זוע are regularly employed together. Cf. Dan 5:19; 6:27; *Tg. Onq.* Deut 2:25.

L. 4 (39:23) יתלה. This *Itpeʿel* renders the *hapax legomenon* 𝔐 תרנה.

L. 4 (39:23) שלט. Borger has demonstrated that שלט (here rendering 𝔐 אשפה) and Akkadian *šalṭu*/*šal(l)aṭu* refer to a 'quiver' or a 'bowcase'.[3]

---

[3] R. Borger, 'Die Waffenträger des Königs Darius', *VT* 22 (1972) 385–98.

L. 5 (39:23) שנן ונזך. שנן is the blade of a weapon, and נזך an Iranian loanword meaning 'lance' (cf. Greenfield and Shaked, 'Three Iranian Words', 40–42). The corrected reading ושנן נזך corresponds precisely to 𝔐 להב חנית, a 'sharp-edged lance'.

L. 5 (39:23) וחרף סיף. Cf. 𝔐 וכידון. It is possible that the translator interpreted 𝔐 להב as a qualifier of both חנית and כידון. חרף, then, is the second translation of להב.

L. 5 (39:25) ולקל קרנא. The translation of 𝔐 39:24 is missing. ולקל קרנא may be the rendering of 𝔐 בדי שפר, but the expression קול שופר also occurs at the end of v 24. The translator either combined the end of v 24 and the beginning of v 25, or employed the same Aramaic rendering for both expressions of 𝔐.

Ll. 6–7 (39:25) ולנקשת זין וזעקת אשתדור / יחדה. Whereas the first two hemistichs of v 25 correspond literally to 𝔐, the third exhibits some small deviations. ולנקשת זין seems to render רעם שרים, but the translator probably interpreted 𝔐 שרים as the pl. participle of שרה, 'to contend'. וזעקת אשתדור renders 𝔐 ותרועה. The verb יחדה, which is missing from 𝔐, is possibly another case of a second translation—here, of 𝔐 יאמר האח, which 𝔗 יימר חדווא also understood as a shout of joy.

L. 7 (39:26) יסתער. A rendering of the *hapax legomenon* יאבר. The verb also occurs in *Tg. 2 Kgs* 6:11, where the subject is the heart of the king of Aram, and the verb is probably used metaphorically (cf. the English verb 'to flutter'). Here the meaning most likely is 'to soar on the winds'.

L. 8 (39:26) לרוחין. Cf. 𝔐 לתימן, 'to the south'. רוחין expresses the meanings 'to the winds' and 'to (all) directions'.

L. 9 (39:27) ועוזא̊. 'And the black eagle' corresponds to 𝔐 וכי, which can be interpreted as the emphatic article (cf. 𝔗 וארום). 𝔊 also mentions a bird, however: γύψ. It is possible that כי was the name of a bird, and that both the Greek and the Aramaic translator thought 𝔐 referred to this כי-bird.[4]

L. 9 (39:28) ויקנ̊ן[. Cf. 𝔐 ויתלנן.

L. 10 (39:29) מ̇ן ת̇]מה י[ח̇צ̇א̊ מ̊אכ̇ל]א. מ̊אכ̇ל]א corresponds to 𝔐 אכל. חצא, 'to peck, pick out', is used as a rendering of 𝔐 נקר in *Tg. Prov* 30:17, a verse describing the eating of birds. That would imply that the author did not grasp the special meaning of חפר, 'to espy' (cf. 𝔗 מאלילי) intended here. מ̇ן ת̇]מה corresponds to 𝔐 משם.

VARIANTS

39:21 (2) 𝔐 יחפרו] 𝔊𝔖𝔙 (יחפור) וחפר

Col. XXXIV (Small scroll, col. vi; Frg. H) Job 40:5-14 (15?)

[לא] א̊סוף̇ *vac* מן ר̊]וחא *va[cat*
6ענא אלהא לאיוב וענ̇א̊ וא̇מר לה 7אסר
נא כגבר חלציך אשאלנך והתיבני פתגם 8האף
תעדא דינה ותחיבנני על דברת די תזכא 9או
הא ד˺ע כאלה איתי לך או בקל כותה תרעם
10העדי נא גוה ורם רוח וזוי והדר ויקר תלבש

---

4 G. R. Driver, 'Job 39:27-28: The *KY*-Bird', *PEQ* 104 (1972) 64–6; M. Dahood, 'Four Ugaritic Personal Names and Job 39:5.26-27', *ZAW* 87 (1975) 220.

[11]העדי נא חמת רגזך וחזא כל גאה והשפלה [12]וכל 7

רמת רוח תתבר והטפי ר֯[שיעין תחו]ת֯יהון [13]וטמר 8

[ה]מ֯ון בעפר { } כח֯[דא אנפי]ה֯ון בקטם תכסה 9

[[14?]]∘∘∘[ ]ה֯[ ]א֯ איתי 10

Mus. Inv. 638
PAM 43.803*, 43.805*

NOTES ON READINGS

Frg. N was placed in the *ed. princ.* in line 8. Though the letters fit, the fragment cannot be placed here on material grounds. Frg. H preserves remnants of lines 9–10.

L. 1 (40:5) אֹ֯סוף [לא]. The traces of *ʾalep* are less clear than those of the following letters. Yet, the left arm and part of the diagonal stroke are recognizable. [ולא] would fit between the right margin and אֹ֯סוף, though the space separating the two words is very narrow; [לא] seems a better reconstruction.

L. 1 (40:6) מן ר֯[וחא. Although the letters are written in line 1, at the same distance from line 2 as the others at the beginning of the line, they should be interpreted as a supralinear addition to line 2, written high because of the empty space.

L. 5 (40:9) תרעם. Only the bottom tip of the *reš* can be seen next to the base of *taw*.

L. 9 (40:13) [ה]מ֯ון. The remains of the first letter could also belong to *taw*, but [ה]מ֯ון makes more sense.

L. 9 (40:13) אנפי]ה֯ון בקטם. Frg. H preserves ה֯ון בק and a small piece of the *ṭet*.

L. 10 (40:14?) א֯[. Or final *nun*.

L. 10 (40:14?) איתי. When enlarged, PAM 43.805 clearly shows that the vertical stroke just before *taw* is another *yod*.

TRANSLATION

1. I will [not] add. *vacat* out of [the] w[ind *vac*]*at*
2. [6]God answered Job and the cloud, and said to him: [7]Gird
3. then your loins like a man; I will question you and you shall answer me. [8]Would you really
4. annul the judgement, and declare me guilty, so that you would be innocent? [9]Or
5. do you perhaps have an arm like a god, or can you thunder with a voice like his?
6. [10]Remove, then, pride and haughtiness, and put on grandeur and majesty and dignity.
7. [11]Remove, then, the heat of your anger, and look at every proud person and bring him down. [12]And all
8. haughtiness will be broken, and extinguish wi[cked people in] their [pla]ce, [13]and hide
9. [th]em in the dust { } toge[ther] cover their [faces] with ashes.
10. [[14?]] [ ] bring

COMMENTS

L. 1 (40:5) אֹ֯סוף [לא]. Cf. 𝔐 ולא אוסיף. Col. XXXVII 5–6 also corresponds to the text of 𝔐 40:5, but here the verse ends with לא אוסף. Presumably, אֹ֯סוף is a scribal error for אוסף.

Ll. 2–3 (40:7) אסר / נא כגבר חלציך אשאלנך והתיבני פתגם. Cf. the identical wording of col. XXX 1 (38:3).

L. 4 (40:8) תעדא. Cf. 𝔐 תפר; ℭ תשני; 𝔖 ܡܒܛܠ ܐܢܬ. There is no reason to assume that the translator objected to the idea that divine judgement could be 'broken'. Both הפר and עדא are used for the meaning 'annul'; cf. Dan 6:9, 13 (*Peʿal* 'to be annulled').

L. 4 (40:8) דינה. Cf. 𝔐 משפטי. The ending of דינה could be either the pronominal suffix or the indicator of the determinate state. Since the translator uses 1st person suffixes in the next hemistich, the latter interpretation is more likely.

L. 4 (40:8) על דברת די. 'So that'. A construction attested in Official Aramaic, but not in the Middle Aramaic dialects.

L. 5 (40:9) הא. This is most likely an interjection, though it does reinforce the interrogative aspect of the sentence. The meaning 'is it that?', listed by Jastrow, is dubious: in some manuscripts of *Tg. Job*, הא is simply an orthographic variant of the interrogative *he*.

L. 5 (40:9) כאלה. This word renders 𝔐 כאל. Since the usual form in the MS is אלהא, one must either assume a scribal mistake by haplography, or an intentional change referring to a god or celestial being. The first assumption is more probable.

L. 6 (40:10) העדי נא. This seems to be a literal translation of 𝔐 עדה נא, but the expressions are opposites. עדה means 'to deck oneself with ornament', but Aramaic העדי means 'to remove'. Cf. *Tg. Zech* 3:4 with the same Aramaic verbs העדי (𝔐 העביר) and הלבש. This interpretation forces a negative understanding of the object גאון וגבה.

L. 6 (40:10) ורם רוח. Cf. 𝔐 גבה. It makes no sense to regard רם as an adjective; it therefore must be a noun, like רמת in line 8.

L. 6 (40:10) וזוי. Cf. 𝔐 והוד. זוי is most likely a scribal mistake for זיו.

L. 6 (40:10) ויקר. The addition of יקר must be attributed to the common association of the words זיו, הדר, and יקר; cf. Dan 4:27, 33; 5:18 (without זיו).

L. 7 (40:11) העדי נא. The expression is used once more, now to render 𝔐 הפץ.

L. 7 (40:12) וכל. Cf. 𝔐 ראה כל. 𝔐 employs ראה in both vv 11b and 12a. The translator combines both hemistichs by substituting *waw* for ראה. 𝔊 omits ראה in both hemistichs.

L. 8 (40:12) רמת רוח. Cf. 𝔐 גאה. There is no need to assume that the translator and 𝔊 (ὑπερήφανος) read גבה. The expressions are synonymous to such an extent that translators (both ancient and modern) do not have to use the same renderings all the time.

L. 8 (40:12) תתבר. Cf. 𝔐 הכניעהו (ℭ ותברניה). The form can be read as a 2nd masc. sing. imperfect *Peᶜal*, or as a 3rd fem. sing. *Itpeᶜel*.

L. 9 (40:13) אנפי]ה̊ון בקטם̇. קטם is the common translation of 𝔐 אפר in the targums; cf. e.g. col. XXXVII 9 (42:6). Because of the common Biblical Hebrew phrase עפר ואפר, the translator probably equated 𝔐 טמון with אפר. In spite of the different wording, the translator expresses the same idea as 𝔐. In the gap one might reconstruct אנפי]ה̊ון with or without the conjunction *waw*.

L. 10 אייתי. The two *yod*s suggest a *Hapᶜel*/*Apᶜel* of אתא, but the spelling is exceptional. Elsewhere in 11QtgJob perfect forms are written with *he* (*Hapᶜel*), so one should identify the form as a 1st sing. imperfect. The final *yod* indicates a final *ī*. The word does not correspond to 𝔐, but perhaps the translator gave a free rendering of the second hemistich of v 14.

VARIANTS

40:6 (1, 2) ועננ̊א̊ (above: מן ר̊[וחא]) 𝔊 (διὰ λαίλαπος καὶ νεφῶν)] 𝔐 מנ סערה

40:12 (8) והטפי 𝔊 (σβέσον = הדעך)] 𝔐 והדך

Col. XXXV (Small scroll, col. vii; Frg. M) Job 40:23-31

[23] 1

ירדנא גאפה יתׄרחץ די יקבלנה אג̊ו̊נ̊א̊ 2

24במטל עינוהי יכלנה כבחכה יזיב אפה 25התגד 3

תנין בחכא או בחבל תחרז לשנה [26]התשוא
זמם באפה ובחרתך תקוב לסתה [27]הימלל
עמך בניח או ימלל עמך בהתחננה לך [28]היקים
קים עמך ותדברנה לעבד עלם [29]התחאך
בה כצׄפר וׄתקטרנה בחוטא לבנתך [30]ויתׄ[ ]ן
]]תין ויׄפׄלגון יתה בארע[[
[31]]]גׄוׄן די נונין[

Mus. Inv. 638
PAM 43.804*, 43.806*

NOTES ON READINGS

Frg. M fits in the first gap in line 8, preserving also the tail of the final *kap* of עמך in line 7. No holes are visible on the front of the stitching; the skin of this sheet overlaps only 3 cm with the wider skin of the following sheet. A clear vertical mark shows the pressure of the stitching in the next revolution; this stripe is 6 cm from the stitching (2 cm less than the stripe on col. XXX, in relation to the stitching which has caused its deterioration).

L. 2 (40:23) אׄגׄוׄגׄאׄ. Apart from the first *ʾalep*, only the bottom parts of several letters can be discerned. The diagonal downstrokes suggest *gimel*s. The legs of final *ʾalep* are fainter than the other traces. The trace of *waw* is uncertain.

L. 8 (40:29) כצׄפר וׄתקטרנה. Frg. M fills the gap in the small scroll. The *waw* is very faint, but it must be a trace; otherwise the space between the two words would be rather long.

L. 8 (40:30) ויתׄ[ ]ן. There is a dark spot before final *nun*, but this is due to a crack in the skin.

L. 9 (40:30) It is unlikely that the trace at the beginning of the line is the remnant of a letter, unless the scribe wrote the letter high above the ceiling line.

L. 9 (40:30) בארע[. The *ʿayin* is clear on the fragment.

L. 10 (40:31)]גׄוׄן. The first letter can be either *gimel* or *nun*. The second is *waw* or *yod*.

TRANSLATION

1. [[23]]
2. the Jordan its bank, he is confident that the fissure will receive him.
3. [24]Can one overpower him by covering his eyes, make his nose bleed as with a hook? [25]Can you draw
4. the crocodile with a hook, or thread his tongue with a rope? [26]Can you put
5. a ring in his nose, and pierce his jaw with your needle? [27]Will he speak
6. gently with you, or will he speak with you in supplication? [28]Will he conclude
7. a pact with you, and will you take him as a slave forever? [29]Can you play
8. with him as with a bird and tie him with a thread for your daughters? [30]And will [ ]
9. [ ] and will they divide him in [the] land [ ]
10. [[31]] of fishes [

Comments

L. 2 (40:23) ירדנא גאפה. It is clear that the translator gave a free rendering of 𝔐. He probably telescoped the two halves of the verse. Because of the strange form גאפה and the severely damaged word at the end of the line, no interpretation can be certain. גאפה has been explained as a *Paʿel* perfect of גוף, 'to enclose', or as an orthographic variant of גיף, 'riverbank'. 𝔊 renders the first part of 𝔐 very freely: 'when there is a flood'; 𝔖 'when the river jumps' (ܢܫܘܪ). 𝔗 employs the verb טלם, 'to oppress', which it always uses to render עשק. There are two arguments in favour of interpreting גאף as a variant of גיף. First, this kind of orthographic variation is less unusual than גאף for גוף. Second, the use of the verb גוף here corresponds with nothing in either 𝔐 or the versions, whereas the image of the Jordan overflowing its bank corresponds to 𝔊, and, possibly, to 𝔖.

L. 2 (40:23) יקבלנה אג̇ו̇נ̇א̇. The clause does not correspond to 𝔐 or any of the versions. The idea is that the hippopotamus can retreat to the fissures alongside the riverbank.

L. 3 (40:24) במטל עינוהי. Cf. 𝔐 בעיניו יקחנו. The expression נטל עינוהי, 'to lift one's eyes', is quite common, and one may interpret the sentence as 'when he (i.e. the hippopotamus) lifts his eyes'. The infinitive in connection with the preposition *bet* (or *kap*) expressing a time-determination is possible, but not common in Aramaic. Alternatively, מטל can be explained as the infinitive of טלל, 'to cover', and *bet* in an instrumental sense. Herodotus *Hist.* 2.70 describes how the Egyptians catch crocodiles, by first covering their eyes with mud.

L. 3 (40:24) יכלנה. The imperfect of either יכל, 'to overcome' (cf. Dan 7:21), or כלא, 'to restrain'. The first meaning is a little more appropriate in the context.

L. 3 (40:24) כבחכה. 'As with a hook'; cf. 𝔐 במוקשים. 𝔖, too, employs the same word (ܒܚܟܬܐ) for מוקשים in v 24, and חכה in v 25.

L. 3 (40:24) יזיב. Cf. 𝔐 ינקב, 'to pierce'. For זוב, only the meaning 'to flow', especially used with regard to blood, is attested. Even though the interrogative particle is missing, it seems logical to understand the verse as a question.

L. 4 (40:25) תנין. Cf. 𝔐 לויתן; 𝔊 δράκοντα; 𝔖 ܬܢܝܢܐ; 𝔗 לויתן.

L. 4 (40:25) תחרז. Cf. 𝔐 תשקיע. The exact sense of השקיע is unknown, but חרז has the meaning 'to perforate, to string (pearls)'. Cf. 𝔗 תקדח, 'to bore, perforate'. 𝔖 three times uses the general word ܐܣܪ: for the last verb of v 24 and for both verbs of this verse.

L. 5 (40:26) זמם. 'Muzzle', 'ring through the nose'. Cf. 𝔐 אגמון; 𝔊 κρίκος, 'ring, nose ring'; 𝔖 ܦܓܘܕܬܐ, 'bridle'; 𝔗 אונקלא, 'hook'. Cf. *Tg. 2 Kgs* 19:28 which also uses זמם (𝔐 מתג) connected with 𝔐 חח.

L. 5 (40:26) ובחרתך. Cf. 𝔐 ובחוח. The word has been analysed as the noun חרת connected with the verb חרת, 'to engrave', with a pronominal suffix, or as an Iranian loanword (from **xurtaka*-) meaning 'thorn'. However, this word first occurs in Middle Persian (*xurdag*) and the meaning 'thorn' is attested only in New Persian (*xurda*). The noun חרת would refer to something sharp (a stylus, needle, or hook) fit for engraving, but also for piercing. 𝔗 renders 𝔐 בחוח with בסילוא ובשירא, 'with a rod and a chain'. שירא is the translation of חח/חוח in e.g. *Tg. 2 Kgs* 19:28 and *Tg. Ezek* 29:4 (*Tg. Ezek* 19:4 has שישלן and *Tg. 2 Chr* 33:11 כירומנקיא 'handcuffs'), whereas סלוא, 'rod, thorn', is the rendering of חוח, 'thorn'. 𝔊 ψελίῳ, 'with a (curb-)chain'.

L. 5 (40:26) לסתה. לסת is the common targumic rendering of 𝔐 לחי.

Ll. 5–6 (40:27) הימלל / עמך בניח או ימלל עמך בהתחננה לך. The order of the two hemistichs is the reverse of that in 𝔐. The translator used ימלל as a rendering both of ידבר and of ירבה. 𝔊 uses only one verb: λαλήσει. There is no need to conjecture that the translator read ידברה instead of ירבה, or that a copyist omitted the word רברבן. The translator simply used a more general expression. For the meaning of התחנן, cf. Dan 6:12.

L. 8 (40:29) בחוטא. This is an addition to 𝔐.

L. 8 (40:29) לבנתך. Cf. 𝔐 לנערותיך. 𝔊 reads ὥσπερ στρουθίον παιδίῳ, 'like a sparrow for a child', combining two interpretations of נער, as 'child' and 'sparrow' (cf. Arabic *nuġar*, 'sparrow, swallow').

L. 8 (40:30) ויתׄ[ ]ן. A verbal form corresponding to 𝔐 יכרו. The meaning of this verb (cf. also Job 6:27) is not certain. Modern scholars suggest 'to barter'. 𝔊 (ἐνσιτοῦνται) and 𝔗 (יעבדון שירותא) interpret it as 'to give a feast'; 𝔖 ܢܬܟܒܪܘܢ. In Job 6:27, 𝔗 employs the verb חשל, 'to scheme', and 𝔊 ἐνάλλεσθε, 'rush against' (but could this be a corruption of a form of ἐναλλάσσω?). There is no way of knowing how the translator interpreted 𝔐 יכרו.

L. 9 (40:30) חין[. The broken word corresponds to 𝔐 חברים, if the translator attempted a literal rending. However, neither 𝔊 (ἔθνη) nor 𝔗 (חכימיא) are literal translations of 𝔐.

L. 9 (40:30) ויפלגון יתה. Cf. 𝔐 יחצוהו. 𝔗 and 𝔖 also use the verb פלג. This is the only occurrence of the particle ית in Qumran Aramaic.

L. 9 (40:30) בארע]. Cf. 𝔐 בין כנענים, which is to be understood as 'among the merchants'. Thus 𝔗 תגריא and 𝔙 *negotiatores*. 𝔊 reads Φοινίκων γένη, possibly a rendering of בית כנענים (cf. 𝔖 [illegible]).

L. 10 (40:31)]גון די נונין[. Since נונין corresponds to 𝔐 דגים, the word ending in גון probably renders 𝔐 צלצל. 𝔗 בגנונא and 𝔖 [illegible] derive this word from צל, 'shadow', whereas 𝔊 renders ἐν πλοίοις ἁλιέων, 'in fishing boats' (cf. also Isa 18:1). Modern scholars interpret both 𝔐 שכות and צלצל as 'harpoons' and 'spears'. Since we do not know how the translator interpreted these words, any reconstruction is very uncertain.

Col. XXXVI (Small scroll, col. viii) Job 41:7-17

[7]גׄבׄוׄהׄ[י] ◦[ ]והׄי שׂ[י]רׄ[יא [8]חדה]
לחדה ידבקן ורוח לׄ[א י]נעול בינה{ו}ן [9]אנתה
לחברתה חענן ולא יתפׄ[ר]שן [10]עטישתה תדלק
נורא בין עינוהי כממח פרׄא [11]מן פמה לפידין
יפקון בלשני אשה ירטון [12]מׄןׄ נחירוה יפק תנן
לכוש יקד ומגמר [13]נפשה גמׄרין תגסא וזיקין
יפקן מן פמה [14]בצורה יבית תקפה וקדמוהי
תרוט עלימו [15]קפלי בשרה דבקין נסיכׄ[ן בה]
כפרזלא [16]ולבׄ[ב]ה]◦◦[ ]דׄ כאבׄןׄ וׄ[
[17?]◦◦◦◦[ ]פח[דו] תבׄ[י]ריא
[ ]לׄ[

Mus. Inv. 638
PAM 43.807

NOTES ON READINGS

The vertical rulings are deeper than on the previous sheet. The vertical ruling is faint, but visible. After the last column of text the skin has also been ruled, but the last vertical ruling cannot be seen. The dimension of the column between the rulings is 7.9 cm (the scribe has written above the ruling in all the lines).

L. 1 (41:7)]◦ [גֿבֿוֿהֿ[י. The letters are hard to identify because only the bottoms remain. The first letter is *ʾalep* or *gimel*. Only the base stroke of the second letter remains. The three vertical strokes standing close to one another suggest a combination of *he* with *yod* or *waw*. Another possible reading is גֿבֿהֿהֿ. The first letter of the next word is in all likelihood *kap*, *mem*, or *pe*. The remains can be seen only in the photograph; they are no longer visible on the manuscript.

L. 1 (41:7) שֿ[י]רֿיא. The first letter is *šin* or *samek*; the following downstroke suggests *dalet* or *reš*. Only *yod* fits in between them.

L. 2 (41:8) לֿ[א י]נעול. The hook of *lamed* is distorted. The *nun* is certain, and almost complete.

L. 2 (41:8) בינה{ו}ן. The erasure between *he* and final *nun* shows that the scribe first wrote בינהון. The upper part of the head of *waw* is still visible.

L. 4 (41:10) פרֿא. The reading is usually transcribed as פ[ר]א, but the photograph clearly shows a vertical trace at the edge of the tear. On the fragment there is now a fold covering the *pe*, such that the *reš* cannot be verified.

L. 5 (41:12) מֿן. Only a small part of the downstroke of final *nun* remains, but the reading is certain.

L. 6 (41:13) גמֿרין. The tip of the left oblique is all that is visible of *mem*.

L. 8 (41:15) נסיכֿ[ן בה]. At the end of the word there is a dark spot which may be the top of final *nun*. There is no trace of a word after נסיכֿ[ן. עלוהי] is impossible; בה] might just fit without leaving any trace at the other side of the lacuna.

L. 9 (41:16)]◦◦[ ]דֿ. The last letter can also be final *kap*. The uppermost tops of two (or three) letters appear at the bottom edge of the scroll.

L. 9 (41:16) כאבֿןֿ. Small parts of final *nun* are still visible.

L. 10 (41:17?)]◦◦◦◦. The narrow, ticked head of the third (fourth?) letter resembles the head of *kap*.

L. 10 (41:17?)]תבֿ[י]ריא. The empty space before *taw* suggests it is the first letter of the word. The next letter is barely legible, but traces of a head, a downstroke, and a base are visible. It might be *bet*, even though its head and base are normally longer. The last letter, *yod*, is rather certain. The short length of the downstroke excludes, e.g. *reš*. The small fragment with ולב cannot be located, and the darkened part in the photograph has been reduced. No new readings can therefore be ascertained for lines 9 and 10.

TRANSLATION

1. [7]His back [ ] his [is] m[a]i[l. [8]One]
2. sticks to the other, and the wind doe[s not] come between them. [9]The one
3. embraces the other, and they do not sep[ar]ate. [10]His sneezing kindles
4. the fire between his eyes, like the shining of dawn. [11]From his mouth flashes
5. come forth, they run with tongues of fire. [12]From his nostrils smoke comes forth,
6. (as from) a burning pot and an incense burner. [13]His breath spews burning coals, and sparks
7. come forth from his mouth. [14]His strength resides in his neck, and before him
8. power runs. [15]The folds of his flesh stick together, cast [on him]
9. like iron. [16]And [his] hea[rt] like a stone, and [
10. [17?] [ ] fe[ar the] brea[kers.
11. [ ] [

COMMENTS

L. 1 (41:7) גֿבֿוֿהֿ[י]. It is not unlikely that the word at the beginning of the line corresponds to 𝔐 גאוה (cf. 𝔗 גיותנות, 'elevations'), possibly an error for גוה, 'his back' (cf. 𝔊 τὰ ἔγκατα αὐτοῦ). The pl. form is somewhat out of the ordinary, and one might also propose the reading גֿבֿהֿהֿ, 'his height, elevation', or a fem. participle of גבה.

L. 1 (41:7)]והי. Nothing corresponds with 𝔐, but cf. 𝔊 σύνδεσμος αὐτοῦ as a rendering of 𝔐 סגור. Probably the translator interpreted the second hemistich as parallel to the first.

L. 1 (41:7) שׁ[י]ר[י]א. 'Coat of mail', as a free rendering of 𝔐 סגור חותם צר, 'shut up tight as with a seal'.

Ll. 1–2 (41:8) חדה] / לחדה ידבקן. Instead of the masc. forms of 𝔐 in vv 8-9, the translator employs fem. forms, possibly referring to a noun, now lost, in line 1. The logical subject is the 'scales' of the crocodile.

L. 2 (41:8) ידבקן. The translator renders 𝔐 יגשו with ידבקן, whereas in the next line he uses the verb חען to render 𝔐 דבק.

L. 2 (41:8) י]נעול. רוח can be masc. and fem. Because both 𝔐 and ℭ use a masc. form, we reconstruct י]נעול.

Ll. 2–3 (41:9) אנתה / לחברתה. The grammatically fem. rendering of 𝔐 איש באחיהו. ℭ also uses the form חבריה.

L. 3 (41:9) חענן. The first attestation in Aramaic of the root חען (Semitic *ḥḏn), 'to embrace'. It corresponds to 𝔐 ידבקו יתלכדו.

L. 3 (41:9) יתפׄ[ר]שן. Cf. 𝔐 יתפרדו; ℭ מתפרשין; 𝔖 ܡܬܦܪܫܝܢ.

L. 3 (41:10) עטישתה. Sing. as opposed to 𝔐 עטישתיו. 𝔊 ἐν πταρμῷ is also sing., whereas ℭ זרירוהי מקקוהי, 'his sputtering, his sneezing', is pl.

L. 4 (41:10) נורא. Once again, the translator interprets 𝔐 אור, 'light', as 'fire'; cf. cols. VIII 3 (24:13) and XXIX 2 (37:11).

L. 4 (41:10) בין עינוהי. Instead of 𝔐 ועיניו.

L. 4 (41:10) כממח פרׄא. The meaning is not certain. 𝔐 reads כעפעפי שחר; 𝔊 εἶδος ἑωσφόρου; ℭ כתמורי קריצתא; 𝔖 ܐܝܟ ܘܠܢܘܗ ܨܦܪܐ. The normal Aramaic rendering of שחר is שפרפרא (ܨܦܪܐ), a word written separately (שפר פרא) in Eastern MSS of Dan 6:20, and as שפר ברא in some MSS of *Tg. Isa* 61:2. Is it possible that פרא, in itself, also means 'dawn'? ממח should be analysed as an infinitive or noun from a root מחא (either the known verb 'to dissolve', or a secondary verb formation of מחא, 'to smite', and perhaps metaphorically 'to flutter one's eyelids'). However, this interpretation is rather far-fetched, and therefore scholars have proposed a number of emendations. The word כממח could be a corruption of כמפח or כמצמח. For lack of a better solution, we prefer the latter. Sokoloff refers to *Lev. Rab.* 24:3 יפקון הכא למחר עם מצימחיה דיומא, 'let them come out here tomorrow at the break (lit. shining) of day'. An alternative to these emendations is to read the two words as one: כממחפרׄא (Jongeling in *ed. princ.*, p. 82). However, the proposed translation, 'as from a crater', is rather unlikely. Of מחפרא (derived from חפר, 'to dig'), only the meaning '(salt) mine' is attested.

L. 5 (41:11) בלשני אשה. Cf. 𝔐 כידודי אש, 'sparks of fire' (𝔖 ܙܒܢܒܪ ܢܘܪܐ). The expression לישנא דנורא is used in *Tg. Esth II* 6:13; cf. also Isa 5:24 לשון אש (𝔖 ܠܫܢܐ ܕܢܘܪܐ); Dan 3:22 שביבא די נורא.

L. 5 (41:12) נחירוה. The *yod* of the suffix has been dropped accidentally, probably due to haplography.

L. 6 (41:12) לכוש יקד. Cf. 𝔐 כדוד נפוח, 'as (from) a burning pot'. In *Tg. Zech* 12:6 (ed. Sperber), לכוש renders 𝔐 כיור (cf. also 3Q15 III 9, and the discussion in *DJD* III, 250–1).

L. 6 (41:12) ומגמר. Cf. 𝔐 אגמן, 'reed'. However, one should most likely emend to ואגם (final *nun* being a result of dittography), a participle of a verb אגם. Cf. also 𝔊 ἀνθράκων. The form מגמר can be a participle of גמר annexed to יקד ('a burning and consuming pot'), but this expression is rather obscure. One should regard it rather as a substantive, 'incense burner'. The preposition in 𝔐 (*kĕ-*, 'as') is missing both here and in 𝔊.

L. 6 (41:13) גמׄרין. Cf. 𝔐 גחלים (ℭ גומרין; 𝔖 ܓܡܘܪܝܢ).

L. 6 (41:13) תגסא. Cf. 𝔐 תלהט. The verb גסא, 'to vomit', is attested in Syriac and Mishnaic Hebrew. This is not merely a free translation, but a change of the image of 𝔐. 𝔊 (ἡ ψυχὴ αὐτοῦ ἄνθρακες), which omits the verb altogether, seems to interpret 𝔐 as in 11QtgJob.

L. 8 (41:15) קפלי בשרה. Cf. 𝔐 מפלי בשרו, 'the folds of his flesh'; 𝔊 σάρκες δὲ σώματος αὐτοῦ; ℭ שלדי בסריה, 'the flakes of his flesh'. The verb קפל means 'to double, fold, roll up'. Although no such noun is yet attested, one might gather that קפל here means 'fold'. On the other hand, *Tg. Job* 41:7 employs the noun קליף ('scale, skin') from קלף, 'to peel'. There is a possibility of a scribal error, קפלי instead of קלפי (*ed. princ.*, p. 83), but in Syriac the verbs are closely related.

Ll. 8–9 (41:15) נסי̇כ̇ין בה] / כפרזלא. Cf. 𝔐 יצוק עליו בל ימוט. It is not certain whether the text really read בה], but this reconstruction conforms to 𝔐 עליו. כפרזלא is a free translation of 𝔐 '(immovable'), possibly brought about by the wording of the next verse.

L. 9 (41:16) ולב̇]בה. The translator added the conjunction.

L. 9 (41:16)]°°[ד̇[. The words in the space between ולב̇]בה and כאב̇ן may correspond to 𝔐 יצוק. The traces at the top of the line (under *śin* and *reš* of בשרה) rule out נסיך, but מ̇ת̇י̇[ס]ד̇[is consistent with these traces; cf. ℭ לביה מתייסד. In order to fill the remainder of the gap, one might add the reconstruction הוא before the participle, but such periphrastic constructions are not used in the text (the only example is the reverse רעין הוא in col. XV 7). If פח[in the next line should be completed as פח]דו[, corresponding to 𝔐 יגורו, than the translator combined the two hemistichs of v 16, the word after כאבן beginning with ו[rendering 𝔐 פלח תחתית (cf. 𝔖 ܨܘܢܡܐ, 'granite').

L. 10 (41:17) פח]דו[. Or י̓פח]דון as a translation of 𝔐 יגורו. However, it is also possible to reconstruct פח]דה[as a rendering of שתו. Cf. 𝔖 ܡܢ ܙܘܥܬܗ, and Job 31:23 where 𝔐 משאתו is translated by ℭ as מן דחלתיה (cf. also 13:11). The illegibility of the first word makes all reconstructions uncertain.

L. 10 (41:17) תב̇י̇]ריא. The word beginning with תב̇י̇[is probably a rendering of 𝔐 משברים. The text of 𝔐 משברים יתחטאו is rather difficult. Modern commentators suggest reading the first word as 'waves, breakers' or emending משברי ים, 'the waves of the sea'. In fact, the text has been understood in this sense by some of the variants of ℭ, which add גללי ימא after מן תבר. One wonders whether תבריא also means 'breakers', or 'the breaking (of the waves)'. *Tg. Ps.-J.* Lev 21:19 might indicate that תביר is a variant of תבר. In that case we might reconstruct תב̇י̇]ריא. Otherwise: תב̇י̇]רותא.

Variants

41:14 (8) תרוט 𝔊 τρέχει (ירוץ)] ידוץ 𝔐 𝔖 ℭ

41:14 (8) עלימו (= דבאה)] דאבה 𝔐 𝔊 (ἀπώλεια) 𝔖 (ܙܘܥܬܐ) ℭ (דבונא)

Col. XXXVII (Small scroll, col. ix; Frgs. J, Q, R) Job 41:25–42:2; 40:5; 42:4-6

] [°ת̇ק] [ת̇ו̇ן] 26? [ר̇ם̇]

והוא מלך על כל רחש *vacat*

[42:1]ענא איוב ואמר קדם אלהא [2]ידעת די כלא

תכול למעבד ולא יתבצר מנך תקף וחכמה

[40:5]חדה מללת ולא אתיב ותרתין ועליהן לא

אוסף [42:4]שמע נא ואנה אמלל אשאלנך

והתיבני [5]למשמע אדן שמעתך וכען עיני

חזתך [6]על כן אתנסך ואתמהא {א̇}ואהוא לעפר

וקטם *va*]*cat* [*va*]*cat*

vacat [7?] °[ ] ו̇[

Mus. Inv. 638
PAM 43.804*, 43.806*, 43.807*, 43.808*

NOTES ON READINGS

Frgs. J (PAM 43.804), R (PAM 43.807), and Q (PAM 43.806) can be joined to the bottom of the scroll. On the first line, nothing is now visible.

L. 1 (41:25)]תׄקׄ°[. Or]תׄקׄ [. To the right of *taw* there is a trace of a slighty diagonal stroke. If the trace is ink, we should read *ʿayin*, *lamed* (several times in this column, its hook extends almost to the baseline), or perhaps *mem*.

L. 1 (41:25)]רׄםׄ[. Only the left tip of the head of the first letter remains.

L. 8 (42:6) אתנסך. Frg. R supplies the missing letters.

L. 8 (42:6) לעׄפר. Frg. Q supplies the base and left part of the head of *pe*, as well as the leg of *reš*.

L. 9 (42:6) וקטם. The last two letters are seen on frg. J.

TRANSLATION

1. [ ] [ ] [26?]high[
2. and he is king over all reptiles. *vacat*
3. 42:1Then Job answered, and said before God: 2I know that all things
4. you can do, and that you are not in want of strength and wisdom.
5. 40:5I have spoken once, and I will not repeat; twice, and to that I will not
6. add. 42:4Hear, and I will speak; I will question you,
7. and you shall answer me. 5By hearsay I have heard of you, and now my eye
8. has seen you. 6Therefore I will be poured out and dissolved, and I will turn into dust
9. and ash(es). *va*[*cat*] *va*[*cat*
10. *vacat* [7? [[ ] [

COMMENTS

L. 1 (41:25?)]תׄקׄ°[. Or]תׄקׄ [. The remains in this line are too meagre to be reconstructed with any certainty. The first two words should correspond to v 25, but neither 𝔐, 𝔗, nor 𝔖 are of much help. Perhaps the translator interpreted משלו as 'his dominion' (cf. 𝔗 שלטניה), and used the noun תקף or adverb תקיף as a rendering (cf. 𝔖 Dan 11:9 ܬܘܩܦܐ; 𝔐 מלכות). It is also possible that he read the first word of v 25 (𝔐 אין) as און or אונו (cf. 𝔖 ܚܝܠܗ): 'and his power on the earth is strong'. But תׄקׄ]ף [could also have been used as a translation of 𝔐 בלתי חת.

L. 1 (41:26)]רׄםׄ[. Cf. 𝔐 גבה?

L. 2 (41:26) רחש. Cf. 𝔐 בני שחץ, literally 'sons of pride' which is usually rendered 'proud beasts'. 𝔗 renders the same expression in 28:8 by בני דאדם and בנייא דאריוון. In 41:26, 𝔗 offers three translations: (1) בני כונרי 'fish' (var. כוורי, נוניא); probably reading or interpreting 𝔐 שחץ as שרץ; cf. also 𝔊 πάντων τῶν ἐν τοῖς ὕδασιν; (2) 'lions', as in 28:8 בני אריון, associating שחץ with שחל; (3) מרי חטופא 'violent men'. 𝔖 ܟܠܗ ܪܚܫܐ has the same interpretation as this text.

L. 4 (42:2) תכול למעבד. Cf. 𝔐 תוכל; 𝔖 ܟܠ ܐܢܬ ܫܟܚ ܠܡܥܒܕ. In Aramaic, יכל with the meaning 'to be able' is an auxiliary.

L. 4 (42:2) יתבצר מנך. The construction יתבצר מן is also used in 𝔖 Gen 11:6.

L. 4 (42:2) תקף וחכמה. A free translation of 𝔐 מזמה.

Ll. 5–6 (40:5) חדה מללת ולא אתיב ותרתין ועליהן לא / אוסף. The text is a rendering of 𝔐 40:5 instead of 𝔐 42:3. The first part of 𝔐 42:3 is, in fact, a slight variation on 𝔐 38:2. Many scholars have had their misgivings about the authenticity of this part of 𝔐 42:3. Here, however, 𝔐 42:3 is omitted altogether, either because it was not included in the text used by the translator, or because he objected to the statement. אסוף in col. XXXIV 1 (40:5) shows that the phrase is also used before 40:6.

Ll. 6–7 (42:4) אשאלנך / והתיבני. Cf. 𝔐 אשאלך והודיעני. The construction also occurs in 40:7, but there (col. XXXIV 3) the translator adds פתגם. In 11QtgJob, התיב is used both with פתגם (cols. XXX 1; XXXIV 3), and without it (col. XXXVII 5 and 7).

L. 8 (42:6) אתנסך ואתמ͏ה͏א. Cf. 𝔐 אמאס ונחמתי. אמאס can be the *Nip*ʿ*al* of מאס II (a secondary root from מסס), 'to flow'. The translator interpreted it in this way. נחמתי is generally understood as the *Nip*ʿ*al* of נחם, 'to repent'. However, the translator read it as the *Nip*ʿ*al* of חמם, 'to be heated'. The root מחו, 'to dissolve', is attested in Mishnaic Hebrew, Syriac, and Ethiopic.

Col. XXXVIII (Small scroll, col. x; Frgs. V, W) Job 42:9-12

[שחיא וצפר נעמתיא ו]עׄבׄדׄו[כדי אמר להון] 1

אלהא ושמע א[ל]הׄא בקלה די איוב ושׁבׄקׄ 2

לאיוב

להון חטאיהון בדילה [10]ותב אלהא ברחמין 3

ויהב לה חד תרין בכל די הוא לה [11]ואתין לות 4

איוב כל רחמוהי וכל אחוהי וכל ידעוהי ואכלו 5

עמה לחם בביתה ונחמוהי על כל באישתה די 6

היתי אלהא עלוהי ויהבו לה גבר אמרה חדה 7

וגבר קדש חד די דהב *vacat* 8

[12]ואׄלׄהׄא בׄרׄךׄ יׄתׄ אׄ[יו]ב באחׄ[רי]לׄ[9

] [ ]עׄ[10

Mus. Inv. 638
PAM 43.808*, 43.809*

NOTES ON READINGS

The ruling is faint but visible, and the scribe has passed beyond it in every line. There is another vertical ruling at 1.8 cm, near the tear which almost split the whole manuscript. From this margin to the end there is 9.5 cm more of skin, ruled but unwritten, meant to serve as a blank handle page. Lines 1 and 9 are no longer visible. Frgs. V and W in PAM 43.808 can be joined to the bottom of the scroll.

L. 1 (42:9) ו]עׄבׄדׄו[. Only the left end of the base of ʿ*ayin* remains presently on the scroll.

L. 2 (42:9) ושׁבׄקׄ. In the preliminary publication, ושׁטׄף was read. Only the base of *bet* is visible, but the characteristic extension of the stroke to the right and the lack of any trace of a downstroke at the left show it is *bet*, not *ṭet*.

L. 9 (42:12) ואׄלׄהׄא. The reading can be established by frg. V, with traces of ʾ*alep*, *lamed*, and *he*.

L. 9 (42:12) בׄרׄךׄ. The heads of the letters can be seen at the bottom of the scroll; the downstroke of *kap* is preserved on frg. W (not included on the plate).

L. 9 (42:12) יתׄ א֯[יו]ב. The letters ית (beneath *dalet* of חד in line 8) are very faint and not easy to read. The same is true of *ʾalep* in א֯[יו]ב.

L. 9 (42:12) באחׄ[רי]ל[. Puech and García Martínez reconstruct באחׄ[ריתא ד]יׄל[ה והוא ל]הׄ, but neither *yod* nor *he* at the end of the line is certain.

TRANSLATION

1. [the Shuhite and Zophar the Naamathite, and] they did [as they were told by]
2. God. And G[o]d listened to the voice of Job and forgave
3. them their sins because of him. [10]And God returned to Job in mercy,
4. and He gave him twice as much of all he had possessed. [11]Then came to
5. Job all his friends and all his brothers and all his acquaintances, and they ate
6. bread with him in his house, and they comforted him for all the evil that
7. God had brought upon him. And each one gave him a ewe,
8. and each a golden ring. *vacat*
9. [12]And God blessed J[o]b in the en[d] [
10. [ ] [

COMMENTS

Ll. 2–3 (42:9) ושׄבׄקׄ / להון חטאיהון בדילה. The clause does not correspond to 𝔐 וישא יהוה את פני איוב, but to 𝔊 καὶ ἔλυσεν τὴν ἁμαρτίαν αὐτοῖς διὰ Ἰώβ. The Aramaic and Greek phrases correspond in some way to 𝔐 42:10 בהתפללו בעד רעהו. The relations among 11QtgJob, 𝔐, and 𝔊 are complicated. 𝔊 also has a rendering of the phrase in 𝔐 42:10, namely εὐξαμένου δὲ αὐτοῦ καὶ περὶ τῶν φίλων αὐτοῦ ἀφῆκεν αὐτοῖς τὴν ἁμαρτίαν (the second part is an addition to 𝔐), whereas 11QtgJob does not translate this clause from 𝔐 42:10. The idiom שבק חטאין also occurs in 4Q**242** (PrNab ar) line 4.

L. 3 (42:10) ותב ^לאיוב^ אלהא ברחמין. This is a free translation which does not correspond exactly to 𝔐 ויהוה שב את שבית איוב or the versions. The expression תב ברחמין also occurs in *Tg. Zech* 1:7.

L. 4 (42:10) חד תרין. Cf. 𝔐 למשנה. In Imperial Aramaic, multiplication is expressed by חד followed by the numeral, whereas the Aramaic of the targums employs על חד; cf. ℭ על חד תרין.

L. 4 (42:11) לות. This is the first example in Aramaic of the independent use of לות with a noun.

L. 5 (42:11) כל רחמוהי וכל אחוהי. 𝔐 and the versions all read 'all his brothers and all his sisters'. The translator omits 𝔐 לפנים.

L. 6 (42:11) ונחמוהי. 𝔐 reads וינדו לו וינחמו אתו.

L. 9 (42:12) ברׄךׄ יתׄ א֯[יו]ב באחׄ[רי. The Aramaic translation changes the construction of 𝔐 ברך יהוה את אחרית איוב.

L. 10 (42:12)]עׄ[. If the reading of *ʿayin* is correct, it may be the first letter of עשר or ען (𝔐 צאן). Puech and García Martínez reconstruct the line: [ארבעת עשר אלפין די] עׄ[ן.

VARIANTS

42:9 (2–3) 𝔐 וישא יהוה את פני איוב] 𝔊 ושׄבׄקׄ / להון חטאיהון בדילה

Unidentified Fragments

The *editio princeps* assigned the siglum A followed by a number to the fragments that were found as separate fragments, and the sigla B, C, D etc. for the fragments that broke off from the small scroll when it was unrolled. PAM 43.800–43.808 show many tiny fragments of the second category placed beneath the unwrapped scroll, none of which is now present on the corresponding Mus. Inv. 638. Like the *editio princeps*, this edition disregards the smallest fragments that preserve only traces, and no complete letters.

Frg. A1

[◦] 1

[◦עוׄן] 2

[◦מחׄ] 3

Mus. Inv. 635
PAM 43.824

NOTES ON READINGS

L. 2 [◦עוׄן]. The first trace is a vertical stroke.

L. 3 [◦מחׄ]. The first trace is rather strange. The last letter looks like *ḥet*, but *he* cannot be excluded.

Frg. A3

[בׯ◦] 1

[דׄ◦◦] 2

[אר] 3

Mus. Inv. 635
PAM 43.824

Frg. A5

[ ] 1

[דנׯ] 2

Mus. Inv. 635
PAM 43.824

Frg. A7

[°אף̊] 1

[מנ̊°] 2

Mus. Inv. 567
PAM 44.114

NOTES ON READINGS

L. 1 [°אף̊]. The trace of the last letter could also belong to final *kap*.

L. 2 [מנ̊°]. The second letter might also be *waw* or *yod*, but the absence of a clear tick rather indicates *nun*. The sharp angle at the upper right of the last letter suggests *pe*, or perhaps *ʾalep*.

Frg. A8

[°] 1

[כב°] 2

Mus. Inv. 581
PAM 44.114

NOTES ON READINGS

The fragment has been removed from Mus. Inv. 567 to the small matchbox with the inventory number 581. The large space before the *kap* may indicate a *vacat* or the right margin, but it is also possible that the right side has faded away as in frg. 4.

L. 2 [כב°]. The slightly convex downstroke of the last letter rules out *waw* or *yod*.

Frg. A9

[כ̊°] 1

[ח̊כ°] 2

Mus. Inv. 567
PAM 44.114

NOTES ON READINGS

Apart from the two last letters of line 2, the traces are very faint or have faded away completely. Four other tiny fragments, with traces but no complete letters, are placed next to this fragment on the plate as it was photographed in PAM 44.114.

L. 2]ח̊כ○[. Part of the left leg and base of the first letter are faintly visible. The last letter may be *samek*, or, slightly less likely, *qop*, *ʿayin* or *šin*.

Frg. A10

]○בׄ○○[

]יע○יׄ ○[

Mus. Inv. 567
PAM 44.114

NOTES ON READINGS

The fragment is very dark, and the different height of the letters on line 2 may be due to superimposed layers. The bottom part of the fragment shows no clear traces.

L. 2]יע○יׄ ○[. After the *ʿayin* the letters are raised half a line, and it is not certain they belong to the same layer. The third letter may be *nun*, *ṣade*, or *taw*.

Frg. A11

]ת̊○○לכ[

]ואתחשך מ̊[

]סׄ ○תרא אׄ[

]תחו○[

]○[

Mus. Inv. 625
PAM 44.116

NOTES ON READINGS

The fragment consists of six pieces on the plate.

L. 1]כל°°ת֯[. The traces between *taw* and *lamed* may belong to two or three letters, the letter preceding *lamed* having a long base. It is not clear where one might place a word-dividing space.

L. 3 °תרא ס֯[. The left part of the head of the letter before *taw* has been preserved. It is not clear whether the *samek* belongs to the same word or is the last letter of the previous one.

TRANSLATION

2.]and it grows dark [

Frg. A12

[°א 1

[נטר֯ת 2

[והי 3

Mus. Inv. 625
PAM 44.116

NOTES ON READINGS

Frgs. A12 and A13 are placed close to one another on the plate, possibly because they belong together. However, the fragments do not seem to join. The blanks at the ends of lines 1 and 3 suggest that the lower fragment preserves the left side of a column.

L. 2 [נטר֯ת. Read either *reš* with a short head or a *waw*.

L. 3 [והי. Or [יהי.

TRANSLATION

1.]
2.]I observed
3.]his[

Frg. A13

]ק֯[1

]°°[2

Mus. Inv. 625
PAM 44.116

Frg. A14

]אלין [1

]∘∘בׄ∘[2

Mus. Inv. 625
PAM 44.116

NOTES ON READINGS

Frgs. A14 and A15, of about the same size and shape, are partially superimposed on the plate.

TRANSLATION

1.]these [

Frg. A15

]∘∘∘[1

]בׄ אוית[2

]לׄ[3

Mus. Inv. 625
PAM 44.116

NOTES ON READINGS

L. 2]בׄ אוית[. The bottom of the *bet* is covered by frg. A14. The skin between *bet* and *ʾalep* preserves no ink, and it is not certain whether to read]בׄ אוית[, or]בׄ[ ]אוית[. Instead of]אוית[one may also read]אוות[.

COMMENTS

L. 2]בׄ אוית[. The last word may be a Hebraism, 'I desired'.

Frg. A16

]ס֯[1
]לא[2
]לישה֯[3
]◦ש[4
]ל[5

Mus. Inv. 625
PAM 44.116

NOTES ON READINGS

L. 3]לישה֯[. The last letter may also be a *ḥet*.

COMMENTS

L. 3]לישה֯[. Reconstruct ח]לישה֯[, 'weak', 'sick' (fem.)?

Frg. A17

]◦ו◦◦[1
]ב֯איש[2
]ארו֯[3
]◦[4

Mus. Inv. 625
PAM 44.116

NOTES ON READINGS

A few tiny fragments with traces have broken off from the main fragment, but it is not clear where they can be joined.

L. 1]◦ו◦◦[. The letter after *waw* has a downstroke and a base, and may be, e.g. *kap*.

TRANSLATION

2.]evil[
3.]for[

Frg. A18

]פׄר֯ה 1

]ו֯ק֯ר֯י֯ן 2

]ן 3

]◦עׄטׄ 4

Mus. Inv. 625
PAM 44.116

NOTES ON READINGS

In PAM 44.116 the fragment displays numerous cracks, and some faint traces might either be ink or cracks in the skin.

L. 1]פׄר֯ה. Or]פׄר֯ה.

L. 2]ו֯ק֯ר֯י֯ן. Only the tick of the first letter remains, and it may also be, e.g. *yod*. The third letter may also be *dalet*, and the fourth *waw*.

L. 4]◦עׄטׄ. The base of *ṭet* has the stance of the right oblique of *šin*, and *šin* is also possible, though difficult.

Frg. A19

]◦ 1

]◦ 2

]◦ 3

Mus. Inv. 625
PAM 44.116

Frg. G

]י֯נׄך ◦[1

PAM 43.803

NOTES ON READINGS

A possible placement may be in col. XXXII 10, joined to frg. F, reading]יׄנך תׄתרחץ ב[ה.

L. 1]יׄנך ◦[. One might perhaps read]תׄך, but the *taw* would be rather narrow. The first letter of the next word is, e.g. *he*, *taw*, or *ḥet*, or *waw* with the leg of another letter.

Frg. N

]◦◦◦[

]◦◦ש◦[

]◦◦◦[

PAM 43.805

NOTES ON READINGS

The *editio princeps* placed this fragment in col. XXXIV, reading]רׄשׄיׄע[ין in line 2 (col. XXXIV 8). This reading is possible, but the shape of the fragment seems to rule out this location.

L. 1]◦◦◦[. The first trace is probably the tail of *qop* or final *nun*, *pe* or *ṣade*.

Frg. O

]תׄפׄיׄשׁ[

PAM 43.805

NOTES ON READINGS

L. 1]תׄפׄיׄשׁ[. The first letter is *nun*, *taw*, or *ṣade*. The second letter has a slightly curved head. It might be *pe*, but *kap* cannot be excluded.

Frg. P

]ו̊נ̊[

]◦ת[

PAM 43.806

Notes on Readings

L. 1]ו̊נ̊[. The first line exhibits a 'ligature' of *nun* or *taw* with *waw* or *yod*. But the traces could also indicate final *mem*.

L. 2]◦ת[. The trace after *taw* seems to belong to a letter with a curved connection of the vertical stroke and base, e.g. *mem*, *pe*, *kap*, or *nun*.

11. 11Qapocryphal Psalms

(PLATES XXII–XXV, LIII)

Previous discussion: J. P. M. van der Ploeg, 'Le Psaume XCI dans une recension de Qumrân', *RB* 72 (1965) 210–7; idem, 'Un petit rouleau de psaumes apocryphes (11QPsAp[a])', in *Tradition und Glaube. Das frühe Christentum in seiner Umwelt. Festgabe für Karl Georg Kuhn*, eds. G. Jeremias, H. W. Kuhn, H. Stegemann (Göttingen: Vandenhoeck & Ruprecht, 1972) 128–39; É. Puech, '11QPsAp[a]: un rituel d'exorcismes. Essai de reconstruction', *RevQ* 14/55 (1990) 377–408; idem, 'Les deux derniers psaumes davidiques du rituel d'exorcisme 11QPsAp[a] IV 4–V 14', *The Dead Sea Scrolls: Forty Years of Research*, eds. D. Dimant, U. Rappaport (STDJ 10; Leiden: E. J. Brill, 1992) 64–89.

Physical Description

ACCORDING to van der Ploeg ('Le Psaume XCI'), this small, heavily damaged, cigar-shaped scroll measured 8.5 cm in height and 3.5 cm in width when acquired. The photograph of the unopened scroll (cf. Pl. LIII) shows that its height, including the pointed protrusions at the top and bottom, actually measured 9.5 cm. After the scroll was opened in the spring of 1963, its width was shown to be 73 cm. The extensive fragmentation of the top and bottom give the opened scroll a zigzag shape. One piece of the opened scroll had broken off and stuck to the next revolution. At a later stage, this fragment (col. III frg. a) became detached. Five other fragments of 11QapocrPs were found among the scattered fragments from cave 11.

The skin is rather thick and coarse and has a large grain. The colour is tan to light brown; the last part of the scroll has several spots which are dark brown. The scroll has been written on one sheet of skin. At its end, a small sheet has been attached to protect it, and to form the handle in which the scroll was rolled. This new sheet is of the same skin (having identical grain, colour, and, apparently, thickness), and measures 7 cm from the stitching to the handle. The stitching is irregular, the string is still attached, and seven holes can be counted. No traces of ruling are visible, but the scribe managed to write quite regular columns. Faint traces of ruling are, however, visible in frgs. 1, 2, and col. I.

Two types of damage can be detected in the scroll. The first is the deposit of a substance which could not be cleaned. It is of a lighter colour than the skin and covers some letters of the upper part of cols. II and III. The second is a perpendicular abrasion and covering with a dark substance which appears in cols. II, IV, and in the margin between cols. IV and V.

Columns and Measurements

Since it is virtually certain that the largest fragment stems from the revolution exterior to the first column of the opened scroll, the present edition renumbers the columns.

TABLE 1: *Numbering of Columns*

Previous Discussion	Present Edition
Frg. A	Col. I
Col. I	Col. II
Col. II	Col. III
Col. III	Col. IV
Col. IV	Col. V
Col. V	Col. VI

Intercolumnar margins have been preserved in frg. 2, and between cols. II through to VI. The left margin of col. VI is preserved until the stitching. It is not certain whether the space at the end of col. I 2 is the beginning of the margin. No top or bottom margins are extant.

The height of the extant fragments and columns is as follows: frg. 1: 5 cm; frg. 2: 5.3 cm; Col. I: 6.9 cm; Col. II: 7.3 cm; Col. III: 8.2 cm; Col. IV: 8.8 cm; Col. V: 8.9 cm; Col. VI: 9.2 cm.

Line height, measured from the top of letters in consecutive lines, is 0.5–0.8 cm, usually *c.*0.6 cm.

Since vertical ruling is lacking, the measurement of columnar width includes the left margin, i.e. measurements are taken from the beginning of one column to the beginning of the next. In addition, the minimal and maximal measurements of blank space between the ends of lines and the next column are added.

TABLE 2: *Measurement of Columnar Widths*

Col.	Width (including left margin)	Left Margin
II	8.5 cm (extant)	1–2.1 cm
III	12.3 cm	0.9–1.8 cm
IV	13 cm	1.6–2.3 cm
V	14 cm	1.7–2.7 cm
VI	16.2 cm (to stitching)	0.8–1.7 cm

The cover sheet in its present state measures 7 cm from the stitching to the handle, but the skin is crumbled and has not been flattened as has the rest of the opened scroll. The length of the opened scroll (the sum of cols. II–VI and the cover sheet) is, therefore, 71 cm.[1]

[1] The difference between the total sum of the columns and the cover sheet (71 cm) and the figure given in the preliminary publications (73 cm) can be attributed to the slight distortion of the actual scroll (the zigzag shape is stretched out too much in the plates, e.g. the revolution preserving the margin between cols. II and III).

Sheets

Cols. II–V belong to the same sheet (64 cm extant to the stitching). The blank cover page at the end belongs to a new sheet (7 cm in crumbled condition). The evidence of faint ruling in frgs. 1, 2, and col. I (as opposed to the lack of ruling in the opened scroll) may indicate they stem from a previous, ruled sheet.

Contents

The manuscript contains the remains of at least three songs against demons. The last song, at the end of the scroll, is a version of Psalm 91, which in some rabbinic texts (e.g. *b. Šebu.* 15b; *y. Šabb.* 6.8b) is called שיר של פגעים, 'the song of the stricken'. The same word ה֯פגועי]ם[is mentioned in col. V 2. One may refer to 11QPs^a XXVII 9–10, which enumerates the songs composed by David and mentions שיר לנגן על הפגועים ארבעה, 'songs to be sung over the possessed: four'.

The preserved text attributes one song to David (col. V 4: לדויד); Psalm 91 may also be ascribed to David (cf. 𝔊). Yet, this is not enough evidence to assume that the manuscript contained the four songs mentioned in 11QPs^a, as the songs of this manuscript are not the only ones dealing with הפגועים. The Songs of the *Maskil* (4Q**510** and **511**) contain different kinds of songs against demons, and the editor, M. Baillet, also referred to 11QPs^a. That composition, however, is attributed to the *Maskil*, not to David. On the other hand, the mention of Solomon in col. II 2 may indicate the scroll did not consist *per se* of four songs of David against the demons, but of a collection of such texts. Some were believed to have been written by David, whereas others were attributed to Solomon, the exorcist *par excellence*.

The last song of the scroll, the version of Psalm 91, begins with col. VI 3. The heading לדויד in col. V 4 introduces the penultimate song. The absence of other formal criteria prevents us from determining the amount and extent of the previous songs. The fact that both the end of col. II and the beginning of col. III seem to refer to God's creative acts, suggests that both columns belong to the same song, and the mention of Solomon in col. II 2 and שדים in line 3 may indicate the beginning of a new song. It is not clear whether that song extended to col. V 3 as Puech suggested, or whether col. IV, which is directed against a particular demon, belongs to another song.

Special Features

The handle with which the scroll was rolled has been preserved. It has the appearance of a stick and is now somewhat curved. Its height measures 4.7 cm, and its diameter is 0.3–0.5 cm.

The end of the skin of the cover sheet has been rolled up tightly (three revolutions can be counted), and the stick has been attached to it with pieces of string on the upper and lower part. The upper string has been preserved, and since it is lower than the top margin, it must be assumed that a hole was cut in the skin through which the string was threaded. The hole can no longer be seen due to the deterioration of the skin.

Palaeography

11QapocrPs is written in a late Herodian formal script (*c*.50–70 CE). The script exhibits a thick *ductus* and a squat configuration, most *keraiai* are fully developed, and *waw* and *yod* are clearly distinct.

The *keraiai* of *gimel*, *zayin*, and medial and final *nun* consist of a thin horizontal stroke attached to the right of the downstroke. A similarly thin horizontal stroke is written across the left arm of *ṭet*.

Dalet and final *kap* are written in two strokes which cross one another. Since the downstrokes of the final letters vary from short to long, and the downstrokes of *dalet*, *waw*, and *reš* occasionally break through the baseline, *dalet* and final *kap* are sometimes very similar.

Taw is mostly written in one stroke, beginning with the left upstroke, resulting in the characteristic triangular wedge on the top, left side (similarly, *samek* and *qop*). However, a few times the wedge is lacking, suggesting that in those cases two strokes were made. The left end of the base of *taw* is sometimes thickened, or even curls upwards. In a number of cases a separate downstroke is added on top of the base (cf. col. IV 12 מתנחך; col. V 4 עת; and, probably, col. IV 5 תקיף).

Orthography

11QapocrPs uses the full spelling with the vowel letters *waw* and *yod* for long *o*, *u*, and *i*. The expanded spelling with final *he* is only used in הואה, the adverb מואדה, and in some 2nd masc. sing. perfect forms (ואמרתה in col. V 5, 11; ח]שקתה in col. VI 12; but קר]את in col. VI 9). The 2nd masc. sing. suffix is written with final *kap*, with the exception of יככה in col. IV 4 (probably influenced by Deut 28:22 𝔐 יככה). Other orthographical features typical of the Qumran scrolls, such as the spelling of כיא, are lacking, and it would appear that the orthography is rather conservative.

Textual Character

The text of Psalm 91 in 11QapocrPs differs in many respects from 𝔐 and the ancient versions. Apart from orthographical variants, several categories of differences may be distinguished:

(1) The use of different words or expressions to convey the same thought, e.g. 11QapocrPs ולוא יגע [נגע for 𝔐 ונגע לא יקרב. In some cases, 11QapocrPs uses a more common word where 𝔐 has a rare expression (e.g. Col. VI 6 [v 4] תשכון for 𝔐 תחסה; Col. VI 10 [v 10] תרא]ה for 𝔐 תאנה אליך) suggesting that 𝔐 preserves the more original text.

(2) Transpositions, e.g. of the two hemistichs of v 6, or of the order of the words within a hemistich. It may be no coincidence that in three examples (11QapocrPs VI 8–9 בעיניך / [תביט רק] and ותרא]ה שלום רשע[ים against 𝔐 רק בעיניך תביט and ושלמת רשעים תראה and VI 10 ו]לוא יגע [נגע for 𝔐 Ps 91:10 ונגע לא יקרב) 11QapocrPs transposes the verb to the beginning of the clause.

(3) Additions in 11QapocrPs, e.g. מבטח in col. VI 4 (v 2b), חסד]ו ע[ליך in line 6 (v 4b). In both cases the addition gives a better parallelism.

(4) A completely divergent text for 𝔐 v 9 and vv 14-16. The wording of v 9 in 11QapocrPs VI 9 is badly preserved, and no conclusions can be drawn. The short text of 11QapocrPs VI 12–13 against the long text of 𝔐 Ps 91:14-16 may possibly be due to a parablepsis between 𝔐 אשגבהו (v 14) and אשביעהו (v 16), but the switch in 𝔐 to the 1st person divine speech and the formulaic expressions in v 15 (cf. Ps 81:8) may also indicate that 𝔐 has an expanded reading where 11QapocrPs preserves a more original form.

Categories (1) and (2) suggest that the wording of 𝔐 is earlier than that of 11QapocrPs, whereas the examples in (3) and (4) may preserve older readings than those of 𝔐.

Mus. Inv. 61, 612, 619, 1032
PAM 42.177, 43. 981*, 43.982–983, 43.984–988*, 44.003*, 44.004*, 44.113*
IAA 563769*

Frg. 1

]וה[1
]כׄב[2
] האׄ[3
]ם ע[4
]דם °[5
]סׄוכות °[6
]לם ו֯[7

Mus. Inv. 619
PAM 42.177, 44.004*

Notes on Readings

The physical characteristics (grain, colour, and shape) and the hand indicate that frg. 1 is part of 11QapocrPs. The fragment shows traces of horizontal ruling. The similar shapes of frgs. 1 and 2 suggest they stem from consecutive revolutions, and the smaller size of frg. 1 may indicate it belonged to the exterior revolution. It is difficult to place frgs. 1 and 2 close to the fragment of col. I, and probably both should be located to the right of that fragment.

L. 2]כׄב[. The first letter may also be *bet*.

L. 5]◦. The bottom part of a slightly slanting downstroke is visible.

L. 6]ס֯וכות. The first letter is *samek* or *qop*. The absence of a trace of the base of the left leg makes *taw* more difficult.

L. 6]◦. The bottom part of a slightly slanting downstroke is visible.

COMMENTS

L. 6]ס֯וכות. A reference to סוכות seems out of place in this text, but it is not clear which other word should be reconstructed.

Frg. 2 i

] 1

]ה 2

]ת 3

]◦יך̇ 4

Mus. Inv. 619
PAM 44.004

NOTES ON READINGS

The physical characteristics and the hand indicate that the fragment is part of 11QapocrPs. The fragment shows traces of horizontal and vertical ruling (the latter only in the second column).

L. 2]ה. The dark trace above *he* is caused by a crack in the skin.

L. 4]◦יך̇. The last letter looks like *dalet*, but the stroke beneath the baseline shows it is a final *kap*. The downstroke does not go straight down, but with a curve; cf. e.g. חושך in col. V 7. The letter at the edge can be *zayin*, *ḥet*, or *šin*.

Frg. 2 ii

ב[5

את [6

שבעים[7

[ ]ל[8

TRANSLATION

7. seventy[

Frg. 3

]◦[1

] למים֯ [2

]אחת̇[3

Mus. Inv. 1032
IAA 563769

NOTES ON READINGS

The fragment was flattened and first photographed in 1997. The identification of the fragment is based upon the hand writing.

TRANSLATION

1.] [
2.] to the water [
3.]one[

Frg. 4

]ת֯[1

] וריק [2

Mus. Inv. 1032
IAA 563769

NOTES ON READINGS

The fragment was flattened and first photographed in 1997. The identification of the fragment is based upon the hand writing.

L. 1]ת֯[. Or *waw* followed by, e.g. *mem*.

L. 2 ו̇ריק. The shortness of the first letter would seem to indicate *yod*, but the head suggests *waw*.

TRANSLATION

1.] [
2.] and empty [

Col. I

]ובוכה֯ו֯ [2

]שבועה֯[3

]ב֯יהוה[4

]ת֯נין [5

א]ת֯ האר֯[ץ 6

] משב֯[יע 7

]את ב[8

]הזואת֯[9

]א֯ת השד[10

]ישב֯[11

Mus. Inv. 612
PAM 44.003

NOTES ON READINGS

The column is composed of one fragment whose shape corresponds closely to that of the following right 'legs' of the 'arches', and it is very probable that it stems from the revolution exterior to the broken one of col. II. In that case, the fragment should be placed close to the left margin of the column. The fragment shows traces of horizontal ruling. It is possible that the words of lines 2–3 (as well as the reconstructed words of lines 4, 6, and 7) are the last of their respective lines. Line 2 corresponds to line 2 of col. II (or some millimetres below col. II 2).

L. 2]ובוכה֯ו֯ [. The three downstrokes at the end of the word must be *he* and *waw*. After the *waw* there is a crack in the skin.

L. 6 האר֯[ץ. The letter after *ʾalep* is more likely to be *reš* than *waw*. There is no trace of any horizontal stroke, but some traces of the head of *waw* should have been preserved.

L. 9]הזואת֯[. *He* and *zayin* are virtually certain. Cf. the long left leg of *he* in line 10.

L. 11]ישב֯[. The first letter is *waw*, *yod*, or *ʿayin*. The last one cannot be *he*. It may be *bet* or *reš*. Reading]ו]ישב֯ or]י]ושב֯ is possible, but there is no trace of the letter before *yod* or *waw*.

TRANSLATION

2.]and the one who weeps for him [
3.]oath[
4.]by YHWH[
5.]dragon [

6.] the ea[rth
7.] exor[cis]ing[
8.] [
9.]this[
10.]the demon[
11.]he will dwell[

COMMENTS

L. 3]שבועׄה[. It seems that this column, like those following, deals with the exorcism of a demon. On the meaning of an oath of cursing, cf. Num 5:21.

L. 5]תׄנין[. 'Snake' or 'dragon'. This may be an allusion to Ps 91:13. Cf. col. VI 12 and possibly col. VI 1.

L. 7 משבׄ]יע. Cf. cols. III 4 and IV 1.

L. 8]את ב[. Several reconstructions are possible, e.g. קר]את ב[יהוה or]את ב[ני.

L. 10]השד. Either sing. or pl.: השד]ים.

L. 11]ישׄבׄ[. Perhaps ו]ישׄבׄ, 'and he will dwell', a form of שבע, or וׄשׄר; cf. col. II 4.

Col. II

1]]שׄם[

2]]הׄ שלומה[ ]ויקרׄ[א

3] הרו]חותׄ[ ]והשדים [

4]] אלׄה [הש]דים וׄשׄ[ר המשט]מה

5] א]שר[ ]לׄ תהׄו[ם]ך

6]]לש◦[ ]הׄגד[ול]וׄהי

7]]◦◦[ ]עמׄו תׄ◦וׄ רפואה

8] על]שמך נשען וקרׄ[א]

9] יש]ראל החזק

10 [ביהוה אלוהי אלים אשר עשה] את השמים

11 [ואת הארץ ואת כול אשר בם א]שׄר הבדיל[בין]

12 [האור ובין החושך]◦ עדׄ[

Mus. Inv. 61
PAM 43.982, 43.983, 44.113*

Notes on Readings

This column is the first of the opened scroll. If the fragment of col. I was positioned at the left side of the column, the width of this column would have measured *c.*11.5 cm in line 4, since the distance between cols. II and III (including the marginal space) measured 12.5 cm. PAM 43.982 and 43.983 show a fragment placed between this column and the next. This location is not correct, and PAM 44.113 shows some letters of the end of col. II 4 which were not visible in the earlier photographs.

L. 1]שׂמ֯[. PAM 43.982 shows a tiny fragment before *šin* which is missing from PAM 44.113. Puech claims its traces are the head of *bet*, turned ninety degrees counter-clockwise, but he only turns the top of the fragment, and not the stroke at the bottom, which he interprets as the base of *bet*. Note also that between this assumed base of *bet* and the next *šin* there are the remains of a vertical stroke. To complicate matters, magnification of the photograph shows that the so-called head of the *bet* seems to consist of three strokes, forming two angles of forty-five degrees. One cannot be sure that all the visible traces are really ink; but it does seem rather certain that the fragment should indeed be turned, in which case the horizontal stroke in the photograph would become a downstroke. The position of this tiny fragment is uncertain. The traces of the letter after *šin* could belong to medial or final *mem*, or several other letters with a downstroke and a base.

L. 2]ה֯. Final *mem* is less likely because of the absence of any trace of a basestroke.

L. 2]ויקר֯[א. *Reš* is more likely than *he*. The distance between *qop* and *reš* is slightly less than between *mem* and *he* of שלומה.

Ll. 4–6 A thin, vertical portion of the skin is damaged, extending from line 4 to 6. The letters in this strip have been partially abraded, and many black dots and strokes that cannot be ink appear in this strip. The same kind of damage can also be seen at the left of col. IV (in the same place in the zigzag pattern). The abrasion at the beginning of col. V is not exactly at the same place in the pattern.

L. 4 ו֯שׂ[ר. Because of the damage to the skin it is difficult to interpret the first letter. The remains look like *yod* (if the dot above the left part of its head is disregarded), but it may also be *waw* with the lower part of the downstroke being abraded. The second letter is *ʿayin* or *šin*/*śin*.

L. 5]ל֯. The vertical stroke after ש]דים in line 4 is probably the head of a *lamed* in line 5. Beneath ים of line 4 there are two traces (the upper one is no longer visible in PAM 44.113, and neither trace is now visible in the fragment). It is not certain whether either of these traces belong to letters; if they do, they were probably supralinear.

L. 6]לש◦[. There is a small space between *lamed* and *šin*, but the letters are too close to belong to different words. The minute trace after *šin* probably belongs to the right part of a head that breaks through the downstroke, e.g. *dalet*.

L. 6]ה֯גד[ול. Not ו]להגד[יל, since the vertical stroke on top of the right leg of *he* is part of a long trail of black dots and strokes, stretching down from line 4 to beyond line 6. The trace after *dalet* is only a dark spot on the edge of the skin.

L. 7]עמו֯. The last letter may also be *yod*.

L. 7 ת֯◦ו֯. The first letter is probably *taw*, but *waw* with *nun* cannot be ruled out altogether. Puech interpreted the next letter as medial *mem*, but that is hardly possible since the stroke reaches the baseline. The slant of the stroke and the barely visible beginning of an upward stroke rather suggest *šin*/*śin*. Note also the remains of a vertical stroke to the right of the next letter.

Translation

1.] [
2. [ ] Solomon,[ ] and he shall invo[ke
3. [the spi]rits, [ ]and the demons, [
4. [ ] These are [the de]mons. And the p[rince of enmi]ty
5. [w]ho [ ] the a[byss]
6. [ ] [ ]the gre[at]

7. [ ] [ ]his nation [ ] cure
8. [ ]relied [upon] your name. And invo[ke]
9. [Is]rael. Lean
10. [on YHWH, the God of gods, who made] the heavens
11. [and the earth, and all that is in them, w]ho separated[ ]
12. [light from darkness] [

COMMENTS

L. 1]שׂמׄ[. Since the only certain letter is *šin*, all reconstructions must be regarded as hypothetical. Therefore, the suggestion that the psalm began here (running from here to col. V 3), and the reconstruction according to col. V 4 (Puech), are unwarranted.

L. 2]שלומה. 𝔐 always writes שלמה, but various *plene* writings are found in the scrolls from the Judaean Desert; cf. e.g. 4QMMT C 18 שלומוה; 3Q**15** V 6; 8–9 שלומו. According to Jewish sources, King Solomon is known for exorcising demons and mastering their harmful influence. Flavius Josephus, commenting on 1 Kgs 5:13, assures his reader that God gave to Solomon the knowledge of the devices to apply against the demons in order to help and cure people. He also composed incantations by which diseases are cured, and he passed on to posterity formulas of exorcism by which those who are possessed by demons may be permanently rid of them (*Ant*. 8.45). Josephus relates how he saw someone called Eleazar exorcise a demon by holding a ring under its nose, and by uttering the name of Solomon and the spells composed by him. Cf. also Wis 7:20.[2] A possible reconstruction of the complete line is [יאמר לחש אשר עש]ה שלומה ויקר]א בשם יהוה 'he shall utter a spell which Solomon made, and he shall invoke the name of YHWH'. In any case, ויקרׄ]א is probably part of an apodosis. The sentence may have begun with a clause comparable to that in col. IV 5, 'when someone is possessed by a demon'. In that case, this line would probably be part of the beginning of a new song.

L. 2 ויקרׄ]א[. Reconstruct, e.g. ויקרׄ]א בשם יהוה] (cf. col. V 4–5). Note, however, Josephus' account, in which Eleazar calls the name of Solomon.

L. 3]הרו]חותׄ. Possible reconstructions of the first part of the line are: [לפלט מכול נגע הרו]חותׄ], 'to set him free from every affliction of the spirits' (Puech), or [לפחד ולבהל כול הרו]חותׄ], 'to frighten and terrify all the spirits' (cf. 4Q**510** 1 5). The first reconstruction gives a column width of *c*.11.5 cm; the second, *c*.11.8 cm.

L. 3 והשדים[. The pl. שדים is used in Deut 32:17 and Ps 106:37. שד is used frequently in rabbinic texts as a name of (the) demons. In this scroll, only the definite plural form has been preserved.

Ll. 3–4 הרו]חותׄ] [והשדים. The clause אלהׄ[השׁ]דים in the next line may suggest that the preceding sentence consisted of an enumeration of 'demons'. Similar enumerations in 4Q**510** 1 5 and 4Q**511** 10 1 suggest a reconstruction like הרו]חותׄ] [והשדים [והלילית] / [והאחים והציים] (Puech).

L. 4 אלהׄ [השׁ]דים. The reconstruction is inspired by the preceding line.

L. 4 ושׂׄ[ר המשט]מה. A tentative reconstruction (Puech); cf. CD XVI 5 מלאך המשטמה.

L. 5 תהׄו]ם. תהום occurs several times in the text. Cf. col. IV 7, 9 (reconstruction).

L. 5 ך[. Because of the repeated mention of the darkness of the abyss or Sheol in cols. IV and V, one may perhaps reconstruct חוש]ך (Puech), חשו]ך (but תהום is fem. in col. IV 9), or וחש]ך (cf. col. IV 8).

L. 6 לשׁ°[. Reconstruct perhaps לשדׄ] or לשדׄ]ים.

L. 6 והׄי[. Reconstruct, e.g. אל]והׄי, 'the gods of' or 'my God', or על]והׄי.

L. 7 עמׄו[. Possibly 'his nation' or the end of a completely different word, e.g. יר]עמו. Unfortunately, the next word is hard to read. If it is a verb, עמו may be a *nomen rectum*, the *regens* being a plural, e.g. בני or פגועי. The fragmentary state of the preceding lines precludes an identification of the person to whom the suffix refers (God or, e.g. Michael).

---

2. For more references to the role of Solomon and the use of his name, cf. E. Schürer, *The History of the Jewish People in the Age of Jesus Christ (175 B.C.–A.D. 135)*, vol. III/I revised and edited by G. Vermes, F. Millard, M. Goodman (Edinburgh: T. and T. Clark, 1986) 375–9.

L. 7 רפואה. 'Cure', 'medicine'; cf. e.g. Jer 30:13; 46:11; Ezek 30:21; Sir 3:26.

L. 8 על] שמך נשען. נשען is a perfect or participle. For נשען, cf. Isa 10:20; 50:10 ('let him trust in the name of YHWH, and rely upon his God'). For similar formulations, cf. 2 Chr 13:18; 14:10 ('O YHWH, our God! for we rely on You, and upon Your name'); 16:7–8. The Name is a protection against demons; cf. e.g. Ps 20:2. The use of the 2nd person suggests that this clause is part of a speech to God. It is, however, uncertain where this speech begins and ends: e.g. should]והי in line 6 be interpreted as אל]והי, 'my God'?

L. 8 וקר[א]. Probably an imperative beginning a new sentence ('Invoke!').

Ll. 8–9 וקר[א] / [ ] יש]ראל. A possible reconstruction of the sentence is: וקר[א] / [אל השמים ובטח על שומר יש]ראל (Puech). The epithet שומר ישראל is not attested in the texts from the Judaean Desert, but it is used in Ps 121:3 in connection with YHWH's creative acts. אלוהי יש]ראל (often used in later magical amulets), or קדוש יש]ראל (cf. e.g. 4Q**176** 8–11 7) also fit.

L. 9 החזק. Probably an imperative, 'Be strong', like וקר[א] in line 8. In the Hebrew Bible this form is attested in 2 Sam 11:25; Ps 35:2; Prov 4:13. The imperative *Qal* is more frequent (cf. e.g. Josh 1:6-7, 9 'be strong and resolute for YHWH your God is with you wherever you go'; Deut 31:6; 1 Chr 22:13; 28:20. The expression החזיק ב-, 'to be strong in', conveys the notion of 'leaning or relying on'.

Ll. 9–10 החזק / [ביהוה אלוהי אלים. A tentative reconstruction (Puech), but a reference to YHWH is very probable. For אלוהי אלים, cf. e.g. 4Q**402** 4 8; 9 2; 4Q**403** 1 i 26; 4Q**511** 16 4.

Ll. 10–12 עשה] את השמים / [ואת הארץ ואת כול אשר בם א]שר הבדיל[בין] / [האור ובין החושך. The reconstruction (Puech) is based on the preserved words, which suggest a reference to God's acts of creation, when God separated (הבדיל) light and darkness. It is possible that the first lines of the next column also refer to God's creative acts; cf. the mention of ארץ and עשה. Yet there, too, the general topic is difficult to ascertain. References to the creative acts of God are also found in later amulets, e.g. Naveh and Shaked, amulet 9.[3]

L. 11 הבדיל[. Cf. the use of this verb in Genesis 1. However, הבדיל is also used in other contexts regarding the separation of Israel from the nations (Lev 20:24), the Levites from their brothers (Num 16:9; Deut 10:8), and that which is pure from the impure (Lev 20:25). Qumran sectarian literature refers to the separation of the community from the rest of Israel (1QS V 1; CD VI 14), and also to the 'separation' (distinction) between the pure and the impure (CD VI 17). הבדיל could be related to demons, being essentially impure, in spite of השמים in the preceding line.

Col. III

[ ]תה[ ]התהומ[ות

הארץ ו°[ה]ארץ מי ע[שה את האותות]

ואת המופ[תים האלה ב]ארץ יהוה הוא[ה אשר]

עשה את ה[אלה בגבור]תו משביע לכול מ[לאכיו]

[וא]ת כול זר[ע הקודש]אשר הת[י]צבו לפני[ו ויעיד א]ת

[כול השמ]ים ו[את כול] הארץ[בהם]אשר יעשו[ ]על

[3] J. Naveh, S. Shaked, *Amulets and Magic Bowls. Aramaic Incantations of Late Antiquity* (Jerusalem: Magnes Press; Leiden: E. J. Brill, 1985).

7 [כול אי]ש֯ חטא ועל כול א֯[דם רשע ו]ה֯ם יודעים

8 [רזי פל]או אשר אינם [ ]ה אם לוא

9 [ייראו]מלפני יהוה ל[ו]להרוג נפש

10 [ ]יהוה ויירא[ו את המכה ה]גדולה הזוא֯[ת]

11 [וירדף א]חד מכם א[לף]°עבד֯י יהו[ה]

12 [ג]ד֯ולה ו֯[ ]ר֯ת[

Mus. Inv. 61
PAM 43.982, 43.983, 43.984, 44.113*

NOTES ON READINGS

PAM 43.983 shows frg. a placed on top of the beginning of col. III, thereby obscuring line 1, the first letter of line 2, and the last two letters of col. II 4. In PAM 44.113, the fragment has been removed. Frg. a fits perfectly with, and partly beneath, the next revolution in the same column. The fragment preserves a portion of the lower layer of the skin (not visible on Plate XXIII), whereas the top of the middle of the column has preserved the surface layer (therefore the join does not appear perfect in PAM 44.113).

L. 1 ה֯תהומ[ו]ת[. The tip of a downstroke before *taw* seems too close to belong to *waw*. A minute speck after the *mem* may be the rest of *waw*.

L. 2 הארץ. It is unlikely that the black spot in front of *he* is the head of *waw*, being too close. It does not correspond to the typical form of the head of *waw*, and there is no trace of a downstroke.

L. 2 ו֯°[. The trace of ink after *waw* should belong to *ʿayin* or *šin*. A *kap* is unlikely; the lower part of the leg and the right part of the base of *kap* should have been preserved.

L. 4 ה֯[אלה. The letter may be *he*, assuming that the crossbar did not extend past the right leg.

L. 4 בגבור]ת֯ו. Instead of *taw*, the first trace may be regarded as the bottom part of a diagonal, hence *ʾalep* or *gimel*, and read the second letter as *nun*, or, with more difficulty, *ṣade*.

L. 4 מ֯[לאכיו]. The broken letter is probably *mem* (cf. מי in line 2); *ṭet* or *pe* are less likely because of the slant of the base.

L. 5 [וא]ת֯. A large part of the left leg of the *taw* is covered by the yellow substance which also covers the beginning of the other lines. The very faint trace at the beginning of the line is not ink, but the lower layer of the skin. The word can be either [א]ת֯ or [וא]ת֯.

L. 5 זר֯[ע הקודש]. זר֯[ע הקדושים] is too long for the gap.

L. 5 ה֯ת֯[י]צ֯בו. The traces may be interpreted as the right end of the crossbar of *he*, the top parts of the legs of *taw*, and the arm of *ṣade*.

L. 6 ו֯[את. *Waw* is the most logical reading. Note, however, that the distance between *waw* and the assumed *ʾalep* is rather large. There is a small dot at the edge which might be the bottom tip of the diagonal, but similar faint traces close to it are definitely not ink.

L. 6 יע֯ש֯[ו. The traces of the second letter suggest *ʿayin* or *šin*. In the gap, there is a small trace, and two smaller specks on the edge of the skin. The trace might be the bottom tip of the left arm of *śin*. Puech reads יש֯[ל]ח֯[ו, which leaves only a small space before על.

L. 7 אי]ש֯. The trace at the very left edge of the line belongs to *zayin*, *ḥet*, final *ṣade*, or *šin*.

L. 7 ו]ה֯ם. The trace before final *mem* seems to be the left end of a crossbar; it lacks the wedge form of *taw*.

L. 11 עבדי°[. Before ʿ*ayin*, there is a horizontal trace on the ceiling line which normally would be interpreted as *he*. The dark area at the bottom shows no trace of the diagonal of *mem*. The head of the last letter suggests it is *yod*, not *waw*. It is tempting to read מׄעבדי יהו[ה], but the trace of the first letter is not common to *mem*.

L. 12 וׄ[. The vertical stroke breaks through the ceiling line, and there is no distinct tick. A *kap* (Puech) is possible, assuming that the head has faded away.

TRANSLATION

1. [ ] [ ]the depth[s
2. the earth and [the] earth. Who ma[de these portents]
3. and won[ders on the] earth? It is he, YHWH[who]
4. made [these through] his [strength,] who summons all [his] an[gels]
5. [and] all the [holy] see[d] to st[a]nd before [him, and calls as witness]
6. [all the hea]vens and[all] the earth[against them]who committe[d]against
7. [all me]n sin, and against all p[eople evil. But] they know
8. his [wonder]ful [secrets] which they do not [ ] If they do not
9. [refrain out of fear]of YHWH from[and] from killing,
10. [ ]YHWH and [t]he[y] will fear tha[t] great [blow.]
11. [O]ne among you [will chase after]a th[ousand] servants of YHW[H]
12. [g]reat and[ ] [

COMMENTS

L. 1]תה[ ]. Read [א]תה[or, e.g. [ה]תה[ומות or [ל]תה[ום (cf. col. IV 7). If [א]תה[, one may reconstruct the preceding line ואמרתה אליו מי] (cf. col. V 5–6).

L. 1]תה[ ]התהומ[ות. The reconstruction [א]תה[עשיתה השמים ו]התהומ[ות וכול אשר בם] (Puech) is problematic, as one would expect the use of the *nota accusativi* after עשיתה.

L. 2 ע]שה את האותות]. אותות and מופתים (line 3) are often used together. עשה is used with מופתים in Exod 11:10.

L. 3 ואת המופ]תים. Probably plural; cf. Deut 7:19; 29:2; 34:11 (the great miracles which God performed on behalf of Israel). In Exod 7:9 there is another kind of מופת which Moses and Aaron must perform in the presence of Pharaoh and which the Egyptian magicians will also be able to perform (cf. vv 11-12). The meaning of the word in this context is not certain. In the Hebrew Bible, מופת does not refer to the wondrous acts of creation.

L. 3 יהוה הואׄ[ה. Here appears the beginning of the answer to the question posed in the previous line, מי ע]שה.

L. 4 משביע לכול. Cf. Ps 145:16 משביע לכול חי רצון, 'you feed every creature to its heart's content', but the genre of 11QapocrPs suggests a reading of משביע, 'adjuring'. The use of the preposition -ל after השביע is not regular; Biblical Hebrew uses a direct object, whereas later stages of Hebrew employ the preposition על.

L. 4–5 לכול מׄ[לאכיו] / [ואׄ]תׄ כול זרׄ[ע הקודש]אשר התׄ[י]צׄבו לפני[ו. The fragmentary state of the lines allows for different reconstructions. Puech suggests the reading משביע לכול מׄ[לאך לעזור] / [א]תׄ כול זרׄ[ע הקודש]אשר התׄ[י]צׄבו לפני[ו, 'adjuring each an[gel to help the holy] race who stand in his presence', referring to the fact that the angels are often told to 'help' the righteous. In this case, the plural of התׄ[י]צׄבו is *ad sensum*. However, [א]תׄ כול זרׄ[ע הקודש may be parallel to לכול מׄ[, either syndetically ([וא]תׄ) or asyndetically ([א]תׄ), and the contents of the adjuration can be expressed by אשר (cf. e.g. Gen 24:3). The length of line 4 demands that either מ[לאך is *nomen regens*, or that one reads a longer word, e.g. מ[לאכיו. If the reconstruction is correct, משביע is first followed by the unusual -ל, then by the normal את. Yet, it should be noted that both objects of משביע have only been preserved in part. (It is possible that the text read לכול מׄ[מזרים / [ואׄ]תׄ כול זרׄ[ע הרשע: God adjures the bastards and the seed of evil to appear before him).

L. 5 ויעיד א[ת. After לפני]ו, a verb that governs a direct object should probably be read. It is not clear whether one should reconstruct a participle like the previous משביע, or a finite verb introducing a new sentence. ויעיד, 'and he will call as witness', makes more sense than וידין. Cf. the parallelism of השביע and העיד in 1 Kgs 2:42, and COMMENTS to line 6.

Ll. 5–6 א[ת / [כול השׄ]מׄים ו]את כול [הארׄץ]. Cf. for the invoking of heaven and earth, Deut 4:26; 30:19; 31:28. The reconstruction א[ת / [בני השׄ]מׄים ו]את כול [הארׄץ (Puech) is improbable, since the expression is בני שמים, not בני השמים.

L. 6 [בהם]. Against the style of Biblical Hebrew, in which העיד ב- is followed by את.

L. 7 [כול אי]שׄ. כול האר]ץׄ is too long for the lacuna.

L. 8 [רזי פל]או. פלאו is regularly used as *nomen rectum* with גבורות, רזי, and מעשי. מעשי only fits if written in small, condensed script. רז is also the object of ידע in other scrolls from the Judaean Desert; cf. e.g. 1QH[a] XII 27–28 (= IV 27–28) כי הודעתני ברזי / פלאכה; 4Q**511** 2 ii 6 [רז]יׄ אלוהים מׄיא ידׄעׄ]; similarly in 1QH[a] XV 27 (= VII 27).

L. 8 אינם [ ]ה. Reconstruct, e.g. אינם [עושים כמו]ה, 'the like of which they cannot do' or אינם [יודעים כמו]ה, 'the like of which they do not know'. Cf. *1 Enoch* 16:3: 'you were in heaven, but the secrets had not yet been revealed to you, and you knew a worthless secret'.

L. 9 [ייראו]. The first word of the line is probably a verb expressing fear, e.g. ייראו, יפחדו, or יבהלו. מלפני is used both with verbs of motion, and with verbs of fearing to indicate the person one fears, whereas ל- with infinitive expresses the action one fears to do. Both constructions are used in Biblical Hebrew with ירא, but not together.

L. 9]להרוג נפש. Cf. Num 31:19; 2 Sam 14:7; Jer 4:31. In the preceding lacuna one may reconstruct another infinitive with an object or two infinitives, e.g. לפגוע באדם, לנגוע באדם, or לאסור אדם (Puech).

L. 10 [ ]יהוה. The missing word is either a verb (*waw* with imperfect) beginning the apodosis, or ול- with infinitive continuing the preceding infinitives. A third possibility, a second imperfect belonging to the protasis, is less likely. Read, e.g. ולחרף]יהוה and וישפוט]יהוה, or preferably וישפטם]יהוה.

L. 10 המכה ה]גדולה הזואׄ[ת]. The reconstruction המכה is based upon col. IV 4. Cf. COMMENTS there.

L. 11 [וירדף א]חד מכם א[לף. Cf. Josh 23:10 איש אחד מכם ירדף אלף; Ps 91:7.

L. 11]◦עבדי יהו[ה]. The reconstruction ושר הצבא]מׄעבדי יהו[ה, 'and the prince of the army is amongst the servants of YHWH' (Puech; cf. col. V 8), is unwarranted and grammatically awkward (בעבדי, not מעבדי, would be expected).

Col. IV

1 [ו]גדול[ ]משביע[

2 והגדול בׄ[ ]תקיף ורׄ[

3 כול הארץ[ ] השמים וׄ[

4 יככה יהוה מ[כה גדול]ה אשר לאבדך[

5 ובחרון אפו[ישלח]עליך מלאך תקיף[לעשות]

6 [כול דב]רו אשר[בלוא] רחמ[ים] עליך אש[ר

7 [ ]עׄל כול אלה אשרׄ[יורידו]ךׄ לתהום רבה

8 [ולשאול] התחתיה ומׄ[ ]◦כב וחשך

9 [בתהום ר]בׄה מואדה [לוא ע]וׄד בארץ
10 [ ]עד עולם ואׄ[ ]בׄקללת האב[דון]
11 [ ]חׄרון אף יׄ[הוה ב]חושך בכׄ[ול]
12 [תעודות]תׄעניות [ ] מתנתך
13 [ ]לׄ[ ]◦[ ]ה הׄ◦[

Mus. Inv. 61
PAM 43.984*, 43.985

NOTES ON READINGS

L. 2 ורׄ[. The absence of any trace on the skin after the vertical stroke of the second letter indicates that it is not *yod*, but probably *reš*.

L. 3]השמים. Dark traces are visible at the right edge of the photographs, but examination of the manuscript reveals that these are not ink.

L. 3 וׄ[. The letter after *waw* has no vertical stroke at the right, i.e. *lamed*, *samek*, *ʿayin*, or *šin*.

L. 5 תקיףׄ[. The long downstroke of final *pe* has been abraded altogether. Only part of the left diagonal stroke is still visible.

L. 5 לעשות]. The small trace at the end of the line is not ink.

L. 6 [כול דב]רו. The reconstruction barely fits in the gap, leaving little space between the two words.

L. 7 יורידו]ךׄ. The last letter is *dalet* or final *kap*. Puech reads [יש]ל[ח]ך, but the trace which he interprets as the top of *lamed* is almost certainly the left tip of the base of *ʿayin* of עליך in line 6.

L. 8 ומׄיׄ[. Or, alternatively, ומׄ[.

L. 8]◦כב. Before *kap* there are two traces. The upper one is compatible with the top of the left arm of *šin*, but the bottom diagonal stroke cannot be part of *šin*. The letter may be *šin* if the bottom stroke is not ink. Alternatively one might regard the letter as *ʿayin* with a rather short base.

L. 9 ר]בׄה. The letter could be either *bet* or *kap*, even though it is larger than the average *bet*.

L. 9 ע]וׄד. The trace before *dalet* is definitely ink; it is probably the left part of the head of *waw* or *yod*.

L. 10 ואׄ[. The small trace after *waw* most likely belongs to a letter without a (right) downstroke: *ʾalep* or *šin*, or, less likely, *qop*.

L. 11 יׄ[הוה. The skin is abraded, either resulting from the breaking off of a fragment or from a scribal correction which failed to cancel the top of the letter.

L. 11 בכׄ[ול. The slightly slanting downstroke after *bet* is curved and could belong to *waw*, *kap*, *mem*, *pe*, or *taw*.

L. 12]תׄעניות [. In spite of the dark spots at the edge of the skin, it is possible to recognize the left downstroke and base of *taw*.

L. 13 הׄ◦[. The *he* is rather peculiar, but the traces fit no other letter. The second letter could be a *waw* preceded by a spot of a dark substance that has not been removed.

TRANSLATION

1. [and] great[ ]adjuring[
2. and the great [ ]powerful and [
3. all the earth[ ] the heavens and[
4. YHWH will strike you with a [grea]t b[low] to destroy you[

5. And in his fury[he will send]against you a powerful angel[to carry out]
6. his [entire comm]and, who[will not show] you mercy, wh[o
7. [ ]over all these, who[will bring] you [down] to the great abyss
8. [and to] the deepest [Sheol.] And [,] and it will be very dark
9. [in the gr]eat [abyss. No any]more on the earth
10. [ ]forever and [ ]by the curse of Ab[addon]
11. [ ]the fury of Y[HWH in] darkness for a[ll]
12. [periods of] humiliation [ ] your gift
13. [ ][ ][ ][

COMMENTS

L. 1]משביע[. The word may be used with the same sense as in col. III 4: YHWH summons an angel or angels to do something. However, since the next lines (4–6) address the demon, it is also possible that the text deals with the adjuration of a demon.

L. 2 תקיף[. This word of Aramaic origin is also found in Qoh 6:10: 'strong', 'cruel'. One may perhaps reconstruct מלאך[תקיף (cf. line 5).

L. 2]ור̇. Read, e.g. ור̇[דף (cf. the reconstruction of col. III 11).

L. 4 יככה יהוה מ[כה גדול]ה אשר לאבדך[. A curse formula; cf. Deut 28:22, 27, 28, 35 (cf. also Num 11:33; Deut 25:2-3; Josh 10:10, 32; Judg 11:33; 1 Sam 6:19; 19:8; 23:5; 1 Kgs 20:21). The words יככה יהוה may indicate that the author was thinking especially of Deuteronomy. The last word of the line may have been לעולם.

L. 5 ובחרון אפו[. The חרון אפו or חרון אף יהוה is mentioned repeatedly in the Hebrew Bible. Cf. e.g. Ps 78:49: 'He inflicted His flaring anger upon them (ישלח בם חרון אפו), wrath, indignation, trouble, a band of deadly messengers (מלאכי רעים)'. מלאך תקיף is reminiscent of Prov 17:11: אך מרי יבקש רע ומלאך אכזרי ישלח בו, 'Ah! An evil man seeks only to rebel, and a ruthless messenger will be sent against him'. In these texts, מלאך is a messenger of YHWH, without the distinction being made between a good and a bad angel ('demon'). מלאך תקיף of **11Q11** could very well be an angel who is sent to combat a demon, like, e.g. Raphael, who catches the demon Asmodeus and chains him in the desert of Upper Egypt (Tob 8:3; ט).

L. 6 כול דב[רו]. Or את דב[רו].

L. 6 אשר[בלוא] רחמ[ים]. Rather than אשר [אין לו] רחמ[ים], which does not fit. For this notion, cf. *1 Enoch* 12:5 'they will have neither mercy nor peace' (cf. 13:2) and *1 Enoch* 68:2-5.

Ll. 6–7 אש[ר. Reconstruct, e.g. אש[ר הואה] / [שליט], 'who is in charge of', but not אש[ר שליט] / [הואה] which is syntactically awkward. Cf. the examples in C. Brockelman, *Hebräische Syntax* (Neukirchen: Kreis Moers, 1956) § 152a (the exception is Gen 7:2 אשר לא טהורה הוא).

L. 7]ע̇ל כול אלה אשר̇[יורידו]ך̇[. Since there seems to be no antecedent to אלה, one may assume that אלה is qualified by the next clause. However, it is also possible that אשר̇ introduces the third qualification of the powerful angel. The missing verb, almost certainly ending with a 2nd masc. sing. suffix, probably expresses the idea of throwing or removing to the abyss. For יורידו]ך̇, which fits neatly in the gap, cf. 1 Sam 2:6; 1 Kgs 2:6, 9; with -ל, e.g. Ezek 28:8. ישליכו]ך̇ is too long, whereas יורו]ך̇ (cf. Job 30:19) is somewhat short. Those who throw are probably angels subservient to the 'powerful angel'.

L. 7 לתהום רבה. Cf. Ps 36:7; Amos 7:4; 1QH[a] XI 31 (III 31).

L. 8 [ולשאול] התחתיה. A reconstruction after the parallelism with לתהום רבה at the end of line 7 and col. V 9 לשאו]ל תחתית]. Cf. Ps 86:13; also Isa 44:23; Ezek 31:14, 16, 18; 32:18, 24; Ps 63:10; 88:7; 139:15.

L. 8 ומ̇[ ]כ◦כב. In spite of the palaeographical difficulties, it is tempting to read the last word as ת]שׁכב. Since the idea expressed in the gap is probably the darkness of Sheol, one may reconstruct ומ̇[עון אור (Puech) or ומ̇[אורות ת]שׁכב. Read alternatively the verb עכב, 'to detain, prevent', and reconstruct e.g. ומ̇[שלת אור]ע̇כב, 'and he will detain the dominion of light'.

L. 8 וחשך. Cf. the partly reconstructed description of the darkness of Sheol in col. V.

L. 9 מואדה. A variant of מאד. Cf. 1QIs[a] XXXIX 26, 29 (Isa 47:6, 9); 1QM XIX 5; XII 13 (מאדה), etc.

L. 9 [ע]וׄד בארץ]. This clause and the next probably describe the everlasting punishment of the demon in Sheol. Reconstruct, e.g. [לוא תשלט ע]וׄד בארץ (Puech) or another verb, e.g. חשב, תרבץ (cf. col. I 11?), etc.

L. 10 [ ]עד עולם. Reconstruct, e.g. [ותאסר]עד עולם, or [ותסגר]עד עולם (cf. *1 Enoch* 21:10), or [מעולם]עד עולם.

L. 10 ואׄ[. Reconstruct, e.g. ואׄ[תה תקלל (*Puʿal*) or, rather, ואׄ[רור אתה.

L. 10 בׄ[קללת. Cf. e.g. Deut 11:26; 28:13; 34:26; Zech 8:13.

L. 10 [האבדון]. 'Destruction', 'Abaddon'. Cf. 4QBer[a] 10 ii 7 השחת ורו[ח האבד]ון. This reconstruction is more likely than [האב]ות, 'the fathers', who heard the cursings of Deuteronomy, pronounced by Moses (van der Ploeg).

L. 11]חׄרון אף יׄ[הוה. Cf. line 5. Reconstruct, e.g. [ותבהל ב]חׄרון אף יׄ[הוה (Puech). Cf. Ps 2:5 ובחרונו יבהלמו, and the use of בהל in 4Q**510** 1 3, 4; 4Q**511** 37 5. However, other verbs expressing punishment or fear are also possible.

L. 11 ב]חושך. Reconstruct a verbal form before ב]חושך, probably 2nd masc. sing. imperfect, e.g. a verb expressing 'dwelling', 'being bound', 'being covered by', 'perish', etc.

L. 12 [תעודות] תׄעניות]. Cf. 4Q**510** 1 7 ותעודות תעניות בני אוׄ[ר]. On this specific meaning of תעודה ('period', instead of 'testimony'), cf. Baillet on 4Q510 1 7 in *DJD* VII.

Col. V

1 [ ]○[ ]ד̊○[ ]○[

2 אשׁ̊ר[ ]הׄפגוע[ים]

3 נדבי א[ר]פׄאל שלמ[ם אמן אמן סלה] *vacat*

4 לדויד עׄ[ל ל]חׄש בשם יהו[ה קרא בכו]ל עת

5 אל הׄשמׄ[ים כי]יׄבוא אליך בליׄ[לה וא]מרתה אליו

6 מי אתה [הילוד מ]אדם ומזרע הקדׄ[ושי]םׄ פניך פני

7 [שו]וׄ וקרניׄךׄ קרני חל[ו]םׄ חושך אתה ולוא אור

8 [עו]ל ולוא צדקה[ ]שׄר הצׄבׄה יהוה [יוריד]ך

9 [לשאו]ל תחתית [ויסגור דל]תי נחושת בׄ[אלה לו]א

10 [יעבור] אור ולוא[יאיר לך ה]שמש אש[ר יזרח]

11 [על ה]צׄדיק לה[ו]אמרתה ה[

12 [הצ]דיק לבואׄ[ ]הׄרע לו ש[ד

13 [א]מת מח○[אשר הצ]דׄקה לו[

14 [ ] ולׄ[ ]ל[ ]ה

Mus. Inv. 61
PAM 43.985*, 43.986

NOTES ON READINGS

L. 1]◦[ ]. The bottom tip of the downstroke belongs to the second letter of the line. The first letter may be *waw* or, more likely, *yod* or *lamed*. The minute dot before the downstroke, if ink, may be the utmost left tip of the head of *yod* or the bottom tip of the diagonal of *lamed*. No traces are visible any longer on the original.

L. 1]ד֯◦[. The first two traces may also be the downstroke and the left end of the head of *reš*.

L. 2]ה֯פגוע[ים. The bottom part of the downstroke before *pe* indicates *waw* or *he*.

L. 3 נדבי א[. There is no space between *yod* and *ʾalep*.

L. 3 שלמ[ם. Note the extremely long base of *mem*.

L. 4 ל]ח֯ש. The small black dot at the edge of the skin may be the bottom tip of the left leg of *ḥet*, but many other letters are also possible.

L. 4 בכו]ל֯. The arm above the ceiling line strongly suggests *lamed*, but in the fragment the trace can no longer be seen.

L. 5 ה֯שמׄ[ים. The traces can also be read as ר֯שפׄ[with medial *pe* (van der Ploeg).

L. 5]י֯בוא. The trace at the edge is most likely to be part of *yod*, even though the stance of the stroke does not correspond exactly to *yod*. However, the fragment is broken at this point, and it is not possible to ascertain if the spot is indeed ink.

L. 6 אתה [. The small vertical stroke after אתה is not ink, but merely a discolouration.

L. 6 הקד֯[ושי]םׄ. Not הקו[דש כ]י֯ (van der Ploeg), which is too long. The trace of the last letter corresponds more closely to final *mem* than to *yod*. At first sight, the letter after *qop* does not resemble *dalet*, since the crossbar normally breaks through the leg. Cf., however, e.g. שדי in col. VI 3.

L. 7 [שו]ו. Or ש]ו֯ו if the faint spot is regarded as part of the head of the first *waw*.

L. 7 וקרנ֯י֯ך. The last two letters are almost completely obscured due to deterioration of the skin.

L. 7 חל[ו]ם֯. The available space and the dot at the end of the word rule out most reconstructions.

L. 8]ש֯ר. Traces of the letter before *reš* consist of a vertical stroke to which a small horizontal stroke is attached to the right; hence, *zayin* or *šin/śin* are the most likely.

L. 8 הצ֯ב֯ה. The second letter is *ʾalep* or *ṣade* (not *šin*!); the third letter is *bet*, *kap*, *mem*, *nun*, *ʿayin*, *pe*, *ṣade*, or *taw*.

L. 9 ב֯[אלה. There is definitely a trace after נחושת, but it is hard to determine whether it is an oblique trace or only a spot, because it is covered by a fold in the skin which cannot be flattened.

L. 10 ה]שמש. The trace before שמש in the photograph is not visible in the manuscript.

L. 13 מח◦[. The left leg of *ḥet* is visible in the manuscript. The small trace after *ḥet* could belong to many letters, e.g. *waw*.

L. 13 לו[. The photograph was taken when the edge of the manuscript was still folded back, hiding the *waw*. Now the fold has been flattened and the *waw* is clearly visible.

L. 14] ול֯[. Puech reads]ו◦[and supralinear לוא. The area between lines 13 and 14 is damaged, and there are several dark traces. *Waw* and *lamed* are possible; *ʾalep* is not likely. The trace which, according to Puech, is part of supralinear *ʾalep*, could also be part of a normal *lamed*.

L. 14]ל[. The trace after *lamed* is not ink.

TRANSLATION

1. [ ] [ ] [ ] [
2. which[ ]the possessed[
3. the volunteers of [Ra]phael has healed [them. Amen, amen. Selah.] *vacat*
4. Of David. A[gainst An incanta]tion in the name of YHW[H. Invoke at an]y time

5. the heav[ens. When]he comes to you in the nig[ht,] you will [s]ay to him:
6. 'Who are you, [oh offspring of] man and of the seed of the ho[ly one]s? Your face is a face of
7. [delu]sion and your horns are horns of ill[us]ion, you are darkness and not light,
8. [injust]ice and not justice.[ ]the chief of the army, YHWH [will bring] you [down]
9. [to the] deepest [Sheo]l, [and he will shut the] two bronze [ga]tes th[rough which n]o
10. light [penetrates,] and [the] sun [will] not [shine for you] tha[t rises]
11. [upon the] just man to [And] you will say: [
12. [the j]ust man, to go[ ] a de[mon] mistreats him, [
13. [of tr]uth from [because] he has [jus]tice [
14. [ ] and [ ] [ ]

COMMENTS

L. 2]הׄפגוע[ים. Cf. 11QPs[a] XXVII 10; 4Q**511** 11 8. One may also read the sing., or a *nomen regens*.

L. 3 נדבי א[. The alternative reading, נדביא[, cannot be explained convincingly. Reconstruct, e.g. נדבי א]מתו; cf. 1QS I 11 הנדבים לאמתו, 'those who volunteer for his truth' (Puech).

L. 3 ר]פׄאל. Raphael may be mentioned here as the angel *par excellence* who heals. Cf. e.g. Tob 3:17; 6:8-9, 17; 11:7-8; *1 Enoch* 20:3.

L. 3 שלמ]ם. If Raphael is the subject, one should reconstruct a pronominal suffix. שלם (*Piʿel*) is used in the sense of 'to heal' (cf. the *Qal* with the meaning 'to be healthy').

L. 3 אמן אמן סלה]. Since the next songs end with these words, they may also be reconstructed here; cf. COMMENTS to col. VI 3.

L. 4 לדויד. The heading of a new psalm. Cf. also the *vacat* at the end of line 3.

L. 4 עׄ]ל. The phrase in the gap may be an analogy to the 'upon' phrases in the headings of many canonical psalms. Alternatively, על may be 'against', in which case one should reconstruct רוח, or another three- or four-letter word referring to evil spirits (e.g. שדים or שטן). עׄ]ל דברי, 'concerning the words of' (Puech) is unlikely, since על דברי (with a proper name, or ספר, ברית, etc.) is not attested as a formula on its own. Another possibility is עׄ]ל פגוע; cf. 11QPs[a] XXVII 9–10 שיר לנגן על פגועים.

L. 4 ל]חׄש. The reconstruction ל]חׄש, 'incantation', 'spell', 'charm', at the end of the lacuna, is quite plausible; cf. Isa 3:3, 20; 26:16; Jer 8:17; Qoh 10:11. However, one may also read ל]חׄש as an imperative *Piʿel*.

L. 4 בשם יהו]ה. An adjunct of ל]חׄש. The name of YHWH is an efficient remedy against pains and dangers; cf. Ps 14:3; 20:2; 118:10; Prov 18:10.

L. 4 קרא. The reconstruction קרא is *exempli gratia*, but note the repeated use of קרא in the scroll.

L. 5 הׄשמׄ]ים. Rather than the reading רשפׄ[. רשף means 'flame', 'lightning', but also fever or pest; cf. Deut 32:24; Hab 3:5 (here 𝔙 translates *diabolus*). According to the rabbinic tradition, רשף can be a name of demons. According to *b. Ber.* 5a, R. Isaac says that the בני רשף of Job 5:7 are the מזיקים, a category of demons; the mediaeval *Targum of Job* agrees with him. In *b. Pesaḥ* 3b, the demons who live on the roof are called רישפי (pl. of רישפא). The spelling of רׄשפׄ[with medial *pe* is problematic since the plural רשפׄ]ים does not agree with the following singular forms. A solution might be to interpret the following as referring to one of the species (. . . 'the roof demons; when one of them comes to you'), but this is unlikely.

L. 5 כי]יׄבוא. The sentence is a conditional clause, but the particle introducing the protasis is missing. Reconstruct כי, or the less usual particle אשר. The latter fits better, but כי is not necessarily too short for the gap.

L. 5 בליׄ]לה. Or בליׄ]על. The choice between the two readings depends on the overall understanding of the text. בליׄ]לה is only possible if the subject was already mentioned in the text, e.g. in the heading. The mention of the night is perfectly possible as it is the most dangerous moment. Belial is not mentioned elsewhere in this psalm (except for col. VI 3 בני בל]יעל which is not pertinent), but nothing in the text opposes this reading.

L. 6 מי אתה. Either simply the question 'who are you?', or 'whoever you are', optionally followed by an attribute qualifying אתה (cf. e.g. Zech 4:7; *KAI* 13 3; 14 4 and 20;[4] in Aramaic: מן את *KAI* 225 5; 226 8; 259 2; cf. also Akkadian *mannu atta*).

L. 6 מי אתה [הילוד מ]אדם. Reconstruct, e.g. [הילוד], 'born', or 'offspring' (with the article as vocative). Usually ילוד is used in a genetival construction, but the reference to two parentages may have provoked the use of the preposition מן. The author holds the view that the evil spirits came (indirectly) into existence through the intermingling of the Watchers and the daughters of men. This solution makes more sense of the phrase 'the seed of the holy ones'. The reconstruction is not compatible with the reading בלי]על in the previous line; one must read בלי]לה. Other reconstructions fail on various grounds. מי אתה [ותירא מ]אדם (van der Ploeg), after Isa 51:12 מי את ותיראי מאנוש ימות, is too long. The same reconstruction with תירא without *waw* fits better, but is syntactically strange. Moreover, a verbal form seems out of place in an address consisting of nominal phrases. Puech ('11QPsAp[a]: Essai de reconstruction') refers to Gen 3:14-15 and 4:11 and suggests מי אתה [ארור מ]אדם. This phrase corresponds nicely to the curses of Belial and his spirits in other Dead Sea scrolls, e.g. 1QS II 4–7; 1QM XIII 4–5; cf. also CD XX 8; 4Q**175** 23. Yet the translation of ארור as a jussive is syntactically unwarranted.

L. 7 [שו]ׄא. The two essential words in the phrases 'your face is the face of . . . and your horns are the horns of . . . ' are broken. [תוה]ׄו (van der Ploeg) is too long (the defective spelling [תה]ׄו is not to be expected). [שו]ׄא, 'delusion', 'futility', fits better (Puech).

L. 7 חל[ו]ׄם. חל[ו]ׄם, 'dream', 'illusion', is a good parallel to [שו]ׄא (cf. Zech 10:2). Both the face and the horns inspire fear. By proclaiming these to be delusionary, the one who speaks these words negates their awesomeness. It is not clear whether these words are believed to state a fact (your appearance is a delusion), or to accomplish a change (that your appearance become nothing but a delusion). Cf. the Akkadian expression noted by Dhorme: 'Witch, like the edge of this seal, may your face become yellow and green!'.[5] The strange appearance of demons is well attested. *B. Pesaḥim* 111b describes the appearance of certain demons: some of them have no eyes, some look like spoons turning in a kettle, others look like goat horns. Other possible reconstructions are חל[כ]ׄה, 'wretch', חל[ו]ׄץ, 'warrior', or perhaps חל[ק]ׄה, 'flattery'. Other words are too long, or are not compatible with the preserved dot at the end of the word.

L. 7 חושך אתה ולוא אור. Cf. Amos 5:18, 20. The demons belong to the darkness; in the Dead Sea scrolls they are the real 'sons of darkness'.

L. 8 [ ]שׂר. Reconstruct in the gap, e.g. נגדך, 'against you' (Puech), יככה, 'he will strike you', or וביד, 'and through'.

L. 8]שׂר הצׄבׄה. For the expression, cf. Josh 5:14-15; Dan 8:11. It refers to the heavenly opponent of Belial and his evil spirits; he is called שר or השר in other Dead Sea scrolls.

L. 8 [יוריד]ך. Cf. col. IV 7. Reconstruct alternatively [יאסר]ך followed by [בשאו]ל (Puech). A verb with *lamed* such as [ישלח]ך is unlikely: there would have been traces of the *lamed* in the previous line.

L. 9 [לשאו]ל תחתית. Cf. Deut 32:22 'For a fire flares in My wrath, it will burn to the bottom of Sheol'; cf. also COMMENTS on col. IV 8.

L. 9 [ויסגור דל]תי נחושת. [סגורה בדל]תי נחושת is slightly too long. For the last two words, cf. Isa 45:2 דלתות נחושה. דלתי would be a dual form, while דלתות in Isaiah is a plural. The theme of demons (or their chief himself) being imprisoned is well attested; cf. e.g. *Jub.* 10:5, 7-8, 11; *1 Enoch* 10:4-5, 12-14; 12:6; Rev 20:1-3; and perhaps 4Q**511** 60 3 ברי]חי כלא.

Ll. 9–10 בׄ[אלה לו]א / [יעבור] אור. The reconstruction of lines 9–11 is based on the assumption that they describe the darkness of the place of imprisonment; cf. *1 Enoch* 10:4-5. Instead of בׄ[אלה לו]א / [יעבור] אור (Puech), בׄ[אלה לו]א / [תראה] אור is possible.

---

[4] H. Donner and W. Röllig, *Kanaanäische und aramäische Inschriften* (Wiesbaden: Harrasowitz, 1962–64).

[5] É. Dhorme, *L'emploi métaphorique des noms de parties du corps en Hébreu et en Accadien* (Paris: Gabalda, 1923) 51.

L. 10 ולוא[יאיר לך ה]שמש. The gap between ולוא[and ה]שמש can be reconstructed in several ways, e.g. יאיר אור (Puech), יהיה לך, יאיר לך (cf. Isa 60:19), or, since שמש can also be feminine, תאיר לך. In view of the following reconstruction, a reading which explicitly addresses the demon is preferred.

Ll. 10–11 אש[ר יזרח] / [על ה]צ֯דיק. Cf. Ps 97:11 אור זרע לצדיק where the versions (𝔊, 𝔙, and 𝔖) suggest אור זרח לצדיק (cf. Ps 112:4).

L. 11 לה֯[. Reconstruct, e.g. לה[איר את פניו (Puech), לה[איר את דרכו, or לה[גיה חשכו (Ps 18:29). The new address to the demon, introduced again by ואמרתה, is badly damaged.

Ll. 11–12 ה[ ]/ הצ]דיק. The beginning of line 12 demands a short word, most likely a preposition, before הצ]דיק. Interesting is Puech's reconstruction, ה[לוא מלאך] / [עם הצ]דיק followed by לבוא֯[במשפט כי ה֯רע לו ש֯]טן, 'is there not an angel with the just man to go to court when Satan mistreats him?'. The angels, in particular the angel of YHWH, protect those who fear God; cf. e.g. Ps 34:8; 91:11; *1 Enoch* 20; 1QS III 24–25. One may consider other reconstructions, e.g. ה[רף וצא] / [מן הצ]דיק, 'desist and come out of the just man' (cf. Luke 4:35), but in that case it is difficult to reconstruct the rest of the line.

L. 12 לבוא֯[. Reconstruct, e.g. לבוא֯[במשפט (Puech). The forensic function of angels is suggested in, e.g. Job 16:19, and is clear from, e.g. *1 Enoch* 8:4; 9:3-4. The example from Enoch is quite appropriate: the angels bring the case of those afflicted by the Watchers and the giants before the Most High. The problem is that בוא במשפט is usually followed by an object introduced by עם or את, and not absolutely (Job 9:32 יחדו implies an opponent).

L. 12]ה֯רע לו.]ה֯רע can be a noun ('the evil'), an adjective, or a *Hipʿil* of רעע (perfect, infinitive, or imperative). Reconstruct perhaps כי]ה֯רע לו (Puech).

L. 12 ש]ד. Or ש֯]טן if one reads בע֯[על in line 5.

L. 13 [א]מת מחו°[. The space before מת suggests [רוח א]מת or [בן א]מת. רוח אמת (or רוח האמת) is mentioned in, e.g. 1QS III 18–19; IV 21, 23. Reconstruct ויצילהו] / [רוח א]מת מח֯[ושך, 'and the spirit of truth will save him from darkness' (Puech), or a phrase more fitting in a forensic context, e.g. ויטהרהו] / [רוח א]מת מח֯ט֯[אתו, 'and the spirit of truth will purify him from his sin' (cf. 1QS III 6–8). Other possibilities are ויציל את] / [בן הא]מת מח֯[ושך, or *lamed* with an infinitive instead of an imperfect form, e.g. ולהציל.

Col. VI

1 [ ]ג[ ]ד[ ]° ל[ ]°ין

2 [ ]תו[ ]יה֯[ ]יה°[ל]ע֯ולם

3 Ps 91 [את כול]בני בל[יעל אמן אמן] סלה [1לדויד יושב]בסתר[עליון בצל] שדי

4 [יתלונן]2האומר [ליהוה מחסי] ומצודת֯[י אלוהי] מבטח [אבטח] בו

5 [3כי ה]֯ואה יצילך מ֯[פח יקו]ש מדבר ה֯ו֯[ות 4ב]אברתו יסך[לך]ותחת

6 [כנפ]יו תשכון חסד֯[ו ע]ל֯יך צנה וסוחרה֯ אמתו סלה *vac* 5לו֯א תירא

7 מ֯פחד לילה מחץ יעוף יומם 6מקטב ישוד[צ]הרים מדבר[בא]פל

8 יהלך 7יפ[ו]ל מצדך אלף ור[בבה מי]מינך אל[יך לו]א יגע 8רק[תביט]

9 בעיניך[ותרא]ה֯ שלום רשע[ים 9קר]את מח[סך]ת מחמדו[10לוא]

10 תרא[ה רעה ו]לוא יגע [נגע באה]ליך 11כ[י מלאכיו]יצוה לך

11 לשומ[רך בדרכי]ך [12]על כפים[ישאו]ך פן[תגוף בא]בן רגל[ך [13]על]

12 *hole* פתן [ואפעה תד]רוך תרמו[ס כפיר] ותנין [[14]ביהוה ח]שקתה ו[יפלטך]

13 *hole* ו[ישגבך [16b]ויר]אך בישוע[תו סלה] *vac]at* *v]aca[t* [

14 ויע[נו אמן אמן] סלה *vaca]t* *v]aca[t* [

15] *v]aca[t* *v]aca[t* [

Mus. Inv. 61, 612
PAM 43.986*, 43.987*

NOTES ON READINGS

L. 1]לֹ ○[. A tiny dot is probably the remains of a letter. There is a space between the dot and *lamed*, but it need not be a space between words.

L. 1]יֹ○ן[. A very small dot beneath the downstroke of *yod* is the left tip of the base of a letter, e.g. *bet* or *nun*.

L. 2]תוֹ[. If the trace to the left of *waw* is ink, it can only be the right end of the base of *bet*. In the manuscript, only the *waw* has been preserved.

L. 2]○יהֹ[. Puech suggests יהו[ה], interpreting the tiny dot as the bottom tip of *waw*, but such short *waw*s are unusual in this text; *yod* would be more likely.

L. 4] מבטח. The reconstruction מבטח[י is only possible if the downstroke of *yod* was considerably shorter than usual, even shorter than *yod* of יסך (line 5).

L. 6 כנפ]יו]. The dark spot at the baseline is not part of the writing.

L. 6 ע]לֹיֹך. A trace on a protrusion of the skin may be part of the upper arm of *lamed*. The head of *yod* is rather small, more like that of *waw*.

L. 7]ישוד. The traces of the first letter are ambiguous. The length of the downstroke corresponds to *waw*, but the large head is more typical of *yod*.

L. 8 תבי[ט. The faint stroke at the end of the line is not ink.

L. 9]מחמדו. Not מחמדך[(van der Ploeg). The downstroke does not break through the bottom line, and there is no indication of the head breaking through the downstroke.

L. 12 פתן. There is a hole to the right of פתן with no ink traces. A similar hole is visible at the beginning of the following line. These were probably already present at the time of writing, and the scribe avoided them, moving the margin farther to the left.

L. 13 ו[ישגבך. The trace on the edge can only be final *pe*, or a long *waw* (cf. line 14). The traces on the edge of the hole are not ink.

TRANSLATION

1. [ ] [ ] [ ] [ ]
2. [ ] [ ] [ ] [for]ever
3. [all]the sons of Bel[ial. Amen, amen.] Selah. [[Ps 91:1]Of David. He that lives]in the shelter[of the Most High, in the shadow of] the Almighty
4. [he stays.][2]He who says [to YHWH: 'My refuge] and [my] fortress,[my God] is the safety in which [I trust.]
5. [[3]For h]e will save you from [the net of the fow]ler, from the calam[itous] pestilence. [[4]With] his feathers he will cover[you]and under
6. his [wing]s you shall stay. [His] kindness [up]on you will be a shield, and his truth a breastplate. Selah. *vac* [5]You shall not fear

7. the dread of night or the arrow that flies by day, [6]the plague that rages at [no]on or the pestilence that [in dark]ness
8. proceeds. [7]A thousand will f[a]ll at your side, and t[en thousand at] your [ri]ght; [y]ou it shall [no]t strike. [8]Only,[look]
9. with your eyes,[and you will see] the retribution of the wicked [ones.] [9]You have [invok]ed [your] shel[ter,] his happiness.
10. You will [not] see[evil, and a plague] will not strike [in] your [ten]ts. [11]F[or] he has commanded [his angels] concerning you
11. to gua[rd you on] your [paths.] [[12]They shall lift] you upon their palms, lest[you strike your] foot [against a st]one. [13] [Upon]
12. cobra [and viper shall you s]tep, you shall tramp[le lion] and dragon. [14]You have [lo]ved [YHWH] and [he will rescue you]
13. and [protect you [16b]and sh]ow you [his] salvation. [Selah] *va[cat v]aca[t*]
14. And [t]he[y] shall an[swer: Amen, amen.] Selah *va[cat v]aca[t]*
15. *v]aca[t v]aca[t*]

COMMENTS

L. 1 [°ין. Perhaps ת]נ֯ין; cf. col. I 5, or ב֯ין].

L. 2 [יה°[ל]ע֯ולם. Reconstruct, e.g. ו]יהו֯[ה יאביד ל]ע֯ולם or ומלאך [יהו֯[ה יאביד ל]ע֯ולם (Puech).

L. 3 [את כול]בני בל֯]יעל. The reconstruction of כול before בני בל֯]יעל[is very likely. This leaves room for a two-letter word, e.g. את or עם. The wording בני בל֯]יעל does not help in determining whether the psalm deals with Belial himself or with a demon.

L. 3 אמן אמן] סלה. Many liturgical compositions end with the formula אמן אמן, e.g. 4Q**504**, 4Q**507–509**. The same words must be reconstructed in line 14 and probably in col. V 3. The combination אמן אמן with סלה is very common in later amulets; cf. e.g. the amulets and fragments in Naveh and Shaked, *Amulets*, where it is either spelled in full, or abbreviated א̇ א̇ ס̇.

L. 3 (91:1) [לדויד. The space between סלה and [יושב is either empty (a *vacat* separating the two songs), or contains another word. In view of col. V 4 and 𝔊, one may reconstruct [לדויד.

L. 4 (91:2) [ליהוה. Reconstructed with 𝔐 and the versions. Note, however, that the addition in the second hemistich of v 2 also allows for the reconstruction [יהוה, in which case [יהוה מחסי] ומצודת֯י and [אלוהי] מבטח [אבטח] בו form two parallel clauses.

L. 4 (91:2) מבטח. It is unlikely that the addition in $\mathfrak{G}^{Lpau}$, βοηθός μου, is related to מבטח. The Lucianic addition is taken, rather, from Ps 18:3 אלי צורי אחסה בו, ὁ θεός μου βοηθός μου καὶ ἐλπιῶ ἐπ' αὐτόν. Note that in 𝔊, βοηθεῖν, βοηθός, etc., never render בטח or one of its derivatives.

L. 8 (91:6) יהלך. Probably read a *Piʿel* instead of 𝔐 *Qal*, which would have been spelled *plene* in this text.

L. 9 (91:8-9) רשע]ים קר[את מח]סך. The text of the first stich of v 9 differs from 𝔐: כי אתה יהוה מחסי. The reconstruction רשע] יהוה קר[את מח]סי (Eißfeldt[6]) does not fit.

L. 9 (91:9) ת[מחמדו]. It is difficult to see how these remains are related to 𝔐 עליון שמת מעונך. The reconstruction שמ]ת מחמדו] 'you have done his happiness', is awkward; שים is not used in such a way.

Ll. 9–10 (91:10) [לוא] / תרא]ה רעה ו]לוא. The text differs from 𝔐 and the versions, and it is not completely clear how line 10 should be reconstructed. One may assume that the verb תרא]ה replaced the unusual wording of 𝔐 תאנה אליך. The reconstruction of the first gap, תרא]ה רע ונגע [לוא (van der Ploeg) only fits if very small spaces (1.5–2 mm) are allowed for between words, whereas this column employs rather large spaces. The alternative reconstruction, תרא]ה בך רע ו]לוא (Puech) fits better, but בך is somewhat awkward and unnecessary. In the reconstruction proposed here, the spaces are rather large (4–

---

[6] O. Eißfeldt, 'Eine Qumran-Textform des 91. Psalms', *Bibel und Qumran. Beiträge zur Erforschung der Beziehungen zwischen Bibel und Qumranwissenschaft. Festschrift Bardtke* (Berlin: Evangelische Haupt-Bibelgesell–schaft, 1968) 82–5.

5 mm), but this is not uncommon in the column. The reconstructed clause]לוא[/ תרא]ה רעה means either 'and you will not see evil', or, elliptically, 'and evil will not be seen', i.e. 'will not appear' (*sc.* to you).

L. 10 (91:10) ו]לוא יגע [נגע באה]ליך. Since נגע barely fits in the first gap before לוא[, it may be restored in the second gap. For נגע נֶגַע, cf. 2 Chr 6:29 (*Piʿel*). That the idea of 𝔐 נגע is expressed by יגע, and that the text used a different noun, cannot be ruled out.

L. 12 (91:13) פתן] ואפעה. 𝔐 reads שחל ופתן, 'lion and cobra', but the versions suggest a word meaning 'viper'. 𝔊 reads βασιλίσκος, which renders אפעה in Isa 59:5. One may either reconstruct according to the versions, or prefer the *lectio difficilior* of 𝔐.

L. 12 (91:13) תרמו]ס כפיר[. The gap is rather large for כפיר, but far too small for an additional word.

L. 12 (91:14)]ביהוה ח[שקתה. The perspective of the text differs from that of 𝔐 כי בי חשק. Another possible reconstruction is]כי בו ח[שקתה.

L. 12 (91:14) ו]יפלטך[. The reconstruction is based upon 𝔐 ואפלטהו.

L. 13 (91:14, 16) ו]ישגבך ויר[אך. Perhaps the eye of the scribe skipped from וישגבך to וישביעך (corresponding to 𝔐 אשגבהו and אשביעהו), but it is also plausible that 11QapocrPs is based upon a shorter version of the end of the psalm.

L. 13 (91:16) סלה]. Cf. the multiple use of סלה in the text (cf. also line 6).

L. 14 ויע]נו אמן אמן[. Cf. Neh 8:6.

VARIANTS

91:1 (3) לדויד] 𝔊 (Αἶνος ᾠδῆς τῷ Δαυιδ)] > 𝔐

91:2 (4) האומר 𝔊 (ἐρεῖ = יאמר)𝔖] אֹמַר 𝔐𝔊[55]

91:2 (4) מבטח] > 𝔐𝔊𝔖

91:3 (5) ה]ואה] הוא 𝔐

91:4 (5) ב]אברתו 𝔐] באברתיו 𝔊𝔖

91:4 (6) תשכון] תחסה 𝔐𝔊(ἐλπιεῖς) Hier (*sperabis*)𝔖(ܬܬܬܟܠ; free translation of תחבה?) 𝔗 (תתרחיץ)

91:4 (6) חסד]ו ע[ליך] > 𝔐𝔊𝔖

91:4 (6) וסוחרה] וסחרה 𝔐

91:4 (6) סלה] > 𝔐𝔊𝔖

91:5 (6) לוא] לא 𝔐

91:6 (7–8) מקטב ישוד[צ]הרים מדבר[בא]פל יהלך] מדבר באפל יהלך מקטב ישוד צהרים 𝔐𝔊𝔖

91:6 (7) ישוד[𝔐] ושד 𝔊𝔖 (ܘܫܐܕܐ)

91:7 (8) יפ]ו[ל] יפל 𝔐

91:7 (8) יגע] יגש 4QPs[b] (י]גש) 𝔐𝔊

91:8 (8–9)] תביט[בעיניך[ ] בעיניך תביט 𝔐

91:8 (9) שלום] ושלמת 𝔐𝔊 (καὶ ἀνταπόδοσιν)

91:8 (9) ותרא]ה שלום רשע[ים] ושלמת רשעים תראה 𝔐𝔊 (καὶ ἀνταπόδοσιν ἁμαρτωλῶν ὄψῃ)

91:9 (9) קר]את מח[סך]ת מחמדו[ ] כי אתה יהוה מחסי עליון שמת מעונך 𝔐

91:10 (10) תרא]ה] תאנה 𝔐𝔊𝔙

91:10 (10) ו]לוא יגע [נגע] ונגע לא יקרב 𝔐𝔊(καὶ μάστιξ οὐκ ἐγγιεῖ)

91:10 (10) באה]ליך 𝔗[MSS]] באהלך 𝔐𝔊𝔖

91:11 (11) לשומ]רך] לשמרך 𝔐

91:13 (12) פתן] ואפעה 𝔊𝔖𝔙] שחל ופתן 𝔐

91:13 (12) תד]רוך] תדרך 𝔐

91:13 (12) תרמו]ס] תרמס 𝔐

12. 11QJubilees

(PLATE XXVI)

Previous discussion: A. S. van der Woude, 'Fragmente des Buches Jubiläen aus Qumran Höhle XI (11QJub)', *Tradition und Glaube. Das frühe Christentum in seiner Umwelt. Festgabe für Karl Georg Kuhn*, eds. G. Jeremias, H. W. Kuhn, H. Stegemann (Göttingen: Vandenhoeck & Ruprecht, 1972) 140–6, pl VIII; J. T. Milik, 'A propos de 11QJub', *Biblica* 54 (1973) 77–8; J. C. VanderKam, *Textual and Historical Studies in the Book of Jubilees* (Missoula, Montana: Scholars Press, 1977) 18–51, 97–9; F. García Martínez, 'Texts from Cave 11', *The Dead Sea Scrolls: Forty Years of Research*, eds. D. Dimant, E. Rappaport (STDJ 10; Leiden: E. J. Brill, 1992) 23.

Physical Description

THE preserved fragments display a variety of colours.[1] Frgs. 1 and 7 are deep brown, but some other fragments are lighter; the lighter colour of frgs. 12 and 13 might indicate their belonging to a different manuscript. The ruling is almost reddish, the grain very fine, and the surface smooth. In its lower section, frg. 9 shows traces of scraping meant to smooth the leather, and the surface is 'carenada' (in parallel stripes). The writing is regular and well calibrated, hanging 0.1 cm below the ceiling line.

Only two fragments, frgs. 8 and 10, preserve a margin, in both cases the right one. Frg. 12 possibly preserves the ruling of the left margin. Frg. 8 shows the beginning of a new sheet and two stitching holes. The margin from the edge to the vertical ruling measures 1.8 cm. The average line-length in the identified and reconstructed fragments varies between 45 and 50 letter-spaces. Since the average width per letter-space is 2–2.1 mm, the width of the columns measured *c.*10 cm.

The average height of a line is 6.5–6.7 mm in frgs. 1–8, 6 mm in frg. 9, and *c.*5.7 mm in frg. 13.

Columns

The preserved fragments do not supply solid evidence enabling a reconstruction of the columns or scroll: most fragments are small, and there is no obvious physical correspondence between the fragments which would indicate successive revolutions.

The Ethiopic text of *Jubilees* provides the only evidence for reconstruction of the text, and therefore of the columns of 11Q**12**. The size of the missing text between frgs. 4 4 and 5 1 is equal to that of the text running from frgs. 1 1 to 4 4. The same amount of text fits between frgs. 8 1 and 9 1.[2] This could mean that frgs. 1–4 belong to one column of 30 lines, and that frgs. 5–7 should be placed two columns further. Frgs. 1–4

---

[1] Some fragment numbers are changed in the present edition.

[2] The calculation is based upon the Ethiopic text in J. C. VanderKam, *The Book of Jubilees. A Critical Text* (CSCO 510; Leuven: E. Peeters, 1989). Frgs. 1 1–4 4 correspond to 42–43 lines of the published Ethiopic text; the text missing between frgs. 4 4 and 5 1 corresponds to 41–42 lines; the text from frgs. 8 1–9 1 has 40–41 lines.

and 5–7 would, thus, originate from two consecutive revolutions, frg. 5 corresponding materially to frg. 1a, and frg. 7 to frg. 2. A missing column is plausible if the scroll was rolled with its end at the interior. Likewise, frgs. 8 and 9 would originate from two consecutive revolutions. In that case, no intervening column existed, as frg. 8 preserves the far right part of the column. A column of 30 lines would imply that the height of the inscribed section of the column measured *c.*20 cm.

Contents

All the identified fragments stem from two sections of *Jubilees*.

TABLE 1: *Contents of 11QJub*

Frg.	*Jubilees*	Frg.	*Jubilees*
1	4:6-11	6	4:31
2	4:13-14	7	5:1-2
3	4:16-17 (or 4:11-12)	8	12:15-17
4	4:17-18 (?)	9	12:28-29
5	4:29-30		

Palaeography

The manuscript is written in a late Herodian formal script, and should therefore be dated close to 50 CE. The hand is rather similar to that of **11Q21** (11QTemple[c]), but small differences between the shapes of some letters can be discerned.

Orthography

The preserved fragments attest the expanded spelling with *he* of pronominal suffixes and pronouns; cf. frg. 7 2 בהמה; frg. 9 5 ע]מׄכה; and 6 לעשו]תׄכה. The 3rd masc. sing. personal pronoun is spelled הואה in frg. 8 5, but הוא in frg. 9 3. The spelling כיא occurs three times, in frgs. 1 6, 5 3, and 6 2. One may also surmise that the scribe used a *plene* spelling, but only one typical *plene* spelling has survived (ריאש]ון in frg. 3 2). The other examples, הכוכבׄ]ים and הכׄוׄכׄ]בים in frg. 8 4 and 6, and יוצא in frg. 9 3, cannot be considered as evidence for a *plene* spelling.

Textual Character

The identified fragments of **11Q12** do not overlap with the text preserved in any of the other copies of *Jubilees* from the Judaean Desert. The text of **11Q12** corresponds closely to that of the Ethiopic translation. In one case, *Jub.* 12:29, the Ethiopic text seems to have one line more than the Hebrew manuscript.

TABLE 2: *Variants between Hebrew and Ethiopic*

Frg.	Hebrew	Ethiopic (retroverted)
1 4	ו]ב֯ארבעה	ובשנה הרביעית
1 7–8	את אחות֯[ו] / [און	את און אחותו
9 5–6	absent	ויתנכה . . . רואיכה

Mus. Inv. 606, 614, 614B, 619, 621B
PAM 42.175, 42.176, 42.177*, 43.980*, 44.004*, 44.006*, 44.008*, 44.117*

Frg. 1 Jub. 4:6-11

1 [הודע]נ֯ו בצ֯[אתנו]
2 [לפני יהוה אלוהינו את כול החטאות]אשר יע֯שו ב֯[שמים]
3 [ובארץ ובאור ובחושך ובכול [7]והיו]אדם ואשתו מ֯ת[אבלים]
4 [על הבל ארבע שבועות *vac?* ו]ב֯ארבעה לשבוע הח[מישי]
5 [שמחו וידע אדם שנית את אשתו]ותלד לו בן ויקרא את שמ[ו שת]
6 [כיא אמר שת לנו יהוה זרע ב]א֯רץ אחר תחת הבל כיא הרגו
7 [קין [8]בשבוע הששי הוליד את אזו]ר֯ה בתו [9]ויקח קין את אחות֯[ו]
8 [און לו לאשה ותלד לו את חנוך בקץ היוב]ל הרביעי *[v]acat*
9 [ובשנת אחת לשבוע הריאשון ליובל החמי]שי נבנו הבתים באר[ץ]
10 [ויבן קין עיר ויקרא את שמה כמו שם ב]נו חנוך *vac* [10]ואד[ם]
11 [ידע את חוה אשתו ותלד עוד תשעה בנים [11]ובשבו]ע֯ הח֯[מישי]

Mus. Inv. 619, 621B
PAM 42.175, 44.004*, 44.117*

Notes on Readings

Frg. 1 consists of two joined fragments, the lower one (frg. 1b) published by van der Woude, the upper one (frg. 1a) referred to by Milik.[3] Because of the absence of margins and the uncertainty about the width of the *vacat* in line 8, one cannot be sure about the placement of the fragment within the column. The reconstruction is based upon the assumption that the next clause begins at the beginning of line 9, but a long *vacat* in the middle of line 8 is also possible.

L. 1 הודע]נׄו. The base of the first letter declines slightly. Other letters such as *kap* or *ʿayin* are possible.

L. 1 בצׄ[אתנו]. A dark stain or tear covers most of the last letter. The only visible stroke can be read as the left arm of *ṣade*. This piece of the fragment is presently absent from the plate.

L. 2 יעׄשו. Most traces are faint, and it takes some effort to discern them. The only certain trace of the second letter can be read as the left arm of *ʿayin*.

L. 3 מׄת[אבלים. A dark stain covers the first letter; most readings are possible.

L. 6 הרגו. Or הרגו[if the fragment is placed more to the right of the column.

L. 7 אחותׄ[ו]. The last letter must be *taw*, but note that the vertical stroke of the head protrudes slightly to the right, beyond the stroke of the right leg.

L. 9 באר[ץ]. On the fragment, one can clearly see a downstroke on the edge, which must be part of the leg of *reš*.

L. 10 *vac*. The small *vacat* is three letter-spaces (6 mm) wide.

L. 11 ובשבו]עׄ. PAM 44.004 shows several traces; some are compatible with *ʿayin*. The edge of the fragment has now receded and broken off.

Translation

1. [ ] we [report,] when [we] co[me]
2. [before YHWH our God, all the sins]which are done in [heaven]
3. [and on earth, and in the light and in the darkness and anywhere. [7]And]Adam and his wife [mourn]ed
4. [for Abel four weeks long. *vacat?* And] in the fourth of the f[ifth] week
5. [they rejoiced. And Adam knew his wife once again]and she gave birth to a son for him, and he named [him Seth]
6. [for he said: 'YHWH has raised up for us] another [seed on] the earth in place of Abel, since [Cain] killed him'.
7. [[8]In the sixth week he became the father of Azu]ra his daughter. [9]And Cain took [his] sister
8. [Awan as his wife, and she gave birth to Enoch for him at the end of the] fourth [jubi]lee. *vaca[t]*
9. [And in the first year of the first week of the fi]fth [jubilee,] houses were built on the ear[th.]
10. [And Cain built a city and named it after] his [so]n Enoch. *vacat* [10]And Ada[m]
11. [knew Eve his wife, and she gave birth to nine more children. [11]And in] the f[ifth wee]k

Comments

L. 2]אשר יעׄשו. Read either a *Qal* or *Nipʿal*. The Ethiopic has *za-yekawwen*.

L. 5 [שמחו וידע אדם שנית את אשתו. The reconstruction (VanderKam, *Textual and Historical Studies*, 18–9) is based upon the longer texts of the Ethiopic variants. The word *ʾAdām* is only attested in MS 12.

L. 5]ותלד לו בן ויקרא את שמ[ו שת]. The main Ethiopic manuscripts have the same text.

---

[3] J. T. Milik, 'A propos de 11QJub', 78: 'je me souviens d'avoir vu, non photographiée, une parcelle de 11Q qui ne contenait que]הׄ לשבוע[et qui se placerait, à mon avis, à la ligne 1 de ce morceau' (i.e. frg. 1b 1).

L. 6 [כיא אמר שת לנו יהוה זרע ב]א֯רץ. Ethiopic *ʾEgziʾabḥēr* renders both יהוה and אלהים. 𝔐 Gen 4:25 reads כי שת לי אלהים זרע.

L. 6 זרע ב]א֯רץ אחר. The Ethiopic manuscripts have the same syntax: *zarʾa westa medr kāleʾa*.

Ll. 6–7 הבל כיא הרגו / [קין]. This is the same wording as 𝔐 Gen 4:25. The Ethiopic manuscripts read *ʾAbēl ʾesma qatalo Qāyan*. The reading of MS 12, which adds *za-qatalo* after *ʾAbēl*, follows the phrasing of 𝔘 Gen 4:25 *la-ʾAbēl za-qatalo Qāyan*, a translation of 𝔊 ὃν ἀπέκτεινεν.

L. 7 (4:8) אזו]ר֯ה. This name is spelled in Ethiopic *ʾAzurā*; and in Greek, ʼΑζουρά; in the Syriac document, 'The Names of the Wives of the Patriarchs according to the book which among the Hebrew is called Jubilees',[4] ܐܙܘܪܐ.

Ll. 7–8 את אחות֯[ו] / [און]. The Ethiopic has changed the order of the words: *la-ʾAwān ʾextu*. The Syriac fragment has the name ܐܣܘܐ, but in Greek, several forms are used: Σαυή, ʼΑσαυνᾶν, ʼΑσαυρᾶν, ʼΑσουάμ, ʼΑσαούλ.

L. 8 [*v*]*acat*. The beginning of a new jubilee warrants the continuation of the text on a new line.

Frg. 2 Jub. 4:13-14

1 [לקח אנוש את אחותו נועם לו לאשה ותלד לו ב]ן בש֯[נה]

2 [השלישית לשבוע החמישי ויקרא שמו קינן [14]ו]ב֯קץ היו[בל]

3 [השמיני לקח לו קינן אשה את אחותו מהללת] לאשה֯[ותלד]

4 [לו בן ביובל התשיעי בשבוע הריאשון בשלו]ש֯ה ל[שבוע]

Mus. Inv. 606
PAM 42.176, 43.980*

NOTES ON READINGS

The fragment was intact in PAM 42.176, broken into two pieces in PAM 43.980, and once again joined on Mus. Inv. 606.

L. 4 (4:14) [בשלו]ש֯ה. The preserved traces of the first letter are only compatible with *šin* or *ṣade*.

TRANSLATION

1. [Enosh took his sister Noam as his wife, and she gave birth to a s]on [for him] in the [third] ye[ar]
2. [of the fifth week. And he named him Qenan. [14]And] at the end of the [eighth] ju[bilee]
3. [Qenan took for himself a wife, his sister Muhallelet] as his wife.[And she gave birth]
4. [to a son for him in the ninth jubilee, in the first week, in the thi]rd (year) of [(this) week]

COMMENTS

A retroversion of the Ethiopic shows that two and a half lines are missing between frgs. 1 and 2. One must assume a long *vacat* of half a line between *Jub.* 4:11 and 12, or place the fragment on a different vertical axis.

---

[4] BM *Additional* 12.154, folio 180; published by A. M. Ceriani, *Monumenta Sacra et Profana* (2 vols.; Milan: Bibliotheca Ambrosiana, 1961–63) 2.IX–X.

Ll. 1–2 [בשׁ]נה] / [השלישית לשבוע]. The preserved letters also allow for the reconstruction [בשׁ]לושה] [לשבוע] /. Cf. the similar construction in frg. 1 4. However, [בשׁ]לושה] / [לשבוע] seems too short compared to the other lines.

L. 3 [לקח לו קינן אשה את אחותו מהללת] לאשה[. Cf. Ethiopic *naš'a lotu Qāynān be'sita Mu'allēlit-hā 'exto lotu be'sita*. This is the long Ethiopic reading, but there are manuscripts dropping the first (17 20 47 63) or second (12 21) *lotu*, *'exto* (20 25), the second *be'sita* (17 63), or the final *lotu be'sita* altogether (21 42[c] 47). The second occurrence of *be'sita* is strange, and therefore it is more likely that the longer text is original. The occurrence of]לאשה[, presumably at the end of the clause, is in itself not indicative of the longer text, but the reconstruction of the lines suggests a long text in Hebrew, too.

Frg. 3 Jub. 4:16-17 (or 4:11-12)

[הרביעי ליובל הזה ותלד לו בן בשבוע הח]מישי [בשנה] 1

[הרביעית ליובל ויקרא את שמו חנוך *vac*[*at* [17]זה ריאש[ון] 2

PAM 42.177

NOTES ON READINGS

Frg. 3 can no longer be located in the museum.

L. 2 *vac*]*at*. The fragment has preserved 0.5 cm of blank space before זה.

TRANSLATION

1. [the fourth (week) of this jubilee. And she gave birth to a son for him in the f]ifth [week, in the fourth year]
2. [of the jubilee, and he called him Enoch. *va*]*cat* [17]He was the firs[t]

COMMENTS

The retroversion of the Ethiopic text suggests that six lines are missing between frgs. 2 and 3. Frg. 3 can also be placed in 4:11-12, immediately following frg. 1, but in that case the retroversion of the Ethiopic results in a line which is longer than those of frg. 1:

[ליובל הח]מישי [לקח שת את אחותו אזורה ובארבעה לו ילדה לו] 1

[את אנוש *va*[*c* [11]זה ריאש[ון קרא בשם יהוה בארץ וביובל השביעי] 2

L. 2 [זה ריאש[ון. Cf. Ethiopic *we'etu qadāmi*; Greek οὗτος πρῶτος; Syriac ܗܢܐ ܫܪܝ ܡܩܕܡܐ:

Frg. 4 Jub. 4:17-18 (?)

1 [ויכתוב בספר אותות השמים כחוק חודשיהמה למע]ן ידְעוֹ [בני]
2 [אדם תקופות השנים כחוקות לכול חודשיהמה 18ריא]שון הוא[ה]
3 [כתב תעודה ויעד בבני אדם בדורות הארץ שבועות]הׄ[יובלים]

Mus. Inv. 621B
PAM 44.117

NOTES ON READINGS

One line is missing between frgs. 3 and 4. Reconstruct e.g. [למד ספר ומדע וחוכמה מן בני אדם הילודים על הארץ].

L. 1 (4:17) ידְעוֹ. The triangular form at the end is typical for the ligature of *ʿayin* with a following downstroke. Two other tips of downstrokes may indicate *waw* and *dalet*. For almost the same distance between *dalet* and *ʿayin*, cf. הדעת in frg. 5 3.

TRANSLATION

1. [And he wrote down in a book the signs of the sky, according to the order of their months, so tha]t [the sons of men] would know
2. [the cycles of the years, according to the orders of all their months. 18He was the [fir]st
3. [to write a testimony, and he testified to the sons of men in the generations of the earth. The weeks of] the [jubilees]

COMMENTS

The sequence ריא]שון הוא[ה] is likely to correspond to 4:12, 17, 18, or 29, but only in the case of *Jub*. 4:18 do the traces of the first line seem to fit. Nevertheless, the remnants of lines 1 and 3 are too meagre to be certain of the identification. Since there may have been a *vacat* before ריא]שון, the lines cannot be reconstructed with certainty.

L. 2 (4:18) ריא]שון הוא[ה]. Contrast the different formula in frg. 3 2 זה ריאש]ון.

Frg. 5 Jub. 4:29-30

1 [ריאשון נק]בׄר ב[אדמה 30ויחצרו לו שבעים שנה מאלף]
2 [השנים כיא] אלף הׄ[ש]נׄיׄםׄ[יום אחד בתעודת השמים לכן]
3 [נכתב על ע]ץׄ הדעת כיא ב[יום אכלכם ממנו תמותו על כן]
4 [לא כלה את]שׄני היום[הזה כיא ימות בו 31במלא היובל הזה]

Mus. Inv. 619
PAM 42.176, 44.004*

NOTES ON READINGS

There are no indications on the fragment regarding its placement within the column. The proposed reconstruction (VanderKam, *Textual and Historical Studies*, 31–4) gives a straight right margin. A join with frg. 6 is textually and materially possible.

L. 2 (4:30)]הׄ[ש]נׄיׄםׄ. A tear in the surface of the skin has peeled off most of the letters. The vertical stroke of the first letter is unlikely to be *nun*: there is no trace of the base, and the upper, almost diagonal, part of the downstroke slants more to the right than would the top of *nun*. The upper part of the trace is more likely to be the protruding right part of the head of *he*.

L. 4 (4:30) שׄני[. The dot on the edge of the fragment comes from the middle bar of the *šin*, and is the only remnant of that letter.

TRANSLATION

1. [the first that was bu]ried in [the ground. [30]And he was seventy years short of one thousand]
2. [years, for] a thousand [y]ears[are one day in the testimony of heaven. Therefore]
3. [is it written about the tr]ee of knowledge: 'For on [the day which you eat from it, you shall die'. Therefore]
4. [he did not complete] the years of [that] day [because he died during it. [31]At the conclusion of this jubilee]

COMMENTS

L. 1 (4:29) ב]אדמה. Ethiopic *westa medr*. Cf. the Greek *Chronicle on Creation*,[5] τοῦτον λέγεται πρῶτον εἰς τὴν γῆν ἐξ ἧς ἐλήφθη ταφῆναι. Both Ethiopic *medr* and Greek γῆ may render either ארץ or אדמה. However, ב]אדמה seems more appropriate here than ב]ארץ. Adam is made from עפר מן האדמה and will be buried באדמה. Cf., however, the reference, earlier in this verse, to Adam's children burying him in the land of his creation (*westa medra feṭratu*).

L. 2 (4:30) אלף הׄ[ש]נׄיׄםׄ[. This kind of construct state is not common with אלף.

L. 2 (4:30) כיא] אלף הׄ[ש]נׄיׄםׄ[יום אחד. Ethiopic reads *ʾesma 1000-ʿāmat (kama) ʾaḥatti ʿelat*, and Syriac ܡܛܠ ܕܐܠܦ ܫܢܝܢ ܫ ܐܝܟ ܝܘܡܐ. It is probable that *kama* (MSS 12 35[c] 39 42 44 47 48 58) is dependent on the reading of Ps 90:4 (𝔊 89:4) כי אלף שנים בעיניך כיום אתמול, 𝔊 ὅτι χίλια ἔτη ἐν οφθαλμοῖς σου ὡς ἡ ἡμέρα ἡ ἐχθές, and 2 Pet 3:8.

L. 4 (4:31) במלא. Cf. Ethiopic *ba-tafṣāmētu*. Or retrovert במלאות, but, in that case, either the line is too long, or the join with frg. 6 is not correct.

Frg. 6 Jub. 4:31

1 [הומת קין] אחריו [בשנה ההיאה ויפול ביתו עליו וימות בביתו]

2 [ויומת באבנ]יׄו כיא [

Mus. Inv. 621B
PAM 44.117

[5] Cf. J. T. Milik, 'Recherches sur la version grecque du Livre des Jubilés', *RB* 78 (1971) 554.

Notes on Readings

Other placements of the fragment may be possible, but this is the only location in the beginning of *Jubilees* which results in an average line length. Moreover, the fragment might be joined to the lower right part of frg. 5.

Translation

1. [Cain was killed] after him [in that year. His house fell on him, and he died in his house.]
2. [And he was killed by] its [stone]s for [

Notes on Readings

L. 1 (4:31) אחריו]בשנה ההיאה. For a discussion of Ethiopic *ba-ʾahadu ʿām*, cf. VanderKam, *A Critical Text of Jubilees*, 30.

Frg. 7 Jub. 5:1-2

[להמה בנים ואלה הנ]פ֯[יל]י֯ם 2 וירב֯[חמס בארץ וכול בשר השחית] 1

[דרכו מאדם עד]בהמה ועד ח֯[יה ועד עוף ועד כול הרומש] 2

[על הארץ וכולם ה]שחיתו דרכם ו֯ח֯[קתם ויחלו לאכול איש את] 3

[רעהו וירב חמס בארץ וכו]ל ◦◦◦[4

Mus. Inv. 619
PAM 42.176, 44.004*

Notes on Readings

L. 1 (5:1) הנ]פ֯[יל]י֯ם. The minute trace at the right may be the tip of the base of *pe*. The *yod* before final *mem* has almost completely disappeared, as has part of the final *mem*. The upper part of the fragment has now become deteriorated and is illegible.

L. 2 (5:2) ח֯[יה. All that remains of the first letter is the downstroke. It could therefore be either *he* or *ḥet*.

L. 3 (5:2) ו֯ח֯[קתם. The first letter could be either *waw* or *yod*. Only the very upper right part of the next letter has been preserved.

L. 4 (5:2)]◦◦◦. The traces are four short vertical strokes, then a small space, one more vertical stroke, and finally a short horizontal stroke, all remains of the tops of letters. The second vertical stroke is slightly slanting down to the right. The traces do not seem to be compatible with any Hebrew word corresponding to the Ethiopic.

Translation

1. [children for them, and these are the g]i[ant]s. 2 And [violence] increased [on the earth, and all flesh corrupted]
2. [its way, from men to]animals, and be[asts and birds and everything that crawls]
3. [on the earth, and they all c]orrupted their way and [their] or[dinance, and they began to eat one]
4. [another. And violence increased on the earth, and al]l [

COMMENTS

A retroversion of the Ethiopic text indicates that seven or eight lines are missing between frgs. 6 and 7, depending on the length of the possible *vacat*s in the text.

L. 1 (5:2) וירבׄ]ה חמס בארץ. Cf. Gen 6:5 רבה רעת האדם בארץ and 6:11 ותמלא בארץ חמס.

Ll. 2–3 (5:2) מאדם עד]בהמה ועד חׄ]יה ועד עוף ועד כול הרומש] / [על הארץ. The fragment also allows one to read determined forms (עד ה]בהמה ועד הׄ]חיה), but both reasons of space and the reading of Gen 6:7 מאדם עד בהמה עד רמש ועד עוף השמים suggest one should reconstruct the undetermined forms.

L. 3 (5:2) ה]שחיתו דרכם וחׄ]קתם. Cf. Ethiopic *ʾamāsanu fenotomu wa-šerʿatomu* (MSS 9 38 lack *wa-šerʿatomu*). Gen 6:12 and *1 Enoch* 8:2 only read 'way(s)'. For *šerʿat* as the translation of חק, cf. 4QJubilees[a] (4Q**216**) II 8 (*Jub.* 1:10).

L. 4 (5:2) וכו]ל ◦◦◦[. The reconstruction of the missing parts of lines 3 and 4 suggests that the text of the fragment corresponds to the first words of Ethiopic *wa-k*^{w}*ellu xelinā ʾaʾmero la-k*^{w}*ellomu ʾegwāla*, 'and every thought of knowledge of all mankind'. None of the words to which *xelinā* might correspond, e.g. הגיון and הגות, מחשבת, עצת, שכל, or דעת, is completely consistent with the traces.

Frg. 8 Jub. 12:15-17

1 ו[ ]
2 עם [תרח אביו בחרן שני שבועי שנים *vacat* [16]ובשבוע הששי]
3 בחמש]ה בו ישב אברם בלילה בראש החודש השביעי להביט אל]
4 הכוכבׄ]ים מערב עד בקר לראות מה מעשה השנה בגשמים ויהי]
5 הואהׄ] יושב לבדו ומביט [17]ויבוא דבר בלבו ויאמר כול אותות]
6 הכׄוׄכׄ]בים

Mus. Inv. 619
PAM 42.177, 44.004*

NOTES ON READINGS

Frg. 8 preserves the beginning of a new sheet. The right edge is folded under. Only two stitching holes are now visible. The line spacing is 0.6–0.7 cm.

L. 1 ו[. The small diagonal trace in the photograph is not ink. The *waw* is complete and immediately after it begins a peeling of the surface of the leather.

L. 6 הכׄוׄכׄ]בים. The downstroke of the second *kap* slants, as in frg. 7 3 דרכם.

TRANSLATION

1. and[ ]
2. with [Terah his father in Haran for two weeks of years. *vacat* [16]And in the sixth week]
3. in [its] fifth (year) [Abram sat down during the night of the first day of the seventh month to observe]

4. the star[s from the evening to the morning to see what would be the nature of the year in relation to the rains. And it happened that]
5. while he[was sitting alone and observing, 17 a voice came to his heart and said: 'All the signs]
6. of the sta[rs

COMMENTS

L. 1 (12:15)]ו. The conjunction *waw* may correspond to either *wa-weludu* or *wa-westa medra Kanāʾan*. The exact length of the reconstruction cannot be calculated because the Hebrew might have read ללכת אל ארץ or ללכת ארצה. Direction was no longer expressed by *he* in this stage of Hebrew, but the author may have been influenced by the text of Gen 11:31. VanderKam (*Textual and Historical Studies*, 40) suggests that the word *medra*, in *wa-xadara westa medra Kārān* in MSS 12 20 25 35 39 42 44 47 48 58, is an addition, and therefore reconstructs the line as: ו]בניו ללכת ארצה לבנון וארצה כנען וישב בחרן וישב אברם[. This gives a total of 52 letter-spaces, which is just slightly more than average.

L. 2 (12:15-16) עם]תרח אביו בחרן שני שבועי שנים *vacat* ובשבוע הששי[. The retroversion of the Ethiopic gives a line of 43 letter-spaces. One must either assume a longer Hebrew text, or a *vacat* of *c*.6 letter-spaces between vv 15 and 16. The probability of a *vacat* is strengthened by the fact that the Syriac text begins a new section with v 16.

Ll. 2–3 (12:16) ובשבוע הששי[/ בחמש]ה בו ישב אברם בלילה בראש החודש השביעי. Cf. Ethiopic *wa-ba-sādes subāʿē ba-ʿāmat xāmesu lotu nabara ʾAbrām ba-lēlit ba-šarqa warx sābeʿ*. Instead of *nabara ʾAbrām*, some manuscripts read *tanšeʾa ʾAbrām wa-nabara* (39 42 47 48 58), *tanšeʾa ʾAbrām* (35), or simply *tanšeʾa* (21). The Syriac has another word order.

L. 3 (12:16) בחמש]ה. Apparently absolute, like ו]בֿארבעה in frg. 1 4.

Frg. 9 Jub. 12:28-29

]]○○○[[1

] v[acat 28 ויהי בשב]עה לשבוע הששי[2

]וידבר עם אביו ויגד לו כיא]הוא יוצא מ[חרן ללכת ארצה[3

]כנען לראותה וישוב אליו 29 ויאמר[לו תרח אֿ[ביו לך בשלום[4

]אל עולם יישיר דרככה ויהוה ע]מֿכֿה ויש[מרכה מכול רע[5

]ולא ימשול בכה כול בני אדם לעשו]תֿכֿה רֿעֿ[6

Mus. Inv. 619
PAM 44.004

NOTES ON READINGS

Frg. 9 consists of two fragments. Frg. a, with the beginning of lines 2 and 3, fits exactly to the right of frg. b. Frg. a can no longer be located. Frg. b has badly deteriorated: it has completely darkened, leaving almost no visible traces of letters, and the lower part has crumbled.

L. 1]∘∘∘[. There are four small traces. The second, a horizontal stroke sloping down to the left, and the third, a slanting vertical stroke, are connected. These two traces are compatible with *šin*, but a ligature is also possible. The first trace seems to be the base of a letter, sloping slightly upwards to the left, as the base of *taw* may do, or perhaps the *keraia* of the left leg of *ʾalep*. The last trace is the bottom tip of a slanting downstroke. It may be the left leg of *he* or *ḥet* if the third trace is the right leg. One may suggest e.g.]אשׂרֿ[, but other readings are also possible.

L. 2 (12:28) ויהי *v*]*acat*. The space between the edge of the fragment and ויהי is somewhat larger than usual. It is plausible that this large space is the last part of a *vacat*.

L. 4 (12:29) אׄ]ביו. The trace close after the *ḥet* of תרח is probably the right arm of *ʾalep*. Note that the width of the spaces varies considerably on this fragment. Cf. e.g. the short space between יוצא and מ]חרן in line 3.

L. 6 (12:30) לעשו]תׄכה. Van der Woude reads]לׄכה, but the vertical stroke above the ceiling line is a crack in the skin. Note also that the horizontal stroke to the right on the ceiling line cannot belong to *lamed*.

TRANSLATION

1.] [
2. [*vaca*]*t* 28And it happened that in the sev[enth (year) of the sixth week]
3. [he spoke with his father and told him that]he was leaving from [Haran to go to the land of]
4. [Canaan to see it, and that he would return to him. 29And] Terah [his] fa[ther said] to him: ['Go in peace.]
5. [May the eternal God make your way smooth, and may YHWH be wi]th you and pro[tect you from all evil]
6. [and may no son of man have power over you to d]o you evil[

COMMENTS

L. 3 מ]חרן. Cf. Gen 12:4. An alternative reading is: מ]ן חרן.

L. 4 לך בשלום[. Cf. Ethiopic *ḥur ba-salām* and Syriac ܙܠ ܒܫܠܡܐ, whereas Gen 12:1 reads לך לך.

L. 5 ויש]מרכה מכול רע[. Cf. Ps 121:7.

L. 6 ולא ימשול בכה כול בני אדם לעשו]תׄכה רׄעׄ[. Ethiopic has a line which is apparently missing in our text: *wa-yahab lā-ʾelēka šāhla wa-meḥrata wa-mogasa ba-qedma ʾella yerēʾeyuka*, 'and may he give you kindness, mercy, and grace before those who see you'.

Unidentified Fragments

Frg. 10

ונקב] 1

עׄל] 2

Mus. Inv. 621B
PAM 44.117

Notes on Readings

The colouring of the skin and of the ruling suggest that frg. 10 belongs to **11Q12**, or, less likely, to **11Q8** (11QPs[d]) A reconstruction according to *Jub.* 2:14, 3:3 (reading ונקב]ה), or 10:15 is difficult, as the traces of the second line do not seem to fit. A join with frg. 5 (ונקב]ר) is materially very improbable, and creates textual problems. Locating it in *Jub.* 10:15 gives no correspondence for the second line.

L. 2 ע̇ל]. Or א̇ל].

Frg. 11

]◦◦[1

]◦ אברם[2

]◦◦[3

Mus. Inv. 614
PAM 42.176, 44.006*

Notes on Readings

More than half of the fragment has lost its surface. The spelling אברם instead of אברהם shows the fragment stems from somewhere between *Jub.* 11:14 and 15:7.

L. 3]◦◦[. The traces, visible in PAM 44.006, are not visible on the actual fragment, and it is not certain that they are ink.

Frg. 12

]עמ̊ה̊ [1

]ה [2

]ל[3

Mus. Inv. 614B
PAM 44.008

Notes on Readings

The fragment is lighter in colour than frgs. 1–11, but darker than frg. 13. Faint vertical traces possibly are remnants of the ruling of the left margin.

L. 1]עמה̇. PAM 44.008 shows only one downstroke after *mem*, indicating *waw* or *yod*, but examination of the fragment shows an additional, fainter downstroke, which would suggest *he*.

Frg. 13

[ויו̇]

[פר א̇]

[ל̇]

Mus. Inv. 619
PAM 42.176, 44.004*

NOTES ON READINGS

L. 1 ויו̇]. The blank space after the second *waw* shows it was not followed by a letter with a vertical stroke. Possible after *waw* are *ʿayin*, *ṣade*, *šin*, or perhaps *lamed* or *qop*.

L. 3 [ל̇]. The horizontal stroke before *lamed* may be a discolouration of the edge of the fragment or the non-serifed head of a letter.

COMMENTS

It is not certain that frg. 13 belongs to 11Q**12**. The colour is lighter than that of the other fragments, and the *ʾalep* is written slightly differently. An alternative identification of the fragment as part of 11Q**8** (11QPsalms[d]) or 11Q**21** (11QTemple[c]) cannot be excluded, but the colour of the fragment is also not compatible with these manuscripts.

Milik's proposition that the fragment corresponds to *Jub.* 3:25-27 is questionable: his readings of lines 1 and 3 do not correspond literally to the Ethiopic text, and a reconstruction would provide lines of more than 60 letter-spaces, whereas all other reconstructed lines of 11Q**12** have an average of *c.*50 letter-spaces or slightly less.[6]

As an alternative, one may consider a correspondence with *Jub.* 14:4-6:

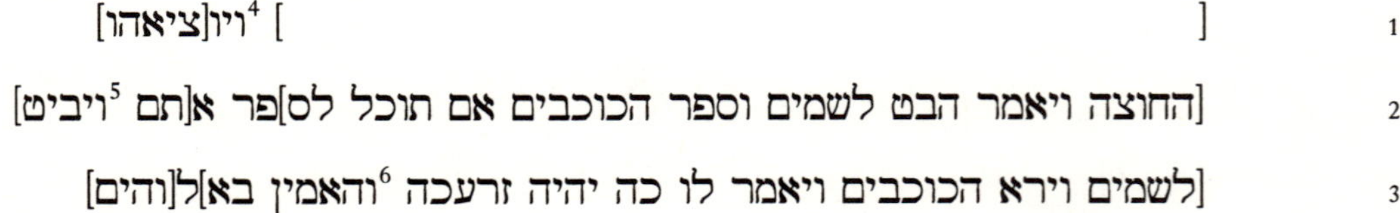

1 [ ]ויו̇[ציאהו][4]

2 [החוצה ויאמר הבט לשמים וספר הכוכבים אם תוכל לס]פר א[תם [5]ויביט]

3 [לשמים וירא הכוכבים ויאמר לו כה יהיה זרעכה [6]והאמין בא]ל[והים]

The lines produced in this reconstruction, however, are longer than in the other fragments. One must also assume a defective spelling, as in 4Q**216** (Jubilees[a]) V–VII.

---

[6] Cf. the discussion in J. C. VanderKam, *Textual and Historical Studies*, 97–8, and *Critical Text of Jubilees*, 19–20.

13. 11QMelchizedek

(PLATE XXVII)

Previous discussion: A. S. van der Woude, 'Melchisedek als himmlische Erlösergestalt in den neugefundenen eschatologischen Midraschim aus Qumran Höhle XI', *OTS* 14 (1965) 354–73; Y. Yadin, 'A Note on Melchizedeq and Qumran', *IEJ* 15 (1965) 152–4; M. de Jonge and A. S. van der Woude, '11Q Melchizedek and the New Testament' *NTS* 12 (1965–66) 301–26; J. T. Milik, '*Milkî-ṣedeq* et *Milkî-reša*ᶜ dans les anciens écrits juifs et chrétiens', *JJS* 23 (1972) 95–112, 124–6; P. J. Kobelski, *Melchizedek and Melchirešaᶜ* (Washington: The Catholic Biblical Association of America, 1981) 3–23, 49–74; É. Puech, 'Notes sur le manuscrit de XIQMelkîsédeq', *RevQ* 12/48 (1987) 483–513; É. Puech, *La croyance des Esséniens en la vie future: immortalité, résurrection, vie éternelle? Histoire d'une croyance dans le Judaïsme ancien.* II: *Les données qumraniennes et classiques* (Paris: J. Gabalda et Cie, 1993) 522–6; F. Manzi, 'La figura di Melchisedek: Saggio di bibliografia aggiornata', *Ephemerides Liturgicae* 109 (1995) 331–49.

Physical Description

THE skin of the manuscript has become brittle and is disintegrating. In many places the written surface has peeled away, revealing the raw skin. The written surface is a clear creamy colour, whereas the underlying layer is dark brown. Frg. 2a has now separated into two parts: the written surface has peeled away from its darker base and the two layers are mounted separately (referred to on Mus. Inv. 579 as frgs. 2A and 2b). Only the outer inscribed layer of some of the fragments has been preserved, and is now mounted on rice paper. Ten fragments can be placed into two consecutive columns (cols. II and III), and it is possible that the remaining fragments also belong to col. III. Frg. 1a preserves an intralinear addition to col. I in its right margin.

The ruling is faint but certain, and easily visible between cols. II and III, where the right rule of col. III and the horizontal lines are visible. The distance between the horizontal lines is 0.5 cm, and the margin between the vertical rulings is 1.5 cm. However, the left alignment of col. II was not respected, and the space between cols. II and III is, in places, as narrow as 0.7 cm.

Measurements of height and width can only be taken from col. II. The calculation of the height of col. II is based upon the assumption that the distance between the left bottom end of frg. 1a and the top of frg. 4a is 2 mm. One more line might be added between these fragments, in which case 5 mm must be added to the measurements. The height of the inscribed section of col. II is 12.5 cm (5 mm per line). Frgs. 1a and 2a preserve *c.*8 mm of skin above the first readable line, and frg. 4b preserves 1.6 cm of the bottom margin. Altogether *c.*14.9 cm has been preserved.

The width of col. II is 14 cm (the maximum width in line 16 is 14.7 cm). There is an average of 73 letter-spaces in the reconstructed lines.

It is likely that frgs. 1a and 2a stem from two consecutive turns of the scroll. The distance between the right edges of these fragments points toward a turn of *c.*13.5 cm. Since the contents seem to stem from the end of a composition, the scroll was probably rolled with the beginning on the interior.

TABLE 1: *Collation of Fragment Numbers*

Previous Frg. Numbers	Present Frg. Numbers
1	1a
2	2a
3	4a
4	5
5	6
6	2b
7	3
8	4b
9	4d
10	4c
11	7
12	1b
13	8
14	9
15	10

Contents

The preserved text of col. II gives an eschatological description of the end of days, the tenth and last jubilee. The events of this period are described by means of thematic *pesharim*; Leviticus 25, Deuteronomy 15, Isaiah 52:7 and 61:1-3, Psalms 7:8-9 and 82:1-2 are quoted or alluded to, and explained with regard to the end of the tenth jubilee. The column focuses on the acts of redemption which will free the sons of light from Belial and the spirits of his lot. These acts will be brought about by Melchizedek, who figures here as a heavenly figure comparable to the Prince of Lights (1QS III 30; CD V 18; 1QM XIII 10), and the archangel Michael (1QM XVII 6–7). The preserved text of col. III and the remaining fragments is very sparse, but almost certainly deals with the final annihilation of Belial and his lot. References to the ramparts of Judah (and Jerusalem?), as well as other construction terms, may be part of a description of a new Jerusalem (cf. 4QCatena[a] = 4QMidrEschat[b] [4Q**177**] IV 9–16).

The contents suggest that the preserved columns belong to the end of a composition. The contents of the preceding text cannot be ascertained. The reference to the ninth and tenth jubilees may indicate that the composition consisted of a survey of the history of the world, culminating in the expected eschatological events. Milik suggested that this manuscript might represent the end of 4QAges of Creation (4Q**180–181**), but it is more likely that 4Q**180** and 4Q**181** belong to two separate compositions, and the correspondences between 11Q**13** and 4Q**180** are outweighed by the differences.[1]

[1] Cf. D. Dimant, 'The "Pesher on the Periods" (4Q180) and 4Q181', *Israel Oriental Studies* IX (1979) 77–102, and R. V. Huggins, 'A Canonical "Book of Periods" at Qumran?', *RevQ* 15/59 (1992) 421–36.

Palaeography

In general, the letters correspond to the type of hand that was described by F. M. Cross as a 'late Hasmonaean or early Herodian book hand' (*c.*50–25 BCE), but Milik observed that the lack of a uniform size of the letters, as well as the relatively archaic forms of some letters, rather suggests an origin in the middle of the first century BCE, perhaps even 75–50 BCE ('*Milkî-ṣedeq* et *Milkî-rešaᶜ* ', 97).

The *lamed* has an idiosyncratic form. Essentially it is semi-cursive, with a very slanting upper arm and in some cases no horizontal stroke at all. Noteworthy is the (often rather long) diagonal tick attached to the left of the top of the upper arm.

Orthography and Morphology

The text is written in the full orthography that is typical of many of the scrolls from Qumran; the *waw* and *yod* are used as vowels, the spelling כיא is used, the independent pronouns are lengthened, as well as the pronominal suffixes for the 3rd person plural (an exception is col. III 8 בלבם), and the pausal form ת]שפוטו is used once.

This orthography is also used consistently in the quotations from the Hebrew Bible. Cf. the following orthographic differences:

Col. II 3	כול	Deut 15:2	כל
Col. II 10 (bis)	אלוהים	Ps 82:1	אלהים
Col. II 10	]בקורב	Ps 82:1	בקרב
Col. II 10	ישפוט	Ps 82:1	ישפט
Col. II 11	ת]שפוטו	Ps 82:2	תשפטו
Col. II 11	עוול	Ps 82:2	עול
Col. II 16	א]ומר	Isa 52:7	אמר

Textual Character

The biblical quotations agree with 𝔐 apart from the orthographical differences, the substitution of אל for 𝔐 יהוה (col. II 4, 11 quoting Deut 15:2 and Ps 7:9), and two small divergences: col. II 3 יד for Deut 15:2 ידו, and col. II 16 הרים instead of Isa 52:7 ההרים. In one case (col. II 25) it is not clear whether the manuscript quotes a text in a form different from 𝔐, or paraphrases the Bible. It seems, however, that the broken text refers to Lev 25:9 in a manner that is closer to 𝔊 than to 𝔐.

Mus. Inv. 579, 621B, 1031, 1032
PAM 43.979*, 44.117*
IAA 563769*

Col. I (Frg. 1)

]שׁוֹן מושה כיא ◦ [ ] ◦◦ [ ]שׁ[12

Mus. Inv. 579
PAM 43.979

Notes on Readings

In the right margin of frg. 1a (col. II) there are traces of a supralinear and, further on, a vertical addition to the previous column (col. I). For similar vertical continuations of supralinear additions cf. e.g. 1QIsa[a] XXVIII, XXX, XXXII, XXXIII; 4QJer[a] III.

L. 12]שׁוֹן. The original is rather well preserved at this point, and the reading is virtually certain (the second letter is a *waw* or *yod*).

L. 12 מושה כיא ◦ [ ] ◦◦ [ ]שׁ[. The words are written vertically, close to the right ruling of col. II. After כיא there is a possible trace of another letter, followed by an abrasion of the surface. Preceding lines 18–20 of col. II faint traces of some letters can be seen. The trace before line 18 is the rather straight head of a letter. The letter preceding line 19 might be *šin*. The following letter is missing, and the last is almost certainly *šin*.

Translation

12.] Moses, because [

Comments

L. 12 The uncertain readings of all words except מושה כיא, and the lack of any context, make reconstructions highly speculative. Examples are מושה כיא [יובל הוא]ה קׄוׄדׄשׁ [תהיה לכמה] (Milik; cf. Lev 25:12a) and המורה הראי]שׁוֹן מושה כיא דׄ[בר (Puech; but דבר is not used in the preserved fragments of this text to introduce a scriptural quotation).

Col. II (Frgs. 1, 2i, 3i, 4)

top margin?

[ ] ◦◦ ◦◦◦◦ מׄ◦◦ עׄלׄ[1

[ ]לׄ וׄאׄשׁר אמר בשנת היובל [הזואת תשובו איש אל אחוזתו 2
ועליו אמר וז]ה

[דבר השמטה] שמוט כול בעל משה יד אשר ישׁה[ברעהו לוא יגוש את רעהו 3
ואת אחיו כיא קרא]שמטה

לׄאׄ[ל פשרו]לׄאׄחׄרית הימים על השבויים אשר[4
]ואשׁר

מׄוׄרׄיׄהׄמה הׄחׄבאׄו וסׄתׄרׄ[ו] ומנחלת מלכי צדק כיׄ[א]◦◦◦◦ וׄהמה 5
נחׄלׄ[ת מלכי צ]דק אשר

6 ישיבמה אליהמה וקרא להמה דרור לעזוב להמה[משא]כול עוונותיהמה
ו[כן יהי]ה הדבר הזה

7 בשבוע היובל הראישון אחר תש[עה ה]יובלים וי[ום הכפ]ורים ה[וא]ה
ס[וף]ה[יו]בל העשירי

8 לכפר בו על כול בני [אור ו]אנש[י]גורל מל[כי]צדק[ ]◦ם עלי[המ]ה
הת[ ]לפ[י]כ[ול עש]ותמה כיא

9 הואה הקץ לשנת הרצון למלכי צדק ולצב[איו ע]ם קדושי אל לממשלת
משפט כאשר כתוב

10 עליו בשירי דויד אשר אמר אלוהים [נ]צב בע[דת אל]בקורב אלוהים
ישפוט ועליו אמ[ר ו]עלי[ה]

11 למרום שובה אל ידין עמים ואשר א[מר עד מתי ת]שפוטו עוול ופני רשע[י]ם
תש[או ס]לה

12 פשרו על בליעל ועל רוחי גורלו אש[ר]◦ים בסו[רמ]ה מחוקי
אל ל[הרשיע]

13 ומלכי צדק יקום נקם משפטי א[ל וביום ההואה יצי]ל[מה מיד]בליעל ומיד כול
ר[וחי גורלו]

14 ובעזרו כול אלי [הצדק וה]ואה א[שר]כ[ול בני אל
והפ[

15 הזואת הואה יום ה[שלום א]שר אמר[ביד ישע]יה הנביא
אשר אמר[מה]נאוו

16 על הרים רגל[י] מבש[ר מ]שמיע שלום מב[שר טוב משמיע ישוע]ה [א]ומר
לציון [מלך]אלוהיך

17 פשרו ההרים[המה] הנביאי[ם]המה א[ ]◦מ[ ]
לכול ◦◦[

18 והמבשר הו[אה]משיח הרו[ח] כאשר אמר דנ[יאל עליו עד משיח נגיד שבועים
שבעה ומבשר]

19 טוב משמי[ע ישועה]הואה הכתוב עליו אשר [

20 לנח[ם] ה[אבלים פשרו]ל[ה]שכילמה בכול קצי הע[ולם

21 באמת למ[ ]מה א[

22 ◦◦[ ]ר הוסרה מבליעל ותש[וב]נק[

23 [ ]במשפט[י] אל כאשר כתוב עליו[אומר לצי]ון מלך אלוהיך
[צי]ון ה[יאה

24]עדת כול בני הצדק המה [מקימ]י[הברית הסרים מלכת]בד[ר֯ך֯ העם ואל]ו[היך֯ ה֯ו֯אה

25]   מלכי צדק אשר יצי[ל]מה מי[ד֯ בליעל ואשר אמר והעברתמה שו]פר ב[כ֯ו֯ל֯
]א[ר֯ץ

bottom margin

Mus. Inv. 579, 1031
PAM 43.979

NOTES ON READINGS

The column is composed of ten fragments, nine of which were presented by van der Woude in the first edition. Frg. 1c, the upper layer of the skin of frg. 1a in lines 18–19, was found in Mus. Inv. 1031, but has not been photographed. The top of frg. 1a might be the top margin, but the area above the assumed first line is too dark, crumbled and abraded to be sure that it contained no writing. The distance between the left bottom part of frg. 1a and the top of frg. 4a is not certain, but the contents of the fragments suggest that no more than one line is missing. The fragments cover 55 to 60 percent of the assumed 25 lines of the column. Some parts of the fragments are abraded or otherwise illegible, but on the other hand several gaps, e.g. in lines 2, 3, 10, 11, and 16 can be reconstructed because they contain scriptural quotations. Altogether, more than 65 percent of the text of the column is certain. The author's literary procedure of quotations from and allusions to specific parts of Scripture may assist in reconstructing even more of the column.

L. 1 [ע֯ל֯ ◦◦מ֯ ◦◦◦◦ ◦◦]. Folds, strokes which need not be ink, and other discolourations complicate the decipherment. It is possible to read]ל֯י֯ם֯ א֯ל֯ו֯ה֯י֯ך֯ מ֯ל֯ך֯ מ֯ל֯◦◦[(Puech), but each letter can be interpreted differently. For example, the alleged tail of the final *kap* of א֯ל֯ו֯ה֯י֯ך֯ could be either a stroke or a small spot; the letter to its right can only be *yod* if its left stroke is covered by a fold; and both traces together can be read as the remains of a single *he*.

L. 2]ל֯. To the left of the dark edge of the fragment there is a lighter stroke that resembles the arm of *lamed*.

L. 2 ו֯א֯ש֯ר. This reading is suggested by the context, but it should be noted that the traces of the letter preceding *reš* are not really consistent with *šin*.

L. 3]דבר. The reading]ד[ב֯ר֯[cannot be substantiated by the fragment or the photograph.

L. 3 ישׂ֯ה[. The abrasion has obliterated most of the *šin*.

L. 4 ל֯]א[ל פשרו]. At the beginning of the line there are some very faint strokes which might be viewed as vestigial remains of the first two (or three) letters. It can be assumed that פשרו was preceded by a large space or small vacat.

L. 4]ל֯א֯ח֯רית. The traces of the first three letters are barely distinguishable.

L. 4]ו֯א֯ש֯ר. The traces of the letter before the *reš* consist of a downstroke with a thickened head and an almost horizontal stroke attached to the right of the downstroke just below the thickened head. It is either *samek* or a *šin* that has turned slightly clockwise because of a fold. The stroke before *ʾalep* suggests *waw*.

L. 5 מ֯ו֯ר֯י֯ה֯מה. The first part of the word is very faint, but *mem* and *reš* are likely. A small stroke following *mem* may be the remnant of the head of *waw*. The first *he* could also be *taw*.

L. 5 ה֯ח֯בא֯ו֯. Only the heads of the first two letters are visible. The third letter is almost certainly *bet* (*kap* would have been larger). The fourth letter has a diagonal (attached to the base of *bet*). The last letter has a rather large head (like *yod*), but a long downstroke (part of the stroke cannot be seen, but the bottom tip is visible).

L. 5 ו֯ס֯ת֯ר֯]ו[. The traces at the beginning of the word cannot be interpreted as *he*; the supposed crossbar clearly does not touch the downstroke. Moreover, the horizontal bar is too long to be the head of *he*. The first trace must be the downstroke of *waw* or *nun*; the next trace looks most like the crossbar of *samek*. The two dots at the end of the word are not necessarily ink, but if so, they probably belong to *he* or final *mem*.

L. 5 ומנחלת. The removal from the fragment of a grain of sand from the left leg of *ḥet* established beyond all doubt that the letter is *ḥet* (Puech). The upper part of the *lamed* is still visible on the fragment above the hole in the skin.

L. 5 ו̊המה oooo[. רוח[ו̊ת̊מ̇ה̊ והמה (Puech) is not completely compatible with the hardly distinguishable traces. It is not certain that the letter preceding המה is *waw*: a small trace attached to the right leg of *he* might suggest a bottomstroke. This part of the manuscript is now completely dark, and no letters are visible.

L. 6 דרור. The photograph shows דרר, but there is a fold in the skin, obscuring the downstroke of *reš* and the head of *waw*.

L. 6 לה̇מ̇ה̊]. The three last letters have been preserved on the small fragment, left of frg. 1b.

L. 6 [כ̇ול. The stance and the position of the downstroke suggest *waw*, rather than the left arm of *ʿayin*.

L. 6 ו]כן יהי[ה̊. The reconstruction ו]יעש[ה̊ is also possible if the letters have been written in somewhat expanded form.

L. 7 ב̊ש̊ב̊ו̊ע̊. Because of a horizontal hole which has stripped the surface of the skin, only the very bottom parts of the letters are visible.

L. 7 ת̊ש̊]עה. Four tiny strokes are probably the tip of the head of *taw* and the uppermost ends of the three arms of *šin*. The interpretation of the dark stroke at the edge of the fragment as part of *ʿayin* is questionable.

L. 7 וי̇]ום. Or וי̇]ו[ם̊] if the tiny speck above the final *mem* at the beginning of frg. 2b 8 is the left bottom angle of a final *mem*.

L. 7 ס̊]וף [ה̊]יו[בל. The two black blots above the ceiling line do not belong to the writing. It is possible that they are the bottom of the legs of *he* (cf. the same distance between *he* and *bet* in היובל at the beginning of the line), but here the hole is broader and it cannot be verified that the two tiny spots are really ink.

L. 8]אור. The photograph does not show a trace of *ʾalep*, but Puech claimed that there are some faint traces on the turnover of the skin. Now only a large hole in the surface of the skin and a smaller hole in the deeper layer of the skin are visible on the fragment. Due to the crumbled state of the fragment it is impossible to measure the distance between the preserved letters accurately.

L. 8 ו[א̇נש]י. The left leg of *ʾalep* is partly obscured by a grain of sand.

L. 8 מל]כי. The flattening of a fold in the skin has confirmed the reading of *mem* and *lamed*. The black vertical traces on the photograph are in fact a crack in the surface layer.

L. 8 [∘ם. The trace preceding *mem* seems to be the upper part of a downstroke slanting slightly to the right.

L. 8 הת]. Puech's claim that the downstroke of a letter forms a ligature with the bottomstroke of *taw*, cannot be verified by the photograph or the original fragment.

L. 8 [לפ̊]י. Following *lamed* two traces are visible. The lower one is in fact the top of a *lamed* on the next line. The upper trace consists of the left end of a horizontal stroke. These two traces are very close, but examination of the fragment reveals that the skin is broken; the piece of skin with the two traces overlaps the one on which the *lamed* of line 8 appears. The horizontal stroke that, in the photograph appears to be part of the head of a letter, is in fact part of the bottom stroke of a possible *pe*.

L. 8 [כ̊]ול. On the bottom edge of the hole in the fragment there is a trace that is consistent with the base stroke of *kap*.

L. 9 צד̊ק. The fold has been flattened, clearly revealing the *qop*. Only the left tick of the *dalet* remains, more clearly visible on the fragment than in the photograph.

L. 9 ו̊לצ̊ב̊]איו ע[ם̊. The dark, slightly diagonal stroke at the beginning is not the diagonal of *gimel* or *ʾalep*, but the lower part of *lamed*. A faint downstroke preceding *lamed* suggests *waw*, but it is not completely certain that this trace is ink. After *lamed* there is a small trace on the ceiling line which could be the left end of the crossbar of *he*. However, beneath this trace there is a horizontal stroke that seems to be the left end of a base stroke. These two traces together suggest *bet*, *kap*, or *ṣade*. The distance between the two traces might seem too small for *kap* or *ṣade*, but the form of the next letter shows that these letters have been compressed. If the letter is *ṣade*, the tiny trace beneath the top stroke of *lamed* could be the tip of the right arm. The form of the last letter has definitely been compressed by the material. *Bet* is more probable than *reš* because of the traces on the bottom line. The broken trace at the beginning of frg. 2b could be the upper end of *waw* or final *nun*, but it could also be the hook of the upper left part of final *mem*.

L. 9 לממׄשׁלת. The second *mem* is only partially preserved, and the surviving traces are also consistent with *pe*. There are only two small traces of *šin*: the bottom end of the downstroke and part of the lower oblique. A vertical, not slanting, bottom part of the downstroke is visible in several *šin*s, especially when the downstroke continues beyond the join with the lower oblique. Milik's reading למפׄעׄל[ו]ת is less compatible with the traces; the small vertical downstroke is not likely to be the bottom part of *lamed*.

L. 10 ו]עׄליׄ[ה]. The traces at the end of the word in the photograph are confusing, suggesting an *ʾalep*, but in the original this part has remained in position after the removal of the surface skin; after cleaning away some impurities, the *yod* seems assured but there is no longer any trace of the *he*.

L. 11 רשע[י]ם. The faint dot above the upper right corner of the hole might be the remnant of a *yod*.

L. 12 רׄוחׄי. The fragment preserves the downstroke and the very right end of the head of *reš*, the bottom tips of *waw*, and the right leg of *ḥet*. Note, however, that this *reš* must have had a very short head; the space between the downstrokes of *reš* and *waw* is only about two thirds of the normal size.

L. 12]◦ים. Milik read [ה]מׄמׄרׄים, placing the two *mem*s of frg. 5 1 here. Puech read הממ]רים, but the first trace seems to be too diagonal to be the tick of the head of *reš*.

L. 12 בסו]רמ[הׄ. A very faint dot and some minute faint strokes might be remnants of *reš* and *mem* or almost any other letter. A faint horizontal stroke is possibly the crossbar of *he*.

L. 13 נקׄםׄ. Only the extreme right part of *qop* and the very left of final *mem* have been preserved. The space is too small for the reading נקׄ[מ]תׄ.

L. 13 יצי[לׄ]מה. Beneath the *bet* of בסו]רמ[הׄ in line 12 there is a trace which seems to be the upper tip of *lamed*.

L. 13 רׄ]וחי. The lower end of the downstroke of a letter is visible. There seems to be a longer stroke along the edge of the fragment, but the black tip is darker than the rest of the stroke.

L. 13 גורלו]. The first line of frg. 3 displays a trace which several scholars regarded as *waw*: גורל[וׄ. However, the trace is not necessarily ink, and רׄ]וחי גורלו written in normally sized letters would not reach it.

L. 14 וה[וׄ]אה א]שר. The first visible trace is the tapered end of a downstroke. The space between this stroke and the next letter also allows for a *reš*. There is only a short space between *he* and the following *ʾalep*.

L. 14 אל. The right tip of the diagonal of the first letter renders חׄ[י]ל an impossible reading. The top of *lamed* touches the downstroke of the *dalet* in line 13.

L. 14 והפׄ[. The fragment shows that the trace above אמר in the following line is not ink, and therefore not the tail of *qop*.

L. 14 The faint traces in the photograph of frg. 3, suggesting *dalet* preceded by another letter, correspond to two cracks in the original.

L. 15 הׄ]שלום א[שר. The two vertical strokes close to one another are probably the legs of *he*. The reconstructed letters fit well in the gap, whereas other suggestions (e.g. הׄ]ישועה א[שר) leave no room for a space before א[שר.

L. 16 רגל[י]. The minute dot in the photograph, which suggests the bottom tip of the right stroke of *yod*, is not visible on the original, which shows an abraded surface.

L. 17 ההרׄיׄם. The fragment has become flattened and traces of the final *mem* are now clearly visible.

L. 17 הׄנביאׄ[ם]. The traces of the first two letters may also be interpreted as *taw*, and the length of the downstroke of the second *yod* is somewhat longer than normal.

L. 17]◦מׄ[. Cf. the *mem* of והמבשר in the following line. The preceding letter is *bet*, *nun*, *pe*, *ṣade*, or *taw*.

L. 17 לכול ◦◦[. The first trace after לכול may not be ink. The other two or three minute traces on the ceiling line are indicative of downstrokes.

L. 18 כׄאשר. A base stroke on frg. 1c suggests one should read כׄאשר, instead of אשר.

L. 18 דנׄ]יאל. The short base of the second letter strongly suggests *nun*, but *kap*, for example, is also possible.

L. 19 טוׄב֯. טוב is certain because of the context, but *bet* is partially lost in the lacuna, and only the bottom of the *waw* has been preserved.

L. 19 הכ֯תוב. Part of *kap*, as well as the complete *taw* and *waw* are supplied by frg. 1c, which is unphotographed.

L. 20 ה]אבלים. The peculiar shape of the *he* is caused by a fold that partially obscures the crossbar.

L. 20 הע]ולם. The traces are distorted in the photograph because the skin was not completely flattened, but both *he* and *ʿayin* are clear in the original.

L. 21 בׄאמת למ֯[. The small dot before *ʾalep* is probably the left end of the base of *bet*. The trace of the first letter of the second word resembles the loop of *lamed*. The next letter is probably *mem* or *pe*, but e.g. *kap, nun*, and *ṣade* are not impossible.

L. 21 The apparent traces above *samek* of סרה on frg. 4a are not ink and do not represent any letter.

L. 21]מׄה֯. Only the tops of the letters are visible, but *mem* is much more probable than *ʾalep*.

L. 22]ר. The letter is clear and almost complete after the flattening of the skin.

L. 22 הוסרה. A crack has caused the loss of the skin between the first *he* and the *samek*, but on the edge, the bottom of the *waw* can still be seen in the original.

L. 22 ותשׁ֯]וב. The trace after *taw* is probably the upper end of the right stroke of *ʿayin* or *šin*.

L. 22]נׄק[. The first letter is probably *nun*, though *ṣade* and *taw* are also possible.

L. 23]במשפט[י] אל. This reading leaves hardly any space between the two words, as, for example, in line 12, מחוקי אל.

L. 24 [בד]ר֯ך֯. The original only shows a trace compatible with the bottom of a final *kap* and the bottom of a *reš* or *dalet*; the space between מלכת and העם though is rather small for the reading of [בד]ר֯ך֯.

TRANSLATION

1. [ ] [
2. [ ] and as for what he said: 'In [this] year of jubilee [each of you shall return to his property', concerning it he said: 'And th]is is
3. [the manner of the remission:] every creditor shall remit what he has lent [his neighbour. He shall not press his neighbour or his brother for it has been proclaimed] a remission
4. of Go[d'. Its interpretation] for the final days concerns the captives, who [ ] and whose
5. teachers have been hidden and kept secret, and from the inheritance of Melchizedek, fo[r] and they are the inheritan[ce of Melchize]dek who
6. will make them return. And liberty shall be proclaimed to them, to free them from [the debt of] all their iniquities. And this [wil]l [happen]
7. in the first week of the jubilee (that occurs) after [the] ni[ne] jubilees. And the D[ay of Atone]ment i[s] the e[nd of] the tenth [ju]bilee,
8. in which atonement shall be made for all the sons of [light and for] the men [of] the lot of Mel[chi]zedek[ ] over [th]em [ ] accor[ding to] a[ll] their [doing]s, for
9. it is the time for the year of grace of Melchizedek and of [his] arm[ies, the nati]on [of] the holy ones of God, of the administration of justice, as is written
10. about him in the songs of David, who said: 'Elohim shall [st]and in the ass[embly of God]; in the midst of the gods he shall judge'. And about him he sa[id: 'And] above [it,]
11. to the heights, return: God shall judge the nations'. And as for what he s[aid: 'How long will you] judge unjustly, and be par[tial] to the wick[e]d. [Se]lah',
12. the interpretation of it concerns Belial and the spirits of his lot wh[o], in [the]ir tur[ning] away from God's commandments to [commit evil].
13. And Melchizedek will carry out the vengeance of Go[d]'s judgements [and on that day he will f]r[ee them from the hand of] Belial and from the hand of all the s[pirits of his lot.]
14. And all the gods [of justice] are to his help; [and h]e is (the one) wh[o] all the sons of God, and he will [
15. This [ ] is the day of the [peace ab]out which he said [through Isa]iah the prophet who said: ['How] beautiful
16. upon (the) mountains are the feet [of] the messen[ger who an]nounces peace, the mes[senger of good who announces salvati]on, [sa]ying to Zion: your God [is king'].

17. Its interpretation: the mountains [are] the prophet[s]; they [ ] every [ ]
18. And the messenger i[s] the anointed of the spir[it], as Dan[iel] said [about him: 'Until an anointed, a prince, it is seven weeks'. And the messenger of]
19. good who announ[ces salvation] is the one about whom it is written [
20. 'To comfo[rt] the [afflicted', its interpretation:] to [in]struct them in all the ages of the w[orld
21. in truth [ ] [
22. [ ] has turned away from Belial and shall retu[rn to] [
23. [ ] in the judgement[s of] God, as is written about him: '[saying to Zi]on: your God is king'. [Zi]on i[s]
24. [the congregation of all the sons of justice, who] establish the covenant, who avoid walking [on the p]ath of the people. And 'your G[o]d' is
25. [Melchizedek who will fr]ee [them from the han]d of Belial. And as for what he said: 'And you shall blow the ho[rn in] all the [l]and (of)

COMMENTS

L. 2 ואׄשר אמר. In 1QpHab the expression ואשר אמר is always followed by a biblical quotation and the word פשרו. In the preserved text of this column the formula appears three times: lines 2, 11, and 25. Only in the second instance has פשרו been preserved (line 12), but it should probably be reconstructed in the two other examples. Note that in both lines 11 and 25 there is a large space in front of ואשר אמר.

L. 2 בשנת היובל. Two biblical texts begin with בשנת היובל, Lev 25:13 and Lev 27:24, but it is certain that the text is quoting the former one. Not only is Lev 27:24 too long, but the column repeatedly refers to Leviticus 25.

L. 2 ועליו אמר. At the end of line 2, וז[ה, the first word of Deut 15:2, which is quoted in line 3, should be reconstructed. The remaining space demands that approximately 9 letters be reconstructed between the two biblical verses, e.g. ועליו אמר or כאשר כתוב.

Ll. 2–4 וז]ה / [דבר השמטה] שמוט כול בעל משה יד אשר ישה[ברעהו לוא יגוש את רעהו ואת אחיו כיא קרא שמטה / לׄאׄ[ל]. The text quotes Deut 15:2. The Greek translations of יובל and שמטה (𝔊 renders in both cases ἄφεσις) show that in the period when the text was written, the originally different concepts could be equated. The text reads יד, whereas 𝔐 has ידו. Also, it is virtually certain that the text read לאל instead of 𝔐 ליהוה. Cf. line 11 אל ידין עמים whereas 𝔐 Ps 7:9 reads יהוה ידין עמים.

L. 4 פשרו]לׄאׄחרית הימים על. In several *pesharim* the expressions פשר הדבר and לאחרית הימים (or על אחרית הימים) are connected, e.g. 4QpIsa[b] (4Q**162**) 1 ii 1, 4QpIsa[c] (4Q**163**) 23 10. Here, the temporal clause לאחרית הימים interrupts the stereotyped sequence פשרו על.

L. 4 השבויים. The word refers to Isa 61:1-3, a section that is repeatedly referred to in this column. A quotation from Isa 61:1-3 may be reconstructed in the gap, e.g. [אשר] אמר עליהמה לקרוא לשבויים דרור], but this is very uncertain. The preserved text of the column uses an expression from Isa 61:1-3 six times, but nowhere does it quote even a complete hemistich (line 4 השבויים; line 6 וקרא להמה דרור; line 9 לׄשנת הרצון; line 13 נקׄםׄ משפׄטׄי א[ל; line 18 מׄשיח הרו[ח]; line 20 לנחׄ[ם] ה[אבלים). Apparently, Isa 61:1-3 is a key passage that was considered to be commonly known. Also, the reconstruction does not really add anything to the text. In the construction פשרו על . . . אשר, אשר introduces a clause that explains or defines the noun introduced by על. Moreover, קרא דרור is mentioned in line 6. Finally, it is not clear how the next almost indecipherable phrase is connected to this reconstruction. Even though part of the line is missing, it is evident that the passage as a whole describes the eschatological return of the exiles to the land of Israel.

L. 4 ואשׄר]. The problems of the reading of the next phrase begin with the last word of this line. It is not clear whether ואסׄר or ואשׄר should be read. If the word is ואסׄר the subject is either Belial (the clause giving a description or explanation of the captivity of השבויים) or Melchizedek (in which case, this is an eschatological description). If the word is ואשׄר, then the clause is probably parallel to the first missing one.

Ll. 4–5 ואשׄר / מׄורׄיׄהמה הׄחׄבאׄו וסׄתׄרׄ[ו]. Suggested alternative readings are: י]אמׄור להיׄוׄתׄמה מן בנׄי השׄמׄ[י]םׄ ומנחלת מלכי צדק, 'and he will declare that they belong to the sons of heaven and to the inheritance of Melchizedek' (Milik, but epigraphically difficult); אשׄר הׄכׄרׄיׄתׄמה מן בנׄי השׄמׄ[י]םׄ ומנחלת מלכי צדק, 'who cut them off from the sons of heaven and from the inheritance of Melchizedek' (Kobelski); ואסר מ(ו)ריהמה מחבאי העצרה ומנחלת מלכי צדק, 'and he will imprison their rebels away from the refugees of the assembly and away from the inheritance of Melchizedek' (Puech 1987); ואשר מוריהמה מדכאי העצרה ומנחלת מלכי צדק,

'and whose teachers are among the oppressed of the assembly and among the inheritance of Melchizedek' (Puech, 1993). In the reading proposed here, it has to be assumed that ומנחלת is the continuation of a term from line 4.

L. 5 ומנחלת מלכי צדק. In this column Melchizedek assumes the role attributed to the archangel Michael in other texts of the same period. For all practical reasons the two figures may be identified (de Jonge and van der Woude, Milik, and Kobelski deal extensively with the figure of Melchizedek in Jewish literature and the New Testament). The background of the expression נחלת מלכי צדק is the biblical view that Israel is the נחלה of God (cf. Deut 32:9; 1 Sam 10:1; Ps 78:71; Isa 19:25 and 47:6 etc.). It refers to the nation as עם, a term which is often used in parallelism with נחלה. A connection with the biblical remarks about the נחלה of the Aaronites and the Levites (cf. Num 18:20; Deut 10:9; 18:2; Josh 13:33) is also possible: usually they are not called the נחלה of God; rather God is their נחלה. Josh 18:7, however, has a different formulation כי כהנת יהוה נחלתו. Like Michael (Dan 10:13, 21; 12:1; *1 Enoch* 20:5), Melchizedek is the guardian and redeemer of Israel. The 'inheritance of Melchizedek' corresponds to the biblical inheritance of God. The substitution of God with Melchizedek is explicit in line 9 and implied in line 13, but this does not mean that Melchizedek is a hypostasis of God.

L. 6 ישיבמה אליהמה. The subject is likely to be Melchizedek, and the object of the verbal form is probably השבויים of line 4. The antecedent of the pronominal suffix of אליהמה is less clear. Does it refer to the 'captives', to the phrase meaning 'he will reconstruct them', or to the נחלת מלכי צדק or another subject in line 5? The expression may at the same time be an allusion to Lev 25:10 ושבתם איש אל אחזתו ואיש אל משפחתו תשבו or 25:13 תשבו איש אל אחזתו.

L. 6 וקרא להמה דרור. Cf. Isa 61:1 (לקרא לשבוים דרור) and Lev 25:10 (וקראתם דרור). In Isa 61:1 the 'anointed' is the subject of קרא, but the distinction between the 'anointed' and Melchizedek has not yet been made in the text. The subject of the verbal form should rather be regarded as indefinite. In Isa 61:1 and Lev 25:10 דרור means 'liberty', but 𝔊 (ἄφεσις) shows that in this period the notion of remission had been added to the term.

L. 6 לעזוב להמ[ה] משא. The notion of דרור as ἄφεσις is made explicit in the next clause, עזב sometimes being rendered by ἀφίημι in 𝔊. The reconstruction משא is based upon Neh 5:10 נעזבה נא את המשא הזה, and upon the expression נשא עון in the Hebrew Bible and Qumran literature (Milik). Also, it provides a link with line 3 משה and ישה.

L. 7 בׄשׄבׄוׄעׄ. Both the surviving traces and the space needed for the first word strongly suggest בׄשׄבׄוׄעׄ, and not בׄשׄנׄתׄ. Here the concept of the weeks (of years) is encountered, known from Dan 9:24-27, *T. Levi* 16:1–18:4, *1 Enoch* 93:1-10; 91:12-17, and 4QAgesCreat (4Q**181**) 2 3.

L. 7 תׄשׄ[ע]ה. Cf. the mention of the tenth jubilee at the end of the line.

L. 7 ו[י]וֹם הכפ[ו]רים. The reconstruction is suggested by לכפר in the next line, and the fact that Lev 25:9 is being referred to.

L. 7 סׄ[וף]ה[יו]בל. Cf. frg. 7 7.

L. 8 בני] אור. A common designation for the members of the Qumran community in 1QS and 1QM. The reconstruction בני [אל] may be considered because of the occurrence of the same expression in line 14 (Milik, Puech). Yet, there it seems to refer to angels, whereas in this line the mention of atonement for angels might be considered less appropriate.

L. 8 ו[אנש]י [ג]ורל מל[כי]צדק. Cf. e.g. 1QS II 2 אנשי גורל אל.

L. 8]ם על[י]ה[מ]ה הת[ ]לפ[י]כ[ול עש]ותמה. The reconstruction ובמר[ו]ם על[י]ה[מ]ה התד[בר]לפ[י גורל]והמה, 'and on the height he will declare in their favour according to their lots' (Puech; cf. 4QAgesCreat [4Q**181**] 1 5 איש לפי גורלו; or at the end: לפ[י כול עש]והמה) is syntactically awkward, and should be dismissed. The most logical reconstruction would be a verb before על[י]ה[מ]ה.

L. 9 לׄשנת הרצון. Another reference to Isa 61:1-3, but whereas Isa 61:2 reads שנת רצון ליהוה, this text has למלכי צדק instead of ליהוה.

L. 9 ולצב[איו ע[ם. ולצב[אותיו ע[ם is too long, and ולצב[אות ע[ם קדושי אל seems somewhat awkward.

L. 10 עליו. The suffix probably refers to Melchizedek, although משפט could also be the antecedent. The author quotes Ps 82:1, which indicates that the first אלוהים of this verse was interpreted as a reference to Melchizedek.

L. 10 ועליו אמׄר. The suffix refers again to Melchizedek.

L. 10 ו[על[י]ה]. The beginning of a quotation of Ps 7:8b-9a. Because of the gap it is uncertain whether the text read ועליה like 𝔐, or עליה. The word עליה refers in this verse to the עדת לאמים of the first hemistich. Apparently the author identified the עדת אל of Ps 82:1 with the עדת לאמים of Ps 7:8.

L. 11 ואשר א[מר עד מתי ת]שפוטו עוול. After the quotation from Psalm 7 the text quotes Ps 82:2.

L. 12 אש]ר [◦ים. The reconstruction אש]ר כולמה היו הממ]רים (Puech) is syntactically difficult; this kind of periphrastic construction is unusual in the Dead Sea Scrolls.

L. 12 בסו[רמ]ה מחוקי. For סור מחוקי cf. Mal 3:7 סרתם מחקי and 1QS I 15 לסור מחוקי אמתו.

L. 12 ל[הרשיע]. The *lamed* at the end of the line is likely to introduce an infinitive.

L. 13 יקום נקם. In view of the other references to Isa 61:1-3, יקום נקם is certainly a reference to Isa 61:2 יום נקם לאלהינו.

L. 13 משפטי א[ל. Cf. line 23 and Ps 19:10 משפטי יהוה אמת.

L. 13 וביום ההואה יצי]ל[מה מיד]בליעל. Cf. e.g. 4QpPs[a] (4Q**171**) 3–10 iv 21 יושיעם אל ו[י]צילם מיד ר[שעי. A *Nipʿal* ינצ]ל[ו is possible, but the *Hipʿil* יצי]ל[מה is a better continuation of יקום. The phrase ביום ההואה fits within the space that is left (ויושיעמה also fits, but is perhaps a little too short). Note, however, that the preserved text twice refers to a day (lines 7 and 15), but that there is no trace of the common formula ביום ההואה. Either וביום ההואה יצי]ל[מה or ביום ההואה ויצי]ל[מה (Puech) may be reconstructed.

L. 14 ובעזרו. For the construction בעזר with a pronominal suffix cf. Ex 18:4, Deut 33:26, Hos 13:9 and Ps 146:5. The pronominal suffix refers to Melchizedek or to another antecedent in the gap of the previous line.

L. 14 אלי]הצדק. Or אלי]המרומים; אלי]קודש is too long. אלי]הצדק may be a reference to Isa 61:3 which reads אילי הצדק. Cf. 4QShirShabb[d] (4Q**403**) 1 i 18; ii 33; 4QShirShabb[f] (4Q**405**) 13 2; 4QShir[b] (4Q**511**) 10 11 for the orthographic variant אילי. Even though the next hemistich in Isa 61:3 clearly indicates that אילי are 'trees', not 'gods', our text may have been an allusion. For אלי]קודש cf. מלאכי קודש in 1QSa II 8–9 and 1QSb III 6, and the very common רוחי קודש.

L. 14 וה[ו]אה א[שר. Or למ]ראה א[בדון (Milik). It is reasonable to assume that ה[ו]אה refers to Melchizedek and that א[שר is followed by a verbal form.

L. 15 הזואת. Probably an adjunct to a preceding noun.

L. 15 יום ה]שלום. Cf. Isa 52:7 which is quoted in this and the next line. יום ה]ישועה is appropriate from a literary point of view (cf. Isa 49:8 where the expression יום ישועה occurs parallel to עת רצון), but is too long. The reconstructions יום ה]הרגה (too long) and יום ה]רגה (cf. 1QH[a] VII 21 [XV 17]) do not relate to Isa 52:7.

L. 15 א]שר אמ[ר   ביד ישע]יה. The usual kind of introductory formula is too short for the space. The formula was possibly extended by an adverbial clause or על with a nominal clause. ביד ישע]יה is to be preferred over בדברי ישע]יה which is common with כתוב.

Ll. 15–16 מה [נאוו על הרים רגל[י] מבש[ר מ]שמיע שלום מב[שר טוב משמיע ישוע[ה [א]ומר לציון [מלך]אלוהיך. A quotation of Isa 52:7. The scribe forgot a *he* of ההרים (in line 17 he correctly writes ההרים).

L. 17 פשרו ההר[י]ם [המה]הנביאי[ם]המה. פשרו ההרים [דברי] הנביאים המה (Kobelski) violates the syntactical rule of the formula. The second המה (ו]המה does not fit) belongs to the next clause.

L. 18 משיח הרו[ח]. A reference to Isa 61:1. The plural 'anointed ones' is used in CD II 12, VI 1, and 1QM XI 7 to denote prophets (compare Ps 105:15 and 1 Chr 16:22). The singular form here may refer to the eschatological prophet referred to in 1QS IX 2 and 4QTest (4Q**175**) 5–8 (cf. de Jonge and van der Woude, p. 306–8).

L. 18 כאשר אמר דנ[יאל עליו עד משיח נגיד שבועים שבעה. The reading דנ[יאל strongly suggests that the remainder of the line quotes part of Dan 9:25 or 26. The clause in Dan 9:25 עד משיח נגיד שבעים שבעה seems quite appropriate and fits very well in the remaining space.

L. 19] אשר. Since the first two words of line 20, לנח[ם] ה[אבלים, seem to be a reference to Isa 61:2, it is possible that this line may also refer to this passage in Isaiah. Hence, e.g. אשר [ישלח להמה לנחם כול אבלים לשום לאבלי ציון] (Puech). However, as commented above (cf. line 4), none of the preserved references to Isa 61:1-3 are introduced by formulas, nor does the preserved text quote complete clauses from these verses.

L. 20 לנח[ם] ה[אבלים. The references to Isa 61:1-3 in this column strongly suggest that the text read האבלים and not some other word. The article is used as in line 18 והמבשר.

L. 20 פשרו [. Or, less likely, a verb, e.g. ויצא (cf. Dan 9:22) or יבוא.

L. 20 קצי הע[ולם. The line may have continued with, e.g., ולהודעמה. השכיל and הודע are often used in parallellism.

L. 22]ר הוסרה מבליעל ותש[וב. The feminine subject of the verbal forms הוסרה and תש[וב may be Zion. The verb שוב is fitting as the opposite of סור.

L. 22]נ֯ק֯[. The letters may belong to a word from the stem נקם, e.g. יום]נ֯ק֯[ם or ב]נ֯ק֯[ם. Reconstruct, e.g., ותש]וב אל אדני ביום]נ֯ק֯[ם, followed by either בליעל ורוחי גורלו or בסוף היובל העשירי (Puech), or, since אדני is not used in the preserved text, ותש֯]וב אל מלכי צדק ב]נ֯ק֯[ם.

L. 23]כאשר כתֹוב עליו. עליו probably refers to Melchizedek, not to המבשר of line 18. It is therefore reasonable to assume that he is mentioned explicitly somewhere in lines 22–23. These two lines seem to resume the theme of line 13.

Ll. 23–24 [צי]ון ה֯[יאה] / [עדת כול בני הצדק. The reconstruction of the first part of line 24 is tentative. The lost text may allude to Isa 1:26 עיר הצדק.

L. 24 המה]מקימ[י הברית. הקים הברית is an activity of the righteous; cf. 1QS V 21–22; VIII 10; 1QSb V 23.

L. 24 הסרים מלכת [בד]ר֯ך֯ העם. Cf. for this common expression Isa 8:11; CD VIII 16; XIX 29; 4QFlor (4Q**174**) 1–3 i 14.

Ll. 24–25 ואל[ו]היך֯ ה֯ואה / [ ] מלכי צדק. The interpretation of אל[ו]היך֯ has not been preserved. It is, however, plausible that the author mentioned Melchizedek. Whatever the horizontal alignment of frg. 4, the reconstruction of the entire clause ואל[ו]היך֯ ה֯ואה / [מלכי צדק אשר יצי]ל[מה מי]ד֯ בליעל is four to six letter-spaces too short. השר, 'the prince' (cf. Dan 12:1) might be added as an epithet of Melchizedek, but הואה also fits after צדק.

L. 25 אשר יצי]ל[מה מי]ד֯ בליעל. Cf. the reconstruction of line 13.

L. 25 ואשר אמר והעברתמה שו]פר ב[כו֯ל֯ [א]ר֯ץ. The long space before ואשר probably indicates a shift of subject. The author seems to quote Lev 25:9, but the text does not correspond completely to 𝔐 which reads first והעברת שופר תרועה בחדש השבעי and at the end תעבירו שופר בכל ארצכם. 𝔊 reads at the beginning of the sentence καὶ διαγγελεῖτε σάλπιγγος φωνῇ ἐν πάσῃ τῇ γῇ ὑμῶν τῷ μηνὶ τῷ ἑβδόμῳ. A retroversion of 𝔊 gives והעברתם שופר תרועה בכל ארצכם בחדש השבעי. The problem in this line is the gap between שו]פר and ב[כו֯ל֯ which only allows for 3 to 4 letter-spaces. תרועה only fits if frg. 4d is moved approximately 0.7 cm to the left, but then a problem is created in lines 23 and 24. Not only the insufficient space between the two fragments, but also the word א]ר֯ץ instead of ארצכם shows that the text is not a literal quotation of any known textual tradition. The gap might be filled by reading שו]פרות or, possibly, שו]פר איל or שו]פר יעל.

Col. III (Frgs. 2ii, 3ii)

1]ם[ ]

2]ודעו ד֯ב֯°°°

3]אל יאו

4]ורוב֯

5]ל֯°°[ ]

6]התור֯ה֯[ע]ל֯יה֯מ֯ה֯

7]יתמכ֯[ו] ב֯ליעל באש֯

8]במזמ[ו]ת֯ בל֯בם ת֯

9]את חומ[ו]ת֯ יה֯ודה ו֯ב֯ר֯[ ]ע֯

10]גדר ולש֯א֯ת ע֯מוד וכ֯פר °[ ]א֯

11]ה֯[ ]

12 [ ]ר̊[ ]°ס̊°°[

13 ה[

14 ה°[

15 בש[

16 מאתים[

17 השבוע[

18 [מח]לקות̊[העתים

19 [ ]ב̊נ̊פ̊[

20 [ ]ה̊י̊[

Mus. Inv. 579
PAM 43.979

NOTES ON READINGS

The only certain fragments of col. III are frgs. 2a ii and 3 ii, both of which have preserved the left side of col. II and the beginning of col. III. It is very difficult to read frg. 2a because only the lower uninscribed layer of almost half of the skin has been preserved. The inscribed surface layer has now become separated (frg. 2b) and appears on the same museum plate as the lower layer (frg. 2a). Frgs. 5, 6, 7, and 8 may also belong to this column, but the original position of none of these fragments can be ascertained (for suggestions, cf. the notes on these fragments).

L. 2 ד̊ב̊°°°[. Nothing can be seen on the original.

L. 4 ורוב̊[. *Bet* is not certain. The photograph suggests a long thick downstroke, but only the upper part belongs to the letter. The reading ורוח̊[is less likely.

L. 5]ל̊°°[. The original suggests that the traces after *lamed* do not belong to *he,* but to two letters.

L. 6 התור̊ה̊[. The fourth letter, of which only the downstroke has been preserved, is probably *reš* or possibly *dalet*. The lower part of the left leg of the final *he* is still visible on the dark part of the skin.

L. 6 ע]ל̊י̊ה̊מ̊ה̊[. The black traces can be interpreted as the bottom part of the loop of *lamed* and *yod*. The traces of the last three letters are quite faint, but they are compatible with this reading, which was proposed by Puech. Objections to this reading are the rather large space (of at least 2 letters) between התור̊ה̊[and ע]ל̊י̊ה̊מ̊ה̊, and that the small black traces between these words might represent letters.

L. 7 יתממ̊[ו] ב̊ליעל. A vertical crack in the skin is visible on the fragment. In the photograph, it appears that the fragment may also possibly have a vertical fold running through several lines, obscuring 1 or 2 letters.

L. 8 במזמ[ו]ת̊. The second *mem* of במזמ[ו]ת̊ is virtually certain, even though only the right downstroke has been preserved. Traces of *taw* are still visible.

L. 8 בל̊בבם. The reading ל]בבם (Puech) cannot be correct because traces of another letter appear between the two *bet*s, probably remains of the loop of *lamed*.

L. 9 חומ[ו]ת̊. חום seems probable in the photograph, but the tiny vertical stroke to the left of the base of *mem* is probably a vestige of the left leg of *taw*, the rest of *taw* and the preceding *waw* being hidden by a fold. Comparison with the surrounding lines shows that חומת̊ is unlikely; the fold must have obscured more than one letter.

L. 9 יה̊ו̊דה. The most probable reading in spite of several difficulties: only two downstrokes of *he* and *waw* can be seen (is one hidden in a fold?), the left tick of the head of *dalet* is much larger than usual and the lower end of its downstroke is strange (is there a fold between *waw* and *dalet*, obscuring the upper part of *waw* and the bottom of *dalet*?), and there is no visible space after the last *he*.

L. 9 ו֯בׄר֯[ ]ע֯[. Immediately after יהׄודה there are traces of three more letters. The last one is almost certainly *reš* (its head is rather large for *waw*) and is connected to the base of the previous letter, which is probably *bet* or *pe*. The downstroke at the beginning could belong to that letter (in which case it is *bet*), but might also be *waw*. Puech's suggestion, כפר (not וכפר!), is not completely impossible. Two letter-spaces after *reš*, there is a thick diagonal stroke which, if ink, might indicate *ʿayin*.

L. 10 ולש֯אׄת. The letter after *waw* is certainly *lamed*. Attached to its loop is a small stroke that could be the upper part of the right stroke of either *ʿayin* or *šin* (*śin*). The stroke before *taw* is too long and not diagonal enough to be the left stroke of *yod*; it is probably the left leg of *ʾalep*.

L. 10 ע֯מוד. Note that on the edge of the light part of the fragment, after *taw* of the previous word, there is a small trace which corresponds to the top of the right arm of *ʿayin*. The rest of *ʿayin* and the right part of *mem* are obscured by a fold.

L. 10 וכׄפר. The second letter is probably *nun* or *kap*; the third one certainly *bet* or *pe*. This word is followed by some indecipherable traces which, if ink, belong to one or two letters.

L. 11]ה֯[. The letter at the end of the line is possibly *he*. The downward stance of the left end of the crossbar rules out final *mem*.

L. 19]בׄנ֯פׄ[. Or]כׄנ֯פׄ[with a rather small *kap*.

TRANSLATION

1. [ ] [
2. and know [
3. God [
4. and the multitude [
5. [ ] [ ] [
6. the law [u]pon them [
7. [they] shall devour Belial with fire [
8. with plots in their hearts [
9. the ramparts of Judah, and [
10. a wall, and to lift up a column and [
11. [ ] [
12. [ ] [ ] [
13. [
14. [
15. [
16. two hundred [
17. the week [
18. [the di]visions [of the times
19. [ ] [
20. [ ] [

COMMENTS

L. 1]ם[ ]. If the reading ב]כו֯ל [א]ר֯ץ at the end of the previous column is correct, then the supplement should be reconstructed at the beginning of this column. It is not certain that this line is the first one of the column, but if it is, a supplement of three or four letters ending with final *mem* should be reconstructed, e.g. [שבי]ם[, though even this might be too long. Somewhere at the beginning of the column פשרו should be reconstructed as the sequel of ואשר אמר in col. II 25.

L. 2 ודעו. The imperative is not part of a scriptural quotation, and is unique in the preserved text which is on the whole descriptive and not parenetic.

L. 3 אל. 'God' or the negative particle. The imperative in line 2 could suggest a preference for the latter possibility, but statistically 'God' is more likely.

L. 6 התורה֯[ע]ל֯יה֯מ֯ה֯[. The clause presupposes a verb and a subject (Melchizedek). Note, however, that the reading התודׄה or התודׄו 'he' or 'they confessed' (or imperative?) is also possible. Cf. with על Lev 16:21

or Neh 1:6. It is tempting to place line 2 of frg. 8 further on in this line, in which case the 'binding' (if that is the correct reconstruction) precedes the burning mentioned in the line 7. Cf. e.g. *1 Enoch* 10:4 'Bind Asael by his hands and feet'.

L. 7 יתממ֯[ו]. Apparently a *Piʿel*. The notion of punishment by fire after the judgement is common. Cf. e.g. *1 Enoch* 10:6, 13-14. On the basis of this line and frg. 8 2, it can be surmised that the beginning of this column deals with the punishment and annihilation of Belial and the evil spirits of his lot.

L. 8 במזמ[ו]ת֯ בל֯בם. Cf. e.g. 4QBer[f] (4Q**280**) 2 6 ו[מ]קימי מזמתכה בלבבמה.

L. 9 את חומ[ו]ת֯ יה֯ודה. The expression 'ramparts of Judah' is not used in the Hebrew Bible. Any reading based upon the following letters is bound to be very hypothetical.

L. 10 ולשׂאׄת עׄמוד. שׂית עמוד, 'to erect a column', is more fitting than נשׂא עמוד, 'to lift up a column', but the trace looks more like *ʾalep*. The building terms חומה, גדר, and עמוד suggest that the episode of the punishments of Belial is followed by one dealing with eschatological constructions.

L. 16 מאתים]. Cf. Dan 12:11 אלף מאתים ותשעים or *1 Enoch* 6:6 (the number of the angels who descended to earth with Semyaza).

L. 18 [מח]לקות֯[העתים. מחלקות העתים occurs regularly in the Qumran Jubilees fragments, and is also the Hebrew title of *Jubilees* (see the discussion of 4Q**228** 1 i 2 in *DJD* XIII, 181). The expression may be a reference to 'the divisions of time', or to *Jubilees*, e.g. [כאשר כתוב בספר] [מח]לקות֯[העתים. If the hypothesis of a quotation from Jubilees is pursued, the end of *Jub.* 50:5 may be the text quoted: 'and the land will be clean from then on till all times' (*watenaṣṣeh medr ʾemweʾetu gizē ʾeska kʷellu mawāʿel)*. If frg. 6 4 corresponds to this line, ה֯[כתוב בספר] [מח]לקות֯[העתים אשר אמר והארץ תטהר מן העת ההיאה עד כול ע]תים פש֯[רו may be tentatively reconstructed. Cf. the cleansing of the earth in *1 Enoch* 10:22 after the punishment of the Watchers.

Frg. 5

1]○ ○[   ]○מ֯[

2]והוא[ה] יגיד֯[

3]בליעל ימ֯רו ○[

4]אׄ○[

Mus. Inv. 579
PAM 43.979

NOTES ON READINGS

Milik's placement of this fragment in col. II 8–11, between frgs. 1 and 2b, is not convincing. It is more likely that the fragment belongs to col. III. If col. III 7 implies the final annihilation of Belial, then the fragment should be placed somewhere in lines 1–6.

L. 1]○מ֯[. The tip of the letter before *mem* seems to belong to a more or less diagonal stroke (e.g. *lamed* or *ʿayin*), rather than to a bottom stroke. The original shows no trace after *mem*.

L. 3 ימ֯רו ○[. The *yod* might also be *waw*. The last trace on the line is ink, and the slanting vertical stroke indicates *dalet*, *he*, *waw*, *ḥet*, *reš*, or *taw*.

TRANSLATION

1.] [   ] [
2.] and he will announce [
3.] (of) Belial shall rebel [
4.] [

Frg. 6

1]ש֯◦[

2] [

3]ה֯ ◦[

4 ע]ת֯ים פש֯]רו

5]במק֯[

Mus. Inv. 579
PAM 43.979

Notes on Readings

The position of this fragment is uncertain. Puech suggests it corresponds in form to frg. 3, and hence places it towards the left of col. III in lines 15–19. This placement can even lead to a hypothetical reconstruction of col. III 18. Yet the correspondence with frg. 3 is doubtful (e.g. if frg. 6 is placed on frg. 3, the letters slope upwards instead of downwards), and frg. 6 might correspond better to the right side of frg. 2a (without the tear). Then, however, the probable placement of frg. 7 cannot be correct.

L. 3]ה֯. Or *ḥet*.

L. 4 ע]ת֯ים. The short base and form of the downstroke suggest *taw*, rather than *nun*.

L. 4 פש֯]רו. The small trace is consistent with *šin*, but also with other letters. There is a rather large space between the two words.

L. 5]במק֯[. *Bet* is very light, but perfectly readable. The small space after *bet* does not warrant the reading]ב מק֯[. The last letter is probably *qop*, but *he* should not be ruled out altogether.

Translation

1.] [
2.] [
3.] [
4. ti]mes. [Its] inter[pretation
5.] in [

Comments

L. 4 ע]ת֯ים. Both עתים, from the reconstruction מח]לקו֯ת העתים (col. III 18) and מאתים (col. III 16) fit here. The large space (or small *vacat*) after this word suggests the beginning of a new sentence. This strengthens the possibility of the reading פש֯]רו. In that case the word ending with תים is likely to be the last word of a quotation. If this line is part of col. III 18, which begins with מח]לקו֯ת עתים, a quotation of the last sentence of *Jub.* 50:5 might be hypothesized. The placement of the fragment is, however, completely uncertain.

Frg. 7

]ר̊°°[1

]מה היא̇[ה 2

]חומת יר̊[ושלם 3

]במועדה[4

]ש הי[5

]ם ו̊י[6

]סוף הי[ובל 7

]ירי [8

י]שׂאנו [9

]ם באלה[10

]ב̇ב[11

Mus. Inv. 579
PAM 43.979

NOTES ON READINGS

The fragment consists of five pieces attached to one another on the museum plate, but the pieces are not aligned correctly in the photograph and on the plate. The two small strokes above הי[of line 5 belong to *ʿayin* and *dalet* of line 4. The position of the fragment within the scroll is not certain. The contours and the form of the fragment correspond most to the left side of frg. 2b, from the tear in line 8 down to the bottom (line 20). If frg. 7 is positioned some 11.5 cm to the left of the left edge of frg. 2b, it would fit just left of the middle of col. III (assuming this column has the same width as col. II). Taking the slight slope of the lines into account, line 1 of the fragment might be part of col. III 6 (this, however, is not certain, and Puech shifts the fragment one line downwards). The fact that this would place חומת יר̊[ושלם in the middle of lines 8 or 9, חומ[ו]ת̊ יהודה being mentioned at the beginning of line 8, strengthens the possibility of this placement.

L. 2 היא̇[ה. The position of the dot beneath the left stroke of *yod* suggests *ʾalep*, rather than e.g. *waw*.

L. 3 יר̊[ושלם. The vertical stroke after *yod* can be read both as *he* and *reš*. Hence, both יה̊[ודה and יר̊[ושלם are possible.

L. 4]במועדה[. Part of *dalet* is obscured in a fold. The two small strokes above הי[in the following line are the bottom tips of *ʿayin* and *dalet*.

L. 6 ו̊י[. The photograph suggests an *ʾalep* after the *waw*, but this appearance has been created by a small erosion on the surface. It is clear in the original that it is a straight stroke, less slanted than the *waw*. Since there is no crossbar, it only can be *waw* or *yod*.

L. 8]ירי [. There is no trace of another letter after the second *yod*. Since there is no evidence of faded letters on this fragment, it may be assumed that ירי is the end of a word.

L. 11]ב̇ב[. Or perhaps]ח̇ב[.

TRANSLATION

1.] [
2.] it is [
3.] the rampart of Jer[usalem
4.] at its appointed time [
5.] [
6.] and [
7.] the end of the j[ubilee
8.] [
9. he] will carry it [
10.] in those[
11.] [

COMMENTS

L. 2 [מה היא̊]ה. If the reading היא̊]ה, and not e.g. היו̊]בל(ים), is correct then the preceding word might belong to a quotation. The word might be חו]מה (cf. the next line), but also any word ending with the 3rd pl. masc. pronominal suffix. Note that in this kind of construction the gender and number of the copula correspond to the following word or clause, not the preceding one.

L. 3 [חומת יר̊]ושלם. The singular form suggests חומת יר̊]ושלם. See חומ[ו]ת̊ יהודה in col. III 9. The fragment may be positioned in such a way that both terms belong to the same line, or the fragment may be shifted one line upwards.

L. 7 [סוף הי]ובל. Cf. col. II 7.

L. 8 [ירי]. Reconstruct e.g. היובל העש]ירי].

Frg. 8

[מלכי] צדק 1

[ת̇קו יד]י 2

[◦דת̇] 3

PAM 43.979

NOTES ON READINGS

The position of this small fragment cannot be ascertained, as its form, contours, and colour are not of much help. Puech tentatively places it in lines 5–7 of col. III (corresponding in form to the part of frg. 2b above the large right hole). At least the sequence of 'binding' the hands (if the reconstruction of line 2 is correct) and throwing in the fire (implied by col. III 7) seems to be appropriate. The fragment has apparently disappeared, since it is not found in Mus. Inv. 579.

L. 1 [מלכי̇]. The bottom part of *lamed* touches the left diagonal of *mem*.

L. 2 יד]י. Several vertical black lines complicate the reading of the second word. Nevertheless, the letters *yod* and *dalet* are almost certain.

L. 3 [◦דת̇]. The first trace could belong to many letters, *ʿayin* being a possibility.

TRANSLATION

1.] Melchi[zedek
2.] the hand[s of
3.] [

COMMENTS

L. 2]ח̇קו. Possible reconstructions include: ינ]ח̇קו 'they will unbind' (scil. e.g. 'the hands of the sons of justice'), יר]ח̇קו 'they will chain' (scil. e.g. 'the hands of Belial and the spirits of his lot'), and יר]ח̇קו *Nipʿal* ('they will be chained').

Frg. 9

]ה̇[1

]◦[2

Mus. Inv. 579
PAM 43.979

NOTES ON READINGS

The tiny fragment has probably become detached from one of the other fragments.

Frg. 10

]רו ול̊[1

]ד̊ אל ב[2

]ם̊ ה̊[3

Mus. Inv. 621B
PAM 44.117

NOTES ON READINGS

Only the upper layer of the fragment has been preserved.

L. 2]ד̊. The crossbar could belong to *dalet* or *reš*.

L. 2 ב[. The dark spot after *bet* in the photograph is not visible in the original.

L. 3 ה̊[. The two separate downstrokes may belong to a *he*, with the crossbar hidden in a crack.

Frg. 11

1]ר̊ה ◦[

2]ותן ב◦[

Mus. Inv. 1032
IAA 563769

Notes on Readings

Two horizontal folds run through the fragment, and obscure the bottom part of line 1.

14. 11QSefer ha-Milḥamah

(PLATE XXVIII)

Previous discussion: A. S. van der Woude, 'Ein neuer Segensspruch aus Qumran (11QBer)', *Bibel und Qumran. Beiträge zur Erforschung der Beziehungen zwischen Bibel- und Qumranwissenschaft. Hans Bardtke zum 22.9.1966*, Hrsg. S. Wagner (Berlin: Evangelische Haupt-Bibelgesellschaft, 1968) 253–8; B. Nitzan, 'Benedictions and Instructions for the Eschatological Community (*11QBer; 4Q285*)', *RevQ* 16/61 (1993) 77–90. W. J. Lyons, 'Possessing the Land: The Qumran Sect and the Eschatological Victory', *DSD* 3 (1996) 130–51.

Physical Description

THE manuscript was extremely well prepared, is very smooth and of a very fine grain.[1] The skin is thicker than average. The colour is light tan with irregular spots of a darker brown colour both on the recto and verso. Frgs. 1d and 2 have darkened, but frg. 2 preserves the original light tan in a few places.

The writing is quite regular, although the scribe began to the right of the ruling of the right margin, and did not care much about the regularity of the left margin. Many of the letters are partially written above the ceiling line.

The colour of the skin and the characteristics of some letters of 11Q**14** are rather similar to those of 11Q**20**, but that text has more widely spaced lines.

Measurements
Intercolumnar margin between frg. 1 i and ii: 1.8–1.9 cm.
Preserved left margin of frg. 1 ii: *c*.0.6 cm.
Bottom margin of frg. 1 i–ii: 3 cm on frg. 1d (probably the complete bottom margin).
Top margin of frg. 1e: 0.8 cm.
Column width: 12.1 cm (frg. 1 ii).
Distance between the lines: 0.7–0.9 cm, with 0.8 cm in the majority of cases.

Columns
The rapid increase of the length of the revolutions on frg. 1, and the short length of the farthest left revolution (*c*.3.6 cm), prove that frg. 1 comes from the end of the manuscript (the interior of the scroll). Since the parallel text of 4Q**285** 1 shows that at least one more line followed after the preserved text of frg. 1 ii, it can be concluded that frg. 1 i–ii preserved the third- and second-to-last columns.

Contents

The manuscript, now named 11QSefer ha-Milḥamah, was provisionally called 11QBerakhot on the basis of the contents of the two largest fragments (frgs. 1a and 1d), before its relation to 4QSefer ha-Milḥamah (4Q**285**) was known. The last columns

[1] The numbering of the fragments has been changed.

(frg. 1 i–ii) describe the end of the eschatological war (the killing of the leader of the Kittim) and a benediction over the eschatological community of Israel. Both columns overlap with fragments of 4Q**285**, a copy of the same work.

The other fragments of 4Q**285** clearly exhibit some kind of relation to the *War Scroll*, and it is not impossible that they belong to the end which was not preserved in 1QM. However, the relation between the manuscripts which are termed as different versions of the *War Scroll* has not yet been clarified. It is not certain which manuscripts offer different editions of the same text, and which are separate compositions on the same topic.

One difference between 4Q**285** and the *War Scroll* is the identity of the main figure; in the latter text, it is the High Priest, whereas 4Q**285** highlights the role of the נשיא העדה, 'the Prince of the Congregation' (but cf. 4Q**285** 5 5 = 11Q**14** 1 i 14). On the other hand, 4Q**285** shows concern for the same topics as the *War Scroll*: the cleansing of the land that has been contaminated by the corpses of the fallen of the enemy, and repentance from sin. It may be assumed that the benediction was the outcome of the cleansing and repentance. Cf. also the same paradigm in *1 Enoch* 10:20–11:2.

Frg. 2 of 11Q**14** might be related to the anthological poem preserved in 1QM XII 8–16, XIX 1–8, and 4QM^b (4Q**492**) 1 1–8. It is interesting to note that frg. 2 probably refers to the three nations mentioned in Sir 50:26, and not to the Kittim featured in the *War Scroll.*

There are no preserved differences between 11Q**14** and 4Q**285**, but there may be a variant in 4Q**285** 1 9. If this line, which reads]מן הארץ ואין דב[ר בארצכ]ם̇ כיא אל ע̊[מכם, is reconstructed on the basis of 11Q**14**, it has fifteen letters more than the average in the preceding lines.

Palaeography

Typologically, the hand should be placed between the hands which Cross called the 'developed Herodian formal script' (*c.*20–50 CE) and the 'late Herodian formal book hand' (*c.*50 CE). The hand has the thick ductus and square configuration of the late formal scripts, but the use of *keraiai* is not as dominant as in other scripts of this type.[2]

---

[2] On the basis of the hand, the present authors also initially identified a small fragment in PAM 44.007 (Mus. Inv. 615) as part of 11Q**14**. However, this fragment, partially covered by another fragment in PAM 44.007, is actually 1Q**44** 6 (cf. *DJD* I and PAM 40.537). In December 1996, the boxes of unphotographed fragments from cave 11 were examined, and the authors requested that photographs be taken of these fragments. Upon examination of the new photographs it became apparent that Box 1063 (IAA 563775) does not contain cave 11 fragments, but small to very small unpublished fragments from cave 1. In IAA 563775, forty-two fragments are displayed, twenty-eight of which are located in PAM 40.476, 40.507, 40.535, 40.537, 40.538, 40.541, and 40.544.

Orthography

The spelling is *plene*, and כיא is preferred to כי. The 2nd masc. pl. affixes do not have the long form with *he*, except for ארצכמה in frg. 1a ii 8, where *he* has been added after the final *mem*.

Mus. Inv. 567, 607, 614, 615
PAM 42.176*, 42.178, 42.179, 43.977*, 44.006*, 44.007*, 44.114*
IAA 525015

Frg. 1 i

Parallel: 4Q**285** 5 (underline)

]]בום 5
]]לו 6
] צמח ד]ויד 7
] [8
] ישעיהו הנביא ונוקפו[9
[סבכי היער בברזל והלבנון באדיר יפול ויצא חו]טר 10
[מגזע ישי ונצר משרשיו יפרה צמ]ח̊ 11
[דויד ונשפטו את [12
] והמיתו נשיא העדה צמח דויד]לה 13
] ם ובמחוללות וצוה כוהן הרואש[14
]]◦פ̊[ ] ח̇ל̊ל̇י 15

bottom margin

Mus. Inv. 567, 607
PAM 42.176*, 42.178, 42.179, 43.977*, 44.114*
IAA 525015

NOTES ON READINGS

The partially preserved column consists of four fragments. The placement of frg. 1d at the bottom left of the column is consistent with the overlap with 4Q**285** 5, and with the physical aspects of the scroll (pattern of damage, length of the revolution). Frg. 1c only appears in the first series of cave 11 photographs, and could not be found in the Rockefeller Museum. The scale of frg. 1c on plate XXVIII differs from that of the other fragments.

L. 6]לו. There is a rather large space between the two letters, but the original clearly shows that no letter appeared in between. The trace on the top edge of frg. 1b is the bottom tip of the *lamed.*

L. 15 [ ]פֿ◦[. The long base stroke may belong to *kap* or *pe*. There is just enough room for *waw* and *lamed* in the gap.

L. 15 חללי. The minute diagonal trace after the first *lamed* might also belong, for example, to *waw*.

TRANSLATION

5. [ ]
6. [ ]
7. [the bud of Da]vid
8. [ ]
9. [the prophet Isaiah: the thickest of the wood will be cut]
10. [with iron, and Lebanon in its grandeur will fall. And a sh]oot [will emerge]
11. [from the stump of Jesse, and a branch will spring from its root the bu]d of
12. [David. And they shall judge]
13. [and the Prince of the Congregation the bud of David, shall kill him,]
14. [and with wounds. And the high priest shall command]
15. [ ] [ ] the dead of

COMMENTS

The overlap with 4Q**285** 5 is very probable, but minimal. The calculation of the width of 4Q**285** 5 is based upon the reconstruction of Isa 10:34–11:1. However, since the size of the spaces between the words in 4Q**285** 5 varies considerably, a reconstruction based upon the number of letter-spaces per line can only be approximate.

L. 11 צמ]חֹ. Cf. 4Q**285** 5 3]צמח דויד ונשפטו את[. In view of the uncertain width of the lines in 4Q**285** 5 (the line-spaces vary considerably), it is not clear how many letter-spaces fit in between יפרה and צמ]חֹ.

L. 15 חללֹי [ ]פֿ◦[. Reconstruct, e.g. נֿפֿ[ול] חללֹי (1QM XIV 3) or וֿכֿ[ול] חללֹי (1QM III 8). Reconstruct after חללֹי, as the first word of the next column, כתיים with 4Q**285** 5.

Frg. 1 ii

Parallel: 4Q**285** 1 (underline)

1]   ]◦[

2]   ]◦◦[   ]וברכם בשֹׁם [אל]

3 [י]שראל וענהֹ] ואמר   ]ישראל ברוכים א[תם]

4 בשם אל עליון ◦[ ] וברוך שם קודש[ו]

5 לעולמי עד וברוכים [ ]תו וברוכים כול

6 מלאכי קודשו *vac*]*at* *vac*[*at*

7 יברך אתכם אל עליון ויאר פניו אליכם ויפתח לכם את

8 אוצרו הטוב אשר בשמים להוריד על ארצכמה

9 גשמי ברכה טל ומטר יורה ומלקוש בעתו ולתת לכם פר[י]

10 תֿנוֹבות דגן תירוש ויצהר לרוב והארץ תנובב לכם פרי

11 [ע]דנים ואכלתם והדשנתם *vac* ואין משכלה בארצכם

12 ולוא מוחלה שדֿפון וירקון לוא יראה בתבואתיה

13 [ואין]כול[נגע ומ]כשול בעדתכם וחיה רעה שבתה מן

14 [הארץ ואין דב]ר בארצכם כיא אל עמכם ומלאכי

15 [קודשו מתיצבי]ם֯ בעדתכם ושם קודשו נֿקרא עליכם

bottom margin

Mus. Inv. 607
PAM 42.178, 42.179, 43.977*

NOTES ON READINGS

The column is composed of four joined fragments: 1a, 1b, 1e, and 1f (for the unphotographed frg. 1f, see below, line 5). A small fragment of *c*.4 mm by 6 mm with an angular trace of almost ninety degrees is visible in PAM 42.179 between lines 11 and 12 (under *dalet*, *pe*, *waw* of שדֿפון), but is no longer present in PAM 43.977.

L. 1]◦[. The original clearly shows traces of ink belonging to final *kap*, *nun* or *ṣade*.

L. 2]◦◦[. The two traces above the *ʾalep* of line 3 are ink. They are the tips of downstrokes.

L. 2 בש֯ם֯. Only the very bottom parts of *šin* and final *mem* have been preserved, but the reading is very probable.

L. 3]ועננ֯. After *nun*, the remains of a downstroke appear.]וענו֯ is also possible.

L. 4]◦. PAM 43.977 suggests *ʾalep*, but the right trace is not ink (cf. PAM 42.179). The left trace is the bottom part of a downstroke slanting very slightly to the left. It might be part of the left leg of *ʾalep* (in which case there was a small space after עליון), but it might also be, for example, the bottom part of the downstroke of *waw* or *reš*. Sometimes in this column the ends of the downstrokes curve slightly to the left.

L. 5] וברוכים. A tiny fragment, frg. 1f, preserving the top of *yod* and final *mem*, has been joined to frg. 1a on Mus. Inv. 607.

L. 8 ארצכמה. The space between the final mem and the *he* suggests the *he* was added as a correction.

L. 9 ומטר. The mem is badly damaged, but the reading is certain.

L. 10 תֿנוֹבות. The right leg of the *taw* is preserved on frg. 1b.

L. 11 [ע]דנים. Examination of frg. 1b shows that the minute speck on the left edge is not ink.

L. 13]נגע ומ[כשול. The space is just large enough for this reconstruction if the words are written close to one another.

L. 13 מן. It is very likely that this is the last word of the line. The blank space between מן and the edge of the fragment is larger than those between other words. Moreover, a word written after מן would have been written in the margin.

Translation

1. [ ] [
2. [ ] [ ] and he shall bless them in the name of [the God of]
3. [I]srael, and he shall begin to speak[and say] Israel, blessed be y[ou]
4. in the name of God Most High [ ] and blessed be [his] holy name
5. for ever and ever; and blessed be[ ] his [ ] and blessed be all
6. his holy angels. *va[cat va]cat*
7. God Most High will bless you and shine his face upon you, and he will open for you
8. his rich storehouse in the heavens, to send down upon your land
9. showers of blessing, dew and rain, the early rain and the latter rain in its season, and to give you frui[t],
10. produce, grain, wine and oil in abundance; and the land will produce for you [d]elightful fruit
11. so that you will eat and grow fat. *vac* And none will miscarry in your land,
12. and none be sick, no blight and mildew will be seen in its grain;
13. [and there will be no stroke or stum]bling at all in your congregation, and wild animals will be absent from
14. [the land; and there will be no plag]ue in your land, for God is with you and [his holy] angels
15. [ar]e [standing] in your congregation and his holy name is invoked over you.

Comments

L. 2]וברכם בשם [אל]. For ברך בשם, cf. Deut 10:8; 21:5; Ps 129:8; 2 Sam 6:18; 1 Chr 16:2; 23:13.

Ll. 2–3 [אל] / [י]שראל. For the epithet in a context of blessing, cf. 1 Chr 16:4 (ליהוה אלהי ישראל); 1QM XIII 1, 2; XIV 4; XVIII 6; 1QS III 24.

L. 3 וענה[. Probably singular as וברכם in line 2.

L. 3] ואמר. The *respondit et dixit* formula requires ואמר after וענה. In PAM 43.325, which shows 4Q**285** 1, Milik placed the small fragment with]לפני[(not]לבני[) before the fragment with]שראל[. The fragment with]לפני[need not, however, be placed in line 1 of 4Q**285** 1. It is possible to reconstruct, e.g. וענה[ואמר לפני כול בני]ישראל, but לפני is very seldom employed with verbs of speech.

L. 3 ברוכים א[תם]. Cf. ברוכים אתם ליהוה in 1 Sam 23:21; 2 Sam 2:5; Ps 115:15. Examples of the blessing of human beings followed by the blessing of God are Gen 14:19-20 ברוך אברם לאל עליון . . . וברוך אל עליון (cf. 1QapGen XX 16) and Jdt 13:18 Εὐλογητὴ συ, θύγατερ, τῷ θεῷ τῷ ὑψίστῳ . . . καὶ εὐλογημένος κύριος ὁ θεός.

L. 4 אל עליון. In the Hebrew Bible, אל עליון only occurs in the section referring to Melchizedek in Genesis 14, and in Ps 78:35. Note the blessing in Gen 14:19 ברוך אברם לאל עליון. In the Dead Sea Scrolls אל עליון appears, e.g. in 1QH XII 31 (IV 31) and XIV 33 (VI 33) and (Aramaic) 1QapGen XII 17; XX 12, 16; XXI 2 (בריך אנתה אל עליון), 20; XXII 15, 16, 21.

L. 4 שם קודש[ו]. Cf. e.g. Ps 105:3 = 1 Chr 16:10 התהללו בשם קדשו; Ps 106:47 = 1 Chr 16:35 להדות לשם קדשך; Ps 145:21 ויברך כל בשר שם קדשו; 1QpHab II 4; 1QSb V 28; CD XX 34.

L. 5 לעולמי עד. The genetival construction עולמי עד is only used once in the Hebrew Bible (Isa 45:17), but is common in Qumran Hebrew, e.g. in 1QH. For the phrase וברוך שם קודש[ו] . . . לעולמי עד, cf. Ps 72:19 וברוך שם כבודו לעולם.

L. 5]תו. Reconstruct, e.g. עד]תו or נחל]תו.

L. 7 יברך אתכם אל עליון ויאר פניו אליכם. Cf. the priestly blessing of Num 6:24-25a יברכך יהוה וישמרך יאר יהוה פניו אליך and 1QS II 2–3.

Ll. 7–8 ויפתח לכם את / אוצרו הטוב אשר בשמים. Cf. Deut 28:12 יפתח יהוה לך את אוצרו הטוב את השמים. Both 11Q**14** and *1 Enoch* 11:1 quote this section of Deut 28:12 and continue with 'to bring down upon the/your earth'. Note also that *1 Enoch* 11:1 τὰ ὄντα ἐν τῷ οὐρανῷ corresponds to אשר בשמים instead of את השמים (𝔐𝔊𝔗).

L. 8 ארצכמה. The spelling is rather unexpected. Elsewhere in this text the suffix -כם is used.

Ll. 8–9 להוריד על ארצכמה / גשמי ברכה. Cf. Ezek 34:26 והורדתי הגשם בעתו גשמי ברכה יהיו. The addition על ארצכמה may come from Deut 11:14 or 28:12.

L. 9 טל ומטר יורה ומלקוש בעתו. Cf. Deut 11:14a ונתתי מטר ארצכם יורה ומלקוש, as well as Deut 28:12; Lev 26:4; Jer 5:24 הנתן גשם וירה ומלקוש בעתו.

L. 10 דגן תירוש ויצהר. Cf. Deut 11:14b ואספת דגנך ותירשך ויצהרך.

Ll. 10–11 פרי / [ע]דנים. עדנים, 'delicacies'; cf. 1QS X 15 להדשן בעדני תנובת תבל.

L. 11 ואכלתם. Cf. Deut 11:15 and Lev 26:5.

L. 11 והדשנתם. A *Hitpaᶜel* form. In the Hebrew Bible אכל is usually followed by שבע. Cf., however, Deut 31:20 ואכל ושבע ודשן.

L. 11 *vac.* A blank space of 0.6 cm separates the two types of benedictions.

L. 11 ואין משכלה בארצכם. Cf. Exod 23:26 לא תהיה משכלה ועקרה בארצך. משכלה is a feminine participle *Piᶜel*: 'a woman who miscarries', or 'a woman bereft of children'.

L. 12 ולוא מוחלה. Cf. Exod 23:25 והסרתי מַחֲלָה מקרבך. In Exodus מַחֲלָה is a noun 'sickness', but here מוחלה must be a *Hopᶜal* participle 'a sick person'.

L. 12 שדפון וירקון. Cf. Deut 28:22; 1 Kgs 8:37; Amos 4:9; Hag 2:17; 2 Chr 6:28.

L. 13 ואין [כול] נגע ומ[כשול. Cf. the parallel text of 4Q**285** 1 8 וא]ין כול נגׄע[. For נגע, cf. 2 Chr 6:28; for ומ[כשול, cf. Ps 119:165 ואין למו מכשול. Van der Woude, who at the time did not know 4Q**285**, reconstructed [אין ש]כול [ואין מ]כשול and referred to Ezek 36:13-14. However, there is insufficient space at the beginning of the line for [אין ש]כול and the alternation of the stems כשל and שכל in Ezek 36:13-14 is textually uncertain.

Ll. 13–14 וחיה רעה שבתה מן / [הארץ]. Cf. Lev 26:6 and Ezek 34:25 והשבתי חיה רעה מן הארץ.

L. 15 ושם קודשו נׄקרא עליכם. Cf. Deut 28:10 כי שם יהוה נקרא עליך.

Frg. 2

top margin?

1]טי הגוי הנב[ל

2 קומה גב]ור שבה פלׄ[שתים

3]◦ונים[

Mus. Inv. 614
PAM 44.006

NOTES ON READINGS

The placement of this fragment is uncertain. The uninscribed top section of the fragment may be the top margin, or a *vacat* in the first line.

L. 2 פל֯]שתים. Or פ֯ק֯[.

L. 3]°ונים[. Before the *waw* the left end of a headstroke remains. Read *bet*, *dalet*, *kap*, or *reš*. This part of the fragment has now broken off from the original. The other trace visible in the upper right portion of the photograph is not ink.

TRANSLATION

1.] of the stup[id] nation [
2. get up he]ro, take the Phil[istines] prisoner [
3.] [

COMMENTS

Only two complete words have been preserved, but it is possible to tentatively reconstruct the other partially preserved ones on the basis of Sir 50:26 and 1QM XII 10.

L. 1 הגוי הנב]ל. Cf. Sir 50:26 גוי נבל הדר בשכם. Cf. also Sir 49:5, Deut 32:6, 21 and Ps 74:18. The reconstruction הגוי הנב]ון, cf. Deut 4:6 עם חכם נבון, is less probable, as עם would be expected instead of גוי.

L. 2 קומה גב]ור שבה פל֯]שתים. Reconstructed on the basis of 1QM XII 10 (the wording is lost in the parallel passage 1QM XIX 2) קומה גבור שבה שביככה. Sir 50:26 not only refers to the גוי נבל, but also to פלשת.

L. 3]°ונים[. The Hebrew of Sir 50:26 reads יושבי שעיר, which 𝔊 incorrectly translates οἱ καθήμενοι ἐν ὄρει Σαμαρείας. On the basis of 𝔊, שומ]ר֯ונים[might be reconstructed.

Frg. 3

1]בו°[

2]קׄח וׄ[

3]°[

Mus. Inv. 607
PAM 42.176, 43.977*

NOTES ON READINGS

L. 1]בו°[. The traces after *waw* may belong to *he* or *ḥet*, or, with more difficulty, to *dalet* with the downstroke of the following letter.

Frg. 4

]◦י כן֯[

] ה֗[

Mus. Inv. 615
PAM 44.007

NOTES ON READINGS

L. 1]◦יכן֯[. Or]◦י כן֯[, based on the small space between *yod* and *kap*. Reconstruct, e.g.,]אח[ר֯י כן֯[.

15. 11QHymns[a]

(PLATE XXIX)

Previous discussion: J. P. M. van der Ploeg, 'Les manuscrits de la Grotte XI de Qumrân', *RevQ* 12/45 (1985) 11.

FOUR fragments have been preserved from 11Q**15**. Frg. 1 contains remnants of six lines and measures *c*.4.5 cm in height and *c*.4.7 cm in width. Frg. 2 measures *c*.4.5 cm in height and *c*.2.5 cm in width, and two smaller fragments (frgs. 3 and 4) each contain only a few letters. The fragments are deep brown, but frg. 1 has a small light brown section, which is possibly the original colour. The grain of frg. 1 is very smooth, and the skin is of an average thickness.

The hand is developed to late Herodian (*c*.50 CE), but quite different from the formal script or bookhand. There is an almost complete lack of rounded forms, the letters having mainly angular strokes. Other features which abound in frg. 1, but are less conspicuous in frg. 2, are the horizontal strokes frequently added to the bases of downstrokes, and the long left-hand strokes (diagonal and base of *mem*, base strokes of *nun* and *kap*; cf. also head of final *mem*) which several times intersect with the following letter. There is no clear distinction between *waw* and *yod*.

The style of the largest fragment is hymnic, and may be compared to the *Hodayot* or to the hymnic sections of 4QBerakhot (4Q**286–287**).

Mus. Inv. 576, 621B, 1025
PAM 42.180, 44.003*, 44.117*
IAA 563765*

Frg. 1

1]ולנו ב◦[
2 א]שר כוננו ידיכ֯הׄ[
3]◦כה ותראה מק◦[
4]בחדריכה בשמותם ב֯[
5]כבודו ומעשיו ועמלו ב֯[
6]אתה בראתה כול רוח 'ל◦◦[

Mus. Inv. 576
PAM 42.180, 44.003*

NOTES ON READINGS

PAM 42.180 preserves several letters and traces on the edge of the fragment which are lost in PAM 44.003. The first line is no longer preserved in Mus. Inv. 576.

L. 1]ולנו. The first two letters are preserved in PAM 42.180.

L. 1 ב◦[. The trace of the second letter could belong to *ʿayin*, *šin*, or, with more difficulty, to *lamed* or *qop*.

L. 2 ידיכ̇ה̊[. Or ידימ̇[.

L. 3]◦כה. PAM 42.180 preserves the long base of the letter preceding *kap*. It probably belongs to *bet*, *kap*, or *mem*.

L. 3 מק◦[. The trace on the left edge is the bottom of a downstroke.

L. 4 ב̊[. There appear to be two traces: a base stroke, and the bottom part of a downstroke. Part of the base stroke extends to the right of the downstroke.

L. 5 ב̊[. A downstroke with traces of a base stroke is visible. The angular join and the size suggest *bet*.

L. 6 רוח ל̇◦◦[. The reading רוח̇ ל◦◦[is also possible. PAM 42.180 shows the heads of two letters after *lamed* (cf. the tiny separated piece in PAM 44.003).

TRANSLATION

1.] [
2. wh]ich your hands have established [
3.] your [ ] and you will show [
4.] in your rooms according to their names [
5.] his glory and his deeds and his labour [
6.] you have created every spirit and [

COMMENTS

L. 1]ולנו. Reconstruct, e.g. כ]ולנו.

L. 2 א]ש̇ר כוננו ידיכ̇ה̊[. Cf. Exod 15:17 מקדש אדני כוננו ידיך, quoted in 4QFlorilegium (4Q**174**) I 3 (= 4QMidrEschat[a] III 3) מקדש] יהוה כ̇ו̇ננו ידיכה.

L. 3 ותראה. Probably a 2nd masc. sing. *Hipʿil*, though the form can be analysed in other ways.

L. 3 מק◦[. Reconstruct, e.g. מקו̊[ם or מקד̊[ש.

L. 5]כבודו ומעשיו ועמלו. The three words may belong to different clauses, ומעשיו ועמלו being the beginning of a new clause, and perhaps corresponding to פעולתה in 1QH[a] (cf. the references in the COMMENTS to line 6).

L. 5 ועמלו. Either 'toil', 'labour', or the result of it, as in 1QS IX 22 הון ועמל כפים.

L. 6]אתה בראתה כול רוח. Cf. e.g. 1QH[a] IX 8–9 (= I 8–9) אתה יצרתה / כול רוח; 1QH[a] VII 26 (= XV 22) אתה יצרתה רוח; 1QH[a] VII 17 (= XV 13) בידך יצר כול רוח.

Frg. 2

1]ט̇ים ◦[

2]ר̊ם למע̇[

3] לשלח̇[

4] לעיני בחיר̊[י

5]ר תבוא ע[

Mus. Inv. 1025
IAA 563765

Notes on Readings

The fragment was first cleaned, flattened, and photographed in 1997.

L. 2 ר̊ם[. Or ד̊ם[.

L. 2 למע̇]. A thin stroke seems to be the remnant of the left arm of *ʿayin*.

Translation

1.] [
2.] for [
3.] to send [
4.] in the presence of [the] chos[en
5.] you will come [

Comments

L. 1 טים[. Reconstruct, e.g. משפ]טים.

L. 2 למע̇]. Reconstruct, e.g. a form of מעשה.

L. 4 בחי̊ר̊]י. Add a suffix, e.g. בחי̊ר̊]יכה, or a noun, e.g. בחי̊ר̊]י צדק.

L. 5 תבוא. Either a 3rd fem. sing. or a 2nd masc. sing. form. One can also read a *Hipʿil* תביא.

Frg. 3

]° פניכה °°[1

Mus. Inv. 621B
PAM 44.117

Notes on Readings

The fragment has broken into two pieces, which are now joined differently in Mus. Inv. 621B.

L. 1 °°[. The traces stem from the head of either one or two letters. In the latter case, the last letter is *waw* or *yod*. The piece with these traces is now joined at the top right side in Mus. Inv. 621B.

L. 1]°. All that remains is part of a vertical stroke, and slightly further left, a dot. The space between the stroke and the dot is very small, and it is not very likely that the dot represents another letter.

Translation

1.] your face [

Frg. 4

1]באזר[וע

Mus. Inv. 621B
PAM 44.117

Notes on Readings

L. 1]באזר[וע. The *bet* is written peculiarly, with the left end of the head turning slightly downwards.

Translation

1.] with [ ] ar[m

Comments

L. 1]באזר[וע. Reconstruct, e.g.]באזר[וע עוזכה (Ps 89:11) or באזר[ועכה (cf. Jer 23:17). Note that in these cases, God's arm is mentioned in relation to his creative acts, which are also mentioned in frg. 1.

16. 11QHymns[b]

(PLATE XXIX)

Previous discussion: J. P. M. van der Ploeg, 'Les manuscrits de la Grotte XI de Qumrân', *RevQ* 12/45 (1985) 12; F. García Martínez, 'Texts from Qumran Cave 11', *The Dead Sea Scrolls: Forty Years of Research*, eds. D. Dimant, E. Rappaport (STDJ 10; Leiden: E. J. Brill; 1992) 24.

THE manuscript consists of three joined fragments. The largest fragment (frg. a) was transcribed from the photograph by van der Ploeg. After the photograph was taken, however, two tiny fragments (frgs. b and c) were joined to the left and the right of the main fragment, on Mus. Inv. 614. The skin has a medium to dark brown colour, with a few darker spots. Horizontal ruling is clearly visible. The skin is thinner than average. The fragment measures 2.5 cm in height and 2.8 cm in width.

As in 11Q7 Psalms[c], the hand is not a completely developed Herodian formal hand. It may be dated to the first half of the 1st century CE as it preserves some 'round' semi-formal traits.

Mus. Inv. 614
PAM 44.006

]◦ אתה יצרתֹ[ה

כ]ול מעשיו בטרם ◦[

]באמתכה כלי ל[

]◦ותו בטר[ם

NOTES ON READINGS

11Q16 consists of three fragments, of which only frg. a has been photgraphed. Frg. b preserves the first two letters of line 2, and frg. c has the last letters of lines 2–4.

L. 1 יצרתֹ[ה. The traces on the border may belong to any letter beginning with a downstroke.

L. 2 ◦[. The skin is very dark, but there seem to be traces of ink in the upper left corner of frg. b.

L. 3 כלי ל[. Van der Ploeg transcribed בלי, but *kap* seems preferable. Frg. c preserves the word-dividing space and the *lamed*.

L. 4]◦ותו. The first trace is the left part of a horizontal head stroke without any tick. Possible are *he*, *kap*, and perhaps *qop*.

TRANSLATION

1.] you have created [
2. a]ll its works before [
3.] in your truth, a tool [
4.] his [ ] befo[re

COMMENTS

L. 1 אהת יצרת̊]ה. Cf. 1QH[a] IX 8–9 (= I 8–9) אתה יצרתה כול רוח; 11Q**15** 1 6]אתה בראתה כול רוח; *1 Enoch* 9:5 'for you have made all things and have power over all'; 84:3 'for you have made and you rule all things'; Rev 4:11 ὅτι σὺ ἔκτισας τά πάντα; 3 Macc 2:3 σὺ γὰρ ὁ κτίσας τὰ πάντα.

L. 2 כ]ול מעשיו בטרם. Cf. 1QH[a] IX 7 (= I 7) ובטרם בראתם ידעתה כול מעשיהם; CD II 7–8 ובטרם נוסדו ידע את מעשיהם; 1QH[a] IX 10–11, 19–20 (= I 10–11, 19–20) בטרם היותם.

L. 3]באמתכה. The word is used regularly in 1QHodayot[a].

L. 3 ל]. This is probably the preposition, to be followed either by a noun or pronominal suffix, or by an infinitive.

17. 11QShirot ʿOlat ha-Shabbat

(PLATES XXX–XXXIV, LIII)

Previous discussions: A. S. van der Woude, 'Fragmente einer Rolle der Lieder für das Sabbatopfer aus Höhle XI von Qumran (11QŠirŠabb)' in *Von Kanaan bis Kerala. Festschrift für Prof. Mag. Dr. J. P. M. van der Ploeg O. P. zur Vollendung des siebzigsten Lebensjahres am 4. Juli 1979. Überreicht von Kollegen, Freunden und Schülern*, eds. W. C. Delsman, J. T. Nelis, J. R. T. M. Peters, W. H. Ph. Römer, A. S. van der Woude (AOAT 211; Kevelaer: Verlag Butzon & Bercker/Neukirchen Vluyn: Neukirchener Verlag, 1982) 311–37, pls 1–6; C. Newsom, *Songs of the Sabbath Sacrifice: A Critical Edition* (HSM 27; Atlanta, Georgia: Scholars Press, 1985) 361–87, pls XVII–XIX; F. García Martínez, 'Texts from Cave 11', *The Dead Sea Scrolls: Forty Years of Research*, eds. D. Dimant, U. Rappaport (STDJ 10; Leiden: E. J. Brill, 1992) 24–5; E. J. C. Tigchelaar, 'Reconstructing *11Q17 Shirot 'Olat ha-Shabbat*', Proceedings of the 1996 International Conference on the Dead Sea Scrolls, eds. D. W. Parry and E. Ulrich (Leiden: E. J. Brill, 1997).

THE interior fragments of the scroll were found rolled in a type of cigar-shaped form (cf. Pl. LIII), but many exterior fragments had already become detached before the interior of the scroll was opened by J. P. M. van der Ploeg in 1963. As a result, the fragments are now to be found on a number of museum plates, of which some contain only fragments of 11Q**17** (Mus. Inv. 565, 609, 618, and 620), and others contain mixed materials (one fragment each on Mus. Inv. 567, 614, and 621B).[1] Five fragments photographed in 1960 in PAM 43.448, and not in 43.992, can no longer be located. Presumably they were already lost when photographs PAM 43.989–992 were taken.

Physical Description

TABLE 1: *Preserved Margins*

Col. or Frg.	Right	Left
IV	•	•
V	•	(•)
VI	•	•
VIII	•	•
IX		•
X	•	•
28	•	
30		• ?

[1] Mus. Inv. 618 contains one hitherto unpublished cave 4 fragment which was previously placed on Mus. Inv. 669.

The colour of the skin is light to dark brown, with stains in some places. The skin itself is very thin and brittle. Both the horizontal and vertical rulings are very clear, and of a reddish colour. Apparently the ruling has not been done 'à la pointe seche', but with a different ink. Under the microscope, it is possible to discern the pigment, and the characteristic relief of the ruling with a sharp instrument is not to be seen. The writing is very small but beautiful. The ink is a deep black, though in the darkened fragments in Box 565, it looks more grey than black.

Measurements

Column height

Col. IV 16.8–18.7 cm (reconstructed for 23–25 lines on the basis of an average line spacing of 0.73–0.75 cm)

Col. VI 14.8–16.8 cm (reconstructed for 19–21 lines on the basis of an average line spacing of 0.78–0.8 cm)

Average number of letter-spaces per line

col. II	102
col. III	56
col. V	85–90?
col. VI	78
col. VII	91
col. VIII	80?

Reconstructed width of columns (without margins)

col. II	*c.*14.5 cm ?
col. III	*c.*8.5–9 cm
col. IV	*c.*17.5 cm
col. V	*c.*12.5 cm
col. VI	*c.*12 cm
col. VII	*c.*14.5 cm
col. VIII	*c.*11.5 cm

Columns

Reconstruction has proceeded from the material evidence of the fragments, especially the margins, but also from the correspondence of horizontal rulings, the altering shape of the fragments of the upper part of the scroll, and, for the other part, the overlap with other copies of the *Shirot*, especially 4Q**405**, but also 4Q**403** and 4Q**404**. Additional evidence for the reconstruction of the scroll is provided by the photographs. The fragments shown in PAM 43.448 had already become detached before the unrolling of the scroll, and therefore probably originate from more exterior revolutions. Note, however, that fragments in PAM 44.006 and 44.007 belong to the interior of the scroll.

There are no remnants of stitching in the form of threads or holes, which would give direct evidence of the size of sheets. However, the patterns of the horizontal ruling lines give indirect evidence; they show that cols. I–III, V–IX, and X, with the blank handling sheet, belong to three different sheets. The pattern of lines of the fragments of col. IV does not correspond to that of cols. I–III or cols. V–IX. Hence, one must assume either that col. IV belonged to a different sheet or that the scribe's ruler was not long enough to rule the whole sheet, i.e. the scribe ruled the sheet in two stages. The first assumption would explain the narrow width of col. III, and the large width of col. IV: col. III would have been the last column of a sheet which had not been neatly divided into equally sized columns, and the large width of col. IV would have been determined by the size of the sheet. The second assumption results in sheets of comparable size, but does not explain the differing widths of cols. III and IV.

Calculation of the number of lines per column is based on the adjacent columns III–VI. Comparison with 4Q**405** suggests that cols. III and IV had 24–25 lines, and cols. V and VI had 18–19 lines. These figures are approximate, as no top and bottom margins of 11Q**17** have been preserved, and because both manuscripts are fragmentary and may have had columns of different lengths and *vacat*s of different sizes. Hence, it is possible that cols. III and IV had as few as twenty-three lines, and cols. V and VI as many as twenty-one lines.

Reconstruction of the columns becomes more tentative as one nears the exterior of the scroll. Reconstruction of col. III, based on a minimal overlap and on the assumption that the text of the eighth Sabbath song is like that of the sixth, results in an atypically narrow column.[2] Though the overlap of col. II with 4Q**403** and 4Q**405** is certain, the horizontal placement of the fragment within the column is uncertain. As a result, the placement of both fragments of col. I in the same column is not entirely certain.

The width of the ten preserved columns measured *c*.1.4–1.5 m, including margins, and excluding the blank handle sheet at the end. Since col. I overlaps with the second half of the middle Sabbath song, the entire scroll, without the handle sheets, probably measured slightly more than 3 metres.

TABLE 2: *Overlap with Other Manuscripts*

11Q**17** (Col.)	4Q**405** (Col.)	Overlap
I	C–D	4Q**404** 5 + 7; 4Q**405** 6 + 83
II	E	4Q**403** 1 ii 18–21; 4Q**405** 8–9 1–6
III	F	4Q**405** 67 + 64
IV	G	4Q**405** 14–15 i
V	H	4Q**405** 15 ii–16 3–7

[2] Widely varying column widths are evident in some manuscripts. Cf. e.g. 4Q**266**, where the extremely narrow frg. 9 iii appears between columns of average width.

11Q**17** (Col.)	4Q**405** (Col.)	Overlap
VI	I	4Q**405** 19
VII	J	4Q**405** 20 ii–22 2–12
VIII	K	
IX	L	
X	M	

TABLE 3: *Old and New Fragment Numbers*

New Numbers (Col., Frg.)	Old Numbers (van der Woude, Newsom)
I 1	not previously published
I 2	frg. o (right)
II 3	frg. o (left)
III 4a	frg. h
III 4b	frg. i
III 4c–e	frg. k (small pieces at bottom)
III 5	frg. r
IV 6	frg. f
IV 7	frg. c
IV 8	frg. e
V 9	frg. b
V 10	frg. k
V 11	frg. m
VI 12	frg. j
VI 13	frg. d
VI 14	frg. g
VI 15	frg. p
VII 16	frg. 3
VII 17	frg. 4
VII 18	frg. a
VIII 19	frg. 5
VIII 20	frg. 6
IX 21a	frg. 8

New numbers (Col., Frg.)	Old numbers (van der Woude, Newsom)
IX 21b	not previously published
IX 22	frg. 7
X 23	frg. 2
X 24	frg. 1
X 25	frg. 9
unidentified frg. 26a	frg. s (top)
unidentified frg. 26b	frg. s (bottom)
unidentified frg. 27	frg. t
unidentified frg. 28	frg. l
unidentified frg. 29	frg. n
unidentified frg. 30	frg. q
unidentified frg. 31	frg. u
unidentified frg. 32	not previously published
unidentified frg. 33	frg. a (lower layer)
unidentified frg. 34	frg. k (left of frg. k)
unidentified frgs. 35–37	not previously published
uninscribed frgs. 38–42	not previously published

Palaeography and Dating

The manuscript reflects a Herodian hand, but the very small, beautiful script (the height of the letters varies from *c*.1.3 to almost 2 mm) displays a rather inconsistent hand. Most letters are written in several different ways; sometimes in the manner of the early Herodian round semi-formal hand (*c*.30 BCE–20 CE), and sometimes in the developed Herodian formal script (*c*.20–50 CE). The inconsistencies in the hand fall into three categories:

1. Strokes that join one another are sometimes written in one move without lifting the pen, and sometimes as two separate strokes. As a result, strokes may be connected by a triangular loop, simply cross one another, or not be joined at all. Thus, for example, the body of medial *mem* can consist of one curved stroke, or two or three separate strokes. Another example is *taw*, the left leg of which may be written either separately, or upward, looping into the crossbar.

2. The characteristic *keraiai* and other ornamental ticks and strokes of the later, formal Herodian script are sometimes lacking or rudimentary; in other places they are very developed.

3. The size and shape of some letters, e.g. *bet*, medial *nun*, or *taw*, may vary from narrow to broad. The variations suggest that, typologically, the hand is transitional, and that the manuscript was written in the first half or first third of the 1st century CE.

ʾAlep is written in several ways, sometimes semi-formal, sometimes more formal. The *keraia* of the right arm has different shapes. At times it is rudimentary, being no more than a thickening at the top, whereas the top sometimes inclines slightly to the left. On the other hand, there are examples of very developed *keraiai* consisting of an angular stroke towards the right. The *keraiai* of the left leg are likewise of different types: sometimes non-existent, and often the bottom of the leg is a mere bulge. When there is a tick, it may extend to the left or, less often, to the right of the bottom of the leg. The left leg mostly inclines, but sometimes it is drawn straight downward. The oblique axis consists, in the majority of cases, of a straight diagonal stroke, but there are examples where it is curved.

Bet is likewise in the process of transition. In most cases it has a straight horizontal or slightly slanting head with a tick at the left end. Yet, there are examples of a two-ticked head, the right, upper shoulder still retaining its tick. In the majority of cases the base stroke is attached to the downstroke, but a few examples show the base stroke extending beyond it. The width and size of the letter vary considerably, irrespective of its form.

By chance, only one *gimel* has been preserved (col. VIII 5 גבורות), which is typically developed Herodian, with a tick at the right side of the top.

Dalet consists of two strokes: the horizontal stroke, sometimes slanting, with a tick at the left, and a straight vertical stroke. The horizontal mostly breaks through the vertical stroke.

He is formed by two or, more often, three strokes. The left leg is drawn separately, and, in many cases, does not meet the crossbar.

In general, *waw* and *yod* are distinguishable by the smaller size of the *yod*. Though, ideally, the head of *yod* is larger, either letter may have a smaller or larger head. The heads are mostly attached angularly, but in some sections (e.g. col. VIII), head and downstroke form a curve.

There are three examples of *zayin*. Those in cols. III 3 and X 8 consist of a downstroke slightly bent to the right at the top. The *zayin* in col. IX 4 seems to have a bulge at the top.

Ḥet is written in two strokes, the head and right leg being formed without lifting the pen.

Ṭet is drawn in two strokes, clearly visible in, for example, col. IX 5: the left arm and base are drawn in one movement, and the curled head and right downstroke in another. The letter is broad and squat; in col. X 3, the left tip of the curled head touches the base. The top of the left arm slightly turns to the right in cols. IV 6 and X 3. In cols. VI 5 and IX 5, 7, the top is thickened to the left.

In some sections of the manuscript, medial *kap* has lost the ticks of its head (thus most *kap*s in col. VII), the head being no more than a short stroke. Final *kap* has a narrow head, with ticks, although sometimes rudimentary. The tip of the often long descender curves slightly to the left.

Lamed displays small differences in its various appearances. Most show a thickening of the top of the upper arm at the left side. Yet, in a few cases, the top of the upper arm leans towards the right without a visible thickening. The size of the hooks varies considerably.

The body of medial *mem* is formed by one, two, or three strokes. As a result, there are very curved forms with hardly any downstroke, as well as angular ones. The top stroke, written separately, sometimes has a tiny hook towards the left.

The shape of final *mem* varies. A few times it is slender and long (e.g. in col. IX 4 קדושים), but more often it takes on a more square shape, hardly any longer than a medial letter. The left end of the head varies from a vertical tick to a slightly descending stroke. The left vertical stroke begins flush with the crossbar, but in a few cases a tick is added above the bar.

The beginning of the downstroke of medial *nun* is sometimes straight, but mostly either thickened or with a bend or small tick towards the right. The length of both the downstroke and the base varies considerably, and either stroke may be twice as long as the other. The top of final *nun* is thickened.

Samek is drawn in a consistent manner. The left leg loops into the crossbar, and the letter is closed.

The top of the right arm of *ʿayin* is either vertical or diagonal from left to right, before going down to the left. The left arm is sometimes thickened.

The head of *pe* occasionally has a thickening, sporadically even an extra stroke towards the right downstroke. Usually the head stroke is diagonal, forming a sharp angle with the downstroke. In a few cases, however, head and downstroke form one curving line, e.g. in col. VII 6]כנפי.

A conspicuous trait present in most examples of *ṣade* is the *keraia*-like leftward stroke attached to the left arm. The right arm can either be straight or angled, the utmost tip being vertical. No final *ṣade* has been preserved.

Two types of *qop* are represented in col. VI 6 מ]חוקק. In the first, the tailstroke is separate from the head stroke. In the second, the tailstroke is attached to the head, both strokes possibly written in one move, the tailstroke being written upwards. The tailstrokes are also of different lengths, as is the optional curve to the left at the bottom of the tailstroke.

Reš is written in one move, mostly with a round shoulder, but occasionally with a slight tick at the right end of the head.

Šin has different forms. Quite often the left downstroke breaks through below the right lower arm. The left downstroke usually has a thickening at the top, towards the left. The top of the right arm is either bent or has a thickening; occasionally, the upper oblique has a thickening, or even a tick towards the right. In a few cases the upper oblique stops short before the left downstroke.

Taw is written in two ways. The left leg is either drawn upward, looping triangularly into the crossbar, or drawn separately, sometimes extending above the crossbar. The letter tends to be rather broad, and quite often the right leg is longer than the left.

Orthography and Morphology

Waw is consistently used to represent *ū* and *ō* of whatever origin (*u*, *ā*). חשני (col. IX 6) seems to be an exception, but the word is probably the plural of *ḥēšen*, not of *ḥōšen*. The vowel letter *yod* represents *ī* and *ē* from *ay*, but not short *i*. מעשי in the construct state may be either singular (cf. 𝔐 מעשה) or plural.

A 'phonetic' spelling of the third masculine singular pronominal suffix appears in cols. VII 6 פנותו] and X 5 תשבוחותו. Similar spellings are also attested in the other *Shirot* manuscripts, e.g. 4Q**405** 15 ii–16: פנו; 20 ii–22 7: לפנו.

Contents

11Q**17** ShirShabb preserves parts of the second section of the composition, which has been called *Shirot ʿOlat ha-Shabbat* in accordance with the headings of the different songs (cf. cols. II 4 and VII 9). Fragments from eight other copies of the composition have been preserved from cave 4, and one from Masada. The combined evidence of the manuscripts shows that the work was composed of thirteen parts, or Sabbath songs. Before all the manuscript evidence was known, it was suggested that the composition consisted of fifty-two songs, one for each Sabbath of the year. The fragments of the blank handle sheet after col. X, as well as the length of the revolutions towards the end of the scroll, attest undeniably that 11Q**17** X and 4Q**405** XXII belonged to the most interior part of the scroll.

An extensive description of the composition and of the individual Sabbath songs has been provided by Newsom. The preserved parts of the columns of 11Q**17** seem to correspond to the following Sabbath songs:

TABLE 4: *Contents of 11Q**17***

Col.	Sabbath Song	Col.	Sabbath Song
I	7	VI	11
II	8 (heading preserved)	VII	11 + 12 (heading of 12 preserved)
III	8	VIII	12
IV	9	IX	13
V	10	X	13

Relation to Other Copies of Shirot ʿOlat ha-Shabbat

The overlap with 4Q**405** shows that there were no major differences between the two manuscripts. This is true both for the preserved text, and for the reconstruction of the scrolls. It is interesting that both 4Q**405** 20 ii–22 9 and 11Q**17** VII 12 have the questionable reading יצא ומבין, which probably should be emended to יצאו מבין. This suggests a close relationship between the two manuscripts.

COMPARISON OF 11Q**17** AND 4Q**400–407**

col. II 5 ב]מ֯ע֯ו֯נ֯י֯ 4Q**405** 8–9 3] במעון 4Q**403** 1 ii 19
col. III 4 בשבע זמ]רות] בשבעה זמ֯ר֯]י 4Q**405** 64 + 67 2 (our reconstruction)
col. VI 6 מ]חוקק] מחוקקי 4Q**405** 19 5
col. VI 7 וצו]ר֯ת] וצורות 4Q**405** 19 7

Mus. Inv. 565, 567, 609, 614, 618, 620, 621B, 1030, 1032, 1034
PAM 42.176*, 42.177, 43.448*, 43.981*, 43.989*, 43.990*, 43.991*, 43.992*, 44.006*, 44.007*, 44.114*, 44.117*
IAA 508046, 525613*, 563759*, 563769*, 563771*

Col. I (Frgs. 1–2)

4]ים מ֯°[ ] האור מ֯[
5] סדרו]תיו סדרו]תיו מבני]ת
6]ש֯י קוד]ש ישמ]יעו תהלי[
7 אל]והים מ°°°[ ]לאלוהי [
8]ושבע °°[ ]משני ר֯[
9]°°° °[א]לוהים ב[

Mus. Inv. 565, 567
PAM 42.176*, 43.448, 43.992*, 44.114*

NOTES ON READINGS

Col. I is composed of two fragments, presumably further apart from one another than suggested in the transcription above. Frg. 1, still intact in PAM 44.114, has now broken into six small fragments (lines 4–6) and one large fragment (lines 7–9). The darkened left part of the fragment (in lines 7–8) does not conform to the shape of the other fragments. On this fragment, though not in the photographs, one can see a vertical trace beginning after the *mem* of the second word in line 7 and running down to the bottom edge, but is it not clear whether the trace is caused by a fold, or whether it indicates two fragments superimposed upon one another. A similar uncertainty occurs in frg. 2. The left edge of frg. 2, in line 4, is not entirely clear: an examination of the fragment suggests that the protruding piece at the left containing the two letters after the *mem* belongs to the fragment (the front shows no trace of a material join, and the back is covered with adhesive tape), but the oldest photograph, PAM 42.176, the reconstruction of col. II, and the comparison with the shape of the other fragments suggest that the left edge runs through the *mem*, and that the other letters on the protruding piece belong to col. II.

L. 4 מׄ◦]. In PAM 44.114 the top of the fragment is distorted, but an examination of the fragment suggests *mem* and the beginning of another letter.

L. 4 האור מׄ]. If frg. 3 is joined here, read: האור מעׄ◦]. It is not certain whether frg. 3 belongs to frg. 2; cf. the general note above.

L. 5 סדרו]תיו. The last letter does not reach the baseline. However, *yod* is usually shorter.

L. 5 מבני]ת. PAM 42.176 suggests the reading מבני אל], but cf. the NOTES ON READINGS to col. II 6.

L. 6 [שׄי. Before *yod* there is a vertical stroke; to its right at the bottom is the left end of a slanting stroke. The two strokes do not completely join, and one may also read e.g. [עׄיׄו.

L. 6 ישמ]יעו. The hook of the *yod* is apparent on the fragment, though not in the photograph.

L. 7 מ◦◦◦]. PAM 44.114 shows traces of three letters after *mem*. The fragment is now black.

L. 9 [◦◦◦ ◦]. The faint head at the right edge possibly belongs to *dalet* or *kap*, or, with more difficulty, to *nun*. Two vertical downstrokes, the first small, the second of normal length, are followed by a curved stroke that is compatible with the left leg of *taw*. Read, e.g. [כׄוׄתׄ, or [נׄיׄתׄ. The upper right part of the next letter is visible, whereas other possible traces seem to be obscured by a fold in the skin.

L. 9 א]לוהים ב]. PAM 42.176 shows a small piece of skin after א]לוהים which preserves part of *bet*. It is not clear, however, whether this small fragment belongs here. It may also be a remnant of frg. 9 which became stuck to frg. 2.

TRANSLATION

4.] [ ] the light [
5. its] beams, [ ] its [beam]s, the structu[re of
6.] hol[y they shall cause to he]ar psalms [
7. G]od [ ] god of [
8.] and seven [ ] second [
9.] [g]od [

COMMENTS

Col. I probably corresponds to the section lost between 4Q**403** i 46 and **1** ii 1. The preceding text of 4Q**403** **1** i 41–46 shows that this section invokes the structural and architectural features of the Temple to join in the praise of God. The last line(s) of frgs. 1–2 may correspond to the first line(s) of 4Q**403** **1** ii, but there is no actual overlap. Three words from lines 4–6 may, however, overlap with 4Q**404** 5 + 7 6–11 and **405** 6 + 83 7–11, which have preserved parts of the text missing from 4Q**403**,[3] but the texts are too fragmentary to reconstruct in such a manner that all three words overlap.

---

[3] One may place 4Q**404** 7 beneath **404** 5 תבני], frg. 7 1 following frg. 5 8. This placement is suggested by three observations. First, the right side of **404** 5 + 7 physically resembles **404** 2. Second, the last line of **404** 7, [ל ברו], could be an overlap of **405** 6 + 83 10–11 [ת קול / ברומ]ם. Third, the mention of סדרות as an architectural term is consistent with the previous mention of other architectural terms such as קירות. The unidentified fragment, 4Q**405** 57, gives a perfect join with 4Q**405** 6 before lines 3–4, and 4Q**405** 58 joins to the right in lines 2–3. 4Q**405** 69 may perhaps be placed above line 1, over בשמח]ת. One may consider the possibility that 4Q**405** 83 should be placed at the right side of the column, in lines 9–12, in which case the joined text seems to overlap with 4Q**404** 5 + 7. A problem with regard to the join of 4Q**405** 6 and 83 is the resulting reading in lines 9–10: אפסי / זמר◦]. There is a small black trace after אפסי which might be the bottom part of a letter, but that would mean an extra word written entirely in the margin. One might also read אפסו, in which case the two words would not belong to a construct chain. The letter following זמר may be *waw*, *yod*, or *taw*.

An additional problem in reconstructing the text is the palaeography of 4Q**404**: the size of the letters differs considerably, and calculations of the number of missing letters are therefore uncertain.

The most conspicuously common word is סדר, in **11Q17** I 5 and 4Q**404** 5 + 7, but it may not reflect an overlap. In the previous lines, the קירות are mentioned twice (4Q**403** 1 i 43 and **404** 5 6), and the same may have been the case with the סדרות.

A second possible overlap involves the more common word האור (**11Q17** I 4). It is probable that the last word of 4Q**404** 5 7 should be read הא]ור, which in turn may overlap with 4Q**405** 6 + 83 9 הא̊]ור. The comparison of 4Q**404** 5 7]בקודש] ∘∘∘∘∘ הא]ור and 4Q**405** 6 + 83 8–9 בקדש קדשים ∘∘] [∘סי / הא̊]ור shows that the texts were not identical. The easiest assumption is that 4Q**404** 5 7 omitted the word קדשים. The overlap of האור with הא]ור of 4Q**404** 5 7 is not completely certain: באור is used some lines earlier, and it is possible that there was yet another use of this word.

The third possible overlap involves ישמ]יעו of **11Q17** I 6, which is also used in 4Q**405** 6 + 83 11. However, the *lamed* in 4Q**405** 6 + 83 12 is not compatible with תהלי.

L. 4]∘ם מ̇ים[. The preserved texts of 4Q**404** 5 and 4Q**405** 6 do not offer a likely overlap. The corresponding text should probably be sought in lost part of the beginning of 4Q**405** 6 7.

L. 4 האור. האור perhaps overlaps with 4Q**404** 5 + 7 7 and 4Q**405** 6 + 83 9. In that case, it is the *nomen rectum* of a construct chain ∘∘] [∘סי האור. The word ending in -סי is possibly an architectural feature. The only word attested in the *Shirot* that graphically fits here is מדרסי, which is a possible, but not completely convincing, reconstruction.

L. 5 סדרו]תיו. After the קירות, now the סדרות of the Temple are called upon to praise God. Both terms are used in 2 Kings 6, the latter word spelled שׂדרת in v 9. The meaning of the word is not certain; it is possible that it is part of the construction of the roof.

L. 5 מבני]ת. The remains of the word may also be read as 'from the sons of', but the context rather suggests a form of מבנית. In that case the word is probably asyndetically juxtaposed to the preceding word. The word may be used in the preceding text, cf. 4Q**403** 1 i 43–44 מבנ]יתו מעשי תבנ̊]יתו] / כ̊[ו]ל̊.

L. 8 מ]שני. Either the adjective משנה ('second', 'double'), or the preposition מן with the numeral.

Col. II (Frg. 3)

Parallels: 4Q**403** 1 ii 18–21 (underline)
4Q**405** 8–9 1–6 (dotted underline)

4 [למשכיל שיר עולת השבת ה]שמ̇י̇נ̇י̊[ת בשלושה ועשרים לחודש השני הללו לאלוהי כול
מ̇רומי רום כול ק̇ד̇ו̇ש̇י̇ עולמי עולמים]

5 [שניים בכוהני קורב סוד שני ב]מ̇ע̇ו̇נ̊י̇ פל[א בשבע
בכול יודעי עולמים ורוממוהו ראשי]

6 [נשיאים במנה פלאיו הללו לאל]אלוהים[שבע̇ כהונת ק̇ורבו̇
רום שבעת גבולי פלא בחוקות]

7 [מקדשיו ראשי נשיאי כהונות פ]לא למלכ̊[י צדק (?)

Mus. Inv. 565
PAM 42.176*, 43.448, 43.992*

NOTES ON READINGS

Col. II is preserved on one fragment, frg. 3, which is visible in PAM 42.176 (where it is attached to the left side of frg. 2). Later photographs show a gradual deterioration of the fragment. The remaining parts of the fragment shift slightly downwards in the later photographs: PAM 43.448 shows the first line broken off, as well as the left part of the last two lines; in PAM 43.992, only the second line of the fragment remains.

The placement of the fragment within the column is problematic. A reconstruction, based upon the assumption that the beginning of the new song started at the right margin, is possible only if the margin between cols. II and III was rather large (*c.*5 cm), and fragments of one revolution are missing. This is not impossible, but one may alternatively reconstruct a *vacat* at the beginning of the first line of the new song, and place the fragment in the middle of the line. If the margins between cols. I and II and between cols. II and III were smaller than those further on, then the fragment might represent the revolution between frgs. 2 and 4.

L. 5 במׄעׄוׄנׄיׄ. Only the left side of *mem* is preserved. The traces that seem to be the right part belong to col. I 4 (cf. NOTES ON READINGS there).

L. 6]אלוהים[. PAM 42.176, which shows the two fragments as they were attached when they came to the museum, has the reading]חיו מבני אלוהים[. The shift in the stance of the ceiling line above אל shows that these letters belong to frg. 3, and not to frg. 2.

L. 7 פ[לא למלכׄ]י צדק. In 4Q**405** 8–9 6, one may read]שׄ [פלׄ]א, but the curved trace which may be *šin* is also compatible with the hook of *lamed*. A minute vertical trace after the second *lamed* is visible.

TRANSLATION

4. [By the instructor. Song of the sacrifice of the] eight[h Sabbath, on the twenty-third of the second month. Praise the God of all the high heavens, all you eternally holy ones,]
5. [second among the priests of the inner sanctum, the second council of the] wonder[ful] dwellings [among the seven among all who have knowledge of eternal things. And exalt him, o you chiefs]
6. [of princes with his wonderful portion. Praise the God] of gods [o you seven priesthoods of his inner sanctum, highness, the seven wonderful territories according to the ordinances]
7. [of his sanctuaries, the chiefs of the princes of the won]derful [priesthoods] of Melch[izedek (?)

COMMENTS

L. 5 ב]מׄעׄוׄנׄיׄ. This is plural, as in 4Q**405** 8–9 3, as opposed to the singular of 4Q**403** 1 ii 19.

L. 7 כהונות פ]לא למלכׄ]י צדק. One may read the last word as]למלךׄ, למלכׄ]ות, למלכׄ]ותו, but in view of the context, למלכׄ]י צדק is very attractive. Cf. also the probable reference to Melchizedek in 4Q**401** 11 3 מלכי צדק כוהן בעדׄ]ת אל[.

Col. III (Frgs. 4a–e, 5)

Parallel: 4Q**405** 64 + 67 (underline)

[ ]◦[ ] 2

[אי זמר]ת עוז ל[אלוהי קודש] 3

[בשבע זמרות נפל]אותיה לברך לׄ[מלך הקודש שבע בשבע ז]מׄרות פלׄ[א] 4

[ ]עׄ שבע תהלי ברׄ[כות כבוד אדון כול אלים שב]ע תהׄ[לי גדל] 5

[צדקו שבע]תהלי רו[ם מלכותו שבע תהלי תשבוחות כבודו שבע תהלי] 6

[הודות נפל]אותיהו [שבע תהלי רנות עוזו שבע תהלי זמרות קודשו] 7

[ ]שבעה בש[בעה דברי פלא דברי רום לנשיאי משני יברך בשם] 8

[כבוד א]דׄון כ[ו]ל א[לים לכול גבורי שכל בשבעה דברי פלא לברך כול] 9

[כוהני]קוׄרב במע[ון פלא בשבעה] 10

[דברי]פׄלא לברך[בשבעה] 11

[דברי פ]לא [ו]ברך לכ[ול] 12

[ ]◦◦◦◦◦[ ] 13

Mus. Inv. 565
PAM 43.448*, 43.992*

NOTES ON READINGS

Col. III is composed of two fragments. Frg. 4 consists of five joined fragments. The two largest, frgs. 4a and 4b, were still partially attached in PAM 43.448, but separated in PAM 43.992 (the top of frg. 4b has now broken off). The three small fragments (frgs. 4c–e) placed near frg. 12 in PAM 43.992 (frgs. 4d and e are upside down) join perfectly with the left side of frg. 4a in lines 4–5. These small fragments have now broken into even smaller pieces. Frg. 5 was photographed only in PAM 43.448 and can no longer be located.

The column preserves part of the eighth Sabbath song and the reconstruction is, to a large extent, based upon the variant text from the sixth Sabbath song (cf. COMMENTS). At several points the reconstruction is uncertain, but the estimated distance between frgs. 4 and 5 in line 4 must be considered correct: it is slightly larger than the gap between the fragments in the next column.

L. 4 לברך. Frg. 4c contains]לב[, frg. 4d:]רך[.

L. 5]עׄ. On the fragment it is possible to distinguish a rounded start going down to the right. An *ʿayin* is almost certain.

L. 5 תהלי ברֹ֯]כות. The left leg of *taw* is preserved at the bottom of frg. 4c; the end of its base and the letters הלי ברֹ֯] are preserved on frg. 4e. Only the downstroke of *reš* is preserved.

L. 6 רו]ם. The left stroke of *waw* is clear; it is certainly not *nun*.

L. 7 נפל]אותיהו. Not נפל]אותיהֹ֯ם. After *he*, the long downstroke with the sharply angled head of *waw* is visible. The reading נפל]אותוהי is very unlikely: the letter before *he* might be a short *waw*, but the last letter cannot be *yod*. This section is no longer visible on the original.

L. 9 א]דון. The reading מֹ֯לֹ֯ך (Newsom) is not possible.

L. 10 קורֹ֯ב. The *reš* resembles a *dalet*. Part of the head of *bet* is obscured.

L. 12 לכ]ול. The upper arm of *lamed* is hardly visible in some of the photographs.

Translation

2. [ ] [
3. [a] powerful [son]g to [the God of Holiness]
4. [with seven wond]erful [songs] to bless the [King of Holiness seven times with seven] wonder[ful so]ngs [
5. [ ] Seven psalms of bl[essing of the glory of the Lord of all Divinities, sev]en psa[lms of magnification of]
6. [his justice, seven] psalms of exal[tation of his kingdom, seven psalms of praise of his glory, seven psalms]
7. [of thanksgiving for] his [won]ders, [seven psalms of rejoicing in his power, seven psalms of songs of his holiness,]
8. [ ] seven times se[ven wonderful words, words of exaltation. Of the deputy princes one will bless in the glorious]
9. [name of the L]ord of a[l]l Di[vinities, all the powerful of intellect with seven wonderful words, to bless all]
10. [the priests of the] inner sanctum in the [wonderful] dwel[ling with seven]
11. wonderful [words] to praise [with seven]
12. [won]derful [words and] he will praise a[ll
13. [ ] [

Comments

Col. III preserves part of the eighth Sabbath song which consists of a description of the psalms and blessings of the seven deputy princes. 4Q**405** 13 shows that the blessings of these deputy princes in the eighth Sabbath song are very similar, but not identical, to the corresponding blessings of the angelic princes in the sixth Sabbath song. Likewise, the text of this column seems to be a variant of the corresponding parts of the sixth Sabbath song which are preserved in MasShirShabb ii 17–26, 4Q**403** 1 i 6–13, and the tiny fragment 4Q**404** 1. It can be calculated that col. III overlapped with 4Q**403** 1 ii 39–44 (or 40–44) of which, however, no text has been preserved. The column deviates from the account of the sixth Sabbath song in several cases, and one can only reconstruct it by assuming that the gaps contained expansions. The following synopsis shows the correspondences and differences.[4]

---

[4] Some of the readings and reconstructions are suggested by É. Puech, 'Notes sur le manuscrit des Cantiques du Sacrifice du Sabbat trouvé à Masada', *RevQ* 48/12 (1987) 575–83. Puech observed the correspondence between frg. 4a and the Masada fragment, but incorrectly tried to place frg. 4a in the sixth song.

Part of the Eighth Song (composite text) 11Q17 III 3–10 and 4Q**405** 64 + 67	Part of the Sixth Song (composite text) MasShirShabb ii 17–26, 4Q**403** 1 i 6–13, 4Q**404** 1
]אי	תהלת זמר בלשון השביעי לנש[יאי רוש]
זמרת עוז ל[אלוהי קודש]	זמר עוז לאלוהי קודש
[בשבע זמרות נפל]אותיה	בשבע[ה זמרי] נ[פ]ל[א]ותיה
לברך ל[מלך הקודש	וזמר למלך הקודש
שבע]בשבע זמרות פל[א]	שבעה בש[בעה ד]ברי זמ[רי פלא]
]ע[ ]	---
שבע תהלי בר[כות כבוד אדון כול אלים]	שבע תהלי ברכותיו
שבע תהלי גד[ל צדקו]	שבע תהלי גדל [צדקו]
שבע]תהלי רו[ם מלכותו]	שבע תהלי רום מלכותו
שבע תהלי תשבוחות כבודו]	שבע תהלי ת[שבוחות כבודו]
שבע [תהלי הודות נפל]אותיהו	שבע תהלי הודות נפלאותיו
[שבע תהלי רנות עוזו]	שבע תה[לי ר]נ[ו]ת עוזו
שבע תהלי זמרות קודשו	שבע תהלי זמר[ו]ת קודשו
	תולדות דב[רי רו]ם [
]שבעה בש[בעה דברי פלא דברי רום	ש[בעה בשבעה דברי פלא דב[רי רו]ם
לנשיאי משני	לנשיאי ר[וש
יברך בשם כבוד א]דון כ[ו]ל א[לים	יבר]ך בשם כבוד אלוהים
לכול גבורי שכל בשבעה דברי פלא	לכ[ול גבורי]שכל[בשבעה] דברי פלא
לברך כול כוהני]קורב במע[ון פלא	לברך כול סודי[ה]ם במקדש[קודשו

L. 3 זמר]ת עוז. The sixth Sabbath song begins the psalm of the seventh prince with תהלת זמר בלשון השביעי לנש[יאי רוש] זמר עוז. Here, the feminine form זמרה is used; cf. also ז]מרות פלא in the next line, and 4Q**405** 64 + 67 1 ז]אי זמרת עוז.]אי in 4Q**405** 67 is not clear; perhaps one should reconstruct נשי]אי with the missing משני added supralinearly.

L. 3 ל[אלוהי קודש]. Cf. MasShirShabb ii 17. The reconstruction, however, may be slightly too long.

L. 4 [בשבע זמרות נפל]אותיה. Or: [בשבעה זמרי נפל]אותיה. The crucial letters showing the gender have not been preserved in the sixth song.

L. 4 לברך ל[מלך הקודש שבע. Cf. MasShirShabb ii 18 וזמר למלך הקודש שבעה.

L. 4 בשבע ז]מׄרות פל[א. 4Q**403** 1 i 7 has בׄ]שבעה ד]בׄרי זמׄ]רי פלא (or, instead of זמׄ]רי, זמׄ]רות). The space at the end of MasShirShabb ii 18 also fits with the reading בשבעה דברי זמרי (with **פלא** in the next line). דברי is omitted in the reconstruction for two reasons. The reading with it demands too much space between the two fragments, and 4Q**405** 64 + 67 2]בשבעה זמרׄ[omits it. **פל]א** may be the last word of the line.

L. 5 עׄ[ ]. A reconstruction of the column shows that this line must have had a longer text than the corresponding text of the sixth Sabbath song. In view of the assumed omission of דברי in the previous line, one may perhaps reconstruct a construct clause beginning with דברי], or a longer clause with שבע תׄ]הלי somewhere in the middle, if the reconstruction of the next clause is incorrect.

L. 5 שבע תהלי ברׄ]כות כבוד אדון כול אלים. The corresponding text of the sixth Sabbath song, שבע תהלי ברכותיו, is too short for the reconstruction of the line and the rest of the column. Newsom suggests that the title מלך כול קדושי עולמים might be a formula of the psalm of the first prince, and ברׄ]כות מלך כול קדושי עולמים would fit neatly in the gap. However, the formula is not attested in the *Shirot* in exactly this form (for מלך כול קדושי, cf. frg. 30; for עולמים as an angelic epithet, cf. 4Q**403** 1 i 13). Moreover, line 9 and 4Q**403** 1 ii 33 show that in the eighth Sabbath song, the title אדון כול אלים was part of the vocabulary used in the sections of the first deputy prince. The reconstruction ברׄ]כות כבוד is based on frg. 30, on the use of כבוד in the blessing of the first angelic prince in the sixth Sabbath song, and on the fact that the other psalms consist of two elements: a noun of praise with another noun as object referring to a property of God.

Ll. 5–6 שב]ע תהׄ[לי גדל] / [צדקו שבע]תהלי רו[ם מלכותו שבע תהלי תשבוחות כבודו. The text of the sixth Sabbath song fits well with the preserved fragments.

Ll. 6–7 שבע תהלי] / [הודות נפל]אותיהו. MasShirShabb ii 21 shows the last word as נפלאותיו. Qimron, *HDSS* 322.142 and 144, seems to claim that the suffix הו- only occurs after *i*, and that other cases are simply misreadings by modern editors of the Aramaic suffix והי-.

Ll. 7–8] / [. שבעה[After קודשו the combined remains of MasShirShabb ii 22–23 and 4Q**403** 1 i 9 show the reading תולדות דׄבׄ]רי רו[ם / ∘∘∘∘∘∘∘שבעה. The reconstruction תולדות דב]רי רו[ם / [לברך בש]בעה (Puech) fits well in the space of both manuscripts of the sixth song, but לברך ב]שבעה בש]בעה is syntactically strange. Here, however, there is not enough space for תולדות דברי רום followed by another word.

L. 8 בש]בעה דברי פלא דברי רום. Cf. MasShirShabb ii 23 בשבעה דברי פלׄא דב]רי and 4Q**403** 1 i 10]ם לנשיאי. The space in 4Q**403** 1 i 10 suggests a short word ending with]ם. Reconstruct 4Q**403** 1 i 9–10 as follows:

[נפלאותיו שבע תהלי רׄ]נׄו[ת עוזו שבע] תהלי זמירו]תׄ קׄודׄשׄוׄ תׄ]ולדות דברי רו]ם[שבעה]

[בשבעה דברי פלא דברי רו]ם לנשיאי ר]וש יברך]בׄשׄםׄ כׄ]בו]ד אלוהים ל]כול גבורי]שׄכׄלׄ[בשבעה דברי]

The gaps at the beginning and end can make it difficult to determine whether a word should come at the end of the line, or at the beginning of a new one, but it is certain that בשבעה does not fit at the end of line 9. Cf., however, a different reconstruction of 4Q**403** 1 i 9–10 in *DJD* XI, 256.

Ll. 8–11 These lines, beginning with לנשיאי, contain the blessing of the first deputy prince. The blessings of the sixth Sabbath song are well enough preserved to determine the elements of their structure. After an introductory phrase mentioning the prince who is to bless, a threefold blessing is described. The first part of the blessing consists of a verb of blessing (יברך), an invocatory phrase, בשם . . . , an indication of those blessed (each time beginning with לכול), and a reference to the words of blessing (בשבעה דברי). The second and third parts of the blessing are less strictly organized, but the typical form consists of a verb of blessing (וברך), an indication of those blessed, and a reference to the words of blessing (בשבעה דברי). In the sixth Sabbath song, several blessings have an expanded structure: a *lamed* clause that indicates the result of the blessing may conclude the second and third parts of the blessing. On the other hand, the indication of those blessed seems to be missing from the second part of the second blessing. The first blessing is peculiar in that the second and third part do not begin with וברך, but with לברך. The words of blessing are also omitted from the third part. (Cf. Newsom for a more extensive discussion of the structure).

L. 8 לנשיאי משני יברך. In the sixth Sabbath song, all the other blessings begin with the determined ordinal number followed by בנשיאי רוש.

Ll. 8–9 [כבוד א]דון כ]ו[ל א]לים / [בשם]. The parallel text in the sixth Sabbath song reads בשם כבוד אלוהים. The same title, אדון כול אׄי[לים, is used in 4Q**403** 1 ii 33, which is probably part of the psalm of the first deputy prince. The title occurs here in the blessing of the first deputy prince. Therefore, one may assume that the eighth Sabbath song used this title in the sections of the first deputy prince.

L. 9 לכול גבורי שכל בשבעה דברי פלא לברך כול]. Cf. the sixth Sabbath song. The word גבורי in the indication of those blessed is a reconstruction.

L. 10 [כוהני]קוׄרב במע]ון פלא. The sixth Sabbath song reads סודיהם במקדש קודשו. The phrases כוהני קורב and סוד are almost synonymous. Cf. e.g. the parallellism in 4Q**403** 1 ii 18–19 (the beginning of the eighth song) כול קדושי עולמי] / עולמים שניים בכוהני קורב סוד שני במעון פלא. In view of 4Q**403** 1 ii 19, we reconstruct במע]ון פלא, but במע[מדיהם may also be possible. One may perhaps reconstruct something like וכול סודיהם במפדש קודשו בשבעה] in the second half of the line, but this seems a little short.

Ll. 10–11 [בשבעה] / [דברי]פׄלא לברך]. The first three words must be the conclusion of the second part of the blessing. לברך] (instead of וברך; similarly in the second part) introduces the third part of the blessing.

Ll. 11–12 [בשבעה] / [דברי פ]לא [ו]ברך לכ]ול. These words presumably represent the end of the first part and the beginning of the second part of the second blessing. Note that the indication of those blessed is missing from the second part of the second blessing in the sixth song.

Col. IV (Frgs. 6–8)

Parallel: 4Q**405** 14–15 i 2–3 (underline)

3 [ ]ב[אל]והי אליׄם[

4 [ ]מעשי לב[ני]אולמי מבׄ[ואי
[

5 [לל]בׄני כבודם [ ]דׄ לבני[
רק]יׄע

6 [מר]אי פלא כׄ[ ]◦י טו[הר
]לחות

7 בהוד תשבׄ[וחות]בׄדמׄוׄ[ת
תשבו]חות

8 אלוהים ◦[
]תׄשבוחות

9 [ ]לׄ[
דמות פלא רוח קו]דש קודשים

10 [מפותח לשון ברך ומדמות אלוהים קול ברך למלך מרוממים והלל
פלאיהם לאל אלים]ים[ ]רׄוקמוׄתׄ[ם]

Mus. Inv. 565, 620
PAM 43.448, 43.991*, 43.992*

NOTES ON READINGS

Col. IV is composed of three fragments (frgs. 6–8) which constitute three legs of the arch form of the upper part of the scroll.

The last two lines of frg. 8 (lines 9–10) indicate an overlap with 4Q**405** 14–15 i 2–3. The line length of the resulting reconstruction suggests that the column measured almost twice the revolution, i.e. *c*.17.5 cm. In that case, one must assume that the right leg of the arch between frgs. 6 and 8 is now lost. The line spaces on frg. 7 show that it is the left leg of either the middle or the right arch of the column. The lack of overlap of the top of the column prevents one from determining whether it should be placed towards the beginning or further to the left of the column.

L. 3]ב[. The head of *bet* is covered by a fold in the skin. The fold is still there and cannot be flattened. Contrary to the photograph, the fragment shows no other traces of letters.

L. 3]אלים֯. A faint discolouration on the edge may be the bottom part of the right downstroke of final *mem*.

L. 4 מעשי[ ]. The space before מעשי[is too large for only *bet*, *kap*, or *lamed*. One must either add an additional *waw* before one of those prepositions, or reconstruct [מ]מעשי.

L. 4 מבׄ]ואי. The minute stroke after *mem* is the bottom part of a downstroke.

L. 5 [לל]בׄני. The space at the beginning of the line is too large for [ל]בׄני.

L. 5 ד֯[. The letter is *dalet* or final *kap*.

L. 5 רק]י֯ע. Before *ʿayin*, appears the bottom part of a downstroke.

L. 6]כׄ. The remains of the letter are compatible with *kap* or *reš*.

L. 6 ◦י[. The upper left part of a downstroke before *yod* has been preserved (clearly seen on the fragment). One may read *šin*, or perhaps *waw*.

L. 6 טו]הר. The trace in the photograph of the partly carbonized piece of skin that is joined to frg. 7, is a crack and not ink.

L. 7 תשבׄ]וחות. The letter after *šin* may also be *waw*.

L. 7 בׄדמ֯ו֯]ת[. The left ends of the head and base of the first letter suggest *bet* (even though the tick is not visible), or, with more difficulty, *kap* or *pe*. The last trace looks like *yod*, but the diagonal stroke at the bottom is peculiar. It may be the tip of the left diagonal of *mem*. The traces after *dalet* look like the utmost top of the head of *reš* or *kap*, but they can also be interpreted as the upper part of *mem*.

L. 8]◦. The trace may be the upper right part of *ʿayin*, or, with more difficulty, *šin*.

L. 8 ת֯שבוחות[. A faint stroke at the edge of the fragment may be the left end of the base of *taw*.

L. 10]ים[. The traces in the photograph are not distinct, unlike those on the fragment. *Mem* is missing the left part of its head and the right part of its base.

L. 10 ר֯ו֯קמות֯[ם][. A small trace may be the far left end of the head of *reš*. The next, almost diagonal trace might be the head of *waw*. *Mem* is clearly followed by *waw* or *yod*. The last letter is problematic. The legs are close to one another, and the head seems to have an indenture. It may be a *taw* that is compressed for reasons of space, or it may merely appear to be compressed due to folding of the skin.

TRANSLATION

3. [ ] [Go]d of gods [
4. [ ] a construction of br[icks] vestibules of en[try
5. [to] their glorious [br]ickwork [ ] brickwork of [va]ult
6. a wonderful [appear]ance [ ] of pur[ity] [ ]

7. with the splendour of prai[ses] in the likene[ss of prai]ses
8. of the divine beings [ ] praises
9. [ ] [wondrous likeness of mo]st holy [spirit
10. [engraved tongue of blessing; and from the likeness of the divine beings comes a sound of blessing for the king of those who exalt, and their wondrous praise is for the God of the gods] [their] multicoloured [ ]

COMMENTS

L. 4 אולמי מבֹ]ואי. Cf. 4Q**405** 14–15 i 4 אולמי מבואיהם and 5 ודמו]תֹ אלוהים חיים מפותח באלמי מבואי מלך].

L. 5 לל]בֹני כבודם]. Cf. 4Q**405** 19 5–6 ב]דני צורות אלוהים מחוקקי סביב ללבני [כ]בֹודם. In view of the mention of engravings in the vestibules of entry in 4Q**405** 14–15 i 5 (cf. previous comment), one may assume that this section has a similar description and that one might reconstruct סביב at the end of line 4.

L. 5 רק]יֹע. This is the only reconstruction which matches the preserved vocabulary of the *Shirot*. Note, however, that the singular form is not congruent with the surrounding plural forms. If the reading is correct, the term probably refers to the vaults of the vestibules.

L. 6 מר]אי פלא]. The 'wonderful appearance' may refer to an engraving in the vault. One may also read כס]אי פלא], but there is no indication that the text here deals with the thrones.

L. 6 לחות[. The word משלחה, 'mission', is used in 4Q**405** 23 i 11 (Newsom, *DJD* XI, suggests that משלוחתו is a different spelling of משלחותו) and 13 in a description of the entering and exiting of the angels through the portals of entrance and the gates of exit. If לחות[is to be reconstructed מש]לחות, one may have a clause parallel to בהוד תשבֹ]וחות in the next line, e.g. בהדר מש]לחות. An alternative reconstruction may be ממו]לחות, 'blended', 'mixed'. Elsewhere in the *Shirot* this word is only used in the construction ממולח טוהר. Cf. COMMENTS on col. VI 4–5.

L. 7 בהוד תשבֹ]וחות. The expression בהדר תשבוחות is used in col. X 4–5 and 4Q**403** 1 i 32.

Ll. 7–8 תשבו]חות / אלוהים. Cf. ת(ו)שבחות כול אלוהים in 4Q**403** 1 i 31–32 and 32–33.

Col. V (Frgs. 9–12)

Parallel: 4Q**405** 15 ii–16 (underline)

2]
תפארת בפרוכת]

3 דֹבירֹ] המלך בדביר פנו רוקמת ת]כול
מֹ]חקת ה מה בדני אלוהים]

4 מעשי]הם כבוד משני עבריהם פרכות]דבירֹ]י הפלא וברכו
לא]לוהי כול[עבריהם]

5 י]שֹמיעו [פלא מביתה ליקרה הדביר במו]צא אול[מי]בדני
פ]לא הודו למלך]

6]הכבו[דֹ]בקול רנה] אלוהים[
]חֹם וצורות [

7 [מ]ראֹ[י]ם ישמעו◦[

]אלו֯הי אלי]ם

8]]כסאי עולמים [

9] ב]ד֯ניהם כרובי[

10]]מוסדי֯ם֯[

]ם֯

Mus. Inv. 565, 620
PAM 43.991*, 43.992*

NOTES ON READINGS

Col. V is composed of frgs. 9–11. Frg. 12, preserving the intercolumnar margin and the right side of col. VI, preserves the last letter of line 10, but not the left ruling of this column. Frg. 9 preserves the right margin of the column (the ruling between lines 3 and 4 is clearly visible on the fragment).

The overlap with 4Q**405** 15 ii–16 shows that 4Q**405** 15 ii–16 (and probably 17), and 4Q**405** 18, 20 i, and 19 belong to consecutive columns.

L. 3]ד֯ביר֯[. The left end of the head and the bottom tip of a downstroke of the first letter have been preserved. The distance between the two traces suggests *dalet*, even though the tick of the head cannot be seen.

L. 4]מעשי֯]הם. The original shows that the traces after *šin* are ink, not a discolouration of the edge of the fragment. The reading of *yod* seems assured. The word should be reconstructed at the end of 4Q**405** 15 ii–16 4.

L. 5] [י]שמיעו. PAM 43.991 shows no trace of *waw* after *ʿayin*, but on the fragment itself, the *waw* is certain and completely preserved. The skin after the *waw* has also preserved the blank space before the next word.

L. 6] [הכבו]ד֯. The downstroke is longer than that of a normal *dalet*, and in isolation one would favour the reading of final *kap*. In PAM 43.991 a small fragment with *yod* and a downstroke has been placed before this letter, but this can hardly be correct.

L. 6]ה֯ם. The first letter resembles *ḥet*. *He* is difficult, but not impossible.

L. 7]מ]רא֯[י. Certain is a diagonal stroke after *reš*, slanting down to the left. If the dark blot below this trace is ink, the letter must be *ʾalep*.

L. 7 ישמעו◦[. The trace after *ʿayin* is not *yod*, but the upper part of the left arm of the *ʿayin*. Following very closely after *waw* is the top of a vertical trace, slanting towards the left. It is consistent with the right arm of *ʾalep*.

L. 7 אלו֯הי. The faint traces after *lamed* are not completely consistent with *waw*, and it is not certain they are evidence of any letter at all. Because of the tear at the end of the word, there appears to be two *yods*; however, one must assume that the *yod* has been torn into two parts.

L. 8] עולמים. It is not certain that the fragment with the last two letters should be placed here. Cf. note on line 9 כר֯ו֯בי[.

L. 9 ב]ד֯ניהם. Before the downstroke of the *nun*, there is a horizontal stroke which possibly is the left end of the head of *dalet*. It is difficult, though not impossible, to combine these traces and read]צ֯ידים.

L. 9 כר֯ו֯בי[. *Reš* and *waw* are preserved on frg. 10b (PAM 43.992). To the left of frg. 10 are several small to very small fragments, not all in their original places. A small fragment with the head of *reš* and the downstroke of *waw* can be shifted to fit between the *kap* of the main fragment and בי. It is not clear from the photograph whether the left parts of the fragments belong to the same layer. The almost continuous ruling of line 9 does suggest that, but the photograph shows a vertical line which is either a large crack or the edge of a fragment. This cannot be checked against the original, since the fragment has now disintegrated.

L. 10]מׄוסדיםׄ[. Or read:]מׄיסדיםׄ[. A *waw* after a *mem* may be either long, stretching towards the baseline as e.g. in col. VII 6 מוש]בו, or short like *yod* as e.g. in col. VII 10 ור[ו]ממוהו]. The trace after *yod* is consistent with the right shoulder of final *mem*; cf. the final *mem* in the previous line.

TRANSLATION

2. [of beauty upon the veil of the]
3. *debir* [of the king in the *debir* of his presence, the mingled colours of] all which is et[ched upon . . .] figures of [gods,]
4. [their] works [are glorious on both their sides the veils of the wonderful] *debir*[s. And they bless the g]ods of all [their sides;]
5. [they] announce [of wonder, inside the precious place, the *debir*, at the ex]it of the vesti[bules] won[derful] forms [give thanks to the king of]
6. [glor]y [with a ringing cry] gods [ ] and figures [
7. [the ap]pea[rance of] they will hear (?) [ ] god of divinitie[s
8. [ ] eternal thrones [
9. [ ] their [f]orms are cherubs of[
10. [ ] foundations [

COMMENTS

L. 3 כול מׄ]חקת[. The *Puʿal* participle of חקה occurs three times in the Hebrew Bible, in each case describing figures carved in relief on a wall or door. In 1 Kgs 6:35 it refers to the cherubs, palm trees, and flowers that were carved on the door of the Temple and covered with gold. In Ezek 8:10, מחקה describes the figures which Ezekiel sees in the defiled Temple of Jerusalem, and in 23:14 the word refers to the figures of the Chaldean men whom Oholibah looks at.

L. 4 מעשי]הם כבוד משני עבריהם. In the next column the appearance of the בדני is referred to by כול מעשיהם. Here, there seems to be no room at the beginning of the line for כול. It is not clear whether משני עבריהם introduces a new clause or belongs to the previous one. Newsom suggests that the two sides referred to are the two sides of the veil, which in Exod 26:31 is described as מעשה חשב, 'cunningly woven'. According to Haran, 'the talmudic sages described *ḥošēb* workmanship as a combination of threads interwoven in such a way that different figures emerge on the two sides of the fabric, whereas in *roqēm* workmanship, taken to be needlework, one figure only emerges, either just on one side, or on both sides of the fabric'.[5] Haran, himself, favours the explanation that חשב workmanship 'contains figures, whereas *roqēm* workmanship involves a mixture of colours and varieties, but has no figures'. Another possibility is to read מעשי] כבוד משני עבריהם, and follow Olyan's suggestion that the *Maʿasim* are an angelic brigade.[6] In that case, 'glorious creatures' is a specification of the more general אלוהים.

L. 4 וברכו לא[לוהי כול]. The subject of וברכו is probably the figures of the divine beings on the veil. The only preserved example of the construction אלוהי כול is in 4Q**400** i 2 אלוהי כול קדושי קדושים, but this may be too long for our line.

L. 5 מביתה ליקרה הדביר במו]צא אול[מי. For the reading and interpretation of ליקרׄהׄ cf. *DJD* XI, but it is not certain how the exit of the vestibules is connected to the preceding description of the veil. אולמי is also mentioned in 4Q**405** 14–15 i 4 and 5.

L. 6]חׄם. The final *mem* is probably the 3rd masc. pl. pronominal suffix. The word ending with *ḥet* must be either a sing. noun, e.g. כו]חׄם, or an infinitive construct, e.g. בשוב]חׄם.

---

[5] M. Haran, *Temples and Temple-Service in Ancient Israel: An Inquiry into the Character of Cult Phenomena and the Historical Setting of the Priestly School* (Oxford: Clarendon, 1978) 160–61.

[6] S. M. Olyan, *A Thousand Thousands Served Him: Exegesis and the Naming of Angels in Ancient Judaism* (Texte und Studien zum Antiken Judentum 36; Tübingen: J. C. B. Mohr, 1993) 42–7.

L. 6 וצורות. The word צורות is used predominantly in the next column, and in the corresponding text of 4Q**405** 19.

L. 7 מ]ראׄ[י. The reconstruction seems the most fitting in this context, which also uses the words צורות and בנדי.

L. 7 ישמעו◦[. The word is awkward, since the preserved parts of the *Shirot* use only the *Hipʿil* of שמע. Perhaps one should read ישמעוׄא[, an unusual—but not impossible—spelling of ישמעו.

L. 9 ב]דׄניהם כרׄובי[. One may reconstruct the word וצורות before ב]דׄניהם; cf. line 7 of the next column.

Col. VI (Frgs. 12–15)

Parallel: 4Q**405** 19 (underline)

2] ◦◦[

3]קׄ ושבחוהו ב]דׄני אלוהׄ[ים רוחי ק]מׄרׄכב[ ]◦ל בׄדני כב[וד מדרס]

4 דבירׄ[י פלא רוחי א]ל[י עולמים] כול בדני דביר מל]ךׄ מעש[י רוחו]ת רקיע פלא מׄ[מולח]

5 טוה[ר רוחי דעת אמת] וצדקׄ[בקודש קודשים צורות אלוהי]ם חיים [צורי רוחות מאיר]ים כול

6 מע[שיהם]רוקמׄ[ה בדני צורות אלוהים מ]חוקק סב[י]ב[ ]צורות[כבוד]

7 למעׄ[שי לבני הוד והדר א]לׄ[ו]היםׄ[חיים כול מעשיהם וצו]רׄת בדניהם מלׄ[אכי קודש מתחת לדב]ירי הׄ[פלא]

8 קול [דממת שקט אלוהים מברכים המלך מהל]לים תמיד כׄ[ו]ל[

9]vac אלוהים]הו במשני מ[

10]]פׄלאׄי הוד והׄ[דר

Mus. Inv. 565, 620
PAM 43.991*, 43.992*

NOTES ON READINGS

Col. VI is composed of four fragments. Frg. 12 preserves the right margin; frg. 15 preserves *c*.0.2 cm of the vertical left ruling after לדב]ירי (line 7).

The correspondence with 4Q**405** 19 helps with determining the width of the revolution of the rolled up scroll at this point. The reconstruction of the text indicates that the distance between the points of correspondence of frgs. 12 + 13 and 14 + 15 is

7.8–8 cm. Note, however, that this column and 4Q**405** 19 do not always have the same text: not only is there one minor spelling difference (מ]חוקק versus מחקקי in line 6), but twice the text of 4Q**405** 19 does not seem to correspond with the gaps in line 6.

L. 2]◦◦[. The two vertical strokes are probably ink (cf. photograph of frg. 15; nothing can now be seen at the top of the fragment), but the horizontal traces are less easy to determine.

L. 3 ק̇[. Comparison with the horizontal ruling lines of frg. 12 shows that the vertical stroke extends beneath the baseline. The trace, therefore, probably belongs to *qop*, and not to *dalet* or *reš*.

L. 3 ב]ד֯ני. The stroke before *nun* is consistent with the left part of the head of *dalet*.

L. 3 אלוה֯]ים. The faint trace at the edge is probaby the lower part of the right leg of *he*.

L. 3]מ֯ר֯כב[. A slightly slanting base stroke is all that remains of the first letter; it could belong to e.g. *bet*, medial *mem*, *nun*, *pe*, or *ṣade*. An *ʿayin* is less likely, since its stroke is more diagonal. Before *kap* the remnant of a horizontal stroke is visible. It might be *he*, in which case one may reconstruct הכב]וד, but then there is hardly any space between the first trace, which should be the last letter of the preceding word, and *he*. Even though one cannot recognize the tick, one may read *reš*.

L. 3]◦ל ב̇דני. The letters דני are visible on frg. 15a. Frg. 15b (the tiny triangular fragment which in the photograph is attached to the fragment with *lamed* does not fit here) shows after *lamed* the remains of the head of a letter which is consistent with *bet*, and a small dot which may be the right end of the head of *dalet*. The space between *lamed* and *bet* is rather small, but not impossible for a word-dividing space. To the right of the upper arm of *lamed* there is a rather long horizontal stroke which is too long for *lamed*. The stroke probably consists of two parts, the left part being the horizontal stroke of *lamed* sloping slightly upwards to the right, and the right part being the head of the preceding letter, possibly *waw* or *kap*. In the manuscript, *lamed* is more than once connected to a preceding *waw*.

L. 6]צורות֯[. The right leg of *taw* is visible on frg. 15a, the upper left part on frg. 15d.

L. 7 וצו]ר֯ת. The trace on the edge of the fragment before *taw* is too thick for the head of *waw* and seems to consist of two parts, the end of a headstroke and a horizontal tick.

L. 7 מל֯]אכי. It is possible that the dark spot at the very edge of the fragment is the far right part of *lamed*. The very thin vertical trace beneath this spot is not likely to be part of a letter.

L. 7 ה̇]פלא[. The traces on frg. 15e may be the crossbar and left leg of *he*.

L. 8 כ̇]ו[ל[. Or כ̇ו֯ל[. Part of a downstroke and the right part of the head of the first letters remain. Since the stroke of the head seems to go slightly upward, *kap* is likely. The upper arm of *lamed* is clearly visible in the carbonized area. The trace to the right of *lamed* may be either the left part of the broken head of *kap* or a remnant of *waw*.

L. 10]פ֯לאי[. A very faint stroke on the edge of the fragment may be the head of *pe*. The final letter may also be *waw*.

TRANSLATION

2. [ ] [
3. [and the f]orms of god[s praise him, spirits of] chariot[ ] the forms of glo[ry, the dais]
4. of the [wonderful] *debir*[s, the spirits of the] eternal [divi]nit[ies, all the forms of the *debir* of the ki]ng. The work[s of the spirit]s of the wonderful firmament are in[termingled]
5. pure[ly, spirits of the knowledge of the truth] and justice [in the holy of holies, images of] living [god]s, [images of shin]ing [spirits]. All
6. [their] con[structions]embroider[ed, forms of the images of the gods, en]graved aro[u]nd [ ] images [of the glory]
7. of the [brick]wor[k of splendour and majesty. Living g]o[d]s [are all their construction and the for]m of their images are [holy] an[gels. Beneath] the [wonderful *deb*]*irs*
8. is the [calm] sound [of murmur, the gods blessing the king prai]sing always a[l]l [
9. *vacat* [gods] him in the second [
10. [ ] wonders of splendour and ma[jesty

COMMENTS

L. 3 קׄ]. There is room for a word of four letters at the beginning of the line.

L. 3 ושבחוהו. 4Q**405** 19 2 reads defectively ושבחהו (indicative or imperative).

L. 3 ב]דׄני. The word בדני, always in the construct state, is attested only in the Songs of the Sabbath Sacrifice and in 1QM V 6 (in the form אבדני) and 9. In both texts it is used alongside צורות; the two words are either synonyms or are closely related. Other parallel nouns, used in similar constructions, are מראי and דמות.

L. 3 רוחי ק. Cf. 4Q**405** 19 2: רוחי קׄ]. One may reconstruct רוחי קודש קודשים as in 4Q**403** 1 ii 7; 4Q**405** 6 5; 22 10; cf. also 4Q**403** 1 i 44; ii 1; 4Q**404** 5 1; 4Q**405** 14–15 i 2; 23 ii 8 רוח קודש קודשים. רוחי קורב קודש קודשים, as in 4Q**405** 14–15 i 4, is also possible.

Ll. 3–4 מדרס] / דביר]י פלא. The exact meaning of מדרס in this context is unknown. For the idea of מדרס cf. Ezek 43:7 את מקום כסאי ואת מקום כפות רגלי.

L. 4 רוחי א]ל[י עולמיםׄ]. Cf. אלי עולמים (MasShirShabb i 10), רוחי עולמים (4Q**403** 1 i 35), and the frequent רוחות אלוהים.

L. 4 בדני דביר מל]ךׄ. For דביר מלך cf. 4Q**405** 14–15 i 7 and 15 ii–16 2. The reading]בׄד]ני in 4Q**405** 19 3 is not certain. The gap between כול and בדני is ten to eleven letter-spaces wide.

L. 4 מעש]י רוחו]ת. Cf. 4Q**400** 1 i 5 כול מעשי רוח. The alternative reconstruction מעש]י רוקמ]ת (cf. 4Q**405** 14–15 i 6 מעשי רוקמות פלא) is less appropriate with רקיע as *nomen rectum*. Since ממולח טהור elsewhere in the ShirShabb modifies the preceding words (cf. 4Q**405** 22 11; 23 ii 10), מעש]י is probably the first word of a new sentence (Newsom). Olyan argues that the מעשים are an angelic order like the *cherub*s or *ophan*s.

Ll. 4–5 מׄ]מולח] / טוה]ר. The phrase occurs once in the Hebrew Bible, in Exod 30:35 קטרת רקח מעשה רוקח ממלח טהור קודש. The use of ממלח in Sir 49:1, and the translation of *Tg*. Exod 30:35 מערב, show that ממלח, 'salted', may also mean 'blended', 'mixed'. Exod 30:34-38 describes the most sacred type of incense which is to be used in the inner part of the sanctuary. In the *Shirot*, the term seems to be used for sacred objects that are connected with the most holy aspects of the divine sanctuary.

L. 5 וצדקׄ] בקודש קודשים. The reconstruction of בקודש is tentative, as the placement of the small fragment 4Q**405** 19b is not entirely certain. קודש קודשים would be a reference to the *debir*.

L. 5 צורות אלוהי]ם חיים [צורי רוחות מאיר]ים. Note the parallelism, the author using the fem. צורות with the masc. אלוהים, and the masc. צורי with the fem. רוחות. The first word of 4Q**405** 19 5 may be read as מאירים (*Hip'il* participle) or מאורים (masc. pl. of מאור). For רוחות מאורים cf. 4Q**405** 14–15 i 5 רוח אורים.

L. 6 מע]שיהם]רוקמׄ]ה. The reconstruction מע]שיהם קודשי דבקי פלא רוחי רוקמׄה], according to 4Q**405** 19 5 (preserved text underlined), is difficult: the gap is five to six letter-spaces too short. Either the scribe of 11Q**17** forgot a word (which may have been added supralinearly), or 4Q**405** had a plus. It is plausible that the word in question (either forgotten or added) is קודשי. Omitting it affects neither the syntax nor the contents of the phrase.

L. 6 מ]חוקק. 4Q**405** 19 5 reads מחוקקי which is more fitting, as it refers to the preceding ב]דני צורות אלוהים.

L. 6 סב]י[ב]]צורות]. 4Q**405** 19 6 reads סביב ללבני [כ]בׄודם צורות, but there is room for one more word of four or five letters in the gap in this column. Since there is no reason for a *vacat*, one may assume either an erasure, an extra word, or a variant text. One may consider the reconstructions סב]י[ב] למעשי לבני כבודם [צורות] (cf. line 7) or סב]י[ב] ללבני כבודם בדני [צורות]. It is not clear from the text of 4Q**405** 19 6 whether לבני refers to the pavement under the throne in the *debir* or (more likely) to the brickwork of the walls of the *debir*.

L. 7 א]לׄ[ו]היםׄ] חיים כול מעשיהם וצו]רׄת בדניהם מלׄ]אכי קודש. The structure of the text is difficult, but seems to display a chiastic pattern: א]לׄ[ו]היםׄ] חיים is parallel to מלׄ]אכי קודש, and כול מעשיהם to צו]רׄת בדניהם. In that case, the antecedent of the pronominal suffixes is probably צורות] כבוד] למעׄ]שי לבני הוד והדר.

L. 7 וצו]רׄת. The parallel text of 4Q**405** 19 7 has the more fitting plural form וצורות, but palaeographically וצור]וׄת is very difficult.

L. 8 קול [דממת שקט אלוהים מברכים. As in 1 Kgs 19:12 קול דממה דקה, the word דממה does not express complete silence, but rather the sound of the rustling of a breeze or the murmuring of voices. 4Q**405** 20 ii–22 indicates that אלוהים מברכים and, further on, מהל]לים, determines the קול [דממת שקט: the blessing of the gods has the sound of rustling or murmuring; cf. lines 7 יפולו לפנו ה֯[כרו]בים וב֯[ר]כ֯ו בהרומם קול דממת אלוהים, ‘the cherubim fall before him and bless, and when they rise, the sound of the rustle of gods (is heard?)’, 12 וקול דממת ברכ בהמון לכתם, ‘and the sound of the murmur of blessing in the tumult of their movement’, and 13 קול גילות רנה השקיט ודממ֯[ת] ב֯ר֯ך֯ א֯לוהים, ‘the sound of glad rejoicing becomes silent, and there is a murmur of blessing of the gods’.

L. 8 מברכים   המלך   מהל]לים. Cf. the pair of participles מברכים ומהללים in 4Q**405** 23 i 9. 4Q**405** 19 8 indicates that between מברכים and ה֯מלך there is room for a four or five letter word (none of the letters can be *lamed*). There is, however, a discrepancy between the two manuscripts with regard to מהל]לים. In 11Q**17** the reconstructed gap between המלך and מהל]לים amounts to eight to ten letter-spaces, but no upper arm of *lamed* is visible in 4Q**405** 19 8 at this approximate distance. The trace of *lamed* under מתחת in 4Q**405** 19 7 is too distant to belong to מהל]לים.

L. 8 מהל]לים תמיד כ֯[ו]ל[. כ֯[ו]ל[may determine the object of the praise or an adverbial clause.

Col. VII (Frgs. 16–18)

Parallel: 4Q**405** 20 ii–22 (underline)

1]
]ו֯ד[

2]]א פ֯נ֯י֯ו֯[ ]ע֯ל
מרום כסא[

3] לו]א֯ יתמהמהו בעומדם [ירי כול כוהני קורב]*vacat*
v]*acat*

4]]◦ם בחוק יתכל[כ]לו לשרת ל◦[מושב ככסא מלכות]ו בדבירי
כבודו לוא ישב[ו

5] מרכבו]ת כבודו [כרו]בי קוד[ש אופני אור בדביר]רוחות אל[והים
]ט֯והר ב◦[

6 [קודש מ]ע֯שי פנותו[ממלכו]ת מוש[בי כבוד למרכבות]כנפי דעת[
ג]בורת פלא[

7 [אמת ו]צדק עולמ[ים מרכבות] כבוד[ו בלכתמה לוא י]סבו לכול ע֯[
י]שרו ל[

8] *vac*[*at*] *vac*[*at*]
vac[*at*

9 [למש]כיל שיר[עולת השבת שתים עשרא בעשרים ואחד לחדש] השלישי [הללו
לאלוהי]שני פ֯ל֯[א]

10 [ור]ו֯ממוהו [כפי הכבוד במשכן אלוהי דעת יפולו לפנו הכרובים ו]ב֯רכו בהרומ֯ם֯[

קול דממת אלוהים נשמע והמון רנה[

11]ברים כנ[פׄיׄהֹ]ם קול דממת אלוהים תבנית כסא מרכבה מברכים ממעל לרקיע
הכרובים והוד רקיע האור ירננו[

12]מתחת מושב כבודו ובלכת האופנים ישובו מלאכי קודש יצ[אׄ ומבין] גלגלי
כבודו כמראי אש רוחות קודש[

13]קדשים סביב מראי שבולי אש בדמות חשמל ומעשי נוגה [ברוקמת כב]וד צבעי
פלא ממולח טוהר רוחות אלוהים[

14]חיים מתהלכים תמיד עם כבוד מרכבות הפלא וקול דממת ב[רך בהמון]לכתם
והללו קודש בהשיב דרכיהם[

15]]ooo[

Mus. Inv. 609, 620
PAM 43.990*, 43.991*

NOTES ON READINGS

Col. VII is composed of frgs. 16–18. Frg. 18 is now reduced to ashes, conserved on rice paper.

L. 2]אׄ פׄנׄיׄוׄ[. Parts of the letters have faded away, and not all traces are necessarily ink. The letter before *nun* looks like a *pe* which was written lower than the other letters. The letter attached to *nun* (the left end of the base has faded away almost completely) is *waw* or *yod*. The last downstroke (the top of which is very faint) may be *waw* or e.g. the right part of *taw*. The trace in the photograph between *ʾalep* and *pe* cannot be seen on the fragment.

L. 4]°ם. The tiny trace at the edge of the fragment cannot belong to *yod*: its position is too low, and the angle of the nib of the pen would have produced a different stroke. Most likely it belongs to the base of a letter (e.g. *bet*, *kap*, *nun*, *pe*, or *taw*), or, with somewhat more difficulty, to *mem* or *ʿayin*.

L. 4 ל°[. After *lamed* one can see the lower part of a downstroke.

L. 4 ישב[ו]. Normally *waw* or *yod* after *bet* are written above the left end of the base, often forming a ligature. Here, no trace of *waw* can be seen. An examination of the fragment, however, shows clearly that the surface of the skin has peeled off just where the base stroke of the *bet* ends (one cannot even know if this stroke is complete); the rest of the skin visible in the photograph is on a different level.

L. 5]טׄוהר. The remains of the letter which must be *ṭet* consist of two strokes very close to one another. The first must be the head, the second the top of the left vertical stroke.

L. 5 ב°[. Attached to the base of *bet* is a downstroke. Possible are *waw*, *reš*, or *taw*. More difficult are *yod* and *dalet*.

L. 6 מ]עׄשי. The *ʿayin* is broken exactly at the point where the left arm joins the diagonal. Hence the remainder of the letter looks very much like *nun*.

L. 6 פנותו[. The space between פנו and תו[is rather large for a space within a word; the reading פני תו[is also possible.

L. 6 ג]בורת. The loose fragment fits before *taw*, with approximately 1 mm between the fragments. Note that the tick of *reš* is preserved before *taw*.

L. 7 עׄ[. Most often in the manuscripts, the tops of the right and left arms of *ʿayin* are more widely spread, but cf. the similarly compact *ʿayin* in line 6 דעת[. Materially, *šin* is also possible.

L. 7]שרו[י. The last letter can also be read as *yod*.

L. 7]ל. The unwritten skin after *lamed* shows that it was not followed by a letter beginning with a vertical stroke. Thin black traces can be seen alongside the diagonal edge of the fragment; an examination of the fragment does not help in determining whether they are ink.

L. 9 פֿלֿ[א]. Definite traces of one or two more letters can be seen after שני[, but their interpretation is difficult. The head of the first letter does not seem to descend to the left as it should if it were *pe*. The horizontal stroke at the end may be the horizontal stroke of *lamed*, but there is no trace of the diagonal.

L. 10 ור[וֿ]ממוהו]. The faint trace before the first *mem* is either a slight discolouration of the skin or part of the tip of *waw*.

L. 11 כנ[פֿיֿה]ם. The first traces may be interpreted as a ligature. In that case, only the left end of the base of e.g. *pe* has been preserved. The meagre traces of the last letter are entirely consistent with *he*.

L. 12 יצ[אֿ ומבין]. The slightly diagonal trace at the right edge of the fragment is more likely the left leg of *ʾalep* than the downstroke of *waw*.

L. 15]◦◦◦[. There are faint traces of the heads (ticks) of three letters.

Translation

1. [ ] [
2. [ ] his face [ ] above the height of the throne [of
3. [ ] they do [no]t delay; when they halt [all the priests of the inner sanctum] *vacat*
4. [ ] by ordinance they are steadfast in the service of [a seat like the throne of] his [kingship] in his glorious *debir*s. They do not sit [
5. [the chariot]s of his glory [ ]hol[y cheru]bs, [shining *ophan*s in the *debir*] spirits of go[ds] purity [
6. [holy. The w]orks of its corners [roya]l, [the glorious] sea[ts of the chariots] the wings of knowledge[ ] wonderful [p]ower [
7. [truth and] eternal justice [his] glorious [chariots. When they move, they do not] turn aside to any [ ] they go [st]raight to [
8. *vacat*
9. [By the instr]uctor. The song [of the sacrifice of the twelfth sabbath, on the twenty-first of] the third [month. Praise the God of] wonder[ful,]
10. [and ex]alt him [according to the glory in the tent of the God of knowledge. The cherubs fall down before him, and] bless. When they rise [the murmuring sound of gods is heard, and there is an uproar of exultation]
11. [when they lift] the[ir win]gs, [the murmuring sound of gods. They bless the image of the throne-chariot above the vault of the cherubs, and they sing the splendour of the vault of light]
12. [beneath the seat of his glory. And when the *ophan*s go forward, the holy angels return.] They [emer]ge from between [its glorious wheels, with the likeness of fire, the spirits of the holy of]
13. [holies. Around them is the likeness of streams of fire, like electrum, and a luminous substance] glor[iously] multi-coloured, wonderful colours purely blended. The spirits of the living]
14. [gods move constantly with the glory of the wonderful chariots. And there is a murmuring sound of bl]essing in the uproar [of their motion, and they praise the holy one on returning to their paths.]
15. [ ] [

Comments

L. 1]וֿד[. Reconstruct e.g.]כב[וֿד or]ה[וֿד.

L. 2]א[פֿניֿו. There is a possibility that the text read]אוֿפֿניֿו[. The suffix of בעומדם in line 3 may then refer to these *ophan*s, or to a composite noun clause to which this word belonged.

L. 2]עֿל מרום כסא[. Cf. e.g. Ezek 1:26 ועל דמות הכסא.

L. 3 לו]א יתמההמו. In view of the negative sense of התמהמה, the reconstruction לו]א is plausible. It is not certain that the following בעומדם should be taken with לו]א יתמהמהו. The preceding lost phrase may have contained בלכת or בלכתם ('when they go they do not tarry'), in which case בעומדם introduces a parallel clause. 4Q**405** 20 ii–22 has a few examples of the construction *bet* with infinitive, followed by a finite verbal form. Cf. lines 7–8 בהרומם קול דממת אלוהים / [נשמע] (rather than ובׄ[ר]כֿו בהרומם), line 9 ובלכת האופנים ישובו מלאכי קודש, lines 12–13 בהרומם ירוממו פלא ובשוכן / [יעמ]וֿדו, and also line 7 of our column בלכתמה לוא י]סבו. The opposite order is attested once in 4Q**405** 20 ii–22 12 והללוֿ קודש בהֿשיב דרכיהם. The verb התמהמה expresses the opposite of haste; cf. e.g. Ps 119:60 חשתי ולא התמהמהתי לשמר מצותיך and 4Q**405** 23 i 11 לוא ירֿוצו מדרך ולוא יתמֿהמהו מגבולו. The expression לו]א יתמהמהו may therefore perhaps refer to the fast movements of the creatures (cherubs) of Ezek 1:14. It is hard to imagine what could be meant by לו]א יתמהמהו בעומדם if one regards this as one clause. בעומדם can be interpreted in several ways (cf. discussion below), but לו]א יתמהמהו, which expresses movement or activity, is hardly compatible with עמד which first of all expresses the lack of movement.

L. 3 בעומדם. עומד can be a noun, the 'place (where one stands)', but in Nehemiah (13:11) and 2 Chronicles (30:16; 35:10) it is used especially in a cultic sense: the 'position', 'post', or 'station' of the priests and Levites within the Temple service. This may also be the meaning of עומדם in 4Q**405** 23 i 6. In that case, לו]א יתמהמהו בעומדם may mean 'they do not tarry at their posts', that is, they do not linger during their cultic tasks. One may also regard בעומדם as an infinitive construct. Though in biblical Hebrew עמד sometimes means 'to rise', it normally refers to the posture of standing (sometimes with the implication of standing still). The verb is often employed in a cultic or liturgical context: 'to stand to serve'. In that case, one might translate לו]א יתמהמהו בעומדם by 'they do not delay when they stand (sc. to serve)'. However, the many references to Ezekiel 1 and 10 suggest another interpretation. בעומדם refers there to the halting of the creatures, the cherubs, and the *ophans* (Ezek 1:21, 24, 25; 10:17). It can hardly be a coincidence that בעומדם is used together with בלכתמה and בהרומם, terms which are used in lines 7 and 10. If בעומדם means 'when they halt', it is probably the first word of a clause, to be followed by a finite verbal form.

L. 3 ירי כול כוהני קורב].]יֿרוֿ כול כוהניֿ קורבֿ of 4Q**405** 21 should be placed somewhere in the gap between] בעומדם and the *vacat*. The expressions כוהני קורב, כוהני קורבו, and כוהני קורב קדושי קדושים occur several times in the *Shirot*, but one may perhaps also reconstruct a participle קורבים or, in the construct state, קורבי (cf. 4Q**400** 1 i 20 כוהני מרומי רום הֿ[קר]בים). Unfortunately, the traces of the first three letters are rather uncertain.

L. 4]°ם בחוק. חוק is probably the divine law or ordinance which regulates the priestly service, but the structure of the clause or clauses is not clear. בחוק may be the last word of a clause that began at the beginning of line 4, or the first word of a new clause, which would imply a very short clause at the beginning of the line. Since both options result in a rather short clause at the beginning of a new subsection, one may consider the possibility that the word ending with *mem* is an adverbially used infinitive construct with the 3rd masc. pl. pronominal suffix, preceded by a noun which is the subject of יתכל[כ]לו, e.g. [המלאכים בלכ]תֿם.

L. 4 יתכל[כ]לו. The *Hitpalpel* of כול is not attested in the Hebrew Bible, but cf. Sir 12:15, 43:3, where it means 'to be steadfast, to endure'; cf. also 4Q**405** 23 i 5.

L. 4 לשרת ל°[. שרת is often used in a cultic context. For שרת with *lamed* to introduce the object cf. Num 4:9; 2 Chr 13:10; 22:8. One may read לשרת לוֿ[, or לשרת ל- with a divine title (with a letter beginning with a downstroke).

L. 4 מושב ככסא מלכות[וֿ. There is room for approximately twelve letter-spaces between ל°[and מושב. The loss of these words prevents an understanding of this phrase, preserved in 4Q**405** 20 ii–22 2. In particular, it is unclear which comparison is made. The following בדבירי כבודו probably qualifies the ככסא מלכות[וֿ, but it cannot be entirely excluded that the words begin a new clause.

L. 4 לוא ישב]ו. This is probably a plural form, as are the other verbs in the column. One may refer to the tradition that no one may sit in the presence of God (cf. *b. Ḥag* 15a; 3 *Enoch* 16), a notion which is not shared by Rev 4:4 (twenty-four elders seated before the throne).

L. 5 מרכבו]ת כבודו]. There is room for a two- or three-letter word at the beginning of the line, probably a preposition, e.g. על or ועל. The same expression is used in 4QBerakhot[a] (4Q**286**) I i 2 ומרכבות כבודכה.

L. 5 כרו]בי קוד[ש אופני אור. This seems to be an enumeration of the divine beings connected to the chariot thrones; cf. 4Q**403** 1 ii 15; 4QBerakhot[a] (4Q**286**) I i 2 ומרכבות כבודכה כרוביהמה ואופניהמה. אור may be read as אוֹר ('light') or אוּר ('flame', 'fire'); cf. Ezek 1:4 which mentions both אש and נגה.

L. 5 בדביר. The reconstruction בדבירי כבודו (cf. line 4) fits exactly in the gap before רוחות[.

Ll. 5–6 ב◦[/ קודש. The word beginning with *bet* is possibly the last but probably the penultimate word of the line (cf. lines 9 and 10).

L. 6 פנותו[. One can also read פני תו[, but in that case the reconstruction of the second word raises problems. In 4Q**403** 1 i 41, כול פנות מבניתו are mentioned, together with the foundations of the Holy of Holies and the pillars of the Temple giving praise to God. The פנות belong there to a series of architectonic items (cf. also the beams and walls in line 43). Here, the פנות may be those mentioned in 1 Kgs 7:34.

L. 6 למרכבות]כנפי. There is room for a four-letter word in the gap.

L. 6 פלא[. There is room for one more word at the end of the line.

L. 7 בלכתמה לוא י]סבו לכול עֹ[. A clear reference to Ezekiel 1 and 10, e.g. Ezek 1:9 לא יסבו בלכתן איש אל עבר פניו ילכו (cf. also 1:12, 17; 10:11). In view of this correspondence, one should probably reconstruct the end as לכול עֹ[בר, 'to any side', rather than לכול עֹ[ולמים, 'forever' (cf. also Isa 47:15 איש לעברו תעו).

L. 9 [למש]כיל שיר[עולת השבת שתים עשרא בעשרים ואחד לחדש] השלישי. The formulaic character of the headings of the songs enables one to reconstruct the heading of the twelfth song. The only optional item in the formula is the number of the month, but here the number השלישי has been preserved.

L. 9 [למש]כיל. A similar formula is used in *Songs of the Sage* (4Q**510** and **511**); cf. e.g. 4Q**511** 2 i 1 למשכיל שיר֯[and 8 4 למשכיל ש]יר שני לפחד מיראיו֯[. There, however, the text continues with a first person recitation. See also the comparable statements in 1QS III 13 למשכיל להבין וללמד את כול בני אור and 1QSb I 1 דברי הברכ]ה[למשכיל לברך את יראי֯ אל (cf. also III 22 and V 20). In all of these cases the works are apparently meant to be recited by the *Maskil* or Instructor. This does not clarify, however, whether למשכיל should be interpreted as 'For the Instructor' or 'By the Instructor'.

L. 9 [הללו לאלוהי. The preserved parts of the *Shirot* in the cave 4 fragments suggest that each song began with הללו אלוהי or הללו לאלוהי. Cf. 4Q**400** 1 1 הללו; 4Q**401** 1 1 הללו לא]לוהי; 4Q**403** 1 i 30 הללו אלוהי מרומים; **405** 8–9 2 הללו לאלוהי כול מ[.

L. 9 שני פלֹ[א][. The words may be part of the divine epithet, but they are more likely part of the vocative. Cf. the structure in 4Q**403** 1 ii 18–20: הללו + object + vocative + ורוממוהו + vocative + הללו + object + vocative. Similarly, 4Q**400** 1 1–2: הללו + [object] + vocative, and MasShirShabb I 9–10: [הללו] + object + vocative + ורוממו + object. שני[may be a complete word or the last part of a longer word. The reconstruction [הללו לאלוהי נשיאי מ]שני פלֹ[א] (tentatively suggested by Newsom) is too short for the line leaving some additional eight letter-spaces. One may fill the gap by reconstructing e.g. [הללו לאלוהי כבוד כול נשיאי מ]שני פלֹ[א], but the deputy princes do not seem to play a role in the following song.

L. 10 [ור]וֹממוהו. For ורוממוהו or ורוממו following הללו, cf. 4Q**403** 1 ii 18–20; MasShirShabb I 9–10; perhaps 4Q**511** 2 i 1–2 (הללו is not preserved in the last two texts).

L. 10 [כ]פי הכבוד. Cf. 4Q**405** 20 ii–22 7 כֹּפֹּי הכבוֹד. הכבוד is probably a divine epithet (cf. *1 Enoch* 9:3; 14:20; 102:3; 104:1; יקרא רבא in 11Q**18**), and may refer to Ezek 1:28.

L. 10 לפנו. This is a phonetic spelling of לפניו (cf. Qimron, §200.18), rather than לפני. Cf. the similar phonetic spelling in 4Q**403** 1 i 43 קירותו.

L. 10 בהרומם֯[. An infinitive construct *Nipʿal* of רמם; cf. Ezek 10:15, 17.

L. 10 בהרומם֯[קול דממת אלוהים נשמע. The clause is probably inspired by Ezek 1:24, which deals with the sounds of the movements of the creatures (the cherubs). Cf. the somewhat similar structure of ברים] בלכתם קול המלה. For the reconstruction נשמע, cf. Ezek 10:5.

L. 11 כנ]פֹיהֹם . Reconstruct ברים (*Hipʿil* infinitive construct with elision of quiescent *he*) rather than ברום (*Qal* infinitive construct).

L. 12]יצ[א̇ ומבין. This is exactly the same reading as in 4Q**405** 20 ii–22 9 which Strugnell and Newsom emended to יצאו מבין. Therefore, either the reading is correct, or both manuscripts are in some way related, both having a wrong reading. It certainly is easier to emend the text.

Col. VIII (Frgs. 19–20)

2]   ]פ̇לא דעת ובינ̇]ה   ]רקיעי פל[א]
3]   ]א̇ באור אור̇ם̇ הוד [   ]כ̇ול תבנית רוחי פל[א]
4]   ]אלוהים נוראי כוח כול [פל]א̇י פלאיהם בכוח אלוהי
5 [עול]מים ומרוממים גבורות אלו[הי   ] מארבעת מוסדי רקיע
6 ה̇פלא ישמ̇[י]ע̇ו̇ מקול משא אלוהים[   ]קיר מברכים ומהללים לאלוהי
7 אלים המ◦[   ] מרומי[   ]◦ מלך הכבוד ◦[   ]למו̇סד̇י פלא
8 למשא מ[   ]◦י אלוהי[   ]ו̇כול אושיהם [   ]ק̇[ו]דש
9 קודשי[ם   ]◦ במש[א   כ]נפיהם מר̇[   ]◦ ר̇ו̇ש[
10 וקרא[ו   ]מעמדי[

Mus. Inv. 609
PAM 43.989*, 43.990*

Notes on Readings

Col. VIII is composed of frgs. 19–20. The middle part of frg. 20 has now broken off, and disintegrated into minute pieces.

L. 2]פ̇לא. The left part of the base of *pe* is visible. The upper arm of *lamed* is very faint.

L. 3]א̇. The stance of the trace at the beginning of the line corresponds most closely to that of the left leg of *ʾalep*.

L. 3]כ̇ול. The downstroke of the *kap* is still visible on the fragment.

L. 4 פל]א̇י. The trace at the edge is identical to the trace at the beginning of line 3.

L. 5 [עול]מים. The reconstruction [מרו]מים is slightly too long.

L. 7 המ◦[. At the edge, a downstroke with the right part of a head has been preserved. The stroke of the head is horizontal and not typical of *waw*. Cf., however, the similar *yod* (or *waw*?) of]ר̇י̇ח in line 4 of the next column. The whole edge is now darkened, and the presence of ink cannot be verified.

L. 7]◦. At the right edge of the fragment are the remains of what probably is the bottom left part of *samek* or *šin*. The base stroke that joins the vertical stroke is too diagonal for final *mem*. The almost diagonal stroke to the left is not ink, but a deep crack in the skin.

L. 7]למו̇סד̇י. The letter after *mem* may be either *waw* or *yod*. For a similar short *waw* cf. [ור]ו̇ממוהו in col. VII 10.

L. 8]◦י. Beneath *yod* appears the left end of the base of a letter.

L. 8]ק̇[ו]דש. The preliminary editions read קו̇דש̇, but there is no certain trace of *waw*.

L. 9 ◦[. The strokes are not entirely consistent with any letter. The downstroke seems to turn at the bottom to the left, giving the impression of a very short base. Above the downstroke there is a horizontal stroke slanting down to the left. It may be *šin* (the right arm breaking through the vertical, not slanting, left arm, with a hook at the top of the left arm) or perhaps *taw* with a very short base, and a hook at the top of the left leg. Unfortunately, this part of the fragment has since broken off, and nothing can be verified.

L. 9 במש]א. Some faint traces may be remnants of *ʾalep*.

L. 9 מר֯]. After *mem* only a slanting vertical stroke remains.

L. 9 ר֯וש] ◦[. Just before *reš* (or *dalet*) there are several traces, at least one of which is certainly ink. The reading]ק֯ד֯וש[(Puech) is not impossible. For the same distance between *qop* and *dalet*, cf. קדושים in IX 4.

TRANSLATION

2. [of] wonder, knowledge, and understand[ing] wonder[ful] vaults
3. [ ] with the light of lights, the splendour [ ] all the figures of the wonder[ful] spirits
4. [ ] gods, awesome in strength, all [ ] their wonderful [won]ders with the strength of the God of
5. [eter]nity, and exalting the powerful works of the Go[d of] from the four foundations of the wonderful vault.
6. They decl[a]re at the sound of the lifting of the gods [ ] blessing and praising the God of
7. the gods [ ] heights [ ] king of glory [ ] for the wonderful foundations
8. for the lifting [ ] gods [ ] and all their foundations [ ] holy of
9. holie[s] at the lifting [up] their [w]ings [ ] head [
10. and [they] call[ ] the stations of [

COMMENTS

One would expect the bottom of the column to overlap with the top of 4Q**405** 23 i. A possible overlap may be line 9 במש]א with 4Q**405** 23 i 1]מ֯שאי֯ה֯[ם. It is also possible that one or more of frgs. 36–41 of 4Q**405** should be placed above 4Q**405** 23 i. There are several graphic overlaps with these fragments. Thus, e.g. 4Q**405** 37 2 מע]מדיה[ם may overlap with line 10]מעמדי֯[, in which case 4Q**405** 37 1] מר]כבות might correspond to line 9 מר֯]. However, מר֯]כבות would not be expected after כ]נפיהם in line 9. Likewise, 4Q**405** 40 3 כ֯נ֯פיהם מ֯] corresponds to line 9, in which case 4Q**405** 40 2 ירומו וכ] should probably be placed after] אושיהם in line 8 (the lines of this column are longer than those of 4Q**405** 23 i, therefore וכ] is not likely to correspond to ו֯כול]). Yet, the lack of any correspondence with 4Q**405** 40 1 ◦◦ם ומ֯◦] at the end of line 7 or the beginning of line 8 would seem to invalidate the overlap.

L. 2 פ֯לא דעת ובינ֯]ה. פ֯לא[is probably the *nomen rectum* of a construct chain. דעת and בינה occur as a pair in 4Q**403** 1 ii 23 (ודעת בינתם); **405** 17 3 (רוחי דעת ובינה); **405** 23 ii 13 (ב]ד֯עת בינתו).

L. 2 רקיעי פל[א]. Since this column follows the text of 4Q**405** 20 ii–22, one may assume that רקיעי פל[א] are not the skies or heavens but the vaults on top of the cherubs. Cf. Ezek 1:22, 25, 26 and 4Q**405** 20 ii–22 8 ממעל רקיע הכרובים, 9 רקיע אור. For the plural form, cf. 4Q**405** 23 i 6, 7, and perhaps also *1 Enoch* 14:11 αἱ στέγαι.

L. 3 א֯[. Before א֯[there is room for six letters. One may reconstruct פל]א֯ preceded by a three-letter word, e.g. עשה פל]א֯]: 'he has made the wonderful vaults wonderful by light of lights'.

L. 3 באור אור֯ים. Elsewhere in the *Shirot* one encounters the phrases באור אורתם (4Q**403** 1 i 45) and אור אורותם (4Q**405** 5 4), a phrase which may be related to אורתום (אור) of 1QH XII 6, 23 (IV 6, 23); XXI 14 (XVIII 29). The אורים here may be 'stars', a reference to the spirits of light (Van der Woude), but it is also possible to understand אור אורים, literally 'light of lights', as the most excellent light. Even though the words at the beginning of the line are lost, it is tempting to connect the phrase באור אורים to the רקיעי פל[א] of line 2. *1 Enoch* 14:11 and 17 describe the glory and grandeur of the roofs and upper storeys of the heavenly buildings in terms of fire and light.

L. 3]כׄול תבנית רוחי פל[א]. The precise meaning of תבנית here is unclear. Possible translations are 'every form (or: figure) of wonderful spirits', or 'the whole structure of wonderful spirits'.

L. 4]אלוהים נוראי כוח. Cf. 4Q**403** 1 i 41–42 [זׄמ]רו / אלוׄ[הים נ]ׄורא כוח[and 4Q**405** 23 i 13 מורא מלך אלוׄהׄים נורא על [כו]ל אלוהים. In these texts the awesomeness refers to God; in 11Q**17** it refers to the gods (angels).

L. 4 פל[אׄי פלאיהם. In view of ומרוממים in line 5 one may perhaps reconstruct מהללים before פל[אׄי.

Ll. 4–5 אלוהי / [עול]מים. Neither here nor further on in line 5 גבורות אלו[ה]י is it clear whether אלוהים refers to God or to the angels.

Ll. 5–6 מארבעת מוסדי רקיע / הׄפלא. It is likely that the vault is here, too, that of the throne chariot, and that the foundations are to be associated with the four cherubs who bear the vault.

L. 6 ישמׄ[י]עׄוׄ מקול. The preposition מן is probably temporal: from the moment of the sound.

L. 6 משא אלוהים[. The use of the noun משא here is possibly a reference to the mention of נשא in Ezekiel 1 and 10. In Ezekiel it is used either in the *Nipʿal* 'to rise (from the ground)', or with wings as its subject. It is not clear whether משא has one of these meanings here, or has the clearly distinct sense of the lifting up of the voice, in this case, in praise.

L. 6]קיר. קיר, 'wall', may refer to the wall of the heavenly *debir* (cf. *1 Enoch* 14:10 καὶ οἱ τοῖχοι τοῦ οἴκου ὡς λιθόπλακες). This is consistent with the mention of other structures of the heavenly Temple (line 5 ארבעת מוסדי רקיע; line 8 אושיהם; cf. also 4Q**405** 23 i 7 שׄעׄריו and 8 פתחי). Yet, as Newsom points out, these architectonic structures are commonly plural, and one should therefore also consider the reconstruction]יׄקיר. Another understanding of the singular is to reconstruct קיר ל[קיר, 'the walls proclaim to one another'.

L. 7]o מלך הכבוד. Reconstruct e.g. קוד]שׄ מלך הכבוד as in col. X 5–6 (cf. NOTES ON READINGS) or ויסׄ[עׄ מלך הכבוד (cf. Ps 24:7, 9 ויבוא מלך הכבוד). The title מלך הכבוד is used five times in Ps 24:7-10. Cf. also 1QM XII 8 and XIX 1 (ומלך הכבוד אתנו); in the *Shirot*; 4Q**403** 1 i 31; ii 25; **405** 16 7.

L. 7]למוסׄדׄי. Read למוסׄדׄי (cf. the mention of the מוסדי רקיע in line 5) or למיסׄדׄי, a *Piʿel* participle of יסד; cf. 4Q**403** 1 i 24 ממיסדי דעת and 17 וׄבׄרׄך ליוסׄדׄ[י הוד] (the parallel text 4Q**405** 3 ii 7 reads וברך ליסודי ה[ו]ד). The broken character of the lines prevents a decision based on the context.

L. 8]oי אלוהי[. Only two construct chains from the preserved parts of the *Shirot* are consistent with]oי: מחני אלוהים and בדני אלוהים. Neither seems to fit here, however.

L. 8]וׄכול אושיהם. אוש is not attested in biblical Hebrew (but cf. אשׁ in biblical Aramaic). The word, which is used commonly in the texts from the Judaean Desert, e.g. 1QH[a] XI 13, 30, 35 (III 13, 30, 35), XV 9 (VII 9), 1QSb III 20, 1Q**36** 17 2, and in mishnaic Hebrew, may be an Aramaism (cf. Qimron, §600). Cf. *1 Enoch* 14:10 καὶ ἐδάφη χιονικά and 4QEn[c] ar (4Q**204**) VI 27 תלג אשׁׄ[וה]י.

L. 9 במש[א. Since the text of 4Q**405** 23 i should come close after the text of this column, one may consider the possibility that]מׄשאיהׄ[ם of 4Q**405** 23 i 1 corresponds to במש[א As the average number of letters per line of 4Q**405** 23 i is slightly less than in this column, the preserved text of 4Q**405** 23 i 2]בעומדם[ ]שבת[should (if there is a correspondence) be placed somewhat more to the right in line 10. However, the pertinent lines in both texts are too fragmentary for any certainty.

L. 9 כ]נפיהם מרׄ[. Reconstruct e.g. כ]נפיהם מרׄ[וממים (Newsom).

L. 9]o רׄוש[. רׄוש[may be reconstructed רׄוש[ם, 'their heads', but one cannot reconstruct על] רׄוש[ם or ע]לׄ רׄוש[ם.

Col. IX (Frgs. 21a–b, 22)

2 [ ]

3 [מנחו]ת רצון המ[ ]כ֯ול מעשיה[ם]

4 [ ]° לזבחי קדושים[ ]ר֯יח מנחותם °°°[

5 [ ]לם ור֯[י]ח נסכיהם למס[ ]ם֯ הטוהר ברוח קוד[ש]

6 [ ]עולמים ב֯[הוד ו]ה֯דר ל°[ ]° פלא ותבנית חשני

7 [פ]ת֯ילי תפ֯ארת[ ]רוקמה כמ֯[עשי אורג]ממולח טוהר צבעי

8 [ו]ה[ו]ד הדר °[ ]°°°[ ]מ֯ו֯ לצורות֯[ ]ש֯א֯ אפוד

9 [ ]מל֯א֯כ֯י֯[קו]ד֯ש֯ו֯

Mus. Inv. 614, 620
PAM 43.989*, 44.006*

NOTES ON READINGS

The column consists of frgs. 21a–b and 22. The comparison of the horizontal ruling lines shows that line 3 corresponds to line 3 of the previous columns.

L. 2 Examination of the fragment suggests that the traces on the loose fragment at the top of frg. 22 are not ink. The two folds are now flattened and the skin is covered with the same granular substance that covers lines 5–6 before the ruling line of the left margin.

L. 3 המ[. One to three letters between *mem* and the edge of the fragment have faded away.

L. 3]כ֯ול. The very left end of the base of a letter is visible beneath *waw*.

L. 4]°. Two dots, one just below the ceiling line, the other on the baseline, are probably the far left ends of the head and base of *bet* or *taw*.

L. 4 קדושים[. A hole appears after the final *mem*; the surface below the hole is abraded.

L. 4]ר֯יח. The middle letter is written somewhat awkwardly with a horizontal head. It may be either *waw* or *yod*.

L. 4 °°°[. The vertical strokes can be interpreted as *waw* with another letter such as *ḥet* or, with more difficulty, *he*. The third stroke, curved to the left, is clear on the fragment (on the edge), and can only belong to a final letter or a *qop*.

L. 5]לם. The vertical black stroke at the edge of the fragment is ink, and is consistent with the upper arm of *lamed*, but it is written very close to the remains of final *mem*.

L. 6 ל°[. The slanting vertical stroke and right part of the base after the *lamed* probably belong to *bet*, *kap*, *nun*, or *pe*. A *mem* is more difficult.

L. 6]°. The trace seems to be the left end of the crossbar or head of a letter.

L. 7 פ]ת֯ילי. Only the left part of *taw* remains; the reading of *nun* is also possible.

L. 7 תפ֯ארת. The *pe* is partially preserved on the edge of frg. 21b.

L. 8 ו]ה[ו]ד הדר. The supralinear *waw* and *dalet* are written above the *he* of ו]הדר.

L. 8]ooo[. Three traces of the tops of letters are visible. The first two are very close together, but cannot belong to the same letter. The last trace is diagonal. It can hardly belong to *ʾalep* (the second trace is too far away to be the tip of the right arm), but possibly is the *keraia* of the right arm of *ʿayin*.

L. 8 מׄוׄ[. If the trace before *waw* (or *yod*?) is ink, it is probably the diagonal of *mem*.

L. 8 שׄאׄ[. The skin is very damaged, and only a few short traces are visible. Close before אפוד there is a trace whose stance suggests the left leg of *ʾalep*. More to the right, two short strokes form a 'v'. This section has since broken away.

L. 9 מלאׄכׄיׄ][. It is hard to determine which traces are ink. After *lamed* there are two diagonal strokes which may belong to *ʾalep*, even though the stroke corresponding to the right arm is longer than average and has no *keraia*. Further to the left appears the base of a letter, followed by a downstroke with possibly a base.

L. 9 קו]דׄשׄוׄ. The top of a vertical stroke with a diagonal stroke to its right suggests *šin*. Before it, a 'T'-like shape is consistent with the upper right part of *dalet* or *he*. The downstroke after *šin* may be *waw* or *yod*.

TRANSLATION

2. [ ]
3. [ ] acceptable [offering]s [ ] all th[eir] works
4. [ ] for the sacrifices of the holy ones [ ] the aroma of their offerings [
5. [ ] their [ ] and the aroma of their libations for [ ] of purity with a spirit of holi[ness]
6. [ ] eternity, with [splendour and] majesty for [ ] wonderful, and the form of the breastplates of
7. [ ] beautiful [th]reads [ ] multicoloured like [woven] wo[rk] purely blended, the colours of
8. [splen]dour [and] majesty [ ] [ ] figures [ ] ephod
9. [ ] angels [ ] his [holi]ness

COMMENTS

L. 3 מנחו]ת רצון. The reconstruction is very plausible in view of the mention of other offerings (all plural) in the next two lines. Cf. also מנח]ת רצון, 'an acceptable offering', as in 1QS IX 5 כנדבת מנחת רצון and CD XI 21 ותפלת צדקם כמנחת רצון. As an alternative one may consider לעשו]ת רצון; cf. Ps 40:9; 103:21; 143:10; Ezra 1:11; 1QS IX 13 לעשות את רצון אל and 23 לעשות רצון בכול משלח כפים.

L. 3 המ][. Reconstruct perhaps המ]לך: offerings acceptable to the king. Cf. also the references to the king in the following passage and in 4Q**405** 23 ii 2, 3, 9, 11.

L. 5 לׄם[. The *mem* is probably the pronominal suffix. עו]לׄם is very unlikely; in the preserved parts of the *Shirot* only the plural עולמים is used.

L. 5 למס]. One may perhaps reconstruct למס]פר (Van der Woude).

L. 6 חשני. The plural, like אפׄודיהם in the following passage (4Q**405** 23 ii 5), may indicate that each of the seven angelic councils had its own priesthood, with one of the seven chief princes officiating as high priest.

L. 7 פ]תׄילי. Cf. פתיל תכלת referred to in Exodus 28 and 39, sections describing the חשן.

L. 7]רוקמה כמׄ]עשי אורג. Cf. 4Q**405** 23 ii 7 רוחות רׄוקמה כמעשי אורג, and 10 וכוׄל מחשביה ממולח טוהר חשב כׄמעשי אורׄג. With the exception of פ]תׄילי, all of the preserved words of this line appear in 4Q**405** 23 ii. Lines 7–9 describe the garments of the spirits.

L. 7 ממולח טוהר. Cf. 4Q**405** 23 ii 10 (see previous comment). On the expression, cf. COMMENTS on col. VI 4–5.

L. 7 צבעי. Cf. 4Q**405** 23 ii 8 (צבעי אור רוח קוׄדש), 9.

L. 8 שׄאׄ אפוד[. Reconstruct perhaps מ]שׄאׄ אפוד, 'the uplifting of the ephod'.

L. 9 קו]דׄשׄוׄ. Or e.g. מק]דׄשׄיׄ, as in 4Q**405** 23 ii 11–12 מקדשי מלכות כׄבודו.

Col. X (Frgs. 23–25)

2 [ ]מ֯ר֯ומי כ[בודו   כב]ו֯דו באׄ◦[
]מת

3 [ש]ל֯[ו]מיו במשפט֯י֯[   ]רחמיו ביקר ◦[
ת]עודותיו

4 [ו]כול ברכות שלומ[ו   כב]וד מעשיו ובאו[ר
]מ֯לה ובהדר

5 תשבוחותו בכול רקי[עי   ]ם אור וחושך ובדני[
]ק֯ודש מלך

6 הכבוד לכול מעשי אמת֯[ו   ]למלאכי הדעת בכול מל[
]הו משאי קודש

7 לכסאי כבודו ולהדום ר֯[גליו   מר]כבות הדרו ולדבירי קו[דשו
]◦ו֯ ולפתחי מבואי

8 [ ]◦ עם כול מוצאי [פנ]ות מבניתו ולכול ז[בולי
ו]להיכלי כבודו ולרקיעי

9 [ ]לכול ד◦[

Mus. Inv. 618
PAM 43.991*, 44.007*

Notes on Readings

The column consists of frgs. 23–25. Vertical ruling marking the right side of the column is clearly visible on frg. 23 between lines 5–7.

The width of the column measures 14.5–15 cm. Therefore, the gaps between the fragments in line 7 are 3.5–4 cm (the second gap being slightly smaller than the first) or *c.*25 letters.

L. 3 [ש]ל֯[ו]מיו. Two traces above the ceiling line are probably remnants of the upper arm of *lamed*. The trace to the right of *mem* is probably a blot of ink, not part of *waw*.

L. 3 במשפט֯י֯[. The photograph suggests that the left arm of *ṭet* touches the curved head of the letter. This impression is caused by an adhesion in the surface of the skin. Now that the fragment is cleaned, it is clear that the left arm, although a little more curved to the right than other examples of *ṭet* in this manuscript, does not join the curved head and is of a regular form.

L. 3]◦. The slanting downstroke curving into a base may belong to *bet*, *ṭet*, *kap*, *mem*, or *pe*.

L. 4]מ֯לה. The first letter may also be *pe*.

L. 6 אמתׄ[ו. The dark stroke along the edge of the fragment is probably the right leg of *taw* which has almost completely disappeared in the vertical scrap.

L. 6 למלאכי[. Not מלאכי[. The *lamed* before *mem* is completely certain, and has been almost completely preserved. Cf. also the dark dot (the bottom of the upper arm) joining the *mem*.

L. 7 ולהדׄום. In spite of an adherence which disturbs the shape of the *dalet*, this reading is more probable than *reš*.

L. 7 רׄ[גליו. A very faint downstroke is consistent with *reš*. The dark spot touching the ceiling line is not ink.

L. 7 °וׄ[. The skin here is somewhat abraded, making it difficult to identify traces before the downstroke. The joint between the downstroke and the horizontal head is more consistent with *waw* than with the left part of *he*. Nothing can be seen at this point on the fragment.

L. 8 °[. The proposal ךׄ[המל] (Newsom) is problematic. The short vertical stroke (*waw*?) is not consistent with final *kap*, there is no trace of the upper arm of *lamed*, and the gap is slightly too large for the reconstruction.

L. 8 מבניתו. In spite of the darkness of the skin all letters are clearly readable. The dark part has now broken away.

L. 9 ד°]. The trace after *dalet* seems to be a diagonal slanting down to the left, compatible with *ʿayin*.

Translation

2. [his] gl[orious] heights [ ] his [glo]ry in [ ] [ ]
3. his [re]pay[men]ts, in the judgements [ ] his compassion, with the honour [ ] his [tes]timonies
4. [and] all the blessings of [his] peace [the glo]ry of his works and with the lig[ht] and with the splendour
5. of his praise in all the vau[lts of] light and darkness, and figures [ ] the holiness of the king
6. of glory towards all the works of [his] truth [ ] for the angels of knowledge, in all [ ] holy upliftings
7. for the thrones of his glory and for the footstool of [his] f[eet cha]riots of his majesty, and for [his] ho[ly] *debirs* [ ] his [ ] and for the entry portals
8. [ ] with all its exits of [cor]ners of its structure, and for all d[wellings of and] for the temples of his glory, and for the vaults of
9. [ ] for all [

Comments

L. 2 מׄרׄומי כ[בודו. The expression probably refers to the heavens.

L. 2 כב[ׄודו באׄ°]. The syntax of the first lines is not clear. In lines 2–3, the words beginning with -ב may be attributes to the preceding noun phrases, but in line 4, ובאו[ר and ובהדר clearly begin new clauses. One may reconstruct באׄו[ר (as in line 4) or באמׄ[ת.

L. 2 מת[. The word is possibly the *nomen regens* of a construct chain. One may perhaps read א]מת, ‘the truth’ (of his repayments).

L. 3 ת]עודותיו. תעודה may simply mean ‘testimony’, but in MasShirShabb i 3, כול תעודות עולמים seem to be the things which were eternally appointed or preordained.

L. 4 ברכות שלומ[ו. Blessing and peace are associated with one another elsewhere in texts from the Judaean Desert (e.g. 1QM I 9; XVII 7), and the words שלום עולמים are the final words of the blessings of the chief princes in the sixth song (4Q**405** 1 i 26). Yet, the reconstruction ברכות שלומ[יו (cf. line 3) may also be possible.

L. 4 מׄלה[. Or פׄלה[. It is not clear which word can be reconstructed to make sense in the (broken) context. In the surrounding lines, the words before the equivalents of ובהדר have a masculine pronominal suffix. The structure of this clause is apparently different. Perhaps the text read א]פׄלה with or without a preceding לוא or בלוא. Cf. the preceding באו]ר and אור וחושך in the next line.

Ll. 4–5 ובהדר / תשבוחותו. In mishnaic Hebrew (it is not attested in biblical Hebrew), the second word is spelled תושבחות, but in texts from the Judaean Desert one encounters both תשבוחות and תושבחות. Cf. the similar phrase in 4Q**403** 1 i 32 בהדר תשבחות and 4QBerakhot[a] (4Q**286**) I i 5 הדר תשבוחות.

L. 5 בכול רקי]עי. Since there are no references in this part of the text to the *debir* or the chariot throne, the רקי]עי are probably the heavens, not the vaults of the throne.

L. 5 אור וחושך. This is the only instance of חושך in the preserved parts of the *Shirot*. The phrase אור וחושך probably has a cosmological, not a dualistic, meaning (cf. the preceding רקי]עי).

L. 6 מעשי אמתׄו[. Cf. e.g. 1QS I 19 (object of מברכים); X 17 (אמת כול מעשיו); 1QM XIII 1, 2 (in both lines object of ברך), 9; XIV 12; 1QH[a] XI 30 (I 30).

L. 6 בכול מל[. Reconstruct e.g. בכול מל]אכותם, 'in all their occupations', or בכול מל]כות כבודו, 'in all His glorious realm' as in 4Q**405** 23 ii 11–12 (the section preceding 11Q**17** X).

L. 6]הו משאי קודש. The first word is probably a verb of praise, e.g. יהללו]הו, ישבחו]הו, or ירוממו]הו. In that case, משאי קודש specifies the manner of praise.

Ll. 7–9 The preserved parts of the lines consist of a series of noun phrases, each of which is introduced by -ל. The sequence of the nouns suggests a movement from that which is nearest to God (the thrones) to the objects further away. The function of the *lamed*s is not clear; perhaps it specifies the grounds for which praise is offered.

L. 7 לכסאי כבודו. The phrase כסא כבוד occurs in Jer 14:21 (כסא כבודך) and 17:12 (כסא כבוד מרום); cf. also Matt 19:28 and 25:31 ἐπὶ θρόνου δόξης αὐτοῦ. It is preferable to understand the form כסאי (cf. also 4Q**405** 23 i 3 כסאיׄכׄהׄ כבודׄ מלכותו) as a masc. construct pl. of כסא, rather than as a special spelling of the singular. A fem. pl. form is used in Biblical Hebrew (כסאות) and Mishnaic Hebrew (כסיות), but the *Shirot* often use masc. pl. forms where Biblical Hebrew uses fem. forms. In view of the following singular הדׄום, one may wonder why כסאי is plural.

L. 7 ולהדום רׄ]גליו. Cf. also 4Q**403** 1 ii 2, and the plural in 4QBerakhot[a] (4Q**286**) I i 1 רגלי כׄבׄודכה והדומי. In the Hebrew Bible, הדם רגליו may refer to the Temple, or more generally to Zion, as the place where God rests (Ps 99:5; 132:7; Lam 2:1; 1 Chr 28:2).

Ll. 7–8 ולפתחי מבואי / [ ]◦. Cf. the references to the portals of entrance in 4Q**405** 23 i 8, 9. The word at the beginning of line 8 may be a synonym of כבודו, קודשו, הדרו, etc.

L. 8 מוצאי [. Cf. 4Q**405** 23 i 8 מוצאי מלׄאכי קודש.

L. 8 פנ]ות מבניתו. Cf. 4Q**403** 1 i 41. Or, alternatively, קיר]ות מבניתו.

L. 8 ולכול ז]בולי. Cf. the use of זבול in 4Q**403** 1 i 41.

L. 8 ו]להיכלי כבודו. היכל is used once more in the preserved text of the *Shirot*, in 4Q**400** 1 i 13 בהיכלי מלך.

L. 8 ולרקיעי. In view of the movement from the throne to items further away, one should understand רקיעי as the heavens.

Unidentified Fragments

Frg. 26a

1]י כׄבוד חׄ[

2]שערי [

Mus. Inv. 1032
PAM 43.448*
IAA 563759*

NOTES ON READINGS

The fragment shown in PAM 43.448, and transcribed by Newsom as frg. s, probably consists of two fragments, partially superimposed. The upper fragment was rediscovered in Box 1032, whereas none of the other 'lost' fragments of PAM 43.448 could be located in the Rockefeller Museum.

L. 1]ח̊. The first downstroke is somewhat diagonal, but the proximity of the next downstroke suggests *he* or *ḥet*.

L. 2]שערי̇. On the basis of PAM 43.448, Tigchelaar, 'Reconstructing 11Q17', suggested the reading ב̇ד̊]בי[רי, and the placement of the fragment in col. IV 12–14, but examination of the recovered fragment and IAA 563759 conclusively reveal the impossibility of that reading, and the unlikelihood of the placement.

TRANSLATION

1.] glory [
2.] gates of [

Frg. 26b

1]י מלך כו[ל
2]ת̊ ∘∘ת̊ אל̇[
3]∘∘∘[

PAM 43.448

NOTES ON READINGS

If frgs. 26a and 26b can indeed be placed together, one should read]שערי מלך כו[ל.

TRANSLATION

1.] king of al[l
2.] [

Frg. 27

]◦◦[1

]◦◦[2

]◦ד֯ני[3

PAM 43.448

NOTES ON READINGS

Newsom read]◦ט[, but if the fragment is rotated as positioned on PAM 43.448, the traces can be read differently. There is a slight possibility that the fragment can be placed below frg. 6, in col. IV reading ב֯א֯]למי,]ם֯[חי]י֯, and]כ]ו֯ד֯ני[(col. IV 12–14).

Frg. 28

ק] 1

ק] 2

משפ]ט 3

ברנות כול֯] 4

כבודו קול ה֯] 5

Mus. Inv. 565
PAM 43.448, 43.992*

NOTES ON READINGS

Frg. 28 shows the right margin of a column. The photograph shows an impurity on the surface, now removed, and not a hole. In spite of the margin, the placement of the fragment is uncertain.

L. 4 כול֯]. The small trace at the far left cannot belong to *waw*, but is consistent with the extreme right part of *lamed*.

L. 5 ה֯]. The distance between the vertical stroke and the dot is consistent with the distance between the legs of *he*. Another possibility is ו֯◦].

TRANSLATION

1. [
2. [

3. judge[ment
4. with the cries of all [
5. his glory, the sound of [

COMMENTS

L. 3 משפ]ט. A form of משפט, sing. or pl., with or without a suffix, is very likely.

Frg. 29

מ]לׄךׄ[1

] רוחו֯ת֯ [2

]פׄלאיהם כולׄ[3

]קודש קודש]ים 3a

]קודש קודׄ]שים 4

קו]ד֯שי]ם 5

Mus. Inv. 565
PAM 43.448, 43.992*

NOTES ON READINGS

From a material point of view, frg. 29 should probably be placed in lines 11–15 (or 12–16) of col. V below frg. 10, or col. VI below frg. 14 (cf. the similar position of the fragments in col. VII).

L. 2 רוחו֯ת֯. After the *ḥet*, the bottom parts of two vertical strokes are visible. The first might very well belong to *waw* or *yod*, but because of the absence of any trace of the left part of *taw* the reading is uncertain.

L. 3a The addition is intralinear, not supralinear.

L. 5 קו]ד֯שי]ם. The letters are written in a dark area of the fragment. The skin in front of the possible *dalet* shows no traces.

TRANSLATION

1. k]ing[
2.] spirits [
3.] their wondrous [ ] all [
3a.] holy of hol[ies
4.] holy of holi[es
5. ho]lie[s

COMMENTS

If the fragment belonged to the bottom half of col. V, there may be overlaps with 4Q**405** 18 and/or 20 i; cf. 4Q**405** 18 1]ר֯ו֯חות[; 3 קו]דשים; and 20 i 2 פל]א֯יהם. Yet, one would rather expect that the fragment corresponded with the text some lines above those fragments from 4Q**405**.

Frg. 30

1]*vacat*

2]מו°°° משבעה

3]°בר מ֯שב֯יעי °מ֯[

4]מלך כול קדושי ע֯ד

5 ת]הלי ברכות כבוד ה֯[

6]ב֯שי °°°°° שבע֯[

PAM 43.448*

NOTES ON READINGS

The fragment can no longer be located and the quality of PAM 43.448 is rather poor. A vertical line at the left side of the fragment in lines 1–2 might be the vertical ruling of the left margin. The photograph suggests that the visible fragment is the top layer of a wad of several fragments.

L. 2]מו°°°. The letter after *mem* may be *waw* or *yod*. The next letter looks most like *ṭet*; *samek* is possible, but more difficult. The following letter looks most like *he*. The final letter might be *reš*. Read e.g. מוטה֯ר֯, but מוס֯ד֯י֯ cannot be excluded.

L. 2 משבעה. Newsom reads the first letter as *bet*, but *mem* is virtually certain. The left diagonal is faint but clear.

L. 3 מ֯שב֯יעי. Both the first and third letters could be either *bet* or *mem*.

L. 3 °מ֯[. The first letter may be *bet*, *kap*, or *pe*. Read ב֯מ֯[ה, 'among them'?

L. 6 °°°°°. The last letters may be חיו, חו, or ני.

TRANSLATION

1.]*vacat*
2. [ ] from seven
3. [ ] from the seventh (?) [
4. k]ing of all the eternally holy ones
5. ps]alms of blessing of the glory of [
6. [ ] seven

COMMENTS

Speculatively, the fragment may overlap with 4Q**403** 1 ii 28–32, in which case it should belong to the bottom of col. II. This assumption is attractive, but there are two problems. Firstly, one must assume a variant text: 4Q**405** 11 does not really overlap. Secondly, the fragments which were under frg. 30 in the wad, would, necessarily, come from preceding columns. A placement at the left side of col. V, approximately beginning at line 11 or 12, is difficult but not impossible.

L. 3]◦בר. One may perhaps read ת]ג֯בר and the next word as בשביעי. In that case, this may be a variant reading of 4Q**405** 11 5 (4Q**403** 1 ii 28).

L. 4 קדושי עד֯. עד is only attested in the first part of the *Shirot*.

L. 5 ת]הלי ברכות כבוד. Cf. 4Q**403** 1 ii 32 תהלת] ב֯רך ב֯[.

Frg. 31

]◦◦[1

]◦◦◦◦[2

PAM 43.448*

NOTES ON READINGS

Frg. 31 can no longer be located. None of the traces can be deciphered. The neat row of traces in line 2 cannot be random, and suggests a line of text. The faint traces closer to the top of the fragment are exactly at the place where a preceding line should have appeared.

Frg. 32

]ח֯מישי[1

]◦ת קודשו פ◦◦ת֯ ד◦[2

]מלך ל֯[3

Mus. Inv. 621B
PAM 44.117*

NOTES ON READINGS

L. 2]◦ת. The trace before *taw* is consistent with e.g. *dalet*, *waw*, or *reš*.

L. 2 פ°°ת֯. Between *pe* and the last letter are traces of two or three letters. The trace before the possible *taw* may be *waw* or the left leg of another letter.

L. 2 ד°[. After *dalet* there is only a trace at the baseline.

L. 3 ל֯[. Apart from the upper arm, there is a trace more to the right. It could be the extreme right part of *lamed*, but that would imply a rather large *lamed*, especially when compared to the *lamed* in the previous word. Otherwise, it might be the tip of the right arm of *ʾalep*, the letters being written in a small and compact script.

TRANSLATION

1.] fifth [
2.] of his holiness, [
3.] king [

COMMENTS

L. 1]ח֯מישי. One would expect the ordinal number to refer to one of the deputy princes of the eighth song. However, the other words of the fragment do not correspond with the words used in the sections regarding the fifth prince. Cf. 4Q**405** 11 4; 13 2–4 and the related sections of the sixth song, 4Q**403** 1 i 3–4, 18–20.

L. 2 פ°°ת֯ ד°[. Read, perhaps, פ֯ר֯וׄכ֯ת֯ דב֯[יר or פ֯ר֯כ֯וׄת֯ דב֯[יר as in 4Q**405** 15 ii–16 3–4.

Frg. 33

]א֯° צׄ°°[1

Mus. Inv. 609
PAM 43.990

NOTES ON READINGS

PAM 43.990 shows that frg. 18 consisted of at least two superimposed layers. Frg. 18 is now reduced to ashes. Frg. 33 comes from the lower layer, although the remains do not seem to conform with the text expected from the layer beneath frg. 18.

L. 1]צׄ°°[. At first sight, the traces seem to indicate צ֯ח֯ד֯[, or, with more difficulty, צ֯ח֯ך֯[(it is not certain that *ṣade* was the first letter of the word, as there are some dark blots before the letter). Yet, the photograph suggests a horizontal stroke at the bottom of the trace which seems to be a left leg of *ḥet*, and possibly צׄו֯ם֯ or צׄי֯ם֯ should be read. Newsom's reading מתוך or בתוך does not match the traces.

Frg. 34

]דׄ֯ך֯ י֯כ֯ב֯[1

Mus. Inv. 565
PAM 43.992

NOTES ON READINGS

Frg. 34 perhaps represents a superimposed layer from the fragments appearing in PAM 43.992 to the left of frg. 10.

L. 1]יׄכׄבׄ. The first letter looks like *pe*, but the base stroke need not be ink.

Frg. 35

]משמע רנהׄ[1

]היו כול ◦[2

Mus. Inv. 614
PAM 42.177, 44.006*

NOTES ON READINGS

The strokes of the letters are thicker than in the other fragments, and perhaps the ticks of *waw* and *yod* are also somewhat different. However, the small size of the letters, the intralinear distance, and the vocabulary of line 1 indicate that the fragment belongs to **11Q17**. The use of a different pen with a thicker nib would explain the differences and would suggest that frg. 35 stems from an earlier part of the manuscript.

TRANSLATION

1.] hearing of a song [
2.] all/everything [

COMMENTS

L. 1]משמע רנהׄ[. The expression is not attested in the preserved fragments of the *Shirot*, but cf. 4Q**401** 14 ii 3]קול רנוׄתׄ[; 4Q**405** 23 i 8 בקול רנה; 4Q**403** 1 ii 12 למשמע אלוהים.

L. 2]היו כול ◦[. Cf. 4Q**402** 4 12 נהיו כול [הוי; MasShirShabb i 1 נהיו כל הוי; 4Q**403** 1 i 35 יהיׄוׄ כׄ[ול אלי. Overlap with 4Q**402** 4 is not impossible, but it is difficult to see where line 1 might fit in 4Q**402** 4.

Frg. 36

]◦[1

כ]בׄוד [2

]ו תש◦[3

Mus. Inv. 1032
IAA 563769

NOTES ON READINGS

L. 1]◦[. The preserved trace is the tail of a letter, e.g. *qop* or final *kap*.

TRANSLATION

1.] [
2. gl]ory [
3.] [

Frg. 37

]מלאכ[י קודש 1

ד]מות כפ֯[2

Mus. Inv. 1034
IAA 563771

NOTES ON READINGS

This very brittle fragment, which was found intact in Box 1034, has broken into several pieces. The transcription is partially based on notes made in the Rockefeller Museum in November 1996, when the fragment was still intact.

L. 1]מלאכ[י קודש. Before the fragment was broken,]מלאכי קו֯[was clearly visible to the naked eye.

L. 2 כפ֯[. Or, with more difficulty, כנ֯[.

TRANSLATION

1.] angel[s of holiness
2. the like]ness of [

COMMENTS

L. 2 כפ֯[. Reconstruct perhaps כפ֯[יהם or כנ֯[פיהם.

Uninscribed Fragments

Frgs. 38–41

Mus. Inv. 1030
IAA 525613

NOTES ON READINGS

The joined fragments are ruled with the same red ink, and with the same pattern of horizontal ruling as col. X. One of the fragments preserves two revolutions, the width of each being 2–2.1 cm. These fragments stem either from the blank handle sheet, or, less plausibly in view of the position at the very end of the scroll, from the unwritten section of a final col. XI.

Frg. 42

Mus. Inv. 1032
IAA 563769

NOTES ON READINGS

The fragment preserves the intercolumnar margin and shows one vertical and two horizontal rulings.

18. 11QNew Jerusalem ar

(PLATES XXXV–XL, LIII)

Previous dicussion: B. Jongeling, 'Publication provisoire d'un fragment provenant de la grotte 11 de Qumrân (11QJérNouv AR)', *JSJ* 1 (1970) 58–64; B. Jongeling, 'Note additionelle', *JSJ* 1 (1970) 185–6; J. P. M. van der Ploeg, 'Les manuscrits de la Grotte XI de Qumrân', *RevQ* 12/45 (1985) 13–14; K. Beyer, *Die aramäischen Texte vom Toten Meer* (Göttingen: Vandenhoeck & Ruprecht, 1984) 222; F. García Martínez, 'The Last Surviving Columns of 11QNJ', *The Scriptures and the Scrolls: Studies in Honour of A. S. van der Woude on the Occasion of his 65th Birthday*, eds. F. García Martínez, A. Hilhorst, C. J. Labuschagne (VTSup 49; Leiden: E. J. Brill, 1992) 178–92, plates 3–9; M. Kister, 'Notes on Some New Texts from Qumran', *JJS* 44 (1993) 282–6; K. Beyer, *Die aramäischen Texte vom Toten Meer: Ergänzungsband* (Göttingen: Vandenhoeck & Ruprecht, 1994) 99–104; F. García Martínez, 'More Fragments of 11QNJ', Proceedings of the 1996 International Conference on the Dead Sea Scrolls, eds. D. W. Parry and E. Ulrich (Leiden: E. J. Brill, 1997).

Physical Description

AT the time of its discovery, 11QNJ was a partially petrified scroll which could not be unwrapped.[1] On the advice of H. J. Plenderleith, a non-petrified protuberance was cut loose, from which all the recovered fragments are reported to originate.

The recovered elements of the scroll are the inscribed fragments which van der Ploeg managed to secure, as well as those which were later separated from the large wad shown in PAM 43.993. Most fragments are dark and brittle on the left and bottom sides, and to a lesser extent also on the right edge. In quite a few cases, remains visible in the photographs no longer appear on the plates. The fragments are light brown in colour, becoming darker toward the edges. The left and bottom edges of the fragments, in particular, are a very dark brown with a shiny, orange tone. Frgs. 30–33 have a somewhat darker colour than the others, and the skin has a different grain. The skin appears to be of an average thickness, *c.*0.3–0.4 mm. Horizontal and vertical dry lines are visible, more clearly so in some lines and fragments than in others.

The petrified pieces of the scroll are preserved in boxes. The pieces displaying special characteristics such as writing or cloth have been photographed in PAM 43.993 and are preserved in Box 578A. Other boxes also contain petrified material which, at

---

[1] Cf. the preliminary report in J. P. M. van der Ploeg, 'Les manuscrits de la Grotte XI de Qumrân'. The following section deals with the physical aspects of the scroll:

'Tout un rouleau du même ouvrage a été retrouvé dans 11Q. Malheureusement il était presque entièrement pétrifié et dur comme la pierre, à tel point qu'il était bien évident qu'il serait impossible de le dérouler ou de le lire. Pendant une de mes trois périodes d'études au Musée Palestinien, le Dr H. J. Plenderleith était là, le même spécialiste qui avait été consulté sur des questions techniques regardant les rouleaux de 1Q et je l'ai consulté sur l'état du rouleau et sur la possibilité éventuelle de le dérouler. Il était d'avis que la seule chose à faire était de découper une protubérance non pétrifiée du rouleau et de considérer tout le reste comme perdu. J'ai estimé pouvoir suivre ce conseil et ainsi j'ai obtenu 26 fragments, correspondant à 25 circonvolutions du rouleau et quelques fragments plus petits. Les plus grands mesurent environ 6x8 cm; un fragment est large de 7,5 cm.

Sur les grands fragments environ quatre mots par ligne ont été conservés; distance des lignes: 7 mm; hauteur moyenne des lettres: 3 mm. Les plus grands fragments ont appartenu à la première partie du rouleau'.

first sight, could be mistaken for stones; four such pieces in Box 578A merit a description. The upper right section of the large wad shown in PAM 43.993 (pl XXXV, frg. 3) is completely petrified and was detached from the rest of the wad. Its right side, with a maximum thickness of 4.3–4.4 mm is completely darkened and has a shiny appearance, similar to that of the left side of some fragments. The left side becomes thinner, literally step by step, revealing many revolutions of the scroll. Writing is preserved on the top and third layers. Two different layers are seen on the surface of the small wad in PAM 43.993 (pl. XXXV, frgs. 1 + 2). Attempts have been made to remove the upper layer, but this petrified wad is very wrinkled and only a few of the pieces could be removed (pl. XXXV, frgs. 1 + 2; pl. XL). This wad has a maximum thickness of 3 mm, and five or six layers can be discerned. Two other pieces preserve part of the now brown cloth in which the scroll was wrapped. The larger petrified piece clearly shows two layers of the enveloping cloth, and together they measure 3 mm in thickness. The smaller piece has parts of cloth attached only to the verso (both pieces appear on plate XL).

The contents of Box 1030, four clean pieces of cloth, one of which is wool, are also possible remnants of the scroll. The cloth pieces are possibly parts of the enveloping wrapper which had partially petrified and adhered to the scroll.[2]

Measurements

No measurements of the unopened scroll have been reported, but according to PAM 43.981 (cf. pl. LIII), it had a height of 10.6 cm. The width of the middle part of the scroll, as shown in this photograph, varies between 3.5 and 3.8 cm.

The height of the largest unbroken fragment (frg. 12) is 8.25 cm, but the joined fragment (frg. 13) has a height of 8.55 cm. The large wad of PAM 43.993, and frgs. 10 and 11, are slightly more than 8 cm in height. Frg. 14 (join of two pieces) measures 7 cm, and all other fragments are between 5 and 6.5 cm. The largest width is attested in frg. 18, *c.*8.8 cm. These figures, compared to those of the unopened scroll, indicate that the report that only a protuberance was loosened, the rest being lost, is not entirely accurate.

Frgs. 6–31 preserve the upper margin, but comparison of the fragments shows that the height of the first line was not the same on all the sheets. Owing to the poor legibility of the ruling lines it is not clear in all cases that the first written line is, in fact, the top line. The largest top margin, 2.4–2.5 cm, is attested in frg. 10, which seems to preserve the top protuberance visible in the photograph of the unopened scroll. It is possible that this fragment preserves the complete top margin. The large top margin of frg. 12 (2–2.1 cm) may include a blank first line.

Intercolumnar margins are preserved on frgs. 10 (probably 2 cm), 12 (1.5–1.7 cm), 14 (*c.*1.9 cm), 16 (1.5–2 cm), 17 (*c.*1.5 cm), 23 (*c.*1.5 cm) and 31 (1.5 cm). The distance between the left ruling and the end of the sheet in frg. 21 is 1.5 cm.

[2] M. Belis, who is currently examining cave 11 materials in the Rockefeller Museum, observed that one of the four pieces is wool. Besides the few pieces of cloth preserved in the museum boxes together with tiny fragments and petrified scroll pieces, many other larger cloths from cave 11 have been stored elsewhere in the museum.

The average space between lines varies between 0.72 and 0.76 cm, and the average height of the letters varies from 0.32–0.35 cm. These measurements are considerably smaller in frgs. 33, 35, 37, and the bottom part of frg. 32 (line spacing is 0.5–0.6 cm and height of letters is 0.25–0.3 cm).

Columns

The exact order of the fragments as they were unrolled from the scroll has unfortunately not been reported. In the preliminary report, van der Ploeg mentions twenty-six fragments from twenty-five revolutions. These figures possibly refer to the twenty-two large fragments in PAM 43.994–44.002, the two fragments in PAM 44.009 which can be joined, and the two large fragments of PAM 43.993. However, the fragments in PAM 43.993 are the upper layers of wads of fragments, and the twenty-five revolutions cannot be subsequent. Mus. Inv. 578, of which PAM 43.993 was taken, was not numbered with a tag, as were the other plates. It seems that the wads, together with smaller uninscribed fragments, were separated from the loosened fragments. Therefore, it is not evident from which part of the scroll these wads came, although it is likely that they belonged to the exterior section.

The arrangement of the fragments on the plates cannot be taken as a precise indication of their original order. In one case the placement on the plates is almost certainly incorrect. The two broken fragments in PAM 43.977 display a superficial resemblance, but a comparison of their shapes with those of other fragments clearly shows that they did not belong to subsequent revolutions, and that the correct fragment (frg. 21) was misplaced.[3] It is possible that at least some of the fragments were arranged by shape, rather than according to their original order.

The combined evidence of the approximate shape of the scroll (a diameter of *c.*3.7 cm, according to the photograph) and the order of the fragments in the photographs, presents severe difficulties. The calculation that the exterior revolutions of the scroll measured 11–12 cm is not compatible with the margins and the contents of the fragments, unless one allows for very irregular column widths. An alternative ordering of the fragments is difficult, since many fragments have more or less the same patterns of damage. The textual evidence rarely helps with the placing of two or more fragments in one column. It is plausible that at the exterior of the scroll the column width measured less than the width of one revolution, so that in most cases a fragment comprised one column.

Since reconstruction of the scroll, or the rearrangement of the fragments in a more plausible order, has been impossible, the presentation of the fragments below agrees, with small exceptions, with the order of the fragments on the museum plates.[4]

---

[3] In a private communication, van der Ploeg allowed for the possibility that one fragment was misplaced.

[4] The PAM photographs display the fragments in the following order (from left to right): PAM 43.994: frgs. 11, 10; PAM 43.995: frgs. 13, 12; PAM 43.996: frgs. 14, 15; PAM 43.997: frgs. 16, 21; PAM 43.998: frgs. 17, 18; PAM 43.999: frgs. 19, 20; PAM 44.000: frgs. 22, 23, 24; PAM 44.001: frgs. 25, 26, 27; PAM 44.002: frgs. 28, 29, 30, 31; PAM 44.009: frg. 32 and other fragments. The present display on the museum plates is the same, wth one exception: Mus. Inv. 570 displays frgs. 27, 26, 25 from left to right. On Mus. Inv. 578, frgs. 6, 7, 8, and 9 and labelled 4, 3, 2, and 1.

The shape of the small wad of PAM 43.993 (frgs. 1 and 2) is unlike that of the other fragments. It is plausible that these fragments came from the exterior of the scroll, and there is a possibility that frg. 3 can be joined to the right-hand side of the wad. Frgs. 3–9 all stem from the large wad visible in PAM 43.993. The increasing size of the hole in the fragments allows the order to be determined.

Frgs. 10–13 and the large wad (frgs. 3–9) have approximately the same shape, but neither the placement of the fragments in relation to the wad, nor the order of the fragments can be established. Since frgs. 10–13 display no trace of the hole of frgs. 4 and 6–9, one should place them further inside than frg. 9. Contrary to what the placement of the fragments on the museum plates suggests, frg. 10 comes from one revolution interior to frg. 9. Frgs. 11–13 cannot be placed in a logical order, suggesting perhaps that they may actually represent three successive revolutions.

Frgs. 16 and 21 are placed together on Mus. Inv. 572, but frg. 16 corresponds closely to frg. 17, and frg. 21 to frgs. 20 and 22. Apart from the different placement of both fragments of Mus. Inv. 572, the order of frgs. 14–31 corresponds to that in PAM 43.994–44.002, even though this may not be precisely the original order.

Contents

The overlap with 2QNew Jerusalem (2Q**24**) in style and vocabulary, as well as content, indicates that the manuscript is a copy of the composition called *New Jerusalem*, copies of which have been found in caves 1 (1Q**32**), 2 (2Q**24**), 4 (4Q**554** and **555**), and 5 (5Q**15**). The combination of the preserved sections shows that the work describes the New Jerusalem and the future Temple, as well as the rituals and offerings which are to be performed in the Temple complex. The text seems to adopt the theme of Ezekiel 40–48: a guiding angel shows the author the city and the Temple, including their architectonic features and measurements. The beginning of the work is set at the outer edge of the city, and it appears that the tour proceeds towards the innermost part of the Temple complex. The remnants of the last preserved column of 4Q**554** refer to an eschatological conflict ('at the end of all'), in which the hostile nations ('Kittim', 'with them Adom and Moab and the sons of Ammon', 'Babel') 'shall do evil to your descendants until the moment that . . . ', but the place and the function of this section within the work are not clear.

It appears that the preserved section of the scroll, or at least from frg. 7 on, deals exclusively with the description of the Temple and the offerings. Owing to the fragmentary state of the scroll and the problems of reconstruction, it is difficult to determine the direction of the 'tour' through the Temple. However, the general direction seems to be from the outside (the wall of the inner court in frg. 6?) towards the inside (the 'throne', probably in the *debir*, in frgs. 31 ii and 32).

An explanation for the almost complete lack of overlap with the other copies of *New Jerusalem* must be based on an understanding of the physical aspects of the scroll. In the *editio princeps*, it was suggested that the exterior of the scroll contained the end of the composition, implying that the beginning of the composition should be sought in the unrecovered interior of the scroll. That, however, is questionable, not only in view of the presumed direction of the 'tour' from the outside to the inside of the Temple, but also because it appears impossible to fit the text of the copies from caves 4 and 5 in the interior of the scroll. Later, the editors considered the possibility that the scroll contained only part of the composition, namely the section dealing with the Temple. However, the evidence of the upper right petrified section of the large wad shows that at least 3 mm of the exterior of the scroll have not been recovered, which implies that at least eight, but probably more, revolutions each 11–12 cm in width, from the beginning of the scroll have been lost.

Palaeography

The fragments display the early Herodian type of script (last part of the first century BCE and the beginning of the first century CE). Their script corresponds to the type termed by Cross as 'round semiformal'. Most letters are virtually identical to those of 4QMMT^{d} (4Q**397**).[5] The most conspicuous differences between 11Q**18** and 4QMMT^{d} are the form of *bet* and the clear distinction between *waw* and *yod*. No final form of *pe* occurs in the fragments. The medial form of *ṣade* is used in final position.

ʾAlep has different shapes in 11Q**18**. The left stroke starts either at or below the top of the diagonal. The stance of the left stroke varies from almost vertical to diagonal. The right stroke descends to the middle of the diagonal or to the bottom right tip.

Bet is written in varying ways. Cases of round and square shoulders indicate that the headstroke and the downstroke were written in one movement. However, many examples show that the scribe, after having drawn the headstroke from left to right, turned back to the left in order to draw the downstroke. The second manner of drawing often results in a concave downstroke. The long base often slants downwards towards the left. In most cases the base extends slightly beyond the meeting point with the downstroke.

Waw has, in most cases, a short and slightly slanting straight hook. Contrary to *yod*, the hook is not written with a triangular loop.

Ṭet is written as in 4QMMT^{d}, but the slant of the base tends to be greater.

Yod has a long hook written with a triangular loop.

Kap is longer than *bet* and its top is considerably narrower. The base stroke which often extends beyond the imaginary baseline sometimes has a slight wave.

Lamed has a curved body as in 4QMMT^{d}, but, incidentally, angular forms with a horizontal and a diagonal stroke occur.

Mem in medial position has the same variants as in 4QMMT^{d}. The final form resembles 4QMMT^{d}, but the vertical stroke on top of the head is in some cases clearly a separate stroke, and not part of the left downstroke.

Samek is distinct from 4QMMT^{d}, as the right downstroke almost immediately starts to curve to the bottom left.

ʿAyin is similar to 4QMMT^{d}, but the top of the left stroke is bent towards the right.

Taw is written as in 4QMMT^{d}, except that the base stroke is often separate, extending to the right beyond the left downstroke.

---

[5] Cf. the description of the script of 4Q**397** by A. Yardeni in E. Qimron and J. Strugnell, *DJD* X (Oxford: Clarendon, 1994) 21–5. In fact, 4Q**397** is more similar to 11Q**18** than to 4Q**27** (4QNum^{b}), on the basis of which Cross described the round semi-formal Herodian hand.

Orthography and Morphology

The *ʾalep* is used as the vowel letter for final [*ā*] in all cases, except for the feminine ending. In the case of numerals with a feminine ending, *ʾalep* is sometimes used instead of *he*; cf. שבעא בשבעא and תלתא in frg.17 ii 1–2 and שבעא in frg.18 2 (but שבעה in line 1). The *ʾalep* is also used to express final [*ē*] of III–*yod* verbs.

The vowel letters *waw* and *yod* are consistently used to indicate long vowels or contracted diphthongs. Two examples of possible defective spellings, סכנתא in frg. 12 i 3 and משרתא[in frg. 15 1, may also be interpreted differently.

Elision of the *ʾalep* occurs in frg. 25 6 ויכלון and in frg. 13 4–5 סתא.

There are no certain examples of assimilation of *nun*. מנצבהון in frg. 14 ii 2 is an example of orthographical, rather than phonological, assimilation.

Original *ś* is spelled with ס in frg. 23 ii 5]סגי֯ and in frg. 13 4–5 סתא. The ש is used in forms of עשר (*passim*) and בשר (frg. 13 6; frg. 25 4).

The 3rd masc. sing. pronominal suffix attached to a plural noun is והי. Twice, the preserved text has עלוי (frgs. 8 3 and 9 4) instead of עלוה]י (frg. 26 2).

The relative pronoun is די, but there are a few possible cases of ד, e.g. in frg. 23 ii 2 ודשלם.

Mus. Inv. 564, 568, 570–575, 578, 578A, 611, 614B, 615, 617, Box 1030
PAM 43.981*, 43.993–44.002*, 44.007–44.009*
IAA 342924*, 508044*

Frg. 1

top margin

1]י֯ן סר֯◦[
2] אר֯עי̇ [
3]כ֯ו֯[

Mus. Inv. 578A
PAM 43.993*
IAA 508044*

NOTES ON READINGS

The fragment must be reconstructed on the basis of two photographs. The right-hand part of the fragment is visible on the wad, as shown in PAM 43.993, but absent in the photograph taken after the separation of the layers of the wad. The removal of the upper fragment has uncovered some letters in IAA 508044, but not all of the upper fragment has been removed, and line 1 remains partially covered.

L. 1]י̊ן̊[. Cf. PAM 43.993.

L. 1]◦ר̊ס. Or]◦ח̊ס, or even]◦ה̊ס, if the downstroke is ink.

L. 2] אר̊עי̇ [. Cf. IAA 508044. The letter between *ʾalep* and *ʿayin* may be *reš* with a broken head.

L. 3]כ̇ו̇[. The first letter may also be *bet* or *pe*, the second one *yod* or the right part of some other letter.

TRANSLATION

2.] below [

COMMENTS

L. 1]◦ר̊ס. If the second letter is a broken *ḥet*, ס̇ח̇ר̇ or ס̇ח̇ר̇[would be possible reconstructions.

Frg. 2

[top margin]

1]◦ה̊יא א◦[

2]◦ח̊תא כ[

3]רתא ◦[

4]◦◦◦[

Mus. Inv. 578A
PAM 43.993*
IAA 508044*

NOTES ON READINGS

The fragment is the upper one of the small wad in PAM 43.993. Part of the fragment has now been detached, resulting in one piece with the remains of lines 1–3 and several snippets (compare pl. XXXV, frgs. 1 + 2 and pl. XL).

L. 1]◦ה̊יא[. The first letter, of which the base and part of the downstroke have been preserved, could be *nun* or *taw*. Of the second letter, only the bottom parts of the legs have been preserved. In view of the distance between these legs and the *yod*, *he* is more likely than *ḥet*. The last two letters are now still superimposed on the next fragment. The skin with the first letters on it has been detached, and seems to have broken into pieces.

L. 1]◦א. The vertical stroke after *ʾalep* suggests *waw*, *yod*, *reš*, or *taw*.

L. 2 אתחׄ○[. The traces of the first letter suggest *nun* or *taw*. The second letter is uncertain. PAM 43.993 clearly suggests *ḥet*, but the second leg is not visible in IAA 508044, therefore suggesting *reš*.

L. 3]○. The vertical stroke on the edge suggests *waw*, *yod*, or *taw*.

L. 4]○○○[. The vertical stroke of the first letter seems to break through the baseline. Read perhaps *qop*. The second letter may be *ḥet*. A vertical stroke is all that remains of the third letter.

Frg. 3

top margin

1]○פׄ○[
2]אׄי○[
3]○מ○[
4]○[

Mus. Inv. 578A
PAM 43.993*
IAA 508044*

NOTES ON READINGS

PAM 43.993 shows the right-hand part of a lower fragment, situated at the upper right of the large wad. Since the first lines of the detached frgs. 6–8 begin *c*.0.9 cm lower than the first line of the upper fragment, these letters cannot belong to the right-hand edge of one of those fragments. The stroke of skin with these letters is now a separate fragment on Mus. Inv. 578A. It is possible that frg. 5 represents the left-hand edge of the same fragment.

A separate layer with a *pe* and the bottom part of a downstroke is attached to, or superimposed upon, this fragment. Comparing the shapes of frgs. 8 and 9 shows that the *pe* fits at the right-hand edge of frg. 8 2 before ותיה[.

L. 1]○פׄ○[. The *pe* (or *waw*) is preceded by a letter with a base stroke.

L. 2]אׄי○[. The *yod* (or *waw*) is preceded by a letter with a base stroke.

Frg. 4

top margin

1] ○○○○ ○○○○ ○מׄ[
2]בׄעׄ ○○ ○○[

3 [○○○○]
4 [ע֯ד֯]
5 [ע֯ו֯ב֯ ב֯]
6 [מרׄ ל○○○]

Mus. Inv. 578A
IAA 508044

The fragment consists of a gelatinous substance, on which no writing can be seen with the naked eye. It is apparent from the shape that this is the remains of another layer of the wad, composed of the fragments of Mus. Inv. 578. The shape conforms most closely to frg. 6, and it is probable that the fragment belonged to one of the layers beneath that fragment. Although the photograph clearly shows both dark and faint traces of letters, the identification of few is certain or even probable.

Frg. 5

3 [○נׄ]
5 [מׄפ֯○]

Mus. Inv. 578
IAA 342924*

NOTES ON READINGS

The thickness of frg. 6, compared with that of the other fragments, implies that there is still an undetached fragment behind it, and the photograph of frg. 6 shows traces, which seem to be ink, written half a line higher than those of frg. 6, at the left-hand side. However, the back is in such a poor state of preservation that separation is likely to be impossible. The position of the traces corresponds to that of frg. 3, and it is possible that frg. 3 and frg. 5 originate from the same layer.

L. 3 [○נׄ]. The faint traces form a perfect *nun*, but it is not certain they are ink.

L. 5 [מׄפ֯○]. The stance of the downstroke of the second letter suggests *pe*, but *kap* is possible if the fragment is distorted.

Frg. 6

top margin

1] מאתין ותמנין אמ̊[ין

2 א]לן̊ פרזיא ליד שור̊[א

3] ד̇רומא ופלג[

4]פ̇רזיא[ ]ח̊[

5]ל[

Mus. Inv. 578
IAA 342924

NOTES ON READINGS

This fragment measures 7 x 4.5 cm. The left side of the fragment is twice as thick as the right side, suggesting that there is another layer underneath. The maximal height of its preserved upper margin is 2 cm. The fragment is very dark and difficult to read with the naked eye, but clear in the infra-red photograph.

The very close physical correspondence of the patterns of damage between frgs. 6–8 and 9 shows that the first line of frgs. 6–8 began 0.9–1 cm lower than that of frg. 9. The fragments certainly belonged to different columns, and presumably to different sheets.

L. 1 אמ̊[ין. It is not evident from the photograph which traces after the *ʾalep* are ink. Material resembling rice paper covers most of the upper left side of the fragment after *ʾalep*.

L. 2 א]לן̊. Only the upper part of the downstroke of the last letter has been preserved. The letter can only be final *nun* or *zayin*.

L. 2 שור̊[א. After the *waw* there remains a slightly curved downstroke. *Reš* is possible, but difficult, since in this hand it usually has a square, not round, shoulder.

L. 3 ופלג[. There may be a trace after the *gimel*, but that is not certain from the photograph.

L. 4]פ̇רזיא[. The upper part of the downstroke of the *pe* is clear. Traces of the head seem to be present on the edge of the fragment.

L. 4]ח̊[. The faint traces at the left of the hole resemble *ḥet*, but it is not certain that they are ink.

L. 5]ל[. There are several dark traces on both sides of the *lamed*, which could be the upper parts of letters if the interlinear space between lines 4 and 5 was smaller than usual.

TRANSLATION

1.] two hundred and eighty cub[its
2. the]se blocks alongside [the] city wall[
3.] the south and half (?) [
4.] the blocks [
5.] [

COMMENTS

L. 1 מאתין ותמנין אמׄ]ין. This measure, 280 cubits or 40 reeds, is not attested for any structure in the other copies of *New Jerusalem*, but it corresponds to the measures of each side of the inner court of the Temple, as deduced by Yadin from the elements provided in the *Temple Scroll* (11Q**19** XXXVI) and 4Q**365a**.

L. 2 פרזיא. In the first part of *New Jerusalem* the פרזיא are blocks of houses in the city. It is not clear whether the fragment refers to blocks attached to the wall of the inner court.

L. 3 ופלג[. Either 'a half', or, less likely, the verb פלג.

Frg. 7

top margin

1] על כול זרע בנׄי [

2]◦א די להוון אכלׄין[

3]ב להון סחור [

4]תׄ מאה וחמש]ין

5]לעׄל[

Mus. Inv. 578
IAA 342924

NOTES ON READINGS

It is not completely clear whether this fragment originates from the revolution between frgs. 6 and 8, or from that between frgs. 8 and 9. The report on the separation of the fragments mentions the first possibility, which is followed here, but the pattern of damage strongly suggests the latter order.

This fragment measures 3.6 x 4.2 cm. The maximal height of its preserved upper margin is 0.9 cm. The blanks at the end of lines 1 and 3 may indicate the end of the line.

L. 1] בנׄי. After the *bet* there is an incomplete letter, of which the base (which continues the base of the *bet*) and part of the downstroke are visible; the peculiar curve of the *nun* cannot be deciphered in this downstroke, and the remaining traces are also consistent with *kap*.

L. 2 ◦א[. The first letter may be *bet* or *reš*.

L. 4 תׄ[. The remnants are the base stroke, written rather close to the *mem* of the next word, and part of the downstroke of the left leg.

L. 5]לעׄל[. Between the *lamed*s, two vertical strokes are visible; the second is angled like the left arm of *ʿayin*.

TRANSLATION

1.] on all the seed of the children of [
2.] which shall eat [
3.] for them around [
4.] hundred and fif[ty
5.] on [

COMMENTS

L. 1 על כול זרע בנׄי. Reconstruct perhaps ישראל after בנׄי. Cf. 11Q**19** XXVII 2 על כול בני ישראל (with כול written above the line). The phrases בני ישראל and זרע ישראל are used in the Bible, but the expression זרע בני is not attested in any text. If the fragment should be located in a description of the inner court of the Temple, א]הרון rather than ישראל should be reconstructed.

L. 2 °א[. The grammatical relation of the word to the next clause is uncertain. A possible reconstruction is בש]ר֯א, 'the [me]at which [. . .] shall eat'.

L. 4]תׄ מאה וחמש]ין. Cf. אמין תלת מאה וחמשין ושבע as the dimensions of each side of the block in 4Q**554** 1 ii 13 and 5Q**15** 1 i 1, but a reference to the blocks is unlikely.

Frg. 8

top margin

1 דהב]טב כולה ארבע רגלו֯הׄ[י

2 פ]ותיה אמה ותרתי עשר֯[ה

3 פתו]רא ועלוי לחמא שויׄו[

4]פוׄתי תרעׄ[ ]ורׄוׄמׄ°°[

5]°° °[

Mus. Inv. 578
IAA 342924

NOTES ON READINGS

The fragment measures 5.3 x 5 cm. The upper margin preserved in this fragment measures 1.5 cm to the clearly visible first ruling line. The left side of the fragment (0.5 cm), as well as the bottom, are dark and wrinkled and illegible on the fragment.

L. 1 רגלו֯הׄ[י. The letter after the *lamed* is either *waw* or *yod*. The next letter has a downstroke and a head, but because of the absence of a trace of the left leg and the relative thinness of the head, *he* is not certain.

L. 2 פ]ותיה. The *pe* and the bottom part of a downstroke which are preserved on the piece superimposed upon frg. 3 (IAA 508044) most probably belong to this word.

L. 2 עשר֯[ה. Faintly visible after the *šin* is the lower part of a downstroke.

L. 3 פתו]רא. It is not clear from the photograph whether the dark stroke on the edge is ink. Read perhaps פת]ו֯רא. The fragment mentioned in the NOTES ON READINGS to line 2 פ]ותיה, has traces which correspond to the left-hand part of *taw*, one line lower down. If the fragment has broken off, פ]ת[ו]רא or פ]תו֯רא are possible readings.

L. 3 שו֯י֯ו֯[. After *šin* three downstrokes, close to one another, are visible. שו֯ם֯[is palaeographically more problematic.

L. 5]°° °[. Maurer[6] reads]ת֯ר֯ע֯ה֯[, but no trace of the *reš* is visible. The other traces may correspond to his reading (but also to other readings).

TRANSLATION

1.] pure [gold,] all of it, i[ts] four legs [
2.] its [w]idth is a cubit. And the twel[ve
3.] the [tab]le, and they had placed the bread upon it [
4.] the width of the door and its height [
5.] [

COMMENTS

All the references of the first three lines of this fragment are compatible with a description of the table for the shewbread.

L. 1 דהב]טב. Cf. Exod 25:23 זהב טהור (*Tg. Onq.* דהב דכי). Apparently טב is used in a general sense to indicate the metal of the highest quality. Cf. e.g. 1 Kgs 6:20, 21; 7:49, 50 MT זהב סגור, *Tg.* דהבא טבא.

L. 1 ארבע רגלו֯ה֯[י. The reference seems to be to the four legs of the table. Cf. Exod 25:26.

L. 2 פ]ותיה אמה. Probably the width of the table for the shewbread. Cf. Exod 25:23 ואמה רחבו. The dimensions in Ezek 41:22 are different.

L. 2 ותרתי עש֯ר[ה. Probably the number of the shewbreads. Cf. Lev 24:5.

L. 3 שו֯י֯ו֯[. The verb possibly had no explicit grammatical subject. Note that most other descriptions concern structures or artefacts, not actions.

Frg. 9

top margin

[סחור לעליתא ד] 1

[אמין עמודין שבעה ת֯] 2

אורכיהון ופו[ת֯יהון אמין שת בשת] 3

[בא ובנא בנין עלוי עמ] 4

[ב֯א וכול בנינא דן] 5

[מ֯קד֯ש֯א ול°ל֯] 6

---

[6] Thanks are due to A. Maurer for providing his unpublished readings and comments on the fragments.

Mus. Inv. 578
PAM 43.993*
IAA 342924*

NOTES ON READINGS

PAM 43.993 (pl. XXXV, frgs. 3 + 9) shows the fragment as the upper layer of the wad, while IAA 342924 (pl. XXXVI, frg. 9) shows the fragment after its detachment. Each photograph shows letters not visible in the other. The transcription is based on the combined evidence. The dimensions are 6.5 x 4.3 cm. The maximal height of the upper margin preserved in this fragment is 1.3 cm.

L. 2 ת֯]. The angular shoulder indicates *taw* or *reš* rather than *dalet*.

L. 3 ופו[ת֯יהון. PAM 43.993 shows a horizontal and vertical trace to the right of *yod*. However, in the original, the *yod* is on the outer edge of the fragment and is incomplete.

L. 4 עמ]. PAM 43.993 shows the *ʿayin* and the downstroke of the second letter. IAA 342924 has lost the *ʿayin*, but preserves almost the complete *mem*.

L. 5 [ב֯א. The first letter may also be *dalet* or *reš*.

L. 6 מ֯קד֯שא. Cf. PAM 43.993 together with IAA 342924. The diagonal trace before *qop* may be the tick of *yod* or the head of *dalet*, but possibly also the diagonal of *mem*. Likewise the trace after *qop* is either *yod* or *dalet*. The *šin* is probable from the combined evidence of the two photographs.

L. 6 ול°ל֯]. IAA 342924 is clearer than PAM 43.993. The skin before the *lamed* is lost in IAA 342924, but the earlier photograph suggests *waw*. The last *lamed* is very faint.

TRANSLATION

1.] around the upper room [
2.] cubits, seven columns [
3. their length and] their [wid]th are six by six cubits [
4.] and a construction built on it [
5.] and this whole construction [
6.] the Temple and [

COMMENTS

L. 3 אמין שת בשת. For these dimensions, cf. Ezek 40:7, 12 (the cells of the gate); 41:1 (the door-posts of the היכל). The same dimensions should probably be reconstructed in 5Q**15** 1 ii 4 with regard to the column in the staircase. The mention of עמודין in line 2 suggests that the dimensions in line 3 refer to the columns. One may possibly reconstuct מרבע, 'square', after בשת, as in 5Q**15** 1 ii 5.

Frg. 10 i

top margin

1]י מין חיין

2]ורא דן דהב טב

3]ין מיא מן

4 [*vacat*

5]○בן כול אבניהון

6]○וך חפא דהב

7]○אה ועש[ר]

8]○[ ]○[

Mus. Inv. 574, 615
PAM 43.994*, 44.007*

NOTES ON READINGS

The upper margin has been preserved up to 1.7 cm. It is now impossible to measure the margin between the columns on the original fragment because the beginning of the second column is carbonized. The photograph shows the distance between the last letters of the right-hand column and the beginning of the left-hand column to vary from 1.2 cm (line 2) to 2.5 cm (line 3). However, טב in line 2 is almost certainly an intercolumnar addition, and אבניהון in line 5 probably spilled into the margin. The endings of lines 1, 3, and 6 suggest a margin of 2 cm.

L. 2 טב. The slightly higher position of the word, the somewhat thinner strokes of the letters, and the probability that the word was written in the intercolumnar margin all suggest that the word was added afterwards as a correction.

L. 5]○בן. The photograph clearly shows a trace before *bet*, but a further identification is impossible. The carbonized part of the fragment has become detached.

L. 6]○וך. The letters are written in a dark area of skin, but the reading is virtually certain.]○ה is not possible because of the upward tick at the left end of the headstroke. This part of the fragment has broken off; the first letter of the line now being *ḥet* of חפא.

L. 7 ועש[ר]. The available space suggests ועש[ר] rather than ועש[רין].

TRANSLATION

1.] living water
2.] this [ ] of pure gold
3.] water from
4.] *vacat*
5.] all their stones

6.] overlaid with gold
7.] and te[n]
8.] [

COMMENTS

L. 1]י. Read e.g. ד]י.

L. 2]ורא. In view of the mention of water, one may perhaps reconstruct כי]ורא, but in the Bible the basin is made of copper (Exod 30:18 *et passim*). In view of the 'stones' of line 5, one may alternatively reconstruct ש]ורא. The reconstruction פת]ורא is unlikely in this context, even though it was made of gold.

L. 3]ין. Reconstruct e.g. נפק]ין.

L. 5]◦בן. Possibly reconstruct ה]ו֯בן. Cf. the COMMENTS on frg. 12 i 7.

L. 5 כול אבניהון. The lack of context makes it impossible to determine the antecedent of the suffix.

L. 7]◦אה. Read perhaps]מׄאה.

Frg. 10 ii

top margin

ארב]עה
מׄ◦[
◦[
ומ◦[
הל◦[
מׄוׄ◦[
וא[
ור◦חׄ[
חד[

Mus. Inv. 572, 574
PAM 43.994*, 44.009*

NOTES ON READINGS

The fragment consists of two pieces. The join proposed in the *ed. princ.* cannot be verified by the originals, as the left-hand part of the main piece is carbonized, and the small pieces of Mus. Inv. 572 have now almost disintegrated, so that nothing can be read any longer. However, because of the shapes of the pieces visible in the photographs and the common right margin, the join is virtually certain. It is not clear

L. 7]בשורתא̊. The reading]בשור תא̊ is difficult because of the absolute form. More likely is a secondary feminine form of שורא (cf. Syriac, which has both forms), or perhaps the noun 'row', but then the determined form is puzzling.

L. 8 בכ̇יור. Read כיור, 'panelling work', rather than כיּוֹר, 'basin'.

Frg. 12 i

top margin

1]◦ מן אלן וערבליא די

2]יא פרישא ודי מעשריא

3]הון פרישא וסכנתא

4] *vacat*

5]כ̇ול רוח מערב

6]◦ שורא

7]ב̊ן̇ הובן

8]בימי̊ן

9]◦◦[

Mus. Inv. 564
PAM 43.995

Notes on Readings

The fragment measures 7.5 x 6.2 cm, including an upper margin of 1.9 cm. The left margin is not visible; the right margin of the next column is very faint, but can be confirmed between lines 5 and 7.

L. 7]ב̊ן̇. Final *nun* is certain; small specks of ink from the tail are visible along the edge of the fragment. The first letter may be *bet* or several other letters. *Mem* is difficult as the top stroke of *mem* is very close to *nun*.

L. 8]בימי̊ן. Only remnants of the last letter remain, and e.g. בימי̊נ̊[ה] is also possible.

L. 9]◦◦[. The first letter may be *waw*, the second e.g. *kap*.

Translation

1.] from these and the sieves which
2.] dedicated and of the tithes
3.] dedicated and arranged
4.] *vacat*
5.] each side, west

6.] the wall
7.]
8.] at the right side
9.] [

COMMENTS

L. 1 וערבליא. For ערבלא (or ארבלא) cf. e.g. *Tg. Amos* 9:9 where it renders MT כברה. Thirteen sieves (נפה) are mentioned in *m. Menaḥ.* 6.7 and 10.4 for the sifting of the grains for the flour of the Omer.

L. 2 פרישא. The root פרש renders the *Hipʿil* and *Hopʿal* of MT רום in the targums, and refers to the 'lifting up', 'taking away' or 'separation', often applied to heave offerings and other things dedicated to God. Cf. also the use of אפרשותא in *Targum Onqelos* for MT תרומה.

L. 3 וסכנתא. The word is problematic. A defective plural form of סכין, 'knife', would be strange in view of the consistent plene spelling. Alternatively, the word may be a participle of סכן, 'to arrange'.

L. 5]כׄול רוח מערב. The syntax is not certain. Either: 'all west side', or 'each side' and 'west', as the start of an enumeration of the sides.

L. 7]בׄן הובן. The meaning of הובן is uncertain. הבנים *qere* (הובנים *ketib*) in Ezek 27:15 is thought to be 'ebony', but this meaning is difficult in frg. 16 i 1. Moreover, not only here (reconstruct א]בׄן הובן), but also in frg. 16 i 1 (reconstruct א]בׄני הובן כולהון) and in frg. 10 i 5 (reconstruct ה]וׄבן כול אבניהון), it is possible to connect הובן with אבן, which would mean that הובן is not 'ebony', but a specification of stones.

Frg. 12 ii

[top margin]

]
]
בׄ]
מׄ]
רו◦]
טׄ◦]
ועלאׄ]
די֯ ◦]

Mus. Inv 564
PAM 43.995

NOTES ON READINGS

L. 5 רו°]. Or רי°]. רא̊] is not possible, since the stroke at the edge seems to slant down to the left.

L. 6 ט°]. The downstroke of the second letter slants slightly more than usual. The lack of a base stroke rules out *bet*. Possible are *waw* and *yod*; more difficult is *reš*.

L. 8 די̊ °]. The *dalet* is certain in the fragment. The slanting downstroke may be *yod* with an abraded head. The faint diagonal trace at the end need not be ink.

TRANSLATION

7. and above [

Frg. 13

top margin

1]בארבע רגלוהי ונשט תורא °[
2 ר]ח̊ע רגלוהי וקרבוהי ומלח כולה̣[
3 ו]ש̊ויה על נורא ואיתי קמח סולת̣[
4 ר]ו̊ב̇ע סתא ואסקה למדבחא כולה̣[
5 רו]ב̇ע סתא ונסך לגוא מורכי̊[ותא
6]א ובשרא מתערב בחדא̣[
7] ר̇יחא *vacat*]
8]מרפסתא ליד יס°[
9]°א̊ ו̊מ̇ב̇° מ°°[
10]°ורנ̊[
11]°[

Mus. Inv. 564, 572
PAM 43.995*, 44.009*

NOTES ON READINGS

The fragment consists of four pieces. Mus. Inv. 572 (PAM 44.009) shows three fragments glued to tissue paper and covered with a white substance on the front. Even though the join of these pieces is not correct, and the traces of two of the fragments are hard to decipher, it is clear that they broke off from the bottom of the main fragment.

L. 1 ונשט. Part of the second letter has been damaged. *Pe* is difficult because of the small space between the downstroke and the following *šin*. Also, the slight curve of the top of the downstroke is consistent with *nun*.

L. 2 ר]חׄע. The first stroke is curved and clearly descending, slanting towards the right. The absence of a trace of the base, as well as the length of the stroke, rules out באר]בׄע. Although there is no trace of a horizontal head, *ḥet* is possible. Otherwise read *šin*.

L. 4 ר]ׄבׄע. The absence of a tick makes א]רׄבע very unlikely. The head and base of the *bet* are slightly sloping, and so *mem* is possible as well.

L. 7 רׄיחא. The bottom of the first letter has broken away, but readings other than *reš* are meaningless. The second letter is clearly *yod*.

L. 8 ליד יס◦[. The space between *dalet* and *yod* is rather small. The trace to the left of *samek* is probably ink.

L. 9 ומׄבׄ◦. The third letter may also be *reš*. There may be a remnant of the base of *bet*. Now this piece of the fragment has broken away. Dots on both pieces suggest another letter after *bet*.

L. 9 מ◦◦[. The head of the letter after the *mem* is short, and has a rounded shoulder. A trace of ink at the bottom left may be part of a base, in which case the letter is probably *bet*. The traces are followed by a thin downstroke and a trace on the ceiling line.

Translation

1.] by its four legs, and stripped the bull [
2. he wa]shed its legs and its intestines, and salted all of it [
3. and] placed it on the fire, and brought fine sifted flour [
4. a fo]urth of a seah, and he brought all of it to the altar [
5. a fou]rth of a seah, and he poured it into [the] troughs [
6.] the [ ] and the flesh were mixed together [
7.] the smell. *vacat*[
8.] the gallery near [
9.] [
10.] [
11.] [

Comments

L. 1]בארבע רגלוהי. Possibly part of a description of tying the four legs of the bull. Cf. *2 Enoch* 59:4 which insists that the four legs should be tied together. Kister, p. 284, also refers to *b.Tamid* 31b.

L. 1 ונשט. Both נשט (cf. Syriac) and פשט can mean 'to strip'. The following *Apʿel* forms ואיתי and ואסקה suggest that the form is a perfect.

L. 2 ר]חׄע רגלוהי וקרבוהי. Cf. *T. Levi* 28 (Bodleian col. d 10–11) רגלין רחיען עם קרביא and 4Q**214** 2 6–7 רגלין רחי]עׄן עם קרביא. קרבין is a Hebrew loanword, 'intestines'. For the combination 'legs and intestines' cf. Lev 1:9, 13 though 𝔐 uses כרעים, 'shins'. Cf. also Josephus *Ant.* III.9.1 §227 τοὺς δὲ πόδας τῶν ἱερείων καὶ τὰ κατὰ νηδὺν.

L. 2 ומלח כולה]. Cf. *T. Levi* 29 (Bodleian col. d 11) וכולהון מליחין במלח and 4Q**214** 2 7 וכׄלׄהׄ]ן מליחין במלח. Cf. Lev 2:13; *m. Zebaḥ.* 6.5; *m. Tamid* 4.3. Josephus *Ant.* III.9.1 § 227.

L. 3 קמח סולת]. Cf. Gen 18:6. Both words are mentioned as separate entities in 1 Kgs 5:2, but it is possible that סולת, 'wheat flour', specifies the more general קמח, 'flour'. סלת is part of the offerings described in Leviticus. Cf. also 2Q**24** 4 4 תמנא סאין סול]תא.

L. 4 סתא. Probably an orthographic variant of סאתא. סאה is a measure of capacity used in biblical Hebrew in connection with grain, but in the Mishnah it also is used for liquids. Since one סאה is two הין, this passage may be connected with the measures of Num 15:9-10. Reconstruct e.g. פיל במשח ר]ׄבע [סתא]. The suggestion in the *ed. princ.*, a defective writing of סיתא or שיתא, 'ewe', requires another reading of the preceding words, and is less likely.

L. 5 רו]ב̊ע סתא. Reconstruct e.g. ואיתי חמר רו]ב̊ע סתא. Cf. Num 15:10.

L. 5 מורכי̊]ותא. מורכיתא, pl. מורכיותא, renders כד, 'jug', and רהטים, 'trough (at a well)', in *Tg. Neof.* Gen 24:20 and 30:38. Here it must be some special receptacle into which the wine libation should be poured.

L. 8 מרפסתא[. Possibly the Aramaic equivalent of Hebrew מרפסת, 'balcony', 'gallery'. Otherwise a participle of רפס, 'to stamp, beat'.

L. 8]◦יס. Reconstruct perhaps יסו̊]ד.

Frg. 14 i

top margin

◦[1

Mus. Inv. 568
PAM 43.996

NOTES ON READINGS

Cf. NOTES ON READINGS on frg. 14 ii.

L. 1 ◦[. Preserved are a base stroke, possibly slightly beneath the baseline, a minute vertical trace on top of the left part of the base and a blot on the edge of the fragment. Only the base stroke is certainly ink. It may belong to *bet*, *ʿayin*, *ṣade* (medial form in final position), or *taw*.

Frg. 14 ii

top margin

גפן כדי פרש מן לולבי̊]א 1

מנצבהון וכלילא חמי̊]שיא 2

גוא כפרה וכלילא שתיתי̊]א 3

שביעיא כדמות נצ ורד[4

להוה לבש כהנא רבא[5

[   ]ים ו̊ב̊כול ע̊ל[6

[   ]לכול ע̊[7

[   ]◦◦[8

Mus. Inv. 564, 568
PAM 43.995*, 43.996*

NOTES ON READINGS

This fragment consists of two pieces. The large one measures 5.2 x 6.8 cm, including an upper margin of 1.3 cm and up to 1.9 cm of intercolumnar margins (until the last letter of the first line of the preceding column). No vertical ruling is visible and the horizontal ruling is very faint. A small piece, measuring 1.5 x 1 cm, can be joined to the bottom.

L. 2 מנצבהון. Or מנצ בהון.

L. 3 שתיתי֯]א. The black trace on the protrusion of the skin is most probably part of *yod*.

L. 4 נצ ורד]. Or נצורד]? נצורד֯] (Beyer) is palaeographically difficult, but not impossible.

L. 5 להוה. It seems that the first letters of lines 5 and 6 are written slightly more to the left than those of the first lines.

L. 5 כהנא. The base of the *nun* and part of the *ʾalep* were preserved on the bottom fragment, but have now broken off.

L. 6 ו֯ב֯כול. Or ב֯כול. The main problem is the two more or less horizontal traces before the *kap*, which do not conform to any letter. The height of the upper stroke is, however, compatible with *bet*. The traces on both fragments may be the top and bottom of *waw*, or both traces may belong to the right-hand side of the *bet*.

L. 8]◦◦[. The traces are no longer visible in the original. The first letter is *ḥet*, *qop*, or *taw*.

TRANSLATION

1. grape, when it comes out from [the] sprouts [
2. from their shoot. And the fif[th] crown [
3. the inside of a cypress flower. And the sixth crown [
4. the seventh (crown) is like the bud of a rose [
5. the high priest will be clothed [
6. [ ] and in all [
7. [ ] for all [
8. [ ] [

COMMENTS

The fragment preserves part of the description of seven crowns, with different decorations, which formed part of the vestments of the high priest. The comparison of the crown with flowers recalls Josephus' description of the crown of the high priest (*Ant*. 3.7.6 §§ 172–7), 'a crown of gold, wrought in three tiers, and sprouting above this was a golden calyx recalling the plant . . . *saccharon*'. Josephus continues with an elaborate botanical description of this plant.

L. 1 גפן כדי פרש מן לולבי֯]א. The expression לולבי גפנים is used in rabbinic literature. Cf. Josephus' similar terminology: ἐκ μέντοι τῶν κλαδῶν ἀνίησι κάλυκα.

L. 2 מנצבהון. This reading is more likely than מנצ בהון. Note that מן is used separately in this text, not assimilated to the noun.

L. 3 גוא כפרה. The גוא is probably the ovary of the plant.

Frg. 15

top margin

]משרתא עוד להן די להוה֯[1

]א וכול די להוון משצין שבעתיהו֯[ן 2

]אחיהון עללין חלפהון ארבע מאה֯ צ֯[3

]אׄ ואמר לׅי לעשרין ושת ◦[4

קד]ישי קדישיא ו֯לא֯[5

ע]לל[י]ן ע֯[6

Mus. Inv 568
PAM 43.996

NOTES ON READINGS

The fragment measures 4.8 x 7.5 cm, including a maximum of 0.8 cm upper margin. The left edge is carbonized and little can be seen.

L. 3 מאה֯ צ֯[. The left edge is carbonized and very dark. The traces after the *ʾalep* correspond more to *he* than to *taw*. The horizontal stroke on the edge may be the right arm of *ṣade*.

L. 4]אׄ. The traces, which in the photograph resemble *yod* and final *nun*, cannot be read this way on the fragment. The surface of the leather has been abraded, but there are clearly three traces, apparently the remains of one single letter, probably an *ʾalep*.

L. 5 ו֯לא֯[. Before *lamed* there is a small gap, and it is also possible that the first letter is *dalet*. Only a tip of the last letter remains, but the thickness and the stance strongly suggest that the trace is the top of the right arm of *ʾalep*.

L. 6 ע֯[. The two tops of the arms have a stance which is compatible with *ʿayin* or, less closely, with *ṣade*.

TRANSLATION

1.] any more, except who is (?) [
2.] and all who will have completed their weeks [
3.] their brothers will enter in their place, four hundred [
4.] and he said to me: 'For twenty six [
5.]the [Ho]ly of Holies, and [
6.] they will [en]ter [

COMMENTS

L. 1]משרתא. The meaning of the word, either a plural participle of שרי or a noun, is not certain. A defective spelling of משריתא, 'camp, resting place', is not likely (Syriac ܡܫܪܝܬܐ, 'field', 'land', is an Akkadian loanword not to be expected in this text). A noun, 'service', or another form related to Hebrew שרת, seems difficult, since Aramaic does not use the root שרת. However, the occurrence of other Hebrew loanwords in this text shows that such a meaning may be possible. Another possibility is to take משרתא for מסרתא, from the root מסר. This is attested in 4Q**534** 1 i 9, in parallelism with חשבון, and in 4Q**536** 2 3 in the expression די מסר לי במנין, 'which count me among the numbers'; the noun משרתא / מסרתא could then be understood as 'the counting'.[7]

L. 1 עוד. Perhaps לא should be reconstructed earlier on in the clause.

L. 1 להן. 'But' or 'for them (fem.)'.

L. 4 לעשרין ושת. 26 = 52/2. The figure possibly refers to the divisions of priests, or to the periods of services.

Frg. 16 i

top margin

]◦ני הובן כולהון

]ל בׄוׄצׄ

כ]תׄפׄן

]◦תׄ

Mus. Inv. 572, 617
PAM 43.997*, 44.009*

NOTES ON READINGS

The fragment consists of three separated pieces on the same plate (measuring approximately 5.5 x 5 cm, including 1.5 cm of upper margin) and another piece (lines 1–2) which also preserves the upper margin. The margin between the columns varies between 1.5 and 2 cm. No rulings (vertical or horizontal) are visible on the fragment.

L. 1]◦ני. The left-hand end of the base of the first letter is visible.

L. 2 בׄוׄצׄ. Preserved are the long headstroke with tick, possibly of a *bet*, a trace which resembles the head of *waw* and traces which conform most closely to the upper part of *ṣade*.

L. 3 כ]תׄפׄן. The traces of the first letter are a downstroke on the edge and a short base stroke. Possible are *nun*, *ṣade*, and *taw* but, because of the straightness of the downstroke, *taw* is most likely. The head of the second letter indicates *yod* or, less convincingly, *pe*. The base stroke, extending towards the final *nun*, could perhaps be the extension of the stroke of the first letter, but is more likely to be the base of *pe*.

L. 4]◦תׄ. *Taw* can be seen clearly in the photograph, but in the original it is very faint.

TRANSLATION

1.] all of them
2.] linen
3. shoulder-]pieces
4.]

---

[7] Cf. A. Caquot, '*4QMess Ar* I i 8–11', *RevQ* 15/57–58 (1991) 148–51.

COMMENTS

The few preserved words suggest that this column continues the description of the vestments of the High Priest, possibly of the Ephod or the breast-piece.

L. 1]°ני הובן. Cf. COMMENTS on frg. 12 i 7.

L. 2 בׄו֯צׄ. Cf. Exod 28:5, 6.

L. 3 כ]תׄפׄן. Cf. Exod 28:7, 12, 25, 27; 39:4, 18, 20 (the shoulder-pieces of the Ephod).

Frgs. 16 ii + 17 i

top margin

ברכה תנינ֯[   ]ל ותודתהון

ופסחיהון ל°[כ]ה֯נׄיא מקבלין

מן ידהון דפ֯שׁ]טו   ]תׄא ל°[ו]ל[א]

עלל לה כול א]נש

ידוהי כול °[

Mus. Inv. 611, 617
PAM 43.997, 43.998

NOTES ON READINGS

The placement of frgs. 16 ii and 17 i in one column is based upon the physical correspondence of frgs. 16 and 17, as well as on the contents of the two fragments.

Frg. 17 measures 7.7 x 5.5 cm, including an upper margin of 1.7 cm. Vertical rulings are visible on both sides of the margin between the column, clearly on the right-hand side of the new column, and fainter but still visible on the left-hand side of the previous column. The distance between the rulings is 1.5 cm. The two first lines of frg. 17 i stop 0.2 cm before the ruling.

L. 2 כ]ה֯נׄיא. The identity of the first two letters is uncertain. It is difficult to ascertain whether the horizontal trace to the right of the *nun*-like letter is the left-hand end of the headstroke of the first letter (in which case the first letter is *he* or *samek*), or the right arm of *ṣade*.

L. 3 דפ֯שׁ]טו. Nothing can now be seen on the original (the left edge is carbonized). According to the photograph, the letter after *dalet* has a downstroke and a short base. The stance of the downstroke corresponds to *pe*, but there is no certain trace of the head. *Nun* is difficult owing to the stance of the downstroke. The last letter seems to be *šin*, with all three arms preserved.

L. 3 It is not clear whether the traces below the last *nun* of line 2 are ink.

TRANSLATION

1. second blessing [ ] and their thank-offerings
2. and their Passover sacrifices [ ] the [pr]iests receiving
3. from their hand which [they] stre[tch out] [and] n[o]

4. per[son] shall enter it [
5. his hands, everything [

COMMENTS

Ll. 1–2 ותודתהון / ופסחיהון. Both terms are mentioned in the list of offerings in 4QReworked Pentateuch[b] (4Q**365**) 23 7.

L. 2]◦ל. Reconstruct e.g. להׄ]ון דברין.

L. 3 דפׄשׄ]טו. The common form of the relative article is די, but both forms, די and -ד, can be used together in one text. One may reconstruct a perfect or participle of פשט, 'stretch forth', 'reach out'.

Ll. 3–4 ו]ל[א] / עלל לה כול אׄ]נש. The reconstruction of the negative particle at the end of line 3 is tentative, but syntactically sound. לה refers either to the Temple or to a specific item in the Temple. For similar prohibitions cf. Deut 23:3-4, 11Q**19** XLV.

Frg. 17 ii

top margin

1 שבעא בשבעא ואׄ[
2 קנין תלתא ורום תרעׄ[יא
3 לכול תרי עשר תרעיׄןׄ[
4 תרתׄין ועובי פותי כותׄ[לא
5 קדמהׄןׄ קנין מאהׄ[
6 [ ]◦[ ]לׄ[

Mus. Inv. 611
PAM 43.998

NOTES ON READINGS

The fragment clearly shows the ruling of the right margin. Some small pieces have broken away from the left edge.

L. 3 תרעיׄןׄ[. The trace on the edge of the fragment may belong to final *nun*, but *ʾalep* is also possible.

L. 5 קדמהׄןׄ. The fourth letter is damaged. The surface is damaged, and what appears as two traces in the photograph, is shown to be just one in the original. The last slanting stroke could be final *nun*.

L. 6]◦[. Both the original and the photograph show only two spots of ink, from the same stroke.

TRANSLATION

1. seven by seven. And [
2. three reeds, and the height of [the] door[s
3. to all twelve doors [
4. two, and the thickness is the width of [the] wal[l

5. the first of them, one hundred reeds [
6. [ ]

COMMENTS

L. 1 שבעא בשבעא. The feminine form of the numeral suggests it was preceded by קנין, not אמין.

L. 1 וא[. Reconstruct e.g. וא]חזיאני.

L. 2 קנין תלתא. Cf. the same measure in 5Q**15** 1 i 10 which describes the twelve gate-houses: קנין תלתה פותי תרעיהון.

L. 2 תרע֯]יא. Or, as in 5Q**15** 1 i 10, תרע֯]יהון.

L. 4 ועובי פותי כות]לא. Cf. 5Q**15** 1 ii 12 where the expression occurs in a description of the measurements of a window, which may be the case here too. Reconstruct, e.g. with 5Q**15** 1 ii 12 רומה אמין תרתין פותיה אמין[/ תרתין עובי פותי כות]לא. It is, however, not clear, how the text could have proceeded from the doors to windows.

L. 5 קדמ֯ה֯ן. The form is grammatically awkward, as one would expect קדמוהן. Neither the meaning of קדם ('before', or 'first'?) nor the antecedent of the feminine suffix is clear.

L. 5 קנין מאה[. A hundred or more (but less than two hundred) reeds equals between seven hundred and one thousand four hundred cubits. This figure is extremely high, and can hardly refer to any structure within the Temple complex.

Frg. 18

top margin

1 כסין שבעה וספלין למרח ש֯ת֯ה֯[
2 ∘י ועליא שבעא דודין תפין על אבׄנ֯[
3]וכ[ולהון תלתין ותרין אלפין ותשע מאה[
4 [ ] *vacat* [
5 [ ]אׄמר לי חזא אנתה ד֯]י
6 [[לבתי חדוא ול[
7 [[ל֯] [לל] [ן֯] ∘∘ל[

Mus. Inv. 611
PAM 43.998

NOTES ON READINGS

The fragment measures 7.5 x 5.8 cm, including a 1.6 cm upper margin. The left edge and the centre have carbonized, and no inscription can be seen. The blank space to the right of line 1 suggests a right margin or *vacat*. The right side of the fragment has broken off, the downstroke of the *kap* of כסין coinciding with the right edge.

L. 1 שׁתׄהׄ]. The right arm and the lower part of the left downstroke of the *šin* are clear. The traces may also correspond with an *ʿayin* and a downstroke, but the trace which would indicate the left arm of *ʿayin* has the wrong stance. The next traces are a downstroke, another downstroke close by with a base stroke, and two more downstrokes.

L. 2 °י. A tiny trace remaining from the head of the first letter is visible; the letter may be *dalet*, but not *lamed*.

L. 2 אבׄנׄיׄ]. The *bet* (or possibly *kap*, as the head is somewhat short) is torn into two pieces; the left ends of the head and of the base are at the left-hand side of the tear. The head of the next letter has not been preserved, and therefore *nun* is not certain. Only the bottom tip of the last letter remains.

L. 3 מאהׄ]. The head of *he* is visible despite the carbonization.

L. 5]אׄמר. The small speck probably belongs to *ʾalep*.

L. 7]לׄ]. A tip at the right edge is consistent with the top of the upper arm of *lamed*.

L. 7 °°ל]. The traces of the heads of the first letters are compatible with *kap* and *waw*.

Translation

1. seven cups, and six bowls to smell [
2. and above are seven cauldrons, placed (for cooking) on stones [
3. [and a]ll of them are thirty two thousand and nine hundred [
4. [ ] *vacat* [
5. [ ] he said to me: 'You are seeing th[at
6. [ ] to the rooms of the joy and to [
7. [ ] [

Comments

L. 1 שׁתׄהׄ]. This numeral corresponds best to the traces, but may be considered doubtful in view of the recurrence of 'seven' in the fragment. As an alternative, one may consider reading the words together: למרחשׁתׄהׄ], cf. rabbinic מרחשת, 'frying pan', but then the function of the preposition -ל is not clear.

L. 2 תפין. Since the noun תפיא denotes the 'fireplace' or 'stove', the word should be interpreted as a passive participle of the denominative verb תפי 'to set on for cooking'.

L. 3 תלתין ותרין אלפין ותשע מאהׄ]. Possibly 32,928 (= 96*7*7*7).

L. 5 חזא אנתה. חזא is more likely to be a participle than an imperative, which would probably have been spelled חזי.

L. 6 לבתי חדוא. Cf. Hatra 107 5–6 *byt ḥdyʾ ʿlyʾ d[y]* [6]*sgyl hyklʾ rbʾ*. The interpretation of several words in this clause is moot, but the *byt ḥdyʾ* is certainly the designation of part of the temple in Hatra, probably on the first floor (*ʿlyʾ*, i.e. a ὑπερῷον, either on the roof, or an upper chamber). The function of the *byt ḥdyʾ* is not known, but Milik argues that the use of the term *byt ḥdyʾ* indicates a room used for religious communal meals.[8] In that case, the בתי חדוא may be related to the בׄ[י]תׄ מושבות of 11Q**19** XXXVII 8.

[8] Cf. the literature referred to in J. Hoftijzer and K. Jongeling, *Dictionary of the North-West Semitic Inscriptions* (Handbuch der Orientalistik. Erste Abteilung: Der Nahe und Mittlere Osten 21; Leiden: E. J. Brill, 1995) 349, 776 (*sub* ḥdy and sgyl); the abbreviation DFD (omitted in the list of abbreviations) refers to J. T. Milik, *Recherches d'épigrafie proche-orientale I. Dédicaces faites par des dieux (Palmyre, Hatra, Tyr) et des thiases sémitiques à l'époque romaine* (Institut Français d'archéologie de Beyrouth Bibliothèque archéologique et historique 92; Paris: Librairie Orientaliste Paul Geuthner, 1972). Cf. also the discussion in K. Dijkstra, *Life and Loyalty. A Study in the Socio-Religious Culture of Syria and Mesopotamia in the Graeco-Roman Period Based on Epigraphical Evidence* (Religions in the Graeco-Roman World 128; Leiden: E. J. Brill, 1995).

Frg. 19

top margin

1]ה תרעיא די לקובל היכלא ל[

2]בׄיומא שביעיא וביום ראשי ח[דשא

3 ק]דיש הוא היכלא ויקרא רבׄ[א

4]לכול עלמין *vacat* [

5]שרי למקרא לי בכתׄ[ב

6]מחזא לי כתב כ[

7]מׄ[ ]ל[ ]ל[

Mus. Inv. 575
PAM 43.999

Notes on Readings

The fragment measures 6.3 x 5.5 cm. Very faint horizontal ruling is visible.

L. 5]שרי. The last letter is certainly *yod*, not *waw*.

L. 5 בכתׄ[ב. The letter after *kap* may also be *mem* or several other letters e.g. *waw*. The small trace on the far left is created by a crack in the leather.

L. 6 כ[. A minute dot after *kap* may be the remains of a letter.

Translation

1.] the doors which are before the Temple [
2.] on the seventh day, and on the first day of the m[onth
3. h]oly is the Temple and the great glory [
4.] for all ages. *vacat* [
5.] he began to read to me from [a] wri[ting
6.] to show me a (*or*: the) writing [
7.] [ ] [ ] [

Comments

L. 1]ה תרעיא די לקובל היכלא. The clause probably refers to the gates in the wall of the inner court. The exact meaning of לקובל in this context is not clear, but it might mean that the gates are directed towards the Temple. One might reconstruct ארבע[ה before תרעיא, in which case the design seems to correspond with that of the *Temple Scroll*.

L. 2]בׄיומא שביעיא. Cf. 4Q555 3 3]פתורא וביומא שב[(PAM 43.610; Beyer J 6 c), but the other lines of this small fragment offer no overlap.

L. 2 וביום ראשי ח[דשא. Jongeling, ‘Note additionelle’, referred to בראשי חדש(י)כם in Num 10:10 and 28:11, and ראשי חדשים in the Mishnah, and suggested taking the singular ביום with a general meaning ‘*au temps de*’, or reading as a collective. It is, however, not clear whether a singular or plural of חדשא should be reconstructed. Cf., however, another still unpublished small fragment probably of 4Q555 (PAM 43.610), consisting of one line reading]◦ׄ חדשא ובׄ◦[.

L. 3 ויקרא רבׄ[א. Cf. *1 Enoch* 14:20 ἡ δόξα ἡ μεγάλη, 104:1 τῆς δόξης τοῦ μεγάλου, and *T. Levi* 3:4 ἡ μεγάλη δόξα. The expression may have been followed by e.g. די אלהא, or is in itself a title of God. Cf. other possible attestations in Kister, p. 286.

L. 5 בכתׄ[ב. The mention of showing a כתב in the next line indicates that the כתב need not be a book, but that it may have been a writing of some kind (an inscription?) in the Temple complex.

Frg. 20

Parallel: 2Q**24** 4 9–16 (underlined)

top margin

1 כו]ל יום שביעי קודם אל דכרׄ[נא

2 לחמא ויסבון לחמא]לברא מן היכלא לימין מערבהׄ[ויתפלג

3 וחזית עד די פ]ליׄג לתמנין וארבעה כהנין שׄ[

3a]מן כול שבעת פלוגת פתורי

4 שביא די בה]ון וארבעת עשר כה[נין

5 כהניא תרתי לחמ]א די הות לבונתא [עליהון

6 חזא הוית עד חדא מן תרתי לחמא י]היבת לכהנא רׄ[בא

7 עמה ואחריתא יהיבת לתנינה די קא]םׄ פנבד ◦[

Mus. Inv. 575
PAM 43.999

NOTES ON READINGS

The fragment measures 5.5 x 5.7 cm, including 1.3 cm of upper margin. The horizontal ruling is very clear in lines 2 and 3, and fainter in lines 1 and 4. The main problem of collating 2Q**24** 4 and this fragment is the uncertainty with regard to the width of the columns in either manuscript. Wise's calculation of a column of 55–60 letter-spaces in 2Q**24** is based on 2Q**24** 1, but a corresponding column of 60–65 letter-spaces in **11Q18** is virtually impossible.

L. 3 פ]ליׄג. The small trace in the photograph, to the bottom right of the right leg of *gimel*, is not ink, in contrast to the trace to the left of the *lamed*, which may belong to *yod*.

L. 3a פתורי. The word seems to be the last one of the interlinear addition, as there are no more traces above the head of the *he* of line 4 כה[נין.

L. 6 רׄ[בא. The upper right part of a letter is consistent with *reš*.

L. 7 ◦[. The head with a tick may belong to *bet*, *reš*, or *taw*.

Translation

1. eve]ry seventh day before God, a memori[al offering
2. bread. And they shall take the bread] outside the Temple, to the right of its west side, [and it shall be divided
3. And while I was watching, it was distrib]uted to the eighty-four priests [

3a.] with everything was satiated the division of the tables of

4. the eldest among th]em and fourteen prie[sts
5. the priests; two bread]s [upon] which was the incense
6. and while I was watching, one of the two breads was g]iven to the h[igh] priest [
7. with him; and the other was given to his deputy who was stan]ding close to him [

Comments

L. 1 כו]ל יום שביעי. The shewbread was changed each Sabbath. Cf. Lev 24:8 ביום השבת ביום השבת יערכנו לפני יהוה תמיד; Josephus *Ant.* 3.10.7 §§ 255–6; and *m. Menaḥ.* 11.7.

L. 1 דכר̇]נא. Or דכר̇]ן. Probably a rendering of 𝔐 אזכרה (Lev 24:7; and also 2:2, 9, 16; 5:12; 6:8; Num 5:26). The targums render this word as אדכרה, but 𝔖 uses ܕܘܟܪܢܐ. The formulation קודם אל דכר̇]נא is almost identical to Lev 6:8 אזכרתה ליהוה. It is tempting to add the words of 2Q**24** 4 9 לחמא ויסבון לחמ]א immediately after this word, in which case the reading would be דכר̇]ן, but this join of the text of the two fragments is not completely certain.

L. 2 לימין מערבה̇]. The suffix of מערבה probably refers to the היכל. לימין can be either 'to the right', or refer to the south. In the latter case, the phrase means 'to the south-west of it'. The reference is not clear because of the broken context. It is probable, but not certain, that line 2 represents the end of the clause which started with 2Q**24** 4 9 ויסבון לחמ]א, in which case the mentioned 'bread' is the old shewbread. The description may be compared to that of *m. Menaḥ.* 11.7 and *m. Šeqal.* 6.4, which refers to three tables of the shewbread. One, of gold, is in the היכל upon which the shewbread lay continually. The other two are in the אולם, one of marble and one of gold: 'on the table of marble they laid the shewbread when it was brought in, and on that of gold when it was brought out'.

L. 2 ויתפלג. Cf. *m. Menaḥ.* 11.7 וחלות מתחלקות לכהנים.

L. 3 פ]לי̇ג. In view of the *plene* writing, a *Peʿil* is more likely than אתפ]לי̇ג.

L. 3 ש̇]. Perhaps reconstruct ש̇]בין (Jongeling).

L. 3a]מן כול שבעת פלוגת פתורי. Since פלוגת is feminine, the word שבעת is unlikely to be the numeral in masculine form. The word is rather the perfect of שבע, 'to be satiated', and the clause seems to state that there was enough shewbread.

Ll. 3a–4 Somewhere in these lines, probably before the interlinear addition, the remnants of 2Q**24** 4 12 ר̇שמרא כ̇] [עי◦] should be reconstructed. The meaning of the word in this context is unclear.

L. 5 תרתי לחמ]א. *m. Menaḥ.* 11.1, 2, 4, 9, and other mishnaic tractates, refer to the biblical חלות by שתי הלחם.

L. 5 די הות לבונתא [עליהון]. Cf. Lev 2:15 ושמת עליה לבנה.

L. 7 פנבד. The word, attested both by this fragment and by 2Q**24**, but unknown from other sources, may perhaps be a Persian loanword. Baillet, 'Fragments araméens', 235, suggested *patipada*, 'in its own place', even though the change from *t* to *n* cannot be explained. Shaked suggests a derivation from Persian **pati-ni-band-*, in which case פנבד might mean 'in close proximity, in association (with the high priest)'.[9]

---

[9] S. Shaked, 'Qumran: Some Iranian Connections', *Solving Riddles and Untying Knots. Biblical, Epigraphic, and Semitic Studies in Honor of Jonas C. Greenfield*, eds. Ziony Zevit, Seymour Gitin, Michael Sokoloff (Winona Lake, Indiana: Eisenbrauns, 1995) 277–81; esp. 280–1 *pnbd*.

Frg. 21

top margin

1] *vacat*

2]◦ר ותרעין תרין

3]ד לתרתי עליתא

4]◦ן̊[ק]נא חד פותי

5]א *vac* וכדן

6]◦ דרגא

Mus. Inv. 572, 617
PAM 43.997*, 44.009*

Notes on Readings

The fragment consists of three pieces. The largest measures 5 x 4.4 cm, including 1.5 cm of upper margin. A smaller piece preserves remains of lines 2–4. The smallest piece in PAM 43.977 (now absent from the plate) belongs to the upper margin and only has a point jalon. The fragment comes from the end of a sheet and has the stitching attached. Six revolutions of string can be counted. The point jalons are traced with the same ink as the writing. Seven are visible, including two on the top where there are no lines of writing. Vertical ruling is faint but visible; the horizontal ruling is not to be seen in this fragment. The distance between the vertical ruling and the end of the sheet is 1.5 cm.

Comparison with the fragments from PAM 43.999 (frgs. 19 and 20), to which the fragment corresponds in shape, suggests that a blank line preceded the first written line.

L. 2]◦ר. Before *reš* the tips of two legs are visible.

L. 6]◦ The abrasion of the surface of the leather prevents identification of the letter.

Translation

1.] *vacat*
2.] and two doors
3.] for the two upper rooms [
4.] one [re]ed; the width of
5.] *vacat* And likewise
6.] the stairs

Comments

L. 4]◦ן̊[. Reconstruct probably a 3rd masc. pl. suffix, in which case the clause had the following structure: 'and the length (*or*: height) of their . . . is one reed'. The measure of one reed corresponds to the height and length of the inside of the rooms or dormitories (חוניא) of the houses in the block (4Q**554** 2 6; cf. 5Q**15** 1 ii 9–10).

L. 5 וכדן *vac.* Probably an introduction to a new item, as in 2Q**24** 1 4 (parallels 4Q**554** 1 ii 15; 5Q**15** 1 i 8), followed by e.g. אחזיאני or אעלני. Also cf., however, 5Q**15** 1 ii 8, in which case the preceding *ʾalep* may belong to a numeral.

Frg. 22

top margin

]◦על ארבע קרנת מדבח̇[א] 1

]י̇ן מנה כול תרבה 2

]◦ תרתין כוליתה 3

נ]שיפה פיל 4

מד]בחא לריח 5

]לקדמין 6

] *vacat* 7

]◦עי̊ן̊ 8

Mus. Inv. 573, 615
PAM 44.000*, 44.007*

Notes on Readings

The fragment consists of two pieces. The top margin is 1.1 cm. The horizontal and left vertical ruling are clearly visible. The distance from the ruling to the edge of the fragment is 1.3 cm.

L. 1 ◦על[. Or על ◦[. The trace or stain beneath *ʿayin* is not part of a letter. The letter before *ʿayin* may be *dalet* or, though more difficult, *kap* or *mem*.

L. 1 ארבע. Both the shape and the ductus of the *ʿayin* suggest that it was added later by another hand.

L. 3 ◦[. Possible are final *mem*, *šin*, or, less likely, *ʾalep*. The dots are no longer in the original, which has lost a little piece here.

Translation

1.] on the four corners of [the] altar
2.] from it all its fat
3.] both its kidneys
4.] the [wh]eat flour soaked
5.] the [al]tar for a smell

6.] first
7.] *vacat*
8.]

COMMENTS

The first three lines of this fragment seem to describe the sin-offerings of Leviticus 4 or Exod 29:10-14. No other fragment fits in the same column, which implies that the width of the column was narrower than the revolution of the scroll.

L. 1]°על ארבע קרנת מדבח̇[א]. The numeral is not mentioned explicitly in Exod 29:12 or Leviticus 4, but cf. Ezek 43:20 על ארבע קרנותיו and 11Q**19** XXIII 12 על ארבע קרנות מזבח.

L. 2]י̇ן מנה. Reconstruct perhaps מפריש]י̇ן מנה (cf. *Tg. Onq.* Lev 4:8 וית כל תרב תורא דחטתא יפריש מניה, and 4:19 וית כל תרביה יפריש מניה).

L. 3]°. Reconstruct יפרי]ש̊?

L. 3 תרתין כוליתה. Cf. Exod 29:13, Lev 3:4; 4:9.

L. 4 נ]שיפה. Cf. Syr. ܢܫܝܦܐ which renders Hebrew סלת.

L. 4 פיל. Renders Hebrew בלול. In the Bible, the expression סלת בלולה is always followed by שמן. Hence במשח should probably be reconstructed in the next line (possibly preceded by a measure). במשח[רבות]א, 'anointing oil' (a targumic translation of שמן משחת-), is used in 4Q**555** 2 2, but the fragments do not seem to overlap.

L. 5 לריח. Reconstruct ניחוח in the next line.

Frg. 23 i

top margin

1]°י̇ן ומן

2]פ̇א

Mus. Inv. 573
PAM 44.000

NOTES ON READINGS

The fragment measures 5.8 x 4.6 cm including 1.3 cm of upper margin in col. i and 0.9 cm in col. ii. Vertical and horizontal rulings are clearly visible in col. ii. In col. i the vertical ruling is visible, but the horizontal ruling on line 1 has faded away. The intercolumnar margin is apparently about 1.5 cm (2 cm on line 1, but this is clearly distorted by the fragment position).

L. 1]°י̇ן. The first trace is formed by two strokes coming from the head of a *bet*, *dalet*, or *reš*.

L. 2]פ̇א. The head may belong to *pe* or *yod*, and the minute trace at the bottom of the diagonal of the *ʾalep* may be part of the base stroke of *pe*.

TRANSLATION

1.] and from
2.]

Frg. 23 ii

top margin

עליהון ל֯]
ו֯דשלם °]
נכסיהון [
ומברכין ב֯°]
כולה סגי֯]
ה֯ן כולה֯]
[י]שראל]

Mus. Inv. 573
PAM 44.000

NOTES ON READINGS

L. 1 ל֯]. The letter is clear on the original fragment, not in the photograph.

L. 2 ו֯דשלם. The first letter may be either *waw* or *yod*. Cf. the *waw* of ומברכין in line 4.

L. 2 °]. A downstroke is visible.

L. 4 ב֯°]. The bottom tip of a downstroke is attached to the base of *bet*.

L. 5 סגי֯]. After *gimel*, only the bottom part of a slanting downstroke has been preserved.

L. 6 ה֯ן. Or perhaps י֯ן[ ]. מ֯ן is very difficult.

L. 7 [י]שראל]. There is probably enough space for one letter, e.g. a *lamed*, before י]שראל].

TRANSLATION

1. upon them [
2. and [
3. their sacrifices [
4. and blessing [
5. it all [
6. if it all [
7. [I]srael [

COMMENTS

L. 2 ו֯דשלם. The relative article (-ד instead of די) with שלם, which may be a noun ('peace', or 'peace-offering', although 'peace-offering' is normally only used in the plural), an adjective, or perhaps a *Paʿel* ('to recompense', 'to acquit a vow').

L. 3 נכסיהון. The feminine noun נכסא, 'slaughter', 'sacrifice', has both masculine and feminine plural forms. The word may also be derived from נכסין, 'herd', 'property', but because of the abundance of sacrificial terms in the other fragments, the former meaning is more likely.

L. 4 ומברכין. Since all certain examples of מן are unassimilated, the reading 'from the knees' is unlikely. A participle, either active or passive, of ברך is more probable.

Frg. 24

top margin

מע]ל שמשא אר[1

]ה דין מן כול ש◦[2

]◦א די ארבעת[3

]על כול זרעא̊[4

]בכול שנא ל̇[5

]כה עללין [6

]כ̊ול די ל[7

Mus. Inv. 572, 573
PAM 44.000*, 44.009*

NOTES ON READINGS

The fragment consists of two pieces. The largest (lines 1–7) measures 5.2 x 3 cm, including 1 cm of upper margin. A small fragment fits at the beginning of lines 5–7. The left side of lines 2–5 has broken off.

L. 2]ה דין. There is a small space between *he* and *dalet*, also permitting the reading]הדין. The trace at the bottom of the right leg of the *he* may be either the bottom tip of the leg, turning more to the left than average, or the end of the base of *bet*, *kap*, *nun*, or *pe*.

L. 2 ש◦[. The fragment now shows no ink after the *šin*, but a little piece may have broken off.

L. 3]◦א. The first letter is *bet*, *dalet*, or *reš*, not *taw*.

L. 5 ל̇[. *Sin* is more probable than *ʿayin*.

L. 7]כ̊ול די. The remnant of the first letter is compatible with *kap*, but also with many other letters. The *lamed* and *dalet* are rather close, suggesting one word.

L. 7 ל[. The thickening of the tip of the tail of final *nun* from the line above is in fact the upper tip of the arm of *lamed*. The *lamed* must have been written immediately after the preceding די; therefore דיל[is plausible.

TRANSLATION

1.] the [su]nset [
2.] judgement (?) from all [
3.] of four [
4.] on all the seed [
5.] in each year [
6.] entering [
7.] all who/which [

COMMENTS

L. 1 מע[ל שמשא. Cf. the references to 'sunset' and 'night' in the following fragments.

L. 1 אר]. Perhaps a form of ארבע (cf. line 3), although its function in the lines is unclear.

L. 2 דין. Perhaps a form from the root דין, 'to judge', whether verbal or nominal, but then the use of the preposition מן is unclear. Alternatively, the preceding *he* may belong to the word, but a *plene* writing of the demonstrative pronoun,]הדין, is not to be expected. Read perhaps ש]הדין, 'witnesses', followed by מן *locale*.

Frg. 25

top margin

1]מן קודשי ישראל[

2]ור ובלילה ה֯[

3]ריתא ויקרא[

4]°בי בשרה די°[

5]°לון עמה ומ[ן

6]ן ויכלון ויש[תון

7]°° ומ֯[

Mus. Inv. 570, 615
PAM 44.001*, 44.007*

NOTES ON READINGS

The fragment consists of two pieces. The larger measures 5.5 x 3 cm, with an upper margin of 1 cm.

L. 2 ה֯[. Also possible, but more difficult, is *ḥet*.

L. 3]ריתא. Though *yod* is more likely, *waw* may also be possible.

L. 4 די°[. The letter after *yod* has a base, visible on the part above the tear.

L. 5]°לון. Part of the head and part of the downstroke of the first letter remain. *Kap* is very difficult. More likely are *he*, *waw*, or possibly *yod* or *samek*.

L. 5 ומ[ן. The space before ומ[ן is slightly larger than elsewhere in this fragment. The small dot at the end of the line is not ink; there is a crack which has caused the spot in the photograph.

L. 6]ן. The remains of the first letter may also belong to *yod*.

L. 7]°°. The last trace may be final *nun*, but it may also be the right part of a letter e.g. *he*, the left part having been abraded. The previous traces must be]ש or]ע°.

L. 7 ומ֯[. The last letter may also be *reš* or *taw*.

TRANSLATION

1.] from the sacrifices of Israel [
2.] and in the night [
3.] the [ ] and the glory [
4.] its flesh which [
5.] with it and from [
6.] they will eat and dr[ink
7.] and [

COMMENTS

L. 1 קודשי. Cf. Hebrew קדשים, 'offerings, votive gifts', but in the targums it is also used to render 𝔐 שלמים. For קודשי ישראל cf. *Tg. Onq.* Lev 10:14 מנכסת קודשיא דבני ישראל (𝔐 מזבחי שלמי בני ישראל).

L. 2]ור. Reconstruct נה]ור?

L. 3 ויקרא]. Either a verbal form of קרי or the noun יקר.

Frg. 26

top margin

]וכול אנשא די יח֯[1

]יתמנון עלוהי[2

]א עד תדנח שמ֯[שא 3

]הי כחדא *vacat*[4

]*vacat* שבעה֯[5

]להוון שב[6

[להו֯]ון[7

Mus. Inv. 570, 572
PAM 44.001*, 44.009*

NOTES ON READINGS

The fragment consists of two pieces. The larger (lines 1–5) measures 4 x 3.5 cm, including an upper margin of 0.8 cm. The second piece (lines 6–7) seems to fit perfectly at the bottom. The join cannot be substantiated by the reading of the pieces, but the join results in a shape very similar to the two other pieces of PAM 44.001.

L. 1 יח֯[. The remains of two legs after the broken *yod* suggest *he*, *ḥet*, or, with more difficulty, *taw*.

L. 3 שמ֯[שא. The small trace after *šin* is probably the lower right part of *mem*.

L. 5 שבעה֯[. The edge of the fragment shows part of a vertical stroke.

TRANSLATION

1.] and all the men who [
2.] they will be appointed over it [
3.] till [the] su[n] sets [
4.] together. *vacat* [
5.] *vacat* Seven [
6.] (to) be [
7.] (to) b[e

COMMENTS

L. 2]יתמנון עלוהי̇[. The meaning depends on the context. If the section deals with the Passover sacrifices, there may be a connection with Exod 12:4 𝔐 תכסו על שה, *Tg. Onq.* תתמנון על אימרא.

L. 3 עד תדנח שמ̇]שא. This and other references to sunset may be pertinent to the time of ritual purity. Cf. Lev 7:15, 22:7, Num 19:7, 4QMMT B 11, 15, and the *Temple Scroll*. Cf. the discussion in *DJD* X, 150–4.

Frg. 27

top margin

כו]ל ישראל ח̇[1

] *vac* וכדי יש◦[2

]ל̇י̇ פסחיא חפ◦[3

עד ת]ד̇נ̇ח שמשא וכו̇[ל 4

]שי שלמיהון[5

]ל̇א̇ לרויו ◦[6

Mus. Inv. 570
PAM 44.001

NOTES ON READINGS

The fragment measures 5.2 x 2.7 cm, including an upper margin of 0.8 cm.

L. 1 ח̇[. Or *he*.

L. 2 *vac* [. It is improbable that the smudge at the right edge is the remains of a letter.

L. 2 יש◦[. Part of a downstroke is apparent just after the *šin*. Possible are *waw*, *yod*, or *reš*; other letters, such as *he*, *ḥet*, or *dalet* would probably have been written at a greater distance from the *šin*.

L. 3]ל̇י̇. The dot on the edge may be the tip of the upper arm of *lamed*. In that case, the next trace must belong to *yod*. If the dot is not ink, the second trace may also be the left part of the crossbar of *he*.

L. 3 חפ◦[. The original fragment shows beyond doubt that the second letter is *pe*. The bottom tip of a downstroke is attached to the base of the *pe*.

L. 6]לׄאׄ. The right part of the line is no longer preserved on the original.

L. 6]○. The letter is probably not *waw*, as the hook of the head comes too far down. More likely is *pe* or *ṭet*.

TRANSLATION

1. al]l of Israel [
2.] *vacat* And as soon as [
3.] Passover offerings [
4. until] the sun sets, and al[l
5.] their peace-offerings [
6.] not (?) for saturation (?) [

COMMENTS

L. 2]○ישׁ. Reconstruct e.g. ישׂ֯]אל or a verbal form.

L. 3]○חפ. Read a form of חפי, 'to cover'?

L. 6]לׄאׄ לרוין. רוי, 'to be saturated', and hence often 'to be drunk', rendering Hebrew שכר.]לׄאׄ may be the negative particle or the end of a definite noun. Is this a warning to be moderate with wine when eating and drinking after the peace-offering (cf. Eli's accusation in 1 Samuel 1)?

Frg. 28

top margin

]לה֯וון דברין בׄ[1

]○בר שבעתׄ[2

]אׄ עד מעל ש]משא 3

]קורבני א[4

]י֯{ן} תורין תר֯]ין 5

]○ין וכו[6

Mus. Inv. 571
PAM 44.002

NOTES ON READINGS

The fragment measures 4.8 x 2.1 cm, including an upper margin of 0.7 cm. Faint ruling is visible in line 1.

L. 1]לה֯וון. A dot of ink remains of the upper arm of the *lamed*. The minute trace before the first *waw* is probably the left end of the crossbar of *he*.

L. 1 בׄ[. The head is somewhat shorter than usual, but the angular tick and the straight head rule out *mem*. Now, only a small dot of the base remains in the original.

L. 2]שבעת̇. The trace above the tear shows that the last letter is *taw* rather than *he*. The shape of the two legs is not compatible with *ʾalep*.

L. 3 א̊[. Even after consulting the original fragment, it is not clear whether the trace is really ink.

L. 4 קורבני[. The first three letters have been written as a correction over an erasure. The original word cannot be ascertained.

L. 5 {ן}י̊[. The trace is followed by a *nun* erased by the corrector, but is still partially visible.

L. 5 תר̊]ין. The downstroke and beginning of the head of the letter after *taw* remain. A very thin trace stands vertically on the head, but this trace cannot be the tick of *mem*.

TRANSLATION

1.] they will take [
2.] seven [
3.] until s[un]set[
4.] offerings of [
5.] tw[o] bulls[
6.] [

COMMENTS

L. 2]שבעת̇. Seven days (Num 28:17) or seven lambs (Num 28:21)?

L. 4]קורבני א. A plausible reconstruction would be קורבני א]להא[, cf. Lev 21:6, 21-22. קורבן is a targumic rendering of אשה ייי (but also of לחם in Lev 21:21-22). In view of line 5 one may have here a description of the offerings of the Feast of Unleavened Bread (cf. Num 28:19).

L. 5 תורין תר̊]ין. Cf. Num 28:11, 19, 27 פרים בני בקר שנים ייי; 11Q**19** XVII 13 (פרים שנים); *Jub*. 16:22 (or 'seven' instead of 'two'). Or reconstruct (less probably) תורין תר̊]י עשר, cf. Num 29:17 and 11Q**19** XXVIII 3.

Frg. 29

top margin

1]ן̊ קודם מד[בחא

2]בון עם עו̇◦[

3]ר̊בון לה [

4]משח וחמ[ר

5]קודמוהי̇[

6 רי]ח ניח̇[וח

Mus. Inv. 571
PAM 44.002

Notes on Readings

The fragment measures 4.7 x 2 cm, including an upper margin of 1 cm.

L. 2]בון[. In the original, there is no ink to be seen before the *bet*. The letter before final *nun* may also be *yod*.

L. 2]◦עוֹ. The small space between the vertical stroke and the trace of the next letter strongly suggest *waw*, but]עתֹ is also possible.

L. 3]רֹבון[. The left end of a head stroke and a vertical, not diagonal, tick remain before *bet*.

Translation

1.] in front of [the] alt[ar
2.] with [
3.] for him/it [
4.] oil; and win[e
5.] in front of him [
6.] a pleas[ant aro]ma [

Comments

L. 1 קודם מד]בחא. Cf. Lev 6:7 𝔐 אל פני המזבח, *Tg. Onq.* לקדם מדבחא; 11QPsalms[a] XXVII 5 (לפני המזבח).

L. 2]◦בון עם עוֹ[. Reconstruct perhaps יקרי]בון עם עוֹגֹ]י לחמא (or מקרי]בין). Cf. Lev 7:13 𝔐 על חלת לחם חמץ יקריב קרבנו. *Tg. Onq.* renders חלת with גריצן.

L. 3]רֹבון[. Possibly a form of הקרב.

L. 4]משח וחמ]ר. Probably not a juxtaposition of 'oil' and 'wine'; rather read וחמ]ר as the beginning of a new clause. Cf. Num 15:4-5 and similar constructions in Numbers 15 and 11Q**19**: 'a cereal offering . . . of flour mixed with . . . oil; and wine for a drink-offering'. In that case, reconstruct e.g. לנסכא after וחמ]ר.

L. 6 רי]ח ניחֹ]וח. The common expression is used five times in Numbers 15 (cf. previous note).

Frg. 30

top margin

1]◦[ ]ין ככול ד◦[

2]ון עוד לויא דבחֹ]ין

3] ולהוה להון ◦[

4]◦◦ מן מועדי אל[

5]ןֹ מא די ל[

6]תרוה◦[

Mus. Inv. 571, 572, 614B
PAM 44.002*, 44.008*, 44.009*

NOTES ON READINGS

When placed together, the six pieces form approximately the same shape as the right fragment of 44.002 (frg. 31). Frgs. 30–32 are darker in colour, and the skin has a different grain.

L. 1 [יׄן. Or [וׄן.

L. 1 ככול. The word is written as a correction over an erasure. The last two letters of the erasure were ון, or perhaps ין. Now the whole darkened area at the left of line 1 has broken away.

L. 1 ד°]. The photograph shows some traces of ink, probably of a downstroke, on the edge of the fragment.

L. 2 דבחׄ]ין. All that remains of the last letter is part of the downstroke. The slight inclination to the right at the top is not consistent with *reš*, but with e.g. *ḥet*.

L. 3 °]. The remaining traces are the downstroke and the extreme right slanting section of the head.

L. 4 [°°. In spite of the discolouration of the leather, a long slanting horizontal stroke is clearly visible. It is less clear whether the tick-like stroke is ink.

TRANSLATION

1.] like all [
2.] while the Levites sacrifice [
3.] and it will be for them [
4.] from the festivals of G[od (?)
5.] what is for[
6.] [

COMMENTS

L. 2 [ון עוד לויא דבחׄ]ין. Both the syntax of the damaged clause and the reconstruction of the last word are uncertain. עוד may mean 'still', 'yet', but ועוד would be expected. Likewise, עוד may be preceded by לא, in the sense of 'no longer', in which case one might reconstruct ולא להו]ן עוד. The reconstruction דבחׄ]ין is not certain; one may interpret the *dalet* as the relative pronoun.

L. 4 מן מועדי אל]. Reconstruct the last word e.g. אל]הא (cf. מועדי יהוה in Lev 23:2, 4, 37, 44).

L. 6 [תרוהי°]. Read e.g. א]תרוהיׄ], 'his places', or another plural noun with a 3rd masc. sing. suffix.

Frg. 31 i

top margin

[תׄ 1

[נׄון 2

[לא 3

Mus. Inv. 571
PAM 44.002

Notes on Readings

The fragment measures 5 x 3.3 cm, including an upper margin of unknown size (1.2 cm to line 2 of col. i). Vertical ruling is visible on both sides; horizontal ruling, on col. ii and in the intercolumnar margin. The distance between the vertical rulings is 1.5 cm.

L. 1 ת̊[. On the fragment, the base stroke of what may be *taw* is visible, slightly descending towards the left.

L. 2 נ̊ו̊ן[. The first letter may also be *taw*, the second perhaps *yod*.

Frg. 31 ii

top margin

ד◦] 1

כורסי̊]א 2

מנה ב̇◦] 3

ידא ח◦] 4

ועל ש̇◦] 5

היכלא̊] 6

ויק◦] 7

Mus. Inv. 571
PAM 44.002

Notes on Readings

L. 1 ד◦]. The downstroke of the second letter seems to have faded away. The remains suggest *yod* or *reš*. If the very thin stroke near the base is ink, *bet* is possible. The dot on the left edge may be the tip of the downstroke of the third letter. Following the taking of the photograph, a piece has broken off the fragment. Now only a small spot of the lower part of the *dalet* remains.

L. 3 ב̇◦]. The *bet* (or *kap*?) seems to have a short base, but the elongation of the base is in the other part of the crack. A tiny dot remains in the original. The photograph shows the bottom tip of a downstroke attached to the base of *bet*.

L. 4 ח◦]. All that remains of the last letter is the bottom part of the downstroke. Read e.g. חד̊]א.

L. 5 ש̇◦]. The first letter has been abraded partially, but the remaining traces may be the right and left arm of *šin*.

L. 7 ויק◦]. A small dot is all that remains of the last letter.

Translation

1. [
2. [the] throne [
3. from it [

4. the hand [
5. and on [
6. the Temple [
7. and [

NOTES ON READINGS

L. 7]○ויק. Reconstruct probably ויקר̊]א; cf. frg. 21 3 where יקרא is mentioned in connection with the היכל. Otherwise,]○ויק might be an imperfect.

Frg. 32

top margin

1]כורסיא [
2]ו̊כ̊תא וישור̊[
3]א היכלא ומן דמ̊[
4 ש]בעת קניה [
5]על ארבע ש̇[
6]ן מן היכלא
6a]ו̊י̇ד אבן דמא○[ומני[
7]ויקדשנה עליה̊[
8]לארבע
9]○י̊ן ויסוד

Mus. Inv. 572
PAM 44.009

NOTES ON READINGS

The upper fragment (lines 1–6) measures 4 x 2.9 cm. The actual colour of all the fragments on this plate is darker than that of the others due to deterioration.

The lower fragment (lines 6–9) measures 1.8 x 2 cm. It is very dark and covered with pieces of the white fibre used to preserve the back. The letters of the main hand are barely discernible, and the letters of the supralinear and intercolumnar addition are even more faint. On the basis of the photograph, it appears that the left end of a column has been preserved on the fragment, and the insertion was continued in the intercolumnar margin.

The join is very plausible: כלא[of the lower fragment supplements היכ] of the upper one. In addition, the traces beneath היכ] are clearly supralinear or intralinear and correspond to the intralinear addition in the lower fragment.

L. 1] כורסיא[. The tear at the bottom of the *samek* has been created by a crack which has separated the far part of the vertical stroke. The trace at the bottom to the left of *samek* is probably part of the diagonal breaking through the vertical stroke. Cf. נכסידון in frg. 23 ii 3.

L. 2 וֹכֹתא[. The first two letters are unclear due to an abrasion of the skin surface. The horizontal stroke at the bottom suggests a base extending beneath the right leg of *taw*. *Bet* and *mem* are far less likely than *kap*. The distance between the remains of the downstroke, which is clear in the original, and *kap* suggests *waw* or *yod*.

L. 2 ישוורֹ]. The traces after the first *waw* are not consistent with *he*. Rather, they suggest two letters, the first one resembling *waw*, the last one also similar to *waw* or perhaps the right part of *reš*.

L. 3 דמֹ]. Or דפֹ].

L. 6a וֹיֹד[. The upper fragment preserves the heads of the two last letters. The reading is based upon the assumption that the two fragments are attached at the left side.

L. 6a דמא°]. Or דמא °]. Only the downstroke of the last letter remains.

L. 6b ומני. The diagonal stroke and the position of the tick show that the second letter cannot be *bet*.

L. 7 ויקדשנה[. The shoulder of the *dalet* seems to be partially covered by an adherence.

L. 9 °יֹןֹ[. The top of the last letter may be somewhat too thick for final *nun*.

TRANSLATION

1.] the throne [
2.] the [ ] and he hastens [
3.] the Temple and from [
4.] its [s]even (*or*: [f]our) reeds [
5.] on four [
6.] from the Temple

6a] stone of [

7.] and he will sanctify it
8.] to four
9.] and the foundation of (?)

COMMENTS

L. 2 וישוורֹ]. The last letter is not certain but, palaeographically and grammatically, a form of שוי is difficult.

L. 3 ומן דמֹ]. Either the preposition followed by a noun or the indefinite personal pronoun with the relative pronoun -ד and a verbal form.

L. 4 ש]בעת. Or אר]בעת.

Frg. 33

1]ל֯ריח ניחוח[

2]◦יא ואיליא ג֯[

3]פרישא על֯[

4]ן֯ כ◦[

Mus. Inv. 572
PAM 44.009

NOTES ON READINGS

The fragment measures 2.3 x 2 cm. No ruling or margins can be seen.

L. 1 ל֯ריח[. *Bet* is much more difficult than *lamed.*

L. 2 ג֯[. The stroke is strictly parallel to the right leg of *ʾalep* but curved inside, which excludes letters other than *gimel.*

L. 4]ן֯. Or]ש֯.

L. 4 כ◦[. The last trace could be the top of the right arm of e.g. *ʾalep* or *šin*, or the top of *nun*..

TRANSLATION

1.] for a pleasant aroma [
2.] and the rams
3.] dedicated [
4.] [

Frg. 34

top margin?

1]◦ אלן [

2]◦ורחׄ[

3]◦◦[

Mus. Inv. 572
PAM 44.009

NOTES ON READINGS

The fragment is dark in colour.

L. 1]◦. *ʾAlep*, *he*, *waw*, and *yod* are possible.

L. 2]◦ורחׄ[. The last letter could also be *gimel*. The tick of the first letter indicates e.g. *bet*, *dalet*, or *reš*.

Frg. 35

1]א מן כול֯[

2]רוחי֯ ע[

Mus. Inv. 572
PAM 44.009

NOTES ON READINGS

The fragment is very dark in colour.

L. 1 כול֯[. The trace of the last letter is also compatible with *šin*.

TRANSLATION

1.] from all [
2.] spirits of [

Frg. 36

top margin?

1]◦רין

2]ש֯[

Mus. Inv. 572
PAM 44.009

NOTES ON READINGS

The blank space at the left side of line 1 is either a *vacat* or the margin. It is not clear from the photograph whether the piece at the right is attached to the larger piece. This fragment is the lightest on Mus. Inv. 572, corresponding in colour to the larger fragments of the manuscript.

L. 1]◦רין. The first trace may be the left arm of *šin*. The small piece at the right may preserve other traces of the same letter. The rather thick vertical stroke above the first letter is most probably the left margin ruling (cf. the rulings on Mus. Inv. 574).

L. 2]ש֯[. Faint traces of the tops of three strokes are visible, consistent with *šin*.

Frg. 37

1]עלון ◦[

2]◦י מ◦[

3]י̊א פחתא̊ ל̊[

4]די ישר̊[

Mus. Inv. 572
PAM 44.009

NOTES ON READINGS

The fragment consists of two pieces placed separately in the photograph. The small piece, printed just beneath the largest fragment in the photograph, fits perfectly to the left of the larger piece. The small piece is now completely dark and illegible.

L. 1]◦. In spite of two downstrokes and a horizontal stroke, the reading is uncertain. *Waw* or *ḥet* is possible, followed by another letter. The curve of the diagonal rules out *ʾalep*.

L. 2 ◦י[. Only a dot of the letter preceding *yod* remains.

L. 2]מ◦. The diagonal stroke after the *mem* may be the tick of *yod*, in which case the downstroke has faded away. The dot at the top of the smallest piece is probably the far left tip of the base of *mem*.

L. 3 פחתא̊. The top of the left leg of the *ḥet* is preserved on the small piece. The two traces after the *taw* are compatible with the left leg and the top of the right arm of *ʾalep*.

L. 4 ישר̊]. The remains of the *šin* on both pieces fit perfectly.

COMMENTS

L. 3 פחתא̊. The meanings 'governor' and 'curse' seem out of place in this composition, but the lack of context precludes determining another meaning.

Additional Fragments

Apart from frgs. 1–4, Mus. Inv. 578A contains fifty additional fragments, the largest being *c*.2.5 x 2 cm and the smallest no larger than 0.2 x 0.2 cm (see pl XL). The largest fragments, some with tissue attached to them, are photographed both in PAM 43.993 and in IAA 508044. Several of these larger fragments seem to be inscribed (visible on IAA 508044), but the letters are very vague and indistinguishable. Most of the small fragments have probably broken away from the two wads of PAM 43.993, and many have traces of just one or two letters.

In addition, Mus. Inv. Box 1030 contains small, unseparated fragments which have not been photographed.

20. 11QTemple[b]

(PLATES XLI–XLVII)

Previous discussion: Y. Yadin, מגילת־המקדש—*The Temple Scroll*, vol. 3 *Supplementary Plates* (Jerusalem: Israel Exploration Society, The Institute of Archaeology of the Hebrew University of Jerusalem, The Shrine of the Book, Hebrew 1977, English 1983), pls. 35*–40*; L. van der Bogaard, 'Le Rouleau du Temple: quelques remarques concernant les "petits fragments"', *Von Kanaan bis Kerala. Festschrift für Prof. Mag. Dr. Dr. J. P. M. van der Ploeg O. P. zur Vollendung des siebzigsten Lebensjahres am 4. Juli 1979. Überreicht von Kollegen, Freunden und Schülern*, eds. W. C. Delsman, J. T. Nelis, J. R. T. M. Peters, W. H. Ph. Römer, A. S. van der Woude (AOAT 211; Kevelaer: Verlag Butzon & Bercker / Neukirchen Vluyn: Neukirchener Verlag, 1982) 285–94; A. S. van der Woude, 'Ein bisher unveröffentlichtes Fragment der Tempelrolle', *RevQ* 13 (1988) 89–92; M. O. Wise, 'A New Manuscript Joint in the "Festival of Wood Offering" (Temple Scroll XXIII)', *JNES* 47 (1988) 113–21; B. Z. Wacholder, 'The Fragmentary Remains of 11QTorah (Temple Scroll)', *HUCA* 62 (1991) 1–116; F. García Martínez, '11QTemple[b]: A Preliminary Publication', *The Madrid Qumran Congress. Proceedings of the International Congress on the Dead Sea Scrolls, Madrid 18–21 March 1991*, vol. 2, eds. J. T. Barrera and L. V. Montaner (STDJ 11, 2; Leiden: E. J. Brill, 1992) 363–90, pls. 9–15; E. Qimron, *The Temple Scroll. A Critical Edition with Extensive Reconstructions* (Judean Desert Studies; Beer Sheva–Jerusalem: Ben-Gurion University of the Negev Press, Israel Exploration Society, 1996); É. Puech, 'Fragments du plus ancien exemplaire du Rouleau du Temple (4Q524)', *Legal Texts and Legal Issues. Proceedings of the Second Meeting of the International Organization for Qumran Studies, Cambridge 1995. Published in Honour of J. M. Baumgarten*, eds. M. J. Bernstein, F. García Martínez, J. Kampen (STDJ 23; Leiden: E. J. Brill, 1997).

Physical Description

THE fragments of 11Q**20** are of a creamy colour with many dark stains. The leather is medium in thickness and the surface is well prepared, with a fine grain. Vertical and horizontal ruling is faint but visible in most of the fragments.

Fifty-eight fragments were photographed separately in the PAM series. IAA photographs have recently been taken of three fragments (frgs. 4b, 7, 42) and two tiny fragments (frgs. 10g, 30b) have been joined on the museum plates without being photographed. A photograph of frg. 14 was not available in time for inclusion in the plates of this volume. Several fragments which were still joined in the earliest photographs have since broken, and are now presented separately on different museum plates. There are forty-two fragments, when counting joined fragments as one. Thirty fragments (frgs. 1–30) can be placed in sixteen separate columns, whereas twelve others (frgs. 31–42) cannot be placed with certainty. Some of these unidentified fragments certainly stem from other columns so that, altogether, one may have the remains of approximately twenty columns.

Yadin, García Martínez, and Wacholder published most of the fragments, but used a different numbering system. To facilitate comparison, the two following tables list the correspondences between the present and previous publications.

TABLE 1: *Identified Fragments of 11Q20*

Present Publication		Previous Publications			Photographs	Mus. Inv.
Frg.	Col.	Yadin	García Martínez	Wacholder		
1a	I	40* 7	26	11	42.178, 43.978	577
1b	I	35* 1	1	2	42.179, 43.976	580
1c+e	I	35* 1	1	3	42.175, 43.978	577
1d	I				44.006	614
2	I	35* 2	2	1	42.178, 43.978	577
3	II–III		3		42.176, 44.114	567
4a	II	35* 3	4	4	43.976	580
4b	II				563769	1032
5	III	40* 14		5	42.178, 44.117	621B
6a	III	36* 1	5	7	42.175, 44.008	614B
6b	III				44.006	614
6c	III		5	6	42.175, 44.008	614B
7	III				508042	577
8a	IV	36* 2	6	8	42.180, 43.975	608
8b	IV	36* 3	6	9	42.177, 43.975	608
9	IV	36* 4	7	10	42.180, 43.978	577
10a	V	37* 1	8	12	42.179, 43.975	608
10b	V	40* 10	24	13	42.178, 43.978	577
10c	VI		8	16	42.179, 43.977	608 1031
10d	VI	37* 3	8	18	42.178, 43.977	607
10e	VI	38* 1	8	19	42.178, 43.977	608
10f	VI	40* 12	8	20	42.178, 43.977	608
10g	VI				not photographed	608
11a	V	37* 2	9	14	42.178, 43.976	580
11b	V	40* 9	23	15	42.178, 43.978	577
12	VI			30	44.008	614B
13	VII	38* 2	10	21	42.178, 43.978, 44.010, 44013	610
14	VIII				589612	1020
15a	IX	38* 3	11	24	42.178, 43.978	577
15b	IX	38* 3	11	25	42.178, 43.978	577
15c	IX		35	34	42.176, 44.008	614B

Present Publication		Previous Publications			Photographs	Mus. Inv.
Frg.	Col.	Yadin	García Martínez	Wacholder		
16	IX		38	26	44.008	614B
17	X	38* 4	12	27	42.177, 43.978, 44.010	566
18	XI			29	42.175, 44.114	567
19	XI				44.005	613
20	XI	40* 5	21	31	42.178, 43.978	577
21	XII–XIII	39* 1	13	32	42.178, 43.976	580
22	XII	40* 3	22	33	42.178, 43.978	580
23a	XII	39* 2	14	36	42.178, 43.976	580
23b	XII	39* 2	14	37	42.178, 43.976	580
23c	XII	39* 3	15	38	42.178, 43.976	580
23d	XII			39	42.177, 44.005	613
24	XII		37	35	42.176, 44.008	614B
25	XIII	39* 4	16	40	42.177, 43.976	580
26	XIV–XV	39* 6	18	42	42.180, 43.978	577
27	XIV		19		44.117	621B
28a	XIV	40* 4	17	43	42.177, 44.006	614
28b	XIV	40* 4	17	44	42.177, 43.978	577
29	XIV				44.114	567
30a	XVI		20	45	42.178, 43.976	580
30b	XVI				not photographed	580
31a				28	42.177, 43.980	606
31b				28	42.177, 44.007	615
32					43.794	1016
33a					42.177, 44.117	621B
33b					42.177, 44.005	613
34					44.005	613
35					44.005	613
36		40* 6	29	22	42.178, 44.006	614
37			30		44.006	614
38			31	46	44.008	614B
39			32	17	44.008	614B
40					44.117	621B
41		40* 8		23	42.178, 43.977	607

Present Publication		Previous Publications			Photographs	Mus. Inv.
Frg.	Col.	Yadin	García Martínez	Wacholder		
42					563769	1032
43					not photographed	580

TABLE 2: *Fragments Previously Identified as 11Q20 and Present Identifications*

Previous Identifications			Present Identifications
Yadin	García Martínez	Wacholder	
40* 13	25	41	11Q**8** 16
40* 11	27		11Q**2** 1
39* 5			11Q**2** 5
40* 15			11Q**14** 1b
	28		11Q**8** 12
	33		11Q**5** F
	34		11Q**27** 2
	36		11Q**8** 11

TABLE 3: *Preserved Margins*

Col./Frg.	Right	Left	Top	Bottom
I	•			•
II		•		
III	•			•
IV		•	•	•
V		•	•	
VI	•		(•)	
VII		•		•
VIII		•		
IX			•	
XI		•		

XII		•	
XIII	•		
XIV	•	•	•
XV	•		•
31		•	
35	•		
37		•	• ?
40		•	• ?

Evidence of stitching can be found on four fragments. On the back of frg. 2 (col. I) appear five stitching holes from the beginning of the sheet. On frg. 8a (col. IV) stitching holes from the end of the sheet can be seen. On frg. 13 (col. VII) can be seen stitching holes and remains of stitching from the end of the sheet. Stitching holes from the beginning of the sheet are visible on frg. 27.

Measurements

The height of the inscribed parts of the columns (without margins) is 27.9 cm for col. I (reconstructed for twenty-six lines on the basis of an extant fragment of 16.9 cm containing the bottom sixteen lines); 27 cm for col. IV (reconstructed for twenty-six lines on the basis of an extant fragment of 20.6 cm containing the top twenty lines); 26.9 cm for col. V (reconstructed for twenty-six lines on the basis of an extant fragment of 17 cm containing the top sixteen lines).

The average line length in **11Q20** is 67 letter-spaces per line.

TABLE 4: *Average Line Lengths (letter-spaces per line)*

Col.	Letter-spaces per Line	Col.	Letter-spaces per Line
I	64	X	54
IV	57	XII	70
V	67	XIV	75
VI	64	XV	82
IX	67	XVI	66

TABLE 5: *Column Widths (excluding margins, in cm)*

Col.	Extant	Reconstructed	Total
I	12.1	4.5	17.6
IV	6.3	8.9	15.2
V	6.2	12.2	18.4

TABLE 6: *Margin Widths (in cm)*

Col.	Right*	Left	Top**	Bottom	Intercolumnar
I	2			2.5	
II					cols. II–III:
III					1.5
IV		2.1	1.5	2.9	
V			1.7		cols. V–VI:
VI			1.4		1.8
VII		1.8***		1.9	
IX			1.3		
XI		2**			cols. XI–XII:
XII					1.4–1.8
XIII					cols. XIII–XIV:
XIV	1.8		2		1.7–2.1
XV			1.7		

*Left and right margin widths are measured from the edge of the sheet to the vertical line.

**The top and bottom margins are all incomplete, except, perhaps, the top margin of col. XIII and the bottom margin of col. IV. The left margin of col. X is possibly incomplete.

***This is an estimated measurement, since the photograph does not show the vertical ruling.

Columns

Comparison with the text of 11Q**19** shows that the number of lines in cols. IV and V is 26. Interlinear spacing in the other columns is, allowing for occasional irregularities, more or less the same as that of cols. IV and V. Therefore, the number of lines in the other preserved columns should probably not exceed 25 to 27. The reconstruction of col. XII demands 26 to 27 lines, that of col. XIV 25 to 26 lines.

The combined evidence of cols. I and IV, belonging to the same sheet, shows that the inscribed part of the columns of this sheet took up between 27.2 and 27.7 cm. The height of the leather was thus at least between 31.6 and 32.1 cm (at least 1.5 cm top margin and 2.9 cm bottom margin in col. IV).

Most of the fragments that have been identified belong to two groups of columns. Cols. I–VI are consecutive, and only two columns are missing between cols. XI–XVI. A precise calculation of the number of columns missing between those groups is impossible, as the text of **11Q19** is very fragmentary in the pertinent section of the scroll, and the absence or presence of *vacat*s, as well as their lengths, differs between the scrolls.

TABLE 7: *Columns of 11Q**20** compared to 11Q**19***

11Q**20**	11Q**19**	
	Preserved Text	Reconstructed Range of Text
	(nine or ten columns of 11Q**20** missing before the first preserved column)	I 1–*c*.XIV 11
I	XV 03–XVI 04; bottom margin preserved	*c*.XIV 11–XVI 04
II	XVI 1–3, 8–11	XVI 04–XVII 11/12
III	XVII 13, XVIII 4–7, XIX 2–9	XVII 11/12–XIX 11
IV	XIX 12–XX 10, 13–16; top and bottom margin preserved	XIX 11–XX 16
V	XXI 01–XXII 5; top margin preserved	XX 16–XXII 6
VI	XXII 6–XXIII 01, 05–5; top margin preserved	XXII 6–*c*.XXIII 17
	(one column of 11Q**20** missing)	*c*.XXIII 17–*c*.XXV 10
VII	XXVII 02–09 ? bottom margin preserved	*c*.XXV 10–XXVII 09?
	(three [?] columns of 11Q**20** missing)	XXVII 09?–*c*.XXXI 2
VIII	XXXI 11–13	*c*.XXXI 2–XXXII 9
IX	XXXII 10–15; top margin preserved	XXXII 10–*c*.XXXIV 06
	(two [?] columns of 11Q**20** missing)	
X	XXXVII 9–XXXVIII 01	
	(three or four columns of 11Q**20** missing)	
XI	XLV 1–4	XLIV 1?–XLV 6?
XII	XLV 9 – XLVI 16	XLV 6?–XLVI 16
XIII	XLVI 16 – XLVII 3	XLVI 16–*c*.XLVIII 5
	(one column of 11Q**20** missing)	*c*.XLVIII 5–L 01/02
XIV	L 02–11, 15 – LI 1; top margin preserved	L 01/02–LI 5
XV	LI 5–17; top margin preserved	LI 5–*c*.LII 20
	(one column of 11Q**20** missing)	
XVI	LIV 19 – LV 06	
	(*c*. eight columns at the end of 11Q**20** missing)	

Palaeography

The manuscript is written in a developed Herodian formal script (*c.*20–50 CE). The hand is very similar to that of the first hand of 1QpHab, and several shared characteristics suggest both manuscripts were copied by the same scribe.

Although the variety of forms of individual letters is somewhat greater in 11Q**20** than in 1QpHab, the letters are very much alike. The major difference is the *bet*, which has two forms in 11Q**20**. The most common form in 11Q**20** is the small *bet* with a slanting, sometimes curved downstroke. *Bet* in 1QpHab corresponds to the less common square form of 11Q**20**.

Neither hand makes a distinction between *waw* and *yod*. A variety of forms appear; short and long downstrokes and short, long, thin, and thick ticks; all forms are used for both *waw* and *yod*. The variety is slightly greater in 11Q**20**.

In addition to the form of the letters, the hands share a number of characteristics. Spaces between words are often minimal. The position of the letters with regard to the horizontal dry lines varies, and in certain cases an 'X' is written at the end of the line at its intersection with the left margin ruling line.

In both manuscripts, the lines are slightly crooked. In 1QpHab, where the ruling lines are very clear, this is less apparent, but it is easy to see how the letters are sometimes written through, and sometimes hanging below the ruling lines.

An 'X' appears at the end of eleven lines in 1QpHab and at the end of two lines in 11Q**20** (cols. IV 9 and V 9). The only common feature seems to be that, in all the cases, the line ends some distance before the margin. The 'X' may indicate that the sentence continues, and that the blank space at the end of the line is not a *vacat*. In both manuscripts, however, there are also similar lines without the addition of an 'X'.[1]

The combination of these shared features suggests that both manuscripts were written by the same scribe.

Additions to the manuscript were written in different hands (cf. TABLE 9).

Orthography and Morphology

The orthography corresponds to that of 11Q**19**: the spelling is *plene*, and the suffixes are of the expanded forms with *he*. Most of the differences between 11Q**20** and 11Q**19** concern the dropping of radical *ʾalep* in 11Q**20**. In col. V 24, the scribe wrote ונשכמה with *samek* for original *śin*. An example of interchange between *mem* and *nun* in final position is attested in col. XII 5 ימי{ן}ם.

[1] The 'X' sign also seems to serve as a line-filler in five texts from Naḥal Ḥever (pap 5/6Ḥev 42, 44, 45, 46, XḤev/Se 21) and in 4Q**252** (courtesy of E. Tov).

TABLE 8: *Orthographic Variants between 11Q**20** and 11Q**19***

11Q**20**		11Q**19**	
I 20	למלו{א}	XV 14	למלא
I 23	ברישונה[	XV 18	בריאש[ונה]
IV 25	האי]לים	XX 15	האי]ל[י]ם or האי]לם
V 8	ריאשונים	XXI 4	ראישונים
V 9	ברישונה	XXI 5	בר[אי]שונ[ה]
XII 4	]כי	XLV 11	כיא
XIV 23	טמים	LI 1	טמאים
XV 3	נפשותיהמה	LI 9	נפשותמה

*Relation to 11Q**19***

11Q**19** and 11Q**20** are clearly two copies of the same work. Although the evidence is restricted and the fragments tend to be clustered around certain columns, the preserved material of 11Q**20** covers almost all the five parts of 11Q**19** and has preserved elements of four of the five sources of 11Q**19** identified by Wilson and Wills and carefully studied by Wise.[2] The only missing element is the Midrash to Deuteronomy, including the King's Law, the absence of which may be due merely to the vagaries of preservation.

An examination of the textual relationship between 11Q**19** and 11Q**20** is difficult because of the fragmentary nature of both texts. The preserved texts of both manuscripts show few, if any, differences, the main variation being related to the length of and presence or absence of *vacat*s. On the other hand, difficulties in reconstructing one of the texts on the basis of the other may suggest differences. In such cases, however, one must take into account the possibility of a variation in the *vacat* sizes, or of lost supralinear or intralinear corrections.

Indirect evidence for the essential correspondence between the two texts can be found in the corrections in 11Q**20**, which frequently attest the text of 11Q**19**.[3]

---

[2] A. M. Wilson, L. Wills, 'Literary Sources in the Temple Scroll', *HTR* 75 (1982) 275–88; M. Wise, *A Critical Study of the Temple Scroll from Qumran Cave 11* (SAOC 49; Chicago: The Oriental Institute of the University of Chicago, 1990).

[3] In the majority of cases, the 11Q**19** text presented here is the one produced by Qimron, *The Temple Scroll*. Occasionally, a reading consisting only of uncertain letters has been omitted. In a few cases, Yadin's reading has been preferred to that of Qimron.

TABLE 9: *Corrections in 11Q20*

11Q**20**	Correction	11Q**19**	
I 20	{א}למלו (erasure of *ʾalep*)	XV 14	למלא
IV 1	שבע^ה (supralinear addition)	XIX 12	שבעה
IV 9	כמשפט (supralinear addition in different ink and different hand)		
IV 24	^לעולם (supralinear addition)		[לעול]ם̇
V 24	ומנחתם^ה (supralinear addition)		
V 24	ונ{ש}סכמה (*samek* superimposed upon *śin*, by the same pen used for the addition to the next line)		
V 25	הכוהנים (supralinear addition with different pen, and possibly in a different hand)	XXII 5	ה]כ̇ו̇ה̇נים
X 5	[מ]קום (supralinear addition in different hand)	XXXVII 9	מק̇ו̇ם
XII 5	ימי{ן}ם (*mem* superimposed upon *nun*)	XLV 12	ימים
XII 11	המקדש (intercolumnar addition in different hand)		
XIII 3	וה|באים (first two letters added to the right of right ruling)		
XV 2	לכ{מ̇}ה (erasure)	LI 7	לכה
XV 7	לכ^מ]ה (supralinear addition)	LI 16	לכמה
Frg. 31 2a	עלידם (interlinear addition in different hand)		
31 4	]∘ש̇∘ת̇מה (addition at end of line in different hand)		
35 2a	כול] (interlinear addition)		

Mus. Inv. 566, 567, 577, 580, 606, 607, 608, 610, 613, 614, 614B, 615, 621B, 1016, Box 1020, 1031, 1032[4]
PAM 42.175, 42.176, 42.177*, 42.178, 42.179, 42.180, 43.794*, 43.975*, 43.976*, 43.977*, 43.978*, 43.980, 44.005*, 44.006*, 44.007, 44.008*, 44.010*, 44.013*, 44.114*, 44.117*
IAA 508042*, 563769*, 589612*

[4] S. A. Reed, M. J. Lundberg, and M. B. Phelps (*The Dead Sea Catalogue. Documents, Photographs and Museum Inventory Numbers* [SBL Resources for Biblical Study 32; Atlanta, Georgia: Scholars Press, 1994] 181, 498) also refer to Mus. Inv. 616 which appears to be missing. Indeed, it cannot be located in the Rockefeller Museum, but since all the photographed 11Q**20** fragments can be located on other museum plates, it seems unlikely that Mus. Inv. 616 contains 11Q**20** material (or even exists).

Col. I Frgs. 1, 2

Parallel: **11Q19** XV 03–XVI 04 (underline)

1–8 [ ]

9 [ ]◦◦[ ]

10 [וה]קריבו על המ[זבח לכול יום ויום]

11 [פר בן בקר אחד איל אחד כבשים בני שנה]שבעה ושעיר ע[זים לחטאת ומנחתמה]

12 [ונסכמה כמשפט הזה *vacat*]ולמלואים איל איל לכ[ול יום ואחד]

13 [וסלי לחם לכול איל ואחד וחצו את]כול האילים והסלים לשבעת[ימי]

14 [המלואים יום ויום כמחלקות הכוהנים] יהיו מקריבים ליהוה עולה[מן האיל ואת]

15 [החלב המכסה את הקרב ואת ש]תי הכליות ואת החלב אשר עלי[הנה ואת החלב]

16 [אשר על הכסילים ואת האלי]ה לעומת עציהה ואת יותרת הכבד[ומנחתו ונסכו]

17 [כמשפט וחלת מצה אחת מ]ן הסל וחלת לחם שמן אחת ורקיק[אחד ושמו הכול]

18 [על החלבים עם שוק התרו]מה אשר לימין ויניפו המקריבים[את האילים ואת]

19 [סלי הלחם תנופה ל]פני יהוה עולה היא אשה ריח ניחוח[לפני יהוה והקטירו הכול]

20 [על המזבח על ה]עולה למלו{א} על נפשותמה שבעת ימי[ם *vac*]*at* [ ]

21 [*vac*[*at* ואם הכוה]ן הגדול[יהיה עומד לכהן]

22 [לפני יהוה ומלא י]דו ללבוש את הבגדים[תחת]אביהו ויקרי[ב פרים שנים אחד על]

23 [כול העם ואחד על הכו]הנים ויקרב את אשר [ל]כוהנים ברישונה[וסמכו זקני הכוהנים]

24 [את ידיהמה על ראו]שו ואחריהמה הכ[ו]הן הגדול וכול הכ[והנים אחר ישחטו את]

25 הפר[לפני יהוה]ולקחו זקני הכוהני[ם] מדם הפר ונתנ[ו על קרנות המזבח באצבעם]

26 מן הד[ם]◦ ישפוכו סביב על ארבע פנות עזרת ה[מזבח]

bottom margin

Average line length: 64 letter-spaces
Mus. Inv. 577, 580, 614
PAM 42.175, 42.178, 42.179, 43.976*, 43.978*, 44.006*
IAA 508042

NOTES ON READINGS

Frg. 1 consists of five joined fragments. Frgs. 1c and 1e seem to be partially joined in PAM 42.175, but in Mus. Inv. 577 (PAM 43.978) they have been separated, flattened, and then incorrectly joined, frg. 1e being placed two lines too high. Frg. 2 should be placed at some distance to the right of frg. 1. It preserves the right margin and part of the stitching, although the string has fallen off. On its back, five stitching holes can be counted. It is not clear, however, whether frg. 2 was positioned to the immediate right of frg. 1 (reading in line 25 הפרׄ ולקחו and in line 26 מן הד]ם [ישפוכו), or at some distance (reading line 25 הפרׄ] לפני יהוה [ולקחו; a reconstruction of line 26 is more difficult).

The calculation of the average line length, based on lines 15–19 and 22–23, is 64 letter-spaces (lines ranging from 62 to 68 letters-spaces).

L. 9]◦◦[. The two vertical strokes belong either to a two-legged letter like *he* or *ḥet*, or to a one-legged letter (*waw*, *zayin*, or *yod*) preceded by *ḥet* or another one-legged letter. The following, slightly sloping base stroke is most consistent with *mem* or *nun*. Read, e.g.]הׄמׄ[.

L. 11 ושעיר. The word has been preserved on two different fragments.

L. 11 עׄ]זים. The tip of the right arm of *ʿayin* is written close after the *reš* on frg. 1a.

L. 17 מ[ן הׄסל. The fragment with final *nun* and *he* is still attached in PAM 42.179, but has broken off in PAM 43.976.

L. 20 למלו{אׄ}. Or: למלואׄ. The reading of the last traces is based upon the photographs, since this segment is now darkened and broken. The remaining traces after the second *lamed* do not correspond to either *he* or *ʾalep*, but to *waw/yod* with the right arm of *ʾalep* (the two traces might also be read as *reš*, but that is improbable). The next word, על, follows closely, leaving hardly any space for *ʾalep*. One must assume either that the *ʾalep* was inserted between למלו and על, but then faded, or that the *ʾalep* of an original למלוא was then partially erased, its right arm remaining. The latter possibility is more plausible than the former.

L. 20 *vac*]*at*. The absence of any traces above]הגדול in line 21 seems to rule out the reconstruction ימ]י המלואים.

L. 22]הבגדיםׄ. A small portion of the top of the final *mem* is still visible on the fragment. The spot is certainly ink.

L. 22 אׄביהו[. Or: אׄבוהי[.

L. 23 ל]כׄוׄהנים. A tiny shred from the upper part of the leather, shown superimposed on the fragment in PAM 42.175, preserves traces which probably belong to *kap* and *waw*.

L. 26 ◦[. The trace belongs to the upper left part of a letter, e.g. final *mem*.

L. 26 ארבע. IAA 508042 clearly shows the left leg of *ʾalep* and the *reš*.

TRANSLATION

1–8. [ ]

9. [ ]

10. [and] they shall offer on the al[tar, day by day]

11. [one young bullock, one ram,] seven [yearling lambs] and a he-[goat for a sin-offering, and their offering]

12. [and their libation according to this regulation. *vacat*] And for the consecration one ram for ea[ch day]

13. [and baskets of bread for each ram. And they shall apportion] all the rams and the baskets for the seven [days]

14. [of the consecration, for every day. According to the priestly divisions] they shall offer to YHWH a burnt-offering [of a ram, and]

15. [the fat which covers the entrails and the t]wo kidneys, and the fat that is upon [them and the fat]

16. [that is upon the loins and the tai]l near its backbone and the appendage of the liver[, and its offering and its libation]
17. [according to the regulation, and one unleavened loaf fr]om the basket, and one loaf of oiled bread, and [one] wafer, [and they shall place it all]
18. [upon the fat with the leg of the wave-offer]ing, the right leg. And those who are offering shall wave [the rams and]
19. [the baskets of bread as a wave-offering be]fore YHWH. It is a burnt-offering, a fire-sacrifice of fragrance appeasing before [YHWH. And they shall offer it all]
20. [on the altar with the] burnt-offering, as a consecration for themselves, seven day[s.] *va[cat*]
21. [*va*]*cat* And when the high [pries]t [stands up to serve as priest]
22. [before YHWH, he shall consecrate] him[sel]f by adorning the vestments [in succession to] his fathers, and he shall offe[r two bullocks, one for]
23. [all the people, and another for the pr]iests, and he shall offer the one [for the] priests first, [and the elders of the priests shall lay]
24. [their hands on] its [hea]d, and after them the high [pr]iest and all the pr[iests. Then they shall slaughter]
25. the bullock [before YHWH] and the elders of the priest[s] shall take from the blood of the bullock and put [with their fingers on the horns of the altar]
26. some of the blo[od] they shall pour around on the four corners of the ledge of the [altar]

COMMENTS

A large part of the terminology of the sacrifice is also found in Jub 21:7–10, part of which is preserved in **4Q219** (4QJub^{d}) I 32–38 and **4Q220** (4QJub^{e}) 1 3–11.[5]

Ll. 12–13 איל איל לכ[ול יום ואחד] / [וסלי לחם לכול איל ואחד. The corresponding text of 11Q**19** XV 3–4 has a supralinear addition between lines 3 and 4. The reconstruction איל איל לכול יום ויום /] [ו]סלי לחם לכול אי[לי המלואים סל אחד לאיל / [ה]אחד (Yadin, Qimron) is much too large too fit in this column, has the awkward formula לאיל האחד, and does not clarify why the copyist missed the added words. According to the tentative reconstruction proposed here the copyist skipped from the first to the second instance of ואחד.

L. 13 [ימי]. This reconstruction, with המלואים] as the first word of line 14, leaves a short gap between the last word and the end of the line. As a result, line 13, with 58 letter-spaces, is considerably shorter than the average (64 to 65 letter-spaces), and somewhat shorter than other short lines of 62 letter-spaces. Another option is that the line ended with המלואים, that word being partially written in the left margin. In that case, we must assume a *vacat* in the first part of line 14.

L. 14 [כמחלקות הכוהנים. Cf. 1 Chr 28:13, 21; 2 Chr 8:14; 31:2. The reconstruction כמחלק[ו]תיהמה is too short for 11Q**19** XV 5 and for this line.

Ll. 14–15 ואת] / [החלב המכסה את הקרב. Reconstructed with, e.g. Exod 19:22 and Lev 3:9; alternatively, one may reconstruct with 4QJub^{e} 1 7 ואת] / [החלב על הקרבים.

L. 16 האלי[ה̊. The reconstruction of תמימה between האליה and לעומת produces excessively long lines, both in this column and in 11Q**19** XV 8.

L. 17 כמשפט וחלת מצה אחת מ[ן הסל וחלת. Neither here nor in 11Q**19** XV 9 is there enough space for the reconstruction כמשפט ולקחו חלת מצה אחת מ[ן הסל וחלת. The text is a quotation of Exod 29:23, which also lacks the verb.

L. 21 לכהן]. Cf. Exod 29:1. Alternatively, reconstruct לשרת].

L. 22 ומלא. Materially this fits better than אשר מלא.

L. 24 הכ[והנים אחר ישחטו את]. הכ[והנים ושחטו את] produces a line which is too short.

L. 26 ◦] ישפוכו. Reconstruct in the gap before]ישפוכו, e.g. ואת הדם.

[5] Cf. *DJD* XIII, 42, 57.

Col. II Frgs. 3 i, 4

Parallel: **11Q19** XVI 1–3, 8–11 (underline)

[top margin]

1] ∘∘ ∘[

2] על] הבוהן

3] [מן השמן

4] [

5] [

6] את כול החלב אשר על הקרב ואת יותרת הכבד ואת שתי הכליות [ואׄתׄ] החלב[

7]אשר עליהנה ואת החלב אשר על הכסילים ואת מנחתו ואת נסכו כמשפט [ויקטי]ר על[

8]המזבח עולה הוא אשה ריח ניחוח ליהוה *vacat* [*vacat*] [

9] *vacat* ואת בשר הפר ואת עורו עם פרשו ישרופו [מחוץ ל]עיר[

Mus. Inv. 567, 580, 1032
PAM 42.176, 43.976*, 44.114*
IAA 563769*

NOTES ON READINGS

Col. II is composed of two fragments. Frg. 3 i is likely to correspond to **11Q19** XVI 1–3, and frg. 4 to 11Q**19** XVI 8–11. A comparison of the line lengths and column height of 11Q**19** and **20** indicates that 11Q**20** II corresponded to 11Q**19** XVI 04–XVII 11 or 12. The comparison with 11Q**19** XVI suggests that frg. 4 should be placed close to the left side of the column in lines 6–9, or, from a material point of view, but less likely, at the right in lines 7–10. The shape of frg. 4a seems to correspond to that of frg. 8b in col. IV, implying a location in lines 9–12. This location is not, however, compatible with the reconstruction of the column. The tiny frg. 4b, found in Mus. Inv. Box 1032, can be joined to frg. 4a.

Line 7, as reconstructed, has 69 letter-spaces. A different horizontal placement of frg. 4 may lead to a slightly different length. An average of 70 letters fits with the reconstruction of the column and the identification of the letters of col. III 2.

L. 1 ∘∘ ∘[. There are three or four traces which seem to be remnants of letters. The vertical stroke above the *bet* and *waw* of הבוהן in line 2 is probably the bottom part of a final *kap*, *nun*, of *qop*, or of a partly faded final *mem*.

L. 6]ואׄתׄ[. Most of *ʾalep*, as well as the right part of *taw*, are preserved on the tiny frg. 4b.

L. 8 *vacat*[. The colour of the trace at the right edge of the fragment is different from the other traces, and it seems unlikely to be ink.

TRANSLATION

1. [ ]
2. [on] the thumb
3. [ ]from the oil
4. [ ]
5. [ ]
6. [all the fat that is upon the entrails and the lobe of the liver and the two kidneys] and [the fat]
7. [that is upon them and the fat that is upon the loins and its offering and its libation according to the regulation.] And he shall bur[n it upon] ,
8. [the altar. It is a burnt-offering, a fire-sacrifice of fragrance appeasing to YHWH. *vacat*] *vacat* [ ]
9. [*vacat* They shall burn the flesh of the bullock, and its hide with its offal] outside the [city]

COMMENTS

It is virtually certain that the first three lines correspond to 11Q**19** XVI 1–3, and contain an abbreviated quotation of Exod 29:20-21. However, as the texts are poorly preserved, it is impossible to reconstruct the lines with any certainty.

L. 2 על]הבוהן. Cf. Exod 29:20 ולקחת מדמו ונתתה על . . . ועל בהן ידם הימנית ועל בהן רגלם הימנית. In this verse, and in all the other biblical uses of בהן, the word is preceded by על and is in the construct state. Both the phrasing ונ]תנו מן הדם in 11Q**19** XVI 2 and the use of the article before בהון show that this text is a modification of Exod 29:20.

L. 3]מן השמן. Cf. Exod 29:21 ולקחת מן הדם אשר על המזבח ומשמן המשחה והזית.

Ll. 2–3 The lines of this column must have had 65 to 75 letters-spaces, whereas the average line length in 11Q**19** XVI is 46 letter-spaces. It is clear that the mentioning of]מן השמן in line 3 should be placed close to the end of 11Q**19** XVI 3. This seems to be in conflict with a reconstruction of 11Q**19** XVI 2–3 which follows 𝔐 by first mentioning the right earlobe, and then the right thumb and big toe. There are several possible explanations. First, this column may have had either a longer text, or a rather long *vacat* where 11Q**19** XVI did not. Second, 11Q**19** XVI may have had the same text, though partially written supralinearly. Third, both texts agree, but did not follow 𝔐. In that case, על הבוהן should probably be placed immediately after ונ]תנו מן הדם [of 11Q**19** XVI 2. The few remnants of the quotation in 11Q**19** XVI and this manuscript show that the quotation of Exod 29:20-21 is abbreviated considerably. 11Q**19** XVI 2–3 shows that the two ולקחת phrases are dropped, and that the object of ולקחת is transferred to the next verb. Also, the replacement of the construct phrases בוהן ידם and שמן משחה by the nouns with the definite article הבוהן and השמן witness the tendency towards condensation. In view of the available space, one may perhaps reconstruct the second part of 11Q**19** XVI 3 as ויז]ו מן הדם ומן השמן עליו ועל בגדיו], in which case the next line would begin with a *vacat*. In view of the required letters between הבוהן [and]מן השמן, however, one should probably prefer a wording in which]מן השמן is placed towards the end, e.g. ויז]ו עליו ועל בגדיו מן הדם ומן השמן]. For this less common word order, cf. Lev 16:19 והזה עליו מן הדם.

L. 6]ואׄתׄ[החלב]. In view of the average line length,]ואׄתׄ[cannot correspond to ואת in the phrase ואת החלב אשר על הכסילים.

Ll. 7–8 כמשפט] ויקטי[ר על] / [המזבח. These four words might just fit at the end of 11Q**19** XVI 9, with the line extending one or two letters further than the other (reconstructed) lines of 11Q**19** XVI.

L. 9 ואת בשר הפר ואת עורו עם פרשו ישרופו]מחוץ ל[עיר]. Cf. Exod 29:14. The space before ואת בשר is probably a *vacat*. One may also reconstruct ל[מחנה] instead of ל[עיר].

Col. III Frgs. 3 ii, 5, 6, 7

Parallel: **11Q19** XVII 13, XVIII 4–7, XIX 2–9 (underline)

1 *va]cat* וכבשים[

2 בׄנׄי֯] שנה שבעה [

3–8] [

9]] ושעי֯[ר עזים לחטאת[

10 [לכפר על כול עם הקהל ומנחתו ונסכו כמשפט עשרון סולת ב]לולה[בשמן רביעית]

11 [ההין ויין לנסך רביעית ההין ע]ל[עם הקהל מכול]

12–20] [

21] ברובע]היום יקרׄ[יבו את עול]תׄ הבכורׄ[ים [

22] שנים עשר כבשים בני שנה]תׄ[מי]מים ומנחתמה ונׄסׄכׄמה כׄ[משפט והניפו]

23] הבכורים]לכׄוהנׄים יהיו ואכלום בחצ[ר הפנימית]

24] לחם הבכורים ואחר]ם לחם חדש אביבות[ומלילות והיה [

25 [היום הזה מקרא קודש חוק עולם לדורותם כול מל]אכת עבודה לוא י[עשו כי חג]

26 [שבועות הוא וחג בכורים לזכרון לעולם *vacat* וספרתמה לכמה מיום]

bottom margin

Mus. Inv. 567, 577, 614, 614B, 621B
PAM 42.175, 42.176, 42.178, 44.006*, 44.008*, 44.114*, 44.117*
IAA 508042

NOTES ON READINGS

Col. III is composed of four fragments. The exact placement of frg. 5 (lines 9–11) is uncertain, though it clearly belongs somewhere in the column. Frg. 6 consists of three joined fragments which are darkened and crumbled, but legible. Frg. 6b has broken into several pieces, of which all but the largest have crumbled, but the join with frgs. 6a and 6c is virtually certain. PAM 42.175 shows frgs. 6a and 6c still partially attached. Frg. 6a is now covered with a protective tissue, and only faint traces can be discerned. The precise positioning of frg. 6 is uncertain, but a position in the left half of the column is probable. Frg. 7 has been removed from the back of frg. 9 and preserves the bottom margin.

No complete line can be reconstructed with certainty. However, the comparison with the text of **11Q19** indicates an average line length of slightly more than 64 letter-spaces.

L. 1 No traces are visible at the beginning of the line. They have either faded away, or a *vacat* should be read.

L. 2 בׄנׄיׄן. The first letter is either *bet* or *reš*; the unticked head of the next downstroke strongly suggests *nun*; the dot at the end is compatible with *yod*.

L. 21 עול[ׄתׄ. The trace near the right edge may be the base of *taw*.

L. 22 תׄ[מי]מים. The traces of a head at the beginning of frg. 6a must belong to *taw*, not to the first *mem*.

L. 22 ונׄסׄכׄמה. Traces of *nun* are visible on frgs. 6b and 6c. Only the right shoulder of *samek* and the tip of the base of *kap* are visible.

L. 26 לכמה. The dot below the *yod* of י]עשו in line 25 might perhaps be the upper part of the *lamed* of לכמה, the rest of the upper arm having faded away. Cf., however, a similar dot to the left of the *lamed* of לוא in line 25.

Translation

1. [and lambs]
2. of [a year seven]
3–8. [ ]
9. [ ]and a he-[goat for a sin-offering]
10. [to atone for all the people of the congregation, and its offering and its libation according to the regulation: a tenth of fine flour m]ixed [with oil, a quarter]
11. [of a *hin*, and wine for a libation, a quarter of a *hin* fo]r [the people of the congregation from all]
12–20. [ ]
21. [in the fourth quarter of] the day [t]he[y] shall of[fer the sacrifice] of the first fruit[s]
22. [twelve] p[er]fect [yearling lambs], and their offerings and their libations according to [the regulation, and they shall lift]
23. [the first fruits] shall be for the priests, and they shall eat them in the [inner] courtya[rd],
24. [bread of the first fruits. Then] new bread, ears of grain [and soft grain. And]
25. [this day will be proclaimed holy, an eternal precept for their generations. T]he[y] shall [do] no [men]ial work [at all, for it is the Feast]
26. [of Weeks, and the Feast of the First Fruits as an eternal memorial. *vacat* And you shall count from the day]

Comments

L. 2 בׄנׄיׄן שנה. In spite of the problem arising from the *vacat* in the first line, the reading בׄנׄיׄן, corresponding to 11Q**19** XVII 13, is the only reading that fits here.

L. 9 ושעיׄר. The word was probably preceded by והקריבו and the mentioning of other animals for slaughter. Read perhaps [והקריבו] at the end of 11Q**19** XVIII 3.

L. 10 לכפר על כול עם הקהל]. The reconstruction לכפר עליהמה (Wacholder) before ומנחתו ונסכו is much too short for both 11Q**19** XVIII 5 and this column. The proposed reconstruction fits perfectly in the line, but may be perhaps slightly too long for 11Q**19** XVIII 5. In that case, one should perhaps omit כול.

L. 11 ע]ל[. Or על כו]ל[.

L. 21 ברובע]היום יקר[יבו. Cf. col. IV 10 and the comments of Yadin on 11Q**19** XX 06.

Ll. 23–24] / [בחצ]ר הפנימית. הפנימית מנחה חד]שׁה / [בחצר] (Yadin) is too long for the space of 11Q**19** XIX 6. בחצר הפנימית ע[םׄ] (Qimron) seems too short.

L. 25 מקרא קודש חוק עולם. The reconstruction of מקרא קודש is not certain, but the space of 11Q**19** XIX 8 shows that, if correct, the following word is more likely to be חוק than חוקות.

L. 25 כי חג]. The gap at the beginning of 11Q**19** XIX 9 is too large for the reconstruction י]עשו חג שבועות]. One must either assume a small *vacat* after י]עשו or a small word, like כי or בו.

Col. IV Frgs. 8, 9

Parallel: **11Q19** XIX 12–XX 16 (underline)

top margin

1]הביאכמה את המנחה חדשה ליהוה את ל[חם הבכורים שבע^ה שבוׄ]עות שבע[
2]שבתות תמימות תהיינה עד ממוחרת השבת ה[שביעית תספורו חמשים[^יום וה]קׄ[ר]בׄתׄמה
3]יין חדש לנסך ארבעה הינים מכול מטות[ישראל שלישית ההין על
4]המטה ויקריבו על היין ביום הזה עולה [ליהוה שנים]ע[שר אילים כול
5]ראשי אלפי ישראל א[ילׄיםׄ ומנחתמה כמשפט שנים
6]עשרונים סולת בלולה בשמן שלישית הה[ין שמן לאיל על הנסך הזה
7]ויקריבו עולה פרים שנים איל אחד וכבש[ים בני שנה שבעה ושעיר
8]עזים אחד לחטאת לכפר על כול עם ה[קׄהל *vacat*
9 [מנחתמ]ה ונסכמה ^כמשפט לפרים ולאיל x
10]ולכבשים ולשעיר עזים אשה ריח ניחוח [לׄיהוה ברובע היום יקריבו
11 [א]תׄ האילים ואת הנסך ויקריבו
12]שלמים [אׄ וכבשים]בני[שנה ארבעה
13]עשר ומנחתמה ונסכמה כמשפט לאילים ו[לׄ]כבשים אחר [העולה יעשום
14 [ואת חלבמה יקט]ירו על המזבח
15]את החלב המכסה את הקרב ואת כול החלב אשר על ה[קׄרבים ואת
16]יותרת הכבד ועל הכליות יסירנה *vac*[*at*
17]ואת החלב אשר עליהנה ואת אשר על הכסילים ואת הא[ליׄה לעומת
18]העצה ויקטירו הכוהנים את הכול על המזבח עם מנחתמ[הׄ ונסכמה
19]אשה ריח ניחוח לפני יהוה *vac*[*at*
20]*vacat?* ותקרב כול מנחה אשר קרב עמה נסך כמשפט וכו[ל מׄנחה
21]אשר קרב עליה לבונה או חרבה יקמוצו ממנה את אזכרתה ויקטירו על[
22]המזבח ואת הנותר מהמה יוכלו בחצר הפנימית מצות יאוכלום הכוהנים לוא[
23]תאכל חמץ ביום ההוא תאכל ולוא תבו[א עׄ]לׄ[יׄ]ו ה[שׄמשׄ *vacat*

]ועל כול קורבנכמה תתנו מלח ולוא ת[שבית ברית מלח לעולם *vacat*

]וירימו ליהוה תרומה תנופה מן האי[לים ומן הכבשים את שוק הימין

]ואת החזה ואת הלחיים ואת הקב[ה ואת האזרוע [ע]ד עצם השכם

bottom margin

Average line length: 57 letter-spaces
Mus. Inv. 577, 608
PAM 42.177, 42.180, 43.975*, 43.978*

NOTES ON READINGS

Col. IV is composed of two fragments. Frg. 8a (lines 1–20) measures 22 x 8.5 cm. It preserves the end of the sheet on which stitching holes can be seen. Remnants of the next layer were attached beneath frg. 9. Frg. 7 was loosened from frg. 9.

The line length of the column is approximately the same as that of 11Q**19** XX. In other cases where the line length of 11Q**20** can be calculated, the lines are longer than those of 11Q**19**. This anomaly may be explained by the fact that this is the last column of the sheet. The average line length is 57 letter-spaces. Lines 2 and 22 are considerably longer (65 and 64 letter-spaces); lines 15, 18, and 26 are shorter (52, 51, and 51 letter-spaces respectively). Reconstruction of the lines suggests an estimated column width (between right margin and left dry line) of 14.5–14.7 cm.

L. 1 שבעה שבו[עות. The *ʿayin* and following *šin* have been written without a separation. The inserted supralinear *he* is clearest in PAM 42.180. This part of the fragment has now broken away.

L. 2 [יום וה]ק[ר]בתמה. The reconstruction [יו]ם והביא[ותמה (Yadin) is impossible on material grounds. The interpretation of the vertical trace as the left leg of the final *mem* of [יו]ם is palaeographically difficult, and allows no plausible reading of the following word. The fragment clearly shows that the stroke is in all respects compatible with the tail of *qop*. יום, found in the corresponding text of 11Q**19**, has been omitted, though it may have been added supralinearly. Thus, [יום וה]ק[ר]בתמה may perhaps be read.

L. 4 [ע]שר. There are no traces whatsoever of *ʿayin*, as the surface of the leather is torn. The distance from the preceding final *mem*, however, allows for the *ʿayin*.

L. 5 אי]לים. Only two points have been preserved after *lamed*, but they are compatible with the reading suggested by Yadin. The dots may be the top of a *yod* and the extreme left part of a final *mem*. ע]ליה (Qimron) is possible, but more difficult, as this would imply a very wide *he*.

L. 6 הה]ין. Peeling of the leather has eradicated the heads of *yod* and final *nun*.

L. 6 על הנסך. There is no space between the two words.

L. 9 כמשפט. The hand of the supralinear insertion is different: the ink is greyer in colour than the deep black of the manuscript and does not cover the leather as well.

L. 12 וכבשים. Of final *mem* only the right leg has been preserved.

L. 14 יקט]ירו. The head of *yod* is rather short, but nevertheless the reading seems to be certain.

L. 15 ה]קרבים. The reading of *qop* is clearest in PAM 42.180.

L. 20 וכו]ל מנחה. Only two small dots of the *mem* have been preserved. There is no real space between *lamed* and *mem*, but that need not imply the reading למנחה].

L. 26 [ע]ד. *ʿAyin* has completely disappeared, as has the lower part of *dalet*. An empty space of 1 cm has also been left before השכם for no apparent reason.

TRANSLATION

1. [on which you brought the new offering to YHWH, the b]read of the firstfruits, seven wee[ks. It will be seven]
2. [full sabbaths up to the morning of the] seventh [sabbath.] You will count fifty [days, and o]f[f]er
3. [new wine for the libation, four *hin* for all the tribes of] Israel, a third of a *hin* for each
4. [tribe. And on that day] all [the heads of the thousands of Israel will offer with this wine an offering] to YHWH: tw[el]ve rams
5. [ra]ms, and their offering according to the regulation, two-
6. [tenths of finest flour mixed with oil, a third of a *h*]*in* of oil for each ram with this libation
7. [and they will offer a burnt-offering: two bullocks, one ram, and] seven yearling [lamb]s and [one] he-
8. [goat, as a sin-offering to atone for all the people of the] assembly. *vacat*
9. [thei]r [offering] and their libation according to the regulation, for the bullocks, the ram, X
10. [the sheep, and the he-goat, a fire-sacrifice of fragrance appeasing] to YHWH. In the fourth quarter of the day they will offer
11. [ ] the rams and the libation. And they shall offer
12. [peace-offerings and four[teen] year[ling] lambs
13. [and their offering and their libation, according to the regulation for rams and] for [sheep. After] the burnt-offering they shall make them
14. [and they shall bur]n [their fat] upon the altar
15. [the fat surrounding the entrails, and all the fat that is upon the] entrails, and
16. [the lobe over the liver, and they shall remove it with the kidneys *va*]*cat*
17. [And the fat that is on top of them and that which is upon the loins, and the t]ail close to
18. [the spine. And the priests shall burn everything upon the altar, with thei]r [offerings] and libations,
19. [a fire-sacrifice of a fragrance appeasing before YHWH. *va*]*cat*
20. [*vacat?* And every offering with which a libation is offered shall be offered according to the regulation. And ev]ery offering
21. [on which frankincense is offered, or if it is a dry offering, they shall collect from it the memorial part, and they shall burn it on]
22. [the altar; and the remains of it they shall eat in the inner courtyard. The priests shall eat it with unleavened bread; not]
23. [with yeast shall it be eaten. On that very same day shall it be eaten, and the] sun [shall not se]t up[on] i[t]. *vacat*
24. [On all your offerings you shall put salt, and] the covenant of the salt [shall not] cease forever. *vacat*
25. [And they shall set aside a contribution for YHWH, a wave-offering from the ra]ms, and from the lambs, the right leg,
26. [the breast, the jawbones, the stoma]ch, and the shoulder blade [u]p to the bone of the upper foreleg.

COMMENTS

L. 1 [הביאכמה את המנחה חדשה ליהוה את ל]חם. The reconstruction of other lines of the column shows that הביאכמה is probably the first word of the line. Preceding these words one should reconstruct וספרתמה לכמה מיום in the last line of the previous column. מיום only fits before הביאכמה if the letters and spaces were written very close together.

L. 1 שב̊ו̊[עות שבע]. Since the reconstruction of line 2 is already longer than any other line of the column, it is most likely that שבע was written at the end of line 1, not at the beginning of line 2.

L. 2 [שבתות תמימות תהיינה עד ממוחרת השבת ה]שביעית. The reconstruction of the beginning of the line seems to demand slightly more space than the other reconstructions, but it is not impossible.

L. 2 [שבתות תמימות תהיינה]. Or reconstruct: [שבתות תמימות תספורו]. If one reconstructs תהנייה, the resulting formula is identical to that of Lev 23:15b-16a: שבע שבתות תמימת תהיינה עד ממחרת השבת השביעת תספרו חמשים

יום. In the quotation of Lev 23:15-16 in 11Q**19** XVIII 10–13, however, ת]ספורו is used instead of תהיינה, corresponding to $\mathfrak{G}^{FMmin}$ ἀριθμήσεις. On the other hand, 11Q**19** XXI 13 uses תהיינה in the same formula.

L. 9 X. Cf. PALAEOGRAPHY.

L. 18 ויקטירו הכוהנים את הכול על המזבח עם מנחתמ]ה֯ ונסכמה. The reconstruction ויקטירו הכול על המזבח עם מנחתמ]ה֯ ונסכמה (Yadin), based upon 11Q**19** XXIII 16–17, is far too short for the line. 11Q**20** may differ from 11Q**19** XXI 7–8, but note that there is space after ויק]טירו in 11Q**19** XXI 7 (in the reconstruction ויק]טירו הכוהנים[, the second *he* of הכוהנים would have been written on the dry line).

L. 20 ותקרב כול מנחה אשר קרב עמה נסך כמשפט וכו]ל מ֯נחה. Yadin's reconstruction of the last words of the line—כמשפט וכול מ֯נחה—fits in 11Q**19** XX 9–10, but is too short for the width of this column, unless one reconstructs a *vacat* either at the beginning of the line or after כמשפט.

L. 22 לוא[. The line is slightly longer than average, but לוא does not fit in the next line. It is possible that יאוכלום was written defectively as יוכלום.

L. 23 *vacat* ה]ש֯מש. The *vacat* is missing in 11Q**19** XX 13.

L. 24 *vacat* [ועל כול קורבנכמה תתנו מלח ולוא ת]שבית ברית מלח לעולם. The first part of the line is a rephrasing of Lev 2:13b על כל קרבנך תקריב מלח. This text has second person plural forms, as in 𝔊, as opposed to the sing. forms of 𝔐. The second part combines the phrasings of Lev 2:13 ולא תשבית מלח ברית אלהיך and Num 18:19 ברית מלח עולם הוא. The beginning of 11Q**19** XX 14 is lost, but Qimron reads [בר]י֯ת מלח֯[לעול]ם֯ at the beginning of the line. Qimron's reading of the letters at the beginning of 11Q**19** XX 14 and 15 is probably based upon a relocation of a piece of text stuck to the verso of the next revolution.

Col. V Frgs. 10 i, 11

Parallel: 11Q**19** XXI 01–XXII 5 (underline)

top margin

1 [ויניפו אותמה תנופה לפני יהוה *vacat?* ולכוהנים י]היה שוק התרומה וחזה

2 [התנופה האזרועו]ת֯ והלחיים והקבאות למנות

3 [לחוק עולם מאת בני ישר]אל ואת השכם ה֯נשאר מן האזרוע

4 [ל]חוק עולם להמה ולזרעמה

5 [ ]ש֯רי האלפים [מן] האילים ומן

6 [הכבשים איל אחד כבש אחד לאהרון ולבנו ולבני לוי אי]ל אחד כבש אחד ולכול
המטה

7 [איל אחד כבש אחד לכול המטות שנים ע]ש֯ר שבטי ישראל ואכלום

8 [בחצר החיצונה לפני יהוה הכוהנ]י֯ם ישתו שמה ריאשונים

9 [והלויים ישראל נ]ש֯יאי הדגלים ברישונה X

10 [שם ואחריהמה כול העם מגדול ו]ע֯ד קטן יחלו לשתות יין חדש

11 [ולאכול ענבים ובוסר מן הגפנים ביו]ם֯ הזה יכפ֯ר֯ו על התירוש

וישמחו

12 [בני ישראל לפני יהוה *vacat?* חוק עולם לדורותיהמ]ה בכול מושבותיהמה ושמחו

13 [ביום הזה במועד החלו לנסך נסך שכר יין חדש על מזבח יהוה] שנה בשנה *vacat*

14 [*vacat* וספרתמה לכמה מיום]הזה שבעה שבועות שבע

15 [פעמים תשעה וארבעים יום שבע שבתות תמימות תהיינה עד ממו]חרת השבת השביעית

16 [תספורו חמשים יום והקרבתמה שמן חדש ממשבות מטות בני יש]ראל מחצית ההין

17 [אחד מן המטה שמן חדש כתית ויקריבו את ראשית היצהר על מזבח העו]ל[ה בכ]ורים

18 [לפני יהוה]ם אילים שנים

19 [וכפ]ר בו על כול העדה לפני

20 [יהוה שלושה עשרונים סולת בלול]ה בשמן הזה מחצית ההין

21 [כמ]שפט עולה הואה אשה ריח

22 [ניחוח ליהוה]השמן הזה יבעירו בנרות

23 [בה]ם שרי האלפים עם נשיאי

24 [כבשים ארבעה עש]ר ומנחתם[ה] ונ{ש}סכמה[כמשפ]ט

25 [לאלים ולכבשים ושחטו בני לוי את וזר]קו [הכוהנים] בני אה[רון את דמם]

26 [על המזבח סביב ואת בשרמה וחלבמה יקטירו על מזבח העולה]

Average line length: 67 letter-spaces
Mus. Inv. 577, 580, 608
PAM 42.178, 42.179, 43.975*, 43.976*, 43.978*

NOTES ON READINGS

The column is composed of two large fragments (frgs. 10a, 10b) and two small fragments (frgs. 11a, 11b). It is possible that frgs. 10b and 11a adjoin. Few lines can be reconstructed with certainty, but the average number of letter-spaces in lines 15–17 is sixty-seven. Since there are no indications that the length of the other lines varied considerably from these three, the present authors are reluctant to adopt the reconstructions of Qimron, most of which result in lines of 50–60 letter-spaces.

L. 2 האזרועות. The left leg of *taw* is best seen in PAM 42.197.

L. 2 והלחיים. The spot after *ḥet* is a crack in the leather, which is responsible also for the anomalous space between the letters.

L. 3 ואת. A double crack in the leather has distorted the shape of *ʾalep*.

L. 3 הנשאר. The surface of the leather has peeled off, abrading the left leg of *he* and the upper part of *nun* and *šin*. The reading, already proposed by Yadin, is nevertheless quite probable. The only anomalous form is the right leg of *he*. The reading is not completely certain, however, and consequently the definition of the שכם as the remains of the upper foreleg (a definition unknown in rabbinic literature) cannot be based on this text.

L. 5 [מן]. The word has disappeared due to the same type of abrasion as noted in line 3.

L. 11 יכׄפׄרו. The skin between *kap* and *waw* is abraded, but two dots of ink remain on the edge of the abraded section.

L. 14]הׄזה. Only the head of *zayin* survives. The small ink dot at the edge of the fragment is the upper left part of the first *he*.

L. 17 בכ[ו]רׄים. Frg. 10a preserves the tops of four (rather than five) letters. Frg. 10b confirms the reading of the last two letters and, indirectly, *reš*.

L. 18 איׄלים. The remains are difficult to read, but this reading is more consistent with the traces than, e.g. [ו]אכולים (Qimron).

L. 19 לפני. The top of the upper arm of *lamed* is visible on frg. 10b.

L. 21 ריח. The dots on the edge of frg. 11a at the ends of lines 21 and 22 are not traces of letters.

L. 24 ומנחתם^ה^ ונ{ש}סכמה[. *He* has been added supralinearly. A second correction in the second word has transformed an original *šin* into *samek*.

L. 25 חור[קׄן. A piece of the skin is folded over, partially covering *qop*.

TRANSLATION

1. [And they shall wave them, a wave-offering before YHWH *vacat?* and for the priests there] will be the leg of the offering and the breast
2. [of the wave-offering the shoulder-blade]s, the jawbones, and the stomachs of the portions
3. [as an eternal law, from the Isra]el[ites], and the upper foreleg that is left from the shoulderblade
4. [as] an eternal law for them and their seed
5. [ ] the heads of thousands [from] the rams and from
6. [the lambs, one ram and one lamb for Aaron and his sons, and for the Levites] one [r]am and one lamb, and for each tribe
7. [one ram and one lamb for all the tribes, the twel]ve tribes of Israel. And they shall eat them
8. [in the outer court before YHWH. The priest]s shall drink there first
9. [and the Levites Israel, the ch]iefs of the battalion first
10. [there, and after them the entire nation, from the oldest] to the youngest, shall start to drink the new wine
11. [and to eat grapes and the unripe fruits from the vines on] this [da]y they shall atone for the new wine, and [they] shall rejoice,
12. [the Israelites before YHWH. *vacat?* An eternal law for thei]r [generations] in all their dwelling places. And they shall rejoice
13. [on this day, at the appointed time when they will have begun to pour out a libation of drink—of new wine—on the altar of YHWH,] year by year. *vacat*
14. [And you shall count from th]is day on] seven weeks seven
15. [times, forty-nine days, they shall be seven full weeks until the mor]ning after the seventh week,
16. [you shall count: fifty days. Then you shall offer new oil from the dwelling places of the tribes of the Is]rael[ites], half a *hin*
17. [from each tribe, new beaten oil, and they shall offer the first (yield) of the oil on the altar of the burnt-]offe[ring, firs]tfruits,
18. [before YHWH.] two rams
19. [and he will ato]ne with it for the whole assembly before
20. [YHWH three-tenths of finest flour mix]ed with this oil, half a *hin*
21. [according to the re]gulation; it shall be a burnt-offering, a fire-sacrifice of a fragrance
22. [appeasing to YHWH.] they shall burn this oil in the lamps

23. [ ] the heads of thousands with the chiefs of
24. [fourte]en [lambs] and their offerings and libations [according to the regulat]ion
25. [for the rams and lambs. And the Levites shall slaughter the and] the priests, the sons of Aa[ron shall sprin]kle [their blood]
26. [against the altar all around, and they shall burn their flesh and their fat on the altar of the burnt-offering]

COMMENTS

L. 1 ויניפו אותמה תנופה לפני יהוה. In view of the formulas in Leviticus and Numbers, it is likely that לפני יהוה came after ויניפו אותמה תנופה.

L. 1 ולכוהנים י]היה. The available space demands three words between לפני יהוה and י]היה. One might reconstruct קודש הואה לכוהנים י]היה on the basis of Num 6:20 (𝔐𝔊 + יהיה), but in view of line 25, Lev 7:30-34, and 10:15, ולכוהנים בני אהרון י]היה is somewhat more likely.

L. 2 האזרועו]ת̇ והלחיים והקבאות למנות. Cf. Deut 18:3 ונתן לכהן הזרע והלחיים והקבה.

L. 3 לחוק עולם מאת בני ישר]אל. Cf. Lev 7:34.

L. 4 ל]חוק עולם להמה ולזרעמה. Cf. Num 18:19.

L. 6 איל אחד כבש אחד לאהרון ולבנו ולבני לוי אי]ל אחד כבש אחד. Cf. Qimron, but the line may be somewhat too long.

L. 6 ולכול המטה. The syntax of this (broken) clause is strange. The similar passage in col. VI 5–6 (11Q**19** XXII 12–13) has the normal expression of the distributive ולכול מטה ומטה.

Ll. 6–7 המטה /[איל. In both 11Q**19** and 11Q**20** there is space for one or two words or a *vacat* between המטה and איל.

L. 11 ולאכול]. The reconstruction of 11Q**19** XXI 7, [יחלו לשתות יין חדש ו]ל[א]כול, leaves no room for a negative particle. The reading ולוא לאכול is therefore improbable.

L. 11 הגפנים ביו[ם̇. The space in the reconstruction between הגפנים and the ביום clause is much larger than in 11Q**19** XXI 7–8. A longer text or a *vacat* must be assumed. In view of the similar passage in 11Q**19** XXII 15–16 (כי ביום הזה יכפרו / [ע]ל[כו]ל[יצ]רה הארץ), one may perhaps reconstruct כי before ביום.

L. 12 לפני יהוה *vacat?* חוק עולם. The reconstruction shows that 11Q**20** had a longer text or, more likely, a *vacat* between לפני יהוה and חוק עולם.

L. 12 חוק עולם לדורותיהמ]ה בכול מושבותיהמה. Cf. Lev 3:17; 23:21; Num 35:29.

L. 13 [ביום הזה. Traces of each of the letters of הזה are visible at the end of 11Q**19** XXI 9.

L. 24 כמשפ]ט]. This is reconstructed according to col. IV 9.

L. 25 לאלים]. The reconstruction of 11Q**19** XXII 3–4 shows that לאלים immediately followed כמשפט or any other word reconstructed after ונסכמה.

L. 25 ושחטו בני לוי את וזר]ק̊ו. The space between לוי and the dry line of the left margin in 11Q**19** XXII 4 allows for approximately 16 letter-spaces. Since the reconstruction of 11Q**19** XXII 5 suggests that the line began with וזרקו, there must be some 13 letter-spaces between את and וזרקו.

Ll. 25–26 וזר]ק̊ו הכוהנים בני אה̊[רון את דמם] / [על המזבח סביב. Cf. Lev 1:11; 3:2, 8, 13.

Col. VI Frgs. 10 ii, 12

Parallel: 11Q19 XXII 6–XXIII 01, 05–5 (underline)

[top margin]

1 כמ[שפט ואת מנחתמה ונסכמה יקטירו על החלבים אשה ריח ניחוח]

2 ליה֯ו֯ה֯[*vacat* וירימו מן האילים ומן הכבשים את שוק הימין ואת חזי]

3 התנופה ולר֯[אשית את האזרוע ואת הלחיים ואת הקבה לכוהנים יהיה למנה]

4 כמשפטמה *vacat*[וללויים את השכם אחר יוציאום אל בני ישראל ונתנו בני]

5 ישראל לכוהנים א[יל אחד כבש אחד וללויים איל אחד כבש אחד ולכול מטה]

6 ומטה איל אחד כבש֯[אחד ואכלום ביום הזה בחצר החיצונה לפני יהוה חוקות]

7 עולם לדורותיהמה[שנה בשנה אחר יואכלו ויסוכו מן השמן החדש ומן הזתים]

8 כי ביום הזה יכפרו ע֯[ל כול יצהר הארץ לפני יהוה פעם אחת בשנה וישמחו]

9 כ֯ול [ב]נ֯י֯ ישראל בכול[מושבותיהמה]

10 [ ]

11 [ואחר מועד יצהר יקריבו]

12 למזב[ח את העצי]ם֯[שנים עשר מטות בני ישראל והיו המקריבים ביום הרישון]

13 מטות֯[לוי]ויהודה וב֯[יום השני בנימין ובני יוסף וביום השלישי ראובן ושמעון]

14 וביום הרביעי יששכר[וז]ב֯ולון ו֯[ביום החמישי גד ואשר וביום הששי דן]

15 ונפתלי *t*] *a* *c*[*a*] *v* הקריבו בחג]

16 העצים עולה ליה[וה שעירי]

17 עזים שנים ל֯[ומנחתמה ונסכמה כמשפט]

18 עול[ה הוא

Average line length: 64 letter-spaces
Mus. Inv. 577, 607, 608, 614B, 1031
PAM 42.178, 42.179, 43.975*, 43.977*, 43.978*, 44.008*

NOTES ON READINGS

Col. VI is composed of frg. 10 ii (with traces on each of the six joined fragments) and frg. 12. Frg. 10c is still partially joined to frg. 10a in PAM 42.179. A large part of the margin on frg. 10c has been transferred to Mus. Inv. Box 1031 and is not photographed in PAM 43.977, but PAM 42.179 has preserved the original form of the fragment. The small frg. 10g (not photographed) has been joined to frg. 10e on Mus. Inv. 608. Frg. 12 should probably be placed *c*.1 cm to the left of frg. 10f. Frg. 41 may perhaps be placed in line 1.

The average line length of lines 3, 5–8 is 64 letter-spaces. This implies that the end of the column should have corresponded approximately to 11Q19 XXIII 17.

L. 1 כמ]שפט. The top of *mem* has suffered damage, but PAM 43.977 confirms the reading.

L. 2 ליהׄוׄהׄ]. Frg. 10c shows the right leg of the first *he*. The five dots on the top of frg. 10d are completely consistent with the lowest parts of the legs of *he*, *waw*, *he*.

L. 3 ולרׄ]אשית. The dot after *lamed* is compatible with the bottom of the leg of *reš*.

L. 8 עׄ]ל. The traces of the preserved letter could also be read as *lamed*.

L. 16 ליה]וה. *Yod* and *he* appear on frg. 10g.

TRANSLATION

1. according to the re[gulation, and they shall burn their offering and libation with the fats a fire-sacrifice of a fragrance appeasing]
2. to YHWH. [*vacat* And they shall set aside from the rams and from the lambs the right leg and the breasts of]
3. the wave-offering, and as the choi[cest part the shoulderblade, the jawbones, and the stomach. It shall be for the priests as a share]
4. according to the regulations concerning them. *vacat* [And for the Levites, the upper foreleg. Then they shall take them out to the Israelites, and they shall give, the]
5. Israelites, to the priests [one] r[am and one lamb, and to the Levites one ram and one lamb, and to each]
6. tribe one ram and [one] lamb. [And they shall eat them on this day in the outer courtyard before YHWH.]
7. Eternal [precepts] for their generations [year after year. Then they shall eat and anoint themselves with the new oil and the olives,]
8. for on this day they shall atone f[or all the virgin oil of the land before YHWH, once a year. And they shall rejoice,]
9. all the [Israel]ites, in all [their dwelling places]
10. [ ]
11. [And after the festival of the virgin oil, they shall bring,]
12. [the twelve tribes of the Israelites, the woo]d to the alta[r as an offering. And they shall offer: on the first day]
13. the tribes [of Levi] and Judah; and on [the second day Benjamin and the sons of Joseph, and on the third day Reuben and Simeon;]
14. and on the fourth day Issachar [and Ze]bulun; and [on the fifth day Gad and Asher; and on the sixth day Dan]
15. and Naphtali. *v*[*a*]*ca*[*t* And they shall offer on the festival]
16. of the wood a burnt-offering for YH[WH he-]
17. goats two for [and their offering and libation according to the regulation]
18. a burnt-offer[ing

COMMENTS

4Q365 (4QReworked Pentateuch[c]) 23 9–11 has a text similar to lines 10–12 of this column, and offers a possible reconstruction for the end of line 10. However, the different context of the sections, as well as the divergent readings, shows that the texts are not parallels. Instead, 4QRP[c] (including, in our opinion, the fragments of 4Q**365a**) contains additional material which was also used in the *Temple Scroll*. The relation between the additional materials of 4QRP[c] and the *Temple Scroll* is disputed. Wise has argued that the the additional materials of 4QRP[c] were sources of the *Temple Scroll*, but the editors of 4QRP[c] suggested that frg. 23 'may at this point be quoting (an unknown portion of) the *Temple Scroll*'.[6]

The pertinent lines of 4QRP[c] are as follows:

9] מ]ׄועד היצהר יקריבו את העצים שנים [

10] °°[י המקרׄיבים ביום הרישׁ[ו]ׄן לוי ° [

11] ראו]ׄבן ושמעון[וב]ׄיום הרבׄ[יעי

L. 2 וירימו מן האילים ומן הכבשים את שוק הימין. This is reconstructed on the basis of 11Q**19** XX 14–15 (cf. 11Q**20** IV 25).

Ll. 13–14 The line length of the reconstructed line 13 is 70 letter-spaces, whereas the average of the reconstructed lines 3 and 5–8 is 64 letter-spaces. The large number is due to the high percentage of narrow letters such as *waw* and *yod* in line 13. On the other hand, line 14, with an equally high percentage of narrow letters, has only 61 letter-spaces, which seems to be somewhat short. The text may have had, e.g. an extra מטות, as in the beginning of line 13.

L. 15 הקריבו בחג[. Or reconstruct ויקריבו על[(Qimron).

L. 17 לׄ[. Reconstruct, e.g. לׄ[חטאת לכפר בהמה על בני ישראל.

L. 18 עול]ה הוא. One may perhaps reconstruct אשה ריח ניחוח ליהוה in the following gap, in which case the sentence continued with פר אחד איל אחד (cf. 11Q**19** XXIII 5–6).

Col. VII Frg. 13

20]קׄ[

21] *vacat*

22]ברׄובׄע הׄי[ו]ם תעלה זואת

23 עו]לת התמיד *vacat*

24]ןׄ שבתון זכׄרון מקרא קודש

25]°°° יעשה לנפש

26 פר אח]ד איל אחד

bottom margin

[6] M. Wise, *A Critical Study of the Temple Scroll*, 50; E. Tov and S. White, '365. Reworked Pentateuch[c]', in *Qumran Cave 4, VIII* (DJD XIII; Oxford: Clarendon, 1994) 295.

Mus. Inv. 610
PAM 42.178, 43.978, 44.010, 44.013*

NOTES ON READINGS

Col. VII, preserved in frg. 13, shows the ends of seven lines from the lower part of the column, the last of a sheet. It preserves the bottom and left margins, and clear traces of its attachment to the next sheet. The contents clearly indicate that the fragment should be located within the section of the *Temple Scroll* that deals with festivals and sacrifices. It is equally certain that frg. 13 does not overlap with the preserved text of 11Q**19**, which suggests that it should correspond to the missing or fragmentarily preserved top lines of one of the columns of 11Q**19** XXIV–XXIX. Yadin's location of frg. 13 24 and 26 in 11Q**19** XXV 4 and 5 is unlikely in view of the expression used in 11Q**19** XXV 5, שבתון זכ]רׄון תרועה מ]קרא קודש, which is characteristic of the New Year Festival, while זכרון without תרועה, as in this fragment, is employed also for other festivals. The only plausible correspondence would be with the eighth day of the Feast of Tabernacles, at the lost beginning of 11Q**19** XXIX. Qimron's suggestion that another column (XXVIIIa) existed before col. XXIX demands a more intensive examination of all the pertinent photographs.

L. 23 עו]לת. The two final letters are completely preserved in the oldest photograph, PAM 42.178, after which a small fragment became detached.

L. 24]ןׄ. Read final *nun* or *šin*. *Dalet* is much more difficult, but not impossible.

L. 25 ∘∘∘[. The tops of two or three letters are visible in some photographs, especially PAM 43.978 and 44.013.

TRANSLATION

20. [ ] [
21. [ ]*vacat*
22. [ ] in the fourth quarter of the d[a]y this shall be offered
23. [ ] the perpetual [burnt-off]ering *vacat*
24. [ ] a great sabbath of memorial, proclaimed holy
25. [ ] shall be done for a person
26. [on]e [bullock,] one ram

COMMENTS

L. 22]ברׄובׄע היׄ[ו]ם. Cf. col. IV 10.

L. 22 תעלה זואת. It is unlikely that תעלה is a noun, e.g. 'channel', as one would then expect determined forms. A *Hipʿil* of עלה, 'you shall offer', is also difficult. A 2nd masc. sing. form is out of place in the section, as far as can be judged from 11Q**19** XXVI and XXVII. The most plausible explanation is a 3rd fem. sing. *Qal* of עלה, with זואת as subject. Cf. Lev 2:12 for this 'passive' meaning of עלה.

L. 25 יעשה לנפש. The lack of context makes an understanding of the reading difficult. יעשה can be a *Qal* or *Nipʿal*. נפש may be a *nomen regens* in a construct state, or absolutely used, e.g. 'for a person'. Read, e.g. כול מלאכת עבודה]אׄשׄ[ר]יעשה לנפש?

Col. VIII Frg. 14

Parallel: 11Q**19** XXXI 11–13 (underline)

[מרובע לכול רוחותיו אחת ועשרים אמה רחוק מהמזבח]חמש[ים] 9

[אמה ורחב הקיר שלוש אמות וגבהו עשרים אמה *vac]at* 10

[*vacat* ה שערים]עשו לה 11

[מהמזרח מהצפון ומהמערב רוחב השערים ארבע אמות וגובהמה]שבע 12

Mus. Inv. 1020
PAM 589612

Notes on Readings

The fragment, mounted on a piece of material and placed in Box 1020, is very worn, with several tears and holes visible. Sixteen lines of 11Q**19** XXXII are missing between this and the next fragments which appear to preserve the top margin of the following column. Since the lines of this fragment are slightly longer than those of 11Q**19** XXXII, one may assume that the first lines of this fragment correspond to line 8, 9, or 10 of the column. The left margin is visible on the left of the fragment, and it is possible, but difficult to judge from the fragment itself, that a trace of the next column can be seen on the left edge.

L. 11 לה֯. A thick horizontal stroke suggests the head of *he*.

Translation

9. [square; all its sides will be twenty-one cubits, at fif[ty cubits distance from the altar,]
10. [and the width of the wall will be three cubits, and its height twenty cubits. *vac]at*
11. [*vacat* gates] shall you make for it,
12. [to the east, the north, and the west; the width of the gates will be four cubits, and their height] seven

Comments

Ll. 10–11 *vacat*. The *vacat* in 11Q**19** XXXI 12 is not visible, since that part of the skin is detached from this column and attached to the next revolution (cf. Yadin Plate 16*, where the reverse writing on the back of col. XXXII shows traces of col. XXX 9), but the evidence of 11Q**20** strongly suggests 11Q**19** also had a *vacat*, albeit much shorter.

L. 11 ה שערים]עשו לה. Yadin reads ו]שׂעׂרים עשו לה in 11Q**19** XXXI 12, whereas Qimron suggests ושלוש]ה שערים עשו לה. The *he* before שערים seems clear, but it is preceded by remnants of letters which do not seem compatible with שלושה.

Col. IX Frgs. 15, 16

Parallel: 11Q**19** XXXII 10–15 (underline)

top margin

]מן הארץ ארבע אמות [מצופות זהב אש]ר יהיו מניחים עליהמה את בגדיהמה אשר[1

]יהיו באים אליהם למע[לה מעׄ]ל [לבׄיתׄ] ה   בבואם לשרת בקודש ועשיתה[2

]תעלה סביב לכיור אצל מזבח [הׄ]עולה הולכת לתחת הכיור ומחלה יורדת למטה[3

]אל תוך הארץ אשר יהיו ה[מים נש]פכים והולכים אליה ואובדים בתוך הארץ ולוא[4

]יהיה נוגעים בהמה כול א[דׄם] כי מדם העולה מתערב במה   [5

Average line length: 67 letter-spaces
Mus. Inv. 577, 614B
PAM 42.176, 42.178, 43.978*, 44.008*

NOTES ON READINGS

Col. IX is composed of two fragments. Frg. 15 consists of three small joined fragments; frg. 16 can be placed beneath frg. 15.

The average line lengths of lines 1, 3–4 is 67 letter-spaces. The exact length of the word beginning with ה- in line 2 is unknown, but the space in 11Q**19** 11 also allows for a reconstruction of the line with 67 letter-spaces. This average would imply that the last line of the column corresponded approximately to 11Q**19** XXXIV 06.

L. 2 למע[לה מעׄ]ל [לבׄיתׄ]. The upper tip of the *lamed* of [לבׄיתׄ] must be positioned just outside the edge of the fragment. The trace before *yod* could belong to many letters. The traces on the left edge are the remains of *bet*, medial or final *mem*, or *taw*.

L. 3 מזבח [הׄ]עולה. The bottom edge shows only the head of a letter. The traces fit, e.g. *taw*, *he*, or *ḥet*. מזב[חׄ] העולה is another possible reading.

L. 4 נש]פכים. The fragment shows the lower tip of the left downstroke of *šin*, not visible in PAM 44.008.

L. 5 א[דׄם]. The left end of a horizontal stroke is visible before *mem*. Although the characteristic tick of *dalet* is missing, it cannot be *yod*. *He* is possible, though difficult.

TRANSLATION

1. [from the ground it will be four cubits] overlaid with gold, [upon] whi[ch they shall place their clothes which]
2. [they shall go u]p with on to[p of the] house [of the   when they go to minister in the Sanctuary. And you shall make]
3. [a channel all around the laver, along the altar of] the [burnt-offering, which shall run beneath the laver, and a shaft shall go down]
4. [into the earth, so that the] water shall be pou[red out and drain into it, and disappear into the earth, and not]
5. [anyon]e[shall touch it, for it is mixed with the blood of the burnt-offering   ]

COMMENTS

L. 1]מצופות. The word is also used in **11Q19** XXXVI 11, XXXIX 3, and XLI 16.

L. 2]לבׄיתׄ[ה. It is not clear which house is meant. Yadin (plate 17*) shows the bottom part of a downstroke attached to the *mem*. Qimron reads הׄכׄיׄוׄ[ר].

Col. X Frg. 17

Parallel: **11Q19** XXXVII 9–XXXVIII 01 (underline)

1 [ושולחנות לפני המושבות בפרור]הׄפנימי אצל קׄ[י]רׄ החׄצרׄ הׄ[חיצון]

2 [מקומות עשוים לכוהנים לזבחיהמה ולב]כורים ולמעשרות *vac* [ולזבחי]

3 [שלמיהמה אשר יהיו זובחים ולוא יתע]רׄבו זבחי שלמי בני ישׄ[ראל]

4 [בזבחי הכוהנים] *vac[at* *vac]at* [ ]

5 [ובארבעת מקצועות החצר לעשות לה]מה [מ]קום לכירים אשר יהיו מבׄ[שלים]

6 [שמה את זבחיהמה ואת החטאות במקצ]וׄע המזרחי צפונה ואתׄ °°[ ]

Average line length: 54 letter-spaces
Mus. Inv. 566
PAM 42.177, 43.978, 44.010*

NOTES ON READINGS

Col. X is preserved in one fragment of almost rectangular shape. The oldest photograph, PAM 42.177, shows the back of a fragment still attached to frg. 16 at the beginning of line 5 and covering part of the first *he*. Apparently, the fragment broke off and it does not appear in later photographs.

The reconstruction of the lines indicates a line length of 54–55 letter-spaces. The vertical position of the fragment is unknown, but the reconstruction of the lines allows for only two horizontal placements, with the more probable one reconstructed here.

The text of **11Q19** indicates that two columns are missing between cols. IX and X.

Ll. 1–6 One may perhaps also reconstruct the lines as follows:

1 [לפני המושבות בפרור]הׄפנימי אצל קׄ[י]רׄ החׄצרׄ הׄ[חיצון מקומות]

2 [עשוים לכוהנים לזבחיהמה ולב]כורים ולמעשרות *vac* [ולזבחי שלמיהמה]

3 [אשר יהיו זובחים ולוא יתע]רׄבו זבחי שלמי בני ישׄ[ראל בזבחי הכוהנים]

4 [*vac[at* *vac]at* ובארבעת]

5 [מקצועות החצר לעשות לה]מה [מ]קום לכירים אשר יהיו מבׄ[שלים שמה את]

6 [זבחיהמה ואת החטאות במקצ]וׄע המזרחי צפונה ואתׄ °°[ ]

The beginning of line 1 presents a problem, however, in this reconstruction: לפני is too short for the space, and ושולחנות לפני is much too long.

L. 2 ולב]כורים. *Bet* has completely disappeared; there are no traces in the empty space before *kap*.

L. 5 [מ]קום. The interlinear spaces are not quite regular, but the space between lines 2 and 3 indicates that line 4 contains a *vacat* and that [מ]קום was written as an interlinear correction by the same copyist.

L. 6 צפונׄה ואתׄ. A small tear in the leather has split the *he*, but Qimron's reading is certain, as opposed to Yadin's צפוני יואן[.

L. 6 ואתׄ ○○[. ואכלו[(Wacholder, Qimron) is impossible. The stroke which is read as the upper arm of *lamed* is not ink, and the surrounding traces cannot be read as *kap* and *waw*.

TRANSLATION

1. [and tables in front of the rooms, in] the inner [colonnade] at the [outer] w[a]ll of the court,
2. [places made for the priests, for their sacrifices, and for the fir]st-fruits and for the tithes, *vacat* [and for their peace]
3. [sacrifices which they shall offer. And] the peace sacrifices of the Is[rael]ites shall not be ming]led
4. [with the sacrifices of the priests. *v*]*ac*[*at*]
5. [And to make for th]em [a p]lace [in the four corners of the courtyard] for the cauldrons where they shall c[ook]
6. [their sacrifices; and the sin-offerings in] the northeast [corn]er, and the [ ]

Col. XI Frgs. 18, 19, 20

Parallel: 11Q19 XLV 03–04; 1–4 (underline)

11 [ ]ל

12 [ ]לבני

13 [ ]לׄ[ ]

14–15 [ ]

16 [מן הפנה הז]ואת עד שׁ[ער]

17 [דן לבני דן ומשער דן עד שער נפתלי לבני נפתלי ומשער נפ]תׄלׄיׄ[עד]

18–20 [ ]

21 [ומ]○באים

22 [שבעים]נׄשכה

23 [וכאשר ו השני י]הׄיה בא

24 [לשמאול ובבואו יצא הרישון מעירי ולוא יהיו מתערבים אלה ב]אלה

25 [ובכליהמה ובא משמר אל מקומו וחנו זה בא וזה יוצא ליום השמיני]

26 [ומטהרים את הנשכות זאות אחרי זאות מעת תצא הראישונה ולוא תהיה]

Mus. Inv. 577, 613, 621B
PAM 42.175, 42.178, 43.978*, 44.005*, 44.117*

NOTES ON READINGS

Col. XI, as reconstructed here, is composed of frgs. 18, 19, and 20; in no case is the placement of the fragments certain. The single complete word of frg. 18 can be placed in various locations in the scroll. Frg. 19 may overlap with the reconstructed formulaic lines of 11Q**19** XLV 03–04, but it also overlaps with 11Q**19** XLI 7–9. In the latter case, its lines would be rather short or long, depending on which example of נפתלי it corresponds to. Because of the absence of a margin, as in frgs. 18 and 20, the placement of frg. 19 in col. XI cannot be considered completely certain. Frg. 20 seems to correspond to 11Q**19** XLV 1–4, as 11Q**19** XLV 3 is the only place in the preserved sections of 11Q**19** with the sequence ה֯יה בא; the occurrence of אלה in the next line seems to support this placement. Moreover, it is very possible that the lost sections of 11Q**19** XLV 1–2 mentioned the storage cells (נשכה). Nonetheless, attempts to reconstruct 11Q**19** XLV 1–2 do not fit this fragment very well.

The reconstructed lines of frgs. 19 and 20 have fewer letter-spaces than do the lines of frgs. 21–24, and the margin of frg. 20 is larger than that of frg. 21. This indicates that frgs. 20 and 21 belong to different columns. A material correspondence may be seen between frgs. 18 and 20, and frgs. 21 and 23b. If so, the reconstruction of the columns should be changed, e.g. by assigning only twenty-five lines to col. XI.

At least two, but probably three, columns are missing between cols. X and XI.

L. 11 ל֯[. Part of the skin surface has abraded, but remnants of *lamed* are still visible.

L. 17 נפ[ת֯ל֯י֯]. Or נפ[ת֯ל֯י. It is not clear from an examination of the fragment whether the dot at the left is ink.

L. 21 ○באים[. A speck of ink in the upper right corner of the fragment belongs to a letter preceding באים. It could be *waw* or *he*.

L. 22 נ֯שכה[. The left end of the base of a letter before *šin* is consistent with *nun*.

TRANSLATION

11. [ ]
12. [ ] for the sons of
13. [ ] [
14–15. [ ]
16. [from th]is [corner] to the ga[te]
17. [of Dan for the sons of Dan. And from the gate of Dan to the gate of Naphtali for the sons of Naphtali. And from the gate of Naph]tali [to]
18–20. [ ]
21. [and] enter
22. [seventy] storeroom
23. [and when the second sh]all enter
24. [to the left. And when he comes, the first shall go out from my city, and one shall not intermingle with] the other
25. [nor with their utensils. And the priestly watch shall come to its place, and they shall camp. As one arrives and one leaves on the eighth day,]
26. [they shall purify the store-rooms, one after another, from the moment when the first goes out, and there shall be no]

COMMENTS

Ll. 12–13]לבני /[ ]ל[. Reconstruct, e.g. with 11Q**19** XLIV 13–14]לבני / [יוסף ולמנשה ולאפרים ומשער יוסף עד שער בנימין לבני קהת מבני ה[ל]ויים[or, alternatively, with the text of 11Q**19** XLIV 9–10.

Ll. 21–23 All attempts to reconstruct these lines are speculative. For the number of lines missing at the top of 11Q**19** XLV, cf. the discussion in NOTES ON READINGS to col. XI.

L. 23 וכאשר ו. Qimron places an unidentified fragment of 11Q**19** in this line and reads וכאשר י[הי]ה בא המש]מר.

L. 24 אלה ב[אלה.]אלה might also correspond to the first אלה, which would make the lines somewhat shorter (*c*.55 letters instead of *c*.60 letters).

Col. XII Frgs. 21 i, 22, 23, 24

Parallel: 11Q**19** XLV 9–XLVI 16 (underline)

1]שמה תערובת *vacat* [

2]ואיש כי יהיה לו מקרה לילה לוא יבוא אל כול המקדש עד אשר ישלים שלושת ימים[

3]וכבס בגדיו ורחץ ביום הראישון וביום השלישי יכבס בגדיו ורחץ ובאה השמש א[ח̇ר

4]יבוא אל המקדש ולוא יבואו בנדת טמאתמה אל מקדשי וטמאו *vacat?* ואיש [כי ישכב

5]עם אשתו שכבת זרע לוא יבוא אל כול עיר המקדש אשר אשכין שמי בה שלוש[ת̇
ימי{ן}ם

6]כול איש עור לוא יבואו לה כול ימיהמה ולוא יטמאו את העיר אשר אני [שוכן בתוכה

7]כי אני יהוה שוכן בתוך בני ישראל לעולם ועד *v[acat*

8]*vacat?* וכול איש אשר יטהר מזובו וספר לו שבעת ימים לטהרתו ויכבס ביו[ם השביעי

9]בגדיו וירחץ את כול בשרו במים חיים אחר יבוא אל עיר המקדש וכול ט[מ̇א לנפש
לוא

10]יבואו לה עד אשר יטהרו וכול צרוע ומנוגע לוא יבואו לה עד אש[ר̇ יטהרו וכאשר

11]יטהר והקריב את]ק לוא יבוא אל
המקדש

12] [ר̊וכל ואל המקדש

13]לוא יבוא [*vacat*

14] [ב̊ה שלנחושת] [

15] ג[ב̊ולו אשר לוא] ישכון כול[

16 [עוף טמא על מקדשי   על גגי השערים אשר [לחצר החי֯[צונה
וכול[

17 [עוף טמא לוא יוכל להיות בתוך מקדשי לעולם ועד כול הימים אשר [אני שוכן[
בתוכם[

18] *vacat*   *v*[*acat*   ]ועשיתה[

19 [רובד סביב לחוץ מחצר החיצונה רחב ארבע עשרה באמה על פי [פ֯תחי השערי[ם
כולמה[

20 [ושתים עשרה מעלה תעשה לו אשר יהיו עולים [ב֯נ֯י יש֯[ראל א[ליו לבוא אל מק[דשי]

21 [*vacat?* ועשיתה חיל סביב למקדש רחב מאה באמה[אשר יהיה[מבדי[ל בין מקדש

22 [הקודש לעיר ולוא יהיו באים בלע אל תוך מקדשי ו[ל[וא יחללוהו [וקדשו את מ[קדשי]

23 [ויראו ממקדשי אשר אנוכי שוכן בתוכמה   *v*]*a*[*cat*   ]

24] *vacat*   ועשיתה להמה מקו[ם יד חוץ מ[ן העיר]

25 [אשר יהיו יוצאים שמה לחוץ לצפון המערב לעיר בתים ומקו[רים ובירות בתוכ֯[מה]

26 [אשר תהיה הצואה יורדת אל תוכמה ולוא תהיה נראה לכול רחוק מן העיר ש[ל[ושת]

Average line length: 70 letter-spaces
Mus. Inv. 577, 580, 613, 614B
PAM 42.176, 42.177, 42.178, 43.976*, 43.978*, 44.005*, 44.008*

NOTES ON READINGS

Frgs. 21 i, 22, 23, 24, 25, and 21 ii overlap with 11Q**19** XLV 9–XLVII 3. Despite the overlap, reconstructions of cols. XI–XII are problematic. A more or less vertical alignment of all the fragments results in twenty-eight lines from frg. 21 i 1 to frg. 21 ii 1, whereas there is no material indication that the column had more than the usual twenty-six lines.[7] A continuous text of 11Q**19** XLVI 01–07 would demand one complete missing line between the last line of frg. 21 i (containing a *vacat*) and the first line of frg. 22. The next problem is the section of uninscribed leather at the top of frg. 23c, which implies either a *vacat* or an unusually large space between two lines.

There are several possible reconstructions of the column with twenty-six lines. Here, frg. 22 has been placed immediately after frg. 21. This assumes that 11Q**19** XLVI had

---

[7] Yadin's reconstruction of the top of 11Q**19** XLV suggests that the columns of the sheet 11Q**19** XLV–XLVIII had twenty-two lines, which would imply that four lost lines (01–04) must be assumed in both 11Q**19** XLVI and XLVII. However, the comparison of 11Q**19** XLVIII with XLIX suggests that the columns of this sheet had more lines. The average distance between the ceiling lines is almost identical (8.34 against 8.26 mm), but sheet 11Q**19** XLV–XLVIII has a large bottom margin, the column ending three lines higher than on the next sheet. Since the next sheet almost certainly had twenty-eight lines, the number of lines in 11Q**19** XLV–XLVIII must be posited as twenty-five.

one or two long *vacat*s, where this text used short *vacat*s. In addition, it is posited here that the third line of frg. 25 belonged to the same line as did the first line of frg. 21 ii, in the following column. Alternatively, one may seek another explanation for the blank space at the top of frg. 22c, allow for the possibility of more than twenty-six lines in the column, or, most radically, regard וה|באים in col. XII as corresponding to יהיו באים of **11Q19** XLVI 17–18.

The average line length, based on the eleven reconstructed lines without *vacat*s, is 70 letter-spaces (range: 68–73 letter-spaces).

L. 3 א]ח֯ר֯. Part of the head and the slanting downstroke of the last letter are preserved and suggest *reš*. Only the bottom tip of the left leg of *ḥet* remains.

L. 5 שלוש]ת֯. The horizontal trace is compatible with the base of *taw*. PAM 42.178 shows that the spot on the edge is not part of a *lamed*.

L. 5 ימי{ן}ם. The final *mem* corrects an original final *nun*.

L. 11 המקדש. The word has been added in the intercolumnar margin by a different hand. Of *šin*, only the two tips of the right and middle arms have been preserved.

L. 12]ר֯וכל. Only the upper half of *kap* has been preserved. The two traces at the beginning cannot be read as *ʾalep*. The reading]י֯וכל is also difficult, as the first trace does not show the leftward tip typical of *yod*. The first trace may be read as the tip of the head of *reš*.

L. 14]ב֯ה. The head of *he* is broken, but the letter is virtually certain. The remnant of a downstroke and the long base before *he* may belong to *bet*, *kap*, or, with more difficulty, to *nun* or *ṣade*.

L. 15 ג]ב֯ולו. The long base stroke before the first *waw* may belong to *bet* or *kap*.

L. 20]ב֯נ֯י. All that remains are the bottoms of the letters. The two base strokes, joined to one another, but clearly two strokes, are compatible with *bet* and *nun*.

L. 20 יש֯]ראל. The stroke after *yod* must belong to *ʿayin* or *šin*, even though the diagonal stroke tends towards the horizontal.

L. 21 אשר. *ʾAlep* has a very clear *keraia*. For an similar *ʾalep*, cf. כאשר in line 10.

L. 22 מ]קדשי[. The photographs show a tiny dot on the edge after *mem*, but its position is not completely compatible with *qop*.

L. 23 *v*]*a*[*cat*. The blank space above the final *ṣade* and the following *mem* of line 24 is 0.8 cm, whereas the interlinear space varies from 0.65 to 0.8 cm. Since the blank space at the bottom of the preceding fragment measures 0.1 to 0.2 cm, one cannot place the fragments beneath one another without assuming a *vacat*.

L. 26 ש]ל֯ושת[. PAM 42.178 proves that the darkened spot on the left edge does not represent a letter.

TRANSLATION

1. [mingling there. *vacat*]
2. [And one who has had a nocturnal emission shall not enter the entire Temple until three days have passed.]
3. [And he shall wash his clothes and bathe on the first day, and on the third day he shall wash his clothes and bathe. And when the sun has set, t]hen
4. [may he enter the Temple. And they shall not enter my Temple with their defiling impurities, and defile it. *vacat?* And a man] who lies
5. [with his wife and has an ejaculation shall not enter the entire Temple city in which I shall cause my name to dwell for thre]e days.
6. [No blind person shall enter it for his entire lifetime, and they shall not defile the city] in [whose] midst [I] dwell,
7. [for I, YHWH, dwell in the midst of the Israelites forever and always. *vaca*]*t*
8. [*vacat?* And any man who purifies himself from his discharge shall count seven days for his purification, and he shall wash on the] seventh [da]y

9. [his clothes, and he shall bathe his body completely in living water. Afterwards he shall enter the city of the Temple. And anyone im]pure through contact with a corpse shall not
10. [enter it until they have purified themselves. And anyone with leprosy or a skin disease shall not enter it, unti]l they have purified themselves and when
11. [he has purified himself, then he shall offer]shall not enter the Temple
12. [ ] trader, and the Temple
13. [he shall not enter] *vacat*
14. [ ] of copper [ ]
15. [ ] its [bor]der so that there does not [sit any]
16. [unclean bird on my Temple on the roofs of the gates of] the ou[ter] courtyard, [and any
17. [unclean bird shall not be able to be in the midst of my Temple, forever and always, for] I dwell [in their midst.]
18. [*vaca*]*t* [And you shall make]
19. [a platform around the outer courtyard, fourteen cubits wide, corresponding to] the openings of [all] the gate[s]
20. [and you shall make twelve steps for it, up]on which the Is[rael]ites[will ascend] to enter [my] tem[ple.]
21. [*vacat?* And you shall make a trench around the Temple, one hundred cubits wide,] which will [separ]ate the [holy] Temple
22. [from the city, and they will not enter my Temple suddenly, thus they will] n[ot defile it.] And they shall sanctify [my] Tem[ple,]
23. [and fear my Temple, for I dwell in their midst. *vac*]*a*[*t*]
24. [*vacat* And you shall make for them latr]ines outsi[de the city]
25. [to which they shall go, outside, to the northwest of the city: houses with bea]ms and pits inside [them]
26. [into which the excreta can drop, without being seen by anyone, at a distance from the city of t]h[ree]

Comments

L. 4 ואיש *vacat?* The reconstruction of the line is 6 to 8 letter-spaces shorter than the average line. The line may have had a longer text, but it is more likely that it had a short *vacat* like **11Q19** XLV 11. Note, however, that though **11Q19** XLV has several short *vacat*s (lines 12 and 17), one cannot be certain that **11Q20** XI contained corresponding *vacat*s.

L. 11 Qimron (p. 64) forgets to reconstruct יטהר והקריב את at the beginning of the line.

L. 12 רׄוכל[. This is perhaps a reference to the absence of traders in the Temple; cf. e.g. Zech 14:21.

L. 13]לוא יבוא. Or a plural form should be reconstructed if רׄוכל[was part of an enumeration of people not allowed in the Temple.

Ll. 13–14 One more line may be missing. Cf. NOTES ON READINGS.

L. 14]בׄה שלנחושת[. The almost completely lost line possibly dealt with a scarecrow which was used to prevent birds from defiling the Temple; cf. Yadin, *The Ṭemple Scroll*, vol. I, 271–2.

L. 15 ג]בׄולו. If the reconstruction is correct, the reference may be to the territory of the Temple complex, or rather to a border wall of the Temple.

L. 16 על גגי על מקדשי. Reconstruct, e.g. על מקדׄ]שי אשר בחצר הפנימית ו[עׄל גגי (Qimron); על מקדׄ]שי ועשיתה שפודים על קיר החצר ועל[גגי (Yadin) is too long for **11Q19** XLVI 2.

L. 17 בתוכם]. As in **11Q19**, or בתוכמה].

Ll. 21–22 The text of **11Q19** XLVI 10–11 seems somewhat short for the available space by approximately one average word. In the proposed reconstruction, the end of line 21 is blank. The word [הקודש] might fit here, but then the beginning of line 22 is too short, in which case a short *vacat* must be assumed.

L. 25 ומקו]ר[ים. It is unlikely that a plural of מקור is meant. One is tempted to relate it to קורה and מקרה, 'beam', as in 11Q**19** XLII 10–11 and XLI 15–16. The word is either a noun, or a participle introduced by an explicative *waw*.

Col. XIII Frgs. 21 ii, 25

Parallel: 11Q**19** XLVI 16–XLVII 3 (underline)

1]אלפים אמה *vacat* וע[ש֯]תה שלושה מקומות למזרח העיר מובדלים זה מזה
אשר יהיו[

2]באים המצורעים והזבים [והאשנים אשר יה]יה להמה מקרה לילה

3 וה[ ]באים[ ]ל֯[

4 רחוק֯ מ[ן

5 וכול ◦[

6 דבר ומש֯[

7 [

8 וחמ[

9 והורדת֯]מה למעלה ולוא למטה

10 עריה֯]מה טהורות וש

Mus. Inv. 580
PAM 42.178, 42.177, 43.976*

NOTES ON READINGS

Col. XIII, as reconstructed here, is composed of frgs. 21 ii and 25. Frg. 25 corresponds to 11Q**19** XLVI 17 (or 16)–XLVII 01 (or 02). Frg. 21 ii must correspond to the first part of 11Q**19** XLVII. It is safe to assume that line 10 overlaps with 11Q**19** XLVII 3. This implies that lines 3–9 correspond to 11Q**19** XLVII 01–07 and 1–2. Nine lines of continuous text of 11Q**19** XLVII should correspond to six lines of col. XII, a column of 70 to 75 letter-spaces per line. However, one extra line in this column may be explained by a long *vacat* where 11Q**19** had a short one. The indentation in the fragment in line 7 prevents one from determining whether this line had text or a *vacat*.

L. 1 וע[ש֯]תה. The second downstroke could be *yod*, *waw*, *dalet*, *reš*, or any letter with two legs, such as *he*, *ḥet*, *taw*, etc.

L. 3 וה|באים]. Although broken, the word is complete. Parts of *yod* are preserved on both sides of the crack. The first two letters are added in the margin and represent a correction. Between וה and באים] is a long vertical stroke. Because of the absence of ticks on this stroke, the reading יהׄו (Qimron) is difficult.

L. 4 רחוקׄ. The traces of *qop* are rather faint. A dark downstroke above it resembles the upper arm of *lamed* (which prompted the reading רחיל in the *ed. prim.*). Nevertheless, the remaining strokes are not compatible with *lamed* and strongly suggest *qop*. The horizontal headstroke clearly breaks through a vertical downstroke on the left.

L. 5]°. The last letter is difficult to read because of a darkened spot on the edge. It could belong to *ʿayin* or *ṣade*.

L. 6 דבר. The first letter might be read as *reš*, but that is more difficult. The last letter is certainly not *dalet*. Hence, the reading רבד (a defective spelling of רובד of 11Q**19** IV 4, 5 and XLVI 5?) is not possible.

L. 6 ומשׄ]. Only the right arm of the last letter is visible. Reading *ʿayin* or *ṣade* is more difficult.

L. 10 עריהׄ]מה. The remnants of the last letter are compatible with both *he* and *kap*.

Translation

1. [thousand cubits. *vacat* And you shall m]ak[e three places east of the city, separated from each other, to which shall]
2. [come the lepers, those afflicted with discharge] and the men who ha[ve had a nocturnal emission
3. And those who | come [
4. far fr[om
5. and all [
6. matter, and [
7. [
8. and [
9. and [you] will lead down [upwards and not downwards
10. and th[eir] cities [pure and

Comments

L. 1 *vacat*. The length of the *vacat* is incertain.

L. 3 וה|באים]. The identification of this word with באים of 11Q**19** XLVI 18 is very unlikely. The first letters are clearly an addition, and do not fit the syntax of the clause of 11Q**19** XLVI 17–18. A far-fetched possibility is that the first letters are יה for יהיו, and that the vertical stroke is meant to separate יה from באים, to prevent the reading והבאים.

L. 4 רחוקׄ מ[ן]. Add perhaps העיר or something similar (cf. col. XII 26 [11Q**19** XLVI 15–16]). The reading רחיל is not only palaeographically unlikely, but seems also not to fit the context.

L. 6 דבר ומשׄ]. One may perhaps reconstruct מכול at the end of line 5; cf. 11Q**19** XLVII 5.

L. 8 וחמ]. Read perhaps וחמ]שים.

Col. XIV Frgs. 26 i, 27, 28, 29

Parallel: **11Q19** L 02–11, 15–LI 1 (underline)

top margin

1 [ע]ד֯ יום

2 [ה יו]ם השביעי

3 [ ]במים

4 [ ]ט֯מאו במת

5 [ ]ואל יואכלו

6 [כול אשר כי מי טהרה מתערובת המת נטמאו] אין עוד

7 [ ]מה עד אשר יזו את השנית ביום השביעי וטהרו בערב בבוא השמש *vac[at*

8 *vacat*] *vacat* וכול איש אשר יגע על פני השדה בעצם אדם[

9 מת ובח֯[לל חרב או במת או בדם אדם מת או בקבר וטהר כחוק המשפט הזה ואם לוא יטהר[

10]כ[משפט] התורה הזואת טמא הוא עוד טמאתו בו וכול האדם אשר יגע בו יכבס בגדו ורחץ[

11 וטהר ל[ערב *vacat* ואשה כי תהיה מלאה וימות ילדה במעיה כול הימים אשר הוא בתוכה[

12 מת תטמ֯[א כקבר [

13 [ ]

14 [ ]

15 וב֯[יו]ם֯ השביעי יזה שנית וכבס בגדיו ורחץ ובאה השמש וטהר *vacat* וכול הכלים ובגדים ועורות[

16 וכול מ[עשה עזים כמשפט התורה הזואת תעשו להמה וכול כלי חרש ישברו כי טמאים המה ולוא[

17 יטהרו[עוד עד לעולם *vacat* כול שרץ הארץ תטמאו החולד והעכבר והצב למינו והלטאה והכח[

18 והחמ֯[ט והתנשמת *vacat* כול איש אשר יגע בהמה במותמה יטמא
עד הערב וכבס]

19 בגדי[ו וכול אשר יפול]

20 עליו מ֯[המה במותמה יטמא מכול כלי עץ או בגד או עור או שק כול כלי אשר
יעשה מלאכה בהמה]

21 במים] יובא וטמא עד הערב וטהר ותשבורו את כול כלי חרש אשר יפול מהמה
אל]תו֯כ֯[ו]

22 וכיא י֯[
]ו֯ וטמ֯[א]

23 עד ה֯[ערב היוצא מהמה
כי]טמים

24]המה ולוא תטמאו בהמה וכול הנוגע בהמה במותמה יטמא עד הערב ויכבס בגדיו
ורחץ במים]

25]ובאה השמש וטהר *vacat*]

26]*vacat* וכול הנושא מעצמותמה ומנבלתמה עור ובשר וצפורן וכבס בגדיו
ורחץ במים]

Average line length: 75 letter-spaces
Mus. Inv. 567, 577, 614, 621B
PAM 42.177, 42.180, 43.978*, 44.006*, 44.114*, 44.117*
IAA 508042, 525015

Notes on Readings

Col. XIV, the first of a new sheet, is composed of five fragments, two of which are joined. The placement of frg. 29 in this column is not completely certain, but very probable: טמים is most likely a variant spelling of טמאים, preserved only in **11Q19** L 18 and LI 1. The irregular interlinear ruling of the fragment corresponds to lines 21–23 (frg. 28b) and the placement fits in the reconstruction of the column.

The small fragment 4Q**524** 2 overlaps with 11Q**19** L 17–LI 01, but the few words in 4Q**524** 2 and 11Q**20** do not overlap.

L. 1 ע[ד֯. The head is not exactly like that of the typical *dalet*; *reš*, though difficult, may also be possible.

L. 5]֯ו אל. Or read]֯י אל.

L. 9 ובח֯[לל. There is a dark spot after *bet*, but the small vertical stroke beneath the spot is possibly the bottom tip of the right leg of *ḥet*.

L. 15]ו֯ב֯[יו֯ם. *Waw* was almost completely hidden in a fold in PAM 42.177, but it is perfectly clear in PAM 44.006, which shows the fragment after it was unfolded. The small trace after *waw* could belong to many letters, but is consistent with *bet*. The distance between the preserved trace on the edge and line 2 suggests that one should read the horizontal trace above the *lamed* of line 2 as the bottom of a final *mem*.

L. 18 והח֯מ֯]ט. The tear between frgs. 28a and 28b runs through all the letters apart from the *waw*. The letter after *he* is most probably *ḥet* with a small blotch on the crossbar. The reading והזב֯]ים is much more difficult. The complete horizontal stroke between *zayin* and *bet* must be dismissed as a blotch, and frg. 28b shows no trace of the base of *bet*.

L. 22]ו֯ וטמ֯[א]. The first two letters are written close together, suggesting the reading]ו֯יטמ֯[א]; however, there are additional instances in this column where the space between words is absent. One may also read]ו֯ יטמ֯[א], or even]ו֯י טמ֯[א].

TRANSLATION

1. [un]til [the] day
2. [ ] the seventh [da]y
3. [ ] in water
4. [ ] impure by a corpse
5. [ ] and they shall not eat
6. [anything that for the water of purification from mingling with a dead person they shall become impure.] No more
7. [until they sprinkle for the second time on the seventh day, and they are pure in the evening, at sunset. *va*[*cat*.
8. *vac*[*at* And any man who in the open field comes across the bones of a]
9. dead person, or one pier[ced with a sword, or a corpse, or the blood of a dead person, or a grave, shall purify himself according to the precept of this regulation. And if he does not purify himself]
10. [according to the] regulation [of this law, he will be impure, his impurity will stick to him, and anyone who comes into contact with him shall wash his clothes, and bathe,]
11. and become pure by [the evening. *vacat* And if a woman is pregnant, and her child dies in her womb, then all the days that it is within her]
12. dead, she shall be impu[re like a grave.
13. [ ]
14. [ ]
15. and on [the seventh da]y [he shall sprinkle himself a second time, and he shall wash his clothes and bathe, and when the sun has set he shall be pure. *vacat* And with all utensils and clothes and skins]
16. and all pr[oducts of goatskin you shall do according to the regulation of this law. And any earthenware vessels shall be broken, because they are impure, and they cannot]
17. become pure [again for ever. *vacat* Everything that creeps on the ground is impure: the rat, the jerboa, and every kind of lizard, the wall-gecko and the gecko,]
18. the great liz[ard and the chameleon. *vacat* Any man who touches them when they are dead shall be impure until the evening. And he shall wash]
19. [his] clothes [And anything]
20. on which [any] of [these falls when they are dead shall be impure, any article of wood or garment or skin or sackcloth, any article that is used for labour,]
21. into water [shall it be plunged, and it shall be impure until the evening, and then it shall be pure, but you shall smash any earthenware vessel] into [which any of these falls.]
22. And when [ ] and it shall be impu[re]
23. until the [evening what issues from them for they] are impure,
24. [and you shall not be contaminated by them. And anyone who touches them when they are dead, shall be impure until the evening, and he shall wash his clothes, and bathe in water,]
25. [and at sunset he shall be pure. *vacat*]
26. [*vacat* And anyone who carries their bones or their corpses, the skin, or the flesh, or the claws shall wash his clothes, and bathe in water]

COMMENTS

L. 2 יו[ם. Probably reconstruct ביו[ם.

L. 3]במים. The word is probably used with the verb כבס or רחץ.

L. 4]ט֯מאו. Reconstruct, e.g. י]ט֯מאו or נ]ט֯מאו.

L. 5]ו֯אל. ואל is used in **11Q19** LXIII 7 ואל תתן, but here it might also be the end of a broken word.

Ll. 7–8 *vacat*. The small *vacat* at the end of line 7, and the large *vacat* at the beginning of line 8 correspond to the rather short *vacat* in **11Q19** L 4.

L. 11 *vacat*. The small *vacat* corresponds to the large *vacat* in **11Q19** L 9.

Ll. 12–14 A reconstruction of these lines based upon the text of **11Q19** L 11–14 (between מת תטמא and וביום השביעי) needs two and a half lines, not three. As a solution one may suggest a *vacat* of approximately half a line in **11Q20**, though it is unclear where it would have been; alternatively, there may have been a longer text in **11Q20**. Another possibility is that the scribe of **11Q20** omitted part of the text, e.g. by skipping from ביום השלישי to ביום השביעי, and that only one line (with a supralinear or intermarginal addition) is missing between frgs. 26 and 27. The text without the clause וביום השלישי יזה ויכבס בגדיו ורחץ fits nicely in lines 12–13.

12 מת תטמ֯[א כקבר כול בית אשר תבוא אליו יטמא וכול כליו שבעת ימים וכול הנוגע בו טמא]

12a [וביום השלישי יזה ויכבס בגדיו ורחץ]

13 [עד הערב ואם לתוך הבית יבוא עמה יטמא שבעת ימים וכבס בגדיו ורחץ ביום הראישון]

In the latter case, however, one must assume that the column had either twenty-five lines, or one or two extra long *vacat*s, as in line 8.

Ll. 18–19 כול איש אשר יגע בהמה במותמה יטמא עד הערב וכבס] / בגדי[ו. Cf. Lev 11:31. Since this clause is too short, one must either assume a longer wording, or a rather long *vacat* before כול. Reconstruct, e.g. ורחץ במים ובאה השמש וטהר after בגדי[ו.

L. 19–20 וכל אשר יפול] / עליו מ֯[המה במותמה יטמא מכול כלי עץ או בגד או עור או שק כול כלי אשר יעשה מלאכה בהמה]. Cf. Lev 11:32. The reconstruction seems, however, a trifle too long. Alternatively, reconstruct ונתן] / עליו מ֯[ים חיים as in Num 19:17.

L. 21 במים] יובא וטמא עד הערב וטהר. Cf. Lev 11:32.

L. 21 ותשבורו את כול כלי חרש אשר יפול מהמה אל]תו֯כ֯[ו. Reconstructed on the basis of Lev 11:33.

L. 22 וכיא]°. The *Temple Scroll* often uses אם where the Hebrew Bible uses כי. For וכיא, cf. the similar use of וכי in Lev 11:37-39. Lev 11:39 is too short for the gap between the two fragments, but the verse may have been expanded.

L. 22 וטמ֯[א]. Or יטמ֯[א] depending on the syntax of the preceding clause.

L. 23 עד ה֯[ערב. The letters should not be identified as corresponding to **11Q19** LI 3 ע֯]ד ה[ערב. An exact calculation of the correspondences of col. XIII with **11Q19** LI is not possible, because the missing text of lines 01–07 may have contained *vacat*s. Long *vacat*s in **11Q19** may be short in **11Q20**, and, less often, short *vacat*s in **11Q19** may be longer in **11Q20**. However, if one compares the line length of both columns, one would expect עד ה֯[to overlap with **11Q19** LI 07, and ע֯]ד ה[ערב of **11Q19** LI 3 to be positioned in the first half of line 25.

L. 23 טמים. This is a variant spelling of טמאים with elision of *ʾalep* after *shewa* (cf. Qimron, *The Hebrew of the Dead Sea Scrolls*, 200.11). **11Q19** LI 1 has טמאים.

Ll. 24–26 The preserved text of **11Q19** LI 2–5 (up to במים, as the next column begins with ובאה) should correspond with lines 24–26 (and perhaps also the end of line 23). A fitting reconstruction is only possible if one assumes a rather long *vacat*, presumably after וטהר.

Col. XV Frg. 26 ii

Parallel: 11Q**19** LI 5–17 (underline)

top margin

1 ובאה השמ[ש אחר יטהר והזהרתמה את בני ישראל מכול הטמאות ולוא יטמאו
בהמה אשר אני מגיד]

2 לכ{מ֯}ה בהר הזה ו[לוא יטמאו כי אני יהוה שוכן בתוך בני ישראל וקדשתמה והיו
קדושים ולוא ישקצו]

3 את נפשותיהמה בכו[ל אשר הבדלתי להמה לטמאה והיו קדושים *vacat*]

4 שופטים ושוטרים[תתן לכה בכול שעריכה ושפטו את העם משפט צדק ולוא
יכירו פנים במשפט]

5 ולוא יקחו שוחד ו[לוא יטו משפט כי השוחד מטה משפט ומסלף דברי הצדק
ומעור עיני חכמים]

6 ועושה אשמ֯ה֯ גדול[ה ומטמא הבית בעוון החטאה צדק צדק תרדוף למען תחיה
ובאתה וירשתה את הארץ]

7 אשר אנוכי נותן לכ֯^{מ}[ה לרשתה כול הימים *vacat?* והאיש אשר יקח שוחד
ויטה משפט צדק]

8 יו[מת ולוא תגורו מננו להמיתו

Average line length: 82 letter-spaces
Mus. Inv. 577
PAM 42.180, 43.978*
IAA 508042

NOTES ON READINGS

L. 2 לכ{מ֯}ה. Traces of the erased *mem* are still visible.

L. 6 אשמ֯ה֯. Most of *mem* and the right part of *he* cannot be seen due to a hole.

L. 7 לכ֯^{מ}[ה. The word has been split; the upper part, showing the top of the upper arm of *lamed* and the upper part of *mem*, which is clearly higher than the other letters of the line, is preserved on the main fragment. On the detached fragment, one can see the lower part of *lamed* and the bottom right part of what is presumably a *kap*. The combination of traces suggests a supralinear *mem* written on top of a *kap*.

TRANSLATION

1. and when the su[n] has set, [then he will be pure. And you shall forewarn the Israelites of all the impurities. And they shall not defile themselves by those things of which I told]
2. you on this mountain, and [they shall not defile themselves, for I, YHWH, dwell in the midst of the Israelites. And you shall sanctify them and they shall be holy. And they shall not make]

3. themselves [detestable] with al[l those things which I have separated for them as unclean. And they shall be holy. *vacat*]
4. [You shall appoint] judges and officers [in all your gates, and they shall judge the people with true justice, shall not show partiality in the judgement,]
5. shall not take a bribe, and [shall not pervert justice. For bribes pervert justice, distort the words of the just person, blind the eyes of wise men,]
6. cause great guilt, [and defile the House with the wickedness of sin. Pursue justice, justice, so that you can live and enter and take possession of the land]
7. which I give to you [as an inheritance for ever. *vacat?* And the person who takes a bribe and perverts just judgement]
8. shall be [put to death, and you shall have no qualms in executing him.

COMMENTS

L. 1 ולוא יטמאו. 11Q**19** LI 6 has a small *vacat* before these words. As the reconstructed line produces a line of average line length for the column, we may assume it had no *vacat*.

L. 2 לכ{מׄ}ה. The corrected form agrees with 11Q**19** 7.

L. 3 *vacat*. The long *vacat* (*c*.30 letters) agrees with the long *vacat* in 11Q**19** 10.

L. 7 לכׄ[ם]ה. Once again, confusion was caused by the alternation of 2nd person singular and plural forms (cf. also line 3).

L. 7 *vacat?*. The reconstruction of the line on the basis of 11Q**19** 16–17 results in a line fourteen letters shorter than the average of 82 letter-spaces. A plausible explanation is the intrusion of a *vacat* which introduces the והאיש clause.

L. 8 להמיתו. After this word, 11Q**19** LI 18 has a long *vacat*. One may plausibly reconstruct a *vacat* in the rest of the line.

Col. XVI Frg. 30

Parallel: 11Q**19** LIV 19–LV 06 (underline)

1]   ואם ישיתכה אחיכה בן אבי]כה או [בן]
2]אמכה או בנכה או בתכה או אשת חיקכה או ריעיכה א]שר כנפשכה בסתר[לאמור]
3]נלכה ונעבודה אלוהים אחרים אשר לוא ידעתמה אתה ואב]ותיכה מאלוהי הׄ[עמים]
4]אשר סביבותיכמה הקרובים אליכה או הרחוקים ממ]כה מקצי הארץ ועד קצ[י הארץ]
5]לוא תאובה לו ולוא תשמע אליו ולוא תחוס עינ]כׄה עליו ולוא תחמל ע[ליו ולוׄא]
6]תכסה עליו כי הרוג תהרגנו ידכה תהיה בו ברא]ישונה להמיתו ויד[כול העם]
7]באחרונה *vacat?* וסקלתו באבנים ומת כי בקש לה]דׄיחכה *vacat* [

Average line length: 66 letter-spaces
Mus. Inv. 580
PAM 42.178, 43.976*

NOTES ON READINGS

The vertical and horizontal positioning of the fragment within the column is uncertain, but a reconstruction of the lines with the fragment in the right part of the column is difficult. A small unphotographed fragment (frg. 30b) has been joined on Mus. Inv. 580.

L. 4 קצ]י. *Qop* and *ṣade* appear on the unphotographed frg. 30b.

L. 5 עינ]כה. The traces before *he* are compatible with the utmost left ends of the head and base of *kap*.

L. 7] *vacat*. It is uncertain whether the absence of traces after לה]ד֯יחכה suggests a *vacat*. In lines 6–7, some letters near the edge have faded away. The same might be the case here.

TRANSLATION

1. [And if your brother entices you—be it the son of] your [father,] or [the son of]
2. [your mother, or your son or your daughter, or the wife of your bosom, or] your soul[mate—]secretly [saying,]
3. [Let us go and worship other gods—whom you did not know before, neither you nor] your fa[ther]s, from the gods of the [nations]
4. [who surround you, either those near to you, or those far from] you, from one end of the earth to [the other—]
5. [then you shall not consent or listen to him. And] your [eye shall not pity] him, nor shall you spare h[im or]
6. [shield him. But you shall surely kill him, your hand shall be the fir]st [to be raised against him] to kill him, and the hand [of all the people]
7. [afterwards. *vacat?* And you shall stone him with stones, and he shall die, because he tried to lead] you astray *vacat*[

COMMENTS

Frg. 30 contains parts of a quotation of Deut 13:7-11. The reconstruction of the (seven) lost lines from the top of 11Q**19** LV strongly suggests that Deut 13:12 was also quoted, before the text continued with Deut 13:13-18 in 11Q**19** LV 2–14. 11Q**19** and 11Q**20** 30 each witness one addition to 𝔐. It is, of course, possible that in the lost sections of the lines there were other variations. Nevertheless, one can plausibly reconstruct the lines not preserved by 11Q**19** on the basis of 𝔐, with the exception of line 7.

L. 1 בן אבי]כה או. The reconstruction of the lines shows that this text must have agreed with 11Q**19** LIV 19 against 𝔐, which omits these words.

L. 6 וידו[. The absence of a trace of *yod* after *dalet* cannot be taken as evidence of the reading וידו[(𝔐) as against וידי[(most 𝔊^mss^), since some of the traces near the edge have faded away.

Ll. 6–7 The text of 𝔐 is too short to fill the gap between the preserved parts of the text. One might reconstruct a small *vacat* after באחרונה or perhaps a longer variant of וסקלתו.

VARIANTS

Deut 13:7 (1) בן אבי]כה או 𝔪𝔊] > 𝔐

13:8 (4) מקצי] מקצה 𝔐𝔊

13:9 (5) על]יו 𝔊 (ἐπ' αὐτῷ)] > 𝔐

Unidentified Fragments

Frg. 31

]נ̇חושת 1

]ט̇פחים 2

]עליהם

]י̊ם את 3

]°ש̊°ת̇מה 4

]ת̇לבו̇ 5

Mus. Inv. 606, 615
PAM 42.177*, 43.980, 44.007

NOTES ON READINGS

Subsequent to the photographing of PAM 42.177, frg. 31 broke into two pieces: frg. 31a was then photographed again in PAM 43.980; frg. 31b in 44.007. The joined fragment preserves the last words of five lines, an intralinear addition, and a left margin. The fragment has tentatively been located by Wacholder in the first lost lines of 11Q**19** XXXVIII, but there is no evidence for this assumption.

L. 3 עליהם. This is an intralinear addition in the scribe's hand, the letters being almost the same size as those of the main text. The word should presumably be read before את of line 3.

L. 3]י̊ם. The trace at the edge is small but cannot be read as *šin*.

L. 4]°ש̊°ת̇מה. The three last letters are written in an entirely different hand. Only the top parts of the preceding letters remain, and it cannot be judged whether those, too, were written in the same hand. The addition is not supralinear or intralinear, but apparently written in a *vacat* at the end of the line.

L. 5]ת̇לבו̇. The head of *taw* and the hook of *lamed* are preserved on a piece of the leather that has almost loosened from the main fragment. It is very difficult to read the remains of the first letter as *ḥet*. There is no indication of a space between *taw* and *lamed*. The *waw* may also be *yod*.

TRANSLATION

1.] copper
2.] handbreadths
3.] on them
4.]
5.]

COMMENTS

Frg. 31 does not seem to correspond to the preserved text of 11Q**19**. The first two lines suggest that the theme of the section is the manufacture of some of the Temple items. The reading of line 5 is uncertain and is therefore of little help.

L. 2]טפחים[. The most probable meaning of the word is ‘handbreadths’, describing the measurements of the item of copper of line 1. Cf. טפחות in Biblical Hebrew, and the masc. pl. form in 1QM V 13, 14, and Mishnaic Hebrew. Another possibility is ‘coverings’; cf. טפחה in Isa 48:13.

L. 3]ים עלידם את. Reconstruct e.g. מניח]ים עליהם את.

L. 5]ת̇לבו̇. Reconstruct, e.g. א]ת̇ לבו̇, or, perhaps, a *Hitpa*ʿ*el* of שלב.

Frg. 32

]מקצוֹעֹ[1

]בֹּדרום[2

]פנוֹתֹ[3

Mus. Inv. 1016
PAM 43.794

NOTES ON READINGS

This fragment, which may perhaps be joined to frg. 40, probably preserves part of the section dealing with the courtyards and the buildings of the Temple (11Q19 XXX–XLV), but does not correspond to the preserved text of 11Q19. The fragment might overlap with the beginning of 11Q19 XXXI, XXXII, or XXXVII.

L. 1]מקצוֹעֹ[. The letter after *ṣade* may also be read as *yod*. Only the upper right part of the last letter is visible. The absence of a downstroke is compatible with ʿ*ayin*.

L. 2]בֹּדרום[. Only the base stroke of the first letter remains. The upper right part of *dalet* is missing and the letter may also be *reš*. *Waw* may be *yod*.

L. 3]פנוֹתֹ[. The word cannot have begun with a *lamed*.

TRANSLATION

1.] angle [
2.] in the south [
3.] corners [

Frg. 33

]ראשית [1

]יטעו בא[2

]פרי בא◦[3

]◦[4

Mus. Inv. 613, 621B
PAM 42.177*, 44.005, 44.117

NOTES ON READINGS

Frgs. 33 was still whole in PAM 42.177, but later broke apart; the two fragments were then placed on different museum plates: frg. 33a in Mus. Inv. 621B, frg. 33b in Mus. Inv. 613.

L. 2]יֿטעו. *Yod* and *waw* cannot be distinguished with certainty.

L. 3]פרי. Or]פרו.

L. 3 באס[. The last letter may be *reš* or *taw*.

TRANSLATION

1.] beginning [
2.] they plant in [
3.] fruit in [
4.] [

COMMENTS

L. 1]ראשית. The only attestation of ראשית in the *Temple Scroll* is in col. VI 3 (11Q**19** XXII 9; but cf. also the reconstruction of col. V 17 = 11Q**19** XXI 15). If the interpretation of the next lines is correct, it might refer to the firstfruits, but elsewhere in the *Temple Scroll* these are called בכורים.

L. 2]יטעו בא[. A form of נטע is more likely than one of טעה. The last word may be בא[רצמה.

L. 3]פרי. Either 'fruit', or a form of כפר.

Frg. 34

1]ם כי [

2]ל[

Mus. Inv. 613
PAM 44.005

NOTES ON READINGS

L. 1 כי [. The long tick suggests *yod*, but כו֯ל cannot be ruled out.

TRANSLATION

1.] for [

Frg. 35

1]וׄכול

2]*vacat*

2a]כול

Mus. Inv. 613
PAM 44.005

NOTES ON READINGS

The vertical ruling is clearly visible on the fragment, and probably represents the right margin. The space between the two words does not correspond to the usual distance between lines in the manuscript; it is plausible that line 2a represents a supralinear addition.

L. 1]וׄכול. The trace before *kap* might belong to several letters. The length of the downstroke of the second *waw* is less likely with *yod*.

TRANSLATION

1. and all [
2. *vacat* [
2a. all [

Frg. 36

1]לׄוׄ[

2]למכונותׄ[

Mus. Inv. 614
PAM 42.178, 44.006*

NOTES ON READINGS

There is no overlap with 11Q**19**, though it might fit in several sections.

L. 2]למכונותׄ[. Or, more difficult, read]למכונהׄ[. There is no space between *lamed* and *mem*, but]ע[ל מכונותׄ cannot be ruled out.

TRANSLATION

1.] [
2.] to the supports [

COMMENTS

L. 2 [למכונות̊]. Cf. e.g. 1 Kgs 7:27-39, where the manufacture of the מכונות, 'trolleys', is described. The general meaning of מכונה, however, also allows for other understandings.

Frg. 37

1 [יהוה

2 [◦ק̊

3 [חת̊

Mus. Inv. 614
PAM 44.006

NOTES ON READINGS

The blank space above the first line indicates a *vacat*, the top margin, or a slightly larger than usual interlinear distance.

L. 1 יהוה. יהיה or והיה are also possible. ל]יהוה is very difficult.

L. 2 [◦ק̊. The length of the head is most compatible with *qop* or *samek*. A tiny trace on the right edge must be the remnant of the preceding letter.

L. 3 [חת̊. The traces of the last letter are most consistent with *taw*, but *bet*, *kap*, and *reš* may also be possible.

TRANSLATION

1.] YHWH
2.]
3.]

Frg. 38

1 [י̊בו̇]

Mus. Inv. 614B
PAM 44.008

NOTES ON READINGS

This tiny fragment has probably broken away from another fragment.

L. 1 [י̊בו̇]. The trace before *bet* is split by a crack in the skin, but looks like the tip of *waw* or *yod*.

Frg. 39

]וׄשוקׄ[1

PAM 44.008

NOTES ON READINGS

Frg. 39 can no longer be located.

L. 1]וׄשוקׄ[. The first letter is probably *waw/yod*, but *he* is not impossible. *Qop* is probable, but *lamed* with final *kap* or *pe* could produce similar traces.

TRANSLATION

1.] and the leg of [

COMMENTS

L. 1]וׄשוקׄ[. In 11Q**19**, only the form שוק is used.

Frg. 40

ע]שרה 1

Mus. Inv. 621B
PAM 44.117

NOTES ON READINGS

The blank space at the top may indicate the top margin. The fragment may perhaps be joined to frg. 32.

TRANSLATION

1. t]en

Frg. 41

]ה רוׄ[1

Mus. Inv. 607
PAM 42.178, 43.977*

NOTES ON READINGS

The grain of the skin, as well as the type of stain, is similar to that of frg. 10c which is on the same museum plate, and not to that of **11Q14**, but none of the letters is typical of **11Q20**. The only plausible explanation is that the letters preserve a correction or addition written in another hand. The large blank space at the top indicates a top or intracolumnar margin, or a *vacat*.

L. 1 [ה רו̊]. The small space between *he* and *reš* need not be a word-dividing space. The last letter is more likely to be *waw/yod* than *zayin*. The reading אש[ה רי̊]ח, and the placement of the fragment in col. X 1, is difficult since there is no trace of *šin*.

Frg. 42

1 [מה בכ]

Mus. Inv. 1032
IAA 563769

Frg. 43

Mus. Inv. 580 displays an uninscribed, unphotographed fragment, 5.5 cm high x 5.5 cm wide. A large part of the surface is abraded. A note in Modern Hebrew states that a piece of the fragment has been used for research.

21. 11QTemple[c]?

(PLATE XLVIII)

Previous discussion: J. P. M. van der Ploeg, 'Les manuscrits de la Grotte XI de Qumrân', *RQ* 12 (1985) 9; B. Z. Wacholder, 'The Fragmentary Remains of 11QTorah (Temple Scroll)', *HUCA* 62 (1991) 1–116; F. García Martínez, 'Texts from Cave 11', *The Dead Sea Scrolls: Forty Years of Research*, eds. D. Dimant, E. Rappaport (STDJ 10; Leiden: E. J. Brill, 1992) 23; E. Qimron, *The Temple Scroll. A Critical Edition with Extensive Reconstructions* (Judean Desert Studies; Beer Sheva–Jerusalem: Ben-Gurion University of the Negev Press, Israel Exploration Society, 1996).

THE physical appearance of the fragments is very similar to those of 11Q**12** *Jubilees*. Frg. 3 has almost the same deep brown colour as 11Q**12** frg. 1, whereas frgs. 1 and 2 are slightly lighter, comparable to some other 11Q**12** fragments. The ruling seems to be identical, and the writing also hangs at the same distance below the ceiling line.

Together the three fragments are a possible witness to a third copy of the *Temple Scroll* from cave 11, but the identification of the fragments is not completely certain. The remains of frg. 1 can be fitted in 11Q**19** III 14–17, though there is little material overlap, but frgs. 2 and 3 do not correspond to the preserved text of the *Temple Scroll*. However, the impossibility of locating the text of the fragments in the known text of *Jubilees*, and the shared vocabulary with the *Temple Scroll*, suggest that they preserve parts missing in 11Q**19**, or belong to a composition dealing with the same subjects as the *Temple Scroll*.

The hand of these fragments is very similar to that of 11Q**12** Jubilees, and it is not impossible that both manuscripts were copied by the same scribe.

Mus. Inv. 567, 614, 619
PAM 44.004*, 44.006*, 44.114*
IAA 525015

Frg. 1

Parallel: 11Q**19** III 14–17 (underline)

1 [וכליה יהיו זה]ב טהור וכו[ל מזבח העולה יעשו נחושת טהור והמכבר]
2 [אשר מלמעלה] לו והכיר וכנו יה[יו נחושת מרוק כמראות לראות פנים]
3 [ ]נחושת ברור[ף ימס
4 [ ] *vacat* [ ]
5 [ת]מיד מאת[בני ישראל
6 [ ]בבית אשר]אשכין[שמי

Mus. Inv. 619
PAM 44.004

NOTES ON READINGS

The identification of the fragment as corresponding to 11Q**19** III 14–17 is based upon the mention of הכיר וכנו (cf. the sequence of objects in Exod 30:27-28 and in 11Q**19** III 13–14), and corroborated by the overlap of some letters.

L. 1 וכו]ל. The head of *kap* is very short, but the letter cannot be *nun*, which has a curve to the right at the top of the downstroke.

L. 3 ברו֯ר]. The downstroke attached to *bet* has a short horizontal stroke at the top which is rather short for *reš*, but *waw* and *yod* are even more unlikely. The angular form of the shoulder of the second *reš* is unusual.

L. 5 ת]מיד. The letter after *mem* is either *waw* or *yod*.

L. 5 מאת]. A short, thick, vertical stroke of ink, without ticks, is placed supralinearly between *ʾalep* and *taw*. It is not clear whether this stroke represents a letter; if so, either *waw* or *yod*.

L. 6 [א֯שכין]. The diagonal stroke of the first letter may belong to *ʾalep* or *mem*. There seems to be the remains of another stroke beneath the diagonal trace, which would indicate *mem*, but this dark trace does not have the same colour as the ink traces.

TRANSLATION

1. [and its vessels shall be of] pure [gol]d and the who[le altar for the burnt offering they shall make of pure bronze, and the grill]
2. [which is on top] of it and the wash-basin and its pedestal shall [be of bronze, polished as a mirror]
3. [ ] pure bronze [
4. [ ] *vacat* [
5. [con]tinually from [the Israelites
6. [in the house where] I shall cause [my name] to dwell [

COMMENTS

L. 1 זה]ב טהור וכו]ל. 11Q**19** III 14 has a *vacat* after טהור.

L. 2 והכיר וכנו. Cf. Exod 30:18 and 28. In the latter verse כיר is written defectively as in this text.

L. 2 יה]יו. Cf. 11Q**19** III 16 יו֯֯[. Qimron's reconstruction should be corrected: והכיר is the last word of 11Q**19** III 5, and line 6 begins with [וכנו יה]יו֯֯.

L. 2 נחושת מרוק כמראות לראות פנים]. Cf. Exod 38:8 and the discussion by Mink.[1]

L. 3 ף ימס. Cf. 11Q**19** III 17. Before the final *pe* there are traces of another letter. There is room for one short word between ברו֯ר] and the word ending with the final *pe*.

L. 4 *vacat*. 11Q**19** III 18 has the remains of three letters, possibly ר֯י֯ב֯, but it is not clear whether they should be placed before or after the *vacat*.

L. 5 ת]מיד מאת] בני ישראל. Cf. 11Q**19** XXIX 5.

L. 6 בבית אשר [א֯שכין] שמי. Cf. 11Q**19** XXIX 3-4, or אשר אשכין עליו את כבודי (11Q**19** XXIX 8-9). Cf. also 11Q**19** XLV 12, LIII 9.

[1] H. A. Mink, 'Die Kol. III der Tempelrolle. Versuch einer Rekonstruktion', *RevQ* 11 (1982–84) 163–81, especially 172–3.

Frg. 2

]°יׄאׄ °ור֯°[

]° ל°°]]וׄהקנים יחׄ°[

]° ככ֯ה יעש]ו

]ל ב°[

Mus. Inv. 614
PAM 44.006

NOTES ON READINGS

The fragment has darkened, part of the surface has eroded, and several traces seem to have faded away. As a result the reading of only a few words is certain, but the mention of the קנים suggests that the fragment could be placed somewhere in 11Q**19** IX.

L. 2]°°ל. The traces after *lamed* may indicate *ṣade* (cf. the examples of *ṣade* in 11Q**12**), in which case one might interpret the following trace as part of *ʾalep*. The space before]וׄהקנים[is rather short, and therefore it is difficult to reconstruct לצׄאׄ]ת]וׄהקנים.

L. 2]°יחׄ. The second letter may perhaps also be *he*. The traces of the third letter may indicate *lamed*.

L. 3 ככ֯ה. The fragment seems to read כרה, but perhaps it should be assumed that the base stroke of the second *kap* has worn away.

TRANSLATION

1.] [
2.] [ ] and the shafts [
3.] thus [t]he[y] shall be made [
4.] [

Frg. 3

]]מ֯ה֯[ ]

לבוא אל עירי [

תרנגול לוא֯ תגד]לו

בכול המקד֯ש֯ °[

המקד֯]ש

Mus. Inv. 567
PAM 44.114*
IAA 525015

Notes on Readings

The fragment consists of two pieces, the smaller one containing the last letters of lines 3–4. Materially the pieces seem to fit, and the letters תגד on the small fragment fit well at the end of line 3. However, the traces in line 4 are difficult to understand as following המקד̊ש.

L. 3 לו̊א̊. The spot close to the horizontal stroke of *lamed* may be the head of *waw*. The next traces may be the *keraia* of the right arm and the bottom part of the diagonal of *ʾalep*.

L. 4]◦. The letter clearly has a horizontal head stroke and a downstroke.

Translation

1. [ ] [
2. to enter my city [
3. a cock you shall not rai[se
4. in the entire Temple [
5. the Tem[ple

Comments

If the identification of the manuscript as a copy of the *Temple Scroll* is correct, one might locate the fragment in the beginning of 11Q**19** XLVIII (Qimron). עירי is used twice at the end of 11Q**19** XLVII (lines 15 and 18), a section dealing with items which should not be brought to the Temple or to the city. In that case the remnants of line 1 might correspond to 11Q**19** XLVII 18 פגוליכמה.

L. 3 תרנגול לו̊א̊ תגד]לו. If the reading is correct, the fragment deals with animals which should not be raised in Jerusalem. תרנגול is probably the object of לו̊א̊ תגד]לו, not of a preceding verb, since the Temple Scroll has a preference for syndetic constructions.

L. 4 בכול המקד̊ש. Cf. 11Q**19** XLV 8 כול המקדש.

22. 11QpaleoUnidentified Text

(PLATE XLVIII)

THE remains of the manuscript consist of seven fragments, three of which (frgs. 1, 2, 5) can no longer be located in the Rockefeller Museum. Frg. 3 is light tan and clearly different from the light brown colouring of frgs. 4 and 6. Frg. 4 seems to be smoother than frg. 3.

The fragments display a regular palaeo-Hebrew hand, somewhat similar to that of 4QpaleoGen-Exod[l] (4Q**11**) and clearly distinct from the palaeo-Hebrew script of 11QpaleoLev[a] (11Q**1**). The height of the letters varies from 1 mm (*taw*) to 2 mm, with the exception of *lamed* (3.5 mm) which reaches up to 3 mm above the ruling line. The distance between the horizontal lines is slightly larger than 8 mm. Frg. 1 shows that the word for God (לאלהיכ) was written with a different colour of ink. The similarity to the hand of 4Q**11** suggests a date within the first half or three quarters of the first century BCE.

Only frg. 1 (1.5 cm high x 7.3 cm wide), frg. 2 (1.4 cm high x 2 cm wide), and frg. 6 contain complete words, but the few remains could not be identified. Most of the Qumran scrolls written in palaeo-Hebrew are biblical, and the few nonbiblical ones (4Q**123–125**) are probably parabiblical (4QParaphrase of Joshua, and two unidentified manuscripts). The first and second verbal forms and pronominal suffixes, suggest that the fragments are hymnal, but the genre may also be considered that of a testament.

Mus. Inv. 614, 1020, 1032
PAM 42.174, 42.175*, 44.006*, 44.117*
IAA 563763*, 563769*

Frg. 1

1 [◦ה̊◦ד̊◦י̊] [◦ו̇◦◦◦◦◦] [◦] [◦]
2 [*vac* תהיה· עדי· נגה· באהבתכ· לאלהיכ· *vac?* ו̊ילב]
3 [תכ· ערכ̊] [ל◦כ◦ ל̊ל]

PAM 42.175

NOTES ON READINGS

L. 1 The upper edge is carbonized, but the bottom parts of some letters are still visible. The *dalet* could also be *reš*.

L. 2 לאלהיכ. The word is written in a different colour ink, probably red, but since the fragment could not be located in the museum, this could not be verified.

L. 2 ו֯ילב[*vac?*. A light area is visible in the photograph between לאלהיכ· and ו֯ילב[. It is not clear whether the section has faded or the surface has peeled off. There is enough space for one or two letters in this light area, but the text may also have had a small *vacat*.

L. 3 ערכ֯[ ]ל◦כׄ◦. There may be room for a word-dividing dot between *kap* and *lamed*. The stroke after the second *kap* might be such a dot, even though the trace is longer (more a stroke than a dot) than elsewhere in the fragments.

TRANSLATION

1.] [ ] [ ] [ ] [
2.] *vac* You shall be a shining ornament because of your love for your God. *vac?* And [
3.] your [ ] [

COMMENTS

L. 2 תהיה·עדי·נגה·באהבתכ·לאלהיכ. For a somewhat similar expression, cf. *T. Abr.* (long recension) 17:7 καὶ τὸ μέγεθος τῆς ἀγάπης σου τῆς πρὸς θεὸν ἐγένετο στέφανος ἐπὶ τῆς ἐμῆς κεφαλῆς.

L. 2 ו֯ילב[. Reconstruct, e.g. ו֯ילב[יש or ו֯ילב[ישכ. For the combination of עדי and לבש, cf. e.g. 2 Sam 1:24 and Isa 49:18.

L. 3 ערכ֯[ ]ל◦כׄ◦. It is probable that the letters belong to two words, and one might read ערכ֯[·]לבׄכׄ·, but no parallel to the expression is known. There does not seem to be enough space to read ערכ֯[·מ]ליׄכ·.

Frg. 2

]·אוהבי·ופק[1

]·הׄייתי[2

PAM 44.006

NOTES ON READINGS

L. 2]·הׄייתי[. The faint trace before *he* may also be part of *waw*. A stroke at the left edge is, if indeed ink, the top part of a *lamed*, in which case one should read]·הׄייתי[·]ל[.

TRANSLATION

1.] who love(s) me, and [
2.] I am (*or*: became) [

COMMENTS

L. 1 ופק[. Reconstruct, e.g. a form of פקד. Cf. Exod 20:5-6 and Deut 5:9-10.

L. 2]·הׄייתי[. Reconstruct, e.g. ואני]·הׄייתי[.

Frg. 3

]◦בו[1

]◦·ת[2

Mus. Inv. 614
PAM 44.006

Notes on Readings

L. 1 [◦בה]. The tiny speck on the right edge is the same colour as the ink.

L. 2 [◦. *Waw* or *qop* is possible.

Frg. 4

[◦◦וד֯ א] 1

Mus. Inv. 614
PAM 44.006

Notes on Readings

The fragment may perhaps be joined to frg. 1, in the first part of line 3.

L. 1 [◦◦וד. In the photograph, the trace before *waw* seems to be triangular, but the fragment shows only the bottom trace. The traces of the first letter are blurred by spots. Read, e.g. [כ֯ב֯וד.

Frg. 5

[תיכ֯ ול] [◦] 1

PAM 44.117

Translation

1.] your[ ]and [

Frg. 6

[◦ו֯ חרפותי] 1

[י֯כ] 2

Mus. Inv. 1020
PAM 42.174
IAA 563763*

NOTES ON READINGS

Frg. 6, the only fragment in PAM 42.174 that does not belong to **11Q1** (11QpaleoLev[a]), is now stored in Box 1020. The traces of the second line are very faint and are not visible on the fragment itself.

TRANSLATION

1.] my reproaches [
2.] your [

COMMENTS

L. 1 חרפותי֯]. In the Hebrew Bible and the Qumran scrolls, חרפה is used almost exclusively in the singular. The plural is used in Ps 69:10, 11; Dan 12:2; and 4Q**200** 1 i 3 (*Tob* 3:6).

Frg. 7

1]יהוה· [

2]ל֯[

Mus. Inv. 1032
IAA 563769

TRANSLATION

1.]YHWH [
2.] [

23. 11QcryptA Unidentified Text

(PLATE XLVIII)

THE skin of 11Q**23** is very similar to that of 11Q**14**. Ruling is faint but visible on some of the fragments.

The hand has been identified as Cryptic A, like those of 4Q**249** *Midrash Sefer Moshe* (4QMSM), 4Q**317** Phases of the Moon, and 4Q**298** Words of the Maskil to All Sons of Dawn.[1] Few letters and traces survive, but it appears that the hand is closer to those of 4Q**249** and 4Q**317**, which are dated to the late 2nd century BCE, than to the somewhat later 4Q**298**.[2]

Mus. Inv. 613
PAM 42.176*, 44.005

Frg. 1

1]°בח[

Mus. Inv. 613
PAM 42.176*, 44.005

NOTES ON READINGS

The uninscribed part of the fragment has become detached since the photographing of PAM 42.176, and does not appear on PAM 44.005.

L. 1 בח[. The *bet* is identical to the examples in 4Q**249** and 4Q**317**, but different from those in 4Q**298**. *Ḥet* is only partially preserved, but the remains match no other Cryptic A letter.

---

[1] The present editors failed initially to recognize the hand, and wish to thank É. Puech for his identification of the fragments as Cryptic A.

[2] Cf. the comparison of the hands in S. Pfann, '4Q298: The Maskîl's Address to All Sons of Dawn', *JQR* 85 (1994–95) 203–35, esp. 216–21.

Frg. 2

[מ◦] 1

Mus. Inv. 613
PAM 42.176*, 44.005

NOTES ON READINGS

L. 1 [מ◦]. The first letter can only be *mem* with the curved descender drawn to the right. The second letter is *ṭet* or *reš*.

Frg. 3

[◦ ◦] 1

[י̊] 2

[א̊ר ◦] 3

[◦ח] 4

Mus. Inv. 613
PAM 42.176*, 44.005

NOTES ON READINGS

L. 2 [י̊. The letter is most probably *yod*, although the angle of the intersecting strokes is wider than in the other Cryptic A MSS.

L. 3 [א̊ר. The first trace may belong to *ʾalep* or *lamed*.

L. 3 ◦]. Possible readings are *ʾalep*, *waw*, *kap*, *ʿayin*, *taw*, or, with more difficulty, *mem*.

L. 4 [◦ח]. The first letter may be *he*, *qop*, or *taw*.

24. 11QUnidentified Text ar

(PLATE XLIX)

THE fragment is a dark reddish brown, and though the black traces of the letters are clearly visible, they are difficult to interpret. A piece of dark tan cloth, partly visible on the museum plate, is attached to the back of the fragment. The fragment has not been smoothed out completely, probably due to the presence of the cloth on the back.

The hand seems to be Hasmonaean, but too few letters have survived to draw further conclusions regarding its date.

Mus. Inv. 567
PAM 44.114*
IAA 525015

Frg. 1

1]ין[
2]ר֯שין לכון ובׄ◦[
3]לכׄון תׄי֯ל֯כׄן ותחׄי[
4]לכ֯ון לה֯◦[

NOTES ON READINGS

L. 2]ר֯שין. The size of the first letter suggests *reš* rather than *yod*.

L. 3 תׄי֯ל֯כׄן. The upper arm of the *lamed* has faded, except for the top which could be mistaken for the tail of the final *nun* of the line above. Also the crossbar is larger than in the other examples of *lamed*, but *samek* is less likely. The letter following *lamed* is either *pe* (in which case the small ascending stroke, if indeed ink, remains unexplained) or a slightly misformed *kap*.

L. 4]לכ֯ון. Or]לה֯ון, but a change of person is unexpected.

L. 4 לה֯◦[. The second letter may also be *ḥet*.

TRANSLATION

1.] [
2.] for you, and [
3.] for you (?) [ ] and [
4.] for you (?), for [

COMMENTS

L. 3 תׄי֯ל֯כ֯ן֯. This reading, as well as תׄי֯ל֯פ֯ן֯ is grammatically anomalous, although possible in Rabbinic Aramaic for תהלכן or תאלפן.

25. 11QUnidentified Text A

(PLATE XLIX)

EIGHT small fragments possibly belong to the same manuscript, as they are all distinct in colour from the rest of the fragments: frg. 1 is light tan; frgs. 2 and 3 display the same tan, but also have creamy white sections, and frg. 4 displays only the creamy white. The fragments have a rather coarse grain. In frgs. 1 and 2, the ink has partially faded away. Four more recently photographed fragments have a similar colour and hand: frg. 5 is light tan, and frgs. 6–8 are whitish.

The hand is early Herodian, but note that the forms of the letters are not completely identical in the fragments.

The words ולא in frg. 1 2 and אלהי[in frg. 3 1 indicate a defective spelling, whereas עינכׄ[ה, frg. 1 2, *si vera lectio*, would attest the long form of the pronominal suffix.

Mus. Inv. 567, 581A, 614, 621B, 1032
PAM 42.178, 44.006*, 44.114*, 44.117*
IAA 525015, 563757*, 563769*

Frg. 1

1 לעממים[
2 ולא עינכׄ[ה
3 [ ]°ר֯וח֯[

Mus. Inv. 567
PAM 42.178, 44.114*
IAA 525015

NOTES ON READINGS

Frgs. 1, 2, and probably also frg. 3, have preserved the right margin.

L. 2 עינכׄ[ה. The fragment clearly shows the base of *kap* extending to the edge of the fragment.

L. 3 [ ]°ר֯וח֯[. The *reš* may also be *bet*, and the *ḥet* possibly *he* or *taw*.

TRANSLATION

1. for the nations [
2. and not your eye [
3. [ ] [

COMMENTS

L. 1 לעממים]. Forms of עם with a reduplication of the last consonant are rare in the Qumran scrolls. Cf. 11QT[a] XXVII 8 עממה; 4QJub[a] (4Q**216**) 2 iv 10 עממי; 4Q**302** 1 i 12 עממים.

L. 2 עינכ]ה. In view of the defective spelling of ולא in frg. 1 2 and אלהי] in frg. 3 1, a long form of the suffix seems irregular. An alternative reconstruction is עינכ]ם.

Frg. 2

על] 1

Mus. Inv. 567
PAM 42.178, 44.114*
IAA 525015

Frg. 3

אלהי] 1

[ ]ל] 2

Mus. Inv. 621B
PAM 44.117

NOTES ON READINGS

L. 1 אלהי]. The word is preceded by the right margin, a *vacat*, or a large space.

Frg. 4

]תْ התורה ואשْ[1

]◦ת לשמْרֹה ◦◦◦[2

]◦ד נْ◦אْ◦[3

]לאْ ◦[4

Mus. Inv. 614
PAM 44.006

Notes on Readings

The fragment has several holes and the surface of the skin has suffered severe damage.

L. 1]ואשׂ̊. Or]ואע̊. The first letter may also be *yod*.

L. 2 ת○[. The *taw* is preceded by a diagonal stroke, which may belong to *ʾalep*, *gimel*, or *mem*.

L. 2 לשמ̊ר̇ה. The skin between *šin* and *reš* is severely damaged. Two faint strokes to the right of the downstroke of *reš* may suggest *mem*, but need not indicate a letter at all. The *reš* is not certain, and its head is slightly different from the *reš* in line 1.

L. 3]○א̊○נ̊ ד○[. The *dalet* and possible *nun* are written close together, and it is not certain that a space should separate them.

Translation

1.] the law and [
2.] to protect him [
3.] [
4.] not [

Frg. 5

1]ו̊ח̊ה [

Mus. Inv. 1032
IAA 563769

Frg. 6

1]נ̊י ז○[
2]ת̊○[

Mus. Inv. 581A
IAA 563757

Frg. 7

]עׄלׄוה[1

Mus. Inv. 581A
IAA 563757

NOTES ON READINGS

L. 1]עׄלׄוה[. The space between *lamed* and *he* seems too small for *yod*.

Frg. 8

]הג◦[1

]ה אר[2

Mus. Inv. 581A
IAA 563757

NOTES ON READINGS

This fragment was stuck to the back of frg. 7, and might therefore belong to a subsequent revolution of the scroll.

26. 11QUnidentified Text B

(PLATE XLIX)

THREE fragments have a similar orange-brown colour, and may share the same hand. It is certain that frgs. 2 and 3 belong to the same manuscript. The thickness of the skin of frg. 1 is average, while that of frgs. 2 and 3 is thicker.

The hand of frg. 1 (and probably also of frgs. 2 and 3) is early Herodian.

Mus. Inv. 567, 621B
PAM 44.114*, 44.117*
IAA 525009, 525011, 525015

Frg. 1

]ולתכם [1

]והתבל[2

Mus. Inv. 621B
PAM 44.117

NOTES ON READINGS

L. 2]והתבל[. Parts of the letters have faded away (e.g. the left leg of *taw*).

TRANSLATION

1.] your [
2.] and [

COMMENTS

L. 1 ולתכם[. Reconstruct, e.g. פע]ולתכם.

L. 2]והתבל[. The word could be a definite noun, a *Hitpa'el*, or an imperfect preceded by the interrogative particle. A possible reading would be והתבל]עה, the *Hitpa'el* of בלע being used in **4Q416** (4QInstruction[b]) 2 iii 8.

Frg. 2

1]יתנׄ[

2]○○[

Mus. Inv. 567
PAM 44.114*
IAA 525011, 525015

NOTES ON READINGS

IAA 525015 is more easily read than PAM 44.114. Some pieces which broke off appear in IAA 525011.

Frg. 3

1]○דנ○[

Mus. Inv. 567
PAM 44.114*
IAA 525009

NOTES ON READINGS

L. 1]○דנ○[. Read, e.g. כ]ו֯דני֯[.

27. 11QUnidentified Text C

(PLATE XLIX)

THE fragments are of a light tan colour with a yellow or orange tone, and the ink has faded slightly.

Mus. Inv. 614B
PAM 44.008

Frg. 1

]עליכה כיא[1

bottom margin?

Mus. Inv. 614B
PAM 44.008

NOTES ON READINGS

The fragment consists of two parts, displayed separately in Mus. Inv. 614B. The fragment probably preserves the bottom margin, though it may also be a blank line.

TRANSLATION

1.] on you, for [

COMMENTS

The words occur in this order in 𝔐 Exod 15:26 and Nah 3:19, but not elsewhere in the Qumran scrolls.

L. 1]עליכה. Most probably the preposition על with suffix, but one may also reconstruct, e.g. נ]עליכה. Cf. e.g. Exod 3:5 של נעליך מעל רגליך כי המקום.

Frg. 2

]שי◦[1

Mus. Inv. 614B
PAM 44.008

NOTES ON READINGS

L. 1]שי◦[. The faint trace after the *yod* in the photograph is not ink.

28. 11QpapUnidentified Text D

(PLATE L)

BOX 988 in the Rockefeller Museum contains eight small and two minute unpublished fragments of 11Q**1**, some small remains of wrappings, one unclassified fragment (11Q**28** 19), as well as two small papyrus fragments. In view of the absence of any other papyrus fragments among the finds in cave 11, the origin of these two fragments may seem suspect, but their placement in the same box as the 11Q**1** fragments warrants their publication as cave 11 fragments. Frg. 2 reveals only faint traces of ink, whereas frg. 1 has some clear traces which are, however, difficult to identify.

Mus. Inv. 988
IAA 563761

29. 11QFragment Related to Serekh ha-Yaḥad

(PLATE L)

THIS fragment is light brown in colour with a coarse grain, and its surface is covered with specks. The top and left of the fragment are abraded, and only a few remnants of three lines are preserved. Only a few letters are legible on the fragment, and the reading is based on the photograph. The few preserved letters suggest a Hasmonaean hand comparable to that described by Cross as a typical Hasmonaean script (*c*.125–100 BCE), but the *keraia*-like form at the right arm of *ʾalep* might suggest a much later Hasmonaean date.

The clause]רׄוחו לבגוׄדׄ in line 2 suggests a relation to the penal codes preserved in 1QS VII and 4QD^e (4Q**270**) 7 i, and the remnants of line 3,]םׄ בראׄ[, suggest that lines 2–3 correspond to 1QS VII 18–19. The difference between this fragment, which reads]רׄוחו לבגוׄדׄ, and 1QS VII 18 רוחו מיסוד היחד לבגוד is comparable to the variants between 4QS^b (4Q**256**) and 4QS^d (4Q**258**) on the one hand, and 1QS on the other. 4QS^b and 4QS^d have a shorter text than 1QS in several places, some explicit references to the *yaḥad* being absent from 4QS^b and 4QS^d. The small amount of legible text does not allow one to conclude whether the fragment is part of a copy of *Serekh ha-Yaḥad*, or from a different composition which relates or refers to it.[1]

Mus. Inv. 615
PAM 44.007

]∘∘∘ ∘[1

]רׄוחו לבגוׄדׄ בׄ[2

]םׄ בראׄ[שונה 3

NOTES ON READINGS

L. 1]∘∘∘ ∘[. Or]∘∘∘∘∘[. All that remains are the bottoms of downstrokes and base strokes.

L. 2]רׄוחו. The first letter is probably *reš*, even though it is slightly different from the *reš* in line 3, or perhaps *kap*.

[1] For a more comprehensive discussion of the relation of the fragment to *Serekh ha-Yaḥad* or the Penal Code section in the *Damascus Document*, cf. E. J. C. Tigchelaar, 'A Newly Identified *Serekh ha-Yaḥad* Fragment from Cave 11?' forthcoming in the Proceedings of the International Congress '50 Years after the Discovery of the Dead Sea Scrolls' (Jerusalem, July 20–25, 1997).

L. 2 ב֯[. Or ל֯[. The long stroke extending upwards above the left side of the crossbar would suggest the upper arm of *lamed*, but the rest of the traces are clearly different from the *lamed* of לבג֯וד֯. The letter is more probably a *bet* as it is consistent with the two other examples in the fragment, albeit with a larger, longer tick.

L. 3 ברא֯[שונה. After *ʾalep*, the bottom tip of a downstroke is visible. It is not clear whether the following dark stroke, which might be the lower oblique of *šin,* is indeed ink.

Translation

1.] [
2.] his spirit to betray [
3.] in the fir[st (year)

Comments

L. 2]ר֯וחו לבג֯וד֯ Cf. 1QS VII 18 רוחו מיסוד היחד לבגוד, VII 23 רוחו לבגוד. In 4Q**270** 7 i 8,]רוחו לבגוד should probably be reconstructed rather than]רוחו מיסוד היחד לבגוד.

L. 3 ברא֯[שונה. Cf. 1QS VII 19 ברישונה.

Reconstruction

2 [והאיש אשר תזוע]ר֯וחו לבג֯וד֯ ב֯[אמת וללכת בשרירות לבו אם]

3 [ישוב ונענש שתי שני]ם֯ ברא֯[שונה

Translation

2. [A man] whose spirit [strays], so as to betray [the truth and to walk in the stubbornness of his heart,
3. [If he returns, he shall be penalized two year]s; in the fir[st (year)

30. 11QUnclassified Fragments

(PLATES L–LI)

Frg. 1

]◦[1

]גבורה מ◦[2

]ח֯◦ב֯◦[3

PAM 44.117

NOTES ON READINGS

The fragment, which can no longer be found in Mus. Inv. 621B, can be interpreted as either Hebrew or Aramaic. The hand resembles that of 11QPs[b], but the *he* is written differently. The remains of line 2 correspond to Ps 65:7-8, Isa 28:6, Jer 10:6-7, and 1QS IV 3. The remains of line 3 are too damaged to give a certain reading. One might read מ]ח֯ש֯ב֯ת֯[(1QS IV 4) or י]ו֯ש֯ב֯י֯[(Ps 65:9), the former corresponding to the traces more closely than the latter.

L. 1]◦[. It is not clear from the photograph whether the horizontal stroke is ink.

L. 2]◦מ. The trace after the *mem*, if ink, suggests *šin* or *ʿayin*.

TRANSLATION

1.] [
2.] might [
3.] [

Frg. 2

]◦[1

] להצׄ[2

]כׄי הא[3

Mus. Inv. 621B
PAM 44.117

NOTES ON READINGS

The fragment is brown with dark spots, and barely legible to the naked eye. The hand is somewhat similar to **11Q8** (Ps[d]) and **11Q12** (Jubilees). A possible correspondence in the Hebrew Bible may be Zeph 1:18 (line 2 להצ֯]ילים [; line 3 יש[ב֯י֯ הא]רץ), but that would imply a rather long line.

L. 2 להצ֯]. The right arm of *ṣade* has a different colour, comparable to the faded right leg of *he* in line 3, and is joined to the preceding *he*. If the stroke is ink the letter could be *nun*.

L. 3 כ֯י֯[. The first letter may also be *bet*; the second could also be *waw*.

Frg. 3

1]°°כ֯ו֯ל֯[

Mus. Inv. 621B
PAM 44.117

NOTES ON READINGS

The fragment is brown, and covered with a white substance. No writing is legible to the naked eye; only by holding a print of the photograph up to a strong light is it possible to identify traces. The bottom of the fragment may preserve the top of a second line.

Frg. 4

1]°ענ [

2]ל[ ]ו ם°[

Mus. Inv. 615
PAM 44.007

NOTES ON READINGS

The fragment is a dark brown colour, and the letters, which are clear in the photograph, are no longer discernible on the fragment.

Frg. 5

]∘∘ג̊[1

] ∘לא[2

Mus. Inv. 615
PAM 44.007

NOTES ON READINGS

Physically, the fragment resembles the 11Q**18** fragments in the same plate, but the *lamed* is quite different from those in 11Q**18**.

L. 2 ∘לא[. The vertical position of the *ʾalep* with regard to the *lamed* is rather high, and one might consider ∘לא̊[, but cf. the trace at the beginning of the line.

Frg. 6

]ל 1

Mus. Inv. 621B
PAM 44.117

NOTES ON READINGS

The fragment as displayed in PAM 44.117 appears to reveal no traces, but when turned 180 degrees, one discerns traces which correspond to part of a *lamed* the size and shape of those in 11Q**20**.

Frg. 7

]רשׁ̊ 1

]ת̇ 2

PAM 42.176

NOTES ON READINGS

The fragment could not be located in the Rockefeller Museum, but a combination of the colour in the photograph and the form of the few letters suggests that it might belong to **11Q8** (Ps^{d}).

L. 1 וש֯]. A trace before the *waw* may be the head of, e.g. *yod*. The trace of the last letter may also indicate *ʿayin*.

Fragments Photographed in 1997 (Frgs. 8–19)

In the boxes of cave 11 materials in the Rockefeller Museum there are hundreds of tiny unsorted, uncleaned, and unphotographed fragments. Most of them do not reveal any writing visible to the naked eye.[1] In autumn 1996, the editors selected from the boxes all fragments which displayed an inscribed text, visible to the naked eye, and requested that they be photographed. In some cases, classification was simple because of the colour of the skin or the characteristics of the hand. In many other cases, identification *in loco* was difficult because of the darkness of the skin and the minimal amount of writing. The fragments were photographed in infra-red in 1997, shortly before this volume was submitted to the publisher.

Frg. 8

] תהׄיה לראו֯[ש 1

]ל◦[2

Mus. Inv. 581A
IAA 563757

NOTES ON READINGS

The hand does not seem to correspond to any of the identified manuscripts, but it is probable that frgs. 8–10 belong to the same manuscript.

L. 1 לראו֯[ש. The presence of a tiny dot on the edge suggests *ʾalep* was followed by a letter with a downstroke, not by *šin*.

TRANSLATION

1.] you will become the he[ad
2.] [

[1] In one case, a dusty reddish fragment was handled with sweaty fingers. The moistened section of the fragment temporarily displayed an inscription, which faded away again as soon as the fragment dried. It is to be expected that infra-red photography of all the tiny fragments would disclose more writing.

Frg. 9

]יֹד באמ◦[1

]ל̊ [2

Mus. Inv. 581A
IAA 563757

NOTES ON READINGS

L. 2]ל̊[. It is not certain whether or not the dark blot is ink.

COMMENTS

L. 1]יֹד באמ◦[. Cf. e.g. Ps 89:50 לדוד באמונתך.

Frg. 10

]מה כיא מ̇[1

Mus. Inv. 581A
IAA 563757

NOTES ON READINGS

A small piece inscribed with]◦ס[is partly attached to the fragment.

TRANSLATION

1.] for [

Frg. 11

[ועל יצוע]י 1

Mus. Inv. 581A
IAA 563757

NOTES ON READINGS

The photograph shows three dots close to the bottom edge, but it is not certain whether they are ink.

TRANSLATION

1.] and on [my] bed [

COMMENTS

L. 1 [ועל יצוע]י. Cf. Ps 63:7 and 1QHª XVII 4 (IX 4).

Frg. 12

1 [בׄתולד]ות

Mus. Inv. 581A
IAA 563757

NOTES ON READINGS

L. 1 בׄתולד]ות. The stroke to the left of *dalet* has a different colour, and does not appear to be ink.

TRANSLATION

1.] in the generation[s of

Frg. 13

1 [בׄ◦◦]

Mus. Inv. 581A
IAA 563757

NOTES ON READINGS

The fragment might belong to 11Q**13**.

L. 1 [בׄ◦◦]. Read perhaps [בׄרׄשׄ].

Frg. 14

]∘∘[1
]רֹב[2
]צ֯[3

Mus. Inv. 1031
IAA 563767

NOTES ON READINGS

L. 3]צ֯[. Or]ב∘[.

Frg. 15

]ה֯וד֯[1

Mus. Inv. 1032
IAA 563769

NOTES ON READINGS

The fragment perhaps belongs to 11Q**8**.

L. 1]ה֯וד֯[. The first letter might also be *qop*.

Frg. 16

top margin

]ל ∘∘[1

Mus. Inv. 1032
IAA 563769

NOTES ON READINGS

The colour of the skin matches that of 11Q**20**, but the upper arm of *lamed* strongly suggests 11Q**6**.

Frg. 17

]למספר ◦[1

]◦ךֹ ה[2

Mus. Inv. 1034
IAA 563771

NOTES ON READINGS

L. 2]◦ךֹ. *Dalet* is more difficult than final *kap*, though in some hands *dalet* might take this form.

TRANSLATION

1.] for the number [

COMMENTS

The remnants may be a quote from Ezek 4:5-6:

]למספר יֹ]מים שלש מאות התשעים יום ונשאת עון בית ישראל וכלית את אלה ושכבת על 1

צ]דֹך ה]ימני 2

Frg. 18

]◦◦[1

]רמ[2

Mus. Inv. 988
IAA 563761

Frg. 19

]ה 1

Mus. Inv. 1020
IAA 563763

Frg. 20

Mus. Inv. 567
PAM 44.114*
IAA 525015

NOTES ON READINGS

There are no traces visible to the naked eye on the fragment, but the photograph displays some ambiguous traces. The letter at the top resembles *mem*, and slightly lower there are traces which suggest *dalet*.

Frg. 21

Mus. Inv. 567
PAM 44.114*
IAA 525015*

NOTES ON READINGS

No traces are visible in the PAM photograph, but in the IAA photograph several traces suggest letters the size of those in 11Q**20**.

Frg. 22

Mus. Inv. 567
PAM 44.114
IAA 525015*

NOTES ON READINGS

No traces are visible on the fragment or the photograph. The thicker than average skin might indicate that it originates from 11Q**2**.

Frgs. 23–26

Mus. Inv. 615
PAM 44.007

NOTES ON READINGS

Neither the fragments nor the photographs display traces which can be interpreted as letters.

Frgs. 27–28

Mus. Inv. 1016
PAM 43.794

NOTES ON READINGS

Neither the fragments nor the photographs display traces which can be interpreted as letters. The shape of frg. 27 corresponds more or less to that of 11Q**3** 3 on the same museum plate.

31. 11QUnidentified Wads

(PLATE LII)

PREVIOUS inventories of the cave 11 materials in the Rockefeller Museum described the contents of Box 563 as tiny unpublished fragments of **11Q17** *Shirot ʿOlat ha-Shabbat*, presumably on account of the hand, the size of the letters, and the thinness and brittleness of the skin. Closer examination of the fragments in the box reveals that it is extremely unlikely that they are remnants of 11Q**17**. The skin is different and the line spacing is only one third the width of that in 11Q**17**.

The most recent examination of the box in December 1996 revealed that the fragments were placed in two parcels of tissue paper, one on top of the other, in a small iron box. The lower parcel consists of a few small wads, some tiny fragments, and thousands of minute pieces ranging from 1 x 1 mm to mere dust particles. On one or two of the tiny fragments, some letters can be seen with the naked eye, but no writing is visible on the small wads. The upper parcel consists of a larger number of small wads and a collection of small fragments, more than half of which contain writing visible to the naked eye. These materials were photographed *recto* and *verso* in the spring of 1996. It is possible that the distribution of the fragments (wads) into two parcels reflects the distinction between inscribed and uninscribed fragments.

The fragments are varying shades of grey in colour. Some of the fragments are covered with spots of a white substance which is probably a type of fungus. The skin, or membrane, is extremely thin (*c*.0.05–0.1 mm; calculation is based on frg. 4 which is 0.3–0.5 cm thick and consists of *c*.6 layers). It is also brittle and loses dust-like specks at a mere touch. All the larger wads consist of multiple layers and, in almost all cases, pieces of the upper layers have peeled away, resulting in the preservation on the *recto* of the readings of several subsequent layers. Frg. 4, with a surface of *c*.1.2 x 1.2 cm, reveals traces belonging to six subsequent layers. Only in a few cases is it possible to distinguish between the layers in the photographs. The side view of the largest wad, frg. 14, suggests folding, not rolling, of the skin, and the indentation in frg. 2 is most probably the result of the pressure of the thread which was wrapped around the folded skin. Several wads (frgs. 4, 5, and 15) are inscribed on both the *recto* and the *verso* of the wad, a phenomenon which is possibly related to the folding of the skin.

The hand is developed Herodian, and despite the tiny size of the letters (*c*.1 mm) the scribe was able to add ticks and *keraiai*. On some fragments, the ink is very clear on the slate-grey skin, whereas in other cases the photographs reveal writing which is barely visible to the naked eye. Frg. 6 has a height of 1.5–1 6 cm and preserves the remains of eight lines, the space between the lines being no wider than 2 mm.

Because of the state of the fragments (wads), they cannot be transcribed. Although some fragments (wads) preserve several lines and letters, these most often stem from multiple layers. In only a few cases have more than two lines containing more than two certain letters been preserved from the same layer. Frg. 6 contains the best preserved single layer, comprising eight lines of two to three letters.

As far as can be judged, these wads are unlike any other manuscripts found in the vicinity of Qumran. The wads have some features in common with the phylacteries, notably the extremely thin and brittle skin, the folding of the material, and the small hand with hardly any space between the lines. The size of the letters and the interlinear distance are comparable to, e.g. 4Q**143** (Phyl P) or 4Q**146** (Phyl S). Unlike most phylacteries, the hand is not semi-cursive, but formal as in 4QPhyl D–F, P, and S, even though none of these phylacteries has a developed Herodian hand. The objections to the identification of the wads as a phylactery are threefold. Most importantly, the dimensions of the wads are incompatible with phylacteries. Frg. 14 measures *c*.1.4 x 1.5 cm, and the largest wad from the lower parcel in the box measures *c*.1.8 x 2 cm, whereas the average size of the phylacteries from cave 4 is *c*.0.5 x 0.5 cm (cf. *DJD* VI, 35, for the exact dimensions of the compartments in which the slips of the phylacteries were kept). Secondly, all the phylacteries were found in *tefillin* boxes, whereas, to our knowledge, no such boxes were found in cave 11. Thirdly, there are too many wads to have belonged to one phylactery.

Alternatively, one may consider the possibility that the remains belong to one or more *mezuzot*. The characteristics of the remains of *mezuzot* are less uniform. Most are made of skin, and at least one (4Q**155**) of membrane, although it is thicker than that of the phylacteries. The dimensions of the wads would be more compatible with *mezuzot* than with phylacteries, but still the objection may be made that the amount of preserved material is too large for one *mezuza*.

In short, only the opening of the very brittle and damaged wads and the recovery of layers with more text would further the identification of the manuscripts.

Mus. Inv. 563
IAA 508046*, 508048*

CONCORDANCES

THESE concordances refer to all the Hebrew and Aramaic words occurring in the texts covered by this volume, together with their respective contexts. All independent words are covered, thus excluding the attached morphemes -ב, -ה, -כ, and -ל. From left to right, each entry contains the reference to the text, parallel if any,[1] lemma, and in-context phrase. The Aramaic lemmas are unvocalized; in the list verbal forms precede nominal forms. The concordances have been prepared by S. and C. Pfann. The volume's editors have reviewed the concordances, and the lemmatizations and readings reflect their preferences.

SIGLA

/	beginning of line
//	beginning of column
א̊	possible letter
א̇	probable letter
^א^	supralinear insertion
{א}	erasure
[א]	reconstructed letter

[1] In the case of 11Q10 tgJob and 11Q13 Jubilees, this column pertains to the MT and the standard edition, respectively; in the case of 11Q20 Temple[b], to 11Q19 Temple[a].

HEBREW CONCORDANCE

Text	Word	Ref.	Location
[ויאמר] לו תרח א]ביו לך בשלום]	אָב	12:29	**12** 9,4
ומלא י]דו ללבוש את הבגדים] תחת]אביהו	אָב	xv16	**20** I,22
/ יככה יהוה מ[כה גדול]ה אשר אבדך[	אבד		**11** IV,4
]בקללת האב[דון	אֲבַדּוֹן		**11** IV,10
]ם לחם חדש אביבות[ומלילות	אָבִיב	xix7	**20** III,24
]אדם ואשתו מת[אבלים / על הבל]	אבל		**12** 1,3
על כפים[ישאונ]ך פן[תגוף בא]בן רגל[ך	אֶבֶן		**11** VI,11
ב]אברתו יסך[לך	אֵבֶר		**11** VI,5
]◦ אברם[	אַבְרָם		**12** 11,2
[יברך בשם / כבוד א]דון כ[ו]ל א[לים]	אָדוֹן		**17** III,9
ועל כול א]דם רשע	אָדָם		**11** III,7
/מי אתה [הילוד מ]אדם ומזרע הקד[ושי]ם	אָדָם		**11** V,6
ואד[ם / ידע את חוה אשתו]	אָדָם	4:10	**12** 1,10
ולוא] / [יהיה נוגעים בהמה כול א]דם[	אָדָם	xxxii15	**20** IX,5
]אדם ואשתו מת[אבלים / על הבל]	אָדָם		**12** 1,3
]·אוהבי·ופק[	אהב		**22** 2,1
תהיה·עדי·נגה·באהבתכ·לאלהיכ·	אַהֲבָה		**22** 1,2
לוא] / תרא[ה רעה ו]לוא יגע [נגע באה]ליך	אֹהֶל		**11** VI,10
וזר]קו הכוהנים בני אה[רון את דמם]	אַהֲרוֹן	xxii5	**20** V,25
בן אבי]כה או [בן / אמכה	אוֹ	liv20	**20** XVI,1
]אולמי מב[ואי]	אוּלָם		**17** IV,4
[ליקרה הדביר במו]צא אול[מי]	אוּלָם		**17** V,5
ויפתח לכם את / אוצרו הטוב אשר בשמים	אוֹצָר		**14** 1ii8
/ יברך אתכם אל עליון ויאר פניו אליכם	אור		**14** 1ii7
חושך אתה ולוא אור	אוֹר		**11** V,7
ב[אלה לו]א / [יעבור] אור	אוֹר		**11** V,10
]ים מ◦[ ] האור מ[	אוֹר		**17** I,4
/]א באור אורים	אוֹר		**17** VIII,3
/]א באור אורים	אוֹר		**17** VIII,3
כב]וד מעשיו ובאו[ר]מלה	אוֹר		**17** X,4
אור וחושך ובדני[ ]קודש מלך / הכבוד	אוֹר		**17** X,5
[בשבוע הששי הוליד את אזו]רה בתו	אזורה	4:8	**12** 1,7
]באזר[וע	אֶזְרוֹעַ		**15** 4,1
ואת האזרוע [ע]ד עצם השכם /	אֶזְרוֹעַ	xx16	**20** IV,26
ואת השכם הנשאר מן האזרוע /	אֶזְרוֹעַ	xxi04	**20** V,3
]אחת[	אֶחָד		**11** 3,3
/ [וירדף א]חד מכם א[לף	אֶחָד		**11** III,11
וחלת לחם שמן אחת ורקיק[אחד	אֶחָד	xv10	**20** I,17
ולבני לוי אי]ל אחד כבש אחד	אֶחָד	xxi1	**20** V,6
ולבני לוי אי]ל אחד כבש אחד	אֶחָד	xxi1	**20** V,6
ולכול מטה] / ומטה איל אחד כבש[אחד	אֶחָד	xxii13	**20** VI,6
פר אח]ד איל אחד /	אֶחָד	xxv5	**20** VII,26
פר אח]ד איל אחד /	אֶחָד	xxv5	**20** VII,26

Text	Word	Ref.	Location
ויקח קין את אחות[ו / און לו לאשה]	אָחוֹת	4:9	**12** 1,7
[הומת קין] אחריו [בשנה ההיאה]	אַחַר		**12** 6,1
/ היובל הראישון אחר תש[עה ה]יובלים	אַחַר		**13** II,7
ואחריהמה הכ[ו]הן הגדול וכול הכ[והנים	אַחַר	xvi01	**20** I,24
ובאה השמש א]חר / [יבוא אל המקדש	אַחַר		**20** XII,3
[זרע ב]ארץ אחר תחת הבל	אַחֵר	4:7	**12** 1,6
פשרו]לאחרית הימים על השבויים אשר[	אַחֲרִית		**13** II,4
]ולמלואים איל איל לכ[ול יום ואחד]	אַיִל	xv3	**20** I,12
]ולמלואים איל איל לכ[ול יום ואחד]	אַיִל	xv3	**20** I,12
וחצו את]כול האילים והסלים	אַיִל	xv4	**20** I,13
]ליהוה שנים [ע]שר אילים	אַיִל	xix16	**20** IV,4
אי]לים ומנחתמה כמשפט	אַיִל	xx01	**20** IV,5
שלישית הה]ין שמן לאיל על הנסך הזה /	אַיִל	xx02	**20** IV,6
לפרים ולאיל · / [ולכבשים ולשעיר עזים]	אַיִל	xx05	**20** IV,9
א]ת האילים ואת הנסך	אַיִל	xx1	**20** IV,11
תנופה מן האי]לים	אַיִל	xx15	**20** IV,25
[מן] האילים ומן / [הכבשים]	אַיִל	xxi06	**20** V,5
ולבני לוי אי]ל אחד כבש אחד	אַיִל	xxi1	**20** V,6
]ם אילים שנים/	אַיִל	xxii01	**20** V,18
א[יל אחד כבש אחד	אַיִל	xxii12	**20** VI,5
ולכול מטה] / ומטה איל אחד כבש[אחד	אַיִל	xxii13	**20** VI,6
פר אח]ד איל אחד /	אַיִל	xxv5	**20** VII,26
אשר אינם [	אַיִן		**11** III,8
ואין משכלה בארצכם / ולוא מוחלה	אַיִן		**14** 1ii11
] אין עוד /	אַיִן	l3	**20** XIV,6
]אשר יעש[ו]על / [כול אי]ש חטא	אִישׁ		**11** III,7
ו]אנש[י]גורל מל[כי]צדק	אִישׁ		**13** II,8
והאנשים אשר יה[יה להמה מקרה לילה	אִישׁ	xlvi18	**20** XIII,2
/ [ע]דנים ואכלתם והדשנתם *vac*	אכל		**14** 1ii11
ואכלום בחצ[ר הפנימית]	אכל	xix5	**20** III,23
ואכלום / [בחצר החיצונה לפני יהוה	אכל	xxi3	**20** V,7
]ואל יואכלו /	אכל		**20** XIV,5
ואל המקדש / [לוא יבוא]*vac*	אַל		**20** XII,12
]ואל יואכלו /	אַל		**20** XIV,5
קרא בכו]ל עת / אל השמ[ים	אֵל		**11** V,5
כי]יבוא אליך בלי[לה וא]מרתה אליו	אֵל		**11** V,5
כי]יבוא אליך בלי[לה וא]מרתה אליו	אֵל		**11** V,5
אל[יך לו]א יגע	אֵל		**11** VI,8
כיא קרא]שמטה / לא[ל	אֵל		**13** II,4
אשר / ישיבמה אליהמה	אֵל		**13** II,6
ע]ם קדושי אל לממשלת משפט	אֵל		**13** II,9
אל ידין עמים	אֵל		**13** II,11
אש[ר]◦ים בסו[רם]ה מחוקי אל ל[הרשיע]	אֵל		**13** II,12

Ref.		Word	Context
13 II,13		אֵל	/ ומלכי צדק יקום נקם משפטי א[ל
13 II,14		אֵל	/ ובעזרו כול אלי [הצדק
13 II,14		אֵל	וה]ואה א[שר]כול בני אל והפ[
13 II,23		אֵל	]במשפט[י] אל כאשר כתוב עליו[
13 III,3		אֵל	/ אל יאו[
14 1ii4		אֵל	/ בשם אל עליון ◦[ ] וברוך שם קודש[ו]
14 1ii7		אֵל	/ יברך אתכם אל עליון ויאר פניו אליכם
14 1ii14		אֵל	כיא אל עמכם
17 III,9		אֵל	[יברך בשם / כבוד א]דון כ[ו]ל א[לים]
17 IV,3		אֵל	[ ]ב[אל]והי אלים[
17 V,7		אֵל	]אלוהי אלי[ם]
17 VI,4		אֵל	רוחי א]ל[י] עולמים[
17 VIII,7		אֵל	]קיר מברכים ומהללים לאלוהי / אלים
14 1ii7		אֶל	/ יברך אתכם אל עליון ויאר פניו אליכם
20 XII,11		אֶל	]ק לוא יבוא אל המקדש /
20 XII,20	xlvi7	אֶל	אשר יהיו עולים]בני יש[ראל א]ליו
20 XII,20	xlvi8	אֶל	לבוא אל מק[דשי]
21 3,2		אֶל	/לבוא אל עירי [
11 II,4		אֵלֶּה	] אלה [הש]דים ושׂ[ר המשט]מה /
11 IV,7		אֵלֶּה	אש[ר /]על כול אלה
13 7,10		אֵלֶּה	]ם באלה[
20 XI,24		אֵלֶּה	ולוא יהיו מתערבים אלה ב]אלה /
13 II,10		אֱלוֹהִים	אלוהים [נ]צב בע[דת אל]
13 II,10		אֱלוֹהִים	]בקורב אלוהים ישפוט
13 II,16		אֱלוֹהִים	[א]ומר לציון [מלך]אלוהיך
13 II,23		אֱלוֹהִים	[אומר לצי]ון מלך אלוהיך
13 II,24		אֱלוֹהִים	ואל[ו]היך הואה / [מלכי צדק
17 I,7		אֱלוֹהִים	אל]והים מ◦◦◦[ ]לאלוהי [
17 I,7		אֱלוֹהִים	אל]והים מ◦◦◦[ ]לאלוהי [
17 I,9		אֱלוֹהִים	]◦◦◦ ◦[א]לוהים ב[
17 II,6		אֱלוֹהִים	[הללו לאל]אלוהים[שבע כהונת קורבו
17 IV,3		אֱלוֹהִים	[ ]ב[אל]והי אלים[
17 IV,8		אֱלוֹהִים	אלוהים ◦[
17 V,4		אֱלוֹהִים	[וברכו לא]לוהי כול[
17 V,6		אֱלוֹהִים	] אלוהים[ ]חם וצורות [
17 V,7		אֱלוֹהִים	]אלוהי אלי[ם]
17 VI,3		אֱלוֹהִים	ק[ושבחוהו ב]דני אלוה[ים
17 VI,5		אֱלוֹהִים	[בקודש קודשים צורות אלוהי]ם חיים
17 VI,7		אֱלוֹהִים	א]ל[ו]הים[חיים כול מעשיהם
17 VII,5		אֱלוֹהִים	]רוחות אל[והים
17 VIII,4		אֱלוֹהִים	/]אלוהים נוראי כוח
17 VIII,4		אֱלוֹהִים	בכוח אלוהי / [עול]מים
17 VIII,5		אֱלוֹהִים	ומרוממים גבורות אלו[הי]
17 VIII,6		אֱלוֹהִים	ישמ[י]עו מקול משא אלוהים[ ]
17 VIII,6		אֱלוֹהִים	]קיר מברכים ומהללים לאלוהי / אלים
17 VIII,8		אֱלוֹהִים	]◦י אלוהי[
20 XVI,3		אֱלוֹהִים	מאלוהי ה[עמים / אשר סביבותיכמה]
22 1,2		אֱלוֹהִים	תהיה·עדי·נגה·באהבתכ·לאלהיכ·
20 I,16	xv8	אַלְיָה	ואת האלי]ה לעומת עציהה
20 IV,17	xx6	אַלְיָה	ואת הא]ליה לעומת / [העצה]
11 III,11		אֶלֶף	/ [וירדף א]חד מכם א[לף
11 VI,8		אֶלֶף	יפ[ו]ל מצדך אלף ור[בבה מי]מינך
12 5,2	4:30	אֶלֶף	כיא] אלף ה[ש]נים[יום אחד
20 V,5	xxi06	אֶלֶף	]שרי האלפים
20 V,23	xxii2	אֶלֶף	]ם שרי האלפים עם נשיאי/
11 III,8		אִם	]ה אם לוא / [וייראו]מלפני יהוה ל[
20 I,21	xv15	אִם	*va[c* ואם[הכוה]ן הגדול[יהיה עומד
11 V,5		אמר	כי]יבוא אליך בלי[לה וא]מרתה אליו
11 V,11		אמר	ו]אמרתה ה[
11 VI,4		אמר	]האומר [ליהוה מחסי] ומצודת[י
13 II,2		אמר	]ל ואשר אמר
13 II,10		אמר	כאשר כתוב / עליו בשירי דויד אשר אמר
13 II,10		אמר	ועליו אמ[ר ו]עלי[ה] / למרום שובה
13 II,11		אמר	ואשר א[מר עד מתי ת]שפוטו עוול
13 II,15		אמר	א]שר אמר[ביד ישע]יה הנביא
13 II,15		אמר	ביד ישע]יה הנביא אשר אמר[
13 II,16		אמר	[א]ומר לציון [מלך]אלוהיך
13 II,18		אמר	כאשר אמר דנ[יאל עליו
13 II,25		אמר	ואשר אמר והעברתמה שו[פר
11 V,13		אֱמֶת	א]מת מח◦[
11 VI,6		אֱמֶת	חסד[ו ע]ליך צנה וסוחרה אמתו סלה
13 II,21		אֱמֶת	/ באמת למ[ ]מה א[
16 3		אֱמֶת	]באמתכה כלי ל[
17 X,6		אֱמֶת	לכול מעשי אמת[ו]למלאכי הדעת
20 XII,17	xlvi4	אֲנִי	אשר]אני שוכן[בתוכם]
20 XV,7	li16	אָנֹכִי	/ אשר אנוכי נותן לכמ[ה לרשתה
11 IV,5		אַף	/ ובחרון אפו[ישלח]עליך מלאך תקיף[
11 IV,11		אַף	]חרון אף י[הוה
17 IX,8		אֵפוֹד	]מו לצורות[ ]שא אפוד /
11 VI,7		אֹפֶל	מדבר[בא]פל / יהלך
20 X,1	xxxvii9	אֵצֶל	בפרור]הפנימי אצל ק[י]ר החצר ה[חיצון
12 1,4	4:7	אַרְבָּע	ו]בארבעה לשבוע הח[מישי / שמחו]
17 VIII,5		אַרְבָּע	מארבעת מוסדי רקיע / הפלא
20 I,26	xvi03	אַרְבַּע	על ארבע פנות עזרת ה[מזבח
20 IV,12	xx2	אַרְבַּע	]א וכבשים [בני] שנה ארבעה / [עשר]
11 I,6		אֶרֶץ	א]ת האר[ץ
11 III,2		אֶרֶץ	/ הארץ ו◦[ה]ארץ
11 III,2		אֶרֶץ	/ הארץ ו◦[ה]ארץ
11 III,3		אֶרֶץ	/ ואת המופ[תים האלה ב]ארץ
11 III,6		אֶרֶץ	ו[את כול] הארץ[בהם
11 IV,3		אֶרֶץ	/ כול הארץ[ ] השמים ו[
11 IV,9		אֶרֶץ	[לוא ע]וד בארץ

Context	Word		Reference
[זרע ב]ארץ אחר תחת הבל	אֶרֶץ	4:7	**12** 1,6
נבנו הבתים באר[ץ]	אֶרֶץ	4:9	**12** 1,9
והעברתמה שו[פר ב]כול [א]רץ //	אֶרֶץ		**13** II,25
להוריד על ארצכםה / גשמי ברכה	אֶרֶץ		**14** 1ii8
והארץ תנובב לכם פרי	אֶרֶץ		**14** 1ii10
ואין משכלה בארצכם / ולוא מוחלה	אֶרֶץ		**14** 1ii11
ואין דב]ר בארצכם	אֶרֶץ		**14** 1ii14
מקצי הארץ ועד קצ[י הארץ	אֶרֶץ		**20** XVI,4
/ יתממ[ו] בליעל באש[	אֵשׁ		**13** III,7
]וכול אושיהם	אשׁ		**17** VIII,8
עולה היא אשה ריח ניחוח[לפני יהוה	אִשֶּׁה	xv13	**20** I,19
אשה ריח / [ניחוח ליהוה	אִשֶּׁה	xxii04	**20** V,21
]אדם ואשתו מת[אבלים / על הבל]	אִשָּׁה		**12** 1,3
[קינן אשה את אחותו מהללת] לאשה[	אִשָּׁה	4:14	**12** 2,3
/ ועושה אשמה גדול[ה	אַשְׁמָה	li14	**20** XV,6
א]שר[ ]ל תהו[ם]ך /	אֲשֶׁר		**11** II,5
א]שר הבדיל[בין / האור ובין החושך]	אֲשֶׁר		**11** II,11
]אשר הת[י]צבו לפני[ו	אֲשֶׁר		**11** III,5
]אשר יעש[ו]על / [כול אי]ש חטא	אֲשֶׁר		**11** III,6
אשר אינם [	אֲשֶׁר		**11** III,8
/ יככה יהוה מ[כה גדול]ה אשר לאבדך[	אֲשֶׁר		**11** IV,4
אשר[בלוא] רחמ[ים] עליך	אֲשֶׁר		**11** IV,6
אש[ר /]על כול אלה	אֲשֶׁר		**11** IV,6
אשר[יורידו]ך לתהום רבה	אֲשֶׁר		**11** IV,7
/אשר[ ]הפגוע[ים	אֲשֶׁר		**11** V,2
אש[ר יזרח] / [על ה]צדיק לה[	אֲשֶׁר		**11** V,10
]אשר יעשו ב[שמים / ובארץ]	אֲשֶׁר		**12** 1,2
]ל ואשר אמר	אֲשֶׁר		**13** II,2
כול בעל משה יד אשר ישה[ברעהו	אֲשֶׁר		**13** II,3
פשרו]לאחרית הימים על השבויים אשר[	אֲשֶׁר		**13** II,4
]ואשר / מוריהמה החבאו וסתר[ו]	אֲשֶׁר		**13** II,4
אשר / ישיבמה אליהמה	אֲשֶׁר		**13** II,5
כאשר כתוב / עליו בשירי דויד אשר אמר	אֲשֶׁר		**13** II,9
כאשר כתוב / עליו בשירי דויד אשר אמר	אֲשֶׁר		**13** II,10
ואשר א[מר עד מתי ת]שפוטו עוול	אֲשֶׁר		**13** II,11
אש[ר]∘ים בסו[רמ]ה מחוקי אל ל[הרשיע]	אֲשֶׁר		**13** II,12
וה]ואה א[שר]כול בני אל והפ[	אֲשֶׁר		**13** II,14
א]שר אמר[ביד ישע]יה הנביא	אֲשֶׁר		**13** II,15
ביד ישע]יה הנביא אשר אמר[	אֲשֶׁר		**13** II,15
כאשר אמר דנ[יאל עליו	אֲשֶׁר		**13** II,18
]הואה הכתוב עליו אשר [	אֲשֶׁר		**13** II,19
]במשפט[י] אל כאשר כתוב עליו[	אֲשֶׁר		**13** II,23
ואשר אמר והעברתמה שו[פר	אֲשֶׁר		**13** II,25
ויפתח לכם את / אוצרו הטוב אשר בשמים	אֲשֶׁר		**14** 1ii8
א]שר כוננו ידיכה[	אֲשֶׁר		**15** 2
ואת החלב אשר עלי[הנה	אֲשֶׁר	xv7	**20** I,15
עם שוק התרו]מה אשר לימין	אֲשֶׁר	xv11	**20** I,18
ויקרב את אשר [ל]כוהנים ברישונה[	אֲשֶׁר	xv17	**20** I,23
אש[ר יהיו מניחים עליהמה את בגדיהמה	אֲשֶׁר	xxxii10	**20** IX,1
אשר יהיו מב[שלים / שמה את זבחיהמה]	אֲשֶׁר	xxxvii14	**20** X,5
עד אש]ר יטהרו	אֲשֶׁר	xlv18	**20** XII,10
וכאשר / [יטהר והקריב את	אֲשֶׁר	xlv18	**20** XII,10
אשר לוא[ישכון כול / עוף טמא	אֲשֶׁר		**20** XII,15
אשר יהיה[מבדי]ל בין מקדש / [הקודש	אֲשֶׁר	xlvi10	**20** XII,21
והאנשים אשר יה[יה להמה מקרה לילה	אֲשֶׁר	xlvi18	**20** XIII,2
/ אשר אנוכי נותן לכמ[ה לרשתה	אֲשֶׁר	li16	**20** XV,7
או ריעיכה א]שר כנפשכה בסתר[לאמור]	אֲשֶׁר	liv20	**20** XVI,2
א]ת האר[ץ	אֵת		**11** I,6
]את ב[	אֵת		**11** I,8
]את השד[	אֵת		**11** I,10
אשר עשה] את השמים / [ואת הארץ]	אֵת		**11** II,10
/ ואת המופ[תים האלה ב]ארץ	אֵת		**11** III,3
יהוה הוא[ה אשר] / עשה את ה[אלה	אֵת		**11** III,4
/ [וא]ת כול זר[ע הקודש]	אֵת		**11** III,5
ויעיד א]ת / [כול הש]מים	אֵת		**11** III,5
]ותלד לו בן ויקרא את שמ[ו שת]	אֵת	4:7	**12** 1,5
ויקח קין את אחות[ו / און לו לאשה]	אֵת	4:9	**12** 1,7
/ יברך אתכם אל עליון ויאר פניו אליכם	אֵת		**14** 1ii7
ויפתח לכם את / אוצרו הטוב אשר בשמים	אֵת		**14** 1ii7
ואת החלב אשר עלי[הנה	אֵת	xv7	**20** I,15
ואת יותרת הכבד[	אֵת	xv8	**20** I,16
ומלא י]דו ללבוש את הבגדים[תחת]אביהו	אֵת	xv16	**20** I,22
ויקרב את אשר [ל]כוהנים ברישונה[	אֵת	xv17	**20** I,23
]ואת[החלב / אשר עליהנה]	אֵת	xvi8	**20** II,6
א]ת האילים ואת הנסך	אֵת	xx1	**20** IV,11
א]ת האילים ואת הנסך	אֵת	xx1	**20** IV,11
ואת / [יותרת הכבד ועל	אֵת	xx6	**20** IV,15
ומן הכבשים את שוק הימין /	אֵת	xx15	**20** IV,25
ואת האזרוע [ע]ד עצם השכם /	אֵת	xx16	**20** IV,26
ואת השכם הנשאר מן האזרוע /	אֵת	xxi04	**20** V,3
ואת ∘∘[	אֵת		**20** X,6
]וקדשו את מ[קדשי]	אֵת	xlvi11	**20** XII,22
ולוא ישקצו] / את נפשותיהמה	אֵת	li9	**20** XV,3
]ים עליהם את /	אֵת		**20** 31,3
/ את חומ[ו]ת יהודה וב֯ר[ ]ע[	אֵת		**13** III,9
/מי אתה [הילוד מ]אדם ומזרע הקד[ושי]ם	אַתָּה		**11** V,6
חושך אתה ולוא אור	אַתָּה		**11** V,7
]אתה בראתה כול רוח גל∘∘[	אַתָּה		**15** 6
]∘ אתה יצרת[ה	אַתָּה		**16** 1
וענה[ואמר]ישראל ברוכים א[תם]	אַתֶּם		**14** 1ii3
בתים ומקו]רים ובירות בתוכ[מה]/	בְּאֵר	xlvi14	**20** XII,25
לבגוד ב[אמת וללכת בשרירות לבו	בגד		**29** 1,2

Ref		Word	Context
20 I,22	xv16	בֶּגֶד	ומלא י]דו ללבוש את הבגדים[
20 XIV,19		בֶּגֶד	יטמא עד הערב וכבס] / בגדי[ו
11 II,11		בדל	א]שר הבדיל[בין / האור ובין החושך]
20 XII,21	xlvi10	בדל	אשר יהיה[מבדי]ל בין מקדש / [הקודש
17 V,5		בדן	]בדני פ[לא
17 V,9		בדן	[ב]דניהם כרובי[
17 VI,3		בדן	ק[ושבחוהו ב]דני אלוה[ים
17 VI,3		בדן	רוחי ק]מרכב[ ]◦ל בדני כב[וד
17 VI,7		בדן	וצו]רת בדניהם מל[אכי קודש
17 X,5		בדן	אור וחושך ובדני[ ]קודש מלך / הכבוד
12 7,2	5:2	בְּהֵמָה	[מאדם עד]בהמה ועד ח[יה ועד עוף]
20 II,2	xvi2	בֹּהֶן	על] הבוהן /
11 V,5		בוא	כי]יבוא אליך בלי[לה וא]מרתה אליו
11 V,12		בוא	הצ]דיק לבוא[
15 2,5		בוא	]ר תבוא ע[
20 IV,23	xx13	בוא	ולוא תבו]א ע[ל]י[ו ה]שמש *vac*
20 XI,21		בוא	ומ]◦באים /
20 XI,23		בוא	וכאשר ו השני י]היה בא / [לשמאול
20 XII,11		בוא	]ק לוא יבוא אל המקדש /
20 XII,20	xlvi8	בוא	לבוא אל מק[דשי]
20 XIII,3		בוא	/ והבאים[ ]ל[
20 XV,1	li5	בוא	/ ובאה השמ[ש אחר יטהר
21 3,2		בוא	/לבוא אל עירי [
15 2,4		בָּחִיר	] לעיני בחיר[י
20 XII,21	xlvi10	בֵּין	אשר יהיה[מבדי]ל בין מקדש / [הקודש
17 VII,12		בֵּין	יצ]א ומבין[גלגלי כבודו
17 VIII,2		בִּינָה	/]פלא דעת ובינ[ה
12 1,9	4:9	בַּיִת	נבנו הבתים באר[ץ]
20 IX,2	xxxii11	בַּיִת	למע]לה מע[ל]לבית[ה
11 I,2		בכה	]ובוכהו [
20 III,21	xix2	בִּכּוּר	ברובע]היום יקר[יבו את עול]ת הבכור[ים
20 IV,1	xix12	בִּכּוּר	את ל]חם הבכורים שבעה שבו[עות
20 V,17	xxi16	בִּכּוּר	בכ]ורים / [לפני יהוה
20 X,2	xxxvii10	בִּכּוּר	לזבחיהמה ולב]כורים ולמעשרות *vac*
11 VI,3		בְּלִיַּעַל	/ [את כול]בני בל[יעל אמן אמן] סלה
13 II,12		בְּלִיַּעַל	/ פשרו על בליעל ועל רוחי גורלו
13 II,13		בְּלִיַּעַל	וביום ההואה יצי]ל[מה מיד]בליעל
13 II,22		בְּלִיַּעַל	/ ◦◦[ ]ר הוסרה מבליעל ותש[וב
13 II,25		בְּלִיַּעַל	אשר יצי]ל[מה מי]ד בליעל
13 III,7		בְּלִיַּעַל	/ יתממ[ו] בליעל באש[
13 5,3		בְּלִיַּעַל	]בליעל ימרו ◦[
20 III,10	xviii6	בלל	סולת ב]לולה[בשמן
20 V,20	xxii03	בלל	בלול]ה בשמן הזה מחצית ההין /
11 VI,3		בֵּן	/ [את כול]בני בל[יעל אמן אמן] סלה
12 1,5	4:7	בֵּן	]ותלד לו בן ויקרא את שמ[ו שת]
12 1,10	4:9	בֵּן	[ויקרא את שמה כמו שם ב]נו חנוך*vac*

Ref		Word	Context
12 2,1	4:13	בֵּן	ותלד לו ב]ן בש[נה / השלישית
13 II,8		בֵּן	/ לכפר בו על כול בני [אור
13 II,14		בֵּן	וה]ואה א[שר]כול בני אל והפ[
20 III,2	xvii13	בֵּן	/ בני[שנה שבעה
20 IV,7	xx03	בֵּן	וכבש]ים בני שנה שבעה
20 V,25	xxii5	בֵּן	וזר]קו הכוהנים בני אה[רון את דמם]
20 VI,9	xxiii01	בֵּן	/ כול [ב]ני ישראל בכול[מושבותיהמה
20 X,3	xxxvii12	בֵּן	ולוא יתע]רבו זבחי שלמי בני יש[ראל]
20 XI,12		בֵּן	]לבני /
20 XII,20	xlvi7	בֵּן	אשר יהיו עולים]בני יש[ראל א]ליו
12 1,9	4:9	בנה	נבנו הבתים באר[ץ]
13 II,3		בַּעַל	כול בעל משה יד אשר ישה[ברעהו
20 V,22	xxii1	בער	]השמן הזה יבעירו בנרות / [בה
15 6		ברא	]אתה בראתה כול רוח ג[ל◦◦[
21 1,3		בָּרוֹר	]נחושת ברור[ף ימס
13 II,24		בְּרִית	המה]מקימ[י] הברית
20 IV,24	xx14	בְּרִית	[ולוא ת]שבית ברית מלח ל[עולם *vac*
14 1ii2		ברך	]וברכם בשם [אל] / [י]שראל
14 1ii3		ברך	וענה[ואמר]ישראל ברוכים א[תם]
14 1ii4		ברך	/ בשם אל עליון ◦[ ] וברוך שם קודש[ו]
14 1ii5		ברך	/ לעולמי עד וברוכים [ ]תו
14 1ii5		ברך	וברוכים כול / מלאכי קודשו *va]c*
14 1ii7		ברך	/ יברך אתכם אל עליון ויאר פניו אליכם
17 III,4		ברך	לברך ל[מלך הקודש]
17 III,11		ברך	[בשבעה / דברי]פלא לברך[
17 III,12		ברך	[בשבעה / דברי פ]לא [ו]ברך לכ[ול]
17 VII,10		ברך	יפולו לפנו הכרובים ו]ברכו
17 VII,14		ברך	וקול דממת ב]רך בהמון [לכתם
17 VIII,6		ברך	]קיר מברכים ומהללים לאלוהי / אלים
14 1ii9		בְּרָכָה	להוריד על ארצכסה / גשמי ברכה
17 III,5		בְּרָכָה	]ע שבע תהלי בר[כות]
17 X,4		בְּרָכָה	[ו]כול ברכות שלומ[ו
17 30,5		בְּרָכָה	ת]הלי ברכות כבוד ה[
20 X,5	xxxvii14	בשל	אשר יהיו מב[שלים / שמה את זבחיהמה]
13 II,16		בשר	רגל[י] מבש[ר מ]שמיע שלום
13 II,16		בשר	מב[שר טוב משמיע ישוע]ה
13 II,18		בשר	/ והמבשר הו[אה]משיח הרו[ח]
12 1,7	4:8	בַּת	[בשבוע הששי הוליד את אזו]רה בתו
20 XII,15		גְּבוּל	ג]בולו
14 2,2		גִּבּוֹר	קומה גב]ור שבה פל[שתים
17 VII,6		גְּבוּרָה	ג]בורת פלא[
17 VIII,5		גְּבוּרָה	ומרוממים גבורות אלו[הי]
30 1,2		גְּבוּרָה	]גבורה מ◦[
11 II,6		גָּדוֹל	]לש◦[ ]הגד[ול]והי /
11 III,10		גָּדוֹל	וייראו[את המכה ה]גדולה הזוא[ת] /
11 III,12		גָּדוֹל	ג]דולה ו[ ]רת[

Reference		Word	Context
11 IV,1		גָדוֹל	/ ו]גדול[ ]משביע[
11 IV,2		גָדוֹל	/ והגדול בֿ[ ]תקיף ורֿ[
20 I,21	xv15	גָדוֹל	*va[c* ואסֿ[הכוה]ן הגדול[יהיה עומד
20 I,24	xvi01	גָדוֹל	ואחריהמה הכֿ[ו]הֿן הֿגדֿול וכול הכ[והנים
20 XV,6	li14	גָדוֹל	/ ועושה אשמֿהֿ גדול[ה
21 3,3		גדל	/תרנגול לוֿאֿ תגד[לו
13 III,10		גָדֵר	/ גדר ולשֿאֿת עֿמוד וכֿפֿר ◦[ ]אֿ[
14 2,1		גוֹי	]טי הגוי הנב[ל
13 II,8		גוֹרָל	ו]אֿנש[י]גורל מל[כי]צדק
13 II,12		גוֹרָל	/ פשרו על בליעל ועל רוחֿי גורלו
14 1ii9		גֶשֶׁם	להוריד על ארצכםה / גשמי ברכה
17 V,3		דְבִיר	תפארת בפרוכת] / דֿבֿירֿ[המלך
17 V,4		דְבִיר	[פרכות]דבירֿ[י הפלא]
17 VI,4		דְבִיר	מדרס] / דבירֿ[י פלא
17 VI,7		דְבִיר	מתחת לדב]ירי הֿ[פלא] / קול [דממת שקט
17 VII,4		דְבִיר	בדבירי כבודו
17 X,7		דְבִיר	מר]כבות הדרו ולדבירי קו[דשו
11 IV,6		דָבָר	[לעשות / כול דב]רו
13 II,6		דָבָר	ו[כן יהי]הֿ הֿדבר הזה
20 XIII,6		דָבָר	/ דבר ומשֿ[
11 VI,7		דֶבֶר	מדבר[בא]פל / יהלך
14 1ii14		דֶבֶר	ואין דב]ר בארצכם
14 1ii10		דָגָן	/ תֿנובות דגן תירוש ויצהר לרוב
20 V,9	xxi5	דֶגֶל	ישראל נ]שֿיאי הדגלים ברישונה
11 V,4		דָוִד	/לדויד עֿ[ל
13 II,10		דָוִד	כאשר כתוב / עליו בשירֿי דויד אשר אמר
14 1i7		דָוִד	[צמח ד]ויד /
20 VI,7	xxii14	דוֹר	חוקות] / עולם לדורותיהמה[שנה בשנה
13 II,11		דין	אל ידין עמים
11 V,9		דֶלֶת	[ויסגור דל]תי נחושת
20 I,25	xvi02	דָם	]ולקחו זקני הכֿוהֿני[ם] מדם הפר
20 I,26	xvi02	דָם	על קרנות המזבח באצבעם] / מן הד[ם
17 IV,7		דְמוּת	]בֿדמֿוֿ[ת תשבו]חות
17 37,2		דְמוּת	ד]מות כפֿ[
13 II,18		דָנִיאֵל	כֿאשר אמר דנֿ[יאל עליו
12 5,3	4:30	דַעַת	[לכן / נכתב על ע]ץֿ הדעת
17 VII,6		דַעַת	]כנפי דעת[
17 VIII,2		דַעַת	/]פֿלא דעת ובינֿ[ה
17 X,6		דַעַת	לכול מעשי אמתֿ[ו]למלאכי הדעת
20 32,2		דָרוֹם	]בֿדֿרום[
13 II,6		דְרוֹר	וקרא להמה דרור
11 VI,12		דרך	[ואפעה תד]רוך תרמו[ס כפיר] ותנין
12 7,3	5:2	דֶרֶךְ	[וכולם ה]שחיתו דרכם וחֿ[קתם]
13 II,24		דֶרֶךְ	הסרים מלכֿת [בד]רֿךֿ העם
14 1ii11		דשן	/ [ע]דנים ואכלתם והדשנתם *vac*
12 1,6	4:7	הֶבֶל	[זרע ב]ארץ אחר תחת הבל

Reference		Word	Context
17 X,7		הֲדֹם	/ לכסאי כבודו ולהדום רֿ[גליו
17 VI,10		הָדָר	]פֿלאֿי הוד והֿ[דר
17 IX,6		הָדָר	]עולמים בֿ[הוד ו]הֿדר ל◦[
17 IX,8		הָדָר	[ה]וד ו]הדר ◦[ ]◦◦◦[
17 X,4		הָדָר	ובהדר/ תשבוחותו בכול רקי[עי]ם
17 X,7		הָדָר	מר]כבות הדרו ולדבירי קו[דשו
11 III,3		הוא	יהוה הואֿ[ה אשר] / עשה את הֿ[אלה
11 VI,5		הוא	ה]וֿאה יצילך מֿ[פח יקו]ש מדבר הֿוֿ[ות
12 4,2		הוא	ריא]שון הוא[ה / כתב תעודה]
12 8,5	12:16	הוא	[ויהי] / הואה[יושב לבדו ומביט]
12 9,3	12:28	הוא	[כיא]הוא יוצא מ[חרן]
13 II,7		הוא	ויֿ[ום הכפ]וֿרים ה[וא]ה סֿ[וף]הֿ[יו]
13 II,9		הוא	כיא / הואה הקֿץ לֿשנת הרצון למלכי צדֿק
13 II,14		הוא	וה]וֿאה א[שר]כֿול בני אל והפ[
13 II,15		הוא	/ הזואת הואה יום הֿ[שלום
13 II,18		הוא	/ והמבשר הו[אה]מֿשיח הרו[ח]
13 II,19		הוא	]הואה הכֿתוב עליו אשר [
13 II,24		הוא	ואל[ו]היךֿ הֿואה / [מלכי צדק
13 5,2		הוא	]והוא[ה] יגידֿ[
20 V,21	xxii04	הוא	כמ]שפט עולה הואה
13 II,23		הִיא	[ציֿ]ון ה[יאה] / [עדת כול בני הצדק
13 7,2		הִיא	]מה היאֿ[ה
20 I,19	xv12	הִיא	עולה היא אשה ריח ניחוח[לפני יהוה
17 IV,7		הוֹד	בהוד תשבֿ[וחות
17 VI,10		הוֹד	]פֿלאֿי הוד והֿ[דר
17 VIII,3		הוֹד	הוד [ ]כֿול תבנית רוחי פל[א]
17 IX,8		הוֹד	[ה]וד ו]הדר ◦[ ]◦◦◦[
11 VI,5		הַוָּה	ה]וֿאה יצילך מֿ[פח יקו]ש מדבר הֿוֿ[ות
12 9,2	12:28	היה	*v[ac* ויהי בשב[עה לשבוע הששי]
13 II,6		היה	ו[כן יהי]הֿ הֿדבר הזה
20 I,14	xv5	היה	] יהיו מקריבים ליהוה עולהֿ[מן האיל
20 III,23	xix5	היה	הבכורים]לכֿוהֿנֿים יהיו
20 V,1	xxi02	היה	י]היה שוק התרומה וחזה / [התנופה
20 X,5	xxxvii14	היה	אשר יהיו מבֿ[שלים / שמה את זבחיהמה]
20 XI,23		היה	וכאשר ו השני י]היֿה בא / [לשמאול
20 XII,21	xlvi10	היה	אשר יהיה[מבדי]ל בין מקדש / [הקודש
20 XIII,2	xlvi18	היה	והאנשים אשר יה[יה להמה מקרה לילה
21 1,2		היה	והכיר וכנו יה[יו נחושת
22 1,2		היה	תהיה·עדי·נגה·באהבתכ·לאלהיכ·
22 2,2		היה	]·הֿייתי[
30 8,1		היה	] תהֿיה לראוֿ[ש
17 X,8		הֵיכָל	ולכול ז[בולי ו]להיכלי כבודו ולרקיעי
20 IV,3	xix15	הִין	שלישית ההין על / [המטה]
20 IV,6	xx02	הִין	שלישית הה]ין שמן לאיל על הנסך הזה /
20 V,16	xxi15	הִין	מחצית ההין / [אחד מן המטה
20 V,20	xxii03	הִין	בלול]הֿ בשמן הזה מחצית ההין /

Ref		Word	Context
11 VI,8		הלך	מדבר[בא]פל / יהלך
13 II,24		הלך	הסרים מלכת [בד]רך העם
17 VI,8		הלל	מהל]לים תמיד כ[ו]לן
17 VIII,6		הלל	]קיר מברכים ומהללים לאלוהי / אלים
11 III,7		הֵם	ו]הם יודעים / [רזי פל]או
13 II,5		הֵם	כי[א]°°°° והמה נחל[ת מלכי צ]דק
13 II,17		הֵם	המה א[ ]°מ[ ] לכול °°[
17 VII,14		הָמוֹן	וקול דממת ב]רך בהמון [לכתם
13 II,16		הַר	[מה]נאוו / על הרים
13 II,17		הַר	/ פשרו ההרים[המה] הנביאי[ם]
20 XV,2	li7	הַר	אשר אני מגיד] / לכ(מ)ה בהר הזה
11 III,9		הרג	ו]להרוג נפש /
12 1,6	4:7	הרג	כיא הרגו / [קין]
11 I,9		זֹאת	]הזואת[
11 III,10		זֹאת	וייראו[את המכה ה]גדולה הזוא[ת] /
13 II,15		זֹאת	/ הזואת הואה יום ה[שלום
20 VII,22		זֹאת	]ברובע הי[ו]ם תעלה זואת /
20 XI,16		זֹאת	מן הפנה הז]ואת עד ש[ער / דן
17 X,8		זְבוּל	ולכול ז[בולי ו]להיכלי כבודו ולרקיעי
20 VI,14		זְבוּלוּן	/ וביום הרביעי יששכר[וז]בולון
17 IX,4		זֶבַח	[ ]° לזבחי קדושים[
20 X,3	xxxvii11	זֶבַח	ולוא יתע]רבו זבחי שלמי בני יש[ראל]
12 3,2	4:17	זֶה	זה ריאש[ון]
13 II,2		זֶה	ועליו אמר וז]ה / [דבר השמטה] שמוט
13 II,6		זֶה	ו[כן יהי]ה הדבר הזה
20 IV,6	xx02	זֶה	שלישית הה]ין שמן לאיל על הנסך הזה /
20 V,11	xxi8	זֶה	ביו]ם הזה יכפרו על התירוש
20 V,14	xxi12	זֶה	*vac* וספרתמה לכמה מיום]הזה
20 V,20	xxii03	זֶה	בלול]ה בשמן הזה מחצית ההין /
20 V,22	xxii05	זֶה	]השמן הזה יבעירו בנרות / [בה
20 VI,8	xxii15	זֶה	/ כי ביום הזה
20 XV,2	li7	זֶה	אשר אני מגיד] / לכ(מ)ה בהר הזה
20 IX,1	xxxii10	זָהָב	מן הארץ ארבע אמות]מצופות זהב
21 1,1		זָהָב	וכליה יהיו זה]ב טהור
20 VII,24	xxv3	זִכָּרוֹן	]ן שבתון זכרון מקרא קודש /
17 III,4		זִמְרָה	[שבע בשבע ז]מרות פל[א]
20 I,25	xvi02	זָקֵן	]ולקחו זקני הכוהני[ם] מדם הפר
11 III,5		זֶרַע	/ [וא]ת כול זר[ע הקודש]
11 V,6		זֶרַע	/מי אתה [הילוד מ]אדם ומזרע הקד[ושי]ם
20 V,4	xxi05	זֶרַע	ל]חוק עולם להמה ולזרעמה /
20 V,25	xxii5	זרק	וזר]קו הכוהנים בני אה[רון את דמם]
13 II,5		חבא	]ואשר / מוריהמה החבאו וסתר[ו]
15 4		חֶדֶר	]בחדריכה בשמותם ב[
20 III,24	xix6	חָדָשׁ	]ם לחם חדש אביבות[ומלילות
20 V,10	xxi7	חָדָשׁ	יחלו לשתות יין חדש/
13 III,9		חוֹמָה	/ את חומ[ו]ת יהודה ובר[ ]ע[

Ref		Word	Context
13 7,3		חוֹמָה	]חומת יר[ושלם
20 II,9	xvi11	חוּץ	ישרופו]מחוץ ל[עיר]
20 XII,24	xlvi13	חוּץ	ועשיתה להמה מקו]ם יד חוץ מ[ן העיר]
20 V,1	xxi02	חָזֶה	י]היה שוק התרומה וחזה / [התנופה
11 II,9		חזק	יש]ראל החזק /
11 III,7		חטא	]אשר יעשו]על / [כול אי]ש חטא
14 1i10		חֹטֶר	ויצא חו]טר / [מגזע ישי
17 VI,5		חַי	[בקודש קודשים צורות אלוהי]ם חיים
12 7,2	5:2	חַיָּה	[מאדם עד]בהמה ועד ח[יה ועד עוף]
14 1ii13		חַיָּה	וחיה רעה שבתה מן / [הארץ
20 XII,16	xlvi3	חִיצוֹן	על גגי השערים אשר]לחצר החי[צונה
20 I,15	xv7	חֵלֶב	ואת החלב אשר עלי[הנה
20 I,17	xv9	חַלָּה	וחלת לחם שמן אחת ורקיק[אחד
11 V,7		חֲלוֹם	וקרניך קרני חל[ו]ם
14 1i15		חלל	]°פ[ ] חללי //
20 V,10	xxi7	חלל	יחלו לשתות יין חדש/
20 XIV,9	l5	חלל	ובח]לל חרב או במת או בדם אדם מת
20 XIV,18	l21	חמט	/ והחמ]ט והתנשמת *vac*
12 1,4	4:7	חֲמִישִׁי	ו]בארבעה לשבוע הח[מישי / שמחו]
12 1,9	4:9	חֲמִישִׁי	לשבוע הריאשון ליובל החמי]שי
12 1,11	4:11	חֲמִישִׁי	/ ובשבו]ע הח[מישי] //
12 3,1	4:16	חֲמִישִׁי	[ותלד לו בן בשבוע הח]מישי
20 XVI,5		חמל	ולוא תחמל ע[ליו
12 8,3	12:16	חָמֵשׁ	[*vac* ובשבוע הששי] / בחמש[ה בו]
17 32,1		חָמֵשׁ	]חמישי [
20 IV,2	xix13	חֲמִשִּׁים	תספורו חמשים[יום
20 VIII,9		חֲמִשִּׁים	רחוק מהמזבח]חמש[ים] /
12 1,10	4:9	חֲנוֹךְ	[ויקרא את שמה כמו שם ב]נו חנוך*vac*
11 VI,6		חֶסֶד	חסד[ו ע]ליך צנה וסוחרה אמתו סלה
20 III,23	xix5	חָצֵר	ואכלום בחצ[ר הפנימית]
20 X,1	xxxvii9	חָצֵר	בפרור]הפנימי אצל ק[י]ר החצר ה[חיצון
20 XII,16	xlvi3	חָצֵר	על גגי השערים אשר]לחצר החי[צונה
13 II,12		חֹק	אש[ר]°ים בסו[רם]ה מחוקי אל ל[הרשיע]
17 VII,4		חֹק	]°ם בחוק יתכל[כ]לו לשרת °[
20 V,4	xxi05	חֹק	ל]חוק עולם להמה ולזרעמה /
12 7,3	5:2	חֻקָּה	[וכולם ה]שחיתו דרכם וח[קתם]
17 V,3		חקק	]כול מ[חקת ה מה בדני אלוהים]
17 VI,6		חקק	בדני צורות אלוהים מ]חוקק סב[י]ב
11 IV,5		חָרוֹן	/ ובחרון אפו[ישלח]עליך מלאך תקיף[
11 IV,11		חָרוֹן	]חרון אף י[הוה
22 6,1		חֶרְפָּה	]°ו·חרפותי[
11 IV,8		חשך	]°כב וחשך / [בתהום ר]בה מואדה
11 IV,11		חֹשֶׁךְ	ב]חושך בכ[ול / תעודות]תעניות
11 V,7		חֹשֶׁךְ	חושך אתה ולוא אור
17 X,5		חֹשֶׁךְ	אור וחושך ובדני[ ]קודש מלך / הכבוד
17 IX,6		חֹשֶׁן	]° פלא ותבנית חשני /

11 VI,12		חשק	[ביהוה ח]שקתה ו֯[יפלטך]
21 1,1		טָהוֹר	וכליה יהיו זה]ב טהור
20 XII,10	xlv18	טהר	עד אש]֯ר יטהרו
20 XIV,11	l8	טהר	יכבס בגדו ורחץ] / וטהר ל[ערב *vac*
20 XIV,17	l18	טהר	ולוא] / יטהרו[עוד עד לעולם *vac*
17 IV,6		טֹהַר	[מר]אי פלא כ֯[ ]◦י טו[הר
17 VI,5		טֹהַר	מ֯[מולח] / טוה[ר
17 VII,5		טֹהַר	]ט֯והר ב◦[/
17 IX,5		טֹהַר	הטוהר ברוח קוד[ש] /
17 IX,7		טֹהַר	]ממולח טוהר צבעי /
13 II,19		טוֹב	ומבשר] / טו֯ב משמי[ע ישועה]
14 1ii8		טוֹב	ויפתח לכם את / אוצרו הטוב אשר בשמים
14 1ii9		טַל	טל ומטר יורה ומלקוש בעתו
20 XII,9	xlv17	טמא	וכול ט]מ֯א לנפש לוא / [יבואו לה
20 XIV,4	l6	טמא	]ט֯מאו במת /
20 XIV,12	l11	טמא	תטמ֯[א כקבר]
20 XIV,22		טמא	/ וכיא י֯[ ]ו֯ וטמ֯[א] /
20 XIV,23		טמא	[כי]טמים / [המה
20 31,2		טֶפַח	]טפחים /
16 2		טֶרֶם	כ]ול מעשיו בטרם ◦[
16 4		טֶרֶם	]◦ותו בטר[ם
13 II,3		יָד	כול בעל משה יד אשר ישה[ברעהו
13 II,13		יָד	ומיד כול ר֯[וחי גורלו]
13 II,25		יָד	אשר יצי]ל[מה מי]֯ד בליעל
13 8,2		יָד	]ת֯קו ידי[
15 2		יָד	א]ש֯ר כוננו ידיכ֯ה֯[
20 I,22	xv16	יָד	ומלא י]ד֯ו ללבוש את הבגדי֯ם[תחת]א֯ביהו
20 XII,24	xlvi13	יָד	ועשיתה להמה מקו[ם יד חוץ מ[ן העיר]
20 XVI,6		יָד	ויד[כול העם / באחרונה ?*vac*]
11 III,7		ידע	ו]ה֯ם יודעים / [רזי פל]או
12 4,1		ידע	למע]ן י֯ד֯ע֯ו֯ [בני / אדם תקופות השנים]
13 III,2		ידע	/ ודעו ד֯ב֯◦◦◦[
13 III,9		יְהוּדָה	/ את חומ[ו]ת֯ יהו֯דה ו֯ב֯ר֯[ ]ע֯[
20 VI,13		יְהוּדָה	מטות֯[לוי]ויהודה
11 I,4		יהוה	]ב֯יהוה[
11 III,3		יהוה	יהוה הוא֯[ה אשר] / עשה את ה֯[אלה
11 III,9		יהוה	]ה אם לוא / [ייראו]מלפני יהוה ל[
11 III,10		יהוה	]יהוה
11 III,11		יהוה	]◦עבדי֯ יהו[ה] /
11 IV,4		יהוה	/ יככה יהוה מ[כה גדול]ה אשר לאבדך[
11 IV,11		יהוה	]ח֯רון אף י֯[הוה
11 V,4		יהוה	ל]ח֯ש בשם יהו[ה
11 V,8		יהוה	יהוה [יוריד]ך / [לשאו]ל תחתית
20 I,14	xv5	יהוה	] יהיו מקריבים ליהוה עולה֯[מן האיל
20 I,19	xv12	יהוה	[ואת / סלי הלחם תנופה ל]פני יהוה
20 IV,4	xix16	יהוה	]ליהוה שנים [ע]שר אילים
20 IV,10	xx06	יהוה	אשה ריח ניחוח]ל֯יהוה
20 VI,2	xxii8	יהוה	אשה ריח ניחוח] / ליהו֯ה֯[*vac*
20 VI,16	xxiii3	יהוה	הקריבו בחג] / העצים עולה ליה[וה
20 37,1		יהוה	] יהוה /
22 7,1		יהוה	]יהוה· [
12 1,8	4:9	יוֹבֵל	בקץ היוב]ל הרביעי *v]ac*
12 2,2	4:14	יוֹבֵל	ו]בקץ היו[בל / השמיני לקח לו]
13 II,2		יוֹבֵל	בשנת היובל [הזואת תשובו איש
13 II,7		יוֹבֵל	היובל ה֯ראישו֯ן אחר֯ ת֯ש֯[עה ה]יובלים
13 II,7		יוֹבֵל	היובל ה֯ראישו֯ן אחר֯ ת֯ש֯[עה ה]יובלים
13 II,7		יוֹבֵל	ה[וא]ה ס֯[וף]ה֯[יו]בל העשירי
13 7,7		יוֹבֵל	]סוף הי֯[ובל
11 VI,7		יוֹם	מחץ יעוף יומם
12 5,4	4:30	יוֹם	[על כן / לא כלה את]ש֯ני היום[הזה]
13 II,4		יוֹם	פשרו]ל֯א֯ח֯רית הימים על השבויים אשר[
13 II,7		יוֹם	וי֯[ום הכפ]ו֯רים ה[וא]ה ס֯[וף]ה֯[יו]בל
13 II,15		יוֹם	/ הזואת הואה יום ה֯[שלום
20 I,20	xv14	יוֹם	למלו֯(א֯) על נפשותמה שבעת ימי֯[ם] *va]c* [
20 III,21		יוֹם	ברובע]היום יקר֯[יבו את עול]ת֯ הבכור֯[ים
20 IV,10	xx06	יוֹם	ברובע היום יקריבו /
20 V,11	xxi8	יוֹם	ביו]ם֯ הזה יכפ֯ר֯ו על התירוש
20 VI,8	xxii15	יוֹם	/ כי ביום הזה
20 VI,14		יוֹם	/ וביום הרביעי יששכר[וז]ב֯ולון
20 VII,22	xxiii8	יוֹם	]בר֯ו֯ב֯ע הי֯[ו]ם תעלה זואת /
20 XII,5	xlv12	יוֹם	אשר אשכין שמי בה שלוש]ת֯ ימי[ן]ם /
20 XII,8	xlv16	יוֹם	ויכבס ביו]ם השביעי / [בגדיו
20 XIV,1		יוֹם	ע]ד֯ יום /
20 XIV,2	l4	יוֹם	יו]ם השביעי /
20 XIV,15	l15	יוֹם	/ וב֯[יו]ם֯[השביעי
14 1ii9		יוֹרֶה	טל ומטר יורה ומלקוש בעתו
14 1ii12		יחל	ואין משכלה בארצכם / ולוא מוחלה
20 V,10	xxi7	יַיִן	יחלו לשתות יין חדש/
12 1,5	4:7	ילד	]ותלד לו בן ויקרא את שמ[ו שת]
11 VI,8		יָמִין	יפ[ו]ל מצדך אלף ור[בבה מי]מינך
20 I,18	xv11	יָמִין	עם שוק התרו]מ֯ה֯ אשר לימין
20 IV,25	xx15	יָמִין	ומן הכ֯ב֯שים את שוק הימ֯ין /
12 1,1		יצא	[הודע]נ֯ו בצ֯[אתנו]
12 9,3	12:28	יצא	[כיא]הוא יוצא מ[חרן]
17 VII,12		יצא	יצ]א֯ ומבין[גלגלי כבודו
11 III,5		יצב	]אשר ה֯ת֯[י]צ֯בו לפני[ו
14 1ii10		יִצְהָר	/ ת֯נובות דגן תירוש ויצהר לרוב
30 11,1		יָצוּעַ	] ועל יצוע[י
16 1		יצר	]◦ אתה יצרת֯[ה
11 VI,5		יָקוּשׁ	ה]ו֯אה יצילך מ֯[פח יקו]ש מדבר ה֯ו֯[ות
17 X,3		יְקָר	ביקר ◦[ת]עודותיו
11 III,10		ירא	וייראו[את המכה ה]גדולה הזוא֯[ת] /

Reference	Alt. ref.	Lemma	Text
11 VI,6		ירא	לוא תירא / מפחד לילה
17 VIII,4		ירא	/]אלוהים נוראי כוח
14 1ii8		ירד	להוריד על ארצכסה / גשמי ברכה
20 XIII,9		ירד	/ והורדת[מה
13 II,5		ירה	]ואשר / מוריהמה החבאו וסתר[ו]
13 7,3		יְרוּשָׁלַיִם	]חומת יר[ושלם
14 1ii12		יֵרָקוֹן	שדפון וירקון לוא יראה בתבואתיה
11 I,11		ישב	]ישב[
17 VII,4		ישב	לוא ישב[ו
11 VI,13		יְשׁוּעָה	/ *vac* ו[ישגבך ויר]אך בישוע[תו סלה]
13 II,16		יְשׁוּעָה	מב[שר טוב משמיע ישוע]ה
13 II,15		יְשַׁעְיָה	א]שר אמר[ביד ישע]יה הנביא
17 VII,7		ישר	י]שרו ל[
11 II,9		יִשְׂרָאֵל	יש]ראל החזק /
14 1ii3		יִשְׂרָאֵל	]וברכם בשם [אל] / [י]שראל
14 1ii3		יִשְׂרָאֵל	וענה[ואמר]ישראל ברוכים א[תם]
20 IV,3	xix14	יִשְׂרָאֵל	ארבעה הינים מכול מטות] ישראל
20 V,3	xxi04	יִשְׂרָאֵל	לחוק עולם מאת בני ישר]אל
20 V,7	xxi3	יִשְׂרָאֵל	[שנים ע]שר שבטי ישראל
20 V,16	xxi15	יִשְׂרָאֵל	שמן חדש ממשבות מטות בני יש]ראל
20 VI,5	xxii11	יִשְׂרָאֵל	ונתנו בני] / ישראל לכוהנים
20 VI,9	xxiii01	יִשְׂרָאֵל	/ כול [ב]ני ישראל בכול[מושבותיהמה
20 X,3	xxxvii12	יִשְׂרָאֵל	ולוא יתע]רבו זבחי שלמי בני יש[ראל]
20 XII,20	xlvi7	יִשְׂרָאֵל	אשר יהיו עולים]בני יש[ראל א]ליו
20 VI,14		יִשָּׂשכָר	/ וביום הרביעי יששכר[וז]בולון
20 I,16	xv8	יֹתֶרֶת	ואת יותרת הכבד[
20 I,16	xv8	כָּבֵד	ואת יותרת הכבד[
15 5		כָּבוֹד	]כבודו ומעשיו ועמלו ב[
17 IV,5		כָּבוֹד	[לל]בני כבודם [
17 V,6		כָּבוֹד	[הודו למלך / הכבו]ד [בקול רנה
17 VI,3		כָּבוֹד	רוחי ק]מרכב[ ]°ל בדני כב[וד
17 VII,4		כָּבוֹד	בדבירי כבודו
17 VII,5		כָּבוֹד	[מרכבו]ת כבודו [
17 VII,7		כָּבוֹד	מרכבות] כבוד[ו
17 VII,13		כָּבוֹד	ומעשי נוגה]ברוקמת כב[וד
17 VIII,7		כָּבוֹד	]° מלך הכבוד
17 X,2		כָּבוֹד	[ ]מרומי כ[בודו
17 X,2		כָּבוֹד	כב]ודו באו°[ ]מת
17 X,4		כָּבוֹד	כב]וד מעשיו ובאו[ר]מלה
17 X,6		כָּבוֹד	]קודש מלך / הכבוד
17 X,7		כָּבוֹד	/ לכסאי כבודו ולהדום ר[גליו
17 X,8		כָּבוֹד	ו]להיכלי כבודו ולרקיעי
17 26a,1		כָּבוֹד	]י כבוד ה[
17 28,5		כָּבוֹד	כבודו קול ה[
17 30,5		כָּבוֹד	ת]הלי ברכות כבוד ה[
17 36,2		כָּבוֹד	כ]בוד [
20 IV,12	xx2	כֶּבֶשׂ	]א וכבשים [בני] שנה ארבעה / [עשר]
20 IV,25	xx15	כֶּבֶשׂ	ומן הכבשים את שוק הימין /
20 V,6	xxi1	כֶּבֶשׂ	ולבני לוי אי]ל אחד כבש אחד
20 VI,6	xxii13	כֶּבֶשׂ	ולכול מטה] / ומטה איל אחד כבש[אחד
20 I,21	xv15	כֹּהֵן	*va[c* ואם[הכוה]ן הגדול[יהיה עומד
20 I,23	xv17	כֹּהֵן	[אחד על / כול העם ואחד על הכו]הנים
20 I,23	xv18	כֹּהֵן	ויקרב את אשר [ל]כוהנים ברישונה[
20 I,24	xvi01	כֹּהֵן	ואחריהמה הכ[ו]הן הגדול וכול הכ[והנים
20 I,24	xvi01	כֹּהֵן	ואחריהמה הכ[ו]הן הגדול וכול הכ[והנים
20 I,25	xvi02	כֹּהֵן	]ולקחו זקני הכוהני[ם] מדם הפר
20 III,23	xix5	כֹּהֵן	הבכורים]לכוהנים יהיו
20 V,25	xxii5	כֹּהֵן	וזר]קו הכוהנים בני אה[רון את דמם]
20 VI,5	xxii11	כֹּהֵן	ונתנו בני] / ישראל לכוהנים
12 8,4	12:16	כּוֹכָב	[להביט אל] / הכוכב[ים מערב עד בקר]
12 8,6	12:17	כּוֹכָב	/ הכוכ[בים]
17 VII,4		כול	]°ם בחוק יתכל[כ]לו לשרת °[
15 2		כון	א]שר כוננו ידיכה[
17 VIII,4		כֹּחַ	/]אלוהים נוראי כוח
17 VIII,4		כֹּחַ	בכוח אלוהי / [עול]מים
11 VI,10		כִּי	כ[י מלאכיו]יצוה לך / לשומ[רך בדרכי]ך
12 1,6	4:7	כִּי	כיא הרגו / [קין]
12 5,3	4:30	כִּי	כיא ב[יום אכלכם ממנו תמותו]
12 6,2		כִּי	[ויומת באבנ]יו כיא [
13 I,12		כִּי	]שון מושה כיא° [ ] °° [ ]ש[
13 II,5		כִּי	כי[א]°°°° והמה נחל[ת מלכי צ]דק
13 II,8		כִּי	כיא / הואה הקץ לשנת הרצון למלכי צדק
14 1ii14		כִּי	כיא אל עמכם
20 VI,8	xxii15	כִּי	/ כי ביום הזה
20 XII,4	xlv11	כִּי	ואיש]כי ישכב / [עם אשתו
20 XIV,22		כִּי	/ וכיא י[ ]ו וטמ[א] /
20,34,1		כִּי	]ם כי [
27 1,1		כִּי	]עליכה כיא [
30 10,1		כִּי	]מה כיא מ[
20 X,5	xxxvii13	כִּיֹּר	[מ]קום לכירים
21 1,2		כִּיֹּר	והכיר וכנו יה[יו נחושת
21 2,3		כָּכָה	]° ככה יעש[ו
11 III,4		כֹּל	משביע לכול מ[לאכיו]
11 III,5		כֹּל	/ [וא]ת כול זר[ע הקודש]
11 III,7		כֹּל	ועל כול א[דם רשע
11 IV,3		כֹּל	/ כול הארץ[ ] השמים ו[
11 IV,7		כֹּל	אש[ר /]על כול אלה
11 IV,11		כֹּל	ב]חושך בכ[ול / תעודות]תעניות
11 V,4		כֹּל	קרא בכו]ל עת / אל השמ[ים
12 7,4	5:2	כֹּל	[וירב חמס בארץ וכו]ל °°°[
13 II,3		כֹּל	כול בעל משה יד אשר ישה[ברעהו
13 II,6		כֹּל	לעזוב להמה[משא]כול עוונותיהמה

13 II,8		כֹּל	/ לכפר בו על כול בני [אור
13 II,8		כֹּל	]◦ם עלי֯[המ]ה הת[ ]לפ֯[י]כ֯[ול עש]ותמה
13 II,13		כֹּל	ומיד כול ר֯[וחי גורלו]
13 II,14		כֹּל	/ ובעזרו כול אלי [הצדק
13 II,14		כֹּל	וה]ו֯אה א[שר]כ֯ול בני אל והפ[
13 II,17		כֹּל	המה א[ ]◦מ֯[ ] לכול ◦◦[
13 II,20		כֹּל	פשרו]ל[ה]שכילמ֯ה בכול קצי הע[ולם
13 II,25		כֹּל	והעברתמה שו[פר ב]כ֯ו֯ל֯ [א]ר֯ץ //
14 1ii5		כֹּל	וברוכים כול / מלאכי קודשו *va]c*
14 1ii13		כֹּל	/ [ואין]כול[נגע ומ]כשול בעדתכם
15 6		כֹּל	]אתה בראתה כול רוח ג֯ל◦◦[
16 2		כֹּל	כ]ול מעשיו בטרם ◦[
17 III,9		כֹּל	[יברך בשם / כבוד א]ד֯ון כ[ו]ל א[לים]
17 III,12		כֹּל	[בשבעה / דברי פ]לא [ו]ברך לכ[ול]
17 V,3		כֹּל	]כול מ֯[חקת ה מה בדני אלוהים]
17 V,4		כֹּל	[וברכו לא]לוהי כול[
17 VI,5		כֹּל	כול / מע[שיהם]רוקמ֯[ה
17 VI,8		כֹּל	מהל]לים תמיד כ֯[ו]ל[
17 VII,7		כֹּל	בלכתמה לוא י]סבו לכול ע֯[
17 VIII,3		כֹּל	הוד [ ]כ֯ול תבנית רוחי פל[א]
17 VIII,4		כֹּל	כול [פל]א֯י פלאיהם
17 VIII,8		כֹּל	]וכול אושיהם
17 IX,3		כֹּל	]כ֯ול מעשיה[ם] /
17 X,4		כֹּל	[ו]כול ברכות שלומ[ו
17 X,5		כֹּל	ובהדר/ תשבוחותו בכול רקי[עי]ם
17 X,6		כֹּל	לכול מעשי אמת֯[ו]למלאכי הדעת
17 X,6		כֹּל	בכול מל[ ]הו משאי קודש
17 X,8		כֹּל	עם כול מוצאי [פנ]ות מבניתו
17 X,8		כֹּל	ולכול ז[בולי ו]להיכלי כבודו ולרקיעי
17 X,9		כֹּל	/ [ ]לכול ד◦[
17 26b,1		כֹּל	]י מלך כו[ל
17 28,4		כֹּל	ברנות כול֯[
17 29,3		כֹּל	]פלאיהם כול[
17 30,4		כֹּל	]מלך כול קדושי ע֯ד /
17 35,2		כֹּל	]היו כול ◦[
20 I,12	xv3	כֹּל	]ולמלואים איל איל לכ֯[ול יום ואחד]
20 I,13	xv4	כֹּל	וחצו את]כ֯ול האילים והסלים
20 I,24	xvi01	כֹּל	ואחריהמה הכ֯[ו]ה֯ן֯ ה֯גד֯ול וכול הכ[והנים
20 IV,4	xix16	כֹּל	כול / [ראשי אלפי ישראל]
20 IV,20	xx9	כֹּל	[וכו]ל מ֯נחה / [אשר קרב עליה לבונה]
20 V,6	xxi1	כֹּל	ולכול המטה /
20 V,12	xxi9	כֹּל	לדורותיהם]ה בכול מושבותיהמה
20 V,19	xxii02	כֹּל	וכפ]ר֯ בו על כול העדה לפני / [יהוה
20 VI,9	xxiii01	כֹּל	/ כ֯ול [ב]נ֯י֯ ישראל בכול֯[מושבותיהמה
20 VI,9	xxiii01	כֹּל	/ כ֯ול [ב]נ֯י֯ ישראל בכול֯[מושבותיהמה
20 XIII,5		כֹּל	/ וכול ◦[
20 XIV,16	l16	כֹּל	/ וכול מ[עשה עזים
20 XV,3	li9	כֹּל	בכו[ל אשר הבדלתי להמה לטמאה
20 35,1		כֹּל	ו֯כול[
20 35,2a		כֹּל	כול[
21 1,1		כֹּל	וכו[ל מזבח העולה יעשו נחושת טהור
21 3,4		כֹּל	/בכול המקד֯ש֯ ◦[
16 3		כְּלִי	]באמתכה כלי ל[
20 I,15	xv7	כִּלְיָה	[ואת ש]תי הכליות
21 1,2		כֵּן	והכיר וכנו יה[יו נחושת
17 VII,6		כָּנָף	]כנפי דעת[
17 VII,11		כָּנָף	ברים כנ]פ֯י֯ה֯[ם
17 VIII,9		כָּנָף	]◦ במש[א כ]נפיהם מר֯[
17 V,8		כִּסֵּא	[ ]כסאי עולמים [
17 VII,2		כִּסֵּא	]ע֯ל מרום כסא[
17 X,7		כִּסֵּא	/ לכסאי כבודו ולהדום ר֯[גליו
11 VI,11		כַּף	על כפיס֯[ישאונ]ך פן[תגוף בא]בן רגל[ך
13 II,7		כְּפוֹר	וי֯[ום הכפ]ו֯רים ה[וא]ה ס֯[וף]ה֯[יו]בל
13 II,8		כפר	/ לכפר בו על כול בני [אור
13 III,10		כפר	/ גדר ולש֯א֯ת ע֯מוד וכ֯פ֯ר ◦[ ]א֯[
20 V,11	xxi8	כפר	ביו]ם֯ הזה יכפ֯ר֯ו על התירוש
20 V,19	xxii02	כפר	וכפ]ר֯ בו על כול העדה לפני / [יהוה
20 VI,8	xxii15	כפר	יכפרו ע֯[ל כול יצהר הארץ
17 V,9		כְּרוּב	[ב]ר֯ניהם כרו֯בי֯[
17 VII,5		כְּרוּב	כרו]בי קו֯ד[ש אופני אור בדביר
13 II,9		כתב	כאשר כתוב / עליו בשירי֯ דויד אשר אמר
13 II,19		כתב	]הואה הכ֯תוב עליו אשר [
13 II,23		כתב	]במשפט[י] אל כאשר כת֯וב עליו[
11 III,8		לֹא	]ה אם לוא / [ייראו]מלפני יהוה ל[
11 V,7		לֹא	חושך אתה ולוא אור
11 V,8		לֹא	[עו]ל ולוא צדקה[
11 V,9		לֹא	ב֯[אלה לו]א / [יעבור] אור
11 V,10		לֹא	ולוא[יאיר לך ה]שמש
11 VI,6		לֹא	לו֯א תירא / מפחד לילה
11 VI,8		לֹא	אל[יך לו]א יגע
11 VI,10		לֹא	לוא] / תרא[ה רעה ו]לוא יגע [נגע באה]ליך
14 1ii12		לֹא	ואין משכלה בארצכם / ולוא מוחלה
14 1ii12		לֹא	שד֯פון וירקון לוא יראה בתבואתיה
17 VII,3		לֹא	לו]א֯ יתמהמהו בעומדם
17 VII,4		לֹא	לוא ישב[ו
20 III,25	xix8	לֹא	כול מל]אכת עבודה לוא י[עשו
20 XII,9	xlv17	לֹא	וכול ט]מ֯א לנפש לוא / [יבואו לה
20 XII,11		לֹא	]ק לוא יבוא אל המקדש /
20 XII,15	xlvi1	לֹא	אשר לוא[ישכון כול / עוף טמא
20 XII,22	xlvi11	לֹא	ו]ל[וא יחללוהו]
20 XV,5	li12	לֹא	/ ולוא יקחו שוחד ו[לוא יטו משפט
20 XVI,5		לֹא	ולוא תחמל ע[ליו

Reference		Lemma	Context
21 3,3		לֹא	/תרנגול לוא תגד[לו
25 1,2		לֹא	/ולא עינכ[ה
25 4,4		לֹא	]לא ◦[
13 III,8		לֵב	/ במזמ[ו]ת בלבם ת[
17 IV,4		לְבֵנָה	[ ]מעשי לב[ני
17 IV,5		לְבֵנָה	[לל]בני כבודם [
17 IV,5		לְבֵנָה	]ר לבני[רק]יע
20 I,22	xv16	לבש	ומלא י]דו ללבוש את הבגדים[תחת]אביהו
20 V,2	xxi03	לְחִי	האזרוע[ו]ת והלחיים והקבאות למנות /
20 I,17	xv10	לֶחֶם	וחלת לחם שמן אחת ורקיק[אחד
20 III,24	xix6	לֶחֶם	]ם לחם חדש אביבות[ומלילות
20 IV,1	xix12	לֶחֶם	את ל[חם הבכורים שבעה שבו[עות
11 V,4		לַחַשׁ	ל[חש בשם יהו[ה
11 V,5		לַיְלָה	כי]יבוא אליך בל[י]לה וא]מרתה אליו
11 VI,7		לַיְלָה	לוא תירא / מפחד לילה
12 1,7	4:8	לקח	ויקח קין את אחות[ו / און לו לאשה]
20 I,25	xvi02	לקח	]ולקחו זקני הכוהני[ם] מדם הפר
20 XV,5	li12	לקח	/ ולוא יקחו שוחד ו[לוא יטו משפט
11 IV,9		מְאֹד	]◦כב וחשך / [בתהום ר]בה מואדה
21 1,5		מֵאַת	ת]מיד מאת[בני ישראל
13 III,16		מָאתַיִם	/ מאתים[
17 IV,4		מָבוֹא	]אולמי מב[ואי]
17 X,7		מָבוֹא	]◦ ולפתחי מבואי
11 VI,4		מִבְטָח	אלוהי] מבטח [אבטח] בו /
17 I,5		מבנית	] סדרו[תיו סדרו]תיו מבני[ת
17 X,8		מבנית	עם כול מוצאי [פנ]ות מבניתו
11 VI,5		מִדְבָּר	ה]ואה יצילך מפח יקו[ש מדבר הו]ות
17 VII,3		מהה	לו[א יתמהמהו בעומדם
17 V,10		מוֹסָד	[ ]מוסדים[ ]ם
17 VIII,5		מוֹסָד	מארבעת מוסדי רקיע / הפלא
17 VIII,7		מוֹסָד	◦[ ]למוסדי פלא
13 7,4		מוֹעֵד	]במועדה
11 III,3		מוֹפֵת	/ ואת המופ[תים האלה ב]ארץ
17 V,5		מוֹצָא	[ליקרה הדביר במו]צא אול[מי
17 X,8		מוֹצָא	עם כול מוצאי [פנ]ות מבניתו
17 VII,6		מוֹשָׁב	מוש[בי כבוד למרכבות]
20 V,12	xxi9	מוֹשָׁב	לדורותיהם]ה בכול מושבותיהמה
20 XV,8	li17	מות	ויטה משפט צדק[/ יו]מת
20 XVI,6		מות	ידכה תהיה בו ברא]ישונה להמיתו
20 I,10		מִזְבֵּחַ	וה]קריבו על המ[זבח לכול יום ויום
20 IV,14	xx4	מִזְבֵּחַ	[ואת חלבמה יקט]ירו על המזבח /
20 VI,11		מִזְבֵּחַ	יקריבו[/ למזב]ח את העצי[ם
13 III,8		מְזִמָּה	/ במזמ[ו]ת בלבם ת[
20 X,6		מִזְרָחִי	ואת החטאות במקצ]וע המזרחי צפונה
13 III,18		מַחֲלֹקֶת	/ [מח]לקות[העתים
11 VI,9		מַחְמָד	קר]את מח[סך]ת מחמדו

Reference		Lemma	Context
11 VI,9		מַחְסֶה	קר]את מח[סך]ת מחמדו
11 VI,7		מַחַץ	מחץ יעוף יומם
20 V,16	xxi15	מַחֲצִית	מחצית ההין / [אחד מן המטה
20 V,20	xxii03	מַחֲצִית	בלול]ה בשמן הזה מחצית ההין /
20 V,15	xxi13	מָחֳרָת	עד ממו]חרת השבת השביעית/
20 V,6	xxi2	מַטֶּה	ולכול המטה /
20 VI,6	xxii13	מַטֶּה	ולכול מטה[/ ומטה איל אחד כבש[אחד
20 VI,13		מַטֶּה	מטות[לוי]ויהודה
14 1ii9		מָטָר	טל ומטר יורה ומלקוש בעתו
11 III,2		מִי	מי ע[שה את האותות]
11 V,6		מִי	/מי אתה [הילוד מ]אדם ומזרע הקד[ושי]ם
11 3,2		מַיִם	] למים [
20 IX,4	xxxii14	מַיִם	יהיו ה]מים נש]פכים והולכים אליה
20 XIV,3		מַיִם	]במים /
20 XIV,21		מַיִם	/ במים[יובא וטמא עד הערב וטהר
11 IV,4		מַכָּה	/ יככה יהוה מ[כה גדול]ה אשר לאבדך[
20 36,2		מְכוֹנָה	]למכונות[
14 1ii13		מִכְשׁוֹל	/ [ואין כול[נגע ומ]כשול בעדתכם
20 I,12	xv3	מְלֹא	]ולמלואים איל איל לכ[ול יום ואחד
20 I,20	xv14	מְלֹא	למלו[א] על נפשותמה שבעת ימי[ם] [*va*]*c*
11 III,4		מַלְאָךְ	משביע לכול מ[לאכיו
11 IV,5		מַלְאָךְ	/ ובחרון אפו[ישלח]עליך מלאך תקיף[
14 1ii6		מַלְאָךְ	וברוכים כול / מלאכי קודשו *va*]*c*
14 1ii14		מַלְאָךְ	ומלאכי / [קודשו מתיצבי]ם בעדתכם
17 VI,7		מַלְאָךְ	וצו]רת בדניהם מל[אכי קודש
17 IX,9		מַלְאָךְ	[ ]מלאכי[קו]דש[
17 X,6		מַלְאָךְ	לכול מעשי אמת[ו]למלאכי הדעת
17 37,1		מַלְאָךְ	]מלאכ[י קודש
20 III,25	xix8	מְלָאכָה	כול מל]אכת עבודה לוא י[עשו
17 IX,7		מלח	]ממולח טוהר צבעי /
20 IV,24	xx14	מֶלַח	[ולוא ת]שבית ברית מלח ל[עולם *vac*
13 II,23		מֶלֶךְ	[אומר לצי]ון מלך אלוהיך
17 VI,4		מֶלֶךְ	כול בדני דביר מל[ך
17 VIII,7		מֶלֶךְ	]◦ מלך הכבוד
17 X,5		מֶלֶךְ	אור וחושך ובדני[ ]קודש מלך / הכבוד
17 26b,1		מֶלֶךְ	]י מלך כו[ל
17 29,1		מֶלֶךְ	מ]לך[
17 30,4		מֶלֶךְ	]מלך כול קדושי עד /
17 32,3		מֶלֶךְ	] מלך לו[
13 II,5		מלכיצדק	ומנחלת מלכי צדק
13 II,5		מלכיצדק	כי[א]◦◦◦◦ והמה נחל[ת מלכי צ]דק
13 II,8		מלכיצדק	ו[אנשי]גורל מל[כי]צדק
13 II,9		מלכיצדק	כיא / הואה הקץ לשנת הרצון למלכי צדק
13 II,13		מלכיצדק	/ ומלכי צדק יקום נקם משפטי א[ל
13 8,1		מלכיצדק	]מלכי[צדק
17 II,7		מלכיצדק	[ראשי נשיאי כהונות פ]לא למלכ[י צדק (?)]

14 1ii9		מַלְקוֹשׁ	טל ומטר יורה ומלקוש בעתו
13 II,9		מֶמְשָׁלָה	ע]ם֯ קדושי אל לממ֯שלת משפט
11 III,9		מִן	]ה אם לוא / [ייראו]מלפני יהוה ל[
11 III,11		מִן	/ [וירדף א]חד מכם א[לף
11 V,6		מִן	/מי אתה [הילוד מ]אדם ומזרע הקד֯[ושי]ם֗
11 VI,5		מִן	ה]ו֯אה יצילך מ֗[פח יקו]ש מדבר ה֯ו֯[ות
11 VI,7		מִן	לוא֗ תירא / מפחד לילה
11 VI,7		מִן	מקטב י֗שוד[צ]הרים
11 VI,7		מִן	מדבר[בא]פל / יהלך
11 VI,8		מִן	יפ[ו]ל מצדך אלף ור[בבה מי]מינך
12 9,3	12:28	מִן	[כיא]הוא יוצא מ[חרן]
13 II,5		מִן	ומנחלת מלכי צדק
13 II,12		מִן	]◦ים בסו[רמ]ה֯ מח֗וקי אל ל[הרשיע]
13 II,13		מִן	ומיד כול ר֯[וחי גורלו]
13 II,22		מִן	/ ◦◦[ ]ר הוסרה מבליעל ותש֯[וב
13 II,24		מִן	הסרים מלכ֗ת [בד]ר֯ך֯ העם
14 1ii13		מִן	וחיה רעה שבתה מן / [הארץ
17 VII,12		מִן	יצ]א֯ ומבין[גלגלי כבודו
17 VIII,5		מִן	מארבעת מוסדי רקיע / ה֯פלא
17 VIII,6		מִן	ישמ֯[י]ע֯ו֯ מקול משא אלוהים[ ]
17 30,2		מִן	]מו◦◦◦ משבעה
17 30,3		מִן	]◦בר מ֯שב֗יעי ◦מ֯[
20 I,17	xv9	מִן	וחלת מצה אחת מ[ן ה֗ס֗ל
20 I,25	xvi02	מִן	]ולקחו זקני הכ֗ו֗ה֗נ֗י[ם] מדם הפר
20 I,26	xvi02	מִן	על קרנות המזבח באצבעם] / מן הד[ם
20 II,3		מִן	]מן השמן /
20 II,9	xvi11	מִן	ישרופו]מחוץ ל[עיר]
20 IV,25	xx15	מִן	ומן הכ֗ב֯שים את שוק הימ֯ין /
20 V,3	xxi04	מִן	ואת השכם ה֗נשאר מן האזרוע /
20 V,5	xxi06	מִן	[מן] האילים ומן / [הכבשים]
20 IX,2	xxxii11	מִן	למע]לה מע֯[ל]לב֗ית֯[ה
20 XII,24	xlvi13	מִן	ועשיתה להמה מקו]ם יד חוץ מ[ן העיר]
20 XIII,4		מִן	/ רחוק֗ מ[ן
20 XIV,20		מִן	יפול] / עליו מ֯[המה במותמה יטמא
20 XVI,3		מִן	מאלוהי ה֯[עמים / אשר סביבותיכמה]
20 XVI,4		מִן	מקצי הארץ ועד קצ[י הארץ
20 V,2	xxi03	מָנָה	האזרועו]ת֗ והלחיים והקבאות למנות /
17 IX,4		מִנְחָה	]ר֗יח מנחותם ◦◦◦[ ] /
20 III,22	xix4	מִנְחָה	ומנחתמה ו֯נ֯ס֯כ֯מה כ֯[משפט
20 IV,5	xx01	מִנְחָה	אי]ל֯י֯ם֯ ומנחתמה כמשפט
20 IV,20	xx10	מִנְחָה	[וכו]ל מ֗נחה / [אשר קרב עליה לבונה]
20 V,24	xxii3	מִנְחָה	כבשים ארבעה עש]ר֯ ומנחתמ֯ה ונ[ש]סכמה[
30 17,1		מִסְפָּר	]למספר ◦[
17 II,5		מָעוֹן	סוד שני ב]מ֗ע֗ו֗נ֯י֯ פל[א
17 III,10		מָעוֹן	[לברך כול / כוהני]קור֗ב במע[ון פלא]
20 IX,2	xxxii11	מַעֲלֶה	למע]לה מע֯[ל]לב֗ית֯[ה
17 VIII,10		מַעֲמָד	]מעמדי[
12 4,1		מַעַן	למע[ן י֯ד֯ע֯ו֯ [בני / אדם תקופות השנים]
15 5		מַעֲשֶׂה	]כבודו ומעשיו ועמלו ב֯[
16 2		מַעֲשֶׂה	כ]ול מעשיו בטרם ◦[
17 IV,4		מַעֲשֶׂה	[ ]מעשי לב[ני
17 V,4		מַעֲשֶׂה	מעשי[הם כבוד משני עבריהם]
17 VI,4		מַעֲשֶׂה	מעש[י רוחו]ת רקיע פלא
17 VI,6		מַעֲשֶׂה	כול / מע[שיהם]רוקמ֯[ה
17 VI,7		מַעֲשֶׂה	]צורות[כבוד] / למע֯[שי לבני הוד והדר
17 VII,6		מַעֲשֶׂה	מ]ע֗שי פנותו[ממלכו]ת
17 IX,3		מַעֲשֶׂה	]כ֯ול מעשיה[ם] /
17 IX,7		מַעֲשֶׂה	]רוקמה כמ֯[עשי אורג
17 X,4		מַעֲשֶׂה	כב]וד מעשיו ובאו[ר]מ֯לה
17 X,6		מַעֲשֶׂה	לכול מעשי אמת֯[ו]למלאכי הדעת
20 XIV,16	117	מַעֲשֶׂה	/ וכול מ[עשה עזים
20 X,2	xxxvii10	מַעֲשֵׂר	לזבחיהמה ולב]כורים ולמעשרות *vac*
11 VI,4		מְצוּדָה	]האומר [ליהוה מחסי] ומצודת֗[י
20 XII,11		מִקְדָּשׁ	]ק לוא יבוא אל המקדש /
20 XII,12		מִקְדָּשׁ	ואל המקדש / [לוא יבוא]*vac*
20 XII,20	xlvi8	מִקְדָּשׁ	לבוא אל מק[דשי]
20 XII,21	xlvi10	מִקְדָּשׁ	אשר יהיה[מבדי]ל בין מקדש / [הקודש
20 XII,22	xlvi11	מִקְדָּשׁ	]וקדשו את מ[קדשי]
21 3,4		מִקְדָּשׁ	/בכול המקד֯ש֯ ◦[
21 3,5		מִקְדָּשׁ	/המק֗ד֯[ש
20 X,5	xxxvii13	מָקוֹם	[מ]קום לכירים
20 XII,24	xlvi13	מָקוֹם	ועשיתה להמה מקו]ם יד חוץ מ[ן העיר]
20 XII,25	xlvi14	מקור	בתים ומקו]רים ובירות בתוכ֗[מה]/
20 X,6		מִקְצוֹעַ	ואת החטאות במקצ]ו֯ע המזרחי צפונה
20 32,1		מִקְצוֹעַ	]מקצוע֯[
20 VII,24	xxv3	מִקְרָא	]ן֯ שבתון זכ֯רון מקרא קודש /
17 IV,6		מַרְאֶה	[מר]אי פלא כ֯[ ]◦י טו[הר
17 V,7		מַרְאֶה	[מ]רא֯[י
13 5,3		מרה	]בליעל י֗מרו ◦[
13 II,11		מָרוֹם	וע֗ליו א֗מ֗[ר ו]ע֗לי[ה] / למרום שובה
17 VII,2		מָרוֹם	]ע֗ל מרום כסא[
17 VIII,7		מָרוֹם	המ◦[ ] מרומי[
17 X,2		מָרוֹם	[ ]מ֯ר֯ומי כ[בודו
17 VI,3		מֶרְכָּבָה	רוחי ק]מ֯ר֯כב[ ]◦ל ב֗דני כב[וד
17 X,7		מֶרְכָּבָה	מר]כבות הדרו ולדבירי קו[דשו
17 VIII,6		מַשָּׂא	ישמ֯[י]ע֯ו֯ מקול משא אלוהים[ ]
17 VIII,8		מַשָּׂא	/ למשא מ[
17 VIII,9		מַשָּׂא	]◦ במש[א כ]נפיהם מר֗[
17 X,6		מַשָּׂא	בכול מל[ ]הו משאי קודש
13 I,12		מֹשֶׁה	]שו֗ן מושה כיא◦ [ ] ◦◦ [ ]ש[
13 II,3		מַשָּׁה	כול בעל משה יד אשר ישה[ברעהו
11 II,4		מַשְׂטֵמָה	] אלה֗ [הש]דים ו֯ש֗[ר המשט]מה /

Reference		Word	Context
13 II,18		מָשִׁיחַ	/ והמבשר הו[אה]מֹשיח הרו[ח]
17 VII,9		מַשְׂכִּיל	/ [למש]כיל
17 35,1		מִשְׁמַע	]משמע רנה[
17 I,8		מִשְׁנֶה	]ושבע ∘∘[ ]משני רֹ[
17 VI,9		מִשְׁנֶה	]הו במשני מ[
13 II,9		מִשְׁפָּט	ע]םֹ קדושי אל לממֹשלת משפט
13 II,13		מִשְׁפָּט	/ ומלכי צֹדק יקום נקםֹ משפטֹי א[ל
13 II,23		מִשְׁפָּט	]במשפט[י] אל כאשר כתֹוב עליו[
17 X,3		מִשְׁפָּט	[ש]לֹ[ו]מיו במשפטֹי[ ]רחמיו
17 28,3		מִשְׁפָּט	משפ[ט
20 IV,5	xx01	מִשְׁפָּט	אי]ליםֹ ומנחתמה כמשפט
20 IV,9	xx05	מִשְׁפָּט	מנחתמ]ה ונסכמה ˻כמשפט˼
20 V,21	xxii04	מִשְׁפָּט	כמ]שפט עולה הואה
20 V,24		מִשְׁפָּט	כמשפ]ט / [לאלים ולכבשים]
20 VI,1		מִשְׁפָּט	// כמ[שפט
20 VI,4	xxii10	מִשְׁפָּט	לכוהנים יהיה למנה] / כמשפטמה *vac*
20 XIV,10	l7	מִשְׁפָּט	/ כ]משפט[התורה הזואת
20 XIV,4	l6	מֵת	]טֹמאו במת /
20 XIV,9	l5	מֵת	יגע על פני השדה בעצם אדם] / מת
20 XIV,12	l11	מֵת	כול הימים אשר הוא בתוכה] / מת
11 IV,12		מַתָּנָה	] מתנתך
13 II,15		נאה	[מה]נֹאוו / על הרים
13 II,15		נָבִיא	ביד ישע]יה הנביא אשר אמר[
13 II,17		נָבִיא	/ פֹשרו ההריֹם[המה] הֹנביאי[ם]
14 2,1		נָבָל	]טי הגוי הנב[ל
13 5,2		נגד	]והוא[ה] יגידֹ[
22 1,2		נגהּ	תהיה·עדי·נגה·באהבתכ·לאלהיכ·
11 VI,8		נגע	אל[יך לו]א יגע
11 VI,10		נגע	לוא] / תרא[ה רעה ו]לוא יגע [נגע באה]ליך
11 V,3		נדב	/נדבי א[
20 XVI,7		נדח	ומת כי בקש לה]דֹיחכה *vac* [
14 1ii10		נוב	והארץ תנובב לכם פרי
20 I,18	xv11	נוף	ויניפו המקריבים[את האילים
13 II,5		נַחֲלָה	ומנחלת מלכי צדק
13 II,5		נַחֲלָה	כיֹ[א]∘∘∘∘ וֹהמה נחֹלֹ[ת מלכי צ]דק
13 II,20		נחם	/ לנחֹ[ם] ה[אבלים
11 V,9		נְחֹשֶׁת	[ויסגור דל]תי נחושת
20 XII,14		נְחֹשֶׁת	]בֹה שלנחושת[ ]
20 31,1		נְחֹשֶׁת	]נחושת /
21 1,3		נְחֹשֶׁת	]נחושת ברוֹרֹ[ף ימס
20 33,2		נטע	]יטעוֹ בא[
20 I,19	xv13	נִיחוֹחַ	עולה היא אשה ריח ניחוח[לפני יהוה
11 IV,4		נכה	/ יככה יהוה מ[כה גדול]ה אשר לאבדך[
11 VI,5		נסך	ב]אברתו יסך[לך
17 IX,5		נֶסֶךְ	]לם ורֹ[י]ח נסכיהם למס[ ]םֹ
20 III,22	xix4	נֶסֶךְ	ומנחתמה וֹנסֹכֹמה כֹ[משפט

Reference		Word	Context
20 IV,6	xx02	נֶסֶךְ	שלישית הה]ין שמן לאיל על הנסך הזה /
20 IV,9	xx04	נֶסֶךְ	מנחתמ]ה ונסכמה ˻כמשפט˼
20 IV,11	xx1	נֶסֶךְ	א]תֹ האילים ואת הנסך
20 IV,18	xx8	נֶסֶךְ	[עם מנחתמ]הֹ ונסכמה /
20 V,24	xxii3	נֶסֶךְ	כבשים ארבעה עש]רֹ ומנחתס˼ה˻ ונ(ש)סכמה[
12 7,1	5:1	נְפִיל	[להמה בנים ואלה הנ]פֹ[יל]יםֹ
11 VI,8		נפל	יפ[ו]ל מצדך אלף ור[בבה מי]מינך
17 III,4		נפלאה	[בשבע זמרות נפל]אותיה
17 III,7		נפלאה	[שבע תהלי / הודות נפל]אותיהו
11 III,9		נֶפֶשׁ	ו]להרוג נפש /
20 I,20	xv14	נֶפֶשׁ	למלו(אֹ) על נפשותמה שבעת ימיֹ[ם] *va]c* [
20 VII,25		נֶפֶשׁ	]∘∘∘ יעשה לנפש /
20 XII,9	xlv17	נֶפֶשׁ	וכול ט]מֹא לנפש לוא / [יבואו לה
20 XV,3	li9	נֶפֶשׁ	ולוא ישקצו] / את נפשותיהמה
20 XVI,2	liv20	נֶפֶשׁ	או ריעיכה א]שר כנפשכה בסתר[לאמור]
20 VI,15		נַפְתָּלִי	וביום הששי דן] / ונפתלי
20 XI,17		נַפְתָּלִי	ומשער נפ]תֹליֹ[עד]
13 II,10		נצב	אלוהים [נ]צֹב בעֹ[דת אל]
11 VI,5		נצל	ה]וֹאה יצילך מֹ[פח יקו]ש מדבר הֹוֹ[ות
13 II,13		נצל	וביום ההואה יצי]לֹ[מה מיד]בֹליעל
13 II,25		נצל	אשר יצי]ל[מה מי]דֹ בליעל
13 II,13		נקם	/ ומלכי צֹדק יקום נקםֹ משפטֹי א[ל
13 II,13		נָקָם	/ ומלכי צֹדק יקום נקםֹ משפטֹי א[ל
20 V,22	xxii1	נֵר	]השמן הזה יבעירו בנרות / [בה
13 II,3		נשא	כול בעל משה יד אשר ישה[ברעהו
13 II,11		נשא	ופני רשע[י]ם תש[או ס]לה
13 III,10		נשא	/ גדר ולשֹאת עֹמוד וכֹפר ∘[ ]אֹ[
13 7,9		נשא	י]שֹאנו [
20 V,9	xxi5	נָשִׂיא	ישראל נ]שֹיאי הדגלים ברישונה
20 V,23	xxii2	נָשִׂיא	]ם שרי האלפים עם נשיאי/
20 XI,22		נִשְׁכָּה	שבעים]נֹשכה /
14 1ii9		נתן	ולתת לכם פרֹ[י]
20 I,25		נתן	ונתנ[ו על קרנות המזבח באצבעם] / מן הד[ם נתן
20 XV,7	li16	נתן	/ אשר אנוכי נותן לכ˻מ˼[ה לרשתה
17 VII,7		סבב	בלכתמה לוא י]סבו לכול עֹ[
17 VI,6		סָבִיב	בדני צורות אלוהים מ]חוקק סב[י]ב
20 I,26	xvi03	סָבִיב	׳שפוכו סביב על ארבע פנות
17 I,5		סְדֵרָה=שְׂדֵרָה	] סדרו[תיו סדרו]תיו מבני[ת
13 II,7		סוֹף	וי[ום הכפ]ורים ה[וא]ה סֹ[וף]הֹ[יו]בל העשירי
13 7,7		סוֹף	]סוף הי[ובל
13 II,12		סור	אש[ר]∘ים בסו[רמ]הֹ מחוקי אל ל[הרשיע]
13 II,22		סור	/ ∘∘[ ]ר הוסרה מבליעל ותשֹ[וב
13 II,24		סור	הסרים מלכת [בד]רֹךְ העם
11 VI,6		סֹחֵרָה	חסד[ו ע]ליך צנה וסוחרהֹ אמתו סלה
20 I,13	xv4	סַל	וחצו את]כֹול האילים והסלים
20 I,17	xv9	סַל	וחלת מצה אחת מ[ן הֹסל

Text	Word		Reference
/ [את כול]בני בל[יעל אמן אמן] סלה	סֶלָה		11 VI,3
חסד[ו ע]ליך צנה וסוחרה אמתו סלה	סֶלָה		11 VI,6
ויע[נו אמן אמן] סלה *va]c va[c a]v* [	סֶלָה		11 VI,14
ופני רשע[י]ם תש[או ס]לה	סֶלָה		13 II,11
תספורו חמשים[יום	ספר	xix13	20 IV,2
]ואשר / מורי̇הׄמה החבאו וסתר[ו]	סתר		13 II,5
יושב]בסתר[עליון בצל] שדי / [יתלונן	סֵתֶר		11 VI,3
או ריעיכה א]שר כנפשכה בסתר[לאמור	סֵתֶר	liv20	20 XVI,2
]∘עבדי יהו[ה] /	עֶבֶד		11 III,11
כול מל]אכת עבודה לוא י[עשו	עֲבוֹדָה	xix8	20 III,25
והעברתמה שו[פר ב]כול [א]רץ //	עבר		13 II,25
]עד עולם וא[	עַד		11 IV,10
[מאדם עד]בהמה ועד ח[יה ועד עוף	עַד	5:2	12 7,2
/ לעולמי עד וברוכים [ ]תו	עַד		14 1ii5
]מלך כול קדושי עד /	עַד		17 30,4
ואת האזרוע [ע]ד עצם השכם /	עַד	xx16	20 IV,26
שם ואחריהמה כול העם מגדול ו]עד קטן	עַד	xxi6	20 V,10
מן הפנה הז]ואת עד ש[ער / דן	עַד		20 XI,16
ע]ד יום /	עַד		20 XIV,1
/ עד ה[ערב	עַד		20 XIV,23
מקצי הארץ ועד קצ[י הארץ	עַד		20 XVI,4
אלוהים [נ]צב בע[דת אל]	עֵדָה		13 II,10
/ [ואין]כול[נגע ומ]כשול בעדתכם	עֵדָה		14 1ii13
ומלאכי / [קודשו מתיצבי]ם בעדתכם	עֵדָה		14 1ii15
וכפ]ר בו על כול העדה לפני / [יהוה	עֵדָה	xxii02	20 V,19
תהיה·עדי·נגה·באהבתכ·לאלהיכ·	עֲדִי		22 1,2
/ [ע]דנים ואכלתם והדשנתם *vac*	עֵדֶן		14 1ii11
[לוא ע]וד בארץ	עוֹד		11 IV,9
] אין עוד /	עוֹד	13	20 XIV,6
[עו]ל ולוא צדקה[	עָוֶל		11 V,8
ואשר א[מר עד מתי ת]שפוטו עוול	עָוֶל		13 II,11
]עד עולם וא[	עוֹלָם		11 IV,10
]תו[ ]יה[ ]יה∘[ל]עולם/	עוֹלָם		11 VI,2
פשרו]ל[ה]שכילמה בכול קצי הע[ולם	עוֹלָם		13 II,20
/ לעולמי עד וברוכים [ ]תו	עוֹלָם		14 1ii5
[ ]כסאי עולמים [	עוֹלָם		17 V,8
רוחי א]ל[י] עולמים[	עוֹלָם		17 VI,4
[אמת ו]צדק עולמ[ים	עוֹלָם		17 VII,7
בכוח אלוהי / [עול]מים	עוֹלָם		17 VIII,5
]עולמים ב[הוד ו]הדר ל∘[	עוֹלָם		17 IX,6
[ולוא ת]שבית ברית מלח ל[עולם *vac*	עוֹלָם	xx14	20 IV,24
ל]חוק עולם להמה ולזרעמה /	עוֹלָם	xxi05	20 V,4
חוקות] / עולם לדורותיהמה[שנה בשנה	עוֹלָם	xxii14	20 VI,7
לעזוב להמה[משא]כול עוונותיהמה	עָוֹן		13 II,6
מחץ יעוף יומם	עוף		11 VI,7
ושעיר ע[זים לחטאת	עֵז	xv2	20 I,11
שעירי] / עזים שנים ל[	עֵז	xxiii4	20 VI,17
זמר]ת עוז ל[אלוהי קודש]	עֹז		17 III,3
לעזוב להמה[משא]כול עוונותיהמה	עזב		13 II,6
/ ובעזרו כול אלי [הצדק	עֵזֶר		13 II,14
על ארבע פנות עזרת ה[מזבח	עֲזָרָה	xvi03	20 I,26
רק[תביט] / בעיניך[	עַיִן		11 VI,9
] לעיני בחור[י	עַיִן		15 2,4
/ולא עינכ[ה	עַיִן		25 1,2
/ עריה[מה טהורות וש	עִיר		20 XIII,10
/לבוא אל עירי [	עִיר		21 3,2
]אשר יעש[ו]על / [כול אי]ש חטא	עַל		11 III,6
ועל כול א[דם רשע	עַל		11 III,7
/ ובחרון אפו[ישלח]עליך מלאך תקיף[	עַל		11 IV,5
אשר[בלוא] רחמ[ים] עליך	עַל		11 IV,6
אש[ר /]על כול אלה	עַל		11 IV,7
/לדויד ע[ל	עַל		11 V,4
חסד[ו ע]ליך צנה וסוחרה אמתו סלה	עַל		11 VI,6
על כפים[ישאונ]ך פן[תגוף בא]בן רגל[ך	עַל		11 VI,11
פשרו]לאחרית הימים על השבויים אשר[	עַל		13 II,4
/ לכפר בו על כול בני [אור	עַל		13 II,8
]∘ם עלי[המ]ה הת[ ]לפ[י]כ[ול עש]ותמה	עַל		13 II,8
כאשר כתוב / עליו בשירי דויד אשר אמר	עַל		13 II,10
ועליו אמ[ר ו]עלי[ה] / למרום שובה	עַל		13 II,10
ועליו אמ[ר ו]עלי[ה] / למרום שובה	עַל		13 II,10
/ פשרו על בליעל ועל רוחי גורלו	עַל		13 II,12
/ פשרו על בליעל ועל רוחי גורלו	עַל		13 II,12
[מה]נאוו / על הרים	עַל		13 II,16
]הואה הכתוב עליו אשר [	עַל		13 II,19
]במשפט[י] אל כאשר כתוב עליו[	עַל		13 II,23
/ התורה[ע]ליהמה[	עַל		13 III,6
להוריד על ארצכםה / גשמי ברכה	עַל		14 1ii8
ושם קודשו נקרא עליכם //	עַל		14 1ii15
]על מרום כסא[	עַל		17 VII,2
וה]קריבו על המ[זבח לכול יום ויום]	עַל		20 I,10
ואת החלב אשר עלי[הנה	עַל	xv7	20 I,15
למלו(א) על נפשותמה שבעת ימי[ם] *c[va*]	עַל	xv14	20 I,20
ישפוכו סביב על ארבע פנות	עַל	xvi03	20 I,26
ע]ל[עם הקהל מכול	עַל	xviii7	20 III,11
שלישית ההין על / [המטה]	עַל	xix15	20 IV,3
שלישית הה]ין שמן לאיל על הנסך הזה /	עַל	xx02	20 IV,6
[ואת חלבמה יקט]ירו על המזבח /	עַל	xx4	20 IV,14
ולוא תבו]א ע[ל]י[ו ה]שמש *vac*	עַל	xx13	20 IV,23
ביו]ם הזה יכפרו על התירוש	עַל	xxi8	20 V,11
וכפ]ר בו על כול העדה לפני / [יהוה	עַל	xxii02	20 V,19
יכפרו ע[ל כול יצהר הארץ	עַל	xxii15	20 VI,8
למע]לה מע[ל]לבית[ה	עַל	xxxii11	20 IX,2

Context	Word	Ref	
יפול] / עליו מ]המה במותמה יטמא	עַל	20 XIV,20	
ולוא תחוס עינ]כה עליו	עַל	20 XVI,5	
ולוא תחמל ע]ליו	עַל	20 XVI,5	
]ום עליהם את /	עַל	20 31,3	
]עליכה כיא [	עַל	27 1,1	
] ועל יצוע]י	עַל	30 11,1	
]ברובע הי]ו]ם תעלה זואת /	עלה	20 VII,22	
] יהיו מקריבים ליהוה עולה] מן האיל	עֹלָה	20 I,14	xv6
עולה היא אשה ריח ניחוח] לפני יהוה	עֹלָה	20 I,19	xv12
]והקטירו הכול / על המזבח על ה]עולה	עֹלָה	20 I,20	xv14
ברובע]היום יקר]יבו את עול]ת הבכור]ים	עֹלָה	20 III,21	xix2
]אחר]העולה יעשום /	עֹלָה	20 IV,13	xx3
ראשית היצהר על מזבח העו]ל]ה	עֹלָה	20 V,17	xxi16
כמ]שפט עולה הואה	עֹלָה	20 V,21	xxii04
הקריבו בחג] / העצים עולה ליה]וה	עֹלָה	20 VI,16	xxiii3
/ עול]ה הוא	עֹלָה	20 VI,18	
עו]לת התמיד *vac* /	עֹלָה	20 VII,23	xxiii8
/ בשם אל עליון ס]] וברוך שם קודש]ו]	עֶלְיוֹן	14 1ii4	
/ יברך אתכם אל עליון ויאר פניו אליכם	עֶלְיוֹן	14 1ii7	
]סס[ ]עמו תסו רפואה /	עַם	11 II,7	
ע]ם קדושי אל לממשלת משפט	עַם	13 II,9	
אל ידין עמים	עַם	13 II,11	
הסרים מלכת [בד]רך העם	עַם	13 II,24	
//לעממים]	עַם	25 1,1	
/ עם [תרח אביו בחרן שני שבועי שנים]	עִם	12 8,2	12:15
]ויהוה ע]מכה ויש]מרכה מכול רע]	עִם	12 9,5	12:29
כיא אל עמכם	עִם	14 1ii14	
עם כול מוצאי [פנ]ות מבניתו	עִם	17 X,8	
]ם שרי האלפים עם נשיאי/	עִם	20 V,23	xxii2
/ גדר ולשאת עמוד וכפר ס[ ]א]	עמד	13 III,10	
לו]א יתמהמהו בעומדם	עמד	17 VII,3	
ואת האלי]ה לעומת עציהה	עֻמָּה	20 I,16	xv8
ואת הא]ליה לעומת / [העצה]	עֻמָּה	20 IV,17	xx7
]כבודו ומעשיו ועמלו ב]	עָמָל	15 5	
ויע]נו אמן אמן] סלה [v]a[c va]c]	ענה	11 VI,14	
ועני]ה] ואמר]ישראל ברוכים א]תם]	ענה	14 1ii3	
]לכן / נכתב על ע]ץ הדעת	עֵץ	12 5,3	4:30
הקריבו בחג] / העצים עולה ליה]וה	עֵץ	20 VI,16	xxiii3
ואת האלי]ה לעומת עציהה	עֵצָה	20 I,16	xv8
ואת האזרוע [ע]ד עצם השכם /	עֶצֶם	20 IV,26	xx16
ולוא יתע]רבו זבחי שלמי בני יש]ראל]	ערב	20 X,3	xxxvii11
מי ע]שה את האותות]	עשה	11 III,2	
יהוה הוא]ה אשר] / עשה את ה]אלה	עשה	11 III,4	
]אשר יעש]ו [על / [כול אי]ש חטא	עשה	11 III,6	
]אשר יעשו ב]שמים / ובארץ]	עשה	12 1,2	
]אחר]העולה יעשום /	עשה	20 IV,13	xx3

Context	Word	Ref	
]ססס יעשה לנפש /	עשה	20 VII,25	
שערים]עשו לה /	עשה	20 VIII,11	
וע]שי]תה שלושה מקומות למזרח העיר	עשה	20 XIII,1	xlvi16
/ ועושה אשמה גדול]ה	עשה	20 XV,6	li14
]ס ככה יעש]ו	עשה	21 2,3	
וי]ום הכפ]ורים ה]וא]ה ס]וף]ה]יו]בל העשירי	עֲשִׂירִי	13 II,7	
]ליהוה שנים [ע]שר אילים	עֶשֶׂר	20 IV,4	xix16
[שנים ע]שר שבטי ישראל	עֶשֶׂר	20 V,7	xxi2
כבשים ארבעה עש]ר ומנחתם ונ]ש]סכמה]	עֶשֶׂר	20 V,24	xxii3
ע]שרה /	עֶשֶׂר	20 40,1	
קרא בכו]ל עת / אל השמ]ים	עֵת	11 V,4	
ע]תים פש]רו	עֵת	13 6,4	
טל ומטר יורה ומלקוש בעתו	עֵת	14 1ii9	
/אשר]]הפגוע]ים	פגע	11 V,2	
]סם עלי]המ]ה הת]]לפ]י]כ]ול עש]ותמה	פֶּה	13 II,8	
לוא תירא / מפחד לילה	פחד	11 VI,7	
ו]הם יודעים / [רזי פל]או	פֶּלֶא	11 III,8	
סוד שני ב]מעוני פל]א	פֶּלֶא	17 II,5	
[ראשי נשיאי כהונות פ]לא למלכ]י צדק [?]]	פֶּלֶא	17 II,7	
[שבע בשבע ז]מרות פל]א]	פֶּלֶא	17 III,4	
[בשבעה / דברי]פלא לברך]	פֶּלֶא	17 III,11	
[בשבעה / דברי פ]לא [ו]ברך לכ]ול]	פֶּלֶא	17 III,12	
[מר]אי פלא כ]]סי טו]הר	פֶּלֶא	17 IV,6	
]בדני פ]לא	פֶּלֶא	17 V,5	
מעש]י רוחו]ת רקיע פלא	פֶּלֶא	17 VI,4	
]פלאי הוד וה]דר	פֶּלֶא	17 VI,10	
ג]בורת פלא]	פֶּלֶא	17 VII,6	
]שני פל]ח]	פֶּלֶא	17 VII,9	
/]פלא דעת ובינ]ה	פֶּלֶא	17 VIII,2	
]רקיעי פל]א]	פֶּלֶא	17 VIII,2	
הוד [ ]כול תבנית רוחי פל]א]	פֶּלֶא	17 VIII,3	
כול [פל]אי פלאיהם	פֶּלֶא	17 VIII,4	
כול [פל]אי פלאיהם	פֶּלֶא	17 VIII,4	
מארבעת מוסדי רקיע / הפלא	פֶּלֶא	17 VIII,6	
ס[ ]למוסדי פלא	פֶּלֶא	17 VIII,7	
]ס פלא ותבנית חשני /	פֶּלֶא	17 IX,6	
]פלאיהם כול]	פֶּלֶא	17 29,3	
קומה גב]ור שבה פל]שתים	פְּלִשְׁתִּי	14 2,2	
על כפים[ישאונ]ך פן[תגוף בא]בן רגל]ך	פֶּן	11 VI,11	
מ]עשי פנותו[ממלכו]ת	פִּנָּה	17 VII,6	
עם כול מוצאי [פנ]ות מבניתו	פִּנָּה	17 X,8	
על ארבע פנות עזרת ה]מזבח	פִּנָּה	20 I,26	xvi03
]פנות	פִּנָּה	20 32,3	
]אשר הת]י]צבו לפני]ו	פָּנֶה*	11 III,5	
]ה אם לוא / [ייראו]מלפני יהוה ל]	פָּנֶה*	11 III,9	
פניך פני / [שו]ו	פָּנֶה*	11 V,6	

Text	Word		Ref.
פניך פני / [שו]ו	פָּנֶה*		**11** V,6
ופני רשע[י]ם תש[או ס]לה	פָּנֶה*		**13** II,11
/ יברך אתכם אל עליון ויאר פניו אליכם	פָּנֶה*		**14** 1ii7
°° פניכה °[	פָּנֶה*		**15** 3,1
[ ]א פניו]	פָּנֶה*		**17** VII,2
[ואת / סלי הלחם תנופה ל]פני יהוה	פָּנֶה*	xv12	**20** I,19
וכפ]ר בו על כול העדה לפני / [יהוה	פָּנֶה*	xxii02	**20** V,19
בפרור]הפנימי אצל ק[י]ר החצר ה[חיצון	פְּנִימִי	xxxvii9	**20** X,1
[אחר ישחטו את] / הפר[לפני יהוה]	פַּר	xvi01	**20** I,25
]ולקחו זקני הכוהני[ם] מדם הפר	פַּר	xvi02	**20** I,25
לפרים ולאיל · / [ולכבשים ולשעיר עזים]	פַּר	xx05	**20** IV,9
ולתת לכם פר[י]	פְּרִי		**14** 1ii9
והארץ תנובב לכם פרי	פְּרִי		**14** 1ii10
]פרי בא°[	פְּרִי		**20** 33,3
/ פשרו על בליעל ועל רוחי גורלו	פֵּשֶׁר		**13** II,12
/ פשרו ההרים[המה] הנביאי[ם]	פֵּשֶׁר		**13** II,17
ע]תים פש[רו	פֵּשֶׁר		**13** 6,4
ויפתח לכם את / אוצרו הטוב אשר בשמים	פתח		**14** 1ii7
]°ו ולפתחי מבואי	פתח		**17** X,7
על פי]פתחי השערי[ם כולמה]	פֶּתַח	xlvi6	**20** XII,19
[פ]תילי תפארת[	פָּתִיל		**17** IX,7
על] / *vac* פתן [ואפעה תד]רוך תרמו[ס כפיר]	פֶּתֶן		**11** VI,12
]שר הצבה	צָבָא		**11** V,8
הקץ לשנת הרצון למלכי צדק ולצב[איו	צָבָא		**13** II,9
]ממולח טוהר צבעי /	צֶבַע		**17** IX,7
יפ[ו]ל מצדך אלף ור[בבה מי]מינך	צַד		**11** VI,8
אש[ר יזרח] / [על ה]צדיק לה[	צַדִּיק		**11** V,11
הצ]דיק לבוא[	צַדִּיק		**11** V,12
רוחי דעת אמת] וצדק[	צֶדֶק		**17** VI,5
[אמת ו]צדק עולמ[ים	צֶדֶק		**17** VII,7
[עו]ל ולוא צדקה[	צְדָקָה		**11** V,8
אשר הצ]דקה לו[	צְדָקָה		**11** V,13
מקטב ישוד[צ]הרים	צָהֳרַיִם		**11** VI,7
כ[י מלאכיו]יצוה לך / לשומ[רך בדרכי]ך	צוה		**11** VI,10
] אלוהים[ ]חם וצורות [	צוּרָה		**17** V,6
]צורות[כבוד] / למע[שי לבני הוד והדר	צוּרָה		**17** VI,6
וצו]רת בדניהם מל[אכי קודש	צוּרָה		**17** VI,7
]מו לצורות[ ]שא אפוד /	צוּרָה		**17** IX,8
[א]ומר לציון [מלך]אלוהיך	צִיּוֹן		**13** II,16
[אומר לצי]ון מלך אלוהיך	צִיּוֹן		**13** II,23
[צי]ון ה[יאה] / [עדת כול בני הצדק	צִיּוֹן		**13** II,23
צמ]ח / [דויד	צמח		**14** 1i11
חסד[ו ע]ליך צנה וסוחרה אמתו סלה	צִנָּה		**11** VI,6
מן הארץ ארבע אמות]מצופות זהב	צפה	xxxii10	**20** IX,1
ואת החטאות במקצ]וע המזרחי צפונה	צָפוֹן		**20** X,6
[ואת החזה ואת הלחיים ואת הקב]ה	קֵבָה	xx16	**20** IV,26
האזרוע]ת והלחיים והקבאות למנות /	קֵבָה	xxi03	**20** V,2
[ריאשון נק]בר ב[אדמה]	קבר	4:29	**12** 5,1
/מי אתה [הילוד מ]אדם ומזרע הקד[ושי]ם	קָדוֹשׁ		**11** V,6
ע]ם קדושי אל לממשלת משפט	קָדוֹשׁ		**13** II,9
[ ]° לזבחי קדושים[	קָדוֹשׁ		**17** IX,4
]מלך כול קדושי עד /	קָדוֹשׁ		**17** 30,4
]וקדשו את מ[קדשי]	קדש	xlvi11	**20** XII,22
/ בשם אל עליון °[ ] וברוך שם קודש[ו]	קֹדֶשׁ		**14** 1ii4
וברוכים כול / מלאכי קודשו *va]c*	קֹדֶשׁ		**14** 1ii6
ושם קודשו נקרא עליכם //	קֹדֶשׁ		**14** 1ii15
]שי קוד[ש ישמ]יעו תהלי[	קֹדֶשׁ		**17** I,6
[ ]ל[דמות פלא רוח קו]דש קודשים	קֹדֶשׁ		**17** IV,9
[ ]ל[דמות פלא רוח קו]דש קודשים	קֹדֶשׁ		**17** IV,9
כרו]בי קוד[ש אופני אור בדביר	קֹדֶשׁ		**17** VII,5
]ק[ו]דש / קודשי[ם	קֹדֶשׁ		**17** VIII,8
]ק[ו]דש / קודשי[ם	קֹדֶשׁ		**17** VIII,9
הטוהר ברוח קוד[ש] /	קֹדֶשׁ		**17** IX,5
[ ]מלאכי[קו]דשו	קֹדֶשׁ		**17** IX,9
אור וחושך ובדני[ ]קודש מלך / הכבוד	קֹדֶשׁ		**17** X,5
בכול מל[ ]הו משאי קודש	קֹדֶשׁ		**17** X,6
מר]כבות הדרו ולדבירי קו[דשו	קֹדֶשׁ		**17** X,7
]קודש קודש[ים	קֹדֶשׁ		**17** 29,3a
]קודש קודש[ים	קֹדֶשׁ		**17** 29,3a
]קודש קוד[שים	קֹדֶשׁ		**17** 29,4
]קודש קוד[שים	קֹדֶשׁ		**17** 29,4
קו]דשי[ם	קֹדֶשׁ		**17** 29,4
]°ת קודשו פ°°ת ד°[	קֹדֶשׁ		**17** 32,2
]ן שבתון זכרון מקרא קודש /	קֹדֶשׁ	xxv3	**20** VII,24
לכפר על כול עם ה]קהל *vac*	קָהָל	xx04	**20** IV,8
מתחת לדב]ירי ה[פלא] / קול [דממת שקט	קוֹל		**17** VI,8
ישמ[י]עו מקול משא אלוהים[ ]	קוֹל		**17** VIII,6
כבודו קול ה[	קוֹל		**17** 28,5
המה]מקימ[י] הברית	קום		**13** II,24
מקטב ישוד[צ]הרים	קטב		**11** VI,7
שם ואחריהמה כול העם מגדול ו]עד קטן	קָטָן	xxi6	**20** V,10
]ויקטי[ר על / המזבח]	קטר	xvi9	**20** II,7
[ואת חלבמה יקט]ירו על המזבח /	קטר	xx4	**20** IV,14
ויקח קין את אחות[ו / און לו לאשה]	קַיִן	4:9	**12** 1,7
בפרור]הפנימי אצל ק[י]ר החצר ה[חיצון	קִיר	xxxvii9	**20** X,1
]בקללת האב[דון	קְלָלָה		**11** IV,10
]° ל°°[]והקנים יה°[	קֵן		**21** 2,2
ו]בקץ היו[בל / השמיני לקח לו]	קֵץ	4:14	**12** 2,2
כיא / הואה הקץ לשנת הרצון למלכי צדק	קֵץ		**13** II,9
פשרו]ל[ה]שכילמה בכול קצי הע[ולם	קֵץ		**13** II,20
מקצי הארץ ועד קצ[י הארץ	קֵץ		**20** XVI,4
מקצי הארץ ועד קצ[י הארץ	קֵץ		**20** XVI,4

Ref.		Word	Context
11 II,2		קרא	]ה֯ שלומה[ ]ויקר֯]א
11 II,8		קרא	על]שמך נשען וקר֯]א[/
11 VI,9		קרא	קר]את מח[סך]ת מחמדו[
12 1,5	4:7	קרא	]ותלד לו בן ויקרא את שמ[ו שת]
13 II,6		קרא	וקרא להמה דרור
14 1ii15		קרא	ושם קודשו נ֯קרא עליכם //
17 VIII,10		קרא	וקרא[ו
20 I,10		קרב	וה]קריבו על המ֯]זבח לכול יום ויום[
20 I,14	xv5	קרב	] יהיו מקריבים ליהוה עולה֯[מן האיל
20 I,18	xv11	קרב	ויניפו המקריבים[את האילים
20 I,22	xv16	קרב	ויקרי[ב פרים שנים
20 I,23	xv17	קרב	ויקרב את אשר [ל]כ֯וה֯נים ברישונה[
20 III,21	xix2	קרב	ברובע]היום יקר֯[יבו את עול]ת֯ הבכור֯[ים
20 IV,2		קרב	וה]ק֯[ר]ב֯תמה / [יין חדש לנסך]
20 IV,10	xx06	קרב	ברובע היום יקריבו /
20 IV,11	xx1	קרב	ויקריבו / [שלמים]
13 II,10		קֶרֶב	]ב֯קורב אלוהים ישפוט
17 III,10		קֶרֶב	[לברך כול / כוהני]קור֯ב במע[ון פלא]
20 IV,15	xx5	קֶרֶב	[ואת כול החלב אשר על ה]ק֯רבים
11 V,7		קֶרֶן	וקרנ֯י֯ך֯ קרני חל[ו]ם֯
11 V,7		קֶרֶן	וקרנ֯י֯ך֯ קרני חל[ו]ם֯
11 VI,9		ראה	ותרא]ה֯ שלום רשע[ים
11 VI,10		ראה	לוא] / תרא[ה רעה ו]לוא יגע [נגע באה]ליך
11 VI,13		ראה	/ *vac* ו[ישגבך ויר]אך בישוע[תו סלה] *va]c*
14 1ii12		ראה	ש֯דפון וירקון לוא יראה בתבואתיה
15 3		ראה	]°כה ותראה מק°[
17 VIII,9		רֹאשׁ	]° ר֯וש[
20 I,24	xvi01	רֹאשׁ	זקני הכוהנים / את ידיהמה על ראו]שו
30 8,1		רֹאשׁ	] תהיה לראו֯[ש
12 3,2	4:17	רִאשׁוֹן	זה ריאש[ון]
12 4,2		רִאשׁוֹן	ריא]שון הוא[ה / כתב תעודה]
13 II,7		רִאשׁוֹן	היובל ה֯ראיש֯ון אח֯ר֯ ת֯ש֯[עה ה]יובלים
20 I,23	xv18	רִאשׁוֹן	ויקרב את אשר [ל]כ֯וה֯נים ברישונה[
20 V,8	xxi4	רִאשׁוֹן	הכוהנ]י֯ם ישתו שמה ריאשונים / [והלויים
20 V,9	xxi5	רִאשׁוֹן	ישראל נ]ש֯יאי הדגלים ברישונה
20 XVI,6		רִאשׁוֹן	ידכה תהיה בו ברא]ישונה להמיתו
29 1,3		רִאשׁוֹן	[ישוב ונענש שתי שני]ם֯ בראי֯[שונה
20 VI,3	xxii9	רֵאשִׁית	ולר֯]אשית את האזרוע ואת הלחיים
20 33,1		רֵאשִׁית	]ראשית [
11 IV,7		רַב	אשר֯[יורידו]ך֯ לתהום רבה
11 IV,9		רַב	]°כב וחשך / [בתהום ר]ב֯ה מואדה
13 III,4		רֹב	/ ורוב֯[
14 1ii10		רֹב	/ ת֯נ֯ובות דגן תירוש ויצהר לרוב
11 VI,8		רְבָבָה	יפ[ו]ל מצדך אלף ור[בבה מי]מינך
12 7,1	5:2	רבה	וירב֯[חמס בארץ]
12 1,8	4:9	רְבִיעִי	בקץ היוב]ל הרביעי *ac*[v]

Ref.		Word	Context
20 VI,14		רְבִיעִי	/ וב֯יום הרביעי יששכר[וז]ב֯ולון
20 IV,10	xx06	רֹבַע	ברובע היום יקריבו /
20 VII,22	xxiii8	רֹבַע	]בר֯וב֯ע הי֯[ו]ם תעלה זואת /
11 VI,11		רֶגֶל	על כפים֯[ישאונ]ך פן[תגוף בא]בן רגל[ך
13 II,16		רֶגֶל	רגל[י] מבש[ר מ]שמיע שלום
17 X,7		רֶגֶל	/ לכסאי כבודו ולהדום ר֯[גליו
11 II,3		רוּחַ	הרו]חות֯[ ]והשדים [
13 II,12		רוּחַ	/ פשרו על בליעל ועל ר֯וח֯י גורלו
13 II,13		רוּחַ	ומיד כול ר֯[וחי גורלו]
13 II,18		רוּחַ	/ והמבשר הו[אה]מ֯שיח הרו֯[ח]
15 6		רוּחַ	]אתה בראתה כול רוח ג֯ל°°[
17 VII,5		רוּחַ	]רוחות אל[והים
17 VIII,3		רוּחַ	הוד [ ]כ֯ול תבנית רוחי פל[א]
17 IX,5		רוּחַ	הטוהר ברוח קוד[ש] /
17 29,2		רוּחַ	] רוחו֯ת֯ [
29 1,2		רוּחַ	[והאיש אשר תזוע]ר֯וחו[
20 XII,12		רוֹכֵל	]ר֯וכל
17 VII,10		רום	/ [ור]ו֯ממוהו [כפי הכבוד
17 VII,10		רום	בהרומם֯[קול דממת אלוהים נשמע
17 VIII,5		רום	ומרוממים גבורות אלו[הי]
17 III,6		רום	[שבע]תהלי רו[ם מלכותו]
20 XIII,4		רָחוֹק	/ רחוק֯ מ[ן
11 IV,6		רַחַם	אשר[בלוא] רחמ[ים] עליך
17 X,3		רַחֲמִים	[ש]ל֯[ו]מיו במשפט֯י[ ]רחמיו
17 IX,4		רֵיחַ	]ר֯יח מנחותם °°°[ ] /
17 IX,5		רֵיחַ	]ל֯ם ור֯[י]ח נסכיהם למס[ ]ם֯
20 I,19	xv13	רֵיחַ	עולה היא אשה ריח ניחוח[לפני יהוה
20 V,21	xxii04	רֵיחַ	אשה ריח / [ניחוח ליהוה
11 4,2		רִיק	] ו֯ריק [
11 VI,12		רמס	[ואפעה תד]רוך תרמו[ס כפיר] ותנין
17 28,4		רִנָּה	ברנות כול֯[
17 35,1		רִנָּה	]משמע רנה[
12 9,6	12:29	רַע	כול בני אדם לעשו]ת֯כ֯ה ר֯ע֯[
14 1ii13		רַע	וחיה רעה שבתה מן / [הארץ
11 V,12		רעע	]ה֯רע לו ש[ד
11 II,7		רְפָאָה	]°°[ ]עמ֯ו ת֯°ו֯ רפואה /
11 V,3		רְפָאֵל	ר]פ֯אל שלמ[ם אמן אמן סלה] *vac*
13 II,9		רָצוֹן	כיא / הואה הק֯ץ֯ ל֯שנת הרצון למלכי צד֯ק
17 IX,3		רָצוֹן	[מנחו]ת רצון המ[
11 VI,8		רַק	רק[תביט] / בעיניך[
17 IV,5		רָקִיעַ	]ר֯ לבני[רק]י֯ע
17 VI,4		רָקִיעַ	מעש[י רוחו]ת רקיע פלא
17 VIII,2		רָקִיעַ	]ר֯קיעי פל[א]
17 VIII,5		רָקִיעַ	מארבעת מוסדי רקיע / ה֯פלא
17 X,5		רָקִיעַ	ובהדר/ תשבוחותו בכול רקי[עי]ם
17 X,8		רָקִיעַ	ולכול ז[בולי ו]להיכלי כבודו ולרקיעי

20 I,17	xv10	רָקִיק	וחלת לחם שמן אחת ורקיק] אחד
17 IV,10		רִקְמָה	]ים[ ]רׄוקמותׄ[ם]
17 VI,6		רִקְמָה	כול / מע[שיהם]רוקמׄ[ה
17 VII,13		רִקְמָה	ומעשי נוגה]ברוקמת כב[וד
17 IX,7		רִקְמָה	]רוקמה כמׄ[עשי אורג
11 VI,9		רֶשַׁע	ותרא]הׄ שלום רשע[ים
13 II,11		רֶשַׁע	ופני רשע[י]ם תש[או ס]לה
11 V,9		שְׁאוֹל	יהוה [יוריד]ך / [לשאו]ל תחתית
20 V,3	xxi04	שאר	ואת השכם הׄנשאר מן האזרוע /
13 II,4		שבה	פשרו]לׄאׄחׄרית הימים על השבויים אשר[
14 2,2		שבה	קומה גב]ור שבה פלׄ[שתים
12 1,4	4:7	שָׁבוּעַ	ו]בׄארבעה לשבוע הח[מישי / שמחו]
12 1,11	4:10	שָׁבוּעַ	/ ובשבו]עׄ החׄ[מישי] //
13 II,7		שָׁבוּעַ	/ בׄשׄבׄוׄעׄ היובל הׄראישׄון
13 III,17		שָׁבוּעַ	/ השבוע[
20 IV,1	xix12	שָׁבוּעַ	את ל]חם הבכורים שבעה֯ שבׄוׄ[עות
20 V,14	xxi12	שָׁבוּעַ	שבעה שבועות שבע / [פעמים
11 I,3		שְׁבוּעָה	]שבועהׄ[
20 V,7	xxi2	שֵׁבֶט	[שנים ע]שׄר שבטי ישראל
20 IV,2	xix13	שְׁבִיעִי	עד ממוחרת השבת ה]שביעית
20 V,15	xxi14	שְׁבִיעִי	עד ממו]חרת השבת השביעית/
20 XII,8	xlv16	שְׁבִיעִי	ויכבס ביו]ם השביעי / [בגדיו
20 XIV,2	l4	שְׁבִיעִי	יו]ם השביעי /
11 I,7		שבע	] משבׄ[יע
11 III,4		שבע	משביע לכול מׄ[לאכיו]
11 IV,1		שבע	/ ו]גדול[ ]משביע[
12 9,2	12:28	שֶׁבַע	*v*]*ac* ויהי בשב[עה לשבוע הששי]
17 I,8		שֶׁבַע	]ושבע °°[ ]משני רׄ[
17 III,5		שֶׁבַע	]עׄ שבע תהלי ברׄ[כות]
17 III,5		שֶׁבַע	[שב]ע תהׄ[לי גדל / צדקו]
17 III,8		שֶׁבַע	[ ]שבעה בש[בעה דברי פלא דברי רום]
17 III,8		שֶׁבַע	[ ]שבעה בש[בעה דברי פלא דברי רום]
17 30,2		שֶׁבַע	]מו°°° משבעה
17 30,3		שֶׁבַע	]°בר מׄשבׄיעי °מׄ[
17 30,6		שֶׁבַע	]בׄשׄי °°°°° שבעׄ[
20 I,11	xv2	שֶׁבַע	כבשים בני שנה]שבעה
20 I,13	xv4	שֶׁבַע	לשבעתׄ[ימי / המלואים יום ויום]
20 I,20	xv14	שֶׁבַע	למלו(אׄ) על נפשותמה שבעת ימׄי[ם] *va*]*c* [
20 IV,1	xix12	שֶׁבַע	את ל]חם הבכורים שבעה֯ שבׄוׄ[עות
20 IV,7	xx03	שֶׁבַע	וכבש]ים בני שנה שבעה
20 V,14	xxi12	שֶׁבַע	שבעה שבועות שבע / [פעמים
20 V,14	xxi12	שֶׁבַע	שבעה שבועות שבע / [פעמים
20 VIII,12		שֶׁבַע	ארבע אמות וגובהמה]שבע /
11 2ii,7		שִׁבְעִים	/ שבעים[
14 1ii13		שבת	וחיה רעה שבתה מן / [הארץ
20 IV,24	xx13	שבת	[ולוא ת]שׄבית ברית מלח ל֯עולם *vac*
20 V,15	xxi13	שַׁבָּת	עד ממו]חרת השבת השביעית/
20 VII,24	xxv3	שַׁבָּתוֹן	]ן֯ שבתון זכׄרון מקרא קודש /
11 I,10		שֵׁד	]אׄת השד[
11 II,3		שֵׁד	הרו]חותׄ[ ]והשדים [
11 II,4		שֵׁד	] אלהׄ [הש]דים וׄשׄ[ר המשט]מה /
11 V,12		שֵׁד	]הׄרע לו ש[ד
11 VI,7		שדד	מקטב ׳ישוד[צ]הרים
11 VI,3		שַׁדַּי	יושב]בסתר[עליון בצל] שדי / [יתלונן
14 1ii12		שִׁדָּפוֹן	שדׄפון וירקון לוא יראה בתבואתיה
17 I,5		שְׂדֵרָה=סְדֵרָה	] סדרו[תיו סדרו]תיו מבני[ת
11 V,7		שָׁוְא	פניך פני / [שו]וׄ
13 II,6		שוב	אשר / ישיבמה אליהמה
13 II,11		שוב	ועׄליו אׄמׄ[ר ו]עׄלי[ה] / למרום שובה
13 II,22		שוב	/ °°[ ]ר הוסרה מבליעל ותשׄ[וב
13 II,25		שׁוֹפָר	והעברתמה שו[פר ב]כׄוׄלׄ [א]רׄץ //
20 IV,25	xx15	שׁוֹק	ומן הכׄבׄשים את שוק הימׄין /
20 V,1	xxi02	שׁוֹק	י]היה שוק התרומה וחזה / [התנופה
20 39,1		שׁוֹק	]וׄשוקׄ[
20 XV,5	li12	שֹׁחַד	/ ולוא יקחו שוחד ו[לוא יטו משפט
12 7,3	5:2	שחת	[וכולם ה]שחיתו דרכם וׄחׄ[קתם]
20 XV,4	li11	שטר	/ שופטים ושוטרים[תתן לכה
13 II,10		שִׁיר	כאשר כתוב / עליו בשירׄי דויד
17 VII,9		שִׁיר	שיר[עולת השבת שתים עשרא
20 XII,4	xlv11	שכב	ואיש]כי ישכב / [עם אשתו
13 II,20		שכל	פשרו]ל[ה]שׄכילמׄה בכול קצי הע[ולם
14 1ii11		שכל	ואין משכלה בארצכם / ולוא מוחלה
20 IV,26	xx16	שְׁכֶם	ואת האזרוע [ע]ד עצם השכם /
20 V,3	xxi04	שְׁכֶם	ואת השכם הׄנשאר מן האזרוע /
11 VI,6		שכן	]ותחת / [כנפ]יו תשכון
20 XII,6	xlv13	שכן	את העיר אשר אני]שוכן בתוכה /
20 XII,17	xlvi4	שכן	אשר]אני שוכן[בתוכם]
21 1,6		שכן	בבית אשר]אׄשכין[שמי
20 XII,14		שֶׁל	]בׄה שלנחושת[ ]
11 VI,9		שָׁלוֹם	ותרא]הׄ שלום רשע[ים
13 II,16		שָׁלוֹם	רגלׄ[י] מבש[ר מ]שמיע שלום
17 X,4		שָׁלוֹם	[ו]כול ברכות שלומ[ו
17 X,3		שְׁלוֹם	[ש]לׄ[ו]מיו במשפטׄי[ ]רחמיו
12 2,4	4:14	שָׁלוֹשׁ	[בשבוע הריאשון בשלו]שׄה ל[שבוע]
20 XII,26	xlvi16	שָׁלוֹשׁ	רחוק מן העיר ש]לׄ[ושת // אלפים אמה
15 2,3		שלח	] לשלחׄ[
17 VII,9		שְׁלִישִׁי	בעשרים ואחד לחודש] השלישי
20 IV,3	xix15	שְׁלִישִׁי	שלישית ההין על / [המטה]
11 V,3		שלם	ר]פׄאל שלמ[ם אמן אמן סלה] *vac*
20 X,3	xxxvii12	שֶׁלֶם	ולוא יתע]רׄבו זבחי שלמי בני ישׄ[ראל]
11 II,2		שְׁלֹמֹה	]הׄ שלומה[ ]ויקרׄ[א
20 V,8	xxi4	שָׁם	הכוהנ]יׄם ישתו שמה ריאשונים /

Reference	Locus	Lemma	Context
11 II,8		שֵׁם	על]שמך נשען וקר[א] /
11 V,4		שֵׁם	ל]חש בשם יהו[ה
12 1,5	4:7	שֵׁם	]ותלד לו בן ויקרא את שמ[ו שת]
14 1ii2		שֵׁם	]וברכם בשם [אל] / [י]שראל
14 1ii4		שֵׁם	/ בשם אל עליון °[ ] וברוך שם קודש[ו]
14 1ii4		שֵׁם	/ בשם אל עליון °[ ] וברוך שם קודש[ו]
14 1ii15		שֵׁם	ושם קודשו נקרא עליכם //
15 4		שֵׁם	]בחדריכה בשמותם ב[
20 V,11	xxi8	שמח	וישמחו / [בני ישראל לפני יהוה ?*vac*
20 V,12	xxi9	שמח	ושמחו / [ביום הזה במועד
13 II,3		שמט	ועליו אמר וז]ה / [דבר השמטה] שמוט
13 II,3		שְׁמִטָּה	כיא קרא]שמטה / לא[ל
11 II,10		שָׁמַיִם	אשר עשה] את השמים / [ואת הארץ]
11 III,6		שָׁמַיִם	ויעיד א]ת / [כול הש]מים
11 IV,3		שָׁמַיִם	/ כול הארץ[ ] השמים ו[
11 V,5		שָׁמַיִם	קרא בכו]ל עת / אל השמ[ים
14 1ii8		שָׁמַיִם	ויפתח לכם את / אוצרו הטוב אשר בשמים
17 II,4		שְׁמִינִי	[למשכיל שיר עולת השבת ה]שמינ[ית
20 I,17	xv10	שֶׁמֶן	וחלת לחם שמן אחת ורקיק[אחד
20 II,3		שֶׁמֶן	]מן השמן /
20 IV,6	xx02	שֶׁמֶן	שלישית הה]ין שמן לאיל על הנסך הזה /
20 V,20	xxii03	שֶׁמֶן	בלול]ה בשמן הזה מחצית ההין /
20 V,22	xxii05	שֶׁמֶן	]השמן הזה יבעירו בנרות / [בה
13 II,16		שמע	רגל[י] מבש[ר מ]שמיע שלום
13 II,19		שמע	ומבשר] / טוב משמי[ע ישועה]
17 I,6		שמע	]שי קוד[ש ישמ]יעו תהלי[
17 V,5		שמע	[י]שמיעו [
17 V,7		שמע	]ם ישמעו°[
17 VIII,6		שמע	ישמ[י]עו מקול משא אלוהים[ ]
11 VI,11		שמר	כ[י מלאכיו]יצוה לך / לשומ[רך בדרכי]ך
12 9,5	12:29	שמר	[ויהוה ע]מכה ויש[מרכה מכול רע]
25 4,2		שמר	]°ת לשמרה °°°[
11 V,10		שֶׁמֶשׁ	ולוא[יאיר לך ה]שמש
20 IV,23	xx13	שֶׁמֶשׁ	ולוא תבו]א ע[ל]י[ו ה]שמש *vac*
20 XV,1	li5	שֶׁמֶשׁ	/ ובאה השמ[ש אחר יטהר
12 2,1	4:13	שָׁנָה	ותלד לו ב]ן בש[נה / השלישית
12 5,2	4:30	שָׁנָה	כיא] אלף ה[ש]נים[יום אחד
12 5,4	4:30	שָׁנָה	[על כן / לא כלה את]שני היום[הזה]
13 II,2		שָׁנָה	בשנת היובל [הזואת תשובו איש אל אחוזתו
13 II,9		שָׁנָה	כיא / הואה הקץ לשנת הרצון למלכי צדק
20 IV,7	xx03	שָׁנָה	וכבש]ים בני שנה שבעה
20 IV,12	xx2	שָׁנָה	]א וכבשים [בני] שנה ארבעה / [עשר]
20 V,13	xxi10	שָׁנָה	] שנה בשנה *vac* /
20 V,13	xxi10	שָׁנָה	] שנה בשנה *vac* /
20 I,15	xv6	שְׁנַיִם	[ואת ש]תי הכליות
20 IV,4	xix16	שְׁנַיִם	]ליהוה שנים [ע]שר אילים

Reference	Locus	Lemma	Context
20 IV,5	xx01	שְׁנַיִם	שנים / [עשרונים סולת בלולה בשמן]
20 V,18	xxii01	שְׁנַיִם	]ם אילים שנים/
20 VI,17	xxiii4	שְׁנַיִם	שעירי] / עזים שנים ל[
20 I,11	xv2	שָׂעִיר	ושעיר ע[זים לחטאת
20 III,9	xviii4	שָׂעִיר	] ושעי[ר עזים לחטאת]
20 IV,7	xx03	שָׂעִיר	ושעיר / [עזים אחד לחטאת
11 II,8		שען	על]שמך נשען וקר[א] /
17 26a,2		שַׁעַר	]שערי [
20 XI,16		שַׁעַר	מן הפנה הז]ואת עד ש[ער / דן
20 XII,19	xlvi6	שַׁעַר	על פי]פתחי השערי[ם כולמה]
13 II,10		שפט	]בקורב אלוהים ישפוט
13 II,11		שפט	ואשר א[מר עד מתי ת]שפוטו עוול
20 XV,4	li11	שפט	/ שופטים ושוטרים[תתן לכה
20 I,26	xvi03	שפך	ישפוכו סביב על ארבע פנות
20 IX,4	xxxii14	שפך	יהיו ה]מים נש[פכים והולכים אליה
11 II,4		שַׂר	] אלה [הש]דים וש[ר המשט]מה /
11 V,8		שַׂר	]שר הצבה
20 V,5	xxi06	שַׂר	]שרי האלפים
20 V,23	xxii2	שַׂר	]ם שרי האלפים עם נשיאי/
17 VII,4		שרת	]°ם בחוק יתכל[כ]לו לשרת °[
20 V,8	xxi4	שתה	הכוהנ]ים ישתו שמה ריאשונים / [והלויים
20 V,10	xxi7	שתה	יחלו לשתות יין חדש/
14 1ii12		תְּבוּאָה	שדפון וירקון לוא יראה בתבואתיה
17 VIII,3		תַּבְנִית	הוד [ ]כול תבנית רוחי פל[א]
17 IX,6		תַּבְנִית	]° פלא ותבנית חשני /
11 II,5		תְּהוֹם	א]שר[ ]ל תהו[ם]ך /
11 III,1		תְּהוֹם	[ ]תה[ ]התהומ[ות
11 IV,7		תְּהוֹם	אשר[יורידו]ך לתהום רבה
17 I,6		תְּהִלָּה	]שי קוד[ש ישמ]יעו תהלי[
17 III,5		תְּהִלָּה	]ע שבע תהלי בר[כות]
17 III,5		תְּהִלָּה	[שב]ע תה[לי גדל / צדקו]
17 III,6		תְּהִלָּה	[שבע]תהלי רו[ם מלכותו]
17 30,5		תְּהִלָּה	ת]הלי ברכות כבוד ה[
20 XII,6	xlv14	תָּוֶךְ	את העיר אשר אני]שוכן בתוכה /
20 XII,25	xlvi14	תָּוֶךְ	בתים ומקו]רים ובירות בתוכ[מה]/
20 XIV,21		תָּוֶךְ	[אשר יפול מהמה אל]תוכ[ו /
30 12,1		תּוֹלָדָה	] בתולד[ות
13 III,6		תּוֹרָה	/ התורה[ע]ליהמה[
25 4,1		תּוֹרָה	]ת התורה ואש[
11 VI,5		תַּחַת	]ותחת / [כנפ]יו תשכון
12 1,6	4:7	תַּחַת	[זרע ב]ארץ אחר תחת הבל
11 IV,8		תַּחְתִּי	/ ולשאול] התחתיה ומי[
11 V,9		תַּחְתִּי	יהוה [יוריד]ך / [לשאו]ל תחתית
14 1ii10		תִּירוֹשׁ	/ תנובות דגן תירוש ויצהר לרוב
20 V,11	xxi8	תִּירוֹשׁ	ביו]ם הזה יכפרו על התירוש
20 VII,23	xxiii8	תָּמִיד	עו]לת התמיד *vac* /

Reference	Parallel	Word	Context
21 1,5		תָּמִיד	ת]מֿיד מאת[בני ישראל
17 VI,8		תָּמִיד	מהל]לים תמיד כֿ[ו]ל[
20 III,22		תָּמִים	[שנים עשר כבשים בני שנה]תֿ[מי]מים
13 III,7		תמם	/ יתממֿ[ו] בֿליעל באשֿ[
14 1ii10		תְּנוּבָה	/ תֿנובות דגן תירוש ויצהר לרוב
20 VI,3	xxii9	תְּנוּפָה	את שוק הימין ואת חזי] / התנופה
11 I,5		תַּנִּין	]תֿנין [
11 VI,12		תַּנִּין	[ואפעה תד]רוך תרמו[ס כפיר] ותנין
17 X,3		תְּעוּדָה	ביקר ◦[ת]עודותיו
11 IV,12		תַּעֲנִית	ב]חושך בכֿ[ול / תעודות]תֿעניות
17 IX,7		תִּפְאֶרֶת	[פ]תֿילי תפֿארת[
11 IV,2		תַּקִּיף	/ והגדול בֿ[ ]תקיף ורֿ[

Reference	Parallel	Word	Context
11 IV,5		תַּקִּיף	/ ובחרון אפו[ישלח]עליך מלאך תקיף[
20 I,18	xv11	תְּרוּמָה	עם שוק התרו]מֿהֿ אשר לימין
20 V,1	xxi02	תְּרוּמָה	י]היה שוק התרומה וחזה / [התנופה
12 9,4	12:29	תֶּרַח	[ויאמר] לו תרח אֿ[ביו לך בשלום]
21 3,3		תַּרְנְגוֹל	/תרנגול לוֿאֿ תגד[לו
17 IV,7		תִּשְׁבָּחָה	בהוד תשבֿ[וחות
17 IV,7		תִּשְׁבָּחָה	]בֿדמֿוֿ[ת תשבו]חות
17 IV,8		תִּשְׁבָּחָה	]תֿשבוחות
17 X,5		תִּשְׁבָּחָה	ובהדר/ תשבוחותו בכול רקי[עי]ם
13 II,7		תֵּשַׁע	היובל הֿראישֿון אחֿרֿ תֿשֿ[עה ה]יובלים

ARAMAIC CONCORDANCE

Ref.	Verse	Lemma	Text
10 XXXI,5	38:28	אב	האיתי למטרא אב
10 XIV,7	29:13	אבד	ברכת א[בד
10 XXVII,7	36:12	אבד	/ ויאבדון מן מ̇[נדעא
10 XVIII,5	31:12	אבדון	הי]א עד / אבדון ת[אכל
10 XV,3	29:25	אבל	]בראש חילה וכגבר די א[בלין ינחם]
10 XXX,4	38:6	אבן	או מן הקים אבן חזיתה
10 XXXI,7	38:30	אבן	כא[בן] מ̇ין התקרמו מנה ואנפי °°°ל̇]
10 XXXVI,9	41:16	אבן	ולב̇[בה]°°[ ]ד̇ כאב[ן ו[
18 10i5		אבן	]°בן כול אבניהון /
18 18,2		אבן	ועליא שבעא דודין תפין על אב̇נ̇י̇]
18 32,6a		אבן	]ו̇י̇ד̇ אבן דמא°[
10 V,4	21:22	אבר	אבר̇[והי
10 XXXV,2	40:23	אגוגא	י̇ת̇רחץ די יקבלנה אג̇ו̇ג̇א̇ /
10 XIII,8	28:27	אדין	באדי̇נ̇[
10 XX,6	32:2	אדין	/ אדין רגז] אליהוא בר ברכאל בוזאה
10 XIII,3	28:22	אדן	/ באדנינא שמענא ש̇[מעה
10 XIV,5	29:11	אדן	/ ת[שמע אדן שבחתני ועין ח̇[זת
10 XXII,2	33:8	אדן	הך אמרת באדני וק̇[ל
10 XXVII,4	36:10	אדן	ויגלא / אדניהון למוסר וא[מר להון
10 XXVII,9	36:15	אדן	]ד̇י אדניהון /
10 XXXVII,7	42:5	אדן	למשמע אדן שמעתך
10 IX,1	24:24	או	התכ[פפו כיבלא יתקפ̇צ̇ון א̇[ו
10 IX,6	25:3	או	] או על מן לא תקו̇ם [
10 XXVI,2	35:7	או	או מא מידך יקבל]
10 XXX,3	38:6	או	או / על מא אשיה אתי̇ד̇ון
10 XXX,4	38:6	או	או מן הקים אבן חזיתה
10 XXXI,5	38:28	או	או מן / ילד̇ [ע]נני טלא
10 XXXI,8	38:31	או	או סיג נפילא ת[פתח]
10 XXXII,8	39:9	או	א̇[ו]היבית על / אוריך
10 XXXIII,8	39:27	או	או על מאמרך יתגב̇ה̇ נ̇שרא /
10 XXXIV,4	40:9	או	או / הא ד̇ר̇ע כאלה איתי לך
10 XXXIV,5	40:9	או	או בקל כותה תרעם /
10 XXXV,4	40:25	או	או בחבל תחרז לשנה
10 XXXV,6	40:27	או	או ימלל עמך בהתחננה לך
10 A,15		אוה	]ב̇ אוית[
10 XXIX,2	37:12	אזל	ואזלין לעבדיהון /
10 VI,5	22:6	אח	א[חיך מגן /
10 XXXVIII,5	42:11	אח	וכל אחוהי וכל ידעוהי
18 15,3		אח	]אחיהון עללין חלפהון ארבע מאה̇ צ̇]
10 IV,5	21:6	אחד	/ ותמהא אחד לי
10 XI,10	27:19	אחד	ש[כב ולא איתחד /
10 XVI,8	30:18	אחד	בסגיא]חיל יאחדון לבו̇[שי]
10 XIX,6	31:29	אחד	/ ואחדת א[

Ref.	Verse	Lemma	Text
10 XXII,4	33:10	אחד	/ ה̇ן עולין השכח אחד לי ה̇[יך
10 XXVII,2	36:8	אחד	א[ח̇ידין בחבלי מסכניא /
10 XXX,4	38:6	אחד	או / על מא אשיה אתי̇ד̇ון
10 XXXVIII,9	42:12	אחרי	/ ו̇אלהא ב̇ר̇ך̇ י̇ת̇ א̇[יו]ב באח̇[רי]ל[
10 XXV,1	34:24	אחרן	ויקים א[חרנין]
10 III,3	20:1	איוב	[ענא צפר נעמתיא ואמר לאיו]ב
10 VIIa,1	23:1	איוב	*v]ac* ענא איוב ואמ̇[ר]
10 XX,4	32:1	איוב	/ הוא איוב זכ̇[י
10 XXI,3	32:12	איוב	/ וארו לא איתי מנכון לא̇[יוב
10 XXIX,5	37:14	איוב	הצת דא איוב
10 XXXIV,2	40:6	איוב	/ ענא אלהא לאיוב וענ̇א̇ ו̇אמר לה
10 XXXVII,3	41:26	איוב	/ ענא איוב ואמר קדם אלהא
10 XXXVIII,2	42:9	איוב	ושמע א[ל]ה̇א בקלה די איוב
10 XXXVIII,3	42:10	איוב	ותב אלהא ל̇איוב̇ ברחמין /
10 XXXVIII,5	42:11	איוב	ואתין לות / איוב כל רחמוהי
10 XXXVIII,9	42:12	איוב	/ ו̇אלהא ב̇ר̇ך̇ י̇ת̇ א̇[יו]ב באח̇[רי]ל[
18 33,2		איל	]°יא ואיליא ג[
10 XXXIII,2	39:20	אימה	/ בס[°]רוהי אימה ודחלה
10 VI,4	22:5	איתי	ל[א איתי /
10 IX,5	25:3	איתי	האיתי רחצן להש[
10 XXI,3	32:12	איתי	/ וארו לא איתי מנכון לא̇[יוב
10 XXIII,10	33:32	איתי	/ הן א[י̇ת̇י̇ מ[לין
10 XXXI,5	38:28	איתי	האיתי למטרא אב
10 XXXIV,5	40:9	איתי	או / הא ד̇ר̇ע כאלה איתי לך
10 V,6	21:25	אכל	ל[א אכל
10 XV,8	30:4	אכל	]ב̇אישה די אכל[ו
10 XVIII,1	31:8	אכל	/ יאכ̇[ל
10 XXXVIII,5	42:11	אכל	ואכלו / עמה לחם בביתה
18 7,2		אכל	]°א די להוון אכלין[
18 25,6		אכל	]ון ויכלון ויש[תון
10 XV,6	30:2	אכף	ידיהון]ל̇א הוא לי צבין ובאכפי̇[הון
18 20,1		אל	כו[ל יום שביעי קודם אל דכר̇[נא
10 IV,8	21:9	אלה	/ אלהא עליהו[ן
10 V,2	21:21	אלה	ארו מא]צ̇בו לאלהא בביתה ו̇[
10 V,3	21:22	אלה	הלא̇[להא
10 VI,1	22:2	אלה	לא[להא /
10 VII,3	22:17	אלה	/ לנא אלה[א
10 VIII,2	24:12	אלה	/ תקבל אלהא[
10 IX,4	25:2	אלה	ארו ש[לטן ורבו עם אלהא
10 IX,7	25:4	אלה	]א̇להא ומא יצדק̇[
10 X,8	27:2	אלה	]ואמר חי אלהא[
10 XI,1	27:11	אלה	בי̇ד̇ אלהא ועבד /
10 XIX,3	31:28	אלה	כד[ב̇ת / לאלהא מעל̇[א

/ להן אלהא חיבנא ולא א̊[נש	אלה	32:13	**10** XXI,5
/ ארו רב אלהא מן אנשא̇[	אלה	33:12	**10** XXII,6
/ א]רו בחדא ימלל אלה[א	אלה	33:14	**10** XXII,8
ב]ת̇ר אלהא *vac*	אלה	34:9	**10** XXIV,3
]ח̊ס לאלהא מן שקר /	אלה	34:10	**10** XXIV,4
]הכען צדא אלהא / ישקר	אלה	34:12	**10** XXIV,6
ולא אמר[ין אן הוא]אלהא / די עבדנה	אלה	35:10	**10** XXVI,4
הא אלהא רב הוא	אלה	36:26	**10** XXVIII,3
וקום הסתכל בגבורת אלהא /	אלה	37:14	**10** XXIX,5
/ הת]נדע מא שויא אלהא עליה֯ו֯ן	אלה	37:15	**10** XXIX,6
ויזעק[ו]ן כחדה כל מלאכי אלהא /	אלה	38:7	**10** XXX,5
/ ענא אלהא לאיוב וענ̇א̊ ו̇אמר לה	אלה	40:6	**10** XXXIV,2
או / הא ד֯ר֯ע כאלה איתי לך	אלה	40:9	**10** XXXIV,5
/ ענא איוב ואמר קדם אלהא	אלה	42:1	**10** XXXVII,3
ו]ע̇ב̇ד̊ו̇[כדי אמר להון] / אלהא	אלה	42:6	**10** XXXVIII,2
ושמע א[ל]ה̇א בקלה די איוב	אלה	42:9	**10** XXXVIII,2
ותב אלהא ֯לאיוב֯ ברחמין /	אלה	42:10	**10** XXXVIII,3
כל באישתה די / היתי אלהא עלוהי	אלה	42:11	**10** XXXVIII,7
/ ו̊א̇להא ב̇ר̇ך̇ י̇ת̇ א̊[יו]ב באח̇[רי]ל[	אלה	42:12	**10** XXXVIII,9
/ אלין מלהתב̇[ה פתגם	אלין	32:1	**10** XX,3
]אלין [	אלין		**10** A,14
א]ל̇ן̊ פרזיא ליד שו̇ר̊[א	אלן		**18** 6,2
]° מן אלן וערבליא די /	אלן		**18** 12i1
]° אלן [	אלן		**18** 34,1
וכ]ולהון תלתין ותרין אלפין	אלף		**18** 18,3
אמתי לנכר[י	אמה	19:15	**10** II,4
] מאתין ותמנין אמ̊[ין	אמה		**18** 6,1
פ]ותיה אמה ותרתי עשר̊[ה	אמה		**18** 8,2
]אמין עמודין שבעה ת̊[	אמה		**18** 9,2
אורכיהון ופו]ת̊יהון אמין שת בשת [	אמה		**18** 9,3
]ת̊והי ארבעא רמין אמין א̇[רבע	אמה		**18** 11,1
ורומה אמין תרתי[ן	אמה		**18** 11,3
]א̇חאך להון ולא יה[ימנון	אמן	29:24	**10** XV,1
ל]ח̇ם ואמרת /	אמר	22:8	**10** VI,7
/ אמרין ל[אלהא	אמר	22:17	**10** VII,2
v[*ac* ענא איוב ואמ̇[ר]	אמר	23:1	**10** VIIa,1
]ואסתכ̇ל מא יאמר ל̇י /	אמר	23:5	**10** VIIa,6
/ קבל למא̇[מר	אמר	24:15	**10** VIII,6
ענא איוב ואמ]ר̊ העד̇[רת	אמר	26:1	**10** IX,10
]ואמר חי אלהא[	אמר	27:1	**10** X,8
/ ואמר לבני[אנשא	אמר	28:28	**10** XIII,9
די למה תאמרו̊ן[	אמר	32:13	**10** XXI,4
הך אמרת באדני וק̇[ל	אמר	33:8	**10** XXII,2
/ ו̇יאמר פצהי מן חב[לא	אמר	33:24	**10** XXIII,1
ויאמ[ר	אמר	33:27	**10** XXIII,5
ארו אמר לא / ישנא גבר מ̊י[	אמר	34:9	**10** XXIV,2
ולא אמר[ין אן הוא]אלהא / די עבדנה	אמר	35:10	**10** XXVI,4
הן תאמר[ ]	אמר	35:14	**10** XXVI,9
ויגלא / אדניהון למוסר וא[מר להון	אמר	36:10	**10** XXVII,4
והוא אמר ישמעון לה	אמר	37:12	**10** XXIX,2
ואמרת עד תנא / ולא תוסף̇[	אמר	38:11	**10** XXX,8
ולקל קרנא יאמר האח	אמר	39:25	**10** XXXIII,5
/ ענא אלהא לאיוב וענ̇א̊ ו̇אמר לה	אמר	40:6	**10** XXXIV,2
/ ענא איוב ואמר קדם אלהא	אמר	42:1	**10** XXXVII,3
]א̇ ואמר לי לעשרין ושת °[	אמר		**18** 15,4
]א̊מר לי חזא אנתה ד̇[י	אמר		**18** 18,5
ויהבו לה גבר אמרה חדה /	אמרה	42:11	**10** XXXVIII,7
/ אן הוית במעבדי ארעא	אן	38:4	**10** XXX,2
/ א]רו אנה ש֯י֯זבת לענא מן °[	אנה	29:12	**10** XIV,6
/ מ̇לי אף אנה	אנה	32:10	**10** XXI,1
/ וא]ח̇וה מלי אף א[נה	אנה	32:17	**10** XXI,9
/ [זכ]י אנה ולא חטא לי ונקא̊[	אנה	33:9	**10** XXII,3
תב]ח̇ר ולא אנה [	אנה	34:33	**10** XXV,9
שמע נא ואנה אמלל	אנה	42:4	**10** XXXVII,6
/ תסוק לשמיא גאותה ואנ]פה לענניא[	אנף	20:6	**10** III,8
א]נ̊פוהי /	אנף	22:8	**10** VI,8
ב]א̊פי הן ימל̇[לן	אנף	27:3	**10** X,10
/ ויחזא אנפוהי באסיא̇[	אנף	33:26	**10** XXIII,4
ויסת]ר̊ אנפוהי	אנף	34:29	**10** XXV,5
/ על אנפי מין	אנף	37:10	**10** XXIX,1
/ על כל די ברא יפקדנון על אנפי תבל	אנף	37:12	**10** XXIX,3
כא[בן] מ̇ין התקרמו מנה ואנפי °°ל̊[	אנף	38:30	**10** XXXI,8
/ ובחיל ינפק לאנפי חרב	אנף	39:21	**10** XXXIII,3
ולא / יזוע ולא יתוב מן אנפי חרב	אנף	39:22	**10** XXXIII,4
/ כל אנש ד̇י[	אנש	19:19	**10** II,8
רמתא ובו]ר̇ אנש תולע̇[תא *vac*	אנש	25:6	**10** IX,9
]אנש רשיעין /	אנש	27:13	**10** XI,3
אנ]ש /	אנש	28:13	**10** XII,9
א]נש / ביתי	אנש	31:31	**10** XIX,7
/ להן אלהא חיבנא ולא א̊[נש	אנש	32:13	**10** XXI,5
/ ארו רב אלהא מן אנשא̇[	אנש	33:12	**10** XXII,6
vac כען אנש̇[	אנש	34:10	**10** XXIV,4
]אנש ישלם לה /	אנש	34:11	**10** XXIV,5
]ך̇ אנש רשיעיא	אנש	34:30	**10** XXV,6
/ ולבר אנש צדקתך	אנש	35:8	**10** XXVI,3
ו]כ̇ל אנשא עלוהי חזין	אנש	36:25	**10** XXVIII,2
ובני אנשא / מרחיק̇[עלוה]̇י יבקון	אנש	36:25	**10** XXVIII,2
די לא אנש בה	אנש	38:26	**10** XXXI,4
ו]ל[א] / עלל לה כול א[נש	אנש		**18** 16ii&17i4
]וכול אנשא די יח̊[	אנש		**18** 26,1
]א̊מר לי חזא אנתה ד̇[י	אנתה		**18** 18,5
/ רוח המכת לאנתתי[	אנתה	19:17	**10** II,6

פ]תיא / לבי בא[נתה	אנתה	31:9	10 XVIII,2
אנתה / לחברתה חענן ולא יתפ[ר]שן	אנתה	41:8	10 XXXVI,2
/ ויחזא אנפוהי באסיא[	אסא	33:26	10 XXIII,4
/ ואף עם אסירין ב[זיקין	אסר	36:8	10 XXVII,2
/ אסר נא כגבר חלצ[י]ך[	אסר	38:3	10 XXX,1
אסר / נא כגבר חלציך	אסר	40:7	10 XXXIV,2
/ ואף ע[ל	אף	32:3	10 XX,8
/ מלי אף אנה	אף	32:10	10 XXI,1
/ וא]חוה מלי אף א[נה	אף	32:17	10 XXI,9
/ ואף עם אסירין ב[זיקין	אף	36:8	10 XXVII,2
אף בהון ימרק ענ[נ]ין]	אף	37:11	10 XXIX,1
פתגם האף / תעדא דינה	אף	40:8	10 XXXIV,3
כבחכה יזיב אפה	אף	40:24	10 XXXV,3
התשוא / זמם באפה	אף	40:26	10 XXXV,5
ומא אפו א[	אפו	17:15	10 I,1
/ ארו אפו לא ת[קצר רוחי	אפו	21:4	10 IV,3
מ]ן אפו יתיבנני פתגם ויש[וא	אפו	24:25	10 IX,2
דהב]טב כולה ארבע רגלוה[י	ארבע		18 8,1
/ ארב[עה	ארבע		18 10ii1
]תוהי ארבעא רמין אמין א[רבע	ארבע		18 11,1
]תוהי ארבעא רמין אמין א[רבע	ארבע		18 11,1
]בארבע רגלוהי ונשט תורא ◦[	ארבע		18 13,1
]אחיהון עללין חלפהון ארבע מאה צ[	ארבע		18 15,3
פ]ליג לתמנין וארבעה כהנין ש[	ארבע		18 20,3
שביא די בה]ון וארבעת עשר כה[נין	ארבע		18 20,4
]◦על ארבע קרנת מדבח[א] /	ארבע		18 22,1
]◦א די ארבעת[	ארבע		18 24,3
]על ארבע ש[	ארבע		18 32,5
]לארבע /	ארבע		18 32,8
ארע]ה ארו מבע רשיע[ין]	ארו	20:5	10 III,6
/ ארו אפו לא ת[קצר רוחי	ארו	21:4	10 IV,3
ארו ידעת[	ארו	21:27	10 V,7
]ארו קשט ודת[	ארו	23:7	10 VIIa,8
/ אתר ערימותא א[רו	ארו	28:20	10 XIII,1
/ בה ארו הוא יצ[	ארו	28:23	10 XIII,4
/ א]רו אנה שיזבת לענא מן ◦[	ארו	29:12	10 XIV,6
] ארו / עבד[ני	ארו	31:15	10 XVIII,7
ארו סברת[	ארו	32:11	10 XXI,1
/ וארו לא איתי מנכון לא[יוב	ארו	32:12	10 XXI,3
/ ארו רב אלהא מן אנשא[	ארו	33:12	10 XXII,6
ארו בכל פ[תגמוהי	ארו	33:13	10 XXII,7
/ א]רו בחדא ימלל אלה[א	ארו	33:14	10 XXII,8
ארו אמר לא / ישנא גבר מ[	ארו	34:9	10 XXIV,2
ארו מ[	ארו	34:33	10 XXV,8
ארו שוא יש[מע אלהא	ארו	35:13	10 XXVI,8
]◦ לה א[רו	ארו	35:14	10 XXVI,10

ארו התרוממו	ארו	36:9	10 XXVII,3
ד]כר ארו רברבין עבדוהי ד[י / חזו המ[ון	ארו	36:24	10 XXVIII,1
ארו / עננ[י] מין ימנא]	ארו	36:27	10 XXVIII,4
ארו (◦)בהון ידין ע[ממין] /	ארו	36:31	10 XXVIII,8
]ארו הוא ידע מדע[א	ארו	37:16	10 XXIX,8
]ארו[	ארו		10 A,17
]ארחך /	ארח	22:3	10 VI,2
]ון בחרת ארחי והוית ר[אש	ארח	29:25	10 XV,2
]ולא / כארחי השתלמת	ארח	33:27	10 XXIII,6
אר]חה ובכל שבילוהי לא הסתכ[לו]	ארח	34:27	10 XXV,3
וארח לעננין קלילין	ארח	38:25	10 XXXI,3
א[ו]היבית על / אוריך	ארי	39:9	10 XXXII,9
]ן וארמלתה לא /	ארמלה	27:15	10 XI,6
/ בפ]ם ארמלה הוית לצלו[	ארמלה	29:13	10 XIV,8
/ לקצוי ארעא י◦[	ארע	28:24	10 XIII,5
ומרא[ ]הוא ארעא עבד /	ארע	34:13	10 XXIV,7
הן למכתש / הן לארעא	ארע	37:13	10 XXIX,4
/ אן הוית במעבדי ארעא	ארע	38:4	10 XXX,2
]כנפ[י]ארע[א]	ארע	38:13	10 XXX,10
ותשוב קדמוהי על ארעא	ארע	38:24	10 XXXI,2
להנחתה על ארע / מדבר	ארע	38:26	10 XXXI,3
]ארעא[	ארע	38:33	10 XXXI,10
ומדרה בארע מליחה /	ארע	39:6	10 XXXII,5
]תין ויפלגון יתה בארע[	ארע	40:30	10 XXXV,9
] ארעי [	ארעי		18 1,2
או / על מא אשיה אתיגדון	אש	38:6	10 XXX,4
וכען עלי תתאשד / [נפשי	אשד	30:16	10 XVI,5
]ת / אשה ישנקנה	אשה	33:25	10 XXIII,2
בלשני אשה ירטון	אשה	41:11	10 XXXVI,5
ליום קרב ואשתדר [	אשתדור	38:23	10 XXXI,1
ולנקשת זין וזעקת אשתדור / יחדה	אשתדור	39:25	10 XXXIII,6
ו]שויה על נורא ואיתי קמח סולת[	אתא		18 13,3
[כחדה / י]תון חתפוהי וכבשו[	אתא	19:12	10 II,2
לס]תרי יתון	אתא	30:13	10 XVI,1
וכע]ן בתקף שחני יתון /	אתא	30:14	10 XVI,2
]◦◦◦[ ]ה[ ]א אייתי /	אתא	40:13	10 XXXIV,10
ואתין לות / איוב כל רחמוהי	אתא	42:11	10 XXXVIII,4
באישתה די / היתי אלהא עלוהי	אתא	42:11	10 XXXVIII,7
] מן את[רה	אתר	18:4	10 I,8
ואתא עד]אתר מדרה	אתר	23:3	10 VIIa,4
את]רי / ספירא[	אתר	28:6	10 XII,2
/ אתר ערימותא א[רו	אתר	28:20	10 XIII,1
וירמא המון באת[ר	אתר	34:26	10 XXV,2
מן פרס / ע[נניא די אתרגו]שתה	אתרגושתא	36:29	10 XXVIII,7
]באיש *v]ac*	באיש		10 III,1
/ בבאיש[תהון	באיש	24:16	10 VIII,8

10 XI,11	27:20	באיש	]כמין באיש[
10 XV,8	30:3	באיש	]באישה די אכל[ו
10 XVI,3	30:14	באיש	תחות]באישה אתכפפת
10 XIX,4	31:29	באיש	ה]ללת / על באישתה[
10 XXVI,8	35:12	באיש	ולא[יענא מן קדם ג]אות / [ב]אישין
10 XXVII,4	36:10	באיש	]הן יתובון מן באישתהון /
10 XXXVIII,6	42:11	באיש	ונחמוהי על כל באישתה
10 A,17		באיש	]באיש[
10 XX,2	31:4	באשוש	/ באשושה
10 XXIX,7	37:17	בדיל	[ב]דיל די לבושך /
10 XXXVIII,3	42:9	בדיל	ושבק / להון חטאיהון בדילה
18 16i2		בוץ	]ל בוצ /
10 XII,7	28:10	בזע	טי]פין / בז[ע
10 XV,2	29:25	בחר	]ון בחרת ארחי והוית ר[אש
10 XXV,9	34:33	בחר	תב]חר ולא אנה [
10 XXXII,7	39:8	בחר	ויבחר לה טורין לרע[יה
10 XXXI,6	38:29	בטן	ומן בטן מן נפק גלידא
10 XXXVI,2	41:8	בין	ורוח ל[א י]נעול בינה(ו)ן
10 XXXVI,4	41:10	בין	עטישתה תדלק / נורא בין עינוהי
10 XXXII,8	39:9	בית	א[ו]היבית על / אוריך
10 XXXVI,7	41:14	בית	בצורה יבית תקפה
10 II,4	19:15	בית	] / ביתי
10 IV,7	21:9	בית	בתיהון[
10 V,2	21:21	בית	ארו מא]צבו לאלהא בביתה ו[
10 XIX,8	31:31	בית	א]נש / ביתי
10 XXXII,5	39:6	בית	די שוית דחשת ביתה
10 XXXVIII,6	42:11	בית	ואכלו / עמה לחם בביתה
18 18,6		בית	] לבתי חדוא ול[
10 I,4	18:1	בלדד	*vac* ענ]א בלדד שוחא[ה
10 IX,3	25:1	בלדד	*va[c* ענא בלד[ד שוחאה ואמר]
10 XXV,7	34:32	בלחוד	]תו לה איחל בלחודוהי /
18 9,4		בנא	]בא ובנא בנין עלוי עמ[
18 9,4		בנין	]בא ובנא בנין עלוי עמ[
18 9,5		בנין	]בא וכול בנינא דן [
10 I,6	18:3	בעיר	לב]עירא דמינא[
10 XXVI,6	35:11	בעיר	די פרשנא מן בע[ירי ארעא
10 XXXVII,4	42:2	בצר	ולא יתבצר מנך תקף וחכמה /
10 XXVIII,3	36:25	בקא	ובני אנשא / מרחיק[עלוה]י יבקון
10 XXXIII,2	39:21	בקע	וחפר בבקע וירוט ויחדא /
10 XXXII,9	39:10	בקעה	וילג[ן] בבקעה / בתריך
10 IX,9	25:6	בר	רמתא וב]ר אנש תולע[תא *vac*
10 XIII,9	28:28	בר	/ ואמר לבני[אנשא
10 XXVI,3	35:8	בר	/ ולבר אנש צדקתך
10 XXVIII,2	36:25	בר	ובני אנשא / מרחיק[עלוה]י יבקון
10 XXXI,9	38:32	בר	]∘∘∘א על בניה תיאש ∘[
10 XXXII,2	39:3	בר	ילדן בניהן ויפלטן /
10 XXXII,3	39:4	בר	יקשן בניהן ויפק[ן
18 7,1		בר	] על כול זרע בני [
18 20,2		בר	]לברא מן היכלא לימין מערבה[
10 XXIX,3	37:12	ברא	/ על כל די ברא יפקדנון על אנפי תבל
10 XXXII,4	39:5	ברחרין	מן שלח פראה ברחרין
10 XXXVIII,9	42:12	ברך	/ ואלהא ברך ית א[יו]ב באח[רי]ל[
18 23ii4		ברך	ומברכין ב∘[
10 XIV,7	29:13	ברכה	ברכת א[בד
18 16ii&17i1		ברכה	// ברכה תניני[
10 XXXV,8	40:29	ברת	ותקטרנה בחוטא לבנתך
10 XXXVI,8	41:15	בשר	קפלי בשרה דבקין נסיכי[ן בה] /
18 13,6		בשר	]א ובשרא מתערב כחדא[
18 25,4		בשר	]∘בי בשרה די∘[
10 XXIV,3	34:9	בתר	ב]תר אלהא *vac*
10 XXXII,7	39:8	בתר	ו]בתר כל ירוק / ירדף
10 XXXII,10	39:10	בתר	וילג[ן] בבקעה / בתריך
10 XXXIV,7	40:11	גאה	וחזא כל גאה והשפלה וכל /
10 XXVI,7	35:12	גאוה	ולא[יענא מן קדם ג]אות / [ב]אישין
10 XXXVI,1	40:31	גב	/ גבוה[י] ∘[ ]והי ש[י]ר[יא
10 XXXIII,8	39:27	גבה	או על מאמרך יתגבה נשרא /
10 XXIX,5	37:14	גבורה	הסתכל בגבורת אלהא /
10 XXIX,7	37:16	גבורה	/ התנ]דע להלבש(ו)א עננה גבורה
10 XIV,2	29:8	גבר	/ ו]חזוני עלומין טשו וגברין ח∘[
10 XV,3	29:25	גבר	]בראש חילה וכגבר די א[בלין ינחם]
10 XXIII,7	33:29	גבר	ג]בר / זמן תרין תלתה
10 XXIV,3	34:9	גבר	ארו אמר לא / ישנא גבר מ[
10 XXV,10	34:34	גבר	מ]לין וגב[ר
10 XXX,1	38:3	גבר	/ אסר נא כגבר חלצ[י]ך[
10 XXXIV,3	40:7	גבר	אסר / נא כגבר חלציך
10 XXXVIII,7	42:11	גבר	ויהבו לה גבר אמרה חדה /
10 XXXVIII,8	42:11	גבר	/ וגבר קדש חד די דהב *vac*
18 13,5		גו	רו]בע סתא ונסך לגוא מורכי[ותא
18 14ii3		גו	/ גוא כפרה וכלילא שתיתי[א
10 XXXIV,6	40:10	גוה	/ העדי נא גוה ורם רוח
18 14ii1		גפן	// גפן כדי פרש מן לולבי[א
10 V,3	21:21	גזר	מני]ן ירחוהי גזירין
10 XXXV,2	40:23	גיף	/ ירדנא גאפה
10 XXX,9	38:11	גל	ג]ללי[ך
10 XXVII,4	36:10	גלא	ויגלא / אדניהון למוסר וא[מר להון
10 XXXI,6	38:29	גליד	ומן בטן מן נפק גלידא
10 XXXVI,6	41:13	גמר	נפשה גמרין תגסא
10 XXXVI,6	41:13	גסא	נפשה גמרין תגסא
10 V,5	21:24	גרם	]ן גרמוהי
10 XVI,7	30:17	גרם	בלילא] גרמי יקדון
18 16ii&17i3		ד־	כ]הניא מקבלין / מן ידהון דפש[טו
18 23ii2		ד־	/ ודשלם ∘[

Reference	Job	Word	Context
10 XXIII,9	33:31	דא	הצת דא [
10 XXIX,5	37:14	דא	הצת דא איוב
18 30,2		דבח	]ון עוד לויא דבח[ין
10 XIV,4	29:10	דבק	/ קל סגנין הטמרו לחנך דב[ק
10 XXXVI,2	41:8	דבק	חדה] / לחדה ידבקן
10 XXXVI,8	41:15	דבק	קפלי בשרה דבקין נסיכ[ן בה] /
10 XXXV,7	40:28	דבר	ותדברנה לעבד עלם
18 28,1		דבר	]להוון דברין ב[
10 I,7	18:4	דברה	] העל דב[רתך
10 XXXIV,4	40:8	דברה	ותחיבנני על דברת די תזכא
10 XXXVIII,8	42:11	דהב	/ וגבר קדש חד די דהב *vac*
18 10i2		דהב	]ורא דן דהב טב /
18 10i6		דהב	]סוך חפא דהב /
18 11,4		דהב	]נאמה וכולה דהב טב די[
18 18,2		דוד	ועליא שבעא דודין תפין על אבני[
10 XXXIII,2	39:20	דחלה	/ בס[ס]והי אימה ודחלה
10 XXXIII,3	39:22	דחלה	יחאך על דחלא
10 XV,7	30:3	דחשת	כ]פן רעין הוא ירק ד[חשת
10 XXXII,5	39:6	דחשת	די שוית דחשת ביתה
10 II,8	19:19	די	/ כל אנש די[
10 III,5	20:4	די	יד]עת מן עלמא מן ד[י]
10 VII,1	22:16	די	/ די מיתו ב[לא
10 VIIa,2	23:2	די	אף יומא דן] מן טלל שעותי די /
10 XIV,7	29:12	די	/ [ד]י לא עדר להו[ן
10 XV,3	29:25	די	]בראש חילה וכגבר די א[בלין ינחם]
10 XV,8	30:4	די	]באישה די אכלו[
10 XXI,4	32:13	די	די למה תאמרון[
10 XXV,1	34:24	די	ר]ברבין די לא סוף
10 XXVI,5	35:10	די	ולא אמר[ין אן הוא]אלהא / די עבדנה די
10 XXVI,5	35:10	די	ודי חלק לנא ל[ ]ס
10 XXVI,6	35:11	די	די פרשנא מן בע[ירי ארעא
10 XXVII,9	36:15	די	]די אדניהון /
10 XXVIII,1	36:24	די	ד]כר ארו רברבין עבדוהי די / חזו המ[ון די
10 XXVIII,4	36:26	די	ומנין שנוהי די לא סוף
10 XXIX,3	37:12	די	/ על כל די ברא יפקדנון על אנפי תבל די
10 XXIX,7	37:17	די	[ב]דיל די לבושך /
10 XXXI,1	38:23	די	/ ד[י מנעת ל[ע]דן ע[קת]א
10 XXXI,4	38:26	די	די לא אנש בה
10 XXXII,5	39:6	די	די שוית דחשת ביתה
10 XXXIV,4	40:8	די	ותחיבנני על דברת די תזכא
10 XXXV,2	40:23	די	יתרחץ די יקבלנה אגוגא /
10 XXXV,10	40:31	די	]גון די נונין[
10 XXXVII,3	42:2	די	ידעת די כלא / תכול למעבד
10 XXXVIII,2	42:9	די	ושמע א[ל]הא בקלה די איוב
10 XXXVIII,4	42:10	די	/ ויהב לה חד תרין בכל די הוא לה
10 XXXVIII,6	42:11	די	באישתה די / היתי אלהא עלוהי
10 XXXVIII,8	42:11	די	/ וגבר קדש חד די דהב *vac*
18 7,2		די	]סא די להוון אכלין[
18 11,2		די	]ינא ליד כותלא די סחר לס[
18 11,4		די	]נאמה וכולה דהב טב די[
18 11,6		די	ד]י עמודין סחר מן תרע לת[רע
18 12i1		די	]ס מן אלן וערבליא די /
18 12i2		די	]יא פרישא ודי מעשריא /
18 12ii8		די	/ די ס[
18 14ii1		די	// גפן כדי פרש מן לולבי[א
18 15,1		די	]משרתא עוד להן די להוה[
18 15,2		די	]א וכול די להוון משצין שבעתיהו[ן
18 18,5		די	]אמר לי חזא אנתה ד[י
18 19,1		די	]ה תרעיא די לקובל היכלא ל[
18 20,5		די	תרתי לחמ]א די הות לבונתא [עליהון
18 24,3		די	]סא די ארבעת[
18 24,7		די	]כול די ל[
18 25,4		די	]סבי בשרה דיס[
18 26,1		די	]וכול אנשא די יה[
18 30,5		די	]ן מא די ל[
18 37,4		די	]די ישר[
10 V,4	21:22	דין	מנדע ו]הוא רמיא מדין
10 XXVIII,8	36:31	דין	ארו [ס]בהון ידין ע[ממין] /
18 24,2		דין	]ה דין מן כול שס[
10 XVIII,6	31:13	דין	]הן אתקצרת / בדין עב[די
10 XXXIV,4	40:8	דין	פתגם האף / תעדא דינה
10 XXVIII,1	36:24	דכר	ד]כר ארו רברבין עבדוהי די / חזו המ[ון
18 20,1		דכרן	כו]ל יום שביעי קודם אל דכר[נא
10 XXXVI,3	41:10	דלק	עטישתה תדלק / נורא בין עינוהי
10 I,6	18:3	דמא	לב]עירא דמינא[
18 14ii4		דמות	/ שביעיא כדמות נצ ורד[
10 V,5	21:25	דן	דן ימות בנפ[ש
10 XVIII,3	31:11	דנא	ד[נא רגז /
18 9,5		דן	]בא וכול בנינא דן [
18 10i2		דן	]ורא דן דהב טב /
18 21,5		דן	]א *vac* וכדן /
10 X,4	26:13	דנח	הד]נח
10 XIX,1	31:26	דנח	/ דנח ולס[הרא
18 26,3		דנח	]א עד תדנח שמ[שא
18 27,4		דנח	עד ת[דנח שמשא וכו[ל
18 21,6		דרג	]ס דרגא /
18 6,3		דרום	] דרומא ופלג[
10 XII,4	28:8	דרך	לא הד]רכה / תנין[
10 XXXIV,5	40:9	דרע	או / הא דרע כאלה איתי לך
10 XXX,6	38:8	דש	/ התסוג בדשין ימא
10 VIIa,8	23:7	דת	]ארו קשט ודת[
10 XXX,8	38:10	דת	ותשוה / לה תחומין ודת[לימא נגר]ין

/ ולהנפקה צמחי דתאה	דתא	38:27	**10** XXXI,5
]העמי לשאול ת[נחתון]	ה־	17:15	**10** I,2
] העל דב[רתך	ה־	18:4	**10** I,7
הלא[להא	ה־	21:22	**10** V,3
האיתי רחצן להש[	ה־	25:3	**10** IX,5
ענא איוב ואמ]ר הע[רת	ה־	26:2	**10** IX,10
]הכען צדא אלהא / ישקר	ה־	34:12	**10** XXIV,6
הבשקר[	ה־	34:17	**10** XXIV,10
] הביומיך מנית /	ה־	38:12	**10** XXX,9
האיתי למטרא אב	ה־	38:28	**10** XXXI,5
היבא ראמ[א ל]מפלחך	ה־	39:9	**10** XXXII,8
א[ו]היבית על / אוריך	ה־	39:9	**10** XXXII,8
] התזיענה בתקף[	ה־	39:20	**10** XXXIII,1
המן חכמתך יסתער נצא	ה־	39:26	**10** XXXIII,7
פתגם האף / תעדא דינה	ה־	40:8	**10** XXXIV,3
התגד / תנין בחכא	ה־	40:24	**10** XXXV,3
התשוא / זמם באפה	ה־	40:25	**10** XXXV,4
הימלל / עמך בניח	ה־	40:26	**10** XXXV,5
היקים / קים עמך	ה־	40:27	**10** XXXV,6
התחאך / בה כצפר	ה־	40:28	**10** XXXV,7
הא כ[ל	הא	33:29	**10** XXIII,7
הא אלהא רב הוא	הא	36:26	**10** XXVIII,3
או / הא דרע כאלה איתי לך	הא	40:9	**10** XXXIV,5
ולקל קרנא יאמר האח	האח	39:25	**10** XXXIII,5
ומרא ה]בלא / [לא] יצתנה	הבל	35:13	**10** XXVI,8
וזוי והדר ויקר תלבש /	הדר	40:10	**10** XXXIV,6
מנדע ו]הוא רמיא מדין	הוא	21:22	**10** V,4
/ בה ארו הוא יצ[	הוא	28:23	**10** XIII,4
והוא חטא[	הוא	31:11	**10** XVIII,4
ומרא[ ]הוא ארעא עבד /	הוא	34:13	**10** XXIV,7
הא אלהא רב הוא	הוא	36:26	**10** XXVIII,3
והוא אמר ישמעון לה	הוא	37:12	**10** XXIX,2
]ארו הוא ידע מדע[א	הוא	37:16	**10** XXIX,8
/ והוא מלך על כל רחש *vac*	הוא	41:26	**10** XXXVII,2
ק]דיש הוא היכלא ויקרא רב[א	הוא		**18** 19,3
/ בפ]ם ארמלה הוית לצלו[	הוא	29:13	**10** XIV,8
]ון בחרת ארחי והוית ר[אש	הוא	29:25	**10** XV,2
אבה]תהון מלמהוא עם כלבי ע[ני	הוא	30:1	**10** XV,5
ידיהון]לא הוא לי צבין ובאכפי[הון	הוא	30:2	**10** XV,6
כ]פן רעין הוא ירק ד[חשת	הוא	30:3	**10** XV,7
/ הוא איוב זכ[י	הוא	32:1	**10** XX,4
והן פתגם חוב להוא / עליה	הוא	37:13	**10** XXIX,4
/ אן הוית במעבדי ארעא	הוא	38:4	**10** XXX,2
[א]ואהוא לעפר / וקטם *vac* [*v*]*ac* *v*]*ac*	הוא	42:6	**10** XXXVII,8
/ ויהב לה חד תרין בכל די הוא לה	הוא	42:10	**10** XXXVIII,4
]°א די להוון אכלין[	הוא		**18** 7,2

/ להוה לבש כהנא רבא[	הוא		**18** 14ii5
]משרתא עוד להן די להוה[	הוא		**18** 15,1
]א וכול די להוון משצין שבעתיהו[ן	הוא		**18** 15,2
תרתי לחמ]א די הות לבונתא [עליהון	הוא		**18** 20,5
]להוון שב[	הוא		**18** 26,6
] להו[ון	הוא		**18** 26,7
]להוון דברין ב[	הוא		**18** 28,1
] ולהוה להון °[	הוא		**18** 30,3
הי]א עד / אבדון ת[אכל	היא	31:12	**10** XVIII,4
ה[יך	היך	21:7	**10** IV,5
/ היך לא [	היך	22:20	**10** VII,6
/ הן עולין השכח אחד לי ה[יך	היך	33:10	**10** XXII,4
/ היכא יפק *vac*	היכא	38:24	**10** XXXI,2
]ה תרעיא די לקובל היכלא ל[	היכל		**18** 19,1
ק]דיש הוא היכלא ויקרא רב[א	היכל		**18** 19,3
]לברא מן היכלא לימין מערבה[	היכל		**18** 20,2
/ היכלא[	היכל		**18** 31ii6
]א היכלא ומן דמ[	היכל		**18** 32,3
]ן מן היכלא /	היכל		**18** 32,6
הך אמרת באדני וק[ל	הך	33:8	**10** XXII,2
ו]הלכת / [מן שמשא	הלך	30:28	**10** XVII,4
ה]ללת / על באישתה[	הלל	31:29	**10** XIX,3
וירמא המון באת[ר	המון	34:26	**10** XXV,2
ד]כר ארו רברבין עבדוהי ד[י / חזו המ[ון	המון	36:24	**10** XXVIII,2
וטמר / [ה]מון בעפר { } כח[דא	המון	40:13	**10** XXXIV,9
]° הן לקד[ם	הן	23:8	**10** VIIa,9
]לנפשי הן לכמ[א	הן	27:3	**10** X,9
ב]אפי הן ימל[לן	הן	27:4	**10** X,10
הן / [	הן	27:14	**10** XI,4
]הן אתקצרת / בדין עב[די	הן	31:13	**10** XVIII,5
ח]ד הן / אמ[נע	הן	31:16	**10** XVIII,8
/ אנה] הן חרגתי לא תסר[דנך	הן	33:7	**10** XXII,1
/ הן עולין השכח אחד לי ה[יך	הן	33:10	**10** XXII,4
הן תאמר[ ]	הן	35:14	**10** XXVI,9
]הן יתובון מן באישתהון /	הן	36:10	**10** XXVII,4
/ הן ישמעון ויעבד[ון	הן	36:11	**10** XXVII,5
הן *vac*	הן	36:29	**10** XXVIII,6
הן למכתש / הן לארעא	הן	37:13	**10** XXIX,3
הן למכתש / הן לארעא	הן	37:13	**10** XXIX,4
הן לכפן וחסרנה	הן	37:13	**10** XXIX,4
והן פתגם חוב להוא / עליה	הן	37:13	**10** XXIX,4
החויני הן ידעת חכמה /	הן	38:4	**10** XXX,2
/ מן שם משחתה הן תנדע	הן	38:5	**10** XXX,3
/ הן כולה[	הן		**18** 23ii6
/ הריתהון פל[טת	הרה	21:10	**10** IV,9
/ שביעיא כדמות נצ ורד[	ורד		**18** 14ii4

10 XXX,4	38:7	זהר	במזהר / כחדא כוכבי צפר
10 XXXV,3	40:24	זוב	כבחכה יזיב אפה
10 XI,7	27:16	זוז	]זוזיא כטינא יסגא /
10 X,2	26:11	זוע	י]זיע ויתמהון מן /
10 XXXIII,1	39:20	זוע	] התזיענה בתקף[
10 XXXIII,4	39:22	זוע	ולא / יזוע ולא יתוב מן אנפי חרב
10 XXXIV,6	40:10	זיו	וזוי והדר ויקר תלבש /
10 XXXIII,6	39:25	זין	ולנקשת זין וזעקת אשתדור / יחדה { }
10 XXVIII,5	36:27	זיק	וזיקי מטר יהכן
10 XXXVI,6	41:13	זיק(ה)	וזיקין / יפקן מן פמה
10 XXXIV,4	40:8	זכא	ותחיבנני על דברת די תזכא
10 IX,8	25:5	זכי	]זכי וכוכביא לא[
10 XX,4	32:1	זכי	/ הוא איוב זכ[י
10 XXII,3	33:9	זכי	/ [זכ]י אנה ולא חטא לי ונקא[
10 XXXV,5	40:26	זמם	התשוא / זמם באפה
10 XXIII,8	33:29	זמן	ג]בר / זמן תרין תלתה
10 XXXI,3	38:25	זמן	מן שויא / למטרא זמן
10 XV,4	30:1	זעיר	וכען ח]אכו עלי זערין מני ביומין[
10 XVII,5	30:28	זעק	]קמת[ו]אזעקת /
10 XXVI,3	35:9	זעק	מן סגיא [עשוקיא יז]עקון
10 XXVI,7	35:12	זעק	תמה יזעקון
10 XXX,5	38:7	זעק	ויזעק[ו]ן כחדה כל מלאכי אלהא /
10 XXXIII,6	39:25	זעקה	ולנקשת זין וזעקת אשתדור / יחדה { }
10 IV,6	21:8	זרע	זרע[הון
10 XX,7	32:2	זרע	מן] / זרע רומא[ה
18 7,1		זרע	] על כול זרע בני [
18 24,4		זרע	]על כול זרעא[
10 VII,5	22:19	חאך	/ ויחאכון ו[
10 XV,1	29:24	חאך	]אחאך להון ולא יה[ימנון
10 XV,4	30:1	חאך	וכען ח]אכו עלי זערין מני ביומין[
10 XXXII,6	39:7	חאך	/ וחאך על מהמא תקף קריא
10 XXXIII,3	39:22	חאך	יחאך על דחלא
10 XXXV,7	40:29	חאך	התחאך / בה כצפר
10 XXIV,5	34:10	חבל	/ ומן לחבל(ה)א מ[רא
10 XXIII,1	33:24	חבל	/ ו'יאמר פצהי מן חב[לא
10 XXVII,2	36:8	חבל	א]חידין בחבלי מסכניא /
10 XXXII,1	39:1	חבל	/ יעלי כפא וחב[ל]י[ ]°[
10 XXXII,3	39:3	חבל	/ וחבליהן תושר
10 XXXV,4	40:25	חבל	או בחבל תחרז לשנה
10 XXIV,1	34:8	חבר	ומתחבר / לעבדי שקרא[
10 XXXVI,3	41:9	חברה	אנתה / לחברתה חענן ולא יתפ[ר]שן
10 XIV,10	29:15	חגיר	ו]רגלין לחגיר [
10 XVIII,8	31:16	חד	ח]ד הן / אמ[נע
10 XXII,8	33:14	חד	/ א]רו בחדא ימלל אלה[א
10 XXXVI,2	41:8	חד	חדה] / לחדה ידבקן
10 XXXVII,5	42:2	חד	/ חדה מללת ולא אתיב
10 XXXVIII,4	42:10	חד	/ ויהב לה חד תרין בכל די הוא לה
10 XXXVIII,7	42:11	חד	ויהבו לה גבר אמרה חדה /
10 XXXVIII,8	42:11	חד	/ וגבר קדש חד די דהב *vac*
18 21,4		חד	]°ן[ק]נא חד פותי /
10 XXXIII,2	39:21	חדא	וחפר בבקע וירוט ויחדא /
10 XXXIII,7	39:25	חדא	ולנקשת זין וזעקת אשתדור / יחדה { }
18 18,6		חדו	] לבתי חדוא ול[
18 19,2		חדש	]ביומא שביעיא וביום ראשי ח[דשא
10 XXI,9	32:17	חוא	/ וא]חוה מלי אף א[נה
10 XXVII,3	36:9	חוא	/ ויחוא להון עבדיהו[ן ועוית]הון
10 XXX,2	38:4	חוא	החויני הן ידעת חכמה /
10 XXI,5	32:13	חוב	/ להן אלהא חיבנא ולא א[נש
10 XXXIV,4	40:8	חוב	ותחיבנני על דברת די תזכא
10 XXIX,4	37:13	חוב	והן פתגם חוב להוא / עליה
10 XXX,3	38:5	חוט	מן נגד עליה חוטא
10 XXXV,8	40:29	חוט	ותקטרנה בחוטא לבנתך
10 XI,2	27:12	חזא	כ]לכון חזיתון
10 XIV,2	29:8	חזא	/ ו]חזוני עלומין טשו וגברין ח°[
10 XIV,5	29:11	חזא	/ ת]שמע אדן שבחתני ועין ח[זת
10 XXIII,4	33:26	חזא	/ ויחזא אנפוהי באסיא[
10 XXIII,7	33:28	חזא	] / בנהור תחזא
10 XXVIII,2	36:24	חזא	ד]כר ארו רברבין עבדוהי ד[י / חזו המ[ון
10 XXVIII,2	36:25	חזא	ו]כל אנשא עלוהי חזין
10 XXXIV,7	40:11	חזא	וחזא כל גאה והשפלה וכל /
10 XXXVII,8	42:5	חזא	וכען עיני / חזתך
18 18,5		חזא	]אמר לי חזא אנתה ד[י
18 19,6		חזא	]מחזא לי כתב כ[
10 XXX,4	38:6	חזית	או מן הקים אבן חזיתה
10 VIII,7	24:15	חטא	/ ויחטא ח[תר
10 XIX,6	31:29	חטא	למחט]א /
10 XVIII,4	31:11	חטא	והוא חטא[
10 XXII,3	33:9	חטא	/ [זכ]י אנה ולא חטא לי ונקא[
10 XXIV,1	34:6	חטא	/ מן חטא
10 XXIV,1	34:7	חטא	]א חטיא
10 XXVI,2	35:8	חטא	[לגבר כות]ך חטיך /
10 XXXVIII,3	42:9	חטא	ושבק / להון חטאיהון בדילה
10 XX,1	31:4	חטה	/ תחות חטא[
10 X,8	27:2	חי	]ואמר חי אלהא[
10 XXIII,9	33:30	חי	בנהו]ר / חיין
18 10i1		חי	]י מין חיין /
10 XV,3	29:25	חיל	]בראש חילה וכגבר די א[בלין ינחם]
10 XVI,8	30:18	חיל	בסגיא]חיל יאחדון לבו[שי]
10 XXXIII,3	39:21	חיל	/ ובחיל ינפק לאנפי חרב
10 XIV,4	29:10	חנך	/ קל סגנין הטמרו לחנך דב[ק
10 XIX,7	31:30	חך	/ חכי למש[אל
10 XXXV,3	40:24	חכה	כבחכה יזיב אפה

Siglum	Ref.	Root	Text
10 XXXV,4	40:25	חכה	התגד / תנין בחכא
10 XXV,2	34:25	חכם	יחכ]ם עבדהון
10 XXVI,7	35:11	חכם	ומן] צפריא / חכמנה
10 XXXIII,7	39:26	חכמה	המן חכמתך יסתער נצא
10 XXX,2	38:4	חכמה	החויני הן ידעת חכמה /
10 XXXVII,4	42:2	חכמה	ולא יתבצר מנך תקף וחכמה /
10 X,4	26:13	חלל	חללת ידה תנין ערק /
10 XXII,9	33:15	חלם	ב]חלמין בחדידי ליליּ[א
10 XII,2	28:4	חלף	/ וחליף]
18 15,3		חלף	]אחיהון עללין חלפהון ארבע מאה צ[
10 XXX,1	38:3	חלץ	/ אסר נא כגבר חלצ[י]ך[
10 XXXIV,3	40:7	חלץ	אסר / נא כגבר חלציך
10 XXVI,5	35:10	חלק	ודי חלק לנא ל[ ]°
10 V,1	21:20	חמה	ומח[מת מרא ישתא]
10 XXXIV,7	40:11	חמה	/ העדי נא חמת רגזך
18 14ii2		חמישי	/ מנצבהון וכלילא חמי[שיא
18 29,4		חמר	]משח וחמ[ר
18 7,4		חמשין	]ת מאה וחמש[ין
10 XXXV,6	40:27	חנן	או ימלל עמך בהתחננה לך
10 XXXII,4	39:5	חנק	וחנקי ערדא מן / שרא
10 XXIV,4	34:10	חס	]חס לאלהא מן שקר /
10 X,1	26:10	חסוך	] על[סי]פי חסוך /
10 XXIX,4	37:13	חסרן	הן לכפן וחסרנה
10 XXXVI,3	41:9	חען	אנתה / לחברתה חענן ולא יתפ[ר]שן
18 10i6		חפא?	]°וך חפא דהב /
10 XXXIII,2	39:21	חפר	וחפר בבקע וירוט ויחדא /
10 XXXIII,10	39:29	חצא	]מן ת[מה י]חצא מאכל[א
10 XXI,2	32:11	חקר	עד תחקרון סוף]
10 XI,5	27:14	חרב	חר]ב יפצון ולא ישבעון /
10 XXVII,6	36:12	חרב	[והן לא ישמ]עון בחרבא יפלון /
10 XXXIII,3	39:21	חרב	/ ובחיל ינפק לאנפי חרב
10 XXXIII,4	39:22	חרב	ולא / יזוע ולא יתוב מן אנפי חרב
10 XXII,1	33:7	חרגה	/ אנה] הן חרגתי לא תסר[דנך
10 XXXV,4	40:25	חרז	או בחבל תחרז לשנה
10 XXXIII,5	39:23	חרף	/ שנן ונזך וחרף סיף
10 XXXV,5	40:26	חרת	ובחרתך תקוב לסתה
10 XIV,3	29:9	חשא	/ ו]רברבין חשו מללא וכף ישון[
10 XXI,7	32:15	חשא	/ והחשיו ונטרת מנהון °[
10 II,1	19:11	חשב	/ ותק]ף עלי רגזה וח[שבני
10 A,11		חשך	]ואתחשך מ[
10 XXX,7	38:9	חתל	ועׄרפלין חותלוהי
10 II,2	19:12	חתף	[כחדה / י]תון חתפוהי וכבשו[
10 VIII,7	24:16	חתר	/ ויחטא ח[תר
10 XXVII,5	36:11	טב	ישלמון]בטב ימהון
18 8,1		טב	דהב]טב כולה ארבע רגלוה[י
18 10i2		טב	]ורא דן דהב טב /
18 11,4		טב	]נאמה וכולה דהב טב די[
10 XVI,4	30:15	טבה	עלי ונדת כ]רוח טבתי ורבותי
10 XXXII,7	39:8	טור	ויבחר לה טורין לרע[יה
10 XVIII,3	31:10	טחן	/ תטחן ל[
10 XI,7	27:16	טין	]זוזיא כטינא יסגא /
10 XII,6	28:10	טיף	טי]פין / בז[ע
10 XXVIII,6	36:28	טיף	ועננוהי יגחתון / ט[יפי מין על]עם סגיא
10 XXXI,6	38:28	טל	או מן / ילד [ע]נני טלא
10 VIIa,2	23:2	טלל	אף יומא דן] מן טלל שעותי די /
10 XXVIII,7	36:29	טלל	/ ע[נניא די אתרגו]שתה מן טלל
10 XIV,4	29:10	טמר	/ קל סגנין הטמרו לחנך דב[ק
10 XXXIV,8	40:13	טמר	וטמר / [ה]מון בעפר { } כח[דא
10 XXXIV,8	40:12	טפא	והטפי ר[שיעין תחו]תיהון
10 XIV,2	29:8	טשי	/ ו]חזוני עלומין טשו וגברין ח°[
10 XXXI,9	38:32	יאש	]°°°א על בניה תיאש °[
10 XXXII,8	39:9	יבא	היבא ראמ[א ל]מפלחך
10 IX,1	24:24	יבל	התכ]פפו כיבלא יתקפצון א[ו
10 IV,4	21:5	יד	/ סימו ידיכון על [פם
10 X,4	26:13	יד	חללת ידה תנין ערק /
10 XI,1	27:11	יד	בי]ד אלהא ועבד /
10 XIX,2	31:27	יד	ל]בי / ונשקת ידי לפ[מי
10 XXVI,2	35:7	יד	או מא מידך יקבל]
18 6,2		יד	א]לן פרזיא ליד שור[א
18 11,2		יד	]ונא ליד כותלא די סחר ל°[
18 13,8		יד	]מרפסתא ליד יס°[
18 16ii&17i3		יד	כ]הניא מקבלין / מן ידהון דפש[טו
18 16ii&17i5		יד	/ ידוהי כול °[
18 31ii4		יד	/ ידא ח°[
10 II,3	19:13	ידע	/ הרחקו וידעי ב°[
10 III,5	20:4	ידע	יד]עת מן עלמא מן ד[י]
10 V,7	21:27	ידע	ארו ידעת]
10 VIIa,3	23:3	ידע	מלוא אנדע ואשכ[חנה] /
10 VIIa,5	23:5	ידע	ואנדע / [
10 XIV,11	29:15	ידע	ל]א ידע[ת
10 XXVIII,4	36:26	ידע	ויומוהי / סגיא[לא ננ]דע
10 XXIX,6	37:15	ידע	/ הת]נדע מא שויא אלהא עליהון
10 XXIX,7	37:16	ידע	/ התנ]דע להלבש(ו)א עננה גבורה
10 XXIX,8	37:16	ידע	]ארו הוא ידע מדע[א
10 XXIX,9	37:19	ידע	ינדע[ ]ל[
10 XXX,2	38:4	ידע	החויני הן ידעת חכמה /
10 XXX,3	38:5	ידע	/ מן שם משחתה הן תנדע
10 XXXII,2	39:2	ידע	ותנדע עדן מולדהין
10 XXXVII,3	42:1	ידע	ידעת די כלא / תכול למעבד
10 XXXVIII,5	42:11	ידע	וכל אחוהי וכל ידעוהי
10 XXXVIII,4	42:10	יהב	/ ויהב לה חד תרין בכל די הוא לה
10 XXXVIII,7	42:11	יהב	ויהבו לה גבר אמרה חדה /

Text	Root	Verse	Reference
מן תרתי לחמא י]היבת לכהנא ר֯[בא	יהב		**18** 20,6
קד]מ֯וני֯ יומי עמ֯[לא	יום	30:27	**10** XVII,4
וכען ח]אכו עלי זערין מני ביומין[	יום	30:1	**10** XV,4
[יאחדונני י]ומי תשבר֯א֯ יאקפוני /	יום	30:16	**10** XVI,6
ותב ליומי עלימ[ותה	יום	33:25	**10** XXIII,3
ישלמון]בטב ימהון	יום	36:11	**10** XXVII,5
ויומוהי / סגיא[לא ננ]דע	יום	36:26	**10** XXVIII,3
] הביומיך מנית /	יום	38:12	**10** XXX,9
ליום קרב ואשתד֯ר֯ [	יום	38:23	**10** XXXI,1
]ב֯יומא שביעיא וביום ראשי ח[דשא	יום		**18** 19,2
]ב֯יומא שביעיא וביום ראשי ח[דשא	יום		**18** 19,2
כו]ל יום שביעי קודם אל דכר֯[נא	יום		**18** 20,1
]תו לה איחל בלחודוהי֯ /	יחל	34:31	**10** XXV,7
ופמ]י֯ אמלא הוכחה	יכח	23:4	**10** VIIa,5
/ במטל עינוהי יכלנה	יכל	40:24	**10** XXXV,3
ידעת די כלא / תכול למעבד	יכל	42:2	**10** XXXVII,4
או מן / יל֯ד֯ [ע]נני טלא	ילד	38:28	**10** XXXI,6
ותנדע עדן מולדהי֯ן	ילד	39:2	**10** XXXII,2
ילדן בניהן ויפלטן /	ילד	39:3	**10** XXXII,2
]ימא ובמנדעה קטל /	ים	26:12	**10** X,3
/ התסוג בדשין ימא	ים	38:8	**10** XXX,6
]בימי֯ן֯ /	ימין		**18** 12i8
]לברא מן היכלא לימין מערב֯ה֯[	ימין		**18** 20,2
]°י֯ן֯ ויסוד /	יסוד		**18** 32,9
]לא אוסף	יסף	34:32	**10** XXV,8
ואמרת עד תנא / ולא תוס֯ף֯[	יסף	38:11	**10** XXX,9
ותרתין ועליהן לא / אוסף	יסף	40:5	**10** XXXVII,6
]י֯ ה֯ת֯ע֯י֯ט(ו֯)ת֯ו֯ן֯[	יעט	21:27	**10** V,8
/ יעלי כפא֯ ו֯ח֯ב[ל]י֯֯[ ]°[	יעל	39:1	**10** XXXII,1
לבנ]ת֯ יענה /	יענה	30:29	**10** XVII,6
ו֯[הו]פ֯ע֯ נ֯הור עננה /	יפע	37:15	**10** XXIX,6
בלילא] גרמי יקדון	יקד	30:17	**10** XVI,7
/ לכוש יקד ומגמר	יקד	41:12	**10** XXXVI,6
[לא / יי]ק֯ר	יקר	33:7	**10** XXII,2
ושניהון / ביקר ועדנין	יקר	36:11	**10** XXVII,6
וזוי והדר ויקר תלבש /	יקר	40:10	**10** XXXIV,6
ק]ד֯יש הוא היכלא ויקרא רב֯[א	יקר		**18** 19,3
]ריתא ויקרא[	יקר		**18** 25,3
/ ירדנא גאפה	ירדן		**10** XXXV,2
ו]בתר כל ירוק / ירדף	ירוק	39:8	**10** XXXII,7
מני]ן ירחוהי גזירין	ירח	21:21	**10** V,3
תמנ]ה֯ [י]ר֯ח֯י֯ה֯י֯ן / שלמין	ירח	39:2	**10** XXXII,1
כ]פ֯ן רעין הוא ירק ד֯[חשת	ירק	30:3	**10** XV,7
/ וחבליהן תושר	ישר	39:3	**10** XXXII,3
י]שראל[	ישראל		**18** 23ii7
]מן קודשי ישראל[	ישראל		**18** 25,1
כו]ל ישראל ה֯[	ישראל		**18** 27,1
]תין ו֯י֯פ֯לגון יתה בארע[	ית	40:30	**10** XXXV,9
/ ו֯אלהא ב֯ר֯ך֯ י֯ת֯ א֯[יו]ב באח֯[רי]ל[	ית	42:12	**10** XXXVIII,9
/ למלכין יתבי֯ ע֯[ל כרסיהון	יתב	36:7	**10** XXVII,1
[כחדה / י]ת֯ון חתפוהי וכבשו֯[	כבש	19:12	**10** II,2
כד]ב֯ת / לאלהא מעל֯[א	כדב	31:28	**10** XIX,2
]מ֯א אעבד / כדי יק[ום אלהא	כדי	31:14	**10** XVIII,7
]*vac* וכדי ישׁ°[	כדי		**18** 27,2
/ להוה לבש כהנא רבא[	כהן		**18** 14ii5
כ]ה֯ניא מקבלין / מן ידהון דפ֯ש֯[טו	כהן		**18** 16ii&17i2
פ]ל֯י֯ג לתמנין וארבעה כהנין ש֯[	כהן		**18** 20,3
שביא די בה]ון וארבעת עשר כה[נין	כהן		**18** 20,4
מן תרתי לחמא י]היבת לכהנא ר֯[בא	כהן		**18** 20,6
]זכי וכוכביא לא֯[	כוכב	25:5	**10** IX,8
במזהר / כחדא כוכבי צפר	כוכב	38:7	**10** XXX,5
]° תרתין כוליתה /	כוליה		**18** 22,3
וזיקי מטר יהכן	כון	36:27	**10** XXVIII,5
/ גוא כפרה וכלילא שתיתי֯[א	כ(ו)פר		**18** 14ii3
או בקל כותה תרעם /	כות	40:9	**10** XXXIV,5
כחדה על [	כחדא	21:26	**10** V,6
במזהר / כחדא כוכבי צפר	כחדא	38:7	**10** XXX,5
ויזעק[ו]ן כחדה כל מלאכי אלהא /	כחדא	38:7	**10** XXX,5
וטמר / [ה]מ֯ון בעפר { } כח֯[דא	כחדא	40:13	**10** XXXIV,9
]א ובשרא מתערב כחדא[	כחדא		**18** 13,6
]הי כחדא *vac*[	כחדא		**18** 26,4
]ל[ ]ן בכי֯ו֯ר֯ °[ ]°[	כיור		**18** 11,8
]ע֯°[ ]כימא	כימה	38:31	**10** XXXI,8
/ כל אנש די֯[	כל	19:19	**10** II,8
כ]לכון חזיתון	כל	27:12	**10** XI,2
/ י]שׁוא בסדא רגלי וסכר כ[ל	כל	33:11	**10** XXII,5
ארו בכל פ[תגמוהי	כל	33:13	**10** XXII,7
הא כ֯[ל	כל	33:29	**10** XXIII,7
אר]ח֯ה ובכל שבילוהי לא הסתכ֯[לו]	כל	34:27	**10** XXV,3
ו]כ֯ל אנשא עלוהי חזין	כל	36:25	**10** XXVIII,2
/ על כל די ברא יפקדנון על אנפי תבל כל	כל	37:12	**10** XXIX,3
ויזעק[ו]ן כחדה כל מלאכי אלהא /	כל	38:7	**10** XXX,5
ו]בתר כל ירוק / ירדף	כל	39:8	**10** XXXII,7
וחזא כל גאה והשפלה וכל /	כל	40:11	**10** XXXIV,7
וחזא כל גאה והשפלה וכל /	כל	40:12	**10** XXXIV,7
/ והוא מלך על כל רחש *vac*	כל	41:26	**10** XXXVII,2
ידעת די כלא / תכול למעבד	כל	42:2	**10** XXXVII,3
/ ויהב לה חד תרין בכל די הוא לה	כל	42:10	**10** XXXVIII,4
ואתין לות / איוב כל רחמוהי	כל	42:11	**10** XXXVIII,5
וכל אחוהי וכל ידעוהי	כל	42:11	**10** XXXVIII,5
וכל אחוהי וכל ידעוהי	כל	42:11	**10** XXXVIII,5
ונחמוהי על כל באישתה	כל	42:11	**10** XXXVIII,6

] על כול זרע בני [	כל		**18** 7,1
דהב]טב כולה ארבע רגלוה[י	כל		**18** 8,1
]בא וכול בנינא דן [	כל		**18** 9,5
]◦בן כול אבניהון /	כל		**18** 10i5
]נאמה וכולה דהב טב די[	כל		**18** 11,4
]כול רוח מערב /	כל		**18** 12i5
ר]חע רגלוהי וקרבוהי ומלח כולה[	כל		**18** 13,2
ר]ובע סתא ואסקה למדבחא כולה[	כל		**18** 13,4
]ים ובכול על[	כל		**18** 14ii6
]לכול ע[	כל		**18** 14ii7
]א וכול די להוון משצין שבעתיהו[ן	כל		**18** 15,2
]◦ני הובן כולהון /	כל		**18** 16i1
ו]ל[א] / עלל לה כול א[נש	כל		**18** 16ii&17i4
/ ידוהי כול ◦[	כל		**18** 16ii&17i5
/ לכול תרי עשר תרעין[	כל		**18** 17ii3
וכ]ולהון תלתין ותרין אלפין	כל		**18** 18,3
]לכול עלמין *vac*[	כל		**18** 19,4
כו]ל יום שביעי קודם אל דכר[נא	כל		**18** 20,1
]מן כול שבעת פלוגת פתורי	כל		**18** 20,3a
]ין מנה כול תרבה /	כל		**18** 22,2
/ כולה סגי[	כל		**18** 23ii5
/ הן כולה[	כל		**18** 23ii6
]ה דין מן כול ש◦[	כל		**18** 24,2
]על כול זרעא[	כל		**18** 24,4
]בכול שנא ל[	כל		**18** 24,5
]כול די ל[	כל		**18** 24,7
]וכול אנשא די יח[	כל		**18** 26,1
כו]ל ישראל ח[	כל		**18** 27,1
עד ת]דנח שמשא וכו[ל	כל		**18** 27,4
]◦[ ]ין ככול ד◦[	כל		**18** 30,1
]א מן כול[	כל		**18** 35,1
כ]לא / ו[ ]◦	כלא	28:11	**10** XII,7
נשמ]תה עלוהי יכלא /	כלא	34:14	**10** XXIV,8
אבה]תהון מלמהוא עם כלבי ע[ני	כלב	30:1	**10** XV,5
/ מנצבהון וכלילא חמי[שיא	כליל		**18** 14ii2
/ גוא כפרה וכלילא שתיתי[א	כליל		**18** 14ii3
]לנפשי הן לכמ[א	כמא	27:3	**10** X,9
/ מלין וכמא לא יתיבנה[	כמא	32:14	**10** XXI,6
על כן אתנסך ואתמהא	כן	42:6	**10** XXXVII,8
]כנפ[י]ארע[א]	כנף	38:13	**10** XXX,10
ויפרוס / כנפוהי לרוחין	כנף	39:26	**10** XXXIII,8
// כסין שבעה וספלין למרח שתה[	כס		**18** 18,1
כ]סי	כסא	36:30	**10** XXVIII,8
אנפי]הון בקטם תכסה /	כסא	40:13	**10** XXXIV,9
וכע]ן בתקף שחני יתון /	כען	30:14	**10** XVI,2
וכען עלי תתאשד / [נפשי	כען	30:16	**10** XVI,5
vac כען אנש[	כען	34:10	**10** XXIV,4
[ ]הכען צדא אלהא / ישקר	כען	34:12	**10** XXIV,6
וכען עיני / חזתך	כען	42:5	**10** XXXVII,7
/ ו]רברבין חשו מללא וכף ישון[	כף	29:9	**10** XIV,3
] וכעבד / כפוהי ישלם לה	כף	33:26	**10** XXIII,5
/ יעלי כפא וחב[ל]י[ ]◦[	כף	39:1	**10** XXXII,1
ב]כפא ישכון ויקנן[ ]◦ ◦[	כף	39:28	**10** XXXIII,9
כ]פן רעין הוא ירק ד[חשת	כפן	30:3	**10** XV,7
הן לכפן וחסרנה	כפן	37:13	**10** XXIX,4
התכ]פפו כיבלא יתקפצון א[ו	כפף	24:24	**10** IX,1
תחות]באישה אתכפפת	כפף	30:14	**10** XVI,3
התכפפת /	כפף	30:15	**10** XVI,3
/ לבש]תני וככתון לבשת [	כתון	29:14	**10** XIV,9
/ כורסי[א	כרסא		**18** 31ii2
]כורסיא [	כרסא		**18** 32,1
]שרי למקרא לי בכת[ב	כתב		**18** 19,5
]מחזא לי כתב כ[	כתב		**18** 19,6
/ תרתין ועובי פותי כות[לא	כתל		**18** 17ii4
כ]תפן /	כתפה		**18** 16i3
/ לעבדי קרית ולא ע[נא	לא	19:16	**10** II,5
/ ארו אפו לא ת[קצר רוחי	לא	21:4	**10** IV,3
ל]א אכל	לא	21:25	**10** V,6
ל]א איתי /	לא	22:5	**10** VI,4
]צהא לא /	לא	22:7	**10** VI,6
/ היך לא [	לא	22:20	**10** VII,6
] או על מן לא תקום [	לא	25:3	**10** IX,6
]זכי וכוכביא לא[	לא	25:5	**10** IX,8
חר]ב יפצון ולא ישבעון /	לא	27:14	**10** XI,5
]ן וארמלתה לא /	לא	27:15	**10** XI,6
ש]כב ולא איתחד /	לא	27:19	**10** XI,10
] / לא י[	לא	28:7	**10** XII,4
/ [ד]י לא עדר להון	לא	29:12	**10** XIV,7
ל]א ידע[ת	לא	29:15	**10** XIV,11
]אחאך להון ולא יה[ימנון	לא	29:24	**10** XV,1
ידיהון]לא הוא לי צבין ובאכפי[הון	לא	30:2	**10** XV,6
ופצא לא / [איתי להון	לא	30:13	**10** XVI,1
מעיני רת]חו ולא / [דמו	לא	30:27	**10** XVII,3
]לא	לא	31:1	**10** XVII,9
/ לא י[בית	לא	31:32	**10** XIX,9
/ וארו לא איתי מנכון לא[יוב	לא	32:12	**10** XXI,3
/ להן אלהא חיבנא ולא א[נש	לא	32:13	**10** XXI,5
/ מלין וכמא לא יתיבנה[	לא	32:14	**10** XXI,6
/ ו]קמו ולא ימללון עוד[	לא	32:16	**10** XXI,8
/ אנה] הן חרגתי לא תסר[דנך	לא	33:7	**10** XXII,1
/ [זכ]י אנה ולא חטא לי ונקא[	לא	33:9	**10** XXII,3
]ולא / כארחי השתלמת	לא	33:27	**10** XXIII,5

Reference	Verse	Word	Context
10 XXIV,2	34:9	לא	ארו אמר לא / ישנא גבר מ֯ן֯ [
10 XXV,1	34:24	לא	ר]ב֯רבין די לא סוף
10 XXV,3	34:27	לא	אר]ח֯ה ובכל שבילוהי לא הסתכ֯[לו]
10 XXV,8	34:32	לא	]לא אוסף
10 XXV,9	34:33	לא	תב]ח֯ר ולא אנה [
10 XXVI,4	35:10	לא	ולא אמר]ין אן הוא]אלהא / די עבדנה לא
10 XXVI,7	35:12	לא	ולא֯ יענא מן קדם ג]אות / [ב]אישין
10 XXVII,10	36:16	לא	]לא֯[
10 XXVIII,4	36:26	לא	ומנין שנוהי די לא סוף
10 XXX,9	38:11	לא	ואמרת עד תנא / ולא תוסף֯[
10 XXXI,4	38:26	לא	די לא אנש בה
10 XXXII,3	39:4	לא	נפקו ולא תבוא / עליהן
10 XXXII,6	39:7	לא	ונגשת שליט לא / ישמע
10 XXXIII,3	39:22	לא	ולא / יזוע ולא יתוב מן אנפי חרב
10 XXXIII,4	39:22	לא	ולא / יזוע ולא יתוב מן אנפי חרב
10 XXXVI,2	41:8	לא	ורוח ל[א י]נעול בינה[ו]ן
10 XXXVI,3	41:9	לא	אנתה / לחברתה חענן ולא יתפ֯[ר]שן
10 XXXVII,4	42:2	לא	ולא יתבצר מנך תקף וחכמה /
10 XXXVII,5	40:5	לא	/ חדה מללת ולא אתיב
10 XXXVII,5	40:5	לא	ותרתין ועליהן לא / אוסף
18 16ii&17i3		לא	ו]ל[א] / עלל לה כול א[נש
18 27,6		לא	]ל֯א לרויו ◦[
10 XIX,1	31:27	לב	ל]ב֯י / ונשקת ידי ל֯פ֯[מי
10 III,3	20:2	לב(ב)	לכן לבבי י[
10 XVIII,2	31:9	לב(ב)	פ]ת֯י֯א / לבי בא[נתה
10 XXVII,7	36:13	לב(ב)	ל]בבהון לרגז / עליהון
10 XXXVI,9	41:16	לב(ב)	ולב֯[בה]◦◦[ ]ר֯ כאב֯ן֯ ו[
18 20,5		לבונה	תרתי לחמ]א די הות לבונתא [עליהון
10 XVI,8	30:18	לבוש	בסגיא]חיל יאחדון לבו[שי]
10 XXIX,7	37:17	לבוש	[ב]דיל די לבושך /
10 XXX,7	38:9	לבוש	בשוית עננ֯י֯[ן ל]בו[שה
10 XIV,9	29:14	לבש	/ לבש]תני וככתון לבשת [
10 XIV,9	29:14	לבש	/ לבש]תני וככתון לבשת [
10 XXIX,7	37:16	לבש	/ התנ]ד֯ע להלבש[ו]א עננה גבורה
10 XXXIV,6	40:10	לבש	וזוי והדר ויקר תלבש /
18 14ii5		לבש	/ להוה לבש כהנא רבא]
10 XXXII,9	39:10	לגן	וילג֯[ן] ב֯בקעה / ב֯ת֯ר֯י֯ך
10 XXI,5	32:13	להן	/ להן אלהא חיבנא ולא א֯[נש
18 15,1		להן	]משרתא עוד להן די להוה[
10 XIX,5	31:29	לוט	]◦א / לוטי
18 30,2		לוי	]ן עוד לויא דבח֯[ין
18 14ii1		לולב	// גפן כדי פרש מן לולבי֯[א
10 XXXVIII,4	42:11	לות	ואתין לות / איוב כל רחמוהי
10 VI,7	22:7	לחם	ל]חם ואמרת /
10 XV,9	30:4	לחם	ועיקרי רתמ]ין לחמהו֯[ן
10 XXXVIII,6	42:11	לחם	ואכלו / עמה לחם בביתה
18 8,3		לחם	פתו]רא ועלוי לחמא שו֯י֯ו֯[
10 VIII,5	24:14	לילא	/ ומסכן ובלי[ליא
10 XXII,9	33:15	לילא	ב]ח֯למין בחדידי ליל֯י֯[א
10 XXVI,6	35:10	לילא	לנצבתנא / בליליא
18 25,2		לילה	]ור ובלילה ה֯[
10 XXXVI,6	41:12	לכוש	/ לכוש יקר ומגמר
10 XI,2	27:12	למה	למה / [
10 XXI,4	32:13	למה	די למה תאמרו֯[ן
10 XXXV,5	40:26	לסת	ובחרתך תקוב לסתה
10 XXXVI,4	41:11	לפיד	מן פמה לפידין / יפקון
10 XXXV,4	40:25	לשן	או בחבל תחרז לשנה
10 XXXVI,5	41:11	לשן	בלשני אשה ירטון
10 I,1	17:15	מא	ומא אפו א֯[
10 VIIa,6	23:5	מא	]ואסתכ֯ל מא יאמר ל֯י֯ /
10 IX,7	25:4	מא	]א֯להא ומא יצדק֯[
10 X,5	26:14	מא	מא עטר מלא נש֯[מע]
10 XVIII,6	31:14	מא	]מ֯א אעבד / כדי יק[ום אלהא
10 XXVI,1	35:6	מא	מא ת֯[עבד לך
10 XXVI,1	35:7	מא	הן זכי]ת֯ מא / תתן לה
10 XXVI,2	35:7	מא	או מא מידך יקבל[
10 XXIX,6	37:15	מא	/ הת]נדע מא שויא אלהא עליה֯ו֯ן
10 XXX,4	38:6	מא	או / על מא אשיה את֯י֯דון
18 30,5		מא	]ן מא די ל[
10 XXXIII,10	39:29	מאכל	]מ֯ן֯ ת֯[מה י]ח֯צ֯א֯ מ֯א֯כ֯ל[א
18 6,1		מאה	] מאתין ותמנין אמ֯[ין
18 7,4		מאה	]ת֯ מאה וחמשי[ן
18 15,3		מאה	]אחיהון עללין חלפהון ארבע מאה֯ צ֯[
18 17ii5		מאה	/ קדמה֯ן֯ קנין מאה[
18 18,3		מאה	תלתין ותרין אלפין ותשע מאה[
10 XXVIII,9	36:32	מאמר	]על מאמרה מ[
10 XXXIII,8	39:27	מאמר	או על מאמרך יתגב֯ה֯ נ֯שרא /
10 III,6	20:5	מבע	ארע]ה֯ ארו מבע רשיע֯[ין]
10 XXXVI,6	41:12	מגמר	/ לכוש יקר ומגמר
10 VI,5	22:6	מגן	א]חיך מגן /
18 13,4		מדבח	ר]ו֯ב֯ע ס֯תא ואסקה למדבחא כולה[
18 22,1		מדבח	]◦על ארבע קרנת מדבח֯[א] /
18 22,5		מדבח	מד]בחא לריח /
18 29,1		מדבח	]ן֯ קודם מד[בחא
10 XXXI,4	38:26	מדבר	להנחתה על ארע / מדבר
10 XXXII,5	39:6	מדר	ומדרה בא֯ר֯ע֯ מליחה /
10 XXVII,8	36:14	מדינה	ו֯◦[מ]דינתהון בממתין /
10 VIIa,4	23:3	מדר	ואתא עד]אתר מדרה
10 XXXVII,8	42:6	מהא	על כן אתנסך ואתמ֯ה֯א
10 XXXII,6	39:7	מהם	/ וחאך על מהמא תקף ק֯ר֯י֯א֯
10 XXVII,4	36:10	מוסר	ויגלא / אדניהון למוסר וא[מר להון
18 30,4		מועד	]◦◦ מן מועדי אל[

Text	Root	Ref.	Scroll
/ מׄנדעי תמיק[ון	מוק	21:3	10 IV,2
רו]בׄע סתא ונסך לגוא מורכי֯[ותא	מורכיות		18 13,5
דן ימות בנפׄ[ש	מות	21:25	10 V,5
/ די מיתו ב֯[לא	מות	22:16	10 VII,1
/ וימות [ ] ישכבון /	מות	34:15	10 XXIV,9
ו֯° [מ]דינתהון בממתין /	מות	36:14	10 XXVII,8
/ תקיף כמח]ז֯יה עקה	מחזיה	37:18	10 XXIX,9
וזיקי מטר יהכן	מטר	36:27	10 XXVIII,5
מן שויא / למטרא זמן	מטר	38:25	10 XXXI,3
האיתי למטרא אב	מטר	38:28	10 XXXI,5
]כׄמי֯ן באישׄ[	מין	27:20	10 XI,11
/ על אנפי מין	מין	37:10	10 XXIX,1
כא[בן] מׄין התקרמו מנה ואנפי °°ל֯[	מין	38:30	10 XXXI,7
]י מין חיין /	מין		18 10i1
]ין מיא מן /	מין		18 10i3
/ במכילה	מכילה	28:25	10 XIII,7
/ רוח המכת לאנתתי[	מכך	19:17	10 II,6
הן למכתש / הן לארעא	מכתש	37:13	10 XXIX,3
ופמ]י֯ אמלא הוכחה	מלא	23:4	10 VIIa,5
ויתמלין [גרמוהי מוח]	מלא	33:25	10 XXIII,2
ויזעק[ו]ן כחדה כל מלאכי אלהא /	מלאך	38:7	10 XXX,5
עד אמת]י֯ תשואׄ סוף למלא֯[	מלה	18:2	10 I,5
מא עטר מלא נשׄ[מע]	מלה	26:14	10 X,5
/ מלי֯[ן	מלה	32:3	10 XX,9
/ מלי אף אנה	מלה	32:10	10 XXI,1
/ למלוהי	מלה	32:12	10 XXI,4
/ מלין וכמא לא יתיבנהׄ[	מלה	32:14	10 XXI,6
/ וא]חׄוה מלי אף א[נה	מלה	32:17	10 XXI,9
/ הן א]י֯ת֯י֯ מ[לין	מלה	33:32	10 XXIII,10
מ]ל֯י	מלה	34:16	10 XXIV,10
מ]לי֯ן ו֯גב֯[ר	מלה	34:34	10 XXV,10
מלוא אנדע ואשכׄ[חנה] /	מלוא	23:3	10 VIIa,3
ינ]עׄול עמי מלוא עדׄ[	מלוא	23:6	10 VIIa,7
ומדרה בארע מליחה /	מלח	39:6	10 XXXII,5
ר]ח֯ע רגלוהי וקרבוהי ומלח כולה[	מלח		18 13,2
/ למלכין יתבׄי ע֯[ל כרסיהון	מלך	36:7	10 XXVII,1
/ והוא מלך על כל רחש *vac*	מלך	41:26	10 XXXVII,2
אמלל / קדמ[והי] / [	מלל	23:4	10 VIIa,4
ב]א֯פי הן ימל֯[לן	מלל	27:4	10 X,10
/ ו]רברבין חשו מללא וכף ישו֯[ן	מלל	29:9	10 XIV,3
/ ו]ק֯מו ולא ימללון עוד֯[	מלל	32:16	10 XXI,8
/ רׄבברן תמלל	מלל	33:13	10 XXII,7
/ א]רו בחדא ימלל אלה[א	מלל	33:14	10 XXII,8
אמ]לל /	מלל	33:31	10 XXIII,9
הימלל / עמך בניח	מלל	40:27	10 XXXV,5
או ימלל עמך בהתחננה לך	מלל	40:27	10 XXXV,6
/ חדה מללת ולא אתיב	מלל	40:5	10 XXXVII,5
שמע נא ואנה אמלל	מלל	42:4	10 XXXVII,6
מ]מ[ונ]ה קשׄיׄטה יפלג	ממון	27:17	10 XI,8
מ]ן אפו יתיבנני פתגם ויש֯[וא	מן	24:25	10 IX,2
] או על מן לא תקוׄם [	מן	25:3	10 IX,6
מ[ן] /	מן	31:32	10 XIX,8
מן[	מן	34:7	10 XXIV,1
מן יתיבנה על עׄם /	מן	34:29	10 XXV,5
מן פרׄס / ע[נניא	מן	36:29	10 XXVIII,6
/ מן שם משחתה הן תנדע	מן	38:5	10 XXX,3
מן נׄגד עליה חוטא	מן	38:5	10 XXX,3
או מן הקים אבן חזיתה	מן	38:6	10 XXX,4
מן שויא / למטרא זמן	מן	38:25	10 XXXI,2
או מן / ילדׄ [ע]נני טלא	מן	38:28	10 XXXI,5
ומן בטן מן נפק גלידא	מן	38:29	10 XXXI,6
ושיקו[ע שמיא] / מ֯[ן ילד]הׄ	מן	38:29	10 XXXI,7
מן שלח פראה ברחרין	מן	39:5	10 XXXII,4
וחנקי ערדא מן / שרא	מן	39:5	10 XXXII,4
] מן את[רה	מן	18:4	10 I,8
יד]עת מן עלמא מן דׄ[י]	מן	20:4	10 III,5
יד]עת מן עלמא מן דׄ[י]	מן	20:4	10 III,5
אף יומא דן] מן טלל שעותי די /	מן	23:2	10 VIIa,2
/ מן קריהוׄן [	מן	24:12	10 VIII,1
י]ז֯יע ויתמהון מן /	מן	26:11	10 X,2
/ א]רו אנה שׄיׄזבת לענא מן °[	מן	29:12	10 XIV,6
וכען ח]אכו עלי זערין מני ביומין[	מן	30:1	10 XV,4
אבה]ת֯הון מלמהוא עם כלבי ע[ני	מן	30:1	10 XV,5
]וׄ מן /	מן	30:30	10 XVII,7
/ אלין מלהתבׄ[ה פתגם	מן	32:1	10 XX,3
/ וארו לא איתי מנכון לאׄ[יוב	מן	32:12	10 XXI,3
/ והחשיו ונטרת מנהון °[	מן	32:15	10 XXI,7
/ ארו רב אלהא מן אנשאׄ[	מן	33:12	10 XXII,6
/ ו֯יאמר פצהי מן חב[לא	מן	33:24	10 XXIII,1
]מן / עולים	מן	33:25	10 XXIII,2
/ מן חטא	מן	34:6	10 XXIV,1
]ח֯ס לאלהא מן שקר /	מן	34:10	10 XXIV,4
/ ומן לחבל(ה֯)א מ֯[רא	מן	34:10	10 XXIV,5
או מא מידך יקבל[	מן	35:7	10 XXVI,2
מן סגיא [עשוקיא יז]עקון	מן	35:8	10 XXVI,3
יצוחון / מן קדם סגיאין	מן	35:9	10 XXVI,4
די פרשנא מן בעׄ[ירי ארעא	מן	35:11	10 XXVI,6
]הן יתוׄבון מן באישתהון /	מן	36:10	10 XXVII,4
/ ויאבדון מן מׄ[נדעא	מן	36:12	10 XXVII,7
ובני אנשא / מרחיקׄ[עלוה]י֯ יבקון	מן	36:25	10 XXVIII,3
די אתרגו]ש֯תה מן טלל	מן	36:29	10 XXVIII,7
וינפק מן / ענן נורה	מן	37:11	10 XXIX,1

Reference	Verse	Word	Text
10 XXX,6	38:8	מן	ב[הנ]גחותה מן רחם תהומא / למפק
10 XXXI,6	38:29	מן	ומן בטן מן נפק גלידא
10 XXXI,7	38:30	מן	כא[בן] מׄין התקרמו מנה ואנפי ∘∘ל̊]
10 XXXIII,4	39:22	מן	ולא / יזוע ולא יתוב מן אנפי חרב
10 XXXIII,5	39:25	מן	ומן / רחיק יריח קרבה
10 XXXIII,7	39:26	מן	המן חכמתך יסתער נצא
10 XXXIII,10	39:29	מן	]מ̊ן̊ ת̊[מה י]ח̊צ̊א̊ מ̊א̊כ̊ל[א
10 XXXIV,1	40:6	מן	מן ר̊[וחא *ac*] *v*
10 XXXVI,4	41:11	מן	מן פמה לפידין / יפקון
10 XXXVI,5	41:11	מן	מ̊ן̊ נחירוה יפק תנן /
10 XXXVI,7	41:13	מן	וזיקין / יפקן מן פמה
10 XXXVII,4	42:2	מן	ולא יתבצר מנך תקף וחכמה /
18 10i3		מן	]ין מיא מן /
18 11,6		מן	ד]י עמודין סחר מן תרע לת̊[רע
18 11,7		מן	]מן תרע לתרע בשורתא̊[
18 12i1		מן	]∘ מן אלן וערבליא די /
18 14ii1		מן	// גפן כדי פרש מן לולבׄי[א
18 14ii2		מן	/ מנצבהון וכלילא חמי[שיא
18 16ii&17i3		מן	כ]ה̊ניא מקבלין / מן ידהון דפ̊ש̊[טו
18 20,2		מן	]לברא מן היכלא לימין מערבהׄ[
18 20,3a		מן	]מן כול שבעת פלוגת פתורי
18 22,2		מן	]ין מנה כול תרבה /
18 23i1		מן	]∘ׄין ומן /
18 24,2		מן	]ה דין מן כול ש∘[
18 25,1		מן	]מן קודשי ישראל[
18 25,5		מן	]∘לון עמה ומן[
18 30,4		מן	]∘∘ מן מועדי אל[
18 31ii3		מן	/ מנה בׄ∘[
18 32,3		מן	]א היכלא ומן ד̊מ̊[
18 32,6		מן	]ן מן היכלא /
18 35,1		מן	]א מן כול̊[
10 XXX,9	38:12	מנא	] הביומיך מנית /
18 26,2		מנה	]יתמנון עלוהי[
10 IV,2	21:3	מ(נ)דע	/ מׄנדעי תמיק[ון
10 X,3	26:12	מ(נ)דע	]ימא ובמנדעה קטל /
10 XXVII,7	36:12	מ(נ)דע	/ ויאבדון מן מׄ[נדעא
10 XXIX,8	37:16	מ(נ)דע	]אׄרו הוא ידע מדע̊[א
10 V,3	21:21	מנין	מני]ן ירחוהי גזירין
10 XXVIII,4	36:26	מנין	ומנין שנוהי די לא סוף
10 XVIII,9	31:16	מנע	ח]ר̊ הן / אמ̊[נע
10 VIII,5	24:14	מסכן	/ ומסכן ובלי[ליא
10 XXV,4	34:28	מסכן	/ ל[היתיה עלוהי קבילת]מׄסכנין
10 XXVII,2	36:8	מסכן	א]ח̊ידין בחבלי מסכניא /
10 XXVII,9	36:15	מסכן	/ ויפרק מ̊[סכנא
10 XIX,3	31:28	מעל	כד]בׄת / לאלהא מעלׄ[א
18 24,1		מעל	מע]ל שמשא אר[
18 28,3		מעל	]א̊ עד מעל ש[משא
18 12i5		מערב	]כׄול רוח מערב /
18 20,2		מערב	]לברא מן היכלא לימין מערבהׄ[
18 12i2		מעשׂר	]יא פרישא ודי מעשריא /
10 V,1	21:20	מפלה	ע]י̊נ̊ו̊הי במפלתה
18 9,6		מקדש	]מ̊קד̊ש̊א ול∘לׄ[
10 XXIV,5	34:10	מרא	/ ומן לחבל{ה̊}א מ̊[רא
10 XXIV,7	34:12	מרא	ומראׄ[ ]ה̊ו̊א ארעא עבד /
10 IX,5	25:2	מרום	ע[בד שלם / במרו]מה
18 13,8		מרפסת	]מרפסתא ליד יס∘[
10 XXIX,1	37:11	מרק	אף בהון ימרק ע̊נ̊נׄ[ין]
18 29,4		משח	]משח וחמ[ר
10 XXX,3	38:5	משחה	/ מן שם משחתה הן תנדע
10 XXII,10	33:15	משכב	במנ]מה על משכבה[
10 XXX,1	38:3	נא	/ אסר נא כ̮גבר חלצ̊[י]ך̊[
10 XXXIV,3	40:7	נא	אסר / נא כגבר חלציך
10 XXXIV,6	40:10	נא	/ העדי נא גוה ורם רוח
10 XXXIV,7	40:11	נא	/ העדי נא חמת רגזך
10 XXXVII,6	42:4	נא	שמע נא ואנה אמלל
10 XXX,3	38:5	נגד	מן נׄגד עליה חוטא
10 XXXV,3	40:25	נגד	התגד / תנין בחכא
10 XXX,6	38:8	נגח	ב[הנ]גחותה מן רחם תהומא / למפק
10 XXXII,6	39:7	נגש	ונגשת שליט לא / ישמע
10 XXIII,7	33:28	נהור	] / בנהור תחזא
10 XXIII,8	33:30	נהור	בנהו]ר̊ / חיין
10 XXVIII,7	36:30	נהור	ופרס נהׄ[ורה /
10 XXIX,6	37:15	נהור	ו̊[הו]פ̊ע̊ נׄהור עננה /
10 XXXV,6	40:27	ניח	הימלל / עמך בניח
10 XXXV,10	40:31	נון	]ג̊ון די נונׄין[
10 VIII,3	24:13	נור	/ קדמוהי לנורה̊[
10 XXIX,2	37:11	נור	וינפק מן / ענן נורה
10 XXXVI,4	41:10	נור	עטישתה תדלק / נורא בין עינוהי
18 13,3		נור	ו]ש̊ויה על נורא ואיתי קמח סולת[
10 XXXIII,5	39:23	נזך	/ שנן ונזך וחרף סיף
10 XXXVI,5	41:12	נחיר	מ̊ן̊ נחירוה יפק תנן /
10 XXXVIII,6	42:11	נחם	ונחמוהי על כל באישתה
10 XVI,9	30:19	נחת	אחתוני [לטינא]
10 XXVIII,5	36:28	נחת	ועננוהי י̮גחתוׄן / טׄ[יפי מין
10 XXXI,3	38:26	נחת	להנחתה על ארע / מדבר
10 XXXV,3	40:24	נטל	/ במטל עינוהי יכלנה
10 XXI,7	32:15	נטר	/ והחשיו ונטרת מנהון ∘[
10 A,12		נטר	]נטרׄת
18 29,6		ניחוח	רי]ח ניחׄ[וח
18 33,1		ניחוח	]לׄריח ניחוח[
10 IV,6	21:7	נכס	/ והסגיו נכסין
18 23ii3		נכס	/ נכסיהון [

Text	Root	Ref.	Location
אמתי לנכר]י	נכרי	19:15	**10** II,4
מן]קדמוהי ינסון	נסא=נשא	27:13	**10** XI,4
קפלי בשרה דבקין נסיכי]ן בה] /	נסך	41:15	**10** XXXVI,8
על כן אתנסך ואתמה̇א	נסך	42:6	**10** XXXVII,8
רו]ב̇ע סתא ונסך לגוא מורכי̇]ותא	נסך		**18** 13,5
העמה ת]נפח ערפלא /	נפח	37:18	**10** XXIX,8
או סיג נפילא ת[פתח]	נפיל	38:31	**10** XXXI,8
[והן לא ישמ]ע̇ון בחרבא יפלון /	נפל	36:12	**10** XXVII,6
וינפק מן / ענן נורה	נפק	37:11	**10** XXIX,1
ב[הנ]גחותה מן רחם תהומא / למפק	נפק	38:8	**10** XXX,7
/ היכא יפק *vac*	נפק	38:24	**10** XXXI,2
/ ולהנפקה צמחי דתאה	נפק	38:27	**10** XXXI,5
ומן בטן מן נפק גלידא	נפק	38:29	**10** XXXI,6
יקשן בניהן ויפק°ן	נפק	39:4	**10** XXXII,3
יקשן בניהן ויפק°ן	נפק	39:4	**10** XXXII,3
/ ובחיל ינפק לאנפי חרב	נפק	39:21	**10** XXXIII,3
מן פמה לפידין / יפקון	נפק	41:11	**10** XXXVI,5
מ̇ן נחירוה יפק תנן /	נפק	41:12	**10** XXXVI,5
וזיקין / יפקן מן פמה	נפק	41:13	**10** XXXVI,7
דן ימות בנפ̇[ש	נפש	21:25	**10** V,5
]לנפשי הן לכמ̇[א	נפש	27:2	**10** X,9
נפשה ג̇מרין תגסא	נפש	41:12	**10** XXXVI,6
המן חכמתך יסתער נצא	נץ	39:26	**10** XXXIII,7
/ שביעיא כדמות נצ ורד]	נץ		**18** 14ii4
לנצבתנא / בליליא	נצבה	35:10	**10** XXVI,5
/ מנצבהון וכלילא חמי[שיא	נצב		**18** 14ii2
/ [זכ]י אנה ולא חטא לי ונקא̇]	נקא	33:9	**10** XXII,3
ובחרתך תקוב לסתה	נקב	40:26	**10** XXXV,5
[ויאחדונני י]ומי תשבר̇א̇ יאקפוני /	נקף	30:16	**10** XVI,6
ולנקשת זין וזעקת אשתדור / יחדה	נקשה	39:25	**10** XXXIII,6
מן]קדמוהי ינסון	נשא=נסא	27:13	**10** XI,4
ותשוב קדמוהי על ארעא	נשב	38:24	**10** XXXI,2
]בארבע רגלוהי ונשט תורא °	נשט		**18** 13,1
נ]שיפה פיל /	נשיף		**18** 22,4
נשמ]תה עלוהי יכלא /	נשמה	34:14	**10** XXIV,8
ל]ב̇י̇ / ונשקת ידי לפ̇[מי	נשק	31:27	**10** XIX,2
או על מאמרך יתגב̇ה̇ נ̇ש̇רא /	נשר	39:27	**10** XXXIII,8
הן זכי]ת̇ מא / תתן לה	נתן	35:7	**10** XXVI,2
ר]ו̇ב̇ע ס̇תא̇ ואסקה למדבחא כולה[	סאה=סתא		**18** 13,4
ר]ו̇ב̇ע ס̇תא̇ ואסקה למדבחא כולה[	סאה		**18** 13,4
רו]ב̇ע סתא ונסך לגוא מורכי̇]ותא	סאה=סתא		**18** 13,5
רו]ב̇ע סתא ונסך לגוא מורכי̇]ותא	סאה		**18** 13,5
להסבעה שיתא ושביקה /	סבע=שבע	38:27	**10** XXXI,4
ארו סברת[	סבר	32:11	**10** XXI,1
/ והסגיו נכסין	סגא=שגא	21:7	**10** IV,6
]וזיא כטינא יסגא /	סגא=שגא	27:16	**10** XI,7

Text	Root	Ref.	Location
/ ב]ך ובסגיא עויתך	סגיא=שגיא	35:6	**10** XXVI,1
מן סגיא [עשוקיא יז]עקון	סגיא=שגיא	35:9	**10** XXVI,3
יצוחון / מן קדם סגיאין	סגיא=שגיא	35:9	**10** XXVI,4
ויומוהי / סגיא[לא נ]דע	סגיא=שגיא	36:26	**10** XXVIII,4
/ ט̇ופי מין על]עם סגיא	סגיא=שגיא	36:28	**10** XXVIII,6
ות°[ה]ת̇תרחץ ב[ה ארו] ס̇גיא /	סגיא=שגיא	39:11	**10** XXXII,10
/ ק̇ל סגנין הטמרו לחנך דב̇[ק	סגן	29:10	**10** XIV,4
/ רשיעין יסגפ̇[ונני	סגף	19:18	**10** II,7
/ י]שוא בסדא רגלי וסכר כ[ל	סד	33:11	**10** XXII,5
/ דנח ולס]הרא	סהר	31:26	**10** XIX,1
/ התסוג בדשין ימא	סוג	38:8	**10** XXX,6
]ס̇יפת /	סוף	31:16	**10** XVIII,9
ספ̇[ו	סוף	31:4	**10** XX,2
/ תסיפון	סוף	32:11	**10** XXI,2
לא] א̇ס̇ו̇ף **	סוף	40:4	**10** XXXIV,1
עד אמת]י̇ תשוא סוף למלא̇]	סוף	18:2	**10** I,5
עד תחקרון סוף[	סוף	32:11	**10** XXI,2
ר]ב̇רבין די לא סוף	סוף	34:24	**10** XXV,1
ומנין שנוהי די לא סוף	סוף	36:26	**10** XXVIII,4
]ב להון סחור [	סחור		**18** 7,3
] סחור לעליתא ד]	סחור		**18** 9,1
ד]י עמודין סחר מן תרע לת̇[רע	סחר		**18** 11,6
]נ̇א ליד כותלא די סחר לי°[	סחר		**18** 11,2
/ ומסטיא]	סטא	28:28	**10** XIII,10
או סיג נפילא ת[פתח]	סיג	38:31	**10** XXXI,8
] על̇] סי[פי חסוך /	סיף	26:10	**10** X,1
/ שנן ונזך וחרף סיף	סיף	39:23	**10** XXXIII,5
/ הסתכל[	סכל=שכל	22:21	**10** VII,7
]ואסתכ̇ל מא יאמר ל̇י /	סכל=שכל	23:5	**10** VIIa,6
]יסתכל *vac*	סכל=שכל	26:14	**10** X,6
ובכל שבילוהי לא הסתכ̇[לו]	סכל=שכל	34:27	**10** XXV,3
וקום הסתכל בגבורת אלהא /	סכל=שכל	37:14	**10** XXIX,5
]הון פרישא וסכנתא /	סכן		**18** 12i3
/ י]שוא בסדא רגלי וסכר כ[ל	סכר	33:11	**10** XXII,5
ר]ו̇ב̇ע ס̇תא̇ ואסקה למדבחא כולה[	סלק		**18** 13,4
ו]ש̇ויה על נורא ואיתי קמח סולת[	סלת		**18** 13,3
כפם כתוני יסנ]פ̇ונני	סנף	30:18	**10** XVI,9
המן חכמתך יסתער נצא	סער	39:26	**10** XXXIII,7
את]ר̇י / ספירא̇]	ספיר	28:6	**10** XII,3
// כסין שבעה וספלין למרח ש̇ת̇ה̇]	ספל		**18** 18,1
/ אנה] הן חרגתי לא תסר̇]דנך	סרד	33:7	**10** XXII,1
ר]ו̇ב̇ע ס̇תא̇ ואסקה למדבחא כולה[	סתא=סאה		**18** 13,4
רו]ב̇ע סתא ונסך לגוא מורכי̇]ותא	סתא=סאה		**18** 13,5
/ צפרי שמיא אסת̇[תרת	סתר	28:21	**10** XIII,2
ויסת]ר̇ אנפוהי	סתר	34:29	**10** XXV,5
לס]ת̇רי יתון	סתר	30:13	**10** XVI,1

Reference	Verse	Word	Context
10 IX,4	25:2	עבד	ע[בד שלם / במרו]מה
10 XIII,6	28:25	עבד	/ במעבדה לרוחא[
10 XIII,7	28:26	עבד	במעבד[ה למטרא דת וארח לעננין]
10 XVIII,6	31:14	עבד	]מא אעבד / כדי יק[ום אלהא
10 XVIII,8	31:15	עבד	] ארו / עבד[ני
10 XXIII,4	33:26	עבד	] וכעבד / כפוהי ישלם לה
10 XXIV,2	34:8	עבד	ומתחבר / לעבדי שקרא[
10 XXV,2	34:25	עבד	יחכ]ם עבדהון
10 XXVI,5	35:10	עבד	ולא אמר[ין אן הוא]אלהא / די עבדנה
10 XXVII,5	36:11	עבד	/ הן ישמעון ויעבד[ון
10 XXVIII,1	36:23	עבד	/ עב[דת עולה
10 XXX,2	38:4	עבד	/ אן הוית במעבדי ארעא
10 XXXVII,4	42:2	עבד	ידעת די כלא / תכול למעבד
10 XXXVIII,1	42:6	עבד	ו]עבדו[כדי אמר להון] / אלהא
10 II,5	19:16	עבד	/ לעבדי קרית ולא ע[נא
10 XI,1	27:11	עבד	בי]ד אלהא ועבד /
10 XVIII,6	31:13	עבד	]הן אתקצרת / בדין עב[די
10 XXIV,7	34:13	עבד	ומרא[ ]הוא ארעא עבד /
10 XXVII,3	36:9	עבד	/ ויחוא להן עבדיהו[ן ועוית]הון
10 XXVIII,1	36:24	עבד	ד]כר ארו רברבין עבדוהי די / חזו המ[ון
10 XXIX,2	37:12	עבד	ואזלין לעבדיהון /
10 XXXV,7	40:28	עבד	ותדברנה לעבד עלם
18 17ii4		עובי	/ תרתין ועובי פותי כות[לא
10 III,7	20:5	עבע	]לעבע תעדא [
10 VIIa,7	23:6	עד	ינ]עול עמי מלוא עד[
10 XVIII,4	31:12	עד	הי]א עד / אבדון ת[אכל
10 XXI,2	32:11	עד	עד תחקרון סוף[
10 XXX,8	38:11	עד	ואמרת עד תנא / ולא תוסף[
18 26,3		עד	]א עד תדנח שמ[שא
18 28,3		עד	]א עד מעל ש[משא
10 III,7	20:5	עדא	]לעבע תעדא [
10 XXXIV,4	40:8	עדא	פתגם האף / תעדא דינה
10 XXXIV,6	40:10	עדא	/ העדי נא גוה ורם רוח
10 XXXIV,7	40:11	עדא	/ העדי נא חמת רגזך
10 XXVII,5	36:11	עדן	ושניהון / ביקר ועדנין
10 XXXI,1	38:23	עדן	/ ד[י מנעת ל]עדן ע[קת]א
10 XXXII,2	39:2	עדן	ותנדע עדן מולדהין
10 XVI,7	30:17	עדק	ועדק[י / לא ישכבון
10 IX,10	26:2	עדר	ענא איוב ואמ]ר העד[רת
10 XIV,7	29:12	עדר	/ [ד]י לא עדר להן
10 XXI,8	32:16	עוד	/ ו]קמו ולא ימללון עוד[
18 15,1		עוד	]משרתא עוד להן די להוה[
18 30,2		עוד	]ון עוד לויא דבח[ין
10 XXXIII,9	39:27	עוזא	/ ועוזא ירים קנ[ה
10 XXVI,1	35:6	עויה	/ ב]ך ובסגיא עויתך
10 XXII,4	33:10	עול	/ הן עולין השכח אחד לי ה[יך
10 XIV,2	29:8	עולים	/ ו]חזוני עלומין טשו וגברין ח∘[
10 XXIII,3	33:25	עולים	]מן / עולים
10 XXIX,9	37:18	עוק	/ תקיף כמח]זיה עקה
10 VII,4	22:18	עטה	/ ועטת רש[יעין
10 XXXVI,3	41:9	עטישה	עטישתה תדלק / נורא בין עינוהי
10 X,5	26:14	עטר	מא עטר מלא נש[מע]
10 IV,7	21:8	עין	/ לעיניהון
10 V,1	21:20	עין	ע]ינוהי במפלתה
10 XIV,5	29:11	עין	/ ת]שמע אדן שבחתני ועין ח[זת
10 XXXV,3	40:24	עין	/ במטל עינוהי יכלנה
10 XXXVI,4	41:10	עין	עטישתה תדלק / נורא בין עינוהי
10 XXXVII,7	42:5	עין	וכען עיני / חזתך
10 I,7	18:4	על	] העל דב[רתך
10 II,1	19:11	על	/ ותק]ף עלי רגזה וח[שבני
10 IV,4	21:5	על	/ סימו ידיכון על [פם
10 IV,8	21:9	על	/ אלהא עליהו[ן
10 V,6	21:26	על	כחדה על [
10 V,7	21:26	על	ע]ליהון
10 IX,6	25:3	על	] או על מן לא תקום [
10 X,1	26:10	על	] על[סי]פי חסוך /
10 XV,4	30:1	על	וכען ח]אכו עלי זערין מני ביומין[
10 XVI,5	30:16	על	וכען עלי תתאשד / [נפשי
10 XVI,10	30:20	על	ע]ליך ∘[
10 XIX,4	31:29	על	ה]ללת / על באישתה[
10 XX,8	32:3	על	/ ואף ע[ל
10 XXII,10	33:15	על	במנ]מה על משכבה[
10 XXIV,8	34:14	על	נשמ]תה עלוהי יכלא /
10 XXV,5	34:29	על	מן יתיבנה על עם /
10 XXVII,1	36:7	על	/ למלכין יתבי ע[ל כרסיהון
10 XXVII,8	36:13	על	ל]בבהון לרגז / עליהון
10 XXVIII,2	36:25	על	ו]כל אנשא עלוהי חזין
10 XXVIII,9	36:32	על	]על מאמרה מ[
10 XXVIII,10	36:33	על	י]שגח על[והי
10 XXIX,1	37:10	על	/ על אנפי מין
10 XXIX,3	37:12	על	/ על כל די ברא יפקדנון על אנפי תבל
10 XXIX,3	37:12	על	/ על כל די ברא יפקדנון על אנפי תבל
10 XXIX,5	37:13	על	והן פתגם חוב להוא / עליה
10 XXIX,6	37:15	על	/ התנ]דע מא שויא אלהא עליהן
10 XXX,3	38:5	על	מן נגד עליה חוטא
10 XXX,4	38:6	על	או / על מא אשיה אתיגדון
10 XXXI,2	38:24	על	ותשוב קדמוהי על ארעא
10 XXXI,3	38:26	על	להנחתה על ארע / מדבר
10 XXXI,9	38:32	על	]∘∘∘א על בניה תיאש ∘[
10 XXXII,4	39:4	על	נפקו ולא תבוא / עליהן
10 XXXII,6	39:7	על	/ וחאך על מהמא תקף קריא
10 XXXII,8	39:9	על	א[ו]היבית על / אוריך

Text	Lemma	Job	Reference
יחאך על דחלא	על	39:22	**10** XXXIII,3
עלוהי יתלה שלט	על	39:23	**10** XXXIII,4
או על מאמרך יתגבה נשרא /	על	39:27	**10** XXXIII,8
ותחיבנני על דברת די תזכא	על	40:8	**10** XXXIV,4
/ והוא מלך על כל רחש *vac*	על	41:26	**10** XXXVII,2
ותרתין ועליהן לא / אוסף	על	40:5	**10** XXXVII,5
על כן אתנסך ואתמהא	על	42:6	**10** XXXVII,8
ונחמוהי על כל באישתה	על	42:11	**10** XXXVIII,6
באישתה די / היתי אלהא עלוהי	על	42:11	**10** XXXVIII,7
] על כול זרע בני [	על		**18** 7,1
]לעל[	על		**18** 7,5
פתו]רא ועלוי לחמא שויו[	על		**18** 8,3
]בא ובנא בנין עלוי עמ[	על		**18** 9,4
ו]שויה על נורא ואיתי קמח סולת[	על		**18** 13,3
ועליא שבעא דודין תפין על אבני[	על		**18** 18,2
]°על ארבע קרנת מדבח[א] /	על		**18** 22,1
// עליהון ל[	על		**18** 23ii1
]על כול זרעא[	על		**18** 24,4
]יתמנון עלוהי[	על		**18** 26,2
/ ועל ש°[	על		**18** 31ii5
]על ארבע ש[	על		**18** 32,5
]ויקדשנה עליה[	על		**18** 32,7
/ ועלא[	עלא		**18** 12ii7
ועליא שבעא דודין תפין על אבני[	עליא		**18** 18,2
] סחור לעליתא ד[	עליה		**18** 9,1
]ד לתרתי עליתא /	עליה		**18** 21,3
ותב ליומי עלימ[ותה	עלימו	33:25	**10** XXIII,3
וקדמוהי / תרוט עלימו	עלימו	41:14	**10** XXXVI,8
י]נעל עמך /	עלל	22:4	**10** VI,3
ינ]עול עמי מלוא עד[	עלל	23:6	**10** VIIa,7
ורוח ל[א י]נעול בינה[ו]ן	עלל	41:8	**10** XXXVI,2
]אחיהון עללין חלפהון ארבע מאה צ[	עלל		**18** 15,3
ע]ללי[ן ע[	עלל		**18** 15,6
ו]ל[א] / עלל לה כול א[נש	עלל		**18** 16ii&17i4
]כה עללין [	עלל		**18** 24,6
יד]עת מן עלמא מן ד[י]	עלם	20:4	**10** III,5
ותדברנה לעבד עלם	עלם	40:28	**10** XXXV,7
]לכול עלמין *vac*[	עלם		**18** 19,4
מן יתיבנה על עם /	עם	34:29	**10** XXV,5
/ ט]יפי מין על]עם סגיא	עם	36:28	**10** XXVIII,6
ארו [°]בהון ידין ע[ממין] /	עם	36:31	**10** XXVIII,8
]העמי לשאול ת[נחתון]	עם	17:16	**10** I,2
י]נעל עמך /	עם	22:4	**10** VI,3
ינ]עול עמי מלוא עד[	עם	23:6	**10** VIIa,7
ארו ש]לטן ורבו עם אלהא	עם	25:2	**10** IX,4
אבה]תהון מלמהוא עם כלבי ע[ני	עם	30:1	**10** XV,5
/ ואף עם אסירין ב[זיקין	עם	36:8	**10** XXVII,2
הימלל / עמך בניח	עם	40:27	**10** XXXV,6
או ימלל עמך בהתחננה לך	עם	40:27	**10** XXXV,6
היקים / קים עמך	עם	40:28	**10** XXXV,7
ואכלו / עמה לחם בביתה	עם	42:11	**10** XXXVIII,6
]°לון עמה ומן[	עם		**18** 25,5
]בון עם עו°[	עם		**18** 29,2
]אמין עמודין שבעה ת[	עמוד		**18** 9,2
ד]י עמודין סחר מן תרע לת[רע	עמוד		**18** 11,6
קד]מוני יומי עמ[לא	עמל	30:27	**10** XVII,4
אבה]תהון מלמהוא עם כלבי ע[ני	ען	30:1	**10** XV,5
vac ענ]א בלדד שוחא[ה	ענא	18:1	**10** I,4
/ לעבדי קרית ולא ע[נא	ענא	19:16	**10** II,5
v[*ac* ענא איוב ואמ[ר]	ענא	23:1	**10** VIIa,1
va[*c* ענא בלד[ד שוחאה ואמר]	ענא	25:1	**10** IX,3
/ ענא אלהא לאיוב ועננא ואמר לה	ענא	40:6	**10** XXXIV,2
/ ענא איוב ואמר קדם אלהא	ענא	41:26	**10** XXXVII,3
/ א]רו אנה שיזבת לענא מן °[	עני	29:12	**10** XIV,6
וקבילת ענין ישמע /	עני	34:28	**10** XXV,4
/ תסוק לשמיא גאותה ואנ]פה לענניא[	ענן	20:6	**10** III,8
וכענן / [עבר מני פורק]ני	ענן	30:15	**10** XVI,4
ארו / ענני[מין ימנא]	ענן	36:27	**10** XXVIII,5
ועננוהי יגחתון / ט[יפי מין	ענן	36:28	**10** XXVIII,5
מן פרס / ע[נניא די אתרגו]שתה	ענן	36:29	**10** XXVIII,7
אף בהון ימרק ענג[ין]	ענן	37:11	**10** XXIX,1
וינפק מן / ענן נורה	ענן	37:11	**10** XXIX,2
ו[הו]פע נהור עננה /	ענן	37:15	**10** XXIX,6
/ התנ]דע להלבש[ו]א עננה גבורה	ענן	37:16	**10** XXIX,7
בשוית עננין [לבו]שה	ענן	38:9	**10** XXX,7
וארח לעננין קלילין	ענן	38:25	**10** XXXI,3
או מן / ילד [ע]נני טלא	ענן	38:28	**10** XXXI,6
/ ענא אלהא לאיוב ועננא ואמר לה	ענן	40:6	**10** XXXIV,2
וטמר / [ה]מון בעפר ( ) כח[דא	עפר	40:13	**10** XXXIV,9
[א]ואהוא לעפר / וקטם *v*]*ac* [*v*]*ac*	עפר	42:6	**10** XXXVII,8
/ ד[י מנעת ל]עדן ע[קת]א	עקה	38:23	**10** XXXI,1
יד]ה / עק[ר	עקר	28:9	**10** XII,6
]א ובשרא מתערב כחדא[	ערב		**18** 13,6
]° מן אלן וערבליא די /	ערבל		**18** 12i1
וחנקי ערדא מן / שרא	ערד	39:5	**10** XXXII,4
/ אתר ערימותא א[רו	ערימו	28:20	**10** XIII,1
העמה ת]נפח ערפלא /	ערפל	37:18	**10** XXIX,8
וערפלין חותלוהי	ערפל	38:9	**10** XXX,7
חללת ידה תנין ערק /	ערק	26:13	**10** X,4
]°אה ועש[ר] /	עשר		**18** 10i7
/ לכול תרי עשר תרעין[	עשר		**18** 17ii3
שביא די בה]ון וארבעת עשר כה[נין	עשר		**18** 20,4

פ]ותיה אמה ותרתי עשר[ה	עשרה		**18** 8,2
]א ואמר לי לעשרין ושת ○[	עשרין		**18** 15,4
אורכיהון ופו]תיהון אמין שת בשת [	פותה		**18** 9,3
○○○○[]פח[דו] תבי[ריא	פחד	41:17	**10** XXXVI,10
נ]שיפה פיל /	פיל		**18** 22,4
מ]מ[ונ]ה קשֻׁטה יפלג	פלג	27:17	**10** XI,8
]תין ויפלגון יתה בארע[	פלג	40:29	**10** XXXV,9
פ]ליג לתמנין וארבעה כהנין ש[	פלג		**18** 20,3
] דרומא ופלג[	פלג		**18** 6,3
]מן כול שבעת פלוגת פתורי	פלוגה		**18** 20,3a
היבא ראמ[א ל]מפלחך	פלח	39:9	**10** XXXII,8
/ הריתהון פל[טת	פלט	21:10	**10** IV,9
ילדן בניהן ויפלטן /	פלט	39:3	**10** XXXII,2
/ בפ]ם ארמלה הוית לצלו[	פם	29:13	**10** XIV,8
ל]בי / ונשקת ידי לפ[מי	פם	31:27	**10** XIX,2
מן פמה לפידין / יפקון	פם	41:11	**10** XXXVI,4
וזיקין / יפקן מן פמה	פם	41:13	**10** XXXVI,7
ואחריתא יהיבת לתנינה די קא]ם פנבד	פנבד		**18** 20,7
]ל ותודתהון / ופסחיהון ל○[	פסח		**18** 16ii&17i2
]לי פסחיא חפ○[	פסח		**18** 27,3
חר]ב יפצון ולא ישבעון /	פצא	27:14	**10** XI,5
ופצא לא / [איתי להון	פצא	30:13	**10** XVI,1
/ וי[אמר פצהי מן חב[לא	פצא	33:24	**10** XXIII,1
/ על כל די ברא יפקדנון על אנפי תבל	פקד	37:12	**10** XXIX,3
מן שלח פראה ברחרין	פרא	39:5	**10** XXXII,4
א]לן פרזיא ליד שור[א	פרז		**18** 6,2
]פרזיא[ ]ה[	פרז		**18** 6,4
נסיכי[ן בה] / כפרזלא	פרזל	41:15	**10** XXXVI,9
מן פרס / ע[נניא די אתרגו]שתה	פרס	36:29	**10** XXVIII,6
ופרס נה[ורה /	פרס	36:30	**10** XXVIII,7
ויפרוס / כנפוהי לרוחין	פרס	39:26	**10** XXXIII,7
פר[ק]ה /	פרק	33:28	**10** XXIII,6
/ ויפרק מ[סכנא	פרק	36:15	**10** XXVII,9
וכענן / [עבר מני פורק]ני	פרקן	30:15	**10** XVI,5
// גפן כדי פרש מן לולבי[א	פרש		**18** 14ii1
די פרשנא מן בע[ירי ארעא	פרש	35:11	**10** XXVI,6
אנתה / לחברתה חענן ולא יתפ[ר]שן	פרש	41:9	**10** XXXVI,3
]יא פרישא ודי מעשריא /	פרש		**18** 12i2
]הון פרישא וסכנתא /	פרש		**18** 12i3
]פרישא על[	פרש		**18** 33,3
כ]הניא מקבלין / מן ידהון דפש[טו	פשט		**18** 16ii&17i3
פ]תיא / לבי בא[נתה	פתא	31:9	**10** XVIII,1
מ]ן אפו יתיבנני פתגם ויש[וא	פתגם	24:25	**10** IX,2
ארו בכל פ[תגמוהי	פתגם	33:13	**10** XXII,7
והן פתגם חוב להוא / עליה	פתגם	37:13	**10** XXIX,4
ואש]אלנך והתיבני ( ) פתגם /	פתגם	38:3	**10** XXX,1

פתגם האף / תעדא דינה	פתגם	40:7	**10** XXXIV,3
פתו]רא ועלוי לחמא שויו[	פתור		**18** 8,3
]מן כול שבעת פלוגת פתורי	פתור		**18** 20,3a
פ]ותיה אמה ותרתי עשר[ה	פתי		**18** 8,2
]פותי תרע[ ]ורומ○○[	פתי		**18** 8,4
/ תרתין ועובי פותי כות[לא	פתי		**18** 17ii4
]○ן[ק]נא חד פותי /	פתי		**18** 21,4
ארו מא]צבו לאלהא בביתה ו[	צבו	21:21	**10** V,2
ידיהון]לא הוא לי צבין ובאכפי[הון	צבין	30:2	**10** XV,6
( ]הכען צדא אלהא / ישקר	צדא	34:12	**10** XXIV,6
]אלהא ומא יצדק[	צדק	25:4	**10** IX,7
/ ולבר אנש צדקתך	צדקה	35:8	**10** XXVI,3
]צהא לא /	צהא	22:7	**10** VI,6
בצורה יבית תקפה	צו(א)ר	41:14	**10** XXXVI,7
צ]דת /	צוד	31:9	**10** XVIII,2
יצוחון / מן קדם סגיאין	צוח	35:9	**10** XXVI,3
התקטר[ראמא ב]צוריה	צור	39:10	**10** XXXII,9
הצת דא [	צות	33:31	**10** XXIII,9
ומרא ה]בלא / [לא] יצתנה	צות	35:13	**10** XXVI,9
הצת דא איוב	צות	37:14	**10** XXIX,5
/ בפ]ם ארמלה הוית לצלו[	צלו	29:13	**10** XIV,8
/ ולהנפקה צמחי דתאה	צמח	38:27	**10** XXXI,5
/ צפרי שמיא אסת[תרת	צפר	28:21	**10** XIII,2
/ ב]צפרין בתרעי קריא בשוק[א	צפר	29:7	**10** XIV,1
ומן] צפריא / חכמנה	צפר	35:11	**10** XXVI,6
במזהר / כחדא כוכבי צפר	צפר	38:7	**10** XXX,5
התחאך / בה כצפר	צפר	40:29	**10** XXXV,8
/ קבל[	קבל	22:22	**10** VII,8
/ תקבל אלהא[	קבל	24:12	**10** VIII,2
או מא מידך יקבל[	קבל	35:7	**10** XXVI,2
יתרחץ די יקבלנה אגוגא /	קבל	40:23	**10** XXXV,2
כ]הניא מקבלין / מן ידהון דפש[טו	קבל		**18** 16ii&17i2
]ה תרעיא די לקובל היכלא ל[	קבל		**18** 19,1
/ קבל למא[מר	קבל	24:15	**10** VIII,6
וקבילת ענין ישמע /	קבלה	34:28	**10** XXV,4
קד]ישי קדישיא ולא[	קדיש		**18** 15,5
קד]ישי קדישיא ולא[	קדיש		**18** 15,5
ק]דיש הוא היכלא ויקרא רב[א	קדיש		**18** 19,3
קד]מוני יומי עמ[לא	קדם	30:27	**10** XVII,4
אמלל / קדמ[והי] / [	קדם	23:4	**10** VIIa,4
]○ הן לקד[ם	קדם	23:8	**10** VIIa,9
/ קדמוהי לנורה[	קדם	24:13	**10** VIII,3
מן]קדמוהי ינסון	קדם	27:13	**10** XI,4
יצוחון / מן קדם סגיאין	קדם	35:9	**10** XXVI,4
ותשוב קדמוהי על ארעא	קדם	38:24	**10** XXXI,2
וקדמוהי / תרוט עלימו	קדם	41:14	**10** XXXVI,7

10 XXXVII,3	42:1	קדם	/ ענא איוב ואמר קדם אלהא
18 17ii5		קדם	/ קדמה̊ן̊ קנין מאה]
18 20,1		קדם	כו]ל יום שביעי קודם אל דכר̇]נא
18 29,1		קדם	]ן̊ קודם מד[בחא
18 29,5		קדם	]קודמוהי̊[
18 22,6		קדמי	]לקדמין /
18 32,7		קדש	]ויקדשנה ̥עליה̊[
10 XXXVIII,8	42:11	קדש	/ וגבר קדש חד די דהב *vac*
18 25,1		קודש	]מן קודשי ישראל[
10 IX,6	25:3	קום	] או על מן לא תקום̇ [
10 XVII,5	30:28	קום	]קמ̇ת̇[ו]אזעקת /
10 XVIII,7	31:14	קום	]מ̇א אעבד / כדי יק[ום אלהא
10 XXI,8	32:16	קום	/ ו]ק̇מו ולא ימללון עוד̇[
10 XXV,1	34:24	קום	ויקים א[חרנין]
10 XXIX,5	37:14	קום	וקום הסתכל בגבורת אלהא /
10 XXX,4	38:6	קום	או מן הקים אבן חזיתה
10 XXXV,6	40:28	קום	היקים / קים עמך
18 20,7		קום	ואחריתא יהיבת לתנינה די קא]ם̇ פנבד
10 XI,9	27:18	קטון	]°°ן כקטותא /
10 X,3	26:12	קטל	]ימא ובמנדעה קטל /
10 XXXIV,9	40:13	קטם	אנפי]ה̊ון בקטם̇ תכסה /
10 XXXVII,9	42:6	קטם	[א̊]ואהוא לע̇פר / וקטם *vac* [*v*]*ac* *v*]*ac*
10 XXXII,9	39:10	קטר	התקטר[ראמא ב]צוריה
10 XXXV,8	40:29	קטר	ותקטרנה בחוטא לבנתך
10 XXXV,7	40:28	קים	היקים / קים עמך
10 XIV,4	29:10	קל	/ ק̇ל סגנין הטמרו לחנך דב̇]ק
10 XXII,2	33:8	קל	הך אמרת באדני וק̇[ל
10 XXXIII,5	39:25	קל	ולקל קרנא יאמר האח
10 XXXIV,5	40:9	קל	או בקל כותה תרעם /
10 XXXVIII,2	42:9	קל	ושמע א[ל]ה̇א בקלה די איוב
10 XIII,8	28:26	קליל	/ קלילין
10 XXXI,3	38:25	קליל	וארח לעננין קלילין
10 III,4	20:3	קללה	ק]ללתי אשמע ורו[ח]
10 XXXIII,9	39:28	קן	/ ועוזא̊ י̊ר̊י̊ם קנ[ה
18 17ii2		קנה	/ קנין תלתא ורום תרע̇]יא
18 17ii5		קנה	/ קדמה̊ן̊ קנין מאה[
18 21,4		קנה	]°ן̊[ק]נא חד פותי /
18 32,4		קנה	ש]בעת קניה [
10 XXXIII,9	39:28	קנן	ב]כ̇פא ישכון ויקנן̊[ ]° °[
18 13,3		קמח	ו]שויה על נורא ואיתי קמח סולת[
10 XXXVI,8	41:15	קפל	קפלי בשרה דבקין נסיכ̇י]ן בה[/
10 IX,1	24:24	קפץ	התכ]פ̇פו כיבלא יתקפ̇צון א̇]ו
10 XIII,5	28:24	קצו	/ לקצוי ארעא י°[
10 XVIII,5	31:13	קצר	]ה̇ן אתקצרת / בדין עב̇]די
10 II,5	19:16	קרא	/ לעבדי קרית ולא ע̇]נא
18 19,5		קרא	]שרי למקרא לי בכת̇]ב

10 XXXI,1	38:23	קרב	ליום קרב ואשתדר̇ [
10 XXXIII,6	39:25	קרב	ומן / רחיק יריח קרבה
18 13,2		קרב	ר]ח̊ע רגלוהי וקרבוהי ומלח כולה[
18 28,4		קרבן	]קורבני א[
10 VIII,1	24:12	קריה	/ מן קריה̊ון [
10 XIV,1	29:7	קריה	/ ב]צ̇פרין בתרעי קריא בשוק[א
10 XXXII,6	39:7	קריה	/ וחאך על מהמא תקף קר̊י̊א̊
10 XXXI,7	38:30	קרם	כא]בן[מ̇ין התקרמו מנה ואנפי °°ל̊[
10 XXXIII,5	39:25	קרן	ולקל קרנא יאמר האח
18 22,1		קרן	]°על ארבע קרנת מדבח̊]א[/
10 XXIV,8	34:13	קשט	/ וקשט תב̇]ל
10 VIIa,8	23:7	קשט	]ארו קשט ודת[
10 XI,8	27:17	קשיט	מ]מ[ונ]ה קשי̥טה יפלג
10 XXXII,3	39:4	קשש	יקשן בניהן ויפקן[
10 XXXII,8	39:9	ראם	היבא ראמ̇]א ל[מפלחך
10 XV,2	29:25	ראש	]ון בחרת ארחי והוית ר̊]אש
10 XV,2	29:25	ראש	]ון בחרת ארחי והוית ר̊]אש
10 XV,3	29:25	ראש	]בראש חילה וכגבר די א]בלין ינחם[
18 19,2		ראש	]ב̇יומא שביעיא וביום ראשי ח[דשא
18 20,6		רב	מן תרתי לחמא י]היבת לכהנא ר̊]בא
10 XIV,3	29:9	רב	/ ו]רבר̥ב̥ין חשו מללא וכף ישוו[
10 XXII,6	33:12	רב	/ ארו רב אלהא מן אנשא̇[
10 XXII,7	33:13	רב	/ ר̊בברן תמלל
10 XXV,1	34:24	רב	ר]ב̇רבין די לא סוף
10 XXVIII,1	36:24	רב	ד]כ̊ר̊ א̊רו רברבין עבדוהי ד̊י̊ / חזו המ̊]ון רב
10 XXVIII,3	36:26	רב	הא אלהא רב הוא
18 14ii5		רב	/ להוה לבש כהנא רבא[
18 19,3		רב	ק]ד̊יש הוא היכלא ויקרא רב̇]א
10 IX,4	25:2	רבו	ארו ש]לטן ורבו עם אלהא
10 XVI,4	30:15	רבו	עלי ונדת כ]רוח טבתי ור̥ב̥ו̥תי
18 13,4		רבע	ר]ו̊ב̊ע ̥סתא ואסקה למדבחא כולה[
18 13,5		רבע	רו]ב̇ע סתא ונסך לגוא מורכי̇]ותא
10 XX,6	32:2	רגז	/ אדין רגז[אליהוא בר ברכאל בוזאה
10 II,1	19:11	רגז	/ ותק]ף עלי רגזה וח[שבני
10 XVIII,3	31:11	רגז	ד]נ̇א רגז /
10 XIX,5	31:29	רגז	]ברגזי /
10 XXVII,7	36:13	רגז	ל]בבהון לרגז / עליהון
10 XXXIV,7	40:11	רגז	/ העדי נא חמת רגזך
10 XII,1	28:4	רגל	/ רגל̇[
10 XIV,10	29:15	רגל	ו]ר̇גלין לחגיר [
10 XXII,5	33:11	רגל	/ י]שוא בסדא רגלי וסכר כ̇ל
18 8,1		רגל	דהב]טב כולה ארבע רגלו̇ה̇[י
18 13,1		רגל	]בארבע רגלוהי ונשט תורא °[
18 13,2		רגל	ר]ח̊ע רגלוהי וקרבוהי ומלח כולה[
10 XXXII,8	39:8	רדף	ו]בתר כל ירוק / ירדף
18 18,1		רוח	// כסין שבעה וספלין למרח ש̊ת̊ה̊[

Reference	Verse	Root	Text
10 XXXIV,1	40:6	רוח	מן ר]וחא vac[v
10 II,6	19:17	רוח	/ רוח המכת לאנתתי[
10 III,4	20:3	רוח	ק]ללתי אשמע ורו[ח]
10 XIII,6	28:25	רוח	/ במעבדה לרוחא[
10 XVI,4	30:15	רוח	עלי ונדת כ]רוח טבתי ורבותי
10 XXXIII,8	39:26	רוח	ויפרוס / כנפוהי לרוחין
10 XXXIV,6	40:10	רוח	/ העדי נא גוה ורם רוח
10 XXXIV,8	40:12	רוח	/ רמת רוח תתבר
10 XXXVI,2	41:8	רוח	ורוח ל[א י]נעול בינה[ו]ן
18 12i5		רוח	]כול רוח מערב /
18 35,2		רוח	] רוחי ע[
18 27,6		רוי	]לא לרויו ◦[
10 XXXIII,2	39:21	רוט	וחפר בבקע וירוט ויחדא /
10 XXXVI,5	41:11	רוט	בלשני אשה ירטון
10 XXXVI,8	41:14	רוט	וקדמוהי / תרוט עלימו
10 XXVII,1	36:7	רום	וכל ר]חימוהי לרחצן ירמון /
10 XXVII,3	36:9	רום	ארו התרוממו
10 XXXIII,9	39:27	רום	/ ועוזא ירים קנ[ה
18 8,4		רום	]פותי תרע[ ]ורומ◦◦[
18 11,1		רום	]תוהי ארבעא רמין אמין א[רבע
18 11,3		רום	ורומה אמין תרתי[ן
18 17ii2		רום	/ קנין תלתא ורום תרע[יא
10 XX,7	32:2	רומאה	מן] / זרע רומא[ה
10 XXVII,1	36:7	רחים	וכל ר]חימוהי לרחצן ירמון /
10 XXVIII,3	36:25	רחיק	ובני אנשא / מרחיק[עלוה]י יבקון
10 XXXIII,6	39:25	רחיק	ומן / רחיק יריח קרבה
10 XXX,6	38:8	רחם	ב[הנ]גחותה מן רחם תהומא / למפק
10 XXXVIII,3	42:10	רחם	ותב אלהא לאיוב ברחמין /
10 XXXVIII,5	42:11	רחם	ואתין לות / איוב כל רחמוהי
18 13,2		רחע	ר]חע רגלוהי וקרבוהי ומלח כולה[
10 XXXII,10	39:11	רחץ	ות◦[ה]תתרחץ ב[ה ארו] סגיא /
10 XXXV,2	40:23	רחץ	יתרחץ די יקבלנה אגוגא /
10 IX,5	25:3	רחצן	האיתי רחצן להש[
10 XXVII,1	36:7	רחצן	וכל ר]חימוהי לרחצן ירמון /
10 II,3	19:13	רחק	/ הרחקו וידעי ב◦[
10 XXXVII,2	41:26	רחש	/ והוא מלך על כל רחש vac
10 XXXIII,6	39:25	ריח	ומן / רחיק יריח קרבה
18 13,7		ריח	] ריחא vac [
18 22,5		ריח	מד]בחא לריח /
18 29,6		ריח	רי]ח ניח[וח
18 33,1		ריח	]לריח ניחוח[
10 V,4	21:22	רם	מנדע ו]הוא רמיא מדין
10 XXXIV,6	40:10	רם	/ העדי נא גוה ורם רוח
10 XXV,2	34:26	רמא	וירמא המון באת[ר
10 XXXIV,8	40:12	רמה	/ רמת רוח תתבר
10 XV,7	30:3	רעא	כ]פן רעין הוא ירק ד[חשת
10 XXXII,7	39:8	רעא	ויבחר לה טורין לרע[יה
10 XXXIV,5	40:9	רעם	או בקל כותה תרעם /
10 II,7	19:18	רשיע	/ רשיעין יסגפ[ונני
10 III,6	20:5	רשיע	ארע]ה ארו מבע רשיע[ין]
10 VII,4	22:18	רשיע	/ ועטת רש[יעין
10 XI,3	27:13	רשיע	]אנש רשיעין /
10 XXV,6	34:30	רשיע	]ך אנש רשיעיא
10 XXXIV,8	40:12	רשיע	והטפי ר[שיעין תחו]תיהון
10 XXIV,2	34:8	רשע	רש]ע
10 XVII,3	30:27	רתח	מעיני רת]חו ולא / [דמו
10 I,2	17:16	שאול	]העמי לשאול ת[נחתון]
10 XIX,7	31:30	שאל	/ חכי למש[אל
10 XXX,1	38:3	שאל	ואש]אלנך והתיבני { } פתגם /
10 XXXIV,3	40:7	שאל	אשאלנך והתיבני
10 XXXVII,6	42:4	שאל	אשאלנך / והתיבני
18 15,2		שבועה	]א וכול די להוון משצין שבעתיהו[ן
10 XIV,5	29:11	שבח	/ ת]שמע אדן שבחתני ועין ח[זת
10 VIII,4	24:13	שביל	/ בשבילוהי ל[
10 XXV,3	34:27	שביל	אר]חה ובכל שבילוהי לא הסתכ[לו]
18 14ii4		שביעי	/ שביעיא כדמות נצ ורד[
18 19,2		שביעי	]ביומא שביעיא וביום ראשי ח[דשא
18 20,1		שביעי	כו]ל יום שביעי קודם אל דכר[נא
10 XI,5	27:14	שבע	חר]ב יפצון ולא ישבעון /
10 XXXI,4	38:27	שבע	להסבעה שיתא ושביקה /
18 20,3a		שבע	]מן כול שבעת פלוגת פתורי
18 9,2		שבע	]אמין עמודין שבעה ת[
18 17ii1		שבע	// שבעא בשבעא וא[
18 17ii1		שבע	// שבעא בשבעא וא[
18 18,1		שבע	// כסין שבעה וספלין למרח שתה[
18 18,2		שבע	ועליא שבעא דודין תפין על אבני[
18 26,5		שבע	]vac שבעה[
18 28,2		שבע	]◦בר שבעת[
18 32,4		שבע	ש]בעת קניה [
10 XXXI,4	38:27	שבק	להסבעה שיתא ושביקה /
10 XXXVIII,2	42:9	שבק	ושבק / להון חטאיהון בדילה
10 IV,6	21:7	שגא=סגא	/ והסגיו נכסין
10 XI,7	27:16	שגא=סגא	]זוזיא כטינא יסגא /
10 XXVI,1	35:6	שגיא=סגיא	/ ב]ך ובסגיא עויתך
10 XXVI,3	35:9	שגיא=סגיא	מן סגיא [עשוקיא יז]עקון
10 XXVI,4	35:9	שגיא=סגיא	יצוחון / מן קדם סגיאין
10 XXVIII,4	36:26	שגיא=סגיא	ויומוהי / סגיא[לא נג]דע
10 XXVIII,6	36:28	שגיא=סגיא	/ ט[יפי מין על]עם סגיא
10 XXXII,10	39:11	שגיא=סגיא	ות◦[ה]תתרחץ ב[ה ארו] סגיא /
10 I,5	18:2	שוא	עד אמת]י תשוא סוף למלא[
10 IX,2	24:25	שוא	מ]ן אפו יתיבנני פתגם ויש[וא
10 XIV,3	29:9	שוא	/ ו]רברבין חשו מללא וכף ישו[ן

Text	Root	Job	Ref.
/ י]שוא בסדא רגלי וסכר כ[ל	שוא	33:11	10 XXII,5
/ התנ]דע מא שויא אלהא עליהו[ן	שוא	37:15	10 XXIX,6
בשוית עננין [לבו]שה	שוא	38:9	10 XXX,7
ותשוה / לה תחומין ודת[לימא נגר]ין	שוא	38:9	10 XXX,7
מן שויא / למטרא זמן	שוא	38:25	10 XXXI,2
די שוית דחשת ביתה	שוא	39:6	10 XXXII,5
התשוא / זמם באפה	שוא	40:26	10 XXXV,4
פתו]רא ועלוי לחמא שוי[ו	שוא		18 8,3
ו]שויה על נורא ואיתי קמח סולת[	שוא		18 13,3
י]שויח על[והי	שוא	36:33	10 XXVIII,10
ארו שוא יש[מע אלהא	שוא	35:13	10 XXVI,8
vac ענ]א בלדד שוחא[ה	שוחי	18:1	10 I,4
/ סימו ידיכון על [פם	שום	21:5	10 IV,4
/ מן שם משחתה הן תנדע	שום	38:5	10 XXX,3
אף יומא דן] מן טלל שעותי די /	שועה	23:2	10 VIIa,2
/ ב]צפרין בתרעי קריא בשוק[א	שוק	29:7	10 XIV,1
]וכתא וישוור[	שור		18 32,2
א]לן פרזיא ליד שור[א	שור		18 6,2
]° שורא /	שור		18 12i6
]מן תרע לתרע בשורתא[	שורה		18 11,7
וכע]ן בתקף שחני יתון /	שחן	30:14	10 XVI,2
/ א]רו אנה שיזבת לענא מן °[	שיזב	29:12	10 XIV,6
ושיקו[ע שמיא] / מ[ן ילד]ה	שיקוע	38:29	10 XXXI,6
]א וכול די להוון משצין שבעתיהו[ן	שיצי		18 15,2
/ גבוה[י] °[ ]והי ש[י]ר[יא	שיר	40:31	10 XXXVI,1
להסבעה שיתא ושביקה /	שית	38:27	10 XXXI,4
או כחדה על עפר נ]שכב *v[ac*	שכב	17:16	10 I,3
ש]כב ולא איתחד /	שכב	27:19	10 XI,10
/ וימות [ ] ישכבון /	שכב	34:15	10 XXIV,9
מלוא אנדע ואשכ[חנה] /	שכח	23:3	10 VIIa,3
/ הן עולין השכח אחד לי ה[יך	שכח	33:10	10 XXII,4
/ הסתכל[	שכל=סכל	22:21	10 VII,7
]ואסתכל מא יאמר לי /	שכל=סכל	23:5	10 VIIa,6
]יסתכל *vac*	שכל=סכל	26:14	10 X,6
ובכל שבילוהי לא הסתכ[לו]	שכל=סכל	34:27	10 XXV,3
וקום הסתכל בגבורת אלהא /	שכל=סכל	37:14	10 XXIX,5
ב]כפא ישכון ויקנן[ ]° °[	שכן	39:28	10 XXXIII,9
מן שלח פראה ברחרין	שלח	39:5	10 XXXII,4
עלוהי יתלה שלט	שלט	39:23	10 XXXIII,4
ארו ש]לטן ורבו עם אלהא	שלטן	25:2	10 IX,4
ונגשת שליט לא / ישמע	שליט	39:7	10 XXXII,6
] וכעבד / כפוהי ישלם לה	שלם	33:26	10 XXIII,5
]ולא / כארחי השתלמת	שלם	33:27	10 XXIII,6
]אנש ישלם לה /	שלם	34:11	10 XXIV,5
תמנ]ה [י]רחיהין / שלמין	שלם	39:2	10 XXXII,2
]שי שלמיהון[	שלם		18 27,5
/ צפרי שמיא אסת[תרת	שמין	28:21	10 XIII,2
ק]ללתי אשמע ורו[ח]	שמע	20:3	10 III,4
מא עטר מלא נש[מע]	שמע	26:14	10 X,5
/ באדנינא שמענא ש[מעה	שמע	28:22	10 XIII,3
/ ת]שמע אדן שבחתני ועין ח[זת	שמע	29:11	10 XIV,5
וישמע]	שמע	31:29	10 XIX,5
ו]ישמענה /	שמע	33:26	10 XXIII,3
וקבילת ענין ישמע /	שמע	34:28	10 XXV,4
ארו שוא יש[מע אלהא	שמע	35:13	10 XXVI,8
/ הן ישמעון ויעבד[ון	שמע	36:11	10 XXVII,5
[והן לא ישמ]עון בחרבא יפלון /	שמע	36:12	10 XXVII,6
והוא אמר ישמעון לה	שמע	37:12	10 XXIX,2
ונגשת שליט לא / ישמע	שמע	39:7	10 XXXII,7
שמע נא ואנה אמלל	שמע	42:4	10 XXXVII,6
למשמע אדן שמעתך	שמע	42:5	10 XXXVII,7
למשמע אדן שמעתך	שמע	42:5	10 XXXVII,7
ושמע א[ל]הא בקלה די איוב	שמע	42:9	10 XXXVIII,2
מע]ל שמשא אר[	שמש		18 24,1
]א עד תדנח שמ[שא	שמש		18 26,3
עד ת]דנח שמשא וכו[ל	שמש		18 27,4
]א עד מעל ש[משא	שמש		18 28,3
ארו אמר לא / ישנא גבר מ[	שנא	34:9	10 XXIV,3
ושניהון / ביקר ועדנין	שנה	36:11	10 XXVII,5
ומנין שנוהי די לא סוף	שנה	36:26	10 XXVIII,4
]בכול שנא ל[	שנה		18 24,5
/ שנן ונזך וחרף סיף	שנן	39:23	10 XXXIII,5
]ת / אשה ישנקנה	שנק	33:25	10 XXIII,2
וחזא כל גאה והשפלה וכל /	שפל	40:11	10 XXXIV,7
{ }[ ]הכען צדא אלהא / ישקר	שקר	34:12	10 XXIV,7
ומתחבר / לעבדי שקרא[	שקר	34:8	10 XXIV,2
]חס לאלהא מן שקר /	שקר	34:10	10 XXIV,4
הבשקר[	שקר	34:17	10 XXIV,10
וחנקי ערדא מן / שרא	שרא	39:5	10 XXXII,5
]שרי למקרא לי בכת[ב	שרא		18 19,5
אורכיהון ופו]תיהון אמין שת בשת [	שת		18 9,3
אורכיהון ופו]תיהון אמין שת בשת [	שת		18 9,3
]א ואמר לי לעשרין ושת °[	שת		18 15,4
// כסין שבעה וספלין למרח שתה[	שת		18 18,1
]ן ויכלון ויש[תון	שתא		18 25,6
/ גוא כפרה וכלילא שתיתי[א	שתיתי		18 14ii3
/ וקשט תב[ל	תבל	34:13	10 XXIV,8
/ על כל די ברא יפקדנון על אנפי תבל	תבל	37:12	10 XXIX,3
/ רמת רוח תתבר	תבר	40:12	10 XXXIV,8
°°°°[]פח[דו] תבי[ריא	תבר	41:17	10 XXXVI,10
ב[הנ]גחותה מן רחם תהומא / למפק	תהום	38:8	10 XXX,6
מ]ן אפו יתיבנני פתגם ויש[וא	תוב	24:25	10 IX,2

Text	Word	Verse	Reference
/ אלין מלהתב[ה פתגם	תוב	32:1	**10** XX,3
/ מלין וכמא לא יתיבנה[	תוב	32:14	**10** XXI,6
ותב ליומי עלימ[ותה	תוב	33:25	**10** XXIII,3
לא[תבה	תוב	33:29	**10** XXIII,8
מן יתיבנה על עם /	תוב	34:29	**10** XXV,5
]הן יתובון מן באישתהון /	תוב	36:10	**10** XXVII,4
ואש]אלנך והתיבני { } פתגם /	תוב	38:3	**10** XXX,1
נפקו ולא תבוא / עליהן	תוב	39:4	**10** XXXII,3
ולא / יזוע ולא יתוב מן אנפי חרב	תוב	39:22	**10** XXXIII,4
אשאלנך והתיבני	תוב	40:7	**10** XXXIV,3
/ חדה מללת ולא אתיב	תוב	40:5	**10** XXXVII,5
אשאלנך / והתיבני	תוב	42:4	**10** XXXVII,7
ותב אלהא לאיוב ברחמין /	תוב	42:10	**10** XXXVIII,3
]ל ותודתהון / ופסחיהון ל◦[	תודה		**18** 16ii&17i1
תו]לעה	תולעה	17:14	**10** I,1
רמתא וב]ר אנש תולע[תא *vac*	תולעה	25:6	**10** IX,9
]בארבע רגלוהי ונשט תורא ◦[	תור		**18** 13,1
]י{ן} תורין תר[ין	תור		**18** 28,5
ותשוה / לה תחומין ודת[לימא נגר]ין	תחום	38:10	**10** XXX,8
/ תחות חטא[	תחות	31:4	**10** XX,1
והטפי ר[שיעין תחו]תיהון	תחות	40:12	**10** XXXIV,8
עלוהי יתלה שלט	תלא	39:23	**10** XXXIII,4
ג]בר / זמן תרין תלתה	תלת	33:29	**10** XXIII,8
/ קנין תלתא ורום תרע[יא	תלת		**18** 17ii2
וכ]ולהון תלתין ותרין אלפין	תלת		**18** 18,3
תמה יזעקון	תמה	35:12	**10** XXVI,7
]מן ת[מה י]חצא מאכל[א	תמה	39:29	**10** XXXIII,10
י]זיע ויתמהון מן /	תמה	26:11	**10** X,2
/ ותמהא אחד לי	תמה	21:6	**10** IV,5
] מאתין ותמנין אמ[ין	תמנין		**18** 6,1
פ]ליג לתמנין וארבעה כהנין ש[	תמנין		**18** 20,3
ואמרת עד תנא / ולא תוסף[	תנא	38:11	**10** XXX,8
תנ]חתי	תנחה	23:2	**10** VIIa,3
חללת ידה תנין ערק /	תנין	26:13	**10** X,4
לא הד]רכה / תנין[	תנין	28:8	**10** XII,5
התגד / תנין בחכא	תנין	40:25	**10** XXXV,4
// ברכה תניני[	תניני		**18** 16ii&17i1
מן נחירוה יפק תנן /	תנן	41:12	**10** XXXVI,5
ועליא שבעא דודין תפין על אבני[	תפא		**18** 18,2
התקלו /	תקל	34:30	**10** XXV,6
/ ותק]ף עלי רגזה וח[שבני	תקף	19:11	**10** II,1
וכע]ן בתקף שחני יתון /	תקף	30:14	**10** XVI,2
]א אתקף ◦[	תקף	30:26	**10** XVII,3
/ וחאך על מהמא תקף קריא	תקף	39:7	**10** XXXII,6
] התזיענה בתקף[	תקף	39:20	**10** XXXIII,1
בצורה יבית תקפה	תקף	41:14	**10** XXXVI,7
ולא יתבצר מנך תקף וחכמה /	תקף	42:2	**10** XXXVII,4
]ין מנה כול תרבה /	תרב		**18** 22,2
ג]בר / זמן תרין תלתה	תרין	33:29	**10** XXIII,8
ותרתין ועליהן לא / אוסף	תרין	40:5	**10** XXXVII,5
/ ויהב לה חד תרין בכל די הוא לה	תרין	42:10	**10** XXXVIII,4
פ]ותיה אמה ותרתי עשר[ה	תרין		**18** 8,2
פותיה אמי]ן תרתין	תרין		**18** 11,3
ורומה אמין תרתי[ן	תרין		**18** 11,3
/ לכול תרי עשר תרעין[	תרין		**18** 17ii3
/ תרתין ועובי פותי כות[לא	תרין		**18** 17ii4
וכ]ולהון תלתין ותרין אלפין	תרין		**18** 18,3
]◦ר ותרעין תרין /	תרין		**18** 21,2
]ד לתרתי עליתא /	תרין		**18** 21,3
]◦ תרתין כוליתה /	תרין		**18** 22,3
]י{ן} תורין תר[ין	תרין		**18** 28,5
/ ב]צפרין בתרעי קריא בשוק[א	תרע	29:7	**10** XIV,1
ודת[לימא נגר]ין ו[תר]עין	תרע	38:10	**10** XXX,8
]פותי תרע[ ]ורומ◦◦[	תרע		**18** 8,4
ד]י עמודין סחר מן תרע לת[רע	תרע		**18** 11,6
ד]י עמודין סחר מן תרע לת[רע	תרע		**18** 11,6
]מן תרע לתרע בשורתא[	תרע		**18** 11,7
]מן תרע לתרע בשורתא[	תרע		**18** 11,7
/ קנין תלתא ורום תרע[יא	תרע		**18** 17ii2
/ לכול תרי עשר תרעין[	תרע		**18** 17ii3
]ה תרעיא די לקובל היכלא ל[	תרע		**18** 19,1
]◦ר ותרעין תרין /	תרע		**18** 21,2
[יאחדונני י]ומי תשברא יאקפוני /	תשבר	30:16	**10** XVI,6
תלתין ותרין אלפין ותשע מאה[	תשע		**18** 18,3

PLATES

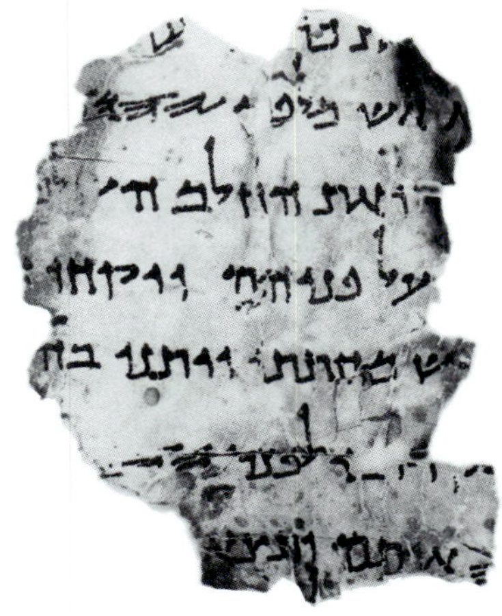

2 (44.011)

1ii 1i

1 (43.978)

4 (42.177)

3 (44.007)

7b (44.114)

7a (43.794)

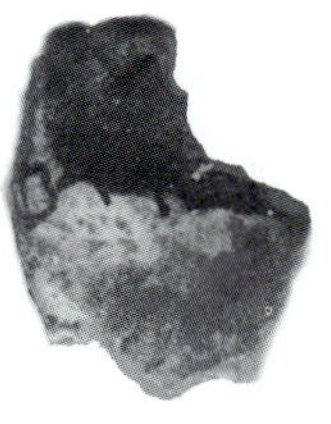

6 (44.114)

5 (43.978)

9ii 9i

9 (44.114)

8 (44.011)

2. 11QLeviticus[b]
PAM 42.177, 43.794, 43.978, 44.007, 44.011, 44.114
Mus. Inv. 566, 567, 577, 615, 1016, 1032

PLATE II

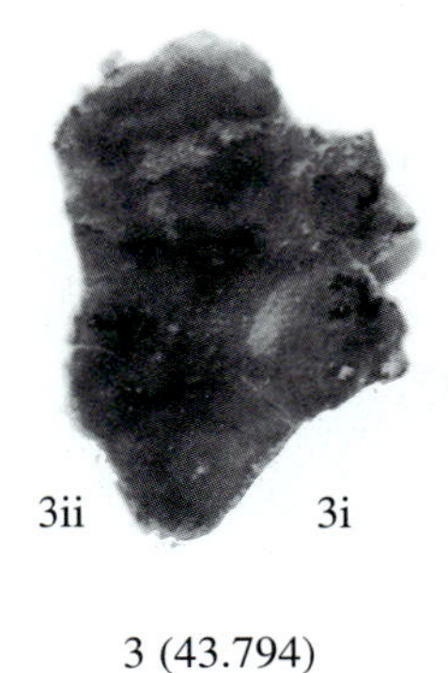

3ii 3i

3 (43.794)

2 (43.794)

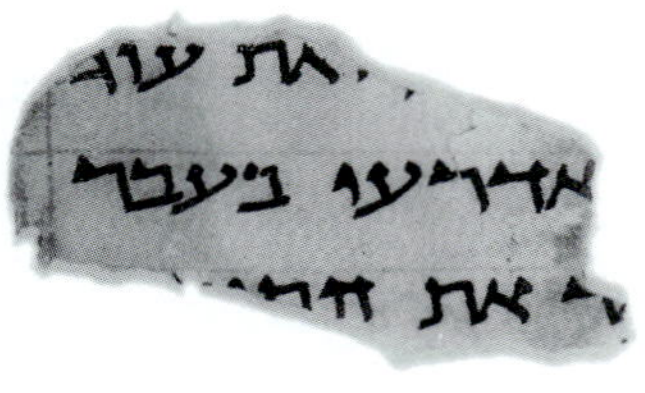

1 (44.003)

3. 11QDeuteronomy
PAM 43.794, 44.003; Mus. Inv. 576, 1016

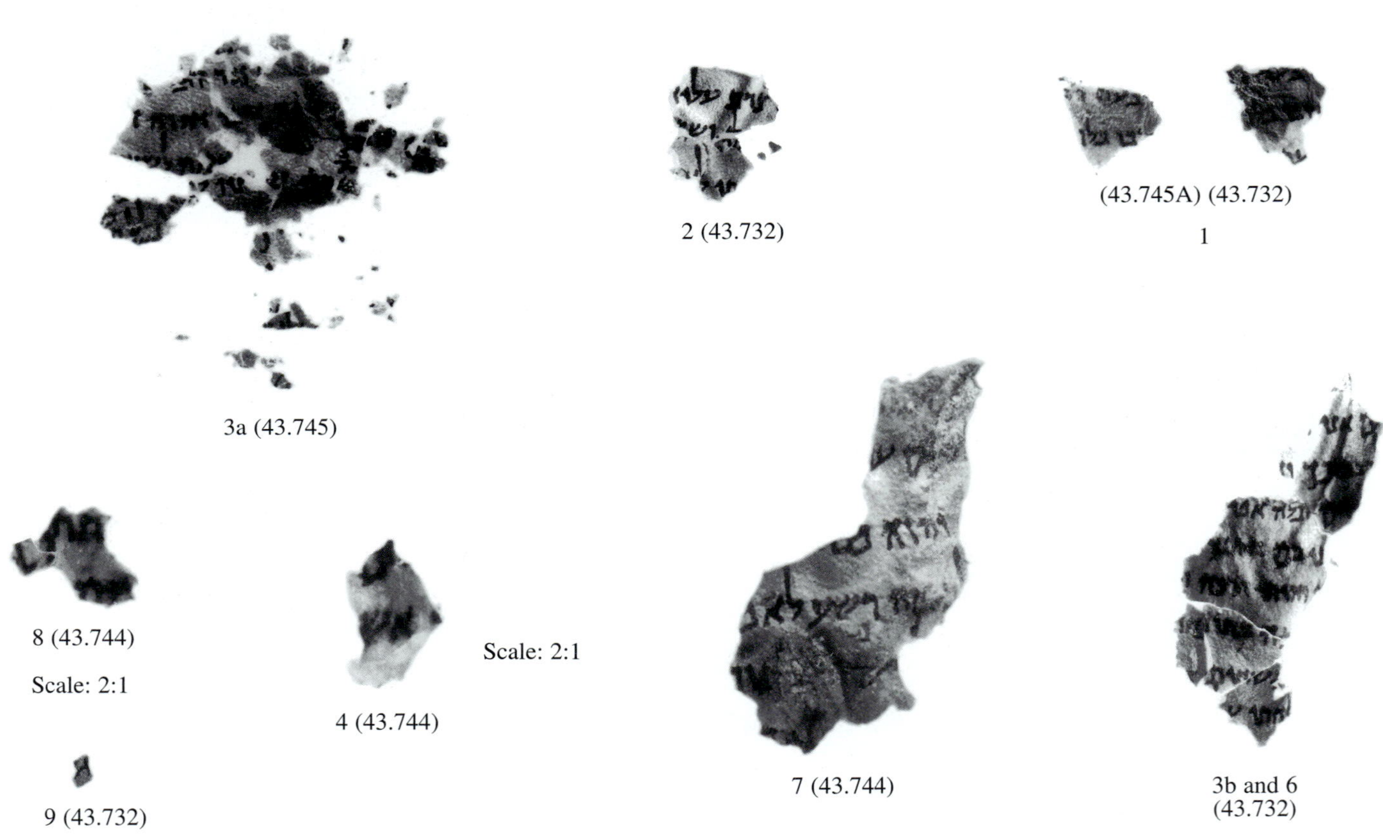

3a (43.745)

2 (43.732)

(43.745A) (43.732)
1

8 (43.744)

Scale: 2:1

4 (43.744)

Scale: 2:1

9 (43.732)

7 (43.744)

3b and 6
(43.732)

4. 11QEzekiel
PAM 43.732, 43.744, 43.745, 43.745A
Mus. Inv. 1010, 1013, 1013A

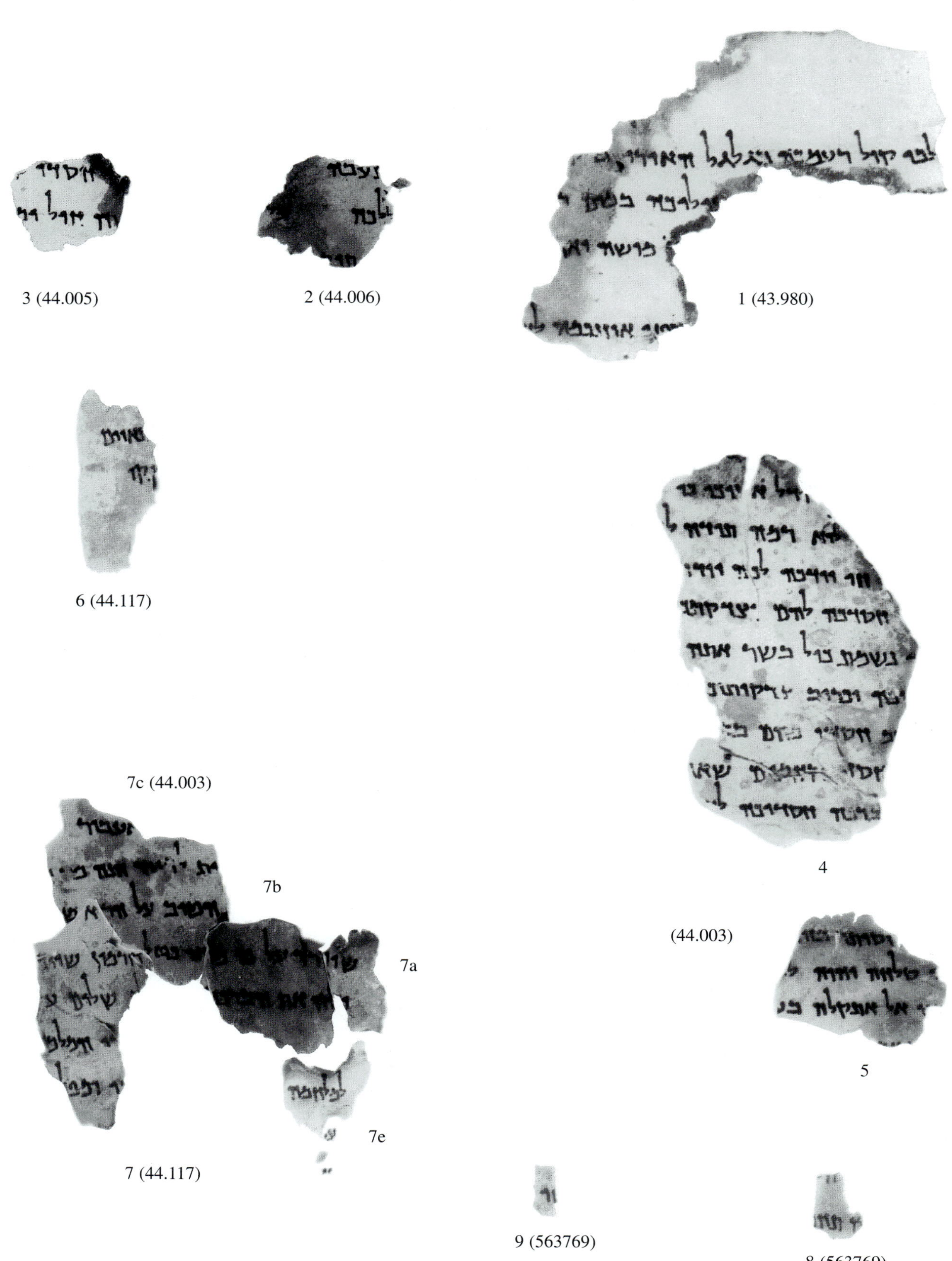

6. 11QPsalms[b]
PAM 43.980, 44.003, 44.005, 44.006, 44.117; IAA 563769
Mus. Inv. 576, 606, 613, 614, 621B, 1032

E

F

0 1 2 3 4 cm

6. 11QPsalms[a] frgs. E, F
SHR 6216; PAM 44.008
Mus. Inv. 614B, 976

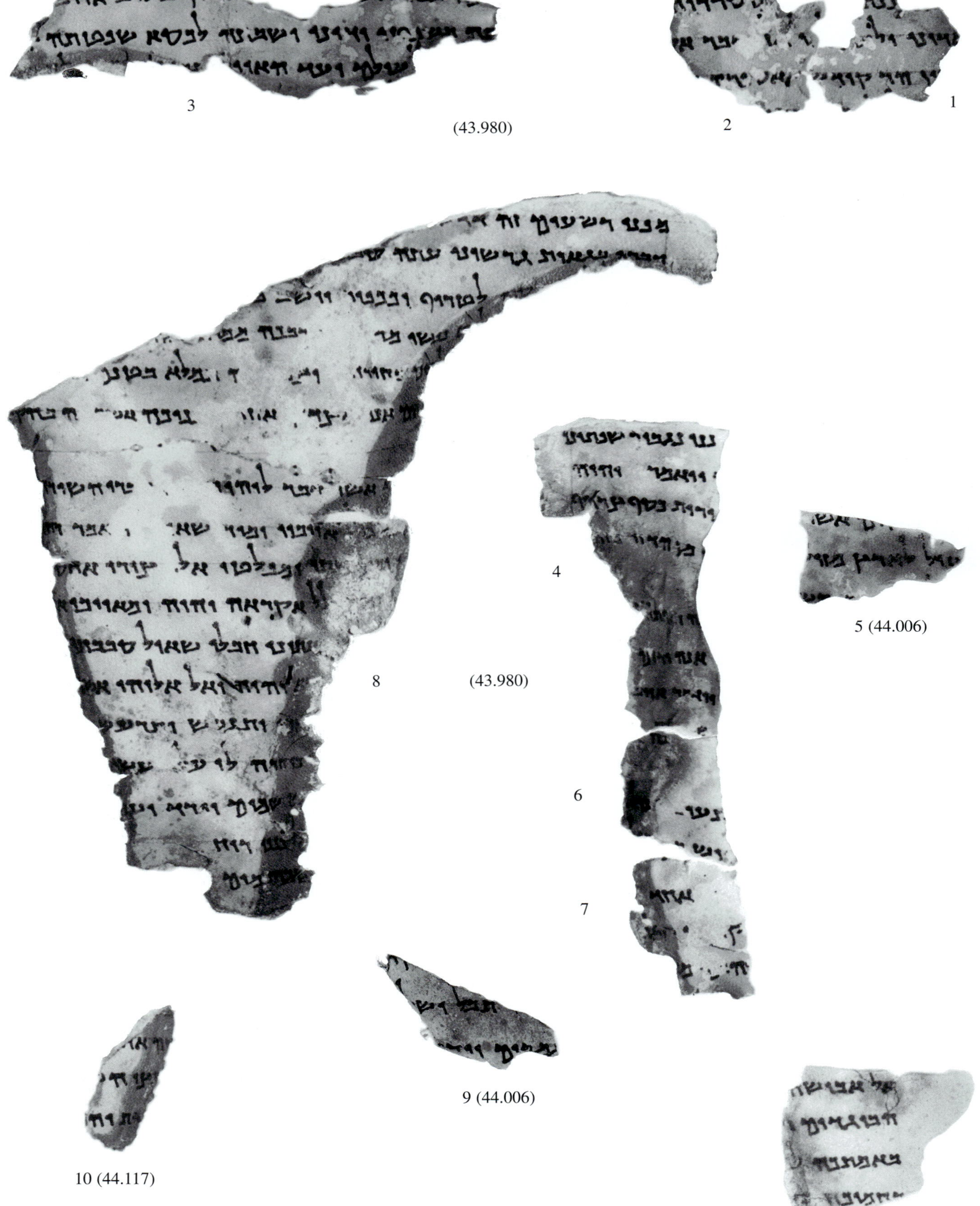

7. 11QPsalms[c]
PAM 43.980, 44.006, 44.117; IAA 522908
Mus. Inv. 606, 614, 621B, 1027

PLATE VII

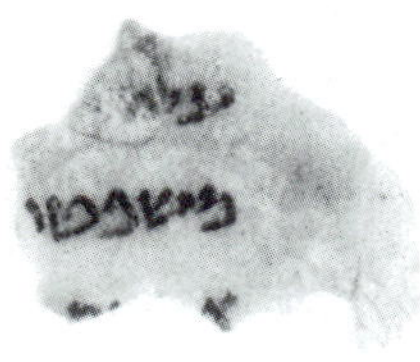
2 (563765)

1 (mirror image)

1 (44.012)

0 1 2 3 4 cm

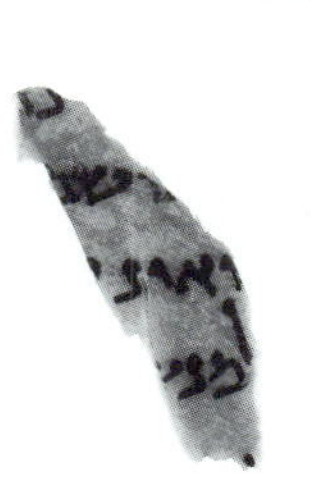
6 (44.006)

5 (44.117)

3 (West Semitic Research No. 629)
(JWS 98)

4 (44.004)

10

9

(44.115)

8 (44.117)

7 (44.115)

8. 11QPsalms[d]
PAM 44.004, 44.006, 44.012, 44.115, 44.117; IAA 563765; WSR 629
Mus. Inv. 569, 619, 621B, 1025

8. 11QPsalms[d]
PAM 43.976, 44.004, 44.005, 44.115, 44.117; IAA 563757, 563769
Mus. Inv. 569, 580, 581A, 621B, 1032

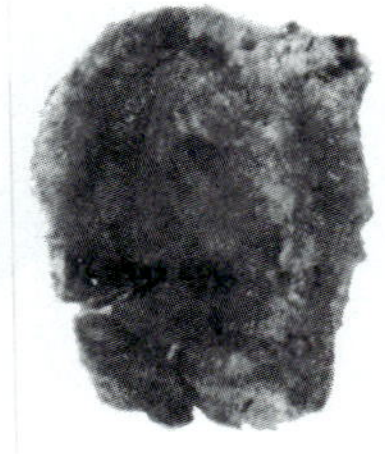

9. 11QPsalms[e]?
PAM 43.794; Mus. Inv. 1016

Col. III

3 (43.823)

Col. II

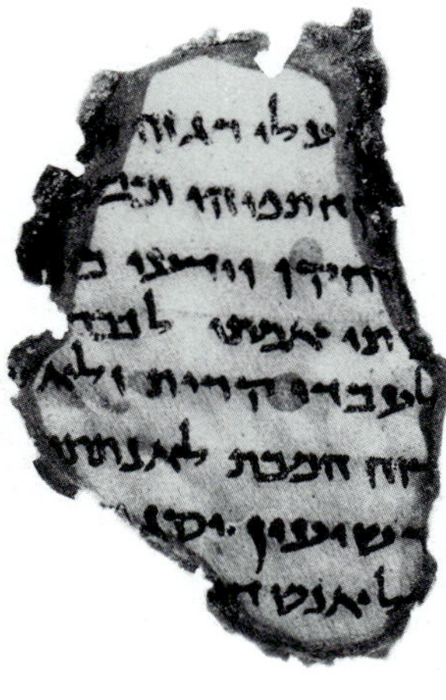

2 (43.823)

Col. I

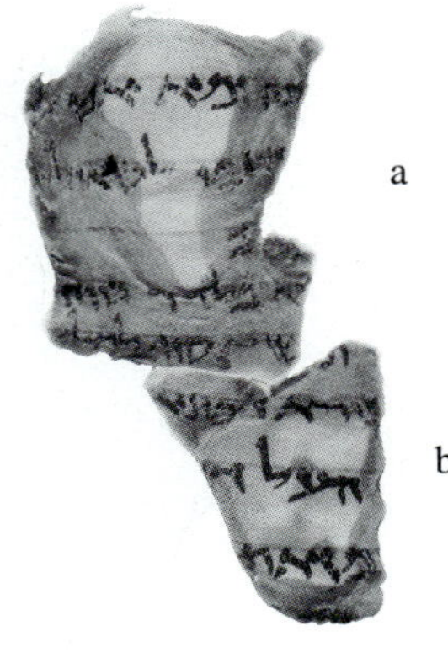

1 (43.824)

Col. V

5 (43.822)

Col. IV

4 (43.822)

10. 11QtargumJob
PAM 43.822, 43.823, 43.824
Mus. Inv. 627, 628, 635

Col. VIIA

6a (SHR 6215)

Col. VII Col. XI

ii i

6 (43.821)

Col. IX

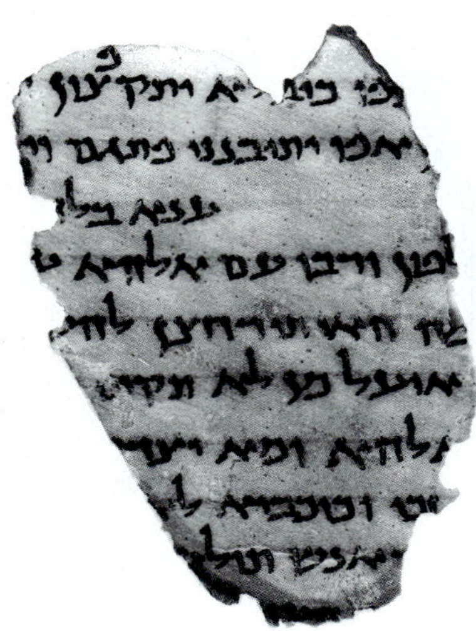

8 (43.820)

Col. VIII Col. VIIB

ii i

7 (43.821)

10. 11QtargumJob
PAM 43.820, 43.821; SHR 6215 (photograph by B. and K. Zuckerman)
Mus. Inv. 633, 636

Col. X

9 (43.820)

Col. XIII

Col. XII

Col. XI

ii i

11 (43.819)

ii i

10 (43.819)

10. 11QtargumJob
PAM 43.819, 43.820
Mus. Inv. 633, 637

PLATE XII

Col. XV

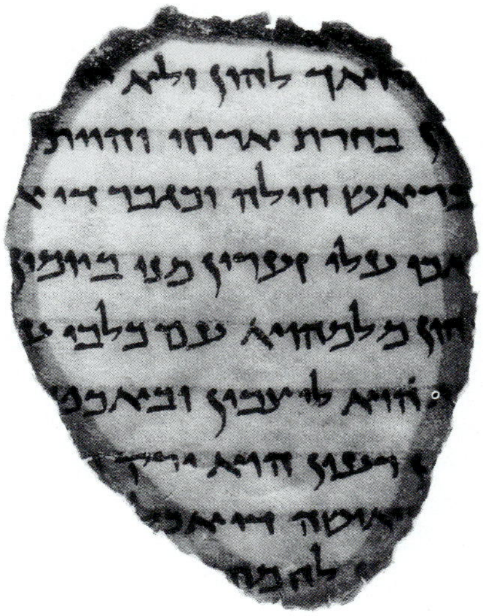

Col. XIV

Col. XVI

13 (43.818)

12 (43.818)

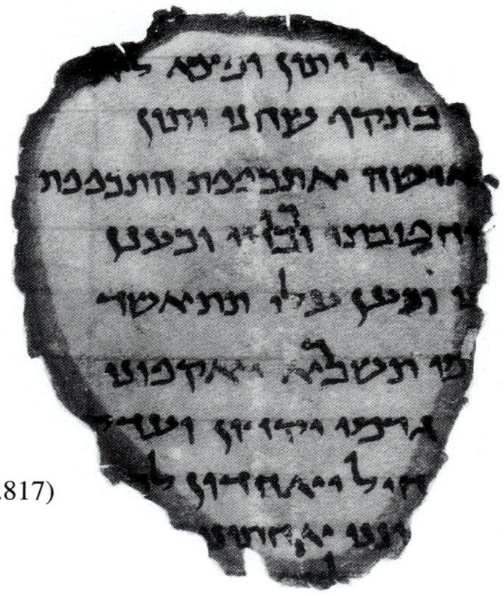

14 (43.817)

Col. XIX

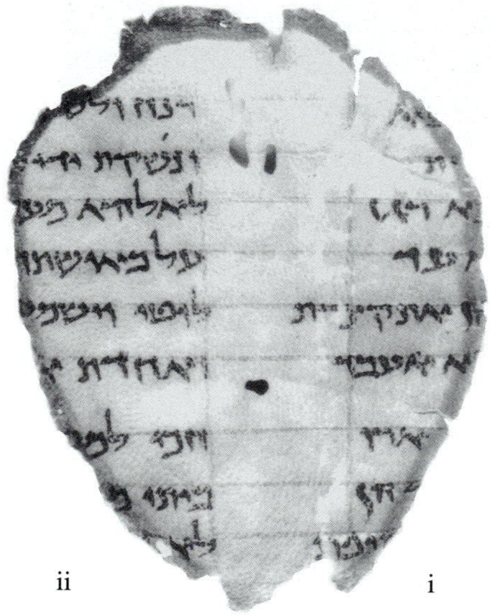

Col. XVIII

Col. XVII

ii

i

ii

i

A6 (44.114)

16 (43.816)

15 (43.817)

10. 11QtargumJob
PAM 43.816, 43.817, 43.818, 44.114
Mus. Inv. 567, 624, 631, 632

Col. XX

Col. XIX

ii

i

17 (43.816)

Col. XXII

Col. XXI

19 (43.815)

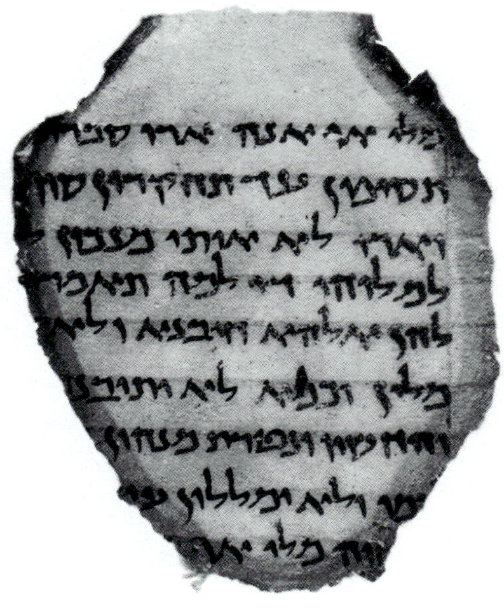

18 (43.815)

10. 11QtargumJob
PAM 43.815, 43.816
Mus. Inv. 624, 634

PLATE XIV

Col. XXIV

21 (43.814)

Col. XXIII

20 (43.814) A4 (43.824)

Col. XXV

23 (43.813)

Col. XXIV

22 (43.813)

10. 11QtargumJob
PAM 43.813, 43.814, 43.824
Mus. Inv. 621, 629, 635

Col. XXVII

ii i

25 (43.812)

Col. XXVI

24 (43.812)

Col. XXVIII

27 (43.810)

Col. XXVII

ii i

26 (43.811)

10. 11QtargumJob
PAM 43.810, 43.811, 43.812
Mus. Inv. 623, 626, 630

PLATE XVI

Col. XXIX

Col. XXX

10. 11QtargumJob
PAM 43.800, 43.801, 43.824
Mus. Inv. 635, 638

Col. XXXI

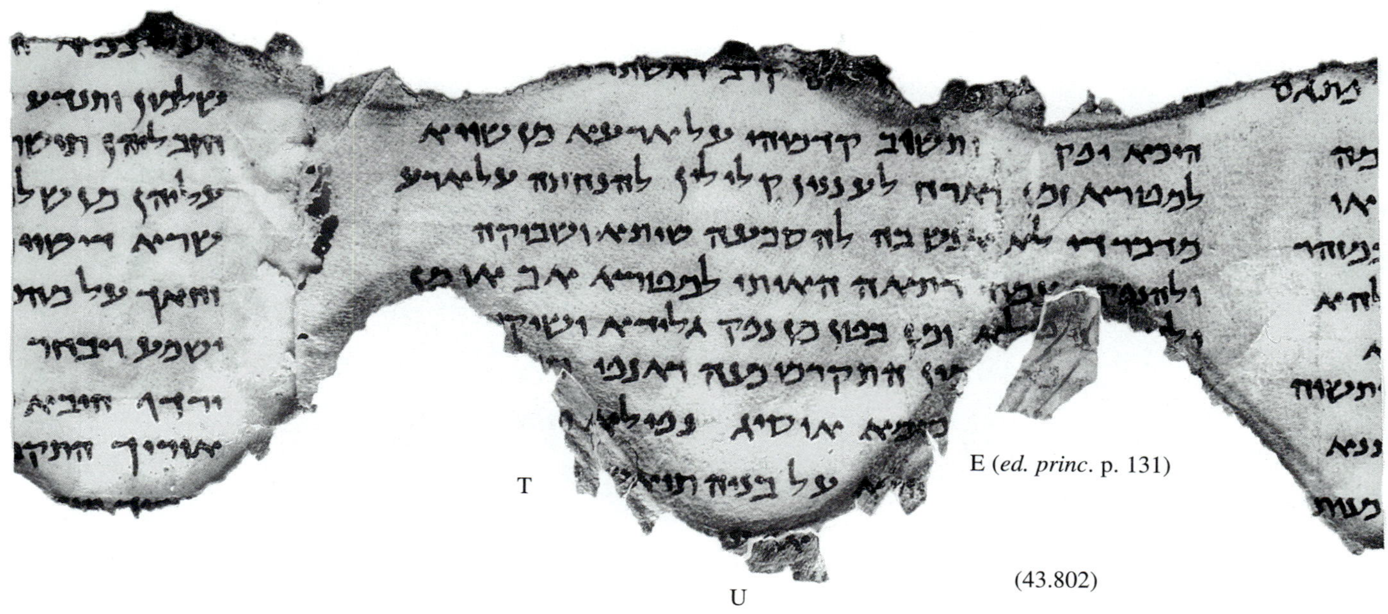

Col. XXXII

10. 11QtargumJob
PAM 43.802, 43.803; Mus. Inv. 638

Col. XXXIII

Col. XXXIV

(43.805)

10. 11QtargumJob
PAM 43.803, 43.804, 43.805; Mus. Inv. 638

Col. XXXV

M (43.804)

(43.806)

Col. XXXVI

(43.807)

10. 11QtargumJob
PAM 43.804, 43.806, 43.807; Mus. Inv. 638

Col. XXXVII

(43.808)

Col. XXXVIII

(43.809)

10. 11QtargumJob
PAM 43.803 43.806, 43.807, 43.808, 43.809
Mus. Inv. 638

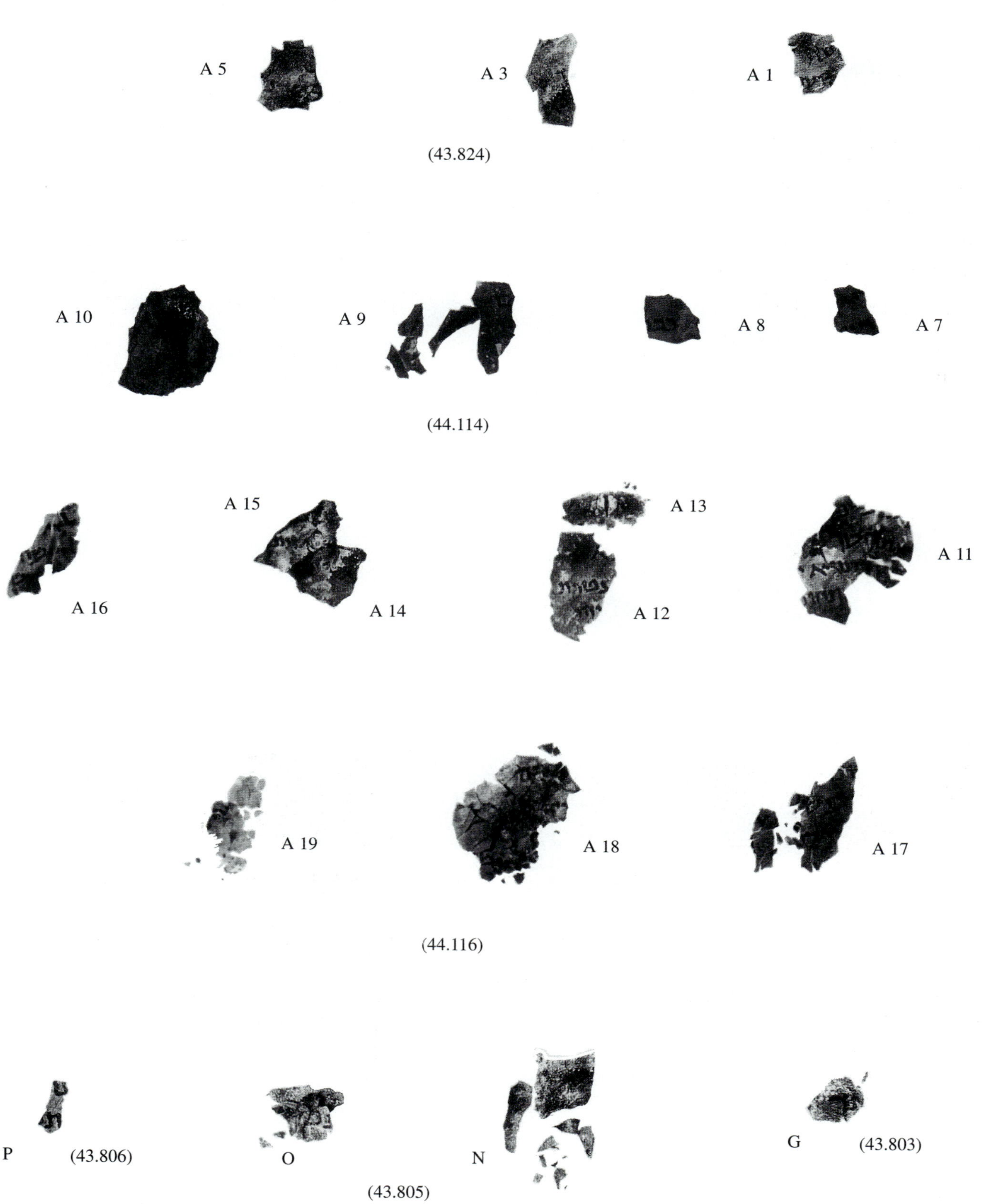

10. 11QtargumJob
PAM 43.803, 43.805, 43.806, 43.824, 44.114, 44.116
Mus. Inv. 567, 581, 625, 635

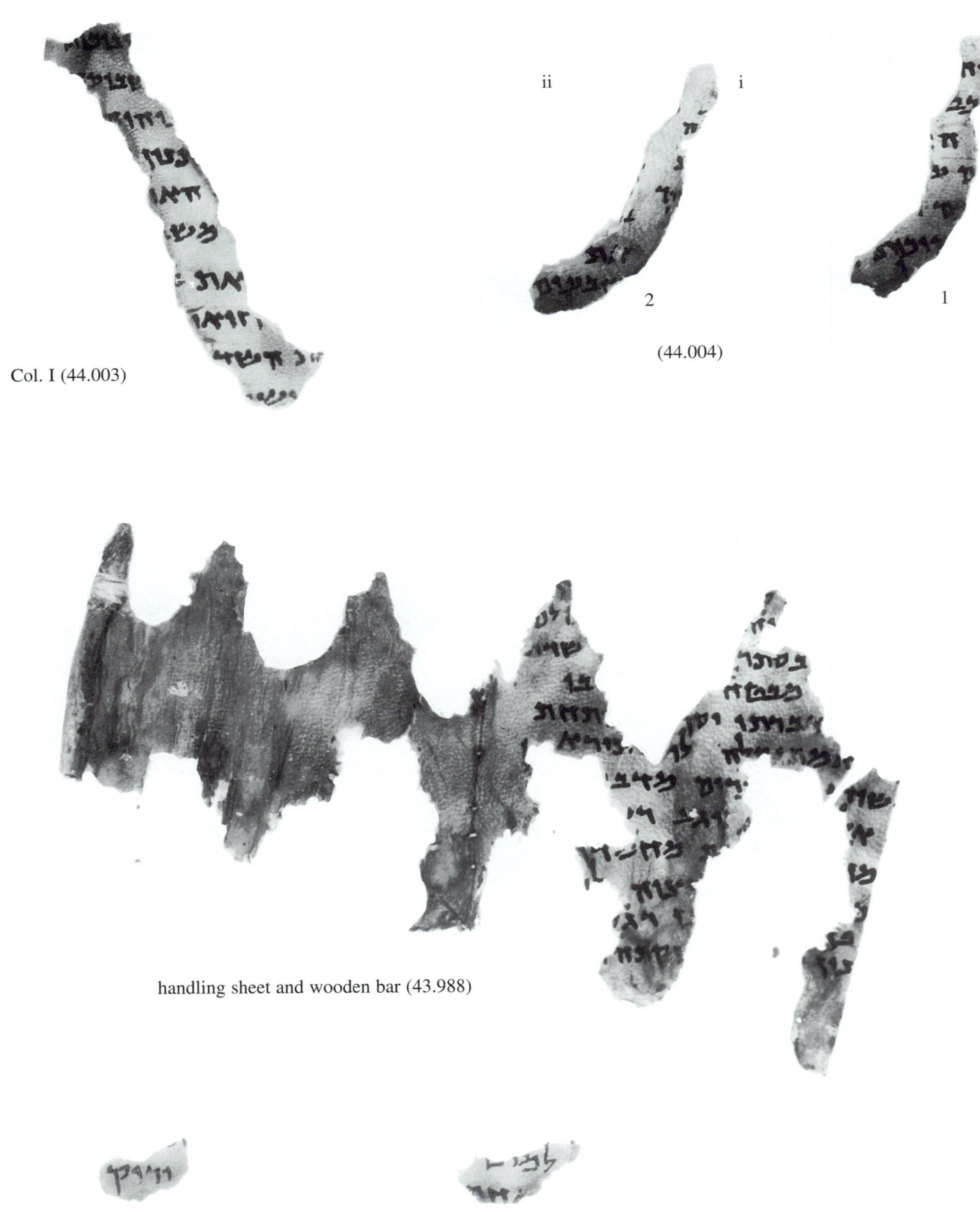

4 (563769) 3

11. 11Qapocryphal Psalms
PAM 43.988, 44.003, 44.004; IAA 563769
Mus. Inv. 61, 612, 619, 1032

11. 11Qapocryphal Psalms
PAM 44.113; Mus. Inv. 61

PLATE XXIV

11. 11Qapocryphal Psalms
PAM 43.984, 43.985; Mus. Inv. 61

Col. VI

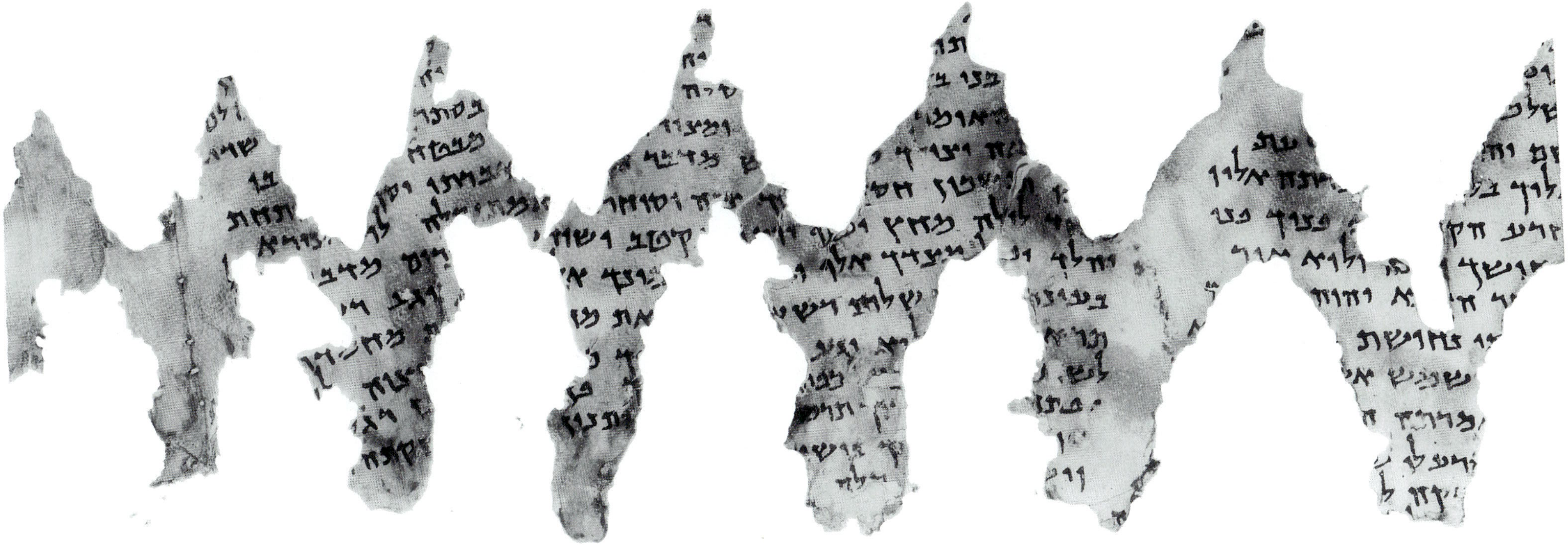

(43.987)

(43.986)

11Qapocryphal Psalms
PAM 43.986, 43.987; Mus. Inv. 61

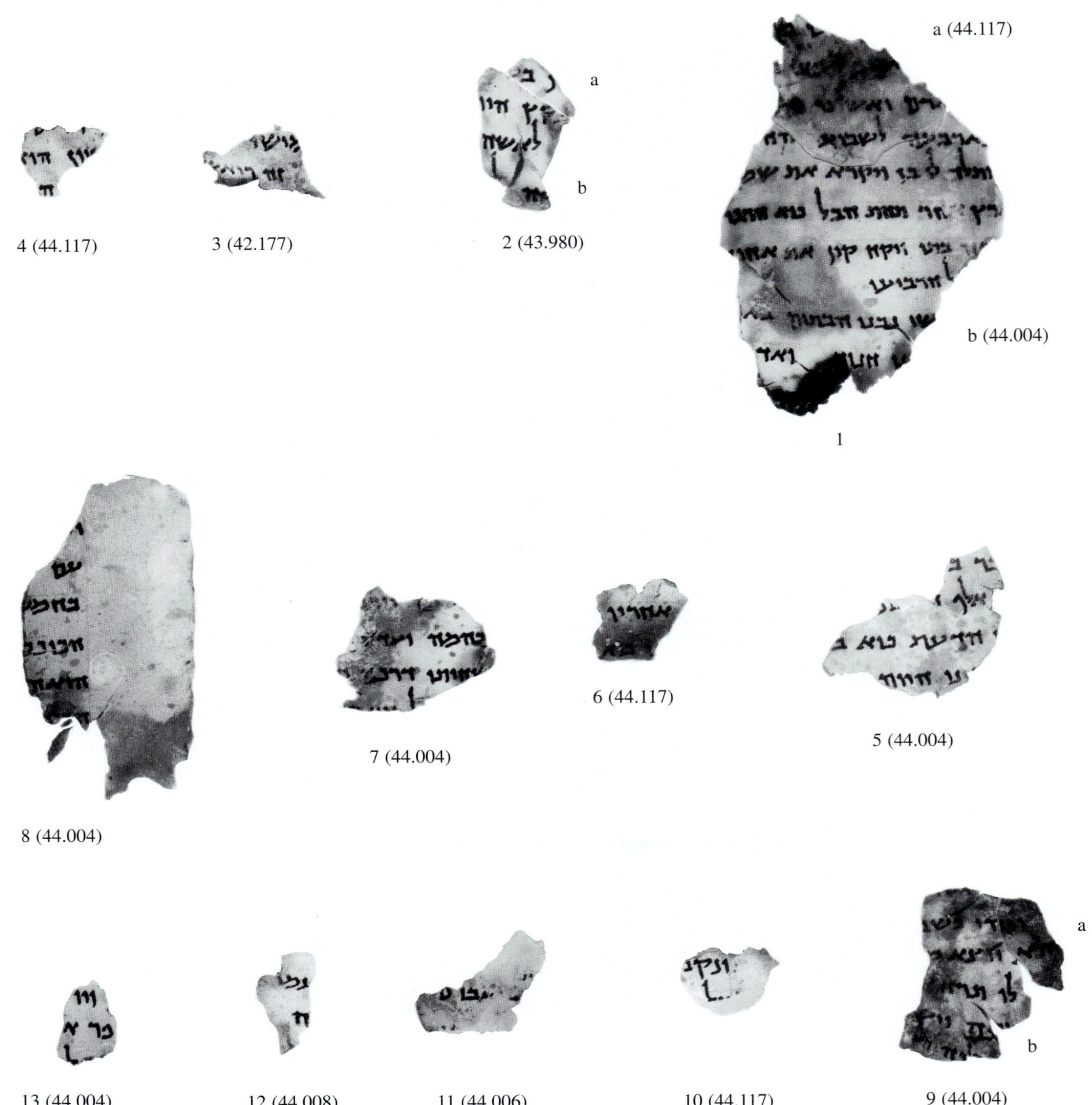

12. 11QJubilees
PAM 42.177, 43.980, 44.004, 44.006, 44.008, 44.117
Mus. Inv. 606, 614, 614B, 619, 621B

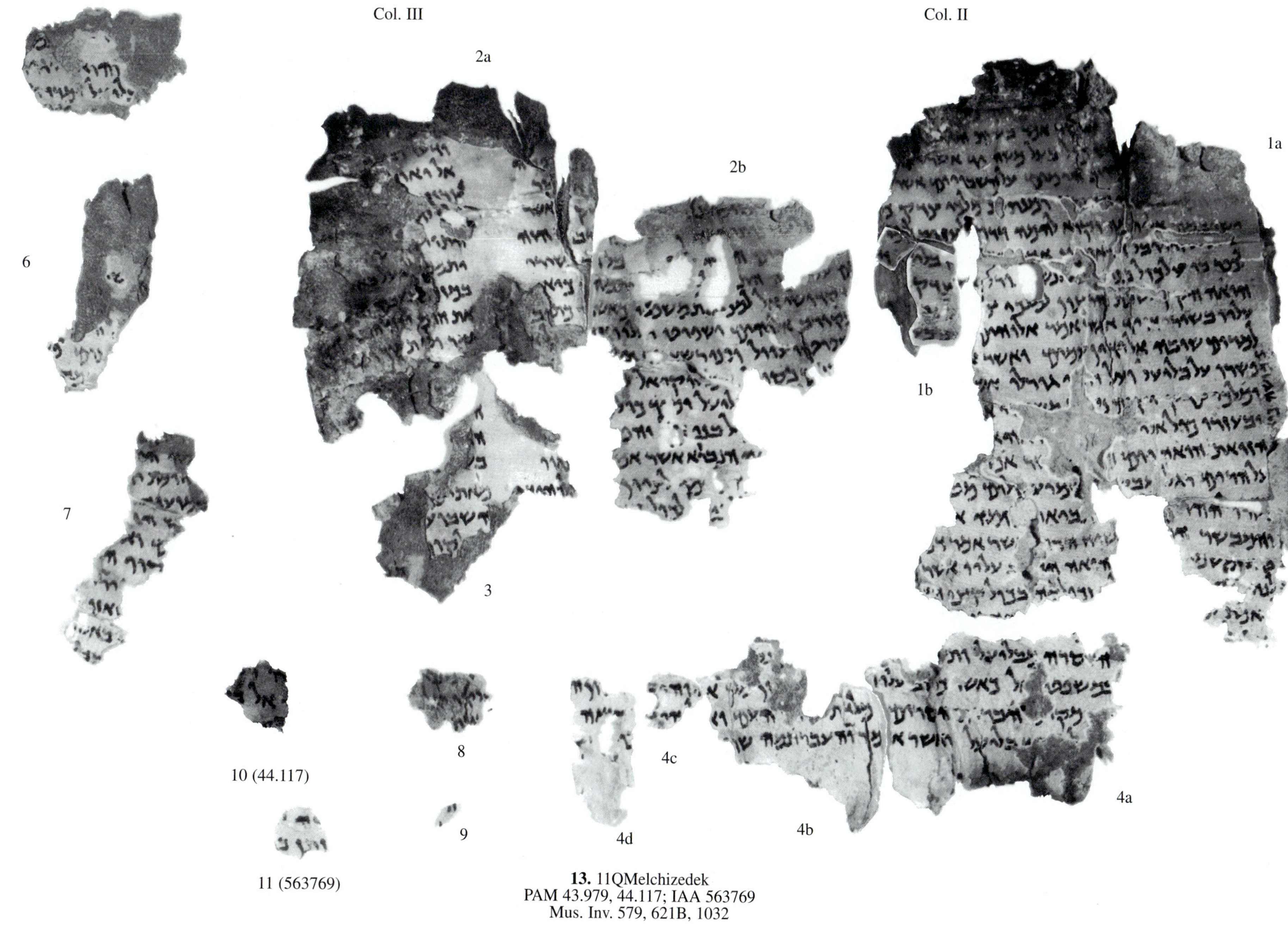

13. 11QMelchizedek
PAM 43.979, 44.117; IAA 563769
Mus. Inv. 579, 621B, 1032

e (43.977) 1ii 1i

b (43.977)

c (42.176)

a (43.977)

d (44.114)

1

0 1 2 3 4 cm

4 (44.007)

3 (43.977)

2 (44.006)

14. 11QSefer ha-Milḥamah
PAM 42.176, 43.977, 44.006, 44.007, 44.114
Mus. Inv. 567, 607, 614, 615

2 (563765)

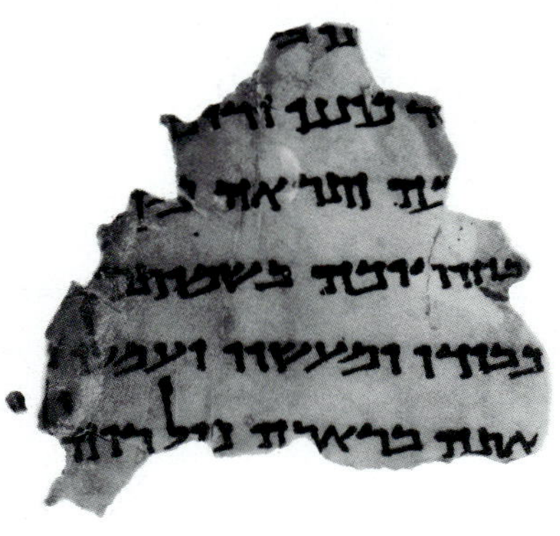

1 (44.003)

4

3

(44.117)

15. 11QHymns[a]
PAM 44.003, 44.117; IAA 563765; Mus. Inv. 576, 621B, 1025

16. 11QHymns[b]
PAM 44.006; Mus. Inv. 614

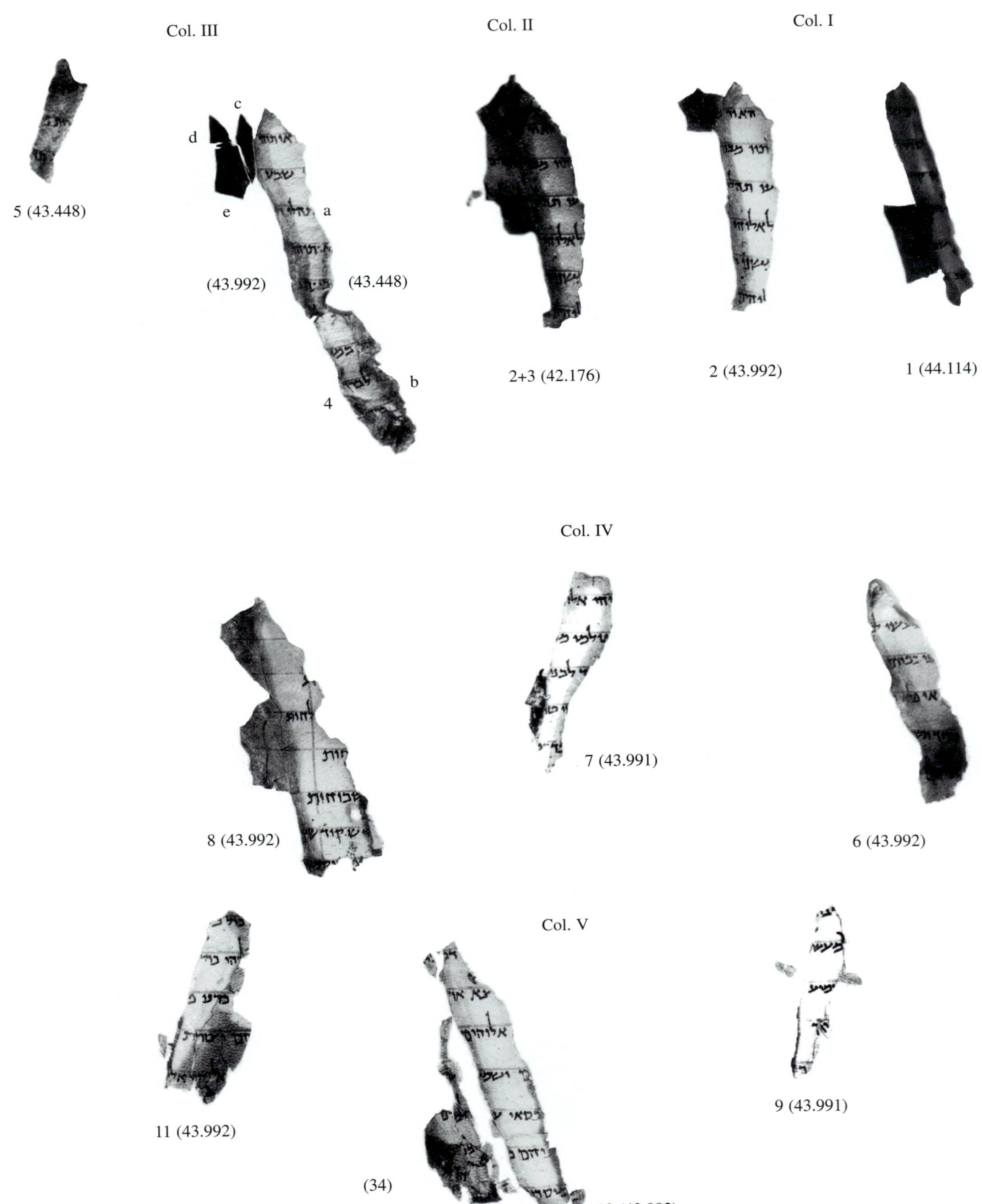

17. 11QShirot ʻOlat ha-Shabbat
PAM 42.176, 43.448, 43.991, 43.992, 44.114
Mus. Inv. 565, 567, 620

Col. VI

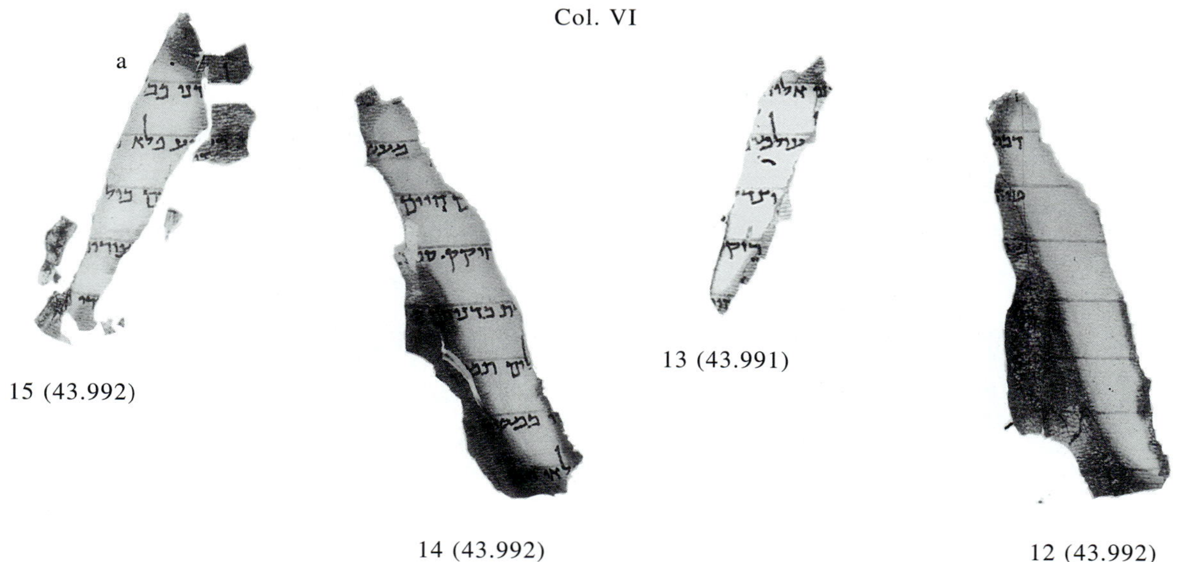

a

15 (43.992) 14 (43.992) 13 (43.991) 12 (43.992)

Col. VII

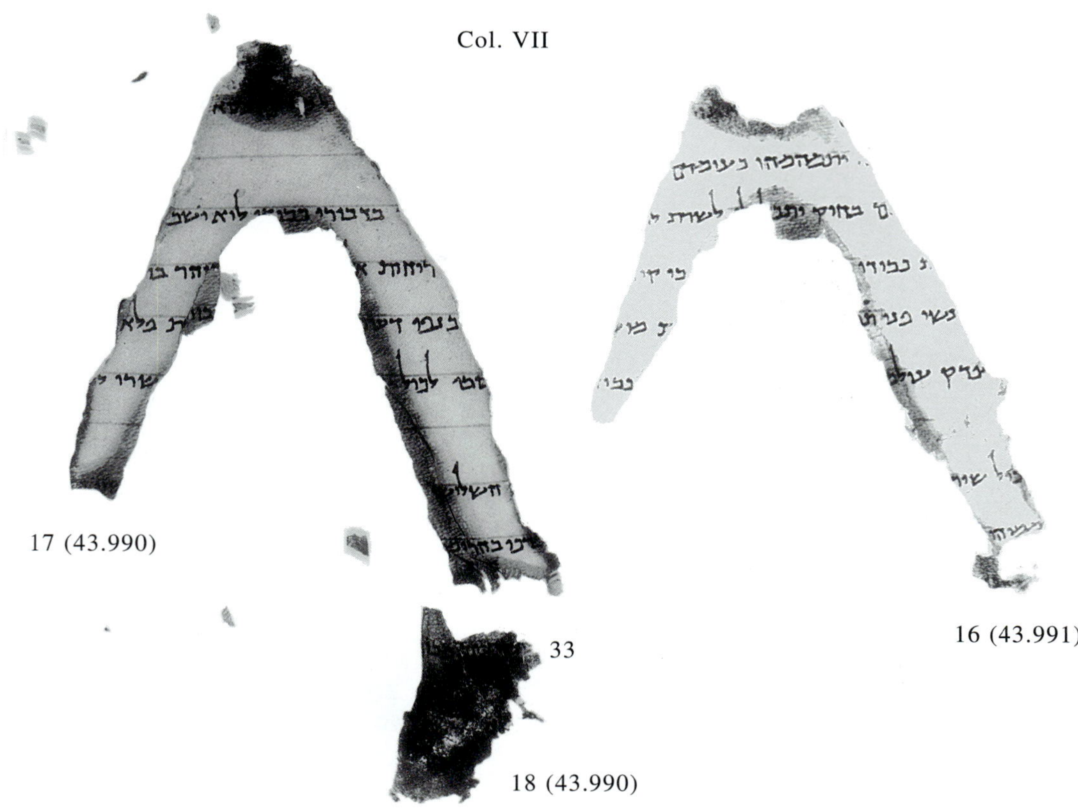

17 (43.990) 33 18 (43.990) 16 (43.991)

17. 11QShirot ʻOlat ha-Shabbat
PAM 43.990, 43.991, 43.992
Mus. Inv. 565, 609, 620

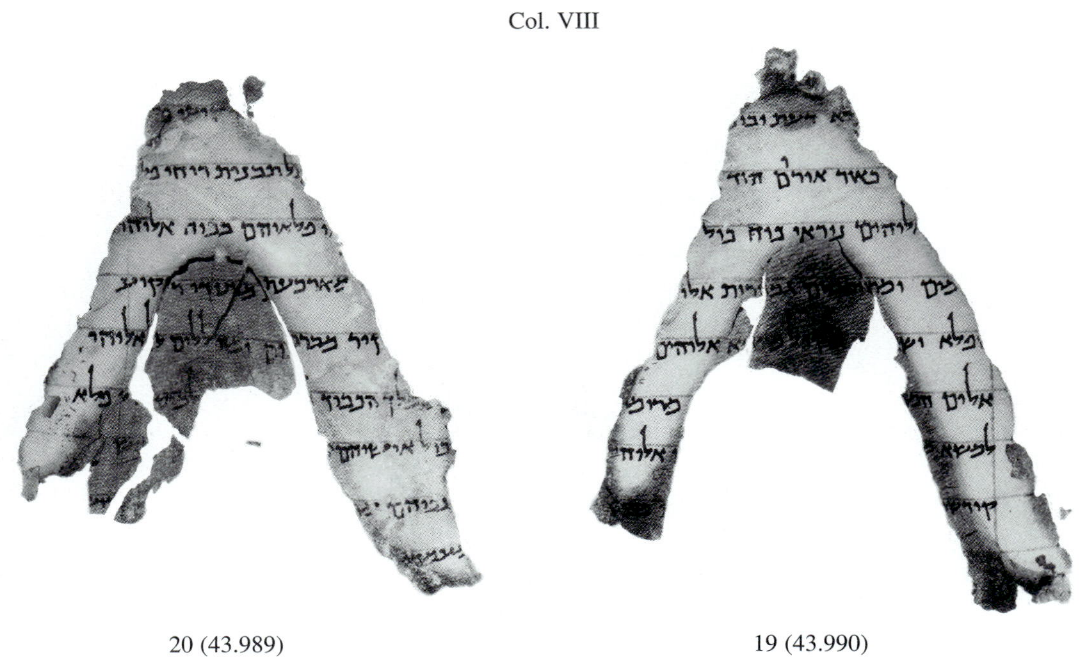

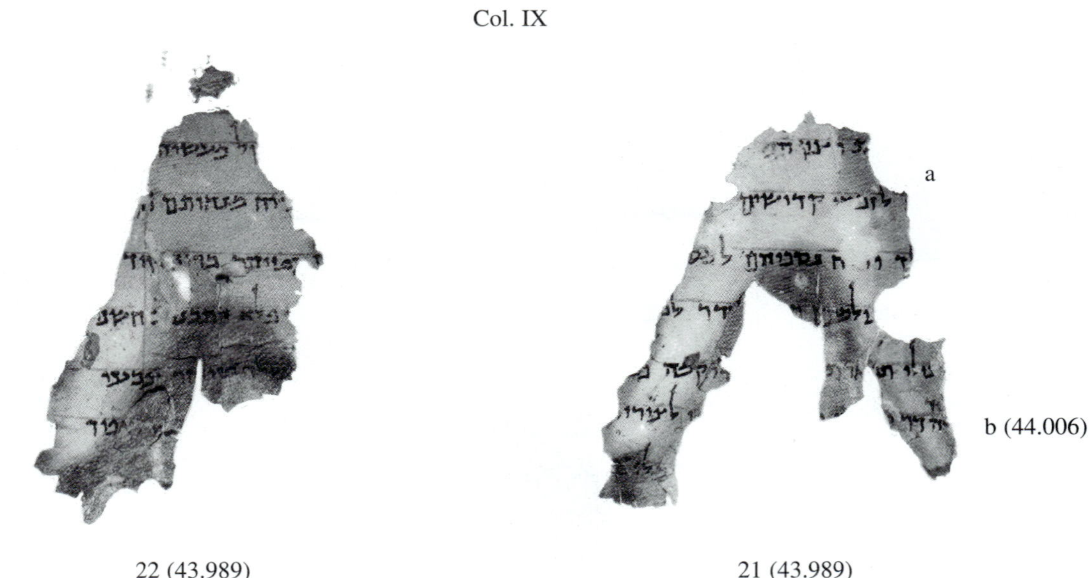

17. 11QShirot ‘Olat ha-Shabbat
PAM 43.989, 43.990, 44.006
Mus. Inv. 609, 614, 620

Col. X

25
(44.007)

24
(43.991)

23
(43.991)

41

40

39

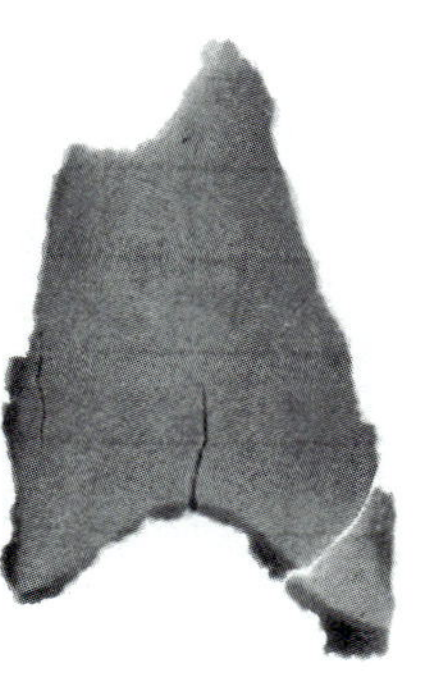

38

end of scroll (525613)

17. 11QShirot ʿOlat ha-Shabbat
PAM 43.991, 44.007; IAA 525613
Mus. Inv. 618, 1030

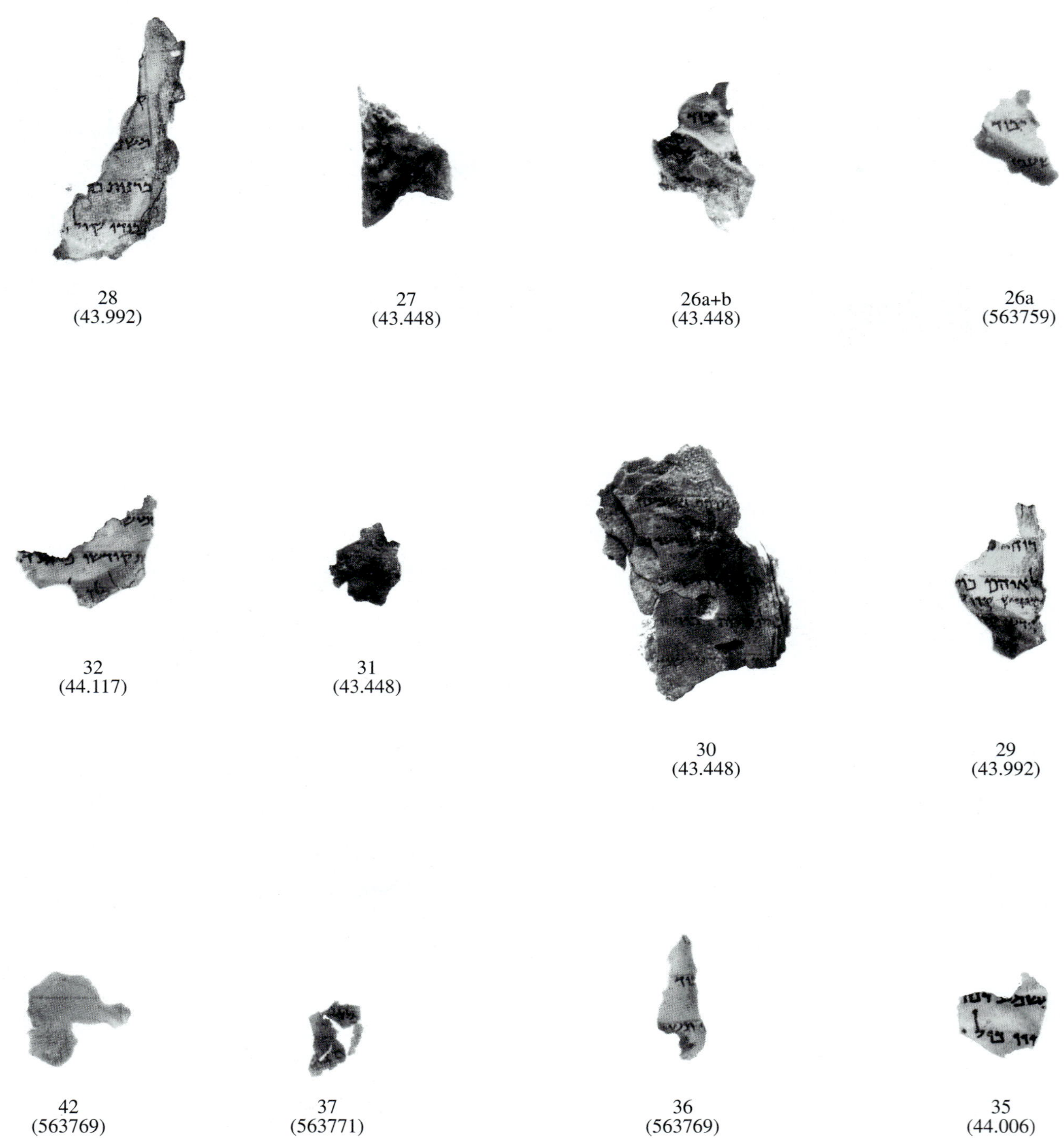

28 (43.992) · 27 (43.448) · 26a+b (43.448) · 26a (563759)

32 (44.117) · 31 (43.448) · 30 (43.448) · 29 (43.992)

42 (563769) · 37 (563771) · 36 (563769) · 35 (44.006)

17. 11QShirot ʿOlat ha-Shabbat
PAM 43.448, 43.992, 44.006, 44.117
IAA 563759, 563769, 563771
Mus. Inv. 565, 614, 621B, 1030, 1032, 1034

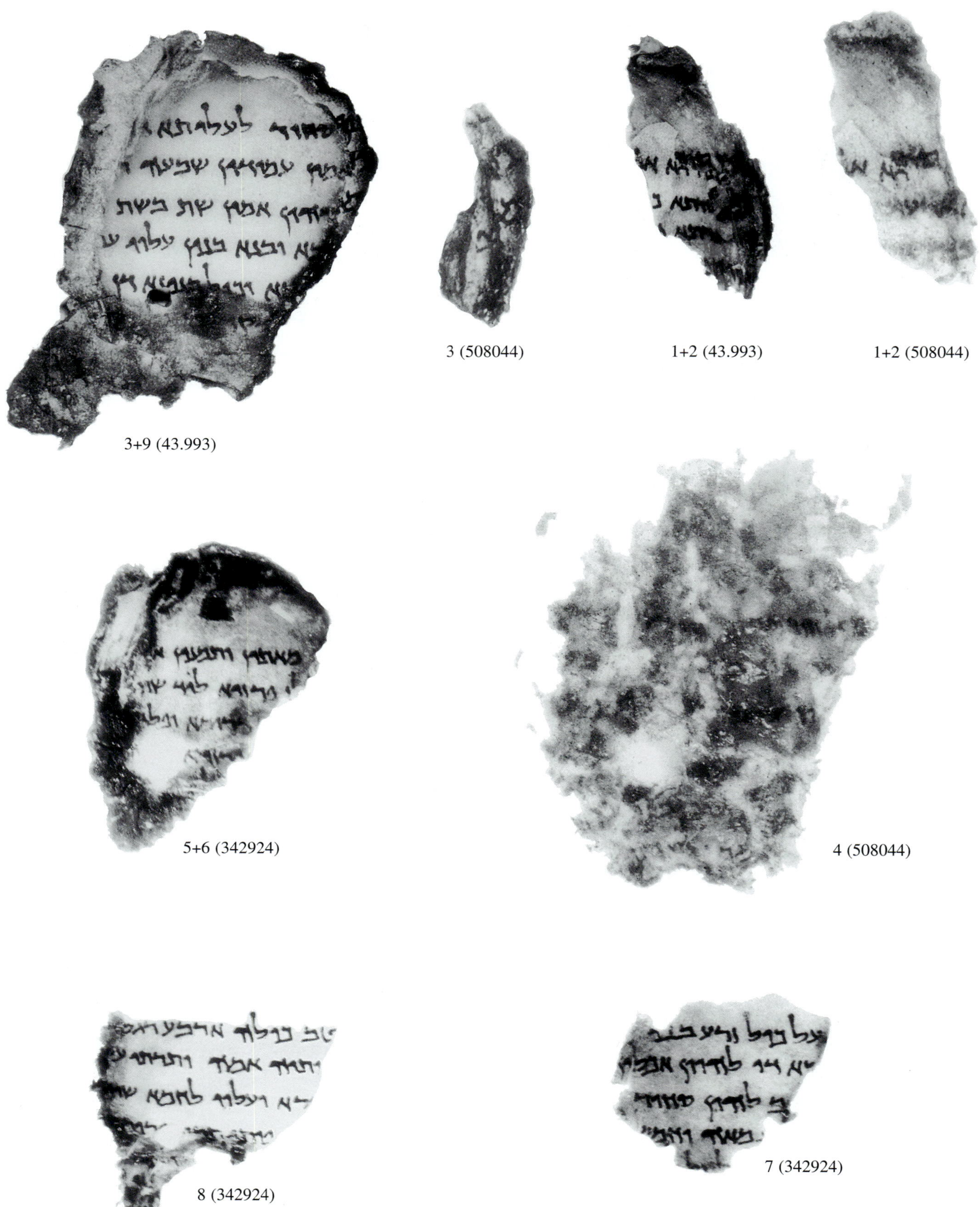

3+9 (43.993)

3 (508044)

1+2 (43.993)

1+2 (508044)

5+6 (342924)

4 (508044)

8 (342924)

7 (342924)

18. 11QNew Jerusalem ar
PAM 43.993, 43.994; IAA 342924, 508044
Mus. Inv. 578, 578A

10ii 10i

(43.994)

(44.007)

(44.009)

10

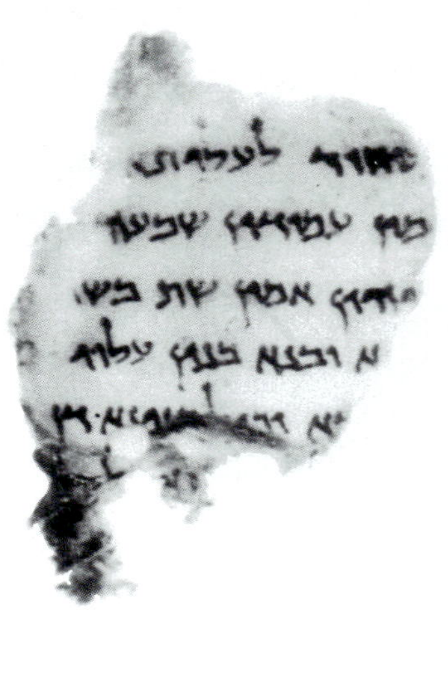

9 (342924)

12ii 12i

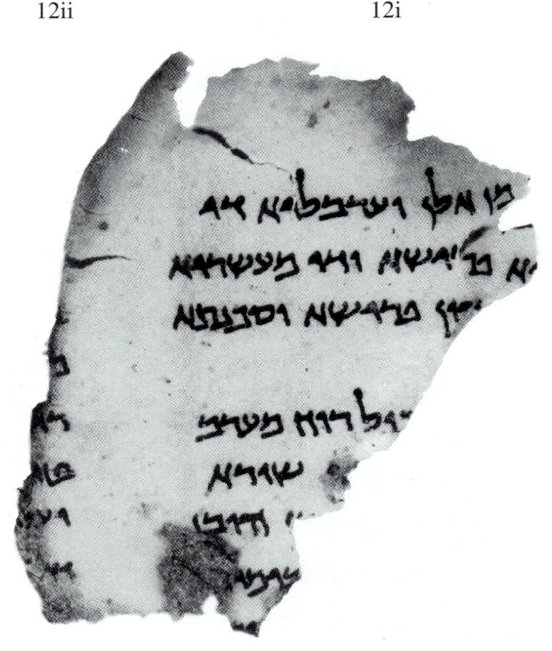

12 (43.995)

11 (43.994)

18. 11QNew Jerusalem ar
PAM 43.994, 43.995, 44.007, 44.009; IAA 342924
Mus. Inv. 564, 572, 574, 578, 615

14ii

14i

(43.996)

(43.995)

14

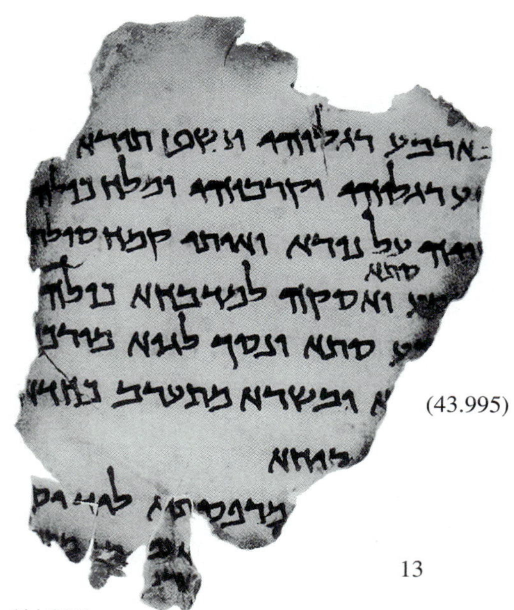

(43.995)

(44.009)

13

15 (43.996)

17ii

17i

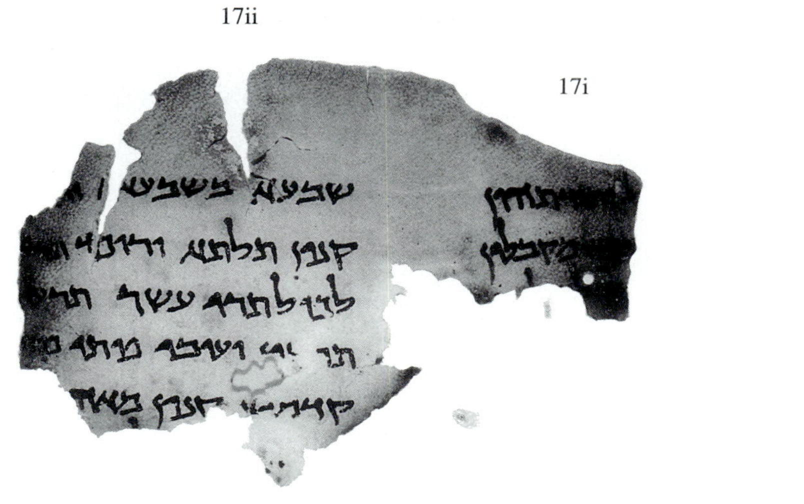

17 (43.998)

16ii

16i

(44.009)

16 (43.997)

18. 11QNew Jerusalem ar
PAM 43.995, 43.996, 43.997, 43.998, 44.009
Mus. Inv. 564, 568, 572, 611, 617

19 (43.999)

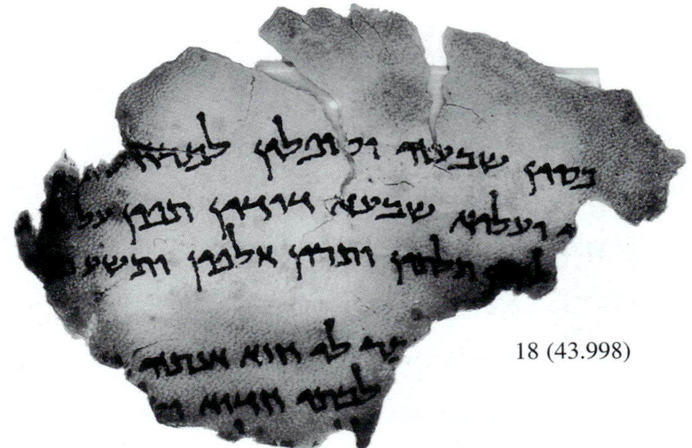

18 (43.998)

(44.009)

21 (44.997)

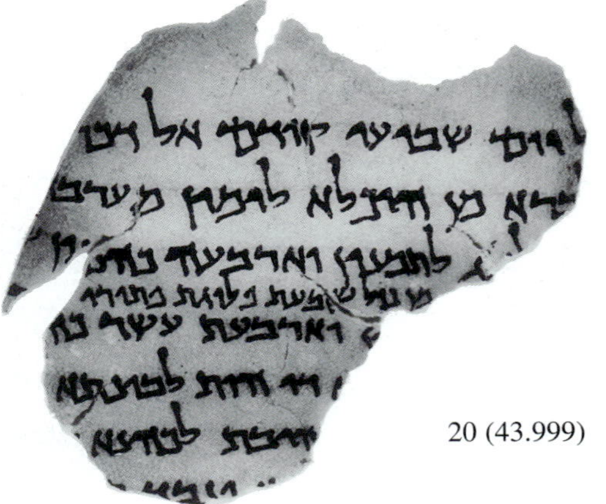

20 (43.999)

23ii 23i

(44.000)

(44.009)

(44.000)

(44.007)

24

23 (44.000)

22

18. 11QNew Jerusalem ar
PAM 43.997, 43.998, 43.999, 44.000, 44.007, 44.009
Mus. Inv. 572, 573, 575, 615, 617

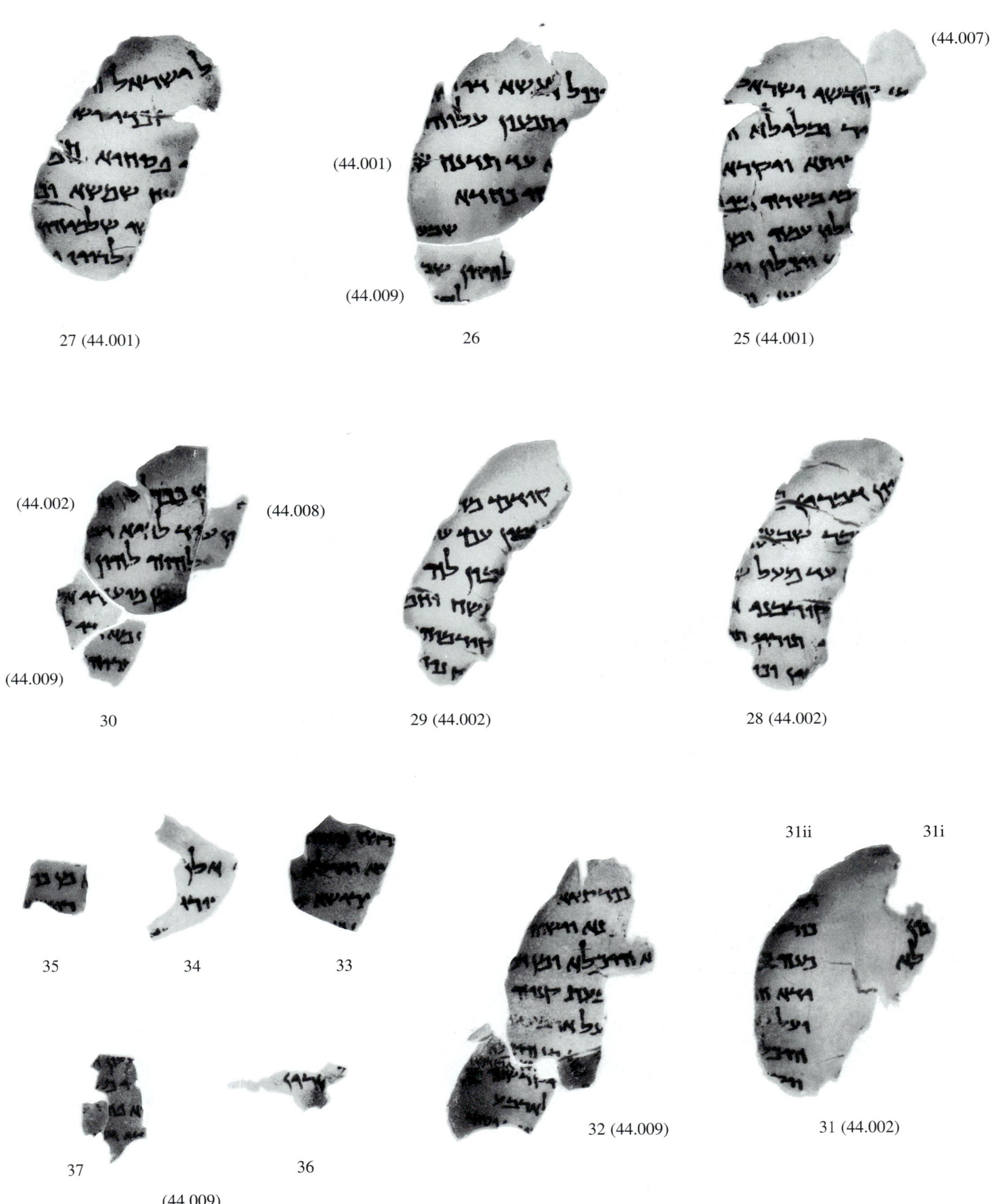

18. 11QNew Jerusalem ar
PAM 44.001, 44.002, 44.007, 44.008, 44.009
Mus. Inv. 570, 571, 572, 614B, 615

18. 11QNew Jerusalem ar
PAM 43.993; IAA 508044; Mus. Inv. 578A

Col. I

20. 11QTemple[b]
PAM 43.976, 43.978, 44.006
Mus. Inv. 577, 580, 614

PLATE XLII

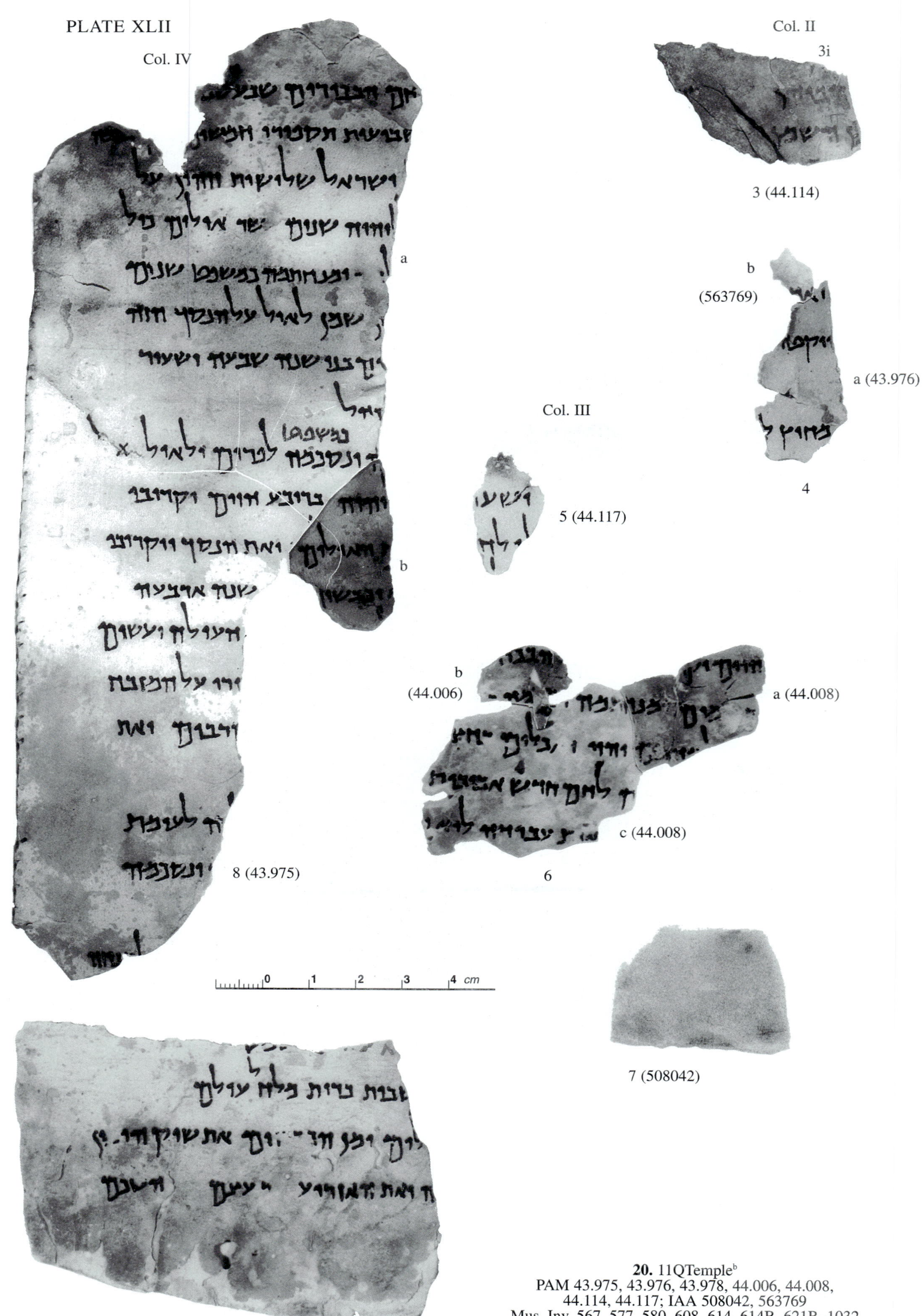

20. 11QTemple[b]
PAM 43.975, 43.976, 43.978, 44.006, 44.008, 44.114, 44.117; IAA 508042, 563769
Mus. Inv. 567, 577, 580, 608, 614, 614B, 621B, 1032

Col. VI

Col. V

c (43.977)

d (43.977)

a (43.975)

12 (44.008)

f

(43.977)

e

b (43.978)

10

a (43.976)

b (43.978)

11

0 1 2 3 4 cm

20. 11QTemple[b]
PAM 43.975, 43.976, 43.977, 43.978, 44.008
Mus. Inv. 577, 580, 607, 608, 614B, 1031

PLATE XLIV

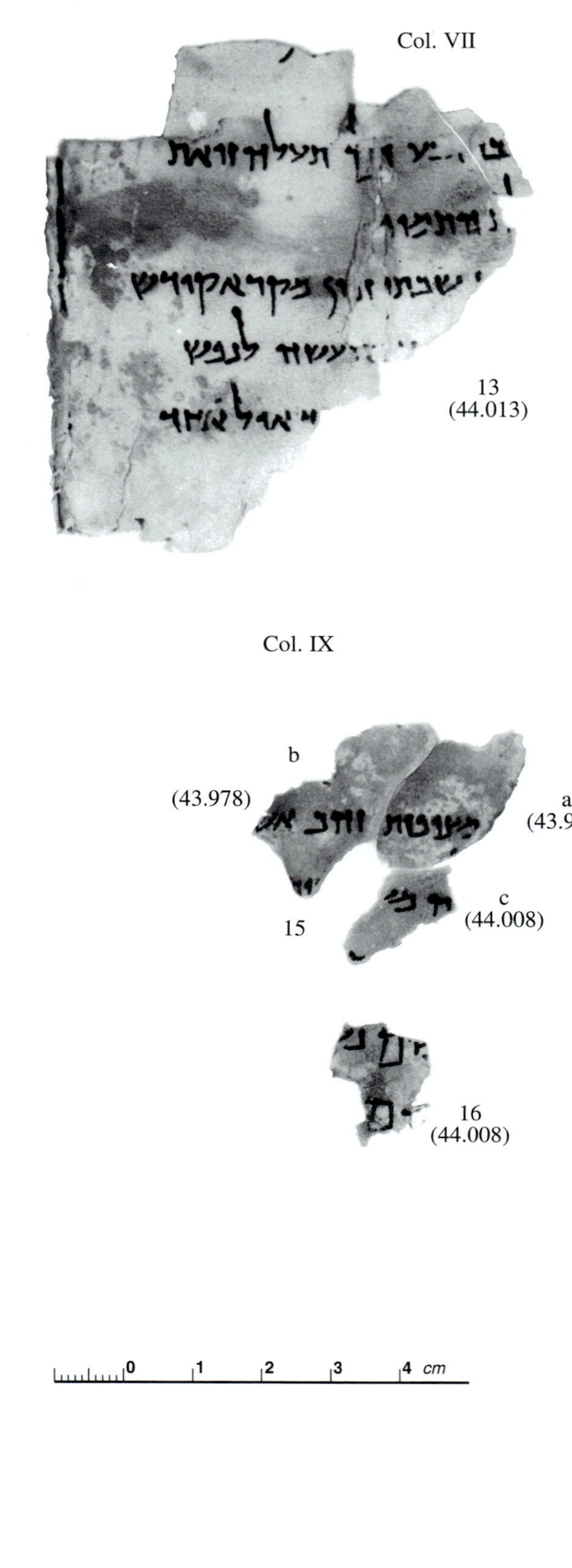

20. 11QTemple[b]
PAM 43.978, 44.005, 44.008, 44.010, 44.013, 44.114; IAA 589612
Mus. Inv. 566, 567, 577, 610, 613, 614B, 1020

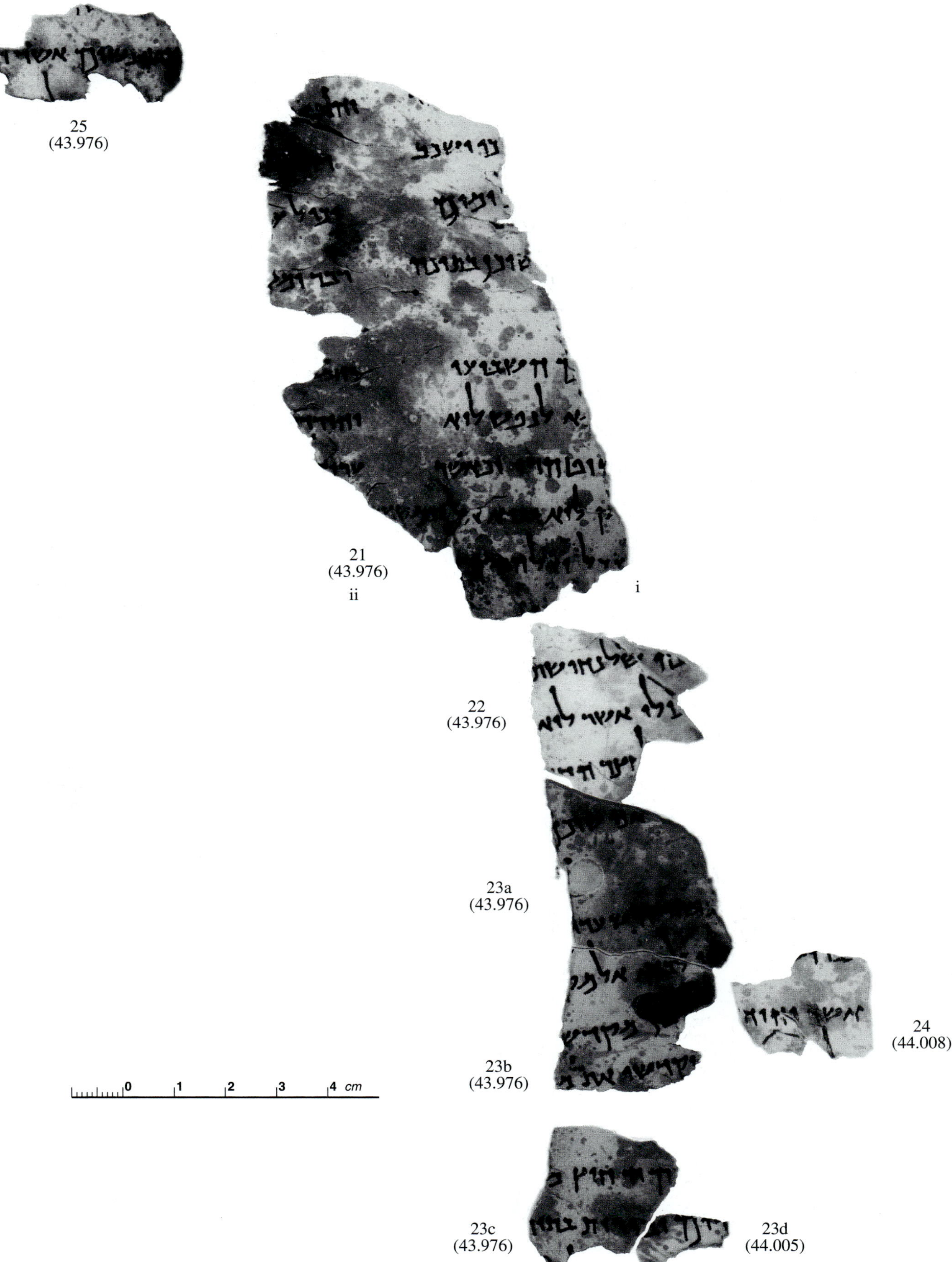

20. 11QTemple[b]
PAM 43.976, 44.005, 44.008
Mus. Inv. 580, 613, 614B

PLATE XLVI

Col. XV

Col. XIV

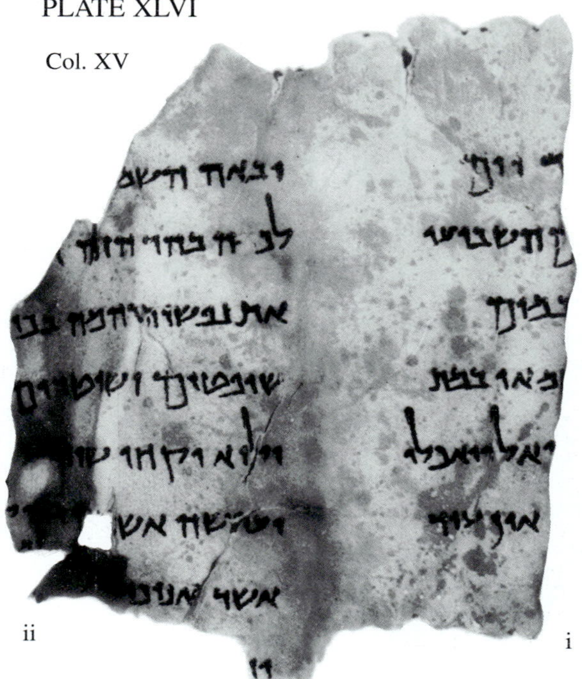

ii

i

26 (43.978)

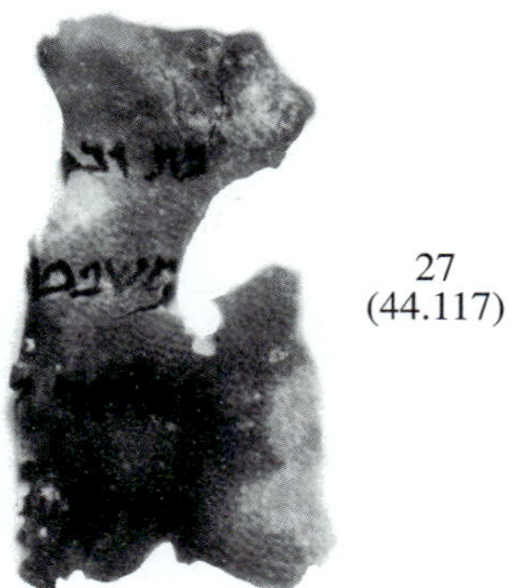

27
(44.117)

0 1 2 3 4 cm

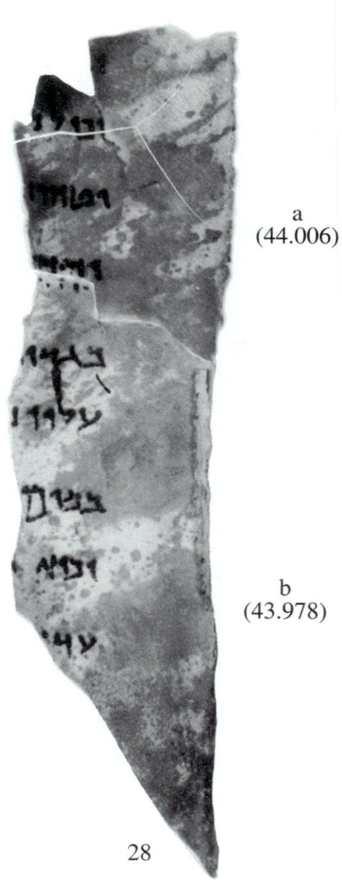

a
(44.006)

b
(43.978)

28

29
(44.114)

20. 11QTemple[b]
PAM 43.978, 44.006, 44.114, 44.117
Mus. Inv. 567, 577, 614, 621B

Col. XVI

31 (42.177)

30 (43.976)

35

34

(44.005)

33 (44.117)

32 (43.794)

40 (44.117)

39

38

(44.008)

37

36

(44.006)

42 (563769)

41 (43.977)

20. 11QTemple[b]
PAM 42.177, 43.794, 43.976, 43.977, 44.005, 44.006, 44.008, 44.117; IAA 563769
Mus. Inv. 580, 606, 607, 613, 614, 614B, 615, 621B, 1016, 1032

3 (44.114)

2 (44.006)

1 (44.004)

21. 11QTemple[c]?
PAM 44.004, 44.006, 44.114
Mus. Inv. 567, 614, 619

3 (44.006)

2 (44.006)

1 (42.175)

7 (563769)

6 (563763)

5 (44.117)

4 (44.006)

22. 11QpaleoUnidentified Text
PAM 42.175, 44.006, 44.117; IAA 563763, 563769
Mus. Inv. 614, 1020, 1032

3

2

1

23. 11QcryptA Unidentified Text
PAM 42.176; Mus. Inv. 613

24. 11QUnidentified Text ar
PAM 44.114; Mus. Inv. 567

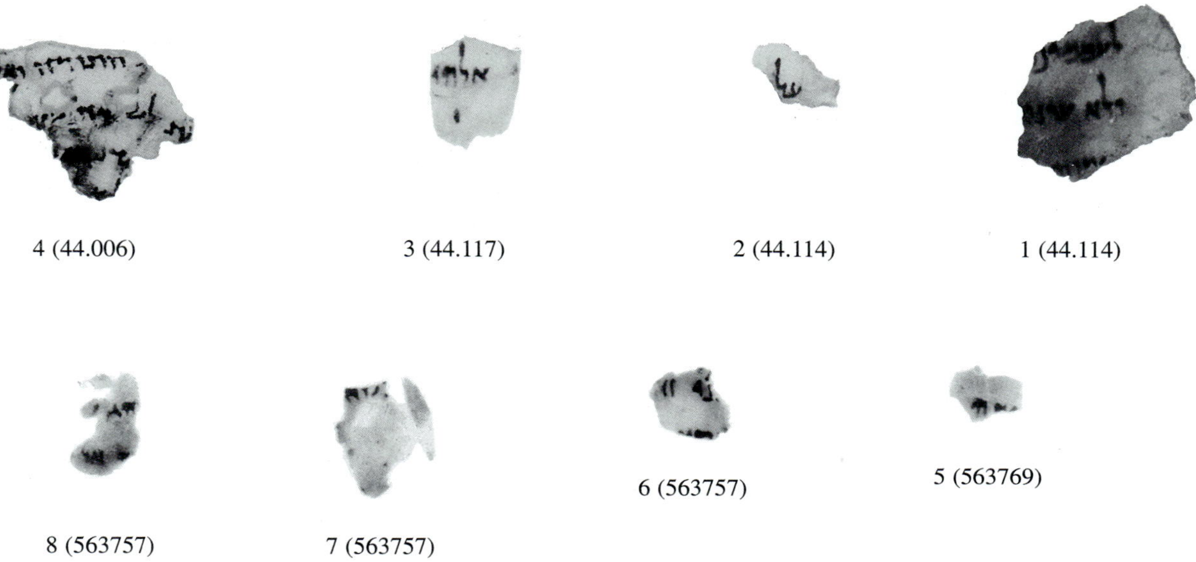

4 (44.006) 3 (44.117) 2 (44.114) 1 (44.114)

8 (563757) 7 (563757) 6 (563757) 5 (563769)

25. 11QUnidentified Text A
PAM 44.006, 44.114, 44.117; IAA 563757, 563769
Mus. Inv. 567, 581A, 614, 621B, 1032

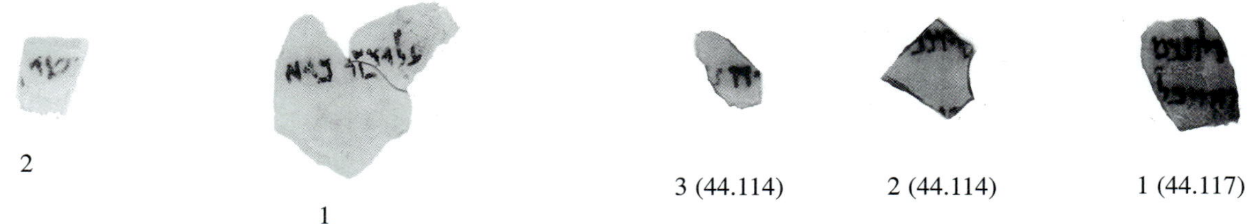

2 1 3 (44.114) 2 (44.114) 1 (44.117)

27. 11QUnidentified Text C
PAM 44.008, Mus. Inv. 614B

26. 11QUnidentified Text B
PAM 44.114, 44.117; Mus. Inv. 567, 621B

28. 11QpapUnidentified Text D
IAA 563761; Mus. Inv. 988

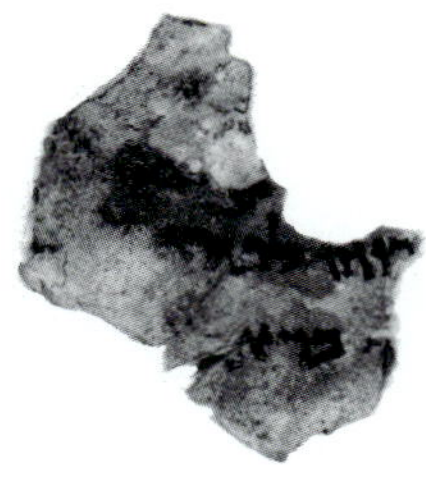

29. 11QFragment Related to Serekh ha-Yaḥad
PAM 44.007. Mus. Inv. 615

4 (44.007)

3 (44.117)

2 (44.117)

1 (44.117)

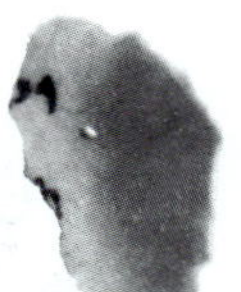

7 (42.176)

6 (44.117)

5 (44.007)

30. 11QUnclassified Fragments
PAM 42.176, 44.007, 44.117
IAA 563757
Mus. Inv. 615, 621B

30. 11QUnclassified Fragments
PAM 43.794, 44.007, 44.114
IAA 525015, 563757, 563761, 563763, 563767, 563769, 563771
Mus. Inv. 567, 581A, 615, 988, 1016, 1020, 1031, 1032, 1034

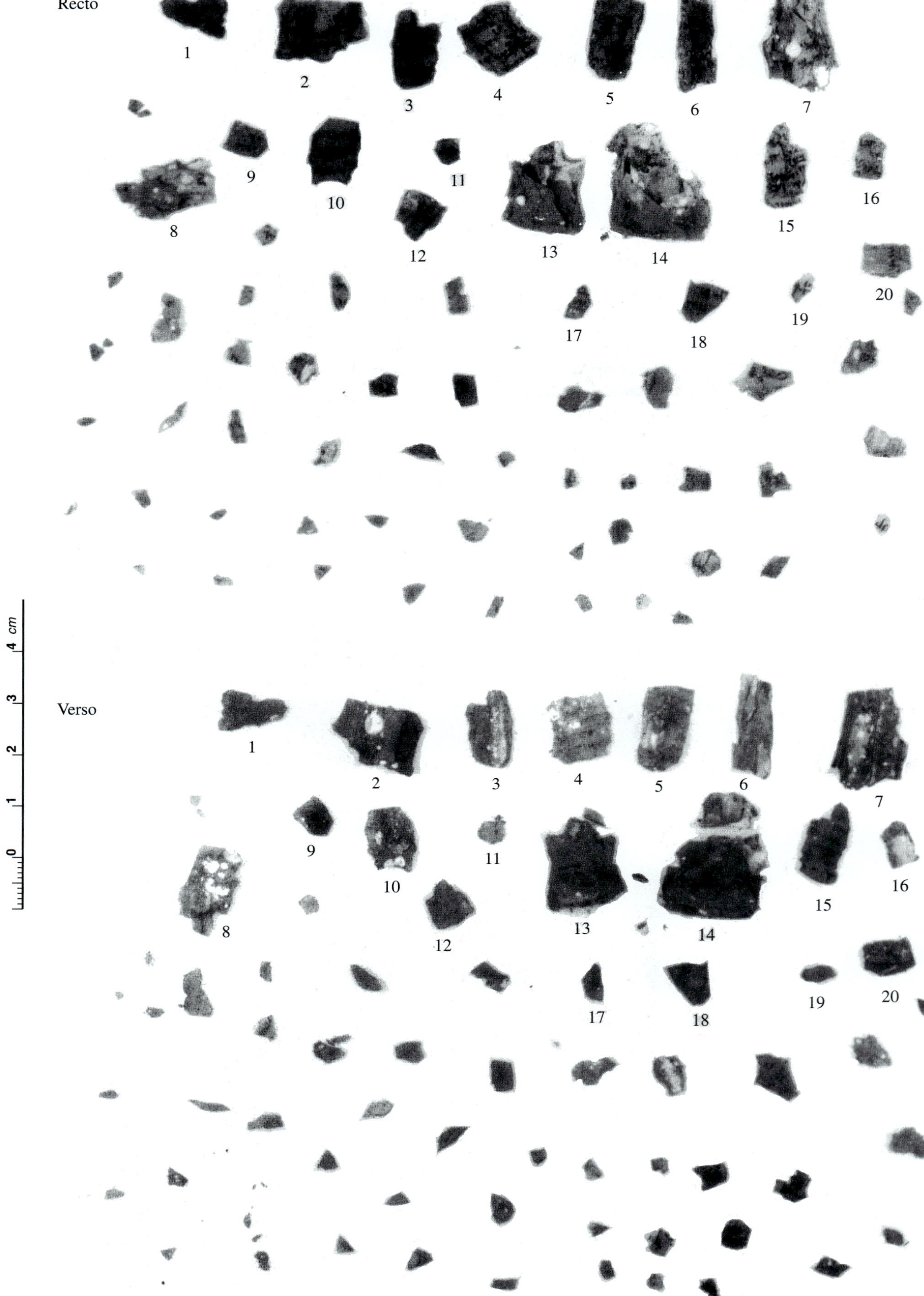

31. 11QUnidentified Wads
IAA 508046, 508048; Mus. Inv. 563

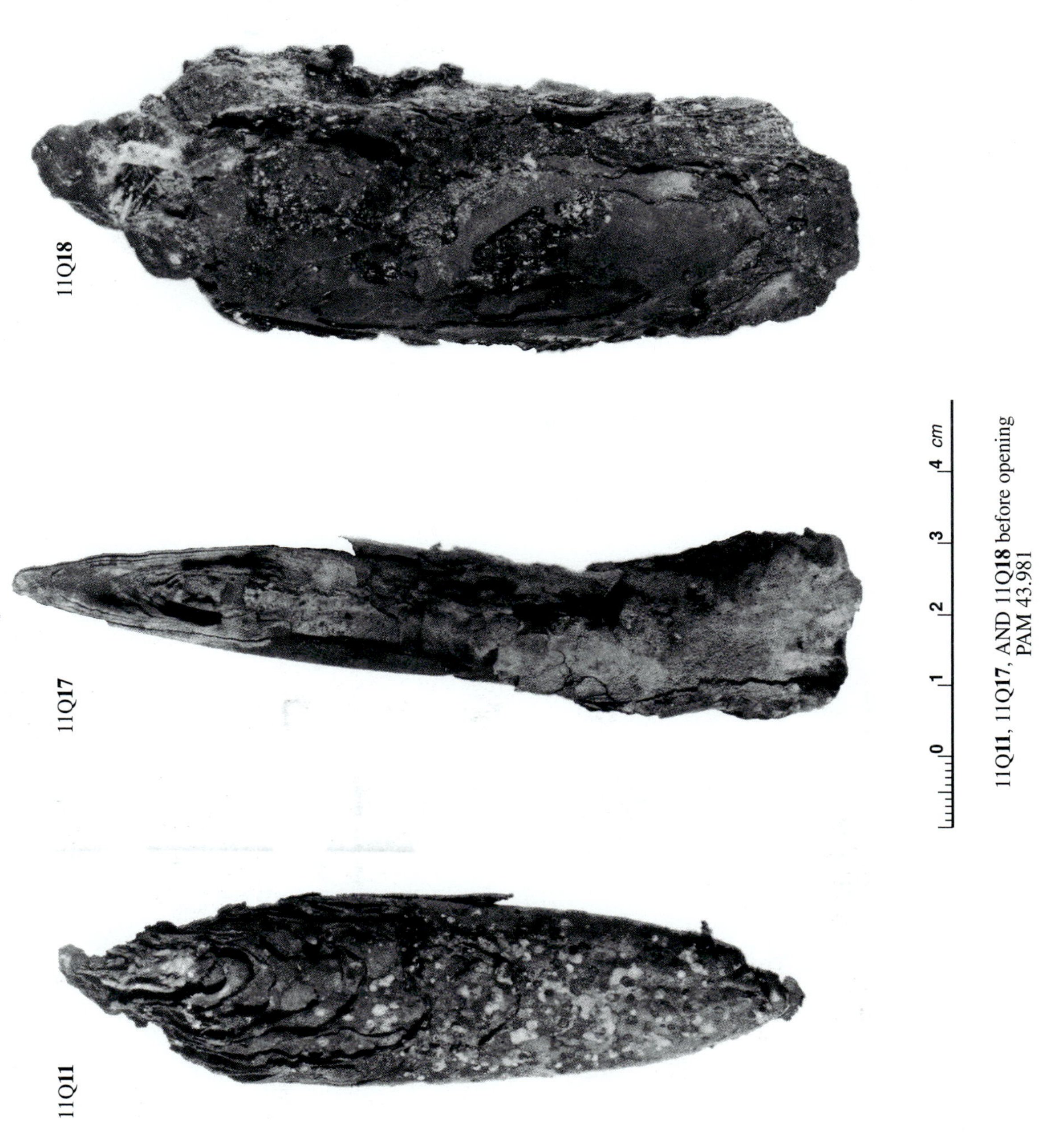

11Q11, 11Q**17**, AND 11Q**18** before opening
PAM 43.981

PLATE LIV

Scale: 2:1

11Q**4** before opening
PAM 43.742

CATHOLIC THEOLOGICAL UNION
3 0311 00111 1074